1. Jan Kochanowski. Sepulchral portrait in the parish church at Zwoleń, about 1610. Photo Stanisław Stępniewski.

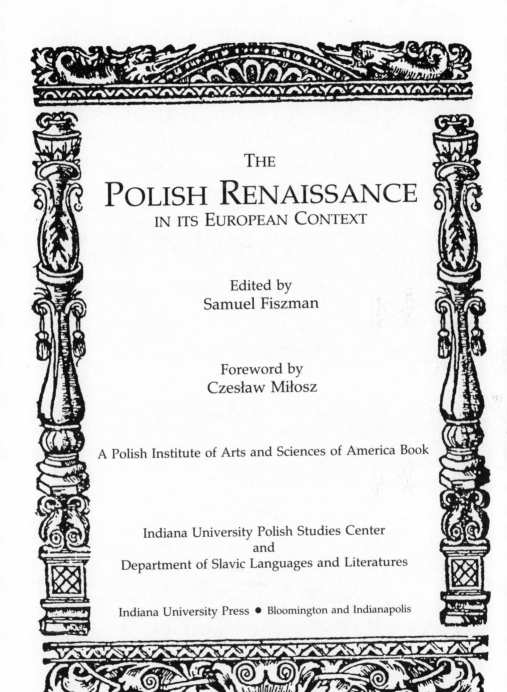

THE
POLISH RENAISSANCE
IN ITS EUROPEAN CONTEXT

Edited by
Samuel Fiszman

Foreword by
Czesław Miłosz

A Polish Institute of Arts and Sciences of America Book

Indiana University Polish Studies Center
and
Department of Slavic Languages and Literatures

Indiana University Press ● Bloomington and Indianapolis

Manufactured in the United States of America

Printed on acid-free paper.

Library of Congress Cataloging-in-Publication Data

The Polish renaissance in its European context / edited by Samuel Fiszman : foreword by Czesław Miłosz.

p.   cm.

"Indiana University Polish Studies Center and the Department of Slavic Languages and Literatures."

Results of a conference commemorating the birth and death of Jan Kochanowski held at Indiana University, May 25-29, 1982; sponsored by Indiana University and Warsaw University.
"A Polish Institute of Arts and Sciences of America book."

Includes index.

ISBN 0-253-34627-4

1. Poland—History—16th century—Congresses. 2. Renaissance—Poland—Congresses. 3. Poland—Relations—Europe—Congresses. 4. Europe—Relations—Poland—Congresses. 5. Kochanowski, Jan, 1530-1584—Criticism and interpretation—Congresses. I. Fiszman, Samuel. II. Kochanowski, Jan, 1530-1584. III. Indiana University, Bloomington. Polish Studies Center. IV. Indiana University, Bloomington. Dept. of Slavic Languages and Literatures. V. Indiana University, Bloomington. VI. Uniwersytet Warszawski.

DK4276.P65 1988
943.8'02—dc19

88-1717
CIP

Table of Contents

Part III. Science and Learning in Renaissance Poland

Part IV. Renaissance Poland and Other Cultures

Part V. Art and Architecture in Renaissance Poland

List of Illustrations

The ornaments in parts I-V are taken from 16th century Polish publications, in part VI from Jan Kochanowski's first editions.

Preface

The publication of this book was made possible through the generous grants of:

The Alfred Jurzykowski Foundation, Inc.
The Joseph B. Slotkowski Publication Fund of the Kościuszko Foundation.
The American Institute of Polish Culture, Inc.
The Rosenstiel Foundation.
Indiana University Office of Research and Graduate Development
Indiana University Dean of the Faculties Multidisciplinary Ventures Fund.

The studies that comprise this volume were originally presented in their initial form at the conference "The Polish Renaissance in its European Context" held at Indiana University, May 25-29, 1982 under the auspices of the academic exchange program between Indiana University and Warsaw University to commemorate the birth (450 years in 1980) and death (400 years in 1984) of Jan Kochanowski, the greatest poet of the Polish Renaissance, and one of the most outstanding European poets of the sixteenth century.

The conference was organized by the Indiana University Polish Studies Center under the direction of Professor Mary Ellen Solt. Professor Samuel Fiszman of the Department of Slavic Languages and Literatures was Conference Chairman with Professor Ian Thomson the Renaissance Studies Program Director. Other organizational tasks were carried out by the Office of International Programs Dean John V. Lombardi and Program Officer Grace Bareikis, as well as by the Warsaw University American Studies Center Director Włodzimierz Siwiński and Assistant Mrs. Wanda Jasińska. The conference was generously sponsored by the National Endowment for the Humanities, and co-sponsored by the Indiana University Office of International Programs, the Department of

Slavic Languages and Literatures, and the Russian and East European Institute.[1]

Preparation of the essays for print that comprise this volume would have
been impossible without the considerable financial assistance that was generously bestowed by the Indiana University President's Council on the Humanities, the Office of Research and Graduate Development, the Office of
International Programs, the Department of Slavic Languages and Literatures,
and the Russian and East European Institute.

The editorial work on the volume was done with the help of the resources
and cooperation of many libraries. These include Indiana University Library
and, particularly due to the subject of the book, Indiana University Lilly Library
which posesses a rich collection of old printings related to the Renaissance in
Poland. Biblioteka Uniwersytecka in Warsaw prepared information on the bibliographies of the contributors, and many illustrations in the volume are based
on its holdings. As well, many illustrations come from the collections of Biblioteka Jagiellońska, and Biblioteka Czartoryskich in Cracow, and Biblioteka
Ossolińskich in Wrocław.

A large portion of the illustrations in the volume were received through the
good offices of Dr. Magdalena Foland-Kugler, Dr. Maria Kowalczyk, Professor
Andrzej Bartnicki, Professor Marian Jakóbiec, and Professor Maria Renata Mayenowa.

The entire preparation of the volume for print was accomplished at the
Department of Slavic Languages and Literatures with the assistance of Dr.
Theodosia Robertson, who is also responsible for the translation from Polish
of several essays and style editing of others, and with the help of Mrs. Mollie
Ducket the secretary of the department. The final stage of the editorial work
was done with the assistance of Dr. Piotr Drozdowski and Mr. Curt Woolhiser.
Mrs. Eleanor Valentine-Jakubiak, Program Assistant of the Polish Studies Cen-
ter participated in both the final editing and production process.

During the course of the organization of the conference and then with the
preparation of the volume for print, and finally in the proof reading, my wife
Alicja Zadrożna Fiszman gave unstintingly of her considerable help, advice,
and encouragement.

To the above mentioned people and institutions who helped in organizing
the conference, and in the preparation of this volume for print and in its
publication, I wish to express my sincere gratitude.

The volume is devoted to Renaissance Polish Culture in many of its major
aspects and as a part of the intellectual movement of humanism in Europe,

---

1. About the conference, see: Jerzy Krzyżanowski, "Kochanowski w Indianie" (Kochanowski
in Indiana), *Przegląd Polski* 11:60 (1982); Aleksander Gieysztor, "O Rzeczypospolitej Królestwa
Polskiego" (On the Commonwealth of the Kingdom of Poland), *Tygodnik Powszechny* no. 34
(1982) and "On the Commonwealth of the Kingdom of Poland," *Dialectics and Humanism*
(1983); William B. Edgerton, "Indiana University Conference on the Polish Renaissance in its
European Context," *Polish Review* 28:1 (1983); and Mary Ellen Solt, "A Good Example of
Polish-American Scientific Cooperation," *Poland* no. 3 (1984).

and its contributors are scholars from the United States and Poland; the author of the Foreward is the Nobel Prize Laureate Czesław Miłosz.

The volume is divided into two parts. The Introduction which constitutes an overview of the cultural achievements of the Polish Renaissance is followed by the first larger part of the volume in which are discussed: the features and development of Polish historical writing in the fifteenth and sixteenth centuries; the economical, social, and political situation in Poland during the Renaissance era, the significance of its heritage for future epochs in Polish history; the religious life of the time, with special emphasis on the Polish Brethern; the particular character of the Reformation in Poland; and the Polish system of law and democracy. The development of science and learning is exemplified by the presentation of the revolutionary ideas in astronomy of Nicholas Copernicus, of the original political thought of Andrzej Frycz Modrzewski, and by the discussion of the growing influence of Renaissance humanism at the Cracow University during the fifteenth century. Among the many problems concerning Poland's cultural relations with other European countries, the volume includes studies on such topics as: Polish Humanism and its Italian sources; the significance of some cultural achievements of sixteenth-century Poland for Eastern Slavic nations; and the circumstances under which the English translation of Wawrzyniec Goślicki's *De Optimo senatore* appeared. The first part of the volume ends with remarks about Polish Renaissance art and architecture.

The first part of the volume provides the context in which the second part adresses the various facets of the work of Jan Kochanowski. It considers his fame, his significance in the development of Polish national literature, the linguistic form of his poetry and its versification, the classical tradition of his work, the particular aspects of his *Fraszka* "On human life," and the poem "The Muse," Kochanowski's sixteenth century editions, his earliest biography, and his influence on Southern and Eastern Slavic cultures.

The aim of the bibliographies of the contributors included at the end of the volume is twofold: to present a selection of their works, and to serve as an additional source of information about publications related to the Polish Renaissance.

The thread which unites these individual essays is the epoch to which they are devoted, and the varied and also different perspective they give to the unique qualities of the Polish Renaissance. However, the essays are also united by their comparative quality and by the common theme of the importance of the ties between Polish culture and the culture of the rest of Europe of the time, as well as the role of Renaissance Poland in the mainstream of Renaissance Europe.

The present volume is the first book in English devoted to the epoch of the Renaissance in Poland in such broad perspective. Nonetheless, it was, for various reasons, impossible to include many noteworthy topics about this period. It is hoped that it will serve as a stimulus for further scholarship and publications devoted to other aspects of the remarkable Polish Golden Age.

Foreword

Czesław Miłosz

To write in the language of Jan Kochanowski. This means to write in Polish and yet to escape in a way many negative and positive associations connected with that word Polish. For a Polish poet the name Kochanowski invokes a homeostasis, an equilibrium broken by the subsequent, turbulent history of that part of Europe. His was after all a time without foreign invasions, heroic struggles, romantic dreams, national humiliation, and self-righteous compensation. At the time Jan Kochanowski was born, 1530 (Pierre Ronsard in France was his elder by six years), all those sad things belonged to the future and he did not taste them in his lifetime. He lived in a huge and prosperous country situated in the center of Europe, strengthened by a formal union between the Kingdom of Poland and the Grand Duchy of Lithuania in 1569 thanks to which the country successfully repelled Ivan the Terrible's attacks against its Eastern fringes. For the most part of Kochanowski's life that state was ruled by Sigismund Augustus, a king who used to say: "I am King of your bodies but not of your consciences," which meant that both Catholics and Protestants could count upon his protection. My final examinations for the baccalaureate, taken in a hall with a portrait of Sigismund Augustus, are for me until today a token of my intention to belong to the spirit of the Renaissance tolerance.

Jan Kochanowski was a Roman Catholic but in his writings we find an ecumenical spirit in this sense at least that he abstained from taking part in the religious controversies of the time. He was perhaps motivated by a skepticism not unlike that of his contemporary Montaigne. Looking from our perspective we can not give an unqualified praise to the sixteenth century skeptics and yet we must have sympathy for them as certainly they acted against the ferocity of European religious wars during the Reformation. Kochanowski after all was brought up as a bilingual humanist writing both in Latin and Polish. His humanism was permeated by the spirit of Erasmus of Rotterdam, a man who

did not go openly to the side of Martin Luther. Both in Poland and other
countries of Europe there were at that time people who hoped to heal the gap
which was opening between Roman Catholicism and the Protestants.

To claim the patronage of Kochanowski is to recognize the role of Italy in
shaping literature of a large part of Europe."An Englishman Italianate is a
devil incarnate" runs an English saying of the sixteenth century. There are no
traces of any devilish influence upon Kochanowski in spite of his many years
spent on studies in Italy, except perhaps his introduction of blank verse (verso
sciolto) into Polish poetry. Like all Italian artists of the Renaissance he was
under the spell of Greek mythology, of Greek and Latin authors, primarily of
Horace. His Songs are Polish embroiderings upon Horatian motifs; his short
Polish epigrams bear a name from the Italian word frasca, a little twig.

I said that Kochanowski wrote before the period of desperate commitments to
the cause of the nation so common in later periods. It doesn't mean that his
poetry deals only with eternal problems of love, death, and the destructive power
of time. Occasionally he used his pen to say something on matters of a civic
concern. But those were not his overwhelming worries.

Linguistically Kochanowski marks the moment of the sudden maturity of the
Polish literary language emerging from its competition with Latin. Kochanowski
read today is closer to modern Polish than Edmund Spenser or Sir Philip Sidney,
some twenty years younger than he, are today to an English reader. Is this
good or bad? I don't know, but the language of another great Polish poet, Adam
Mickiewicz (1798-1855) is a perfect continuation of Kochanowski's language.

To be a Polish poet is, let me be frank, a harsh experience. It is to bow daily
under the burden of innumerable deaths in torture of men, women, and children,
and to bear in addition a tragic division of the victims into Jews and non-Jews.
Kochanowski gives to a poet who writes in his language a reprieve from his
feelings of guilt. After all Kochanowski's honest craftmanship, his pursuit of
artistic perfection have been vindicated by the permanent value of his poems.

Introduction

Numerous are the diverse manifestations of Poland's presence as a state and as a cultural center in humanist Europe. The importance of Poland of the Jagiellons as a political power, the importance of the University of Cracow as an international center of learning, and the importance of Polish scholars and writers in the intellectual movements of humanist Europe was considerable and is reflected in an imposing amount of published scholarly works, literary works, and letters—that favorite genre of the humanists.

The fifteenth century is marked by the flourishing of the University of Cracow, the first printings, the early development of humanism in Poland, and by increasingly lively relations with universities and humanists of other European countries. These relations had already been initiated in previous centuries when Polish students began to travel the roads to Paris, Bologna, and Padua. Among these thirteenth-century scholars were: Wincenty Kadłubek Bishop of Cracow, author of the *Chronicles*, important both for Polish history and literature, and Martinus Polonus, author of the widely read *Chronicles of Popes and Emperors*, a work known in numerous copies and later published several times in the fifteenth and sixteenth centuries.

In the mid-fourteenth century, Prague became an important destination for Polish student travel. Matthaeus de Cracovia earned his Master of Philosophy at the University of Prague; he became professor of theology there as well, and then later, professor and rector at the University of Heidelberg. He authored theological works, known first in manuscript copies and then later printed, which contain elements of the doctrine of conciliarism. This doctrine was propagated at the University of Cracow in the first half of the fifteenth century, a fact apparent from the positions taken by the University's representatives at the Council of Constance and particularly of Basel. Two outstanding participants at the Council of Constance studied at Prague and at Padua: Paweł Włodkowic and Andrzej Łaskarz. Their participation was noteworthy, particularly because of the pronouncement of Paweł Włodkowic (Paulus Vladimiri), Rector of the University of Cracow. Defending Poland against charges made by the Teutonic Knights that Poland collaborated with pagans, Paweł Włodkowic enunciated the principle that Christianity cannot be imposed by force, and that pagan nations also have the right to their independent existence. It should be noted that in the next century a Spanish theologian, Francisco de Vitoria, proclaimed a similar idea in connection with the subjugation of the American Indians.

In Poland, the implications of this advanced doctrine of the rights of nations would underlie the conviction that the individual has a right to his own beliefs. This concept aided the development of religious tolerance, one of sixteenth-century Poland's most essential features and one which distinguishes her in the European context of the time.

Conciliarism in the fields of theology and canon law, the concept of legal equality among nations in the field of law, Aristotelianism in the fields of philosophy, and in both the natural and social sciences, the enormous work in arranging the codices of sources of Polish history upon which Jan Długosz based his great work, the *Annales*—all are achievements and intellectual trends connected in great part with the activity of the University of Cracow, re-established in 1400. The humanist Aeneus Silvius Piccolomini, later Pope Pius II in his work *De Europa* (1458) praised "Cracow, the celebrated capital of the Kingdom where the school of liberal art flourished." The fields in which the University became particularly famous, however, were mathematics and astronomy. A department of mathematics and astronomy was established at the University in 1410 and by mid-century, a department of astrology as well; this department also enriched the achievements of the Cracow school of astronomy. The influence of this school was immediately apparent in the second half of the fifteenth century when its graduates took teaching positions at the Universities of Prague, Padua, and especially at the University of Bologna, where the chair of astronomy and mathematics was held by Polish scholars for several decades. Among the most famous of these was Marcin Bylica, who in the years 1463-64 lectured at Bologna on astronomy and astrology. In 1464, Bylica began to work in Rome with the most eminent astronomer and mathematician of the day, Johannes Regiomontanus; the result of their collaboration was a small volume by Regiomontanus, *Dialogus inter Vienennsem et Cracoviensem*. . . . The two scholars continued to work together in Hungary, where both had been invited to the newly founded University at Pozsony. During these same years, the University of Cracow became an international center of astronomical and mathematical studies, educating future professors in these fields for such universities as Heidelberg, Wittenberg, and Vienna. It was during this flowering of the Cracow school of astronomy that Nicolaus Copernicus studied at the University (1491-95).

The above achievements and intellectual trends associated with the University of Cracow clearly indicate the changes denoting the beginning of humanism in Poland which in the second half of the fifteenth century increasingly affected other fields. Thus, philological study increased at the University of Cracow, so that by the end of the century, the University had gained international recognition in this field as well. Laurentius Corvinus, whose works include

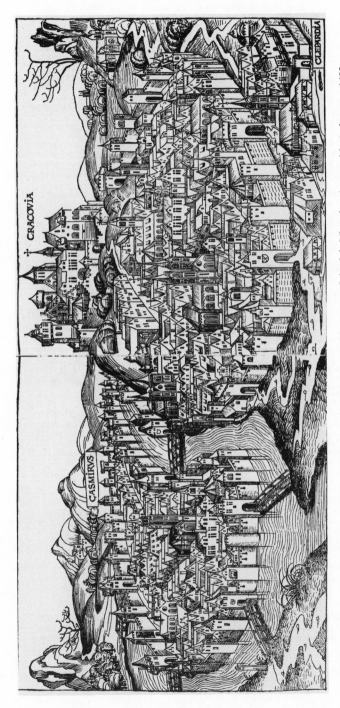

2. The panorama of Cracow at the end of the XV century. Woodcut in Hartmann Schedel, *Liber chronicarum*, Norimbergae, 1493 (Indiana University Lilly Library, Bloomington).

¶ Sanctus Stanislaus episcopus

¶ De sancto Stanislao episcopo Cracouiensi patrono Sarmacie

Oiuus Stanislaus vir magne apud deu auctoritatis tocius sarmacie patronus z signifer. Natus anno salutis nostre M.viij. in rure quod Szeppanowo vocant nobilibus ac claris parentibus. quoz cura fuit in templis diuino seruicio incumbere. z cu pijs placare precibus. Is du in iuuentutem deuenisset patris monitu in celebre gymnasium parisius deuenit vbi optimaz litterarum studijs summa opera dabat. vnde multis virtutibus floruit. sacro aut diuinoqz iuri precipue insistebat. non ea qua huius etatis iurisperiti questus causa solet vt maiorum dignitatu honore adipisceret. sed vt si quando locus statui sue aut coditioni sue ferre posset vt tantu miseris quantum potentibus. orphano pupilloque iustitiam administraret. z vnicuiqz equo pondere quod suu esset subente id legere deret. Tandem paternas sedes rediens Cracouiam inclita Sarmacie vrbem deuenit. Illic ob virtutem z scientia sua canonicali dignitate fungitur. Mortuoqz antistite celestis numinis prouidentia in presulis sedem declaratus fuit. Huic du ampliare. Empto tandem rure a quodam milite. eoqz mortuo amici illius villam eande iure hereditario a diuo presule repetere conabant. At ille testimoniu huius stipulationis emptionisqz proferre non potuit. nam bij qui huius rei satis edocti fuerant propter illoz impotentia latebant. Air ergo sanctus orationibus ac ieiunijs incumbit. confisusqz summi dei potentia. qui se iam diu munitu cognouerat accedens ad tumulus defuncti militis a quo rus illud emerat. z euoluto lapide et arena pia z deuota oratione deu obtestabatur. et mortuu illu per quatuor annos in vita reduxit. Euqz coram tyranno Boleslao apud que tale ius agebatur constituit. Astantibus illic suis aduersarijs ceterisqz regni optimatibus. quo se emisse villam aperte demostrauit. Iamqz seuus Boleslaus fedo turpiqz luxu insistebat. ac omne in suas gentes psidiam z tyranni dem exercebat. ac illustres viros egregiosqz ciues nefandis dirisqz supplicijs excruciabat. Stanislaus vero christi vates haud longius id ferendum existimabat. itaqz regem intrepidus adiens vt talib cepis desineret illum obiurgabat. At ille magis indies facinus exercebat. Tandem a presule in sententiam excoiunicationis poit. quare tyrannus boleslaus ignarus pre furore quid ageret dimisit satellites suos vt psulem quocunqz esset loco trucidarent. Eo tempore diuus Stanislaus in sacellu diui Michaelis quod super rupellam in Casimiro vrbe conditu est deuenerat gratissimu illic deo offerens sacrificiu. hunc in locum du ministri regij deuenissent. iamqz ter ingredi templu conarentur. ter iterum pulsi diuina potentia in tergum cadebant. Id postqz ad regias aures deuentum fuisset magno fremitu rex Boleslaus in sacellum pperat. vbi sanctum presulem iam sacrificia offerentem immani verbere ac seuissimis ictibus trucidat. Tandem per ministros in frusta partitus extravrbe deijcit vt volucres illud vncis rostris deuellerent. sed diuina sic agente prouidencia aquile illic aderant que preciosum corpus in vnum collegerunt summaqz diligentia id seruabant quousqz ciues ipi maximo venerandoqz ritu in rupellam honorifice sepelirent. Tande in hunc ru sanctoz relatus vt premissum est in arce regia ad templu diui wentzeslai deduct[us] in aurea tumba multis miraculis coruscat. quem populus multo thure ac precibus indies veneratur

¶ De Cracouia vrbe regia Sarmacie

Cracouiam vrbem regiam insigni huic operi inserendam haud absurdum esse duxi. Nam celebris germanie ciuitas e teste Ptolomeo optimo lucidiorisqz cosmographo. q ea Cozrodunu appellat. Strabo aut germania diffunit quu Rhenus z Albis in se clauserint. Nos ea causa sane non indigna vrbem sarmatie foro censemus. Hanc a prima eius origine repetendas satis digna esse putaui. Sed ne prolixiori ambiguaue oratione narrando fabulari videar breuiter de eius situ quippiam narrare constitui. Cracouia igitur illustris vrbs sarmatie qua poloniam vocant ad rippam Istule no longe ab eius fontibus sita. Hec a Cracco primo duce sarmacie condita fuisse z eam suo nomine celebrasse multi retulere. Hec altis primu menibus cingit. ppugnaculis z celsis turribus. post paruo muro z ob vetustatem ruituro similis. Tande valles ac fosse vt imminentibus hostibus facilior aditus prohibeatur. Hec quedam piscinarijs aquis replete quedam virgultis frutice ac graminibus virent. Post aggerem vero qui valli imminet amnis non late fluens Rudys dictus totam ciuitatem circumluit. Hic rotarum orbes agitat qui Cererem satis continent et emoliunt. Deducitur tandem per subterraneos cuniculos z cannas toti vrbi satis vndarum prebet. Por te vrbis septem. In ea vero plurime pulcherrime ac egregie ciuium domus. Ac plurima ingentia templa precipui diue virginis Marie in medioyqbis extat cum duabus ardua celsisqz turribus. Sut z illic multa monasteria. vbi multus deuotozum religiosozumque patru cetus fulget. Ad edem nanqz gloriosissime trinitatis sic vocatam est celebris ordo predicatozu. In ea vero sacra ede multe sanctitatis vir beatus Iacinctus non du in numerum sanctozum relatus magnis miraculis redolet. diui Dominici comes. Qui adbucvi uens tres mortuos in vitam reduxit. Ad templu vero sancti Francisci est ordo fratrum minoz non reformatus. Ac cetera multa monasteria. Est et templu non longe a porta Istule quod ad sanctas Annam vocant. vbi beatus Cantus celebris huius vrbis gimnasij doctoz multis miraculis z prodigijs fulget. Quis no du in cathalagum sanctozu ascriptus sit. Hanc iuxta sacra edem situatu est ingens celebze gymnasiu multis clarissimis doctissimisqz viris pollens. vbi p plurime ingenue artes recitantur. Studiu eloquentie poetices philozophie ac phisices. Astronomice tamen studiu maxime viret. Nec in tota germania (vt ex multozu relatione satis mihi cognitum est) illo clarior reperitur. Illic iam maxime phebus colitur. qui z cozu cruda elimat

3. Hartmann Schedel, *Liber chronicarum*, Norimbergae, 1493. The page containing the encomium to Cracow and the University (Indiana University Lilly Library, Bloomington).

many poems, textbooks of Latin versification, and geography—*Cosmographia* (1496)—was the most eminent of the Silesian humanists who lectured at the University of Cracow. Another was Caspar Ursinus Velius, who studied Greek at the University and later became a well-known poet and historian, and tutor to the future emperor Maximilian II. During a two year stay in Cracow, the major German humanist Konrad Celtis (Conradus Celtes) attended lectures by Wojciech (Adalbert) of Brudzewo on astronomy and mathematics, and founded *Sodalitas Litteraria Vistulana*, a humanist society, in Cracow. It is believed that he sent material to Hartmann Schedel for the chapter on Poland in his chronicle *Liber chronicarum* (1493). Schedel's work contained two well-known panoramas of fifteenth-century Cracow and an encomium to Cracow and "the renowned University distinguished by its most illustrious learned men, where many of the liberal arts are taught: rhetoric, poetry, philosophy, and physics. Astronomy, however, flourished there the most." Among the German humanists who were attracted by the fame of the University of Cracow, Heinrich Bebel should be mentioned. A German poet and future professor of oratory and poetics at the University of Tübingen, he went to Cracow to study under Corvinus.

Several Italian humanists also participated in the cultural life of Cracow in those days. The most famous was Filippo Buonaccorsi, called Callimachus, a poet, historian, and diplomat who lectured at the University, became a tutor to the sons of King Kazimierz IV (Jagiellończyk), and remained in Cracow for the rest of his life. Callimachus, author of Poland's first humanist biography, *Vita et mores Gregorii Sanocei* (1476), as well as elegies, love epigrams, and political and historical writings, contributed to the development of humanism in Poland and to increased Italian-Polish cultural contacts. The correspondence of Aeneas Sylvius Piccolomini, with the Bishop of Cracow, Cardinal Zbigniew Oleśnicki, exemplifies even earlier Italian-Polish links dating from mid-century. Dedications by Italian humanists to their Polish humanist friends date from the end of the fifteenth century and the beginning of the sixteenth. Examples of these are the dedications of Philippo Beroaldo to the Royal Secretary, Paweł Szydłowiecki, and to the Bishop of Płock, Erazm Ciołek, as well as that of Aldo Manuzio to the Bishop of Poznań, Jan Lubrański.

Students, poets, and scholars from Switzerland were especially numerous in Cracow. Rudolf Agricola—to mention only one of them—became professor of poetics at the University. In 1518 the wandering English humanist and admirer of Erasmus of Rotterdam, Leonard Coxe, also arrived in Cracow. Before commencing his lectures, he delivered a lengthy and very interesting encomium to the University subsequently published under the title *De Laudibus Celeberrimae Cracoviensis Academiae* (1518). In his oration he lauded the University's professors and the various disciplines cultivated there.

In Poland, as elsewhere in Europe, printing was a factor which stimulated the spread of humanism. In Cracow, the first printings appeared between 1474 and 1477. Some years later successful printing houses were established, and

DE laudibus Celeberrimæ Cracouiensis Academiæ, LEONardi Coxi Britãni, Octauo Idus Decẽbris habita Oratio. Anno. 1518.

RVDOLFVS AGRICOLA IVNIOR POETA IMPE/ ratorijs manibus coronatus, ob amore inclytæ Academiæ Cracouiensis carmen hoc Peoniaim subito faciebat.

Deuola in ætherios felix Academia tractus,
  Ad Tartessiacum, Gargaridumcæ solum.
Vnipedes Blemyes, medijs Nasomenes harenis
  Et Thocaros, Phrunos: Sauro natasæ uagos.
Iure tuum nomen merito, laudesæ perennes
  Septenum a primo climate clima tonat.
Artibus ingenium docile illustrare beatis,
  Instruis & uitam moribus egregijs.
Schemata Romanæ linguæ, uocesæ latinas
  Grammaticęcæ tropos, verbacæ culta doces
Et pleno ardentes Demosthenis ore loquelas,
  Artecæ Rhetoricaicum Cicerone loqui.
Zenonis ricas, perplexa sophismata soluis,
  Quid verum & falsum quidcæ repugnet agis,
Archesilaus amat cuiritæ moenia Crocæ,
  Ex Asia physicam quippe minore tulit.
Ipsa doces primas naturæ noscere partes
  Stellaticæ uias, splendidacæ astra poli.
Dyctacæ peruigilierum quæ sit proportio rerum,
  Musica quas uoces pulchra, potensæ canit.
Et uarios cerræ tractus & dñnata mundi,
  Aequedistantés signifecicæ gradus.
Quamcæ Hyperionij sit declinatio solis,
  Descensus qualis rite docere soles.
Et decreta patrum, sacratacæ iura tonantis,
  Scripturæ ante alias sensa profunda sacræ.
Non inuenta modo diuinitus, altacæ mentis
  Humanæ referas dogmata, docta parens
Circumfer proprios ergo paucosæ clientes
  Dicto quisne omnes enumerare potest.
Hinc sacer atcæ miser contra qui dixeris esto
  Pauper in exilio, semilacercæ graui.

4. Leonard Coxe, *De laudibus Celeberrimae Cracoviensis Academiae…Oratio*, Cracoviae, 1518. The English wandering humanist and enthusiastic Erasmianist delivered this oration before commencing his lectures at Cracow University where he stayed until 1519, and returned for the academic years 1525-27 (Biblioteka Czartoryskich, Kraków). Reprinted from Henryk Barycz, *Szlakami dziejopisarstwa staropolskiego*, (Wrocław: Ossolineum, 1981). Photo A. Wierzba.

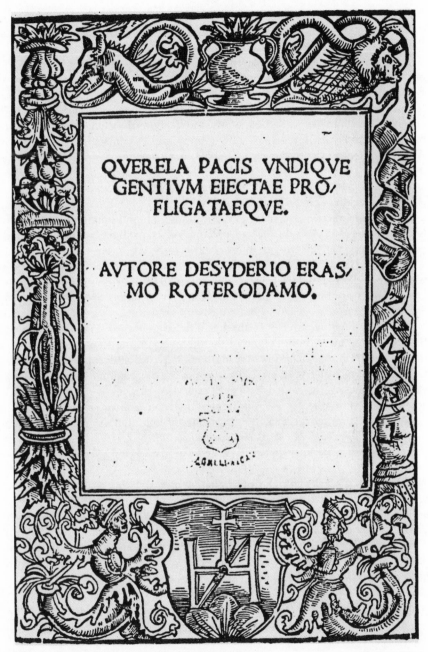

5. Erasmus of Rotterdam, *Querela pacis undique gentium eiectae profligataeque*, Cracoviae, 1518. One of the numerous works of Erasmus published in Cracow, (often soon after first editions) in Latin and also in Polish translation (Biblioteka Jagiellońska, Kraków). Reprinted from *Erasmiana Cracoviensia*, (Kraków: Uniwersytet Jagielloński, 1971).

the production of beautiful books, not only in Latin and in Polish, began on a scale quite large for those times. The first printings in cyrillic, as well as the first book in Hungarian, were done in Cracow.

Cracovian printers soon appeared in other countries, practicing the beautiful art of book printing, and even founding printing houses themselves. Associated with the renowned Neapolitan printing house of Mathias Moravus were Johannes Adam de Polonia—of whose work only two incunabula printed in 1478 survive—and Stanislaus Polonus, whose publications done together with Meinrad Ungut in Seville in the years 1490-99 and later by himself in Seville and in Alcala de Henares in the years 1499-1504, are considered some of the finest printings produced in Europe at this time for the beauty of their type, the arrangement of capitals on their title pages, and for their illustrations.

When speaking about the development of pre-Copernican astronomy at the University of Cracow, two more eminent names should be mentioned. Jan of Głogów (Głogowczyk), whose lectures Copernicus, in all probability, attended, was a professor at the University for nearly forty years. He wrote numerous works in the fields of philosophy, logic, astronomy, astrology, geography, in which he also discussed the important position of the sun among other planets. His commentary *Introductorium compendiosum in tractatum 'Spherae' Johannis de Sacrobosco* (Cracoviae, 1506) to the handbook on astronomy of Joannes Sacrobosco, twice re-edited and published also in Strassburg in 1518, included the first published mention in Poland of the discovery of the New World. Among the numerous works in astronomy, mathematics, and philosophy of the above mentioned Wojciech (Adalbert) of Brudzewo, the most significant was his *Commentariolum super 'Theoricas novas planetarum' Georgii Purbachii* written in 1482 and published in Milan in 1495, in which the inconsistencies existing between various astronomical facts in Ptolemys' theory were emphasized. This commentary on Peurbach's *Theoricae novae planetarum* of c. 1472, became the accepted text on planetary theory at Cracow while Copernicus was a student there.

The outstanding development of Polish geography and cartography is well represented in the works of a friend of Copernicus, Bernard Wapowski, who assisted in supplying the map of Poland and neighboring countries for the 1508 Rome edition of Ptolemy's *Geography*, prepared by Marco Beneventano.

Exemplifying the high standard of Polish printing and testifying to the further development of historical science in Poland in the humanist spirit is a work by the professor and rector of the University of Cracow, Maciej of Miechów (Miechowita): *Chronica Polonorum* (Cracoviae, 1521), continued by the historian, economist, and Royal Secretary, Jodocus Ludovicus Decius (Decjusz).

Polish philological achievements in the area of Greek are also connected with the name of Copernicus. This area of philology is well-represented by his translation into Latin of the letters of Theophylaktos Simokattes (Cracoviae, 1509), and by the first Latin translation of Aithiopika of Heliodoros of Emesa (1552) made by Stanisław Warszewicki, a pupil of Melanchthon and student together with Jan Kochanowski at the University of Padua. The translation is particularly important in that it became the basis for translations of Heliodoros into various European languages.

The name of Decius and that of the young Jan Łaski (future religious reformer) are connected with the subject of Erasmus of Rotterdam's close and numerous contacts with Poles, and the enormous influence which Erasmianism exerted upon Polish culture. Close correspondents with Erasmus included, besides Decius and Łaski, Primate Jan Łaski, Chancellor Krzysztof Szydłowiecki, Bishop of Cracow Piotr Tomicki, poet and primate Andrzej Krzycki, poet and diplomat Jan Dantyszek, as well as King Sigismund the Old and others. In addition to letter writing, Erasmus expressed his friendship for his Polish correspondents in his works dedicated to them.

During the first half of the sixteenth century the Polish Renaissance is illuminated by the brilliant name of Nicolaus Copernicus (Mikołaj Kopernik). In his dedication to Pope Paul III of his work *De Revolutionibus orbium coelestium, Libri VI* (Basileae, 1543)—one of the most admirable documents of the Renaissance epoch, Copernicus wrote:

> I can readily imagine, Holy Father, that as soon as some people hear that in this volume, which I have written about the revolutions of the spheres of the universe, I ascribe certain motions to the terrestrial globe, they will shout that I must be immediately repudiated together with this belief. For I am not so enamored of my own opinions that I disregard what others may think of them. I am aware that a philosopher's ideas are not subject to the judgment of ordinary persons, because it is his endeavor to seek the truth in all things, to the extent permitted to human reason by God. Yet I hold that completely erroneous views should be shunned. Those who know that the consensus of many centuries has sanctioned the conception that the earth remains at rest in the middle of the heaven as its center would, I reflected, regard it as an insane pronouncement if I made the opposite assertion that the earth moves. Therefore I debated with myself for a long time whether to publish the volume which I wrote to prove the earth's motion. . . .
>
> Perhaps there will be babblers who claim to be judges of astronomy although completely ignorant of the subject and, badly distorting some passage of Scripture to their purpose, will dare to find fault with my undertaking and censure it. I disregard them even to the extent of despising their criticism as unfounded. For it is not unknown that Lactancius, otherwise an illustrious writer, but hardly an astronomer, speaks quite childishly about the Earth's shape, when he mocks those who declared that the Earth has the form of the globe. Hence scholars need not be surprised if any such persons will likewise ridicule me. Astronomy is written for astronomers. To them my work

AD SANCTIS´
SIMVM DOMINVM PAV.
LVM III. PONTIFICEM MAXIMVM,
Nicolai Copernici Præfatio in libros
Reuolutionum.

ATIS equidem, Sanctifsime Pater, æ=
ftimare poſſum, futurum eſſe, ut ſimul
atcʒ quidam acceperint, me hiſce meis li
bris, quos de Reuolutionibus ſphæraru
mundi ſcripſi, terræ globo tribuere quoſ
dam motus, ſtatim me explodendum
cum tali opinione clamitent. Necʒ enim
ita mihi mea placent, ut nō perpendam,
quid alij de illis iudicaturi ſint. Et quamuis ſciam, hominis phi
loſophi cogitationes eſſe remotas à iudicio uulgi, propterea
quòd illius ſtudium ſit ueritatem omnibus in rebus, quatenus
id à Deo rationi humanę permiſſum eſt, inquirere, tamen alie
nas prorſus à rectitudine opiniones fugiendas cenſeo. Itacʒ cū
mecum ipſe cogitarem, quàm abſurdum ἀκρόαμα exiſtimatu
ri eſſent illi, qui multorum ſeculorum iudicijs hanc opinionē
confirmatam norūt, quòd terra immobilis in medio cœli, tan
quam centrum illius poſita ſit, ſi ego contra aſſererem terram
moueri, diu mecum hæſi, an meos cōmentarios in eius motus
demonſtrationem conſcriptos in lucem darem, an uero ſatius
eſſet, Pythagoreorum & quorundam aliorum ſequi exemplū,
qui non per literas, ſed per manus tradere ſoliti ſunt myſteria
philoſophiæ propinquis & amicis duntaxat. Sicut Lyſidis ad
Hipparchum epiſtola teſtatur. Ac mihi quidem uidentur id
feciſſe : non ut quidam arbitrantur ex quadam inuidentia
communicandarum doctrinarum, Sed ne res pulcherrimæ, &
multo ſtudio magnorum uirorum inueſtigatę, ab illis contem
nerentur, quos aut piget ullis literis bonam operam impende=
re, niſi quæſtuoſis, aut ſi exhortationibus & exemplo aliorum
ad liberale ſtudium philoſophiæ excitentur, tamen propter
ſtupidita

6. The first page of Copernicus' letter to Pope Paul III (in Nicolai Copernici Torinensis, *De revolutionibus orbium coelestium, Libri VI,* Norimbergae, 1543 (Indiana University Lilly Library, Bloomington).

too will seem, unless I am mistaken, to make some contribution also to the Church, at the head of which Your Holiness now stands. (Translated by Edward Rosen).

These noble and courageous words testify, of course, to the courage of Copernicus himself, who, after years of hesitation, at the urgent request of his friends decided to bring out an edition of his revolutionizing work. At the same time these words exemplify the atmosphere of that time in Poland, the atmosphere of freedom and intellectual liberty.

In the history of Polish culture the year 1543 was a remarkable one. The appearance of Copernicus' work opened a new epoch in the perception of the universe. With the publication of the satirical work by Mikołaj Rej (called the father of Polish literature), *Krótka rozprawa między trzema osobami Panem, Wójtem a Plebanem* (A short conversation among three persons a Squire, a Bailiff, and a Parson) (Cracow, 1543), a new epoch of literature written in Polish began.

In the same year Andrzej Frycz Modrzewski (Andreas Fricius Modrevius), one of the most original political and social writers of the Renaissance, published his first treatise, *Ad Sigismundum Secundum Augustum . . . Lascius sive de poena homicidi, Oratio prima* (Cracoviae, 1543), in which he protested against social discrimination in the punishment of murder. Modrzewski's main work, *Commentariorum de Republica emendanda libri quinque* (Basileae, 1554, 1559), intended to embrace the entire system of the state in order to introduce reforms in the spirit of Christian morality and humanism, constitutes a significant and lasting contribution to European political and social thought of the Renaissance.

In the first half of the sixteenth century Latin poetry still flourished in Poland. Of the most famous poets writing exclusively in Latin were: the aforementioned Andrzej Krzycki (Cricius), a typical court poet known in humanistic circles; Jan Dantyszek (Dantiscus), who wrote patriotic and religious poems, and Klemens Janicki (Janicius), *poeta laureatus* (a title bestowed on him in Padua), the author of remarkable autobiographical elegies. Dantiscus played a notable role in Poland's international political and cultural relations at this time. One of the most accomplished diplomats of his day, and Polish ambassador at Madrid and Brussels, Dantiscus was not only a poet, but first of all a patron of scholars and writers. He was a friend and correspondent with the most outstanding personages of the time, such as Melanchthon, Erasmus of Rotterdam, and Sir Thomas More. While in the Netherlands, Dantiscus entered into close contact with the most prominent scholars there, such as Jan van der Campen, professor of Hebrew at Louvain. Dantiscus both encouraged van der Campen to undertake a poetic paraphrase in Latin of the Psalms, and then aided in their publication. The Psalms enjoyed immediate popularity, were printed numerous times, and translated into many languages. Dantiscus counted among his friends and proteges: Gemma Frisius, mathematician and geographer; Conrad Goclenius, professor of Latin literature; Jan Secundus, poet and medal maker; the German poet, Eoban Helius Hessus, who dedicated many of his works to Dantiscus; and many others.

The sixteenth century in Poland—the Renaissance or the Golden Age—is also the period of the Reformation. In the second half of the century, various currents of the Reformation movements were widespread in Poland, finding many adherents among powerful political figures as well as in intellectual circles. The spread of the Reformation in Poland was facilitated by the policy of religious tolerance then unique in Europe. Many specific features of the conditions existing in Poland, such as the Polish parliamentary system, astounded West European observers and travelers. Perhaps most remarked upon was Poland's religious tolerance, and the great diversity of faiths which lived together in peace and worshipped unimpeded. Fynes Moryson, in a chapter of the *Itinerary* (1617) of his journey to twelve European countries including Poland in 1593, wrote on this subject: "No people in the world are so much infected with the variety of opinions in Religion. Insomuch as it is proverbially sayd that if any men haue lost his Religion, he may find it in Poland, if it be not vanished out of the world."

The resolution of the Diet of 1555, reaffirmed and extended by the resolution of the so-called confederation of Warsaw in 1573, assured full freedom of religious confession in Poland.

The Reformation strongly influenced the cultural life of the country. In the disputes between different denominations, the need to appeal to the mass of the faithful caused a shift from Latin to Polish in religious writings. The most important results of this were the new translations of the Bible into Polish. A Lutheran translation of the New Testament was published in 1551-53. The first complete Catholic Bible in Polish was edited by Jan Nicz (called Leopolita) in 1561. The Calvinist translation of the Bible was published in 1553. The translation by the Arians was edited in 1572. A second Catholic Bible by Jakub Wujek appeared in 1599.

Calvinism played a particularly conspicuous role in the Reformation movement in Poland. This was due in great part to the fact that Calvinism gained many adherents among the politically influential magnate and gentry families, but also in some degree to the fact that the most eminent Polish religious reformer of the time, Jan Łaski, was closest in spirit to Calvinism. Calvin himself attached great significance to the growth of his church in Poland; he had high hopes for it, even anticipating the conversion of King Sigismund II August. Calvin's correspondence with the King and with leaders and organizers of the Calvinist Church in Poland testify eloquently to those hopes.

Theodor Bèze, at first chief assistant to Calvin and then his successor as head of the Reformed Church, continued Poland's close ties with Calvinism. A poet, theologian, professor of Greek at the Academy of Lausanne, and later professor of theology and rector of the Academy of Geneva, Bèze displayed a lively interest in the Reformation movement in Poland. He taught many of the large group of Polish Calvinists and conducted a voluminous correspondence with Poles. In his eulogies to church reformers, *Icones* (1580), he included a praise of Jan Łaski (Joannes a Lasco), entitled: "*Christianissimi apud Polonos restituti instauratores praecipui."* Prominent in the Reformation movement and organizer of Reformed congregations in England, Holland, and Germany, Jan Łaski returned to Poland toward the end of his life and worked there for the unification of the Reformed churches into a national church.

The spread of Calvinism in Poland, combined with the numerous groups of young Polish Calvinists studying in Basel and Geneva, stimulated increased Polish-Swiss cultural contacts in the mid-sixteenth century, as dedications inscribed in the works of Celius Secundus and Zacharias Ursinus testify.

Among the various trends in the Polish Reformation, the small religious movement known as the Polish Brethren, the Arians, Socinians, or Antitrinitarians, was the most radical in its new understanding of Christian doctrine and also in the field of social and political reform. Some of their adherents were theologians and writers whose contributions to Polish literature were outstanding. Their founders included people from different countries: from Italy, such as Faustus Socinus, from Switzerland, and elsewhere. They came to tolerant Poland, where their faith was not persecuted as a heresy. In their main center in Raków, they organized a flourishing Academy and a very active publishing house. The origin of their ideas lay in Renaissance rationalism. Along with Antitrinitarianism and the use of reason in the interpretation of the Holy Scripture, one of their basic convictions, which is repeated in the works of Faustus Socinus, Johann Crelius, and Samuel Przypkowski and which had repercussions in other countries as well, was religious tolerance. "We do not grant," wrote Przypkowski, "anyone the liberty to violate, in private or in public, the freedom of conscience, nor the liberty to propagate religion by force and violence."

The growing Counter Reformation forced the Polish Brethren to leave Poland. Some of them migrated to Holland, where they published in Amsterdam in 1665-1668 eight large volumes under the title *Bibliotheca Fratrum Polonorum,* containing the works of their most outstanding thinkers. The ideas of the Polish Brethren had great impact on the religious movements in the Netherlands and England, and their influence is visible especially in John Locke's *Letters on Toleration* and in the theological work of Isaac Newton. The Polish Brethren are considered to be predecessors of the Unitarian Church.

Poland's close cultural connections with Italy, already established in earlier centuries, flourished in the sixteenth century with particular vigor. One of the many examples of such connections in the second half of the sixteenth century are the letters of Paolo Manuzio to various prominent Poles; especially noteworthy are Manuzio's letters to the young Jan Zamoyski, future chancellor, hetman, and founder of the Academy of Zamość, and to Andrzej Patrycy Nidecki, philologist, humanist, and publisher of a work highly valued in the humanist world, a collection of unknown fragments of Cicero, accompanied by a superb commentary: *Fragmentorum M. T. Ciceronis . . .* (1561).

Michele Giovanni Bruto, an Italian historian forced to leave Italy because of his Reformation sympathies, arrived in Poland as had many of his predecessors.

He became secretary to King Stefan Batory and wrote a history of Hungary under the King's direction.

Cultural relations with the Netherlands, especially with the circle around Erasmus of Rotterdam dating from mid-century and subsequently developed and expanded by Dantiscus, are continued in the latter sixteenth century by Justus Lipsius, the most outstanding Dutch humanist after Erasmus. His many Polish friends included Jan Zamoyski, and the scholars and writers connected with the Zamość Academy, as well as the outstanding poet, Szymon Szymonowicz.

Sebastian Petrycy, professor at the University of Cracow and the most outstanding exponent of Renaissance Aristotelianism in Poland, represents the latter sixteenth-century development of Polish science. His translations of Aristotle's *Politics*, *Ethics*, and *Economics* continues the old tradition of social aristotelianism at the University of Cracow. The further development of Polish historiography is connected with the name of Marcin Kromer, a humanist educated at Cracow and Bologna, diplomat, and Royal Secretary. His extensive history of Poland to 1506, *De origine et rebus gestis Polonorum* (1555), beautifully written in the spirit of Renaissance historiography and intended for foreign readers, was highly respected both in Poland and in other countries, as was his *Polonia sive de situ* . . . (1577), a kind of encyclopedia containing a geographical, social, and political description of Poland.

The latter sixteenth century and beginning of the seventeenth are marked by a growing interest of other countries in Poland, its history, government, geography, and daily life. This is confirmed by the numerous reprints and translations of works about Poland and its contemporary life, as well as chapters on Poland in works on European history, on the governmental systems of European nations, and on the most important contemporary European events, of works containing impressions of European travel. This growing interest in Polish affairs is represented by the works of Jean Bodin, Giovanni Botero, Fynes Moryson and others. It is also confirmed by the increasingly numerous and more accurate maps of Poland in geographical works. Examples are Sebastian Münster's *Cosmographia universalis* of 1550, containing a chapter (dedicated to King Sigismund II August) on the Polish kingdom appended to the map of Poland and Hungary, the *Theatrum orbis terrarum* of Abraham Ortelius (1570), containing a map of Poland by Wacław Grodecki, and George Braun's *Civitates orbis terrarum* (1574-1618), containing magnificent color panoramas of Polish cities including laudatory texts. Outstanding among these is the magnificent view of Cracow, "Cracovia Metropolis Regni Poloniae." This large collection of views is a further visual proof of European interest in Poland and Poland's role in sixteenth-century Europe. Lastly, mention should be made of one of the editions of Ambrogio Calepino's *Dictionarum decem linguarum* (1594), the first edition to include the Polish, Hungarian, and English languages.

In the Polish Renaissance three of the best-known names who bear especially vivid witness to the exceptionality of this age in Poland are Nicolaus Coper-

7. One of the two panoramas of Cracow at the end of the XVI century. Engraving in George Braun, Franz Hogenberg, *Civitates orbis terrarum*, Cologne, 1574-1618 (Indiana University Lilly Library, Bloomington).

nicus, Andrzej Frycz Modrzewski, and Jan Kochanowski. Kochanowski, the greatest poet of the Polish Renaissance, admirably represents the spirit of his age in Poland. All Kochanowski's writings manifest both his organic ties with European Renaissance culture and his uniqueness—his original approach to humanist values such as individualism, formal perfection, and concern for moderation. Among the Renaissance poets Kochanowski is one who perhaps best personified the spirit of the high ideal of the Renaissance: moderation and harmony.

During the age of the Renaissance, Polish culture developed in lively and intimate connection, and in manifold intellectual exchanges with other national cultures through frequent close contacts with their outstanding representatives. Poland participated in a creative way in the formation of this age. The unique and original features of Poland's Renaissance culture arose from the spirit of democracy, freedom, and tolerance. This is Poland's contribution to what we consider the achievements of the European Renaissance and humanism.

In the year 1524, Erasmus of Rotterdam wrote to the Archbishop of Canterbury, William Warham, "Polonia mea est." Poland was well-disposed to Erasmus, as indeed she was toward the noblest expressions of political, social, and moral thought of Western European humanism, fostering such thought herself and enriching it with lasting values. Awareness of her creative participation and her full membership in the Western European circle of culture remains today, as in centuries past, a living tradition in the consciousness of the Polish nation.

Samuel Fiszman

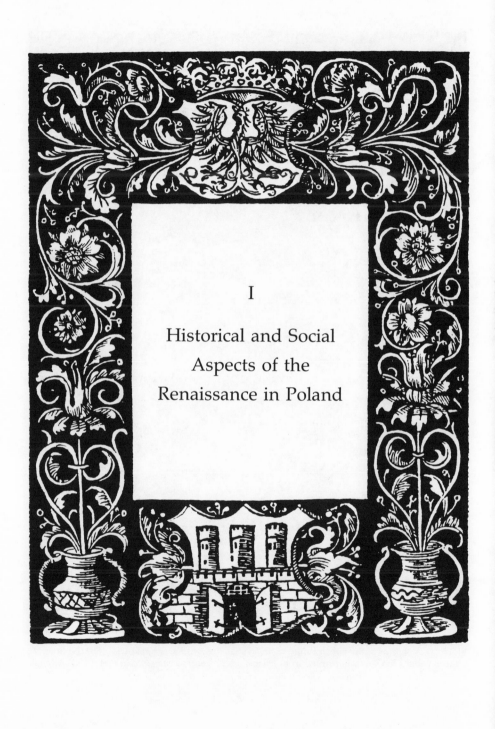

I

Historical and Social
Aspects of the
Renaissance in Poland

8. The coat of arms of the Polish Kingdom in Mikołaj Rej *Postilla*, w Krakowie, 1557 (Biblioteka Czartoryskich, Kraków). Reprinted from *Polonia typographica saeculi sedecimi*, vol. 9, ed. Alodia Kawecka-Gryczowa (Wrocław: Ossolineum, 1974).

1

Polish Historians and the Need for History in Fifteenth- and Sixteenth-Century Poland

Aleksander Gieysztor

The beginnings of the modern understanding of the world and society, nature and man date back in Poland as elsewhere to the fifteenth century. The polemics concerning the place of Jan Długosz and his works in the history of historiography indicate that it is difficult to accept a clear boundary between the Polish autumn of the Middle Ages and the early Renaissance.[1] His *Annales seu cronicae incliti Regni Poloniae*, written in the third quarter of the fifteenth century, have some pre-Renaissance characteristics.[2]

The first pre-Renaissance feature is the pragmatic attitude of the author towards his task of writing in the political service of the kingdom. This attitude, visible throughout this very large work, is also expressed in the foreword, a kind of a peculiar treatise on the theory of history as understood by the author. "From among all the sciences which serve to shape the mind there is none, in my opinion," wrote Jan Długosz, "which shines so marvelously nor has such value as history. For it is from it that we learn to live honestly, it is from it that we gather our largest benefits and at the same time, experiencing greater pleasure, we induce in ourselves the desire to imitate good acts while arousing disgust in bad ones."[3] History of this kind was a historian's obligation towards his own country: "each one has a debt to repay to his motherland, as much as one can afford depending on his capabilities and strength."[4] This debt Długosz repaid both with his work in the chancellery and in diplomacy and in his works on the history of the whole people of Poland from their beginnings to the Jagiellonians, and all this written against the background of general history.

Another characteristic which distinguishes him from previous chroniclers is his academic training, his inquisitiveness in searching for and enlarging his source base, together with the inclusion of the geographical picture of his country when writing down its history. No lesser importance should be attached to the ancient models, from Livy up to some of the contemporary Italian writers who opened the author's eyes to the possibilities of the construction and style of exposition and the pragmatic perspective of associating events.[5]

Długosz did not work in a vacuum. The fifteenth century brought to life an intellectual stratum connected primarily with Cracow University where historical consciousness pulsated, finding expression in collections of manuscripts, hagiographic, genealogical, and biographical writings. This historical consciousness can even be found in university lectures on the early thirteenth century chronicle of Master Vincent (Wincenty Kadłubek), where it was perceived as a model of style and a way for shaping the knowledge of the past.[6] The end of the fifteenth century brought a program of new synthesis, formulated within the circles of the intellectual and political elite and evolving mainly through the initiative of Piotr of Bnin, a bishop of Włocławek; Filippo Buonaccorsi Callimachus (Kallimach) was commissioned to draw up the program.[7]

Studies on Polish historiography and historical consciousness in Poland of the Golden Age, conducted during the last twenty five years, reveal a multidimensional presence of history in the intellectual life of the times. Homage was paid to the muse Clio, first of all by those who were greater or lesser professionals, i.e., historians studying Poland and its neighbors. The first royal historiographer, Mikołaj Rożemberski, was to undertake a salaried job in the year 1502; Bernard Wapowski became the next one in 1529.[8] The revolution in printing not only drastically enlarged the circle of consumers of the works of the small number of Polish historians, but it also especially affected the vast ancient classical historical literature—literature which shaped the cultural appetites of the contemporary intellectual elite and stratum of educated people already quite large in sixteeth-century Poland and Lithuania. Together with the works of modern historians from other countries, it created one of the pillars of the historical culture of the time upon which rested its arches and vaults.

Figurative art was one such arch; its iconography was characterized by the presence of the historical element, to mention only the series of monarchs' portraits at the Wawel castle or the paintings of battles (beginning with the Battle of Orsza with Muscovy in 1514).[9] Another such arch supporting contemporary culture consisted of *belles-lettres*, which began in 1516 with the Latin epos *Bellum Prutenum* by Jan of Wiślica about the Battle of Grunwald in 1410. Also included here is Maciej Stryjkowski's work in poetry and prose, *O początkach . . . sławnego narodu litewskiego . . .* (On the origins . . . of the famous Lithuanian nation . . .), written in the last quarter of the sixteenth century and finally published just some years ago.[10]

We will focus our comments on the pursuit of history by the historians themselves and especially on their theoretical reflection. One of the best experts on the subject, the late Stanisław Herbst, compared the then emerging feeling of historical perspective with the already established perspective in drawing and painting.[11] Measured historical time was formed by smaller or greater epochs, even if these only embraced the reigns of consecutive monarchs, and by concentrating the interests of the reader on a chronological series of events. It offered an insight into past history. In 1555 Marcin Kromer divided Polish history into three periods: the first, from the beginnings of Poland until the end of the division into duchies, the second, embracing the history of the unified kingdom until the death of Ladislaus III (Władysław Warneńczyk), and the third period, leading only up to 1506—the author carefully avoiding presentation of contemporary history.[12]

Another characteristic of historical writings was the desire to portray the past realistically, which was achieved by overburdening the general picture with details rightly or wrongly considered to be important. Considered important were those details relating especially to politics, which was understood as a struggle for power within the state and between states. Thus, we have two basic orientations in historiography: monarchic and noble, both valuing the hard facts of the past. "History as it was," *uti gestae fuerint*, was formulated three centuries before Leopold Ranke by Francesco Robortello in 1548, and it was incorporated into the theory and practice of Polish historians searching within the available sea of facts.[13] Such a state of mind prompted the need for continuous search for new source materials. Jan Długosz consciously presented this need in his works and among his successors the same need took on various forms. We have an enormous collection of about seven thousand public documents and political correspondence covering the reign of Sigismund I the Old (Zygmunt Stary) and collected by Stanisław Górski, who died in 1572 (the collection is known as *Acta Tomiciana*).[14] Initiated by Queen Bona, this collection is an example of the close attention which contemporary historical primary sources received at the time.

Historical writers assumed similar duties. Maciej, a burgher from Miechów (known as Miechowita), and a rector of Cracow University, followed the path of continuation and adaptation of the works of Długosz. He was the author of the geographical work describing the countries under the reign of the Jagiellonians (1517) and of the first printed Polish chronicle (1519) conceived as a textbook. In it he also boldly included current history, a decision which led to the confiscation of the four last sheets, which were reedited in the next edition (1521) and rewritten by Jan Łaski, Chancellor of the Crown.[15] Jodocus Ludovicus Decius (Decjusz), a royal diplomat and economist, turned out to be more cautious and closer to the views of the lords of the Royal Council. He is the author of a well-informed account of the first ten years of the reign of Sigismund the Old, included as the third part of the work entitled *De vetustatibus Polonorum* (1521).[16]

One should recall with praise the historical work of Stanisław Orzechowski, a talented political firebrand from the middle of the century. His *Annales Polonici ab excessu Divi Sigismundi Primi*, dated 1554, testify to his full mastery of the principles of Italian historical writing, but also reveal in particular the personal talent of the author.[17] Świętosław Orzelski, a diligent though uncreative author of two interregna (1572-76) histories,[18] was no match for King Stefan Batory's secretary, Reinhold Heidenstein. The latter was able to brilliantly apply the models of antiquity to the description of the wars with Moscow.[19] Orzelski also had to surrender the field to at least two others, Krzysztof Warszewicki (Varsevicius)[20] and Jan Dymitr Solikowski.[21]

Writings on both Polish and general history did not—with two exceptions—offer such possibilities as did current history with its political excitement. Those two honorable exceptions were: Marcin Kromer, a thorough writer with a gift for synthesis [22] and Maciej Stryjkowski who successfully utilized his impressive multilingual research capabilities not so much in the service of Clio, but of the Polish Calliope. Only today after its publication can we fully appreciate his verse and prose text.[23] Others satisfied themselves with the hardly ambitious task of compiling compendia: Stanisław Sarnicki (1587)[24] or Jan Herburt, whose shortened version of Kromer (1571)[25] was translated twice by Frenchmen. While with the exception of Stryjkowski, all those mentioned wrote in Latin, the *Kronika Wszytkiego Świata* (Chronicle of all the world) by Marcin Bielski (1551) and the *Kronika Polska* (Polish chronicle) added by his son, Joachim, in 1597, captured the interest of the nobility and gentry.[26]

Historical culture in countries under Jagiellonian rule came into existence through readings of Polish historians, sometimes of Italian and German writers, but as it has been already mentioned, it was influenced to a greater degree by readings of Roman and Greek historians. Works of the ancient world became the subject of serious studies in Poland. Andrzej Patrycy Nidecki was noted as a collector of the writings of Cicero. Benedykt of Koźmin published Cicero, Cornelius Nepos, and Pliny. In the middle of the sixteenth century, Herodotus was lectured on at Cracow University, and Andrzej Kochanowski tried his talent in translating Livy.[27] Roman law, another vital source of knowledge about the ancient world and its institutions, was studied by scholars in Cracow, Wilno, Toruń and Zamość.[28] There was a great flow of foreign editions of classics into Polish libraries, and the works of ancient historians appeared not only in private collections of such professionals as Maciej Miechowita, whose collection included practically every name from the ancient world. Such works were also present in the collections of such enlightened amateurs as Krzysztof Szydłowiecki, the Great Chancellor of the Crown and palatine of Cracow, or Piotr Tomicki, the bishop of Cracow and the vice-chancellor of the Crown.[29]

In this way, through readings and writing, views concerning the tasks of history took shape. These tasks can be and should be deciphered from the works of historians and writers. In them one can also find a writer's political and ethical reflections on his own work. But in the sixteenth century in Poland attempts were also made to formulate a theory of history.[30] This field was represented by a number of writers, none of whom, interestingly enough, was known as an author of works on either general or Polish history. The Polish authors of methodological statements on history were not writers of historical works; rather, they were attentive and critical readers of them. Thus, they were less interested in how to write history and more in how and what to read in history, mainly ancient history.

A concise and brief treatise by Stanisław Iłowski (1557) begins a series of such publications. The author, the son of a palatine of Płock, studied in Cracow, Padua, Paris, and Basel, where he gathered materials for his planned book, *De perfecto historico*. Although it remained under the influence of the work of Francesco Robortello (1548), *De perfecto historico* set its own requirements for history. And so Iłowski demanded from historians that they express themselves clearly in a language *potius quae est mathematicorum* and not one full of rhetoric. This seems to be an astonishingly prophetic demand for the formalization of the language used in historical writings. Among Iłowski's normative postulates, the following demands are worth mentioning: feats of the enemy should not be passed over in silence; do not judge people, because the evaluation of their behavior should be left up to the reader; do not moralize, for that is the task of philosophers, and not historians. In conclusion, there is a list of suggested readings, where, alongside the ancient authors, we find a few contemporary names, including Paolo Giovio and Sebastian Münster. There we also find instructions on how to take notes while reading and on putting together *locos virtutum communes*, i.e., behavioral stereotypes. The whole work is characterized by a large dose of common sense, expressed also in the warning not to take history literally as *magistra vitae*. "Let history be a simple story of public or private events relating to the same or different purpose through sustaining the chronological order of facts," wrote Iłowski, proclaiming a kind of teleology of the historical work and its chronological structure allowing the sequence of events in time and also the transitions of cities, states, and kingdoms to be shown.[31]

There existed at the same time another well-established convention of perceiving history as a set of pedagogical directives transmitted to the receiver through developed forms of rhetoric. In Poland this tendency was represented by Giovanni Michele Bruto, an Italian historian brought to Cracow by King Stefan Batory. In 1582 he published a treatise the aim of which was to point "the way and the idea on how to read writers." As to writing history, the author, referring to the king, called for praise of the intellectual freedom of a historian and defended the choice of a foreigner to the office of royal historiographer. The treatise, however, is mainly a stimulus for reading the works of renowned authors. These include classical writers and Niccolo Machiavelli as well. The conclusions stemming from Bruto's reflections can be summarized as the recognition of the practical benefits of history for the choice of directions in life and politics.[32]

The third text on the theory of history is a university speech presented by Jan Firlej, the son of the castellan of Radom. He also praises history as necessary *ad prudentiam politicam acquirendam*, but like Iłowski he appreciates history as a record of events, worth remembering and learning if only for themselves.[33]

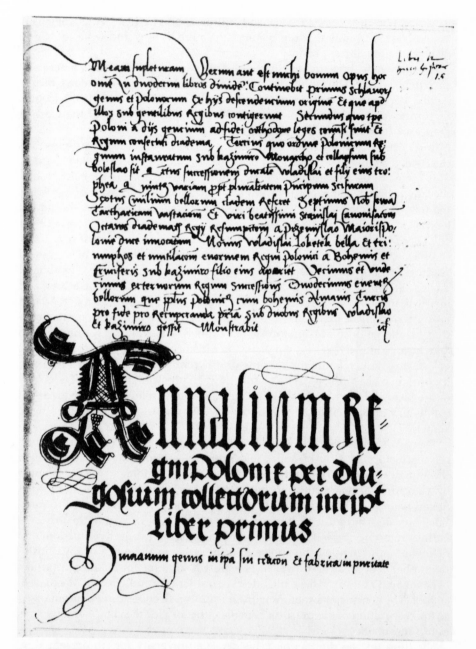

9. Jan Długosz, *Annales seu Cronicae incliti Regni Poloniae*. The page with the beginning of the first book in the manuscript copy—the so-called *Codex Regius* (Biblioteka Narodowa, Warszawa). Reprinted from Joannis Dlugossi, *Annales ...*, vol. 1-2 ed. Jan Dąbrowski (Varsaviae: PWN, 1964).

10. Maciej z Miechowa, *Chronica Polonorum*, Cracoviae, 1521. The title page (Indiana University Lilly Library, Bloomington).

11. Marcin Kromer, *De origine et rebus gestis Polonorum. Libri XXX*, Basileae, 1555. The title page. (Biblioteka Uniwersytecka, Warszawa). Photo Andrzej Bodytko.

12. Marcin Bielski, *Kronika, to jest Historia świata* (The Chronicle that is the History of the World), w Krakowie, 1564. The first page of the chapter describing Columbus' sailing. (Biblioteka Uniwersytecka, Warszawa). Reprinted from *Odrodzenie w Polsce*, vol. 2, part 2, ed. Bogdan Suchodolski (Warsaw: PIW, 1956).

We should conclude with the recollection of an author of remarkable intellectual stature and influence during his lifetime. In the 1610 posthumous edition of the collected lectures of Bartholomaeus Keckermann, a Gdańsk philosopher and educator, we find a very profound reflection on history. An advocate of what today we call political science, he demanded the inclusion of history in it: "without methodically conducted readings of historiographical works it is impossible to gain political foresight and carry out actions beneficial for the country." Far from offering naive advice about what to read, Keckermann points out the advantages of the comparative method. "If it is necessary to give advice to the Polish *res publica*," he writes, "it should be compared with the republics of Sparta, Rome, Venice and others and after comparing the existing forms we can offer some salutory advice also to the Polish *res publica*." This method he passed on to his pupils, among whom Mikołaj Siennicki wrote about Sparta, comparing it with Poland. Keckermann's treatise *De natura et proprietatibus historiae* had the characteristics of mature scientific work written by a professional philosopher. Such postulates about historiography as *universalia ex singularibus*, the requirements of erudition on the part of historians, the demand for integral history embracing the history of the school, law, grammar, philosophy, rhetoric, medicine, painting, sculpture, and printing are astonishing in their scope and maturity of expression. They were presented from the point of view of an observer of history and historiography and were quickly forgotten.[34]

The presence of theoretical reflection in the historical culture of the sixteenth century is evidence that the feeling of ties existing between history and current life was very much alive. It also reflects a faith in the didactic role of historiography. In this case the transmitting element was undoubtedly the political awareness of the citizens of the Jagiellonian state in the sixteenth century which sought in both Polish and general history points of reference and state and national self-identification. Observation of reality, including the past, and the conclusions drawn in accordance with rules set by the historian were to be useful instruments of the citizen's education. An acquaintance with national history both ancient and modern became a duty of the educated man. At the same time, he had to bear in mind the achievements of the ancient world which also offered material for reflection, material of an entirely secular nature. The laicization of historiography in the sixteenth century is seen especially clearly in comparison with Długosz. The sixteenth-century aim of a humanistically balanced approach on the part of the historian is vividly expressed in the ending of the long title of Maciej Stryjkowski's work: "from God's inspiration and from truly diligent experience." This does not mean an indifference of historians towards complex matters of faith. It also does not mean that they were fully critical, nor that they gave up ancient and later collective myths, especially the national supermyth about the first ruler Lech or the conviction of the Sarmatian origins of Poles or the Roman origins of Lithuanians.[35] Polish historiography of the sixteenth century was characterized by its own stylization of historical substance and by a very optimistic evaluation of its own creative value to society. As the above-mentioned Stryjkowski overzealously wrote: "one example from history concerning either domestic matters or war is worth more than a thousand problems raised by the best philosophers."[36]

Or as Jakub Górski more modestly, and following the Aristotelian *topos*, wrote in 1597: "who does not know history, and does not read what happened in the world, is ever as a small child."[37] The need for history had become an important part of intellectual perception.

Notes

1. See Maria Koczerska, "Mentalność Jana Długosza w świetle jego twórczości" (Jan Długosz's mentality in the light of his work), *Studia Źródłoznawcze* (hereafter *St. Źr.*), vol. 15, 1971, pp. 109-140; *Długossiana. Studia historyczne w pięćsetlecie śmierci Jana Długosza* (Długossiana: Historical studies on the five hundredth anniversary of the death of Jan Długosz) (Nakł. Uniwersytetu Jagiellońskiego, Warsaw: PWN, 1980); Władysław Tomkiewicz, "Przełom renesansowy w świadomości społeczeństwa polskiego XV i XVI wieku" (The renaissance turning-point in the consciousness of Polish society in the fifteenth and sixteenth centuries), in *Renesans. Sztuka i ideologia* (Warsaw: PWN, 1976), pp. 9-17, believes that the crucial point in historiography is marked by the names of Miechowita and Decjusz and their publications, 1517-1521.

2. Particularly pointed out by Ignacy Zarębski, "Problemy wczesnego odrodzenia w Polsce. Grzegorz z Sanoka-Boccaccio-Długosz" (Problems of the early Renaissance in Poland: Gregory of Sanok, Boccaccio, Długosz), *Odrodzenie i Reformacja w Polsce*, vol. 2, (Warsaw: PWN, 1957), pp. 5-12; *idem*, "Chronographia Regni Poloniae Jana Długosza a Giovanni Boccaccio," *St. Źr.*, vol. 18, 1973, pp. 181-189.

3. "Ex omnibus enim literis, que ad humanitatis comparata sunt studia, nulle michi splendidius relucere atque excellere vise sunt quam que rerum gestarum ordinem nobis commendant. Ex illis enim ad recte vivendum imbuimur, et singulares fructus et egregiam quandam iocunditatem comparamus, studio imitacionis accendimur et a pravis in recta revocamur." *Ioannis Dlugossi Annales seu cronicae incliti Regni Poloniae*, lib. 1-2, ed. Joannes Dąbrowski, Vanda Semkowicz-Zaremba (Varsoviae: PWN, 1964), p. 56.

4. "Unusquisque enim tantum in patriam debitor est quantum ingeni sui vires valent axsolvere." *Dlugossi Annales*, p. 61.

5. Cf. Wacława Szelińska, *Chorographia Regni Poloniae Jana Długosza* (Cracow: Wydawnictwo Wyższej Szkoły Pedagogicznej, 1980); Aleksander Gieysztor, "Polski homo mediaevalis w oczach własnych" (The Polish *homo mediaevalis* as seen by himself), in *Polaków portret własny* (Cracow: Wydawnictwo Literackie, 1979), pp. 19-31.

6. See Jacek Wiesiołowski, *Kolekcje historyczne w Polsce średniowiecznej XIV-XV w.* (Historical collections in medieval Poland, 14th-15th Centuries) (Wrocław: Ossolineum, 1967); Marian Zwiercan, *Komentarz Jana z Dąbrówki do kroniki mistrza Wincentego zwanego Kadłubkiem* (Jan of Dąbrówka's commentary on the chronicle of Master Vincent) (Wrocław: Ossolineum, 1969); Józef Szymański, "O recepcji Kroniki Wincentego w środowisku krakowskim w XV w.," (On

the reception of Vincent's chronicle in 15th century Cracow) *St. Źr.*, vol. 20, 1976, pp. 114-122; Maria Koczerska, "Piętnastowieczne biografie Zbigniewa Oleśnickiego," (Fifteenth-century biographies of Zbigniew Oleśnicki) *St. Źr.*, vol. 24, 1979, pp. 5-82; Jacek Banaszkiewicz, "Historia w popularnych kompilacjach, tzw. Poczet królów polskich," (History in popular compilations: The so-called gallery of Polish kings), in *Kultura elitarna a kultura masowa w Polsce późnego średniowiecza* (Wrocław: Ossolineum, 1978), pp. 211-229. See *Sztuka i ideologia XV w.* (Art and ideology in the fifteenth century), ed. Piotr Skubiszewski (Warsaw: PWN, 1978).

7. Bronisław Nadolski, *Kierunki rozwojowe dziejopisarstwa staropolskiego* (Directions of development in old Polish historical writings) (Lwów, 1938); Henryk Barycz, *Szlakami dziejopisarstwa staropolskiego. Studia nad historiografią w. XVI-XVIII* (Investigating old Polish historical writing: Studies in the historiography of the 16th-18th centuries) (Wrocław: Ossolineum, 1981), pp. 16ff.

8. Barycz, p. 18.

9. Stanisław Herbst, *Potrzeba historii czyli o polskim stylu życia* (The need for history, or on the Polish way of life), vol. 2, (Warsaw: PIW, 1978), pp. 501-502; Stanisław Mossakowski, *Sztuka jako zwierciadło czasu* (Art as the mirror of time) (Warsaw: Arkady, 1980), pp. 95-150.

10. Cf. Jan z Wiślicy, *Nowy Korbut*, vol. 3, *Piśmiennictwo staropolskie* (Old Polish literature) (hereafter *NK*) (Warsaw: PIW, 1965), pp. 399-401; on history and literature's historical consciousness, cf., Jan Malicki, *Mity narodowe. Lechiada* (National myths. Lechiada) (Wrocław: Ossolineum, 1982).

11. Herbst, vol. 1, p. 110.

12. Martinus Cromerus, *De origine et rebus gestis Polonorum libri XXX*, Basileae, 1555 (1558, 1568, 1582); Polish translation by Marcin Błażewski, 1611; *NK*, vol. 2, pp. 412-419.

13. *De facultate historica*, Florentiae, 1548.

14. Cf. *NK*, vol. 2., pp. 226-229.

15. *Tractatus de duabus Sarmatiis Asiana et Europiana et de contentis in eis*, Cracoviae, 1517 (ed. 1518, 1521, 1532, 1537, 1542, 1582), Polish translation by Andrzej Glaber of Kobylin, 1535; *Cronica Polonorum*, Cracoviae, 1519 (1521, 1582), Polish translation by Stanisław Chwalczewski before 1549, ed. 1824.

16. Cf. *NK*, vol. 2, pp. 120-123.

17. *NK*, vol. 3, pp. 47—57.

18. ed. 1917; *NK*, vol. 3, pp. 59-60.

19. *De bello Moscovitico commentariorum libri sex*, Cracoviae, 1584 (1588, 1600, 1672); posthumous edition, *Rerum polonicarum ab excessu Sigismundi Augusti libri XIII*, Francoforti, 1672.

20. *Turcicae tres*, Pragae, 1589, and *Turcicae quatuordecim*, Cracoviae, 1595; *Rerum polonicarum liber XIII* (ed. Florence 1827); cf. *NK*, vol. 3, pp. 376-380.

21. *Commentarius brevis rerum polonicarum a morte Sigismundi Augusti . . .*, Gedani, 1647; *NK*, vol. 3, pp. 270-275.

22. Cf. Barycz, pp. 83ff. on the beginnings and the reception of Kromer's work.

23. Maciej Stryjkowski, *O początkach, wywodach, dzielnościach, sprawach rycerskich i domowych sławnego narodu litewskiego, żemojdzkiego i ruskiego, przedtym nigdy od żadnego ani kuszone, ani opisane, z natchnienia Bożego a uprzejmie pilnego doświadczenia* (On the beginnings, origins, virtues, military and domestic affairs of the glorious Lithuanian, Samogitian, and Rus' nation, previously by no one either attempted or described, from God's inspiration and truly diligent experience) ed. Julia Radziszewska (Warsaw; PIW 1978); Prior to this publication Stryjkowski was known primarily as the author of a chronicle in prose with some poetical inclusions, . . . *Kronika polska, litewska, zmódżka, i wszystkiej Rusi* (A chronicle of Poland, Lithuania, Samogitia and all Rus') (Królewiec, 1582). About this chronicle, see Aleksandr Ivanovich Rogov, *Russko-pol'skie kul'turnye sviazi v epoxu vozrozhdenija (Stryjkovskii i ego Xronika)* (Russian-Polish cultural connections in the Renaissance Period: Stryjkowski and his chronicle) (Moscow, 1966); Juliusz Bardach, *Studia z ustroju i prawa Wielkiego Księstwa Litewskiego (XIV—XVII w.)* (Studies on the political system and law of the Grand Duchy of Lithuania) (Warsaw: PWN, 1970), pp. 68-85.

24. *Annales sive de origine et rebus gestis Polonorum et Lituanorum libri octo,* Cracoviae, 1587; *NK*, vol. 3, pp. 216-219; Barycz, pp. 52f. on the king's and Jan Zamoyski's orders and the disappointment of the author, and on Jan Kochanowski's polemics with Sarnicki's views about old Polish history.

25. *Chronica sive Historiae Polonicae compendiosa . . . descriptio.* Basileae, 1571 (1584, 1609, 1615, 1643, 1658); *NK*, vol. 2, pp. 257-259; Barycz, pp. 162f.

26. *NK*, vol. 2, pp. 24-31. Another way of considering the past was heraldry and genealogy of noble families and clans treated as a specific historical and literary branch of writing. Bartosz Paprocki, *Gniazdo cnoty* (The nest of virtue), Cracow, 1578; *Herby rycerstwa polskiego* (The arms of the Polish knighthood), Cracow, 1584; cf. *NK*, vol. 3, pp. 81-85.

27. Paweł Rybicki in *Historia nauki polskiej* (The History of Polish Science), vol. 1 (Wrocław: Ossolineum, 1970), pp. 365f; cf. vols. 6, 7 (1974-5). Bio-bibliographical information s.v.

28. Rybicki, *Historia,* p. 379f.

29. Leszek Hajdukiewicz, *Biblioteka Macieja z Miechowa* (The library of Maciej of Miechów) (Wrocław: Ossolineum, 1960), and *Księgozbiór i zainteresowania bibliofilskie Piotra Tomickiego na tle jego działalności kulturalnej* (Piotr Tomicki's library and bibliophilic interests in the context of his cultural activities) (Wrocław: Ossolineum, 1961); Barycz, p. 79.

30. Marceli Handelsman, *Zagadnienia teoretyczne historii* (Theoretical problems of history) (Warsaw, 1919), p. 37f.; Aleksandr Gieysztor, "Teorija istoricheskoj nauki v Pol'she XVI v." (The theory of historical science in 16th-century Poland), in *Kul'turnye sviazi narodov Vostochnoj Evropy v XVI v.* (Cultural ties between the peoples of eastern Europe in the 16th century) (Moscow, 1976), pp. 32-43.

31. "De historica facultate libellus," in Demetrius Phalereus, *De elocutione liber,* Basileae, 1557; *NK*, vol. 2, pp. 277-278; Barycz, pp. 43-44; Janina Czer-

niatowicz, Bronisław Nadolski in *Polski Słownik Biograficzny* (Polish biographical dictionary), vol. 10, 1962-1964, pp. 160-161.

32. *De historiae laudibus sive de certa via et ratione qua sunt rerum scriptores legendi*, Cracoviae, 1582; Barycz, pp. 49-50.

33. *Oratio de studio historico*, (Heidelberg, 1604); *Historia nauki polskiej*, vol. 6, pp. 156-7.

34. *De natura et proprietatibus historiae commentarius*, Gedani, 1610; *Historia nauki polskiej*, vol. 6, pp. 293-4; Bronisław Nadolski, *Życie i działalność uczonego gdańskiego Bartłomieja Keckermanna* (The life and work of the Gdańsk scholar Bartholomeus Keckermann) (Toruń: Towarzystwo Naukowe w Toruniu, 1961).

35. Tadeusz Ulewicz, "Zagadnienie sarmatyzmu w kulturze i literaturze polskiej. Problematyka ogólna i zarys historyczny" (The problem of Sarmatism in Polish culture and literature: General problems and historical outline), *Zeszyty Naukowe Uniwersytetu Jagiellońskiego*. 59. *Prace Historycznoliterackie*, no. 5, 1963.

36. Stryjkowski, p. 39.

37. Jakub Górski, *Rada Pańska* (Council of Lords), ed. Wiktor Czermak (Cracow, 1892), p. 54.

2

Polish Society and Power System in the Renaissance

Antoni Mączak

The title of this essay intentionally limits the scope of our discussion to society on the territory of the Polish-Lithuanian Republic and excludes problems of language and national consciousness. Further, the term Renaissance is used to define the epoch under consideration, even though there may be some doubt whether this phenomenon constitutes an adequate eponym for the period in Poland. Therefore, we shall consider the Renaissance here as standing only for a broad chronological frame for that period beginning at the close of the fifteenth and ending in the first half of the seventeenth century at the latest. But a description of Polish society within that period of time requires certain additional points of reference. It also demands a separation of theses which have been accepted on the basis of thorough research from those which only fill in gaps and seal up cracks in our knowledge—though we often fail to differentiate between these two.

Michael Postan used to say that there were probably only two historical events which had not been explained by the "rise of the middle classes": the October Revolution in Russia and the partitions of Poland. And indeed, that interpretation has not been useful as a master key with which to open up all the puzzles of Poland's historical development.[1] On the contrary, in Poland we have become accustomed to a conception which posits a steady, long-term polarization of wealth within society, beginning in the Middle Ages and going on up to the time of the national uprisings in the nineteenth century. Examined in the context of a shorter period, this thesis does not arouse any reservations and the evidence collected in its support is quite imposing. But when approached from a longer time perspective the following question arises: if the process of polarization lasted so long, then does it not mean that Polish society at the threshold of the modern era would have been very egalitarian? An affirmative answer would contradict the direct information we have about that period.

Another question arising from comparisons over a long period of time concerns relative economic development. Stagnation and economic recession, once considered the result of destruction suffered during the wars and invasions of the mid-seventeenth century, had begun earlier, both in rural districts and in towns. Thus, the period in question has come to be considered by historians a high point in the development of Polish society in pre-partition times.[2] I do not propose to reject this conclusion, but certain gaps in this picture should be examined. The cohesion of Polish society and the Polish power system in Renaissance times must be reexamined in order to decide whether it should be treated as a system of hypotheses or as a system of proven facts.

Economically, the nearly 150 years under review witnessed the development of the serf labor system and of the export of grain. Contrary to popular views, the interrelationships between those two phenomena are neither simple nor obvious. First, serf labor manorial farms appeared prior to the demand from overseas; secondly, they developed in other places than those from which the floating of goods to Gdańsk was most convenient. Leonid Żytkowicz has remarked that the development of serf labor and demesne farming has been most marked in places where peasant farms were very small, that is, where they constituted potential reservoirs of labor;[3] in modern terms one may speak about disguised unemployment. These were not the regions from where the transport was the easiest. Were a map of demesne farms to be drawn and interpreted, many complicating factors would appear. There is no simple or unequivocal explanation for convergences of demographic, social, market, legal, and political structures. Any attempt at elucidation can be treated only as an introductory simplification.

Against this background, of particular significance is another hypothesis of the same scholar linking the choice of serf labor as a form of rent with the low yield ratios of grain. When the expected yield ratio was about three and the farming technique was unable to eliminate huge fluctuations in crops, the increasing claims of landowners could not be met by rises in money rents but only by increased serf labor.[4] Seen from this angle, the sixteenth century is no longer a time of efficient agriculture: soon its yield dropped by one-third following unfavorable structural changes in the agrarian economy. The matter is even further complicated by organizational and social changes whose importance had nothing to do with labor productivity and technique.

The origin of the drive to raise rents which emerged at the turn of the fifteenth and in the early years of the following century is still unexplained. Why were the landlords no longer satisfied with money rents used increasingly in Poland since the thirteenth century? Jerzy Topolski has proposed a hypothesis which cannot be presented briefly without undue simplification. It consists in a specific rivalry between the nobility and the middle class all over Europe. The development of the urban economy and the growing wealth of the patriciates and the merchant classes were endangering the status of landowners, forcing them to look for effective forms of intensive exploitation of the properties and tenants.[5] With respect to the Polish territories, this argument in my opinion lacks justification, for where the rivalry between the gentry and the towns was clearly noticeable, and the towns could not only impress but also directly threaten the nearby landowners—that is, in Royal Prussia on the Lower Vistula—serfdom and serf labor were both weak and late in development.[6]

Several factors may have accounted for the drive to raise rents and the dissatisfaction with them. Where mass socio-economic phenomena are concerned, a specific factor such as demand may not always act directly. Imitation becomes an autonomous factor, all the more so, as not every restructuring of a landed estate turns out to be both effective and advantageous from the point of view of its owner's interests. The manner in which those interests could be met when the estate concerned was vast differed radically from that applicable to a single manor property. Great landowners established connections with the Gdańsk, Königsberg (Królewiec), or Riga markets and usually maintained them permanently.[7] Small landowners (with the exception of the Lower Vistula region) began to imitate them only around the middle of the sixteenth century. Considered here is trading on a scale of some importance both as concerns the volume of goods exported and the number of producers. It remains an open question whether they established any permanent contacts with their customers-merchants in Gdańsk and if so, when, and to what extent.

During the fifteenth and early sixteenth century gentry in many regions could still increase their income by enlarging the land under cultivation through settling new tenants and in that way clearing more land. Characteristically, seeing to these matters was considered by the squires to be the main duty of the village reeve (Pol. *sołtys*; Lat. *scultetus*). However, the *sculteti* were not always interested in making their lords richer and tended "*sicut vermes in parietibus*" ("like worms eating wood") to take over untenanted wasteland and till it themselves. In these cases, a well-to-do landowner, wanting to raise his income, had to eliminate as a competitor the reeve who was not content with his income from administration of justice, village inn, mill, etc.

The raising of money rents was a difficult process where the population was scarce, and there was, consequently, a low supply of tenants wanting to rent a holding. If the rent was to be raised sufficiently high, an adequate supply of money was necessary. Here a feedback situation can be seen, for the development of money rents conditioned, and contributed to, a faster circulation of money. The simplest solution seemed to force the peasant to work in the landlord's fields. This made it possible to use the reserves of manpower, to lower capital expenditure to a minimum, and to develop wasteland. It should be noted that every acre of demesne brought to the squire or the landlord much more than the same acreage of his tenants' farms. This fact played a significant role in the small squires' calculations. The negative consequences of such a system emerged only after many decades. The tenants had felt them earlier: in some regions there was a clear slump in demand for cheap sorts of textiles already in the 1580's, and this seriously affected local industries. The landowners felt the depression rather later, as a matter of fact, only in the following century when market disturbances coincided with desertions of peasants and when there was already a marked drop in yields; some observers attributed that phenomenon to the low quality of tools and draft animals brought to the demesne by impoverished serfs.[8] Yet the sixteenth century had managed serf labor quite well.

I shall pass over the relatively well-known mechanism of economic regression, pointing only to some of its consequences. First, it was precisely about the middle of the sixteenth century that Polish society came into contact with western Europe in many spheres and on a fairly large scale. In terms of economics, it was exactly the scale that was significant. Secondly, all the economic processes in the country favored the great landowners, the magnates.

International commercial relations do not function on the principle of conjoint vessels. The opening of a flow of goods does not necessarily mean the equalization of living standards and/or the convergence of management systems. Compared with several Central European countries such as Silesia, Upper Hungary (i.e., Slovakia), Bohemia, or Saxony with their rich mineral deposits and thriving urban centers, Poland of the sixteenth century was a poor country. Polish scholars are correct when they emphasize the monocultural character of her economy. But we often do not realize how poor this country was as a whole in comparison to its principal trading and political partners.[9] This fact is verified by examining the expenses undergone by travelers in Europe in the sixteenth century. The map of the costs of living is very differentiated. The countries on the Rhine and the Upper Danube, the towns of Switzerland, Lombardy, central Italy, England and of many provinces of France were expensive. Less so was the North, while for Westerners the East was simply cheap. The costs depended upon the prices of products and on the quality of services. Low prices indicate weakly developed markets, low demand, and a poorly developed money economy. In the then northeast Germany, Denmark, or Poland the infrastructure, that is, roads and other transport facilities, inns, etc., was little developed, and towns worth that name were scarcer. Fynes Moryson was so impressed by his observations there that he ventured to formulate a general law of living costs in their relation to the strength of states. "And in truth," he wrote after having seen more countries than even the "well traveled" among his contemporaries, "myselfe having in Poland and Ireland found a strange cheapnesse of all such necessaries, in respect they want and the more esteeme silver, this observation makes me of an opinion much contrary to the vulgar, that there is no more certaine signe of a flourishing and rich commonwealth, than the deare price of these things (excepting the yeares of famine), nor any greater argument of a poore and weake State, than the cheape price of them."[10] But it is not the impressions of travelers that are of importance here; they only pinpoint phenomena which are more difficult to grasp on the basis of other sources (although, incidentally, Moryson supplies copious quantitative data which are astonishingly exact and endorse his view).

Significant here are the consequences of such a state of affairs. Low prices multiplied by low productivity and subsistence economy, taking into account a relatively sparse population, indicate the country's poverty. In the sixteenth and seventeenth centuries the plentifulness of food was quoted as a favorable symptom, yet the figures are contradictory. Władysław Czapliński has pointed out that the polemical pamphlets of the early seventeenth century also speak of famines, while Andrzej Wyczański, in presenting the high calorie content of the food consumed by at least some groups of the rural population (manorial servants and laborers), has shown that it contained only an insignificant amount of fat and proteins.[11] This seems to confirm the hypothesis put forward long ago by Marian Małowist that the situation of tenants in the money-rent period was so favorable that the pressure of the serf labor system made itself felt only at the turn of the sixteenth century or even in the seventeenth. But what is the connection with the low yields mentioned previously?

Discussions about the economics in the sixteenth century, conducted both in those times and by contemporary students of the Renaissance period center upon the paramount criterion of *supply*, not of demand, as determining what is currently thought to denote prosperity. This criterion is characteristic of pre-industrial economies (and can be applied to contemporary non-capitalist economies as well). Polish early modern writers are often intoxicated with the abundance of grain in the country, of its timber and wool. But even among them there are those who express their anxiety because of the unfavorable structure of foreign trade and the prices of imported goods. A study of prices confirms this anxiety, often dressed in moralizing guises, and suggests certain conclusions.

In the field of continental trade, Poland sold her products cheaply while she bought industrial goods, spices, and overseas foodstuffs dearly. Although the huge demand for Polish goods assured that the entire volume of goods delivered to the ports would be sold, the long-term consequences were not favorable. As the export of Polish raw materials and food facilitated the industrialization and expansion of the European West, so it increased at the same time the difference between the development levels of Poland (and other countries in a similar position) and of the European core. More immediately, trading was taken over by foreigners who drew principal profits from it and controlled the levers of trade. When the intermediary was a city of the Commonwealth, that is, Gdańsk, it acted in this—and only in this—respect like an outside partner, vitally interested in the development of trade but in a way detrimental to the advancement of the hinterland.[12]

In the sphere of political confrontation, since the volume of fine metals in circulation was relatively small, the means at the disposal of the central authorities were proportionately low and certain constitutional factors further reduced them. This adversely affected Poland's combat readiness. At a time when armies grew in numbers, when artillery was getting more guns, when firearms for the infantry were in general use and navies were beginning to emerge, war became a genuinely royal pastime because it was extremely costly. What is more, armed forces in the otherwise generally cheap and relatively poor countries of the eastern part of Europe were no less expensive than in the West. No goods had as large a market as the soldier's services, and throughout the continent the prices for mercenaries were more constant than the prices of other goods.

This should be kept in mind when examining the social and political structure of the kingdom. The decentralization trends, active since the close of the sixteenth century, and the earlier extensive fiscal privileges of the nobility significantly diminished the part of the national income paid into the treasury. We know that this income, particularly in its money sector, was low. It is widely known how disproportionate were the armed forces of the partitioning powers to those of the Commonwealth in the eighteenth century. Two hundred years earlier the ratio of the forces was different but in relation to the European powers there was already a greater difference than would seem natural simply from the comparison of differences in the population of the respective countries.

Particularly important was the distribution of national income and national wealth. The expansion of the serf labor economy meant a drop in the peasants' share of both wealth and income. Of a similar character, *mutatis mutandis*, was the economic recession of towns beginning in the early seventeenth century;[13] this, however, is more difficult to determine. But even within the nobility itself changes occurred of no less importance. Scanty but univocal evidence indicates that a process of concentration of landed property was steadily taking place, possibly accelerated under the Vasas (1587-1668).[14] This adversely affected small landowners (having one or a few manors) who would lose their lands to their richer neighbors. On the other hand, there was no drop in the number of petty squires and noble freeholders (*szlachta zagrodowa* or homestead gentry) who were spread not only throughout Mazovia and Podlasie (which were proverbial petty-gentry regions), but also all over the other provinces. Thus, while in political life the gentry was winning a measure of independence and even actively opposing the magnates, in the economic sphere the supremacy of the magnates was a foregone conclusion.

An assessment of Polish society during the Renaissance depends upon whether the historian is searching for the origins of developments which dominated the seventeenth century or whether he seeks to compare it to the prevailing contemporary features in Europe. Renaissance Poland was a society at a crossroads. Socio-economically, the Renaissance constituted primarily a transition period between the late Middle Ages and the seventeenth century, a transition period which in Poland was determinative for the future.[15] Hence, the sixteenth century seems to have left less specific and lasting features than the succeeding one. It was both a relic of the Middle Ages and an augury for the next difficult century with its drop in the population, economic depression, and money crisis. There are obviously good reasons for emphasizing the spread of literacy, printing presses, the progress and peculiar values of Polish Renaissance art, a fruitful match of Italian influences with local patronage and taste. However, the economic historian cannot close his eyes to the portentous increase of serfdom and its influence upon the urban economy. The latter half of the sixteenth century was a time when all those various social phenomena counterbalanced one another in a particularly favorable way. In the economy, the growth of demesne farms and the favorable (at the very close of the century) terms of trade led to an increase in the incomes of all the landowners with a surplus of marketable produce; there were as yet no visible negative results of the beginning pauperization of the peasantry (although this still needs further study) and concentration of estates at the hands of the magnates.

In political life, the *executio iurium* movement was finding massive support among the gentry, contributing to a high level of political involvement among this class. *Executio iurium*, or "execution of laws", was a movement among gentry represented in the *Sejm* or Diet or the Chamber of Deputies who sought—either with or without the king—to strengthen the state against the magnates. The rising tide of the Reformation and its subsequent ebb, together with serious problems facing the gentry in connection with three free royal elections, educated the gentry politically. The influx of new families into the elite, both secular and ecclasiastical, the opening, especially under King Stefan Batory, of prospects for advancement through distinguished military service, constituted a *novum*, favorable at the time, but which in the long run could not stop decentralizing and oligarchic trends.

The same developments brought a change in cultural life which seems as obvious as it is difficult to perceive. Political and religious writings, prints, and leaflets, family records (*silvae rerum*) all indicate intellectual activity much more widespread than before. Trips to north Italian universities, to Wittenberg and Königsberg (chartered 1544, and where Poles were particularly numerous and influential), and to other schools of international repute, both Protestant and Catholic (Strasbourg, Leyden, Louvain, Orleans), were more frequent at the close of the sixteenth and the beginning of the next century than before or after. The young Polish nobleman traveling with his governor through Europe between 1560 and 1650, met friends everywhere, as did his English counterpart.

International cultural relations were only a spectacular symptom of a much deeper phenomenon: the general spread of education. More recent studies of the Catholic school system in the second half of the sixteenth century indicate large numbers of parish schools. Historians tend to agree that this was no mere statistical fiction and that children of various classes, who were later to follow different paths, were taught the rudiments of knowledge there. The spread of education is, however, another characteristic paradox of Polish Renaissance society. The development of elementary education coincided with the trend to pull down the peasants to a level comparable in some respects with slavery, while the gentry was increasingly monopolizing the better and middle ranking positions in many spheres of life, such as the Church or the law.[16]

Cōmune incliti Polonie Re
gni priuilegium cōstitutionũ
z indultuũ publicitus decretorum approbatorũq3.cum
nōnullis iuribus tā diuinis ꝗ humanis pSere
nissimum principē et dñm dominũ Alexādrum
deigratia Regem polonie magnumduce Lith-
zvanie Russie iPrussieꝗ dñm et heredē rc. Non
tamen in illudipsum priuilegiũ sed motu pprio
regio serenitatis sue p adhortationē p istructiõe
Regnicolarũ.proꝗregni eiusdē.ac iustitie statu
feliciter dirigēdis eidē priuilegio ānexis z ascri-
ptis.Mandāreꝗ sacra eadem Maiestate accu-
ratissime castigatis.

13. Jan Łaski, *Commune incliti Poloniae Regni privilegium*, Cracoviae, 1506. Title page with the woodcut: Chancellor Jan Łaski presenting King Aleksander the Jagiellon with the collection of statutes of Polish public and judicial law which was drawn up on the initiative of the *Sejm* and the king's recommendation. (Biblioteka Uniwersytecka, Warszawa). Photo Andrzej Bodytko.

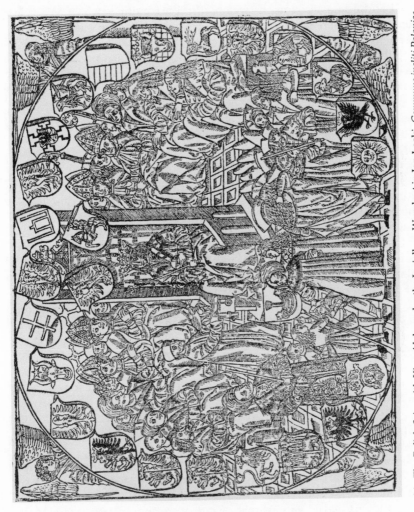

14. The Polish *Sejm* with King Aleksander the Jagiellon. Woodcut in Jan Łaski, *Commune incliti Poloniae Regni privilegium*, Cracoviae, 1506 (Biblioteka Uniwersytecka, Warszawa). Photo Andrzej Bodytko.

The spread of education was in part a response to the intellectual successes of Protestantism. This can be seen in the mushrooming of Jesuit colleges which began at the close of the sixteenth century. Next to the increase in printed matter the religious and political conflicts of the time spawned a mass of pamphlets, handwritten and included in family *silvae rerum*. The *word*, that is news, opinions, witticisms, seemed worthier of recording than the *figure*, that is, household and estate accounts, as well as fiscal accounting, which as a rule were kept badly. Where such accounts were being kept, no one seemed to care to preserve them thoroughly.

Among the specific features of Renaissance society in Poland and Lithuania was the coexistence of various faiths. The tradition of the neighborly political coexistence of Catholics and Orthodox Christians had created a precedent which proved very valuable when it became necessary to establish relations between Catholicism and several Protestant denominations.[17] Religious tolerance—or as Juliusz Bardach more aptly terms it, religious freedom—constitutes a particularly cherished element of the Polish civilization of the Renaissance. An extremely complex phenomenon, the future of the Reformation (and religious freedom) was decided at the close of the reign of Sigismund Augustus (Zygmunt August, d. 1572). While toying with the idea of a national church, he nevertheless did not secularize Church estates (a fact emphasized by Jarema Maciszewski).[18] The Protestants were divided, so that even when the Lutherans and the Calvinists allied, the Unitarians were excluded. The election of a Protestant king was never seriously envisaged; Protestants always voted for Catholic zealots (Henri de Valois, Stefan Batory, Sigismund Vasa) in order to avoid having a Habsburg on the throne. The political freedoms of heretic noblemen were a consequence of the political system; its alternative was the recognition of strong prerogatives for a central authority, which meant absolutism. On the other hand, the gentry could not imagine the republic without a king, and as has been emphasized in oral discussions by Włodzimierz Dworzaczek, many of the less determined and more easily influenced people considered that the order of the world required a harmonious coexistence between their own faith and the ruling Church; the multitude of Protestant denominations in Poland was their weakness, the popular mind still was not ripe for separating the Church from the State. And the nobles in Poland-Lithuania liked their State; they knew it was *theirs*.

Irrespective of the choice of years from which to date the economic decline of the Commonwealth, bright lights still dominate the shadows in the late sixteenth century. This applies particularly to towns. In early modern European societies the towns played various roles. Crafts were concentrated there (or at least the management of cottage industries located in the countryside); trading was also centered there, for just as the weekly fair was a privilege chartered to a town or its owner, so a brisk market was a very important part of town economic life. But in the fourteenth and fifteenth centuries Central European towns had also won an important political status. With strong economic assets, strong against knights and dukes always in need of credit, aided by the unstable balance between the rulers and the estates, many cities were able to attain a significant, sometimes even a decisive role in the state. As for the area in question, evidence of this may be found in their function of guarantor of international agreements, in the political and military activity of the Hanseatic cities, and particularly in the role played by Prussian towns in the victory of Poland over the Teutonic Order. In the Renaissance this splendid stage in the towns' political development was completed. In Poland only the towns of Royal Prussia backed by their wealth and the tradition of resistance to the Teutonic Order, still enjoyed a political balance with the gentry in their province, but after the Union of 1569 they, too, were not included in the representation of their province in the *Sejm* or Diet. According to a hypothesis put forth by Konstanty Grzybowski, the Polish towns in the fifteenth century were not so much excluded from the Sejm as they themselves did not wish to be represented in it for, according to prevailing political concepts, participation in the debates would bind them to abide by the resolutions voted during the session. [19]

It might be said that the great cities of Germany and Italy had also lost their political position, that in the West the trend was even more evident either because of suppressed revolts (as in Spain), or because of the loss of real if never formal sovereignty (as in the case of Hanseatic towns), or else because of changes in the political system (as in Florence under the grand dukes). But in these cases the economic functions of towns differed from those in Poland. In the West, towns limited in the sphere of politics developed economically. In Poland, on the other hand, the prime feature of towns was a lack of capital and their defensive attitude in the face of the openly or indirectly hostile policy of the gentry. Apart from a few, mostly Prussian larger cities, and apart from large emporia, the towns were receding in importance. The new function of some towns as centers of big estates was one clearly subordinated to the interests of the landed gentry. [20] In Renaissance Poland politics and economy became linked because in the latter part of the sixteenth century the towns of the Commonwealth—with the notable exception of Gdańsk—gave up trying to influence politics of the state through their natural means: money.

Many elements of the economic life upon which Polish Renaissance society was based were determined geographically. This accounts in particular for variations in the intensity of economic life. Poland-Lithuania lay in a transition zone; her geo-economic position has been discussed recently by Immanuel Wallerstein, using the concepts of core, semi-peripheries, and peripheries, and by Artur Attman in connection with the intercontinental circulation of precious metals. [21] These theories will not be discussed here. Instead, I shall concentrate on the interplay of geographical determinants and the factors of politics and constitution.

What in the Empire of the early sixteenth century and in the Duchy of Prussia several decades later was a kind of utopia, the dream of some dreamers and ideologues, came true in Poland: a democracy of, or perhaps for, the gentry,

a *monarchia mixta* with a particularly strong position for the Chamber of Deputies. It is easy to draw in Poland the same lines of class conflicts that are
well known from other countries: landowners and the peasantry, noblemen
and townspeople, the feudal elite (the magnates) and the lesser gentry, etc.
However, these took on specific features when a strong central authority was
lacking. While this did occur in several other countries as well, the difference
in the trends was crucial: in Poland, the state was weakening from the close
of the Renaissance discussed here, while elsewhere it was gaining in strength.

European princes based their power on a more or less skillful playing off of
the estates. The Polish Jagiellons had difficulties in this game and during the
whole of the fifteenth century conceded more and more freedoms to the nobility. This was by no means unique in Europe, but the Jagiellons found themselves in the sixteenth century in Poland with no levers to use for the
strengthening of their position. The first years of the century witnessed a
dramatic parliamentary struggle between the magnates entrenched in the Senate and the rank and file nobility defending—and in fact increasing—the constitutional role of the Chamber of Deputies. From that time on, kings could
support only one of these parties and use it for their own goals, or (from the
end of our period) to create their own regalist (i.e., royalist) party. Already
Sigismund Augustus, a master of parliamentary tactics, could choose only
between the senators and the *executio iurium* party of the gentry.[22] No longer
was there any question of intervention in the lord's jurisdiction over his tenants.
What was probably still more important, the king had a limited choice of his
officials.

The prosopographic research into power elites in Poland has only just come
into its own. Evidence is lacking for prosopographical studies similar to those
of Lawrence Stone or G.E. Aylmer for England, or Knud J.V. Jespersen et al.,
for Denmark.[23] Yet without doubt the host of royal servants did not increase
and close their ranks in Poland, and some crucial offices—like that of the *starosta
grodowy*, responsible for the law and order in a district and representing the
king's will there—was becoming a mere member and representative of the local
establishment. Zbigniew of Tęczyn in 1485-1496 and Ambrose Pampowski in
1504-1510 as royal *capitanei* (*starostowie*) in Malbork (Marienburg) represented
the earlier concept of that office.[24] Several persons are also known who identified themselves strongly with royal power and the state as such. And yet
neither the schools nor the royal court became training grounds for the cadres
in administration. It seems that much more attention is due to particular offices
not only in relation to their function but also as keystones of developed power
structures. We shall return to this when discussing patronage. What is clear
is that while efficient collective governing bodies composed both of noblemen
and professional commoners are developing in Vienna (or Prague), in Berlin
(or Königsberg), in Stockholm, Munich, and Madrid, the trend in Poland is
the reverse.

Little systematic research has been done to explain this difference. Here it
should be stressed only that neither the leaders of the Chamber of Deputies

nor the magnates entrenched in the Senate strove towards building up a strong central apparatus for the Commonwealth, and kings had no means to do so. The reasons for this lie in the intertwining of questions of public law and socio-economic structures. The system of elective monarchy together with the imposition by the nobility of conditions embodied in the *Articuli Henriciani* and the *pacta conventa*, functioned in a singular way. In the Commonwealth, a "domain state," practically the only form of high favor to bestow upon a royal supporter or servant was a royal domain. During the fifteenth and early sixteenth centuries numerous such grants turned into estates "hereditary and feudal"; from 1504 the last Jagiellons and the *executio iurium* party attempted to turn the tide, but even their obvious successes could not change the system. All advancement, all personal political success stories gave the nobleman-politician a seat in the Senate and led him straight to the group of magnates. Monarchies in which the Church estates had been secularized had similar problems, and the future of the confiscated monastic property (and partly that of the bishoprics) can be compared with the history of royal grants in Poland. The program aiming at recuperation of the royal domain partly squandered during former reigns, although pursued vigorously by the Chamber of Deputies, could not result in an affluent treasury: unlike the later Swedish *reduktionen*, the reform of the 1560's in Poland was not completed by enacting an efficient fiscal control.[25] Surveys of the royal domain under the elective kings testified not only to the depression of peasant farming and expansion of demesne farms, but first and foremost to the helplessness of the control system of the royal *fiscus*.

That failure of fiscal reforms—of the domain under Sigismund Augustus, and of taxation under Stefan Batory and Sigismund III—had crucial importance for the subsequent evolution of the power system in the Commonwealth. The kings had neither the fiscal basis for constitutional reforms, nor the broad political support, and being elected, had no adequate charisma to pursue their rather moderate absolutist aims. It would be an exaggeration to maintain that in the sixteenth century royal power in Poland was particularly weak. But while it was not, the period witnessed the consolidation of the system which developed in the next century. In the seventeenth century the great lord became, according to Tadeusz Manteuffel, "not so much a citizen of the Commonwealth as the absolute ruler of a territory, sometimes large, sometimes less so, within its borders."[26]

The social and political system of the Commonwealth can be approached from several angles, each revealing different parts of the reality. True, suffrage and elegibility for regional diets (*sejmiki*) were enjoyed by more people than anywhere else even well into the nineteenth century, with the possible exception of Stuart England. But did this give large groups of voters the possibility to influence the government policies constructively? It seems that in everyday circumstances—outside periods of particular political activity culminating in armed congresses of the gentry (*rokosze*)—the direction of politics was determined by the interests of the great nobles and the agreements reached by them, while the support gained by them of the gentry public opinion was achieved mainly at the expense of the state. As dignitaries of the realm, the magnates were able to secure for their adherents and clients life tenure of royal estates, incomes, and posts in the administration.

"The disruption of authority," wrote Manteuffel, "suffered by Poland at the turn of the sixteenth century (the exact dating is still a matter of controversy) caused: first, the independence of the great lords; secondly, their taking over governmental functions within their estates; thirdly, the creation between the magnates and the poor gentry of a personal relationship based on a pledge of loyalty (servants bound to their master by the ceremony of handshake), or by life tenure held by the grace of the lord; fourthly, the spread of conditional property in the form of endowments granted to the handshake-servants (ręko-dajni)."[27] All this was reminiscent of feudal social forms during the high Middle Ages in the West rather than of changes which in modern times have led the most advanced societies to capitalist relations. Similar forms of patronage were characteristic of many (if not all) European societies in the Renaissance, but during the seventeenth century they would peter out in the West, while they would flourish in Poland-Lithuania.[28]

Social barriers were another factor adversely affecting the socio-economic evolution of the Commonweaith. The percentage of the gentry in the popu-lation was very considerable and the fluidity between the estates greater than the law would permit. Yet, this social mobility had no positive impact. In England the value of her social structure consisted, among other things, in the fact that the barriers between the nobles and the commoners were fluid, existed within families, and that money made possible the advancement of a person and his family. Another example in Europe of the time is the number of Genoese financiers who were promoted by scores to Neapolitan counts, marquesses, and princes. By comparison, in Poland the social promotion of bankers and merchants to the higher spheres ended with the Boners and the Morsztyns of Cracow as early as the first half of the sixteenth century, and with the Werdens of Gdańsk slightly later. On the other hand, there was a mass influx into the lowest strata of the gentry, presented so vividly by Walerian Nekanda Trepka in his Liber Chamorum.[29] A specific rag-tag gentry was being created from towns-folk, village reeves, millers, or peasants.

During the sixteenth century the path of social advancement became closed to the peasants. By the end of the century the class of well-to-do tenants having considerable means at their disposal who engaged in certain market opera-tions—the Polish yeomen farmers or fermiers—disappeared. As Janusz Tazbir has pointed out, in the Polish versions of the life of the Spanish saint, Isidore the Plowman, of the first half of the seventeenth century, the information about his having been appointed farm manager was omitted: as the path of promotion closed to the peasants, so ended the dreams about it.[30] The chances of advancement through the Church were also diminishing. Of less importance seems the fact that in the seventeenth century there were no outstanding prelates of commoner origin as there had been in the previous century. More significant for the social structure was the number of sons of poor gentry families who increasingly occupied the posts of parish priests formerly accessible to townsfolk and even to peasant sons.[31]

The picture presented here is a complex one. Rather than repeat conventional descriptions of the period, less well-known matters and rarely posed questions have been stressed. Polish Renaissance society has been painted in contrasting tones, producing the effect of light and shade. If the latter dominates,it is because the sixteenth century created a social and political framework which in the next period became filled with a content of backward characteristics, thus darkening the image of the Golden Age. Emphasis has been laid on matters relating to the nobility because it was they who decided the form of the state. Poland's position in the world system meant that the extremely important factor of the relative poverty of the country was to a large extent geographically determined. In the Polish economy and society of four hundred years ago the slow flow of money in the country's economic arteries, the weak and uneven amount of it at the disposal of the economy, and vulnerability in the face of wealthier trading partners were to turn in the next century into helplessness in the face of mighty partners in the European political game.

Notes

1. It may be indirectly useful to refer to the totally different case of Tudor England. See Jack H. Hexter, "The Myth of the Middle Class in Tudor England," in *Reappraisals in History* (Evanston: Northwestern University Press, 1961).

2. There is something of a general consensus on that question based principally on the estimates of grain yield ratios. For a typical view, see Jerzy Topolski, "Economic Decline in Poland from the Sixteenth to the Eighteenth Centuries," in Peter Earle, ed., *Essays in European Economic History 1500-1800* (Oxford: Clarendon Press, 1974), pp. 127-142.

3. The best overview of the Polish agrarian economy is Leonid Żytkowicz's "The Peasant's Farm and the Landlord's Farm in Poland from the Sixteenth to the Middle of the Eighteenth Century," *Journal of European Economic History* 1, no. 1 (1972): 135-154 (see p. 140). However, in its footnotes the author much underquoted his own contributions.

4. Leonid Żytkowicz, "Z badań nad wydajnością pracy w rolnictwie feudalnym" (Studies on the productivity of labor in feudal agriculture), *Kwartalnik Historii Kultury Materialnej* 17, no. 3 (1969): 549.

5. Jerzy Topolski, *Narodziny kapitalizmu w Europie XIV-XVII wieku* (The birth of capitalism in Europe. 14th-17th Centuries) (Warsaw: PWN, 1965), and more recently in a very brief form, "Wielki przewrót w gospodarce europejskiej w XVI wieku: przyczyny rozwoju i struktura gospodarki folwarczno-pańszczyźnianej" (The great revolution in the European economy in the 16th century: the origins and the structure of serf-manorial economy). *Gospodarka Polska a europejska w XVI-XVII wieku* (Polish and European economy in the 16th-17th centuries) (Poznań: Wydawn. Poz-

nańskie, 1977), pp. 71-84. In the latter paper Jerzy Topolski does not stress the merchant-nobleman rivalry.

6. For a survey of the very particular and characteristic socio-economic and political structure in Royal Prussia, see Gerard Labuda, ed., *Historia Pomorza* (History of Pomerania), vol. 2, pt. 1 (Poznań: Wydawn. Poznańskie, 1976), pp. 201-318, 355-404.

7. See for bibliography Antoni Mączak, "Agricultural and Livestock Production in Poland: Internal and Foreign Markets," *Journal of European Economic History* I, no. 3 (1972): 671-680; Antoni Mączak, "Money and Society in Poland-Lithuania in the Sixteenth and Seventeenth Centuries," *Journal of European Economic History* 6, no. 1 (1976).

8. On the demand for textiles: Antoni Mączak, *Sukiennictwo wielkopolskie XIV-XVII wieku* (Clothmaking in Great Poland of the 14th-17th centuries) (Warsaw: PWN, 1955), pp. 243-299; on the demand for tools and the crisis in the iron industry: Benedykt Zientara, *Dzieje małopolskiego hutnictwa żelaznego XIV-XVII w.* (History of the Little Poland iron industry, 14th-17th centuries) (Warsaw: PWN, 1954), pp. 185-267.

9. I am following here my own argument presented in "Money and Society."

10. Fynes Moryson, *An Itinerary, Containing His Ten Years' Travel . . .*, vol. 4 (Glasgow, 1908), p. 70. On early modern travelers' ability to appreciate, and their interest in economic phenomena, see Antoni Mączak, "Progress and Underdevelopment in the Eyes of Renaissance and Baroque Man," *Studia Historiae Oeconomicae* 9, 1974.

11. Andrzej Wyczański, *Polska w Europie XVI stulecia* (Poland in 16th century Europe) (Warsaw: Wiedza Powszechna, 1973), pp. 70-73.

12. Maria Bogucka, "Die Bedeutung des Ostseehandels für die Aussenhandelsbilanz Polens in der ersten Hälfte des 17. Jahrhunderts," in Ingomar Bog, ed., *Der Aussenhandel Ostmitteleuropas 1450-1650* (Cologne: Böhlau Verlag, 1971), pp. 47-55; Maria Bogucka, "Merchants' Profits in Gdańsk Foreign Trade in the First Half of the 17th Century, *Acta Poloniae Historica* 23 (1971): 73-90.

13. Andrzej Wyrobisz, "Small Towns in the 16th and 17th centuries," *Acta Poloniae Historica* 34 (1978): 153-163.

14. Antoni Mączak, "Zur Grundeigentumsstruktur in Polen im 16. bis 18. Jahrhundert," *Jahrbuch für Wirtschaftsgeschichte* 1967, pt. 4.

15. Antoni Mączak, "Przełom stulecia przełomem losów Rzeczypospolitej." (The turn of the century: The turning point of the Commonwealth's destiny), in *Przełom wieków XVI i XVII w literaturze i kulturze polskiej* (Wrocław: Ossolineum, 1984), pp. 33-46.

16. See Jerzy Kłoczowski, ed., *Kościoł w Polsce* (The Church in Poland) 2 (Cracow: Znak 1970), *passim*; also Włodzimierz Dworzaczek, "La mobilité sociale de la noblesse polonaise aux XVIe et XVIIe siècles," *Acta Poloniae Historica* 36 (1977): 147-162.

17. The question of religious tolerance has been studied thoroughly by Janusz Tazbir. See his *A State Without Stakes.Polish Religious Toleration in the Sixteenth and Seventeenth Centuries* (Warsaw: PIW, 1973).

18. Jarema Maciszewski, *Szlachta polska i jej państwo* (Polish nobles and their state) (Warsaw: Wiedza Powszechna, 1969), ch. 7 and 8.

19. Konstanty Grzybowski, *Teoria reprezentacji w Polsce epoki Odrodzenia* (Theory of representation in Poland in the Renaissance) (Warsaw: PWN, 1959), pp. 112-120.

20. Andrzej Wyrobisz, "Small Towns".

21. Immanuel Wallerstein, *The Modern World-System, Capitalist Agriculture and the Origins of the European World Economy in the Sixteenth Century* (New York: Academic Press, 1974), chapter 2; Artur Attman, *The Russian and Polish Markets in International Trade, 1500-1650* (Göteborg: The Institute of Economic History of Gothenburg University, 1973); Artur Attman,*The Bullion Flow Between Europe and the East 1000-1750* (Göteborg: Kungl. Vetenskaps- och Vitterhets-Samhället, 1981), pp. 59-92.

22. We share the late Konstanty Grzybowski's high opinion of Sigismund Augustus' parliamentary tactics. See his *Teoria reprezentacji w Polsce epoki Odrodzenia*; for a bibliography of Polish parliamentarism, see S. Russocki, "Le Système représentatif de la république nobiliaire de Pologne," in *Der moderne Parlamentarismus und seine Grundlagen in der ständischen Repräsentation* (Berlin: Duncker und Humblot, 1977).

23. L. Stone, *The Crisis of the Aristocracy, 1558-1641* (Oxford: Clarendon Press, 1965); G.E. Aylmer, *The King's Servants: The Civil Service of Charles I, 1625-1642* (New York: Columbia Univ. Press, 1961). Knud J.V. Jespersen, ed., *Rigsråad, adel og administration 1570-1648* (Odense: Odense Universitetsforlag, 1980). Danish and Swedish collective biographies on the sixteenth and seventeenth centuries have been increasing in the 1980's.

24. Karol Górski, *Starostowie malborscy w latach 1457-1510* (The starosts of Malbork in 1457-1510) (Toruń: Towarzystwo Naukowe w Toruniu, 1958); Jacek Wiesiołowski. *Ambroży Pampowski — starosta Jagiellonów* (Ambroży Pampowski — a *starosta* of the Jagiellons) (Wrocław: Ossolineum, 1978).

25. On the *reduktionen*, see the best essay in English, by K. Agren: "The *reduktion*," in *Sweden's Age of Greatness, 1632-1718*, M. Roberts, ed. (London: Macmillan, 1973), pp. 237-284.

26. Tadeusz Manteuffel, "Problem feudalizmu polskiego" (The question of Polish feudalism), *Przegląd Historyczny* 37 (1948): 62-71.

27. Tadeusz Manteuffel, "The Question."

28. Roland Mousnier, *Les Institutions de la France sous la monarchie absolue 1598-1789*, vol. 1 (Paris: Presses universitaires de France, 1974), p. 84. (Roland Mousnier has returned to this subject in several of his books). Walter T. MacCaffrey, "Place and Patronage in Elizabethan Politics," in S. T. Bindoff, J. Hurstfield, C.H. Williams, eds., *Elizabethan Government and Society, Essays Presented to Sir John Neale* (London: Athlone Press University of London, 1981), pp. 95-125; See also Antoni Mączak ed., *Klientele systeme in Europa der Frühen Neuzeit* (Munich: R. Oldenbourg Verlag, 1987)

29. Walerian Nekanda Trepka, *Liber generationis plebeanorum ("Liber chamorum")* (Wrocław: Ossolineum, 1963), pt. 1.

30. Janusz Tazbir, "The Cult of St. Isidore the Farmer in Europe," in *Poland at the 14th International Congress of Historical Sciences in San Francisco. Studies in Comparative History* (Wrocław: Ossolineum, 1975), p. 107.

31. On social advancement through the Church and the careers of the lesser nobility, see Jerzy Kłoczowski, ed., *Kościół w Polsce*, vol. 1.

3

The Political Heritage of the Sixteenth Century and its Influence on the Nation-building Ideologies of the Polish Enlightenment and Romanticism

Andrzej Walicki

The topic of this paper is too broad for the presentation of a rich panorama of facts; it compels one, instead, to strive for generalizations. It seems proper, therefore, to start with a fundamental question about the nature of the political heritage of the Polish Renaissance.

The sixteenth century was, as we know, the Golden Age of Poland, the full flower of ancient Polish freedom, the finest page in the history of that peculiarly Polish political structure called the "democracy of the gentry." What kind of democracy, or what kind of freedom did it represent? Was it a deviation from a "normal" development, a relic of medievalism which, in specific circumstances, and for some time, proved to be compatible with political and cultural growth but in the final result led the Polish state towards self-destruction? Or was it an anticipation of modern democracy and constitutional freedom?

It is obvious that the "democracy of the gentry" was restricted, by definition, to one estate only; some historians, especially German and Russian, have concluded from this that it was in fact a form of absolute (although collective) political power. On the other hand, it is undeniable that sixteenth-century Poland was, as R.H. Lord put it, "the freest state in Europe, the state in which the greatest degree of constitutional, civic and intellectual liberty prevailed."[1] The number of "active citizens," voting and eligible to vote, was much greater in Poland than in the West. The Polish gentry was an extremely numerous group; in the sixteenth century 11 to 13 percent of the total population of the Polish-Lithuanian Commonwealth consisted of noblemen who were represented in parliament, whereas in sixteenth-century England the corresponding figure was only 5 percent. From this point of view, earlier Polish democracy was impressive even if measured by nineteenth-century standards: the Polish romantic poet, Zygmunt Krasiński, was right to remind Lamartine, who had called Poland "an aristocracy without a people," that in the bourgeois France of Louis Philippe only 1.5 percent of the population had the right to vote. It might be added that, after 1572, every Polish noble was an "elector" of the king and could become king himself.[2]

It is possible, and quite easy, to multiply arguments for each point of view. But in order to achieve a better understanding of the specific features of the ancient Polish freedom, a more philosophical approach could be applied. It would be useful to look at Polish freedom from the point of view of the famous typological distinction put forward by Benjamin Constant: the distinction between "ancient," or democratic freedom on the one hand, and "modern," or liberal freedom on the other.

Briefly, the first freedom was a political or public freedom, consisting in the decentralization of sovereignty, in the active participation of every citizen in the exercise of political power; the second was a civil or private freedom, limiting the scope of political power by stable laws, which would safeguard inalienable individual rights—among them property rights and free economic activity. The first was a freedom *in* politics, the second freedom *from* any kind of political interference. The first, in juridical language, was unthinkable without subjective rights in the sphere of public law, whereas the second stressed private law and apolitical civil rights. The first conception was concerned with the problem of the source of political power, the second with the problems of its scope, its limits. The first set forth the idea of a *free state*, i.e., of the sovereignty of the people; the second insisted rather on *freedom from the state*, on "limited government," i.e., on the limited character of sovereignty, whether royal or popular.

The validity of the historical generalization implied by the terms "ancient" and "modern" freedom is questionable: it might be argued that "modern" freedom was not unknown in the ancient world. This problem, however, is irrelevant if we use the two concepts in their typological rather than their historical sense. The important thing is that the difference between the two kinds of freedom, and even the possibility of a sharp conflict between them, was undeniable, although both were proclaimed simultaneously by the French revolution.[3] Among the people to emphasize this difference was the young Marx who, unlike Constant, declared himself in favor of the "ancient" freedom. Analyzing the French "Declaration of the Rights of Man and of the Citizen," he extolled the rights of the citizen, i.e., the rights of man as a member of a political community, and strongly condemned the rights of man, i.e., the rights of man as a *bourgeois*, a member of civil society. The first, in his eyes, implied heroic virtues, readiness to sacrifice private interest, whereas the second were simply "the rights of egoistic man," separated from other men and from the community, withdrawn into the confines of his private interests.[4]

There can be no doubt, I think, how we should classify the sixteenth-century Polish freedom: it was surely the "ancient," democratic, "republican" freedom,

freedom of political decision-making, and not the "modern" liberal freedom, finding its main outlet in private economic activity. The Polish noble was not a "private" man: "private men" were plebeians,[5] nobles were part of the Res publica, "noble blood" was seen as an attribute of public service and authority.[6] Privacy was not considered to be an inseparable part of freedom; the word "privacy" has no equivalent in the Polish language, because the word "pry- wata," from the same root, denotes something different—not a positive value, but an unworthy, condemnable private particularism. The proper field in which to exercise one's freedom was the Res publica, "Rzeczpospolita." The popularity of this word, as Claude Backvis has rightly noted, has prevented, or rather retarded for centuries the emergence of the Polish word for "state."[7] Res publica, as conceived by sixteenth-century Poles, was compatible with royalty, although incompatible with royal absolutism; therefore, Poland was, in this sense, equally as "republican" under the Jagiellons as under the elected kings. The greatest political thinker of the Polish Renaissance, Andrzej Frycz Modrzewski (Andreas Fricius Modrevius), defined a republic as a "community of people bound by law" and "established for the sake of a good and happy life."[8] It was, in his view, the sphere of active public life, as opposed to the sphere of private, family life; a "matter of common concern," a "common wealth," as opposed to the pursuit of individual interests.

The two concepts of freedom are often contrasted as "negative" and "pos- itive" freedom: liberal freedom, freedom from the state, is presented as "neg- ative," while democratic freedom, the freedom to take part in political decisions, is already a form of "positive" freedom, i.e., "the freedom which consists in being one's own master."[9] It would be unfair, however, to conclude from this that in the liberal conception freedom was understood as a passive state, as mere leisure. True, it was "negative" in relation to the state but, historically speaking, the demand for "freedom from the state" was born among people who wanted to be their own masters in the sphere of private economic activity, for whom "negative freedom" was only a precondition for controlling their own lives and realizing their own plans. Both the democratic and the liberal conception of freedom presuppose a conscious and autonomous will; this is even more true for liberalism than for democracy. The liberal conception is more individualistic: it recognizes the exerciser of an autonomous will in the individual endowed with inalienable, prepolitical rights, whereas the demo- cratic conception sees individual men as members of a given body politic. The ethos of democracy is collectivistic: Polish nobles exercised their freedom in public, in tumultuous gatherings—in provincial dietines (sejmiki), in the Diet (Sejm), and finally, on the election field. In contrast to this, the ethos of classical liberalism was deeply rooted in the self-reliant, disciplined individualism of the Puritans—hard-working people, inner-directed and not afraid of loneliness, multiplying their wealth and seeing their successes as the result of divine grace.

The function of the liberal notion of inalienable subjective rights was to limit the scope of all kinds of political power, including the power of the democratic majority. As we know, fear of the "despotism of the majority" was not alien to the Polish "democracy of the gentry"—on the contrary, Polish nobles of the sixteenth and seventeenth centuries could be accused of rather exaggerating this danger. They felt deeply that the opinions of the majority were liable to quick changes, sometimes under the influence of accidental circumstances, that majority decisions could be as arbitrary and unjust as the decisions of absolute rulers, and that a majority in the Diet could always be manipulated by a clever king and thus could not be considered a sufficient safeguard of freedom. However, the constitutional device which was to protect Polish freedom against the possible arbitrariness of a parliamentary majority was quite different from the principles of liberal constitutionalism (which, of course, developed much later, in post-absolutist Europe). It consisted, as is known, in the principle of unanimity whose converse side was the notorious right of *liberum veto*. This right, which proved so fatal to the Polish state, was already theoretically acknowledged, or implied, in the sixteenth century, although in practice it was exercised for the first time in 1652.[10] It stemmed from a conviction that majority decisions are valid only if nobody contradicts them (*nemine contradicente*), i.e., if the minority, at the final stage, agrees to accept the will of the major part of the assembly.

Thus, unlike later liberal doctrine, Polish political doctrine protected the rights of the minority without limiting the scope of political power. The liberals maintained that certain spheres of life, above all economic life regulated by private law, ought to be placed outside the scope of political decision-making. The theorists of the Polish democracy of the gentry did not share this view: they insisted instead that all political decisions must have the consent of the entire body of citizens. It is not surprising, therefore, that Andrzej Maksymilian Fredro, a seventeenth-century apologist for the *liberum veto*, should be a follower of mercantilism, advocating political interference in the economic sphere and even treating private property as a right which might be suspended or withdrawn in the interests of the public good.[11] Indeed, why should the Polish gentry, who saw themselves as constituents of political power, proclaim principles limiting the scope of political power? In order to protect their freedom as independent parts of the body politic they proclaimed instead the maximum decentralization of sovereignty, endowing each member of the Diet with the royal right of veto. In contrast to this, liberalism was not the product of an estate holding political power; it was the ideology of private producers and merchants, interested above all in economic freedom and, consequently, in clearly dividing the state from "civil society."

The specific features of the democracy of the gentry were reflected in its attitude towards the reception of Roman law. Max Weber has established that professional jurists trained in Roman law, especially in Roman private law, were of tremendous importance for the development of capitalism and liberalism in the West. In Poland, however, Roman law, although propagated by the Catholic Church, was actively resisted by the gentry and not allowed to take root. The reasons for this were first, the fear that Roman law might be used by the adherents of royal absolutism and, secondly, a negative attitude towards professional jurists. This is understandable: the gentry, as collective sovereign, did not want the laws of their Commonwealth to be interpreted or commented upon by an independent "caste" of learned professionals. This attitude, I should add, was as a rule quite compatible with the habit of quoting from Cicero and with a profound admiration for the republican traditions of ancient Rome.[12]

In order to achieve a better understanding of the Polish democratic tradition, it is necessary to dismiss the widespread view treating the *liberum veto* as a strange curiosity, devoid of any positive function. In fact there was nothing "self-evident" about the "majority principle;" on the contrary, in the early stages the principle of unanimity in representative institutions was the rule rather than the exception. This has already been demonstrated by Władysław Konopczyński, although he himself stressed the negative aspect of the functioning of the unanimity principle in the Polish-Lithuanian Commonwealth.[13] A new approach to this problem is to be found in the works of Claude Backvis and Zbigniew Ogonowski.[14] Their findings may be summarized as follows:

If a "free protest" was voiced by a deputy in the Diet, the Diet was automatically dissolved and all laws passed during the session were annulled. Every member of the Diet knew that to make use of the right of veto would not only prevent the legislation which his constituency did not desire, but cancel desired legislation as well. The Polish-Lithuanian Commonwealth was not a city-republic, like Venice, but a great agricultural state whose parliament was based upon the principle of territorial representation. This entailed two dangers: the danger of ignoring the specific needs and interests of a given province and, on the other hand, the danger of an excessive provincialism. The first of these was prevented by the principle of unanimity which effectively protected provincial independence; because of this the Commonwealth was a very attractive state, capable of spreading by voluntary union. The second danger was for a long time prevented by the grave consequences of resorting to the right of veto. A deputy from Pomerania might be indifferent to the fate of the Ukraine, but he would not dare to oppose contributing to the defense of Ukrainian lands against the Tartars if this would be tantamount to dissolving the Diet. A further restraint was the realization that next time a deputy from the Ukraine might oppose the defense of Pomerania against Brandenburg.

The demand for unanimity combined with the threat of veto had yet another positive function. It prevented the polarization of opinions in the Diet, strengthening instead the will for mutual understanding, the awareness that it was in the interests of all deputies to reach agreement through compromise. The Polish Diet could not be divided into organized parties, struggling with each other; it was not a "machine for voting" but rather a complex laboratory in which the "general will"—in Rousseau's sense—was being produced. No wonder that Rousseau, the theorist of the "general will," as opposed to the "spirit of parties," was so sympathetic towards the institutions of ancient Poland.[15]

Needless to say, the ideal of unanimity was based upon the assumpton that the essential values and interests of all citizens (i.e., the gentry) were the same and that everybody was ready not to insist on his particular interests if the common good required it. In other words, the democracy of the gentry could function well, or at least relatively well, only if there was enough civic virtue and enough rational understanding of common interests. Mickiewicz idealized this aspect in describing the political system of ancient Poland as one based entirely upon moral factors, such as "good will," "enthusiasm," and "exaltation." It is obvious, however, that "ordinary" parliamentary systems which openly legitimize conflicting interests and resolve debates by the simple "mechanical" means of counting votes are much more stable, less dependent on subjective factors, and better adjusted to the complex differentiated nature of modern societies.

Let us turn now to the problem of the nation-building processes and the national consciousness in Poland.

In the vast literature on nationalism two theses are widely accepted: first, that modern nations are the products of capitalist development; second that modern national consciousness is a correlate of the process of democratization. The first thesis claims that the growing socialization of production and large-scale economic integration destroys the barriers dividing provinces and estates, increases horizontal and vertical social mobility, intensifies contacts between different people who, by the same token, discover the importance of a commonly understood national language, unifies laws, and, finally, creates national markets and nation-states. The second thesis maintains that the idea of national sovereignty is closely bound up, logically and historically, with the democratic idea of the sovereignty of the people, that the development of a national consciousness depends on the numbers of politically active or, at least, politically conscious people, i.e., on the degree of political and social democratization.

It is evident that the strong, deeply-rooted traditions of the democracy of the gentry greatly influenced the processes of nation-building in Poland, especially in the sphere of national consciousness. Their effects, I think, were at once positive and negative. In order to understand them properly it is necessary to make some conceptual distinctions.

At the beginning of this century Friedrich Meinecke introduced the famous distinction between "political" and "cultural" nationalism. In his view, "political" nationalism derived from the spirit of 1789, from the idea of self-determination and the sovereignty of the nation, that is, of the *political* nation striving to form its own political constitution and to direct its own political destiny. In contrast to this, *cultural* nationalism strives for national individuality, characteristic of anti-Enlightenment German thought. A similar distinction was made later by Hans Kohn, the most prolific American specialist in the theory and history of nationalism. Kohn claimed that nationalism in Europe from its very beginnings was divided into two diametrically opposite types: Western nationalism and the nationalism of Central and Eastern Europe. The first was a political concept, a product of the Enlightenment, implying a legal, rational democracy; the second was a product of romanticism, centered around "the irrational, pre-civilized folk concept," emphasizing ethnic, linguistic and cultural differences and supporting anti-democratic, authoritarian attitudes.[16]

The importance of the Polish democracy of the gentry for the comparative history of nationalism consists in providing an important correction to these theories. The case of Poland shows, first, that the "political" type of nationalism was much older than the French Enlightenment and revolution and, secondly, that its birthplace was not the West but East-Central Europe. If Hans Kohn is right in maintaining that the "Western" type of nationalism was bound up with the idea of the sovereignty of the people, with government by consent and a constitutional conception of the state, and that it was incompatible with an absolutist monarchy and inconceivable without the idea of political democracy,[17] it follows that conditions for this type of national consciousness were much better in the Polish-Lithuanian Commonwealth than in Western Europe. If "nationalism" means that loyalty to the nation comes before loyalty to the king or multiple loyalties to supra-national feudal authorities, the Polish gentry was "nationalistic" from the beginnings of "gentry democracy," and Frycz Modrzewski (who advocated, among other things, treating burghers and peasants as equal before the law and establishing a Polish national church) should be recognized as one of the first great theorists of "political" nationalism.

It is worthwhile to add that the opposition between "political" nationalism on the one hand, and "linguistic" or "cultural" nationalism on the other, must lead to the conclusion that the "nationalism" of the sixteenth-century Polish gentry was more consistently "political," more indifferent to linguistic and cultural differences, than the variety of nationalism which emerged from the French Revolution. The Polish-Lithuanian Commonwealth was a multi-ethnic and multi-cultural state, a state in which six languages (Polish, Latin, Ruthenian, German, Armenian, and Hebrew) were recognized as official,[18] whereas the post-revolutionary French state, both under the Jacobins and under Napoleon, quite ruthlessly carried out a policy of enforcing a linguistic and cultural homogeneity. The gentry of the Commonwealth, irrespective of their native language or ethnic background, considered themselves as constituting one political nation. The difference between "nationhood" and ethnicity could be made clear by defining oneself, or another man, as "*gente Ruthenus (vel Lithuanus, etc.), natione Polonus*"; it could also be blurred, as was done by the theory claiming that all nobles of the Commonwealth were descendants of the ancient Sarmatians. As time went on, cultural factors played an increasingly important role, as was shown in the voluntary polonization of the Lithuanian, Ruthenian, and (partially) German nobles. Nevertheless, the "nation of the gentry" always defined its identity by referring to the *political* tradition of its Commonwealth. It was, thus, a political nation, based (to quote Meinecke) "on the unifying force of a common political history and constitution," and desiring "to direct its own political destiny."[19] Even the word "nation" was used in Poland as a political and legal category: it denoted a collective sovereign, a community of people endowed with political rights and organized as a state.

The idea of the "sovereignty of the nation of the gentry" in its relation to the king paved the way for modern ideas of national sovereignty and the right to national self-determination—ideas which appeared in Poland earlier than in any other European country and, as has been shown by Jean Fabre, had some influence on the republican current in the French Enlightenment.[20] This is quite understandable: as soon as Polish political freedom became endangered from outside rather than from inside, the entire libertarian tradition of the "gentry democracy" produced powerful arguments for national independence. The fragility of Polish independence of the eighteenth century gave birth to a rich theoretical literature dealing with the problems of the law of nations. A physiocrat, Hieronim Stroynowski, put forward a theory that every nation had four natural rights: (1) the right to free and independent existence, (2) the right to defend itself by force, (3) the right to the certainty that international agreements would not be violated, and, finally, (4) the right to demand help from other nations.[21] Similar ideas were developed by many other Polish jurists of the Age of Enlightenment.[22] It should be stressed that the right to self-determination was never restricted, explicitly or implicitly, to European peoples: Polish public opinion did not sympathize with the ideology of colonialism and took the part of the distant colonized peoples.[23] After the second partition of Poland, Hugo Kołłątaj, a leading political thinker of the Polish Enlightenment, formulated the common conviction of his generation thus:

> That every nation should be free and independent, that every nation should be allowed to embrace that form of government which it prefers and that no foreign nation is entitled to interfere in its constitutional development—this is the first and most important maxim of the law of nations, so evident in the light of our century that no proofs are needed to justify it. A nation which has no right to rule in its own country is not a nation.[24]

It is a commonplace that in the eighteenth century the Polish "democracy of the gentry" degenerated into anarchy, actively supported by the neighboring absolute monarchies whose hirelings used the right of veto to block all attempts at progressive legislation. The necessary reforms came too late to save the existence of the Polish-Lithuanian state. Nevertheless, as Rousseau had rightly predicted, it was easier to swallow Poland than to digest it.[25] Maurycy Mochnacki, the romantic literary critic who in the uprising of 1830-31 emerged as an outstanding intellectual leader of the Left, asserted with good reason that after the downfall of the state the republican traditions of the gentry democracy, quite irrespective of their functioning in the recent past, did much to support the inner vitality of the nation and the spirit of resistance against the partitioning powers. If Poland had been an absolute monarchy, he argued, its society would have become passive, devoid of civic spirit and unable to defend itself. In other words, the downfall of the Polish state would then have meant the dissolution of the Polish nation. If Poland had "not yet been lost" (to quote from the Polish national anthem), it was because a large percentage of its population felt itseif to be a nation, endowed with an inalienable right to sovereignty.[26]

Many contemporary historians fully agree with this view. Janusz Tazbir has pointed out that in the changed conditions even the ancient vices of the gentry showed their positive side: stubborn conservatism changed into a stubborn determination to preserve national tradition and identity, the long-established habit of opposing royal power became resistance to the foreign yoke, and so forth.[27]

Thus we may conclude that the "democracy of the gentry," whose "golden age" coincided with the Golden Age of Poland, greatly contributed to the formation of the modern Polish nation. Its main legacy, the twin ideas of the "sovereignty of the people—sovereignty of the nation," were easily modernized, that is, applied to the entire population of the country, and not to one estate only. In the last decades of the "gentry republic" an impressive re-emergence of active patriotism took place and the partitioning powers proved unable to break it. The tradition of independence and active citizenship, the long-established habit of distinguishing between "a nation" and "a mere state," enabled nineteenth-century Poles to feel themselves to be a "historical nation," although one temporarily (and illegitimately) deprived of its own statehood.

However, there was also the other side of the coin. For a long time—much too long—the democratic tradition existed in Poland without capitalism and without the liberal values bound up with it. The underdevelopment of modern social structures was paralleled by a psychological unpreparedness for the requirements of modernity. Poland had not passed through the school of liberal individualism, had not developed such "bourgeois" values as economic capacity and industriousness, self-reliance in economic life, thrift, and so forth. Its elite remained faithful to the values characteristic of the nobility, such as honor, courage in open fight (as distinct from civil courage), freedom conceived as participation in political power; it did not pay much attention to the prosaic, down-to-earth concerns of private law and could hardly understand Napoleon's famous dictum that the essence of freedom is a good Civil Code.[28] The democratic ideologies of the Polish intelligentsia remained significantly related to the "democracy of the gentry" in their emphasis on disinterestedness and sacrifice; even peaceful "organic work," in order to be accepted, had to take the form of, or at least be presented as, a disinterested public service, a patriotic duty. Thus, the Polish democratic tradition could contribute very little to the release of the economic energy of the nation; moreover, its inherent hostility towards "bourgeois-liberal" values created psychological obstacles for genuine economic modernization.

We face, therefore, a seeming paradox which explains, I think, a great deal in Polish history. The same national tradition functioned in two different ways

IOANNIS SARII
ZAMOSCII
DE SENATV ROMANO
L I B R I   D V O.

ex libris f' fridicum Holzinag congregationis f'mauri ordin. f' Benedicti

Index auctorum, & rerum memorabilium.

CVM PRIVILEGIO.

Venetiis, apud Iordanum Ziletum. M. D. LXIII.

15. Jan Zamoyski, *De Senatu Romano libri duo*, Venetiis, 1563. The title page of the study of the young Jan Zamoyski, the future Royal Chancellor and Hetman, written under the influence of Carlo Sigonio, his professor of Roman Law at Padua (Bibliothèque Polonaise, Paris). Reprinted from Joseph A. Teslar "Shakespeare's Worthy Consellor," *Sacrum Poloniae Millenium*, vol. 7, Rome, 1960.

16. *Konstitucie Seymu walnego Warszawskiego*, Roku Bożego, 1578. (The Constitutions of the general assembly of the *Sejm* in Warsaw in the Year of Our Lord, 1578). The title page of the resolutions (acts) passed by the *Sejm* during its session in Warsaw in 1578. After each session of the *Sejm*, these acts were published, before 1543 in Latin, later in Polish. (Biblioteka Czartoryskich, Kraków) Reprinted from *Polska i jej dorobek dziejowy*, ed. Henryk Paszkiewicz (London: Orbis, 1956).

in the process of forming the modern Polish nation. With respect to such preconditions of modern nationhood as active citizenship and political nationalism, centered on the question of national independence, its role was both considerable and positive. At the same time, with respect to capitalist development—a development so essential for modern national formations—its role was much smaller, ambiguous, sometimes simply negative. True, it paved the way for "bourgeois development" to the extent that it was universalized, i.e., that the "democracy of the gentry" became transformed into a democracy embracing the entire nation, removing the barriers between estates. However, it was inherently unable to further capitalist development in a positive way. According to Mochnacki, Polish democracy, in contrast to the Western form, strove not for liquidation of the nobility, but for the ennoblement of the entire nation. To a certain extent this striving proved successful, and the consequences of this lie at the roots of some notorious weaknesses of Poland as a national organism.

Let us turn now to a question relevant to the history of ideas; what impact had the political legacy of the "Golden Age" on Polish thinkers of the Enlightenment and romanticism?

It was at once highly significant and relatively insignificant. It was unexpectedly small, relatively insignificant, because knowledge of the legacy of political writers of the Renaissance was scanty. Their works, as a rule, were not reprinted and even the titles were therefore largely unknown. Tadeusz Mikulski has tried to show the importance of Frycz Modrzewski for the Polish Enlightenment but has in fact shown a very different picture. In spite of the fact that an abridged Polish version of Modrzewski's *De Republica emendanda* was reprinted by the Piarists (Wilno, 1770), it had virtually no place in the mainstream of heated discussion which paved the way for the Constitution of 3 May 1791. The same is true of the first half of the nineteenth century, and eloquent testimony to this is the conspicuous absence of the outstanding political theorists of the "Golden Age" from Mickiewicz's Paris lectures on Slavic literature. Much better known were the sixteenth-century ideologists of the Counter Reformation, such as Cardinal Hosius (Stanisław Hozjusz) and the famous Jesuit Piotr Skarga, whose memory was kept alive by the Church. Significantly enough, the heritage of the progressive sixteenth-century thinkers was systematically if briefly discussed in the *Piśmiennictwo polskie w zarysie* (Outline of Polish literature) (1845) by Edward Dembowski, one of the most radical revolutionaries of the romantic epoch. Dembowski, however, just because of his revolutionary radicalism, was inclined to stress that the "democracy of the gentry" was only relativeiy progressive and therefore did not refer to its legacy in his works on political philosophy or in his articles on political and social problems of the day.

Nevertheless, Mikulski was right in asserting that the Polish Enlightenment felt itself to be a continuation and a further development of the Polish Renaissance.[29] The same, although in a slightly different sense, can be said about Polish romanticism. The legacy of individual political thinkers of the Polish Renaissance might be relatively unknown or underestimated, but the political institutions of the "gentry democracy" were well-known, thoroughly studied, and the sixteenth century was universally recognized as the best period in Polish history. Enlightenment thinkers, as a rule, regarded the "Golden Age" as a sound combination of freedom under the law with a powerful state, whereas the romantics, especially romantic poets, idealized even the excesses of "ancient Polish freedom" and saw the "democracy of the gentry" as a powerful manifestation of the unique Polish national spirit. In both cases, the age of Kochanowski was felt to be of crucial importance for an understanding both of Poland's past and Poland's future.

The great movement for reform which, after several decades of lethargy, emerged in eighteenth-century Poland is usually described as royalist, striving to strengthen royal power, while the conservative opposition to reform is often identified with the "republican party."[30] This is only partially true and therefore often misleading. The leaders of the "party of reform," in spite of their efforts to eliminate free elections, confederations, the *liberum veto* and other attributes of "golden freedom," were closer to republicanism than to genuine monarchism. This was explicitly acknowledged by Hugo Kołłątaj when he said that even the hereditary king of Poland would not be a monarch, i.e., a sovereign, because sovereignty would rest with the nation.[31] Indeed, the Constitution of 3 May made the king entirely dependent on the Diet; the royal title was made hereditary, the unanimity principle was replaced by the principle of the majority vote, but the final result was very far from a genuine strengthening of royal power. The real power was vested in the Diet, conceived as both the legislative and the ruling body, while the hereditary king remained in fact the first official of the Commonwealth.[32]

True, there was a small minority in the party of reform which adhered to the principles of genuine monarchism. Their main representative was Stanisław Staszic, a man born into a bourgeois family in western Poland and representing the viewpoint of the burghers. He evolved the theory that absolute monarchy represented a higher stage of development than "feudal republicanism," of which the retarded and degenerate form was, in his eyes, the "democracy of the gentry." It says much, however, that he did not dare to proclaim this theory before the final partition of Poland. In his works addressed to the deputies preparing the plan of constitutional reform for Poland, he was careful to emphasize that in itself republicanism was the best form of government and that the need to strengthen royal power was due mainly to external dangers.[33]

The difference between Staszic, the spokesman of the burghers, and Kołłątaj, the chief architect of the Constitution of 3 May, is well illustrated by their respective views on the sixteenth century: Staszic sympathized, of course, with the monarchs who tried to strengthen their authority, whereas Kołłątaj identified himself with Samuel Zborowski, a nobleman who was executed for violent rebellion and became venerated as a martyr and a symbol of "golden freedom."[34]

The case of the "republican party" is equally ambivalent. The majority of eighteenth-century Polish republicans were conservatives, praising old national traditions (so-called "Sarmatism") and combining ardent republicanism with equally ardent Catholicism and hostility to everything foreign. Nevertheless, it would be a vulgar oversimplification to dismiss their ideology as merely "feudal" and, therefore, having nothing in common with the building of the modern nation. The republicans kept alive the legal concept of the nation as a body of citizens endowed with political rights; they claimed that people living under a monarchy, even a parliamentary monarchy like Britain's, cannot constitute a nation,[35] and, therefore, they deeply sympathized with "bourgeois" revolutions. Thus, for instance, Kazimierz Pułaski, one of the leaders of the Confederation of Bar (seen by some historians as a reactionary movement), became a hero of the American Revolution, and Seweryn Rzewuski, an ardent opponent of the Constitution of 3 May and a leader of the Targowica Confederation, wholeheartedly rejoiced at the downfall of the monarchy in France, seeing this event as a glorious victory for the French nation.[36] So we may say that even conservative Polish republicans were fully conscious that the state had to be thoroughly modernized, both politically and socially, but tried to achieve this aim without betraying republican tradition. Michał Wielhorski, the intellectual leader of the Bar Confederation and the author of the book, *O przywróceniu Dawnego Rządu Według Pierwiastkowych Rzeczypospolitey Ustaw* (On the Restoration of the Ancient Government in Accordance with the Fundamental laws of the Republic) (1775), was inspired by John Locke and some thinkers of the French Enlightenment and, in his turn, inspired Rousseau to write his famous *Considérations sur le gouvernement de Pologne*. It should be stressed in the present context that by the "ancient government" whose restoration and modernization was advocated in his book he meant the institutions of the "gentry democracy" of Kochanowski's age. An even more striking example of the combination of "ancient Polish republicanism" with the "new republicanism" was Wojciech Turski—an admirer of revolutionary France who, in a dramatic speech in the French Convention, appealed to the Jacobins to help the Poles save their freedom.[37]

It should also be remembered that in the last years of the Polish-Lithuanian Commonwealth the quasi-royalist "party of reform" and a significant section of the "republican party" came closer together and that the Constitution of 3 May was, to a certain extent, the work of both. True, the opponents of the Constitution, who organized the conservative, pro-Russian Targowica Confederation, defined themselves as defenders of republican and national values, but this should not obscure the fact that there was also a progressive variety of republicanism and an "enlightened" version of "Sarmatism." Another important fact was the quick appearance of a "new republicanism," free from any significant connections with "Sarmatian" traditionalism. Tadeusz Koś-

ciuszko, the leader of the great national uprising which followed the second
partition of Poland, was a republican in the American sense and, as such,
carefully avoided committing himself to the defense of the "monarchical" May
Constitution.[38]

One of the most controversial innovations of this Constitution was that
political rights (as distinct from civil rights) were made dependent on the
ownership of land: this meant that some burghers were raised to the status of
"active citizens," while the landless gentry, extremely numerous in Poland,
were deprived of their share in political decision-making.[39] This measure was
levelled against certain big magnates who were skillful in using the landless
gentry as their political clients (in the ancient Roman sense of the word). The
architects of the Constitution wanted to place the decisive political influence
in the hands of the middle gentry and in this way replace eighteenth-century
anarchy by a healthy "gentry democracy," such as had existed in the "Golden
Age." They wished also to modernize the nation by replacing "the nation of
the gentry" by "a nation of proprietors." The main advocate of this idea was
Kołłątaj, a firm supporter of absolute private property. He went so far as to
proclaim that all property ought to belong to private persons, that no land
should be public property, and that the possession of every piece of land should
be secured by contract or clear title.[40]

No wonder, then, that the petty and landless gentry could not accept a law
which violated the most cherished principle of the gentry democracy—the
principle of the political equality of all the nobles. Their political rights were
not restored either by the Napoleonic Constitution of the Grand Duchy of
Warsaw or by that of the Congress Kingdom—on the contrary, both constitutions introduced property qualifications which discriminated against not only
the landless gentry but smallholders of gentle birth as well. This greatly contributed to the growing radicalization of the poor gentry, i.e., of the overwhelming majority of the noble estate. The former clients of reactionary magnates
were transformed into radical democratic nationalists to whom only a democratic, modernized and independent Poland could restore their lost political
rights as fully franchised, influential citizens.[41]

This process of political and social radicalization was greatly accelerated by
the defeat of the November uprising of 1830. After the liquidation of the autonomous institutions of the Congress Kingdom, Polish patriots had almost
nothing to lose and everything to gain. This was especially true of the thousands
of political exiles who settled in France and started the great debate about the
past and the future of Poland. For them the only hope was the revolutionary
overthrow of the "Old World"—the world whose main pillar was the Holy
Alliance of the three absolute monarchies which had partitioned Polish lands
and strangled Polish freedom.

Under these new conditions the Constitution of 3 May and the progressive
tradition bound up with it were monopolized by the right wing of the Polish
national-liberation movement.[42] It was represented in exile by the followers of

Prince Adam Czartoryski, head of the insurrectionary national government in 1831. His followers declared themselves in favor of a strong constitutional monarchy and naturally tried to justify their political program by a suitable interpretation of Polish history. Janusz Woronicz, theorist of the "Monarchical and Insurrectional Party of 3 May," tried to minimize the achievements of the sixteenth-century "democracy of the gentry," attributing the greatness of Poland's "Golden Age" to monarchical principles. The historian Karol Hoffman went even further: royal absolutism was for him a necessary phase of normal historical evolution while the Polish "democracy of the gentry" represented a historical anomaly, a deviation from the norm due to retarded development.

Quite different was the position of Joachim Lelewel—the greatest Polish historian of the romantic epoch and chief representative of the Left in the insurrectionary government. As an ardent republican and democrat, he criticized the May Constitution not only for its "monarchism" but also because it had made "active citizenship" dependent on property. In his view, the democratic principles of the ancient republic of the gentry should have been made a universal condition by means of which all inhabitants of Poland were given equal political rights, quite irrespective of their status, ethnic background, or property qualifications. He wrote a special treatise on the "lost citizenship" of the Polish peasants and demanded that their lost rights should be fully restored. According to his historical theory, the democratic-republican principles were inherent in ancient Slavic communalism and, as such, were part of the common heritage of all Slavic nations. He put special emphasis on the existence of a republican tradition in Russia, exemplified by the flourishing city-republics of Pskov and Novgorod, and spoke sympathetically of the Decembrists, who had tried to restore the "ancient Russian freedom." On the whole, however, Russia was for him a sad example of a Slavic country in which the democratic traditions of ancient Slavdom had been cruelly suppressed by absolutism. The case of Poland was entirely different: here the ancient Slavic principles had been weakened by western feudalism and Catholicism, but had later reemerged and reestablished themselves in the form of "gentry democracy." True, ancient Slavic freedom was confined there to one estate only. Nevertheless, Lelewel argued, the natural tendency of "gentry democracy" was to enlarge freedom, not restrict it. If this truly Slavic tendency had not prevailed and resulted in the general democratization of the Commonwealth, it was due to the kings who never lost monarchical leanings, and to the magnates who distorted the egalitarian principles of the gentry republic while paying it lip service.

Such a conception combined severe criticism of the Polish past with an extreme romantic idealization of it. The objects of criticism were kings and magnates; the objects of idealization were the poor gentry with their dietines and other republican institutions. The Commonwealth of the "Golden Age" was seen as something unique in world history—as the only case of a large agrarian country organized in a republican way. This emphasis on the agrarian character of Poland was combined with a strange indifference to the decline of Polish cities. Lelewel (who came from a polonized German family) even thought that the development of Polish cities, whose inhabitants were often of German background, may have led to a dangerous increase of German influence in Poland.[43]

In the political life of the émigrés, Lelewel represented the most moderate Left. Much more radical was the Polish Democratic Society (Towarzystwo Demokratyczne Polskie, or TDP), the best organized and most numerous party of Polish democrats in exile. Its ideologists were influenced at first not so much by Polish republican traditions as by the modern French republicanism of Robespierre, Marat, and Saint-Just. Jan Nepomucen Janowski, the son of a simple peasant, emphasized that a true republic is inconceivable without a true democracy and thence concluded that neither the Polish oligarchy nor magnates nor even the "gentry republic" of the Golden Age deserved to be called "republics" in the proper sense of the term; he even claimed that a true democratic republic had never yet existed. A few years later, however, the ideologists of the TDP (including Janowski) became more sympathetic toward the Polish past and put more emphasis on the native sources of their thought. In the "Great Manifesto" of 1836 they paid tribute to the tradition of Polish "gentry republicanism." Following Lelewel, they stressed the alleged causal relation between ancient Slavic communalism and the Polish gentry's love of freedom. Their criticism of the May Constitution was even sharper than Lelewel's because they saw the espousal of royalism as contrary not only to the Polish national spirit but to the spirit of the age as well. The "gentry republic," especially the Commonwealth of the Golden Age, was in their eyes superior to the Western absolute monarchies of that time. At the same time, however, they saw "gentry democracy" as far removed from genuine democracy and refused to extol or continue any traditions specific to the gentry as a separate social estate.

Edward Dembowski, an outstanding Left-Hegelian philosopher and the leading spirit of the revolutionary movement in Poland, who was to become the virtual leader of the Cracow uprising of 1846, should be placed even more to the left than the TDP: he combined a democratic radicalism, especially pronounced in his approach to the agrarian question, with a romantic socialism demanding, although not immediately, the complete abolition of private property.[44] His *Outline of Polish Literature*, mentioned above, contains a philosophy of Polish history which could be described as translating Lelewel's historical views into the speculative language of Hegelianism. The whole span of Polish history and literature is here presented as self-estrangement of the dormant national spirit through the process of "latinization," followed by the process of returning to itself on the higher level of self-awareness—a process which entered its final stage in the literary and revolutionary activity of the romantic epoch. The sixteenth century, called "the epoch of splendor," is seen in this perspective both as the culminating point of "Latinization" and as the first important step towards a national self-awakening. This is because the victory of the "democracy of the gentry" was a victory for the Slavic tendency within the latinized culture, a victory for democracy, although confined to one estate only. It is the "democracy of the gentry" which explains, in Dembowski's eyes, the splendid flowering of Renaissance culture, including, of course, Kochanowski's poetry. It is natural, therefore, that he devotes relatively more space to such progressive political thinkers of the Golden Age as Frycz Modrzewski, Andrzej Wolan, whom he praises for his fight against the Jesuits, Wawrzyniec Goślicki (Laurentius Grimalius Goslicius), the author of "the famous and important book" De optimo senatore,[45] and many others. In the religious sphere he sees an anti-Latin and, therefore, more nationalist tendency in Protestantism, especially in the radical Reformation represented by the Socinians or Polish Brethren. The victory of the Jesuit Counter Reformation is regarded by him as the beginning of a cultural and political decline. In some cases, however, he is not consistent. Stanisław Orzechowski (Orichovius), for instance, one of the main pillars of the Counter Reformation, is treated most sympathetically and judged as "undeniably progressive for his time."[46] The obvious reason for this rather strange appraisal is Orzechowski's adamant republicanism.[47]

In this way "gentry republicanism" was "rehabilitated" by progressive romantic thinkers, and the eighteenth-century "party of reforms" fell into disfavor because of its real or alleged monarchism. As a rule, the more radical a given thinker was, the more critical was his attitude towards the Polish Enlightenment. Dembowski, for instance, dismissed the Polish "age of light" as aping everything French. The reforms initiated and carried out by the leaders of the Enlightenment, including the May Constitution, were, in his view, destructive to Poland because they led to the replacement of the republican form of government by a constitutional monarchy.

The great messianic poets, Adam Mickiewicz and Juliusz Słowacki, combined idealization of ancient Polish republicanism with an extreme form of romantic hero-worship. They believed in the crucial role of great divinely inspired men in history; in matters of faith they were awaiting a personal Messiah and in politics they set all their hopes on charismatic leadership. The idea of charismatic authority enabled them to recognize the need for a truly strong personal leadership, as advocated by the monarchists, without making any concessions to rationalist, Enlightenment-inspired criticism of "Polish anarchy." Strong leadership, they argued, does not consist in dynastic principle, enlightened absolutism, or "majority" rule in the Diet. The early Poles, like other Slavic nations (with the important exception of Russia), lacked great divinely-inspired leaders; this was their misfortune, but they were right in rejecting the doctrines of the West.

According to Mickiewicz, the essence of the ancient Commonwealth was an attempt to base society exclusively upon the inner impulses of its members, upon their "good will" strengthened by "enthusiasm and exaltation."[48] Free elections (before their degeneration in the eighteenth century) were in his eyes full of religious meaning. Their results were regarded as a decree of Providence, as a miracle, and not as an outcome of deliberate effort. Because of this voters were forbidden to divide into parties and to organize electoral campaigns, which could distort the spontaneous generation of a common will.[49] Praising ancient Polish freedom, for its moral, not merely "mechanical," unification of society led Mickiewicz to defend the *liberum veto*. For him the right of veto was perfectly compatible with charismatic leadership because freedom was perfectly compatible with divine inspiration: if the leader was truly charismatic, no one would, as a rule, oppose his decisions, and if anybody dared to use his right of veto, it would mean that his spirit was stronger than the spiritual power of the leader and, consequently, that he himself had the right to impose his will. Similar views were voiced by Słowacki, who called himself "a republican in spirit." From his point of view, the *liberum veto* was a precious device by means of which the true spiritual hierarchy was able to defend itself against a false, artificial, material hierarchy. In ancient Poland, in sharp contrast to Western bourgeois republicanism, lesser spirits, although in the majority, could not rule over nobler ones who, on the contrary, were assured of the right to oppose the will of the majority. Interestingly, this approaches the view of Andrzej Maksymilian Fredro, who also saw the veto as the special privilege of intellectual and moral superiority.[50]

The idea of spiritual leadership conflicts with the modern principle of the impersonal rule of law; it conflicted also with the legal convictions characteristic of the "democracy of the gentry." Mickiewicz and Słowacki were fully aware of this. For Mickiewicz, written laws were a rationalistic device and his ideal Poland was a country which could dispense with them. Słowacki, in turn, contrasted "the dead force" of positive laws with the higher "laws of the spirit" as exemplified, in his view, by the sixteenth-century aristocratic rebel, Samuel Zborowski, whose execution by Chancellor Zamoyski (the incarnation of the soulless state law) became the topic of one of his mystical dramas.

The third messianic poet, Zygmunt Krasiński, idealized Poland's past in a more conventional way. He glorified the piety of the ancient Poles, their tolerance and love of freedom, and emphasized their knightly generosity, nor did he hesitate to claim that Poland had "left the whitest page in the history of Europe—least defiled by crime and most Christlike."[51] It is interesting, however, that in his youth he inclined to a very different view. Thus, in a letter of 1836 to his father, he described the Poles as a bleak, lazy nation, lacking true "organicity," energy, and creativeness.[52] He attributed this to the absence of powerful social struggles in Polish history resulting from the complete domination exercised by the gentry from the sixteenth century. He even explained the sixteenth-century religious toleration in Poland as the result rather of a lack of strong convictions than of a genuine respect for freedom.

It only remains to consider briefly the fate of two conceptions of a nation: the conception of a multilingual and multi-ethnic political nation, typical of the Polish Golden Age, and the conception of a "nation of proprietors," put forward by the eighteenth-century reformers.

Polish Enlightenment thinkers, like Kołłątaj, defined a nation as a political category, not as an ethnic or linguistic community. At the same time, like the

French Jacobins, they insisted that modern nationhood demands legal, linguistic and cultural homogeneity. The same view was later held by the democratic radicals from the TDP, for whom all kinds of "provincialism" and "separatism" were, by definition, reactionary and incompatible with the centralizing tendency of progress. They did not define a nation by linguistic criteria and, just because of this, demanded the restoration of the Polish-Lithuanian state with its historical borders; on the other hand, unlike the sixteenth-century gentry, they were firmly convinced that the official language of the Polish state ought to be Polish and that the laws of the country should be unified. A different attitude was represented by Lelewel, Mickiewicz, and other Poles from the ethnically mixed eastern territories, who were proud of the cultural diversity of their homeland and wanted to preserve it. For Lelewel, as for the sixteenth-century Poles, the Polish nation consisted of Mazovians, Lithuanians, Ruthenians, and so forth; even Polish Germans were in his eyes simply German-speaking Poles.[53] Notwithstanding these differences, both Lelewel and the ideologists of the TDP represented a *political* variety of nationalism. The romantic nationalism of the messianic poets, who defined a nation as a "community of kindred spirits realizing a common historical mission," was also very different from the ethnic and linguistic nationalism allegedly characteristic of East-Central Europe. The sweeping generalizations of Hans Kohn have little relevance to the Polish nationalism of the Enlightenment and of the romantic epoch.

The Enlightenment thinkers' conception of a "nation of proprietors" was an attempt to redefine the concept of a "political nation" in the "bourgeois" spirit and so to secure the dominance of that part of the gentry which could be transformed into a class of modern landowners. In this sense it was a step towards "bourgeois" liberalism; at the same time, however, it was a major departure from the democratic principle of political equality among the gentry. As I have already mentioned, the mass of poor and landless gentry were not easily reconciled to their new degraded status; they preferred rather to share their political rights with other poor and landless people than to be deprived of them in favor of landowners. That is why the idea of a "nation of proprietors" was never accepted by democratic national-liberation movements in partitioned Poland. After the November uprising the rejection of this idea became bound up with a more or less determined rejection of the notion of "absolute" private property. Lelewel, Mickiewicz, and other romantic interpreters of Polish history saw the concept as something alien to the Polish national spirit, and even the ideologists of the TDP defended private property very half-heartedly, stressing that what they meant was only a conditional right which could always be suspended for the sake of the common good. The agrarian socialists, like Stanisław Worcell and other leaders of the "Communities of Polish People," proclaimed that private property was "the center of all evil which oppresses mankind."[54] All these attitudes were combined with a conscious anti-Western-ism and anti-liberalism, that is, an outright condemnation of "bourgeois"values. The socialists did not hesitate to declare that the old, feudal aristocracy was better than the "new aristocracy of money" and that the only function of the liberal doctrine of inalienable "human rights" was to sanctify egoism, especially the dirty, divisive egoism of private property. Equally anti-liberal was the ethos of romantic nationalism: against subjective legal rights it set moral duties and preached a noble disinterestedness, selflessness, and boundless sacrifice in the service of national aims.

It should be added that, in the stateless conditions of existence in Poland, it was difficult for Polish patriots, deeply imbued as they were with the knightly traditions of the gentry, to find a legal outlet for patriotic public activity. The ethos of public service in the political sphere, characteristic of the ancient democracy of the gentry, became transformed, very one-sidedly, into the ethos of an open struggle on the battlefield, in accordance with the gospel of heroism preached by the great romantic poets. Under the influence of messianic ro-manticism the very idea of a nation became unduly spiritualized, divorced from empirical reality; patriotism was identified as service of the glorious "national idea," which was found in the past and would be triumphant again in the future, rather than with the prosaic daily task of making life more bearable in the present. The view that it is possible to serve one's nation by furthering worthy individual interests in the sphere of civil society appeared only with the so-called "Warsaw positivists" and even then proved to be short-lived.

In this way, the legacy of the gentry democracy, combined with the legacy of romantic nationalism, created important psychological obstacles to the emergence and respectability of "bourgeois virtues" in Poland. Cyprian Nor-wid, on the eve of the desperate uprising of 1863, summarized the position by contrasting "Poland as a society" and "Poland as a nation." According to his famous diagnosis, the Poles were supreme as a nation because their patriotism in crucial moments was superb; they were least admirable as a society because they were deficient in the virtues of will and character indispensable to normal, everyday life. Let me quote:

This is Polish society!—this is the nation which is undeniably great as far as *patriotism* is concerned but which *as a society* represents noth-ing.
    Everything which concerns patriotic and historical feelings is so great and so noble in this nation that I am ready to raise my hat before an urchin of Warsaw—but everything which one can expect not from patriotism, not from *national* but from social feelings is merely budding here and so insignificant, almost mean, that I fear even to think of it! [. . .]
    We are no *society* at all.
    We are a great *national banner*.[55]

Notes

1. Charles Homer Haskins and Robert Howard Lord, *Some Problems of the Peace Conference* (Cambridge: Harvard University Press, 1920), pp. 22-23.

2. See Wacław Lednicki, *Life and Culture of Poland as Reflected in Polish Literature* (New York: Roy, 1944), pp. 3-4.

3. Cf. Gustav Radbruch, in *The Legal Philosphies of Lask, Radbruch and Dabin* (Cambridge: Harvard University Press, 1950), pp. 101-110.

4. Cf. Karl Marx, "On the Jewish Question," in Karl Marx, Friedrich Engels, *Collected Works*, vol. 3 (London, 1975), pp. 162-164.

5. See Andrzej Frycz Modrzewski, *De Republica emendanda*, Bk. II, "On Laws," chapter 3. In Lech Szczucki (ed.), *Filozofia i myśl społeczna XVI wieku* (Philosophy and social thought of the 16th century) (Warsaw: PWN, 1978), pp. 258ff (hereafter referred to as Szczucki).

6. *The Cambridge History of Poland: from Origins to Sobieski* (Cambridge: The University Press, 1950), p. 440 (chapter written by J. Siemieński).

7. See Claude Backvis, *Szkice o kulturze staropolskiej* (Essays on old Polish culture) (Warsaw: PIW, 1975), p. 475.

8. See Szczucki, p. 245.

9. Isaiah Berlin, *Four Essays on Liberty* (London-Oxford-NewYork: Oxford University Press, 1969), p. 131.

10. Cf. Konstanty Grzybowski, *Rzeczy odległe a bliskie*, (Those who are distant and yet close) (Warsaw: Książka i Wiedza, 1969), p. 143.

11. See Zbigniew Ogonowski, Introduction to *Filozofia i myśl społeczna XVII wieku* (Philosophy and social thought of the 17th century) (Warsaw: PWN, 1979), pp. 30-311 (hereafter referred to as Ogonowski).

12. See Backvis, *Szkice o kulturze staropolskiej*, pp. 556-558.

13. See Władysław Konopczyński, *Liberum veto* (Cracow, 1918).

14. See Claude Backvis, "Wymóg jednomyślności a wola ogółu" (The requirement of unanimity and the general will), *Czasopismo prawno-historyczne* 27, no. 2 (1975); Zbigniew Ogonowski, "W obronie liberum veto" (In defense of the *liberum veto*), *Człowiek i Światopogląd* 4 (1975).

15. See Jerzy Michalski, *Rousseau i sarmacki republikanizm* (Rousseau and Sarmatian republicanism) (Warsaw: PWN, 1977).

16. For a detailed critical discussion of Meinecke's and Kohn's theories see my book, *Philosophy and Romantic Nationalism: the Case of Poland* (Oxford: Clarendon Press, 1982), pp. 64-69 (hereafter referred to as Walicki, *Philosophy*).

17. See Hans Kohn, *The Idea of Nationalism*, 6th ed. (New York: Macmillan, 1956), pp. 2 and 103; also Hans Kohn, "Nationalism," in *International Encyclopedia of the Social Sciences*, ed. D. L. Sills, vol. 11, 1968.

18. See *The Cambridge History of Poland*, p. 438.

19. Friedrich Meinecke, *Cosmopolitanism and the National State* (Princeton: Princeton University Press, 1970), p. 10.

20. See Jean Fabre, *Lumières et romantism: énergie et nostalgie de Rousseau à Mickiewicz* (Paris: C. Klicksieck, 1963), pp. 131-49.

21. See Hieronim Stroynowski, *Nauka prawa przyrodzonego, politycznego, ekonomiki politycznej i prawa narodów* (The science of natural law, political law, law of political economy, and the law of nations), 3rd ed. (Wilno, 1791).

22. Such as Kajetan Skrzetuski, Wincenty Skrzetuski, Antoni Popławski, and others. Cf. Stanisław Hubert, *Poglądy na prawo narodów w Polsce czasów Oświecenia* (Opinions on the law of nations in Poland during the time of the En-

lightenment) (Wrocław: Ossolineum, 1960). This humanitarian tradition in the law of nations in Poland can be traced back to Paulus Vladimiri (Paweł Włodkowic), who at the Council of Constance (1415-1417) defended the thesis that even pagan peoples ought to be treated as legitimate subjects of the law of nations and that therefore their conversion to Christianity by force, as practiced by the Teutonic Knights, should not be allowed.

23. See Janusz Tazbir, *Rzeczpospolita szlachecka wobec wielkich odkryć* (The gentry republic in relation to the great discoveries) (Warsaw: Wiedza Powszechna, 1973), pp. 203-204.

24. Hugo Kołłątaj, et al., *O ustanowieniu i upadku Konstytucji polskiej 3 maja 1791 roku* (On the establishment and collapse of the Polish constitution of 3 May 1791) (Paris, 1868) (First ed. Metz, 1793), p. 5.

25. In his *Considérations sur le gouvernement de Pologne*.

26. See Maurycy Mochnacki, *Pisma wybrane* (Selected writings) (Warsaw: Książka i Wiedza, 1957), p. 358.

27. Janusz Tazbir, *Kultura szlachecka w Polsce* (Gentry culture in Poland) (Warsaw: Wiedza Powszechna, 1978), pp. 71-73.

28. As reported by Mme de Staël: "La liberté c'est un bon code civil."

29. Tadeusz Mikulski, *Ze studiów nad Oświeceniem. Zagadnienia i fakty* (Studies on the Enlightenment. Problems and facts) (Warsaw: PIW, 1956), p. 159. The term "Renaissance" was, of course, of later origin.

30. For a more detailed analysis of the idea of a nation in the Polish thought of the Enlightenment, see my study, "Idea narodu w polskiej myśli oświeceniowej" (The idea of the nation in Polish Enlightenment thought), *Archiwum Historii Filozofii i Myśli Społecznej*, vol. 26, 1980 (hereafter referred to as Walicki, "Idea narodu").

31. See Hugo Kołłątaj, *Listy Anonima i Prawo polityczne narodu polskiego* (Letters of Anonymous and Political law of the Polish nation) (Warsaw: PWN, 1954), vol. 2, pp. 47-48.

32. See Bogusław Leśnodorski, *Dzieło Sejmu Czteroletniego* (The Work of the Four Year Diet) (Wrocław: Ossolineum, 1951), pp. 295-98.

33. Cf. Walicki, "Idea narodu," pp. 54-74. See also Claude Backvis, "Quelques observations à propos du rapport de Bogdan Suchodolski sur le mouvement des idées en Pologne pendant la seconde moitié du XVIIIe siècle," in *Le mouvement des idées dans les pays slaves pendant la seconde moitié de XVIIIe siècle*. Collana di "Richerche Slavistiche," no. 2 (1962), pp. 129 and 131.

34. Kołłątaj, *Listy Anonima*, vol. 1, pp. 352-353.

35. See, for instance, Adam Wawrzyniec Rzewuski, *O formie rządu republikańskiego myśli* (Thoughts on the republican form of government) (1790), vol. 2, pp. 73-74.

36. See Seweryn Rzewuski, *O sukcesji tronu w Polszcze rzecz krótka* (A short essay on succession to the throne in Poland) (1789), p. 25.

37. See Walicki, "Idea narodu," pp. 51-4.

38. He thought that after the victory of the uprising the form of government in Poland would be chosen (once more!) by a freely elected, representative Diet.

39. According to Leśnodorski, *Dzieło Sejmu Czteroletniego*, p. 18.

40. Kołłątaj, *Listy Anonima*, vol. 1, p. 340; vol. 2, p. 308.

41. Cf. Hipolit Grynwasser, *Demokracja szlachecka* (Gentry democracy) (Warsaw: PIW, 1948) (first ed. 1918).

42. For a detailed analysis of the controversy over republicanism and monarchism after 1831, see Walicki, *Philosophy*, pp. 311-41.

43. See Marian Henryk Serejski, *Joachim Lelewel* (Warsaw: PWN, 1953), pp. 102-103.

44. Cf. Walicki, *Philosophy*, pp. 207-25.

45. Edward Dembowski, *Pisma* (Writings) (Warsaw: PWN, 1955) vol. 4, p. 208.

46. Ibid., pp. 204-208.

47. Under Orzechowski's influence the Catholic Church in Poland, including the powerful order of Jesuits, became favorable to the "republicanism of the gentry." In spite of his theocratic leanings, Orzechowski's personal attitude towards the hierarchy of the Church was defiantly nonconformist, as shown in the case of his marriage. This fact also influenced Dembowski's judgement.

48. Adam Mickiewicz, *Dzieła* (Works) (Warsaw: Czytelnik, 1955), vol. 10, p. 44.

49. Ibid., pp. 42-43.

50. See Ogonowski, p. 304.

51. Zygmunt Krasiński, *Pisma* (Writings) (Warsaw, 1912), vol. 7, p. 99.

52. See Józef Kallenbach, *Zygmunt Krasiński* (Lwów, 1904), vol. 2, pp. 290-92.

53. It is interesting to note that this view was fully shared by Engels. Cf. Karl Marx, Friedrich Engels, *Collected Works* (New York, 1976-), vol. 7, p. 339.

54. See Peter Brock, *Polish Revolutionary Populism* (Toronto, Buffalo: University of Toronto Press, 1977), p. 17.

55. Cyprian Kamil Norwid, *Pisma wszystkie* (Complete works) (Warsaw: PIW, 1971-76), vol. 9, pp. 63-64.

NEW CONSTITUTION

OF THE

GOVERNMENT of POLAND,

ESTABLISHED

BY THE REVOLUTION,

THE THIRD OF MAY, 1791.

THE SECOND EDITION.

L'ONDON:
PRINTED FOR J. DEBRETT,
OPPOSITE BURLINGTON HOUSE, PICCADILLY.
M.DCC.XCI.

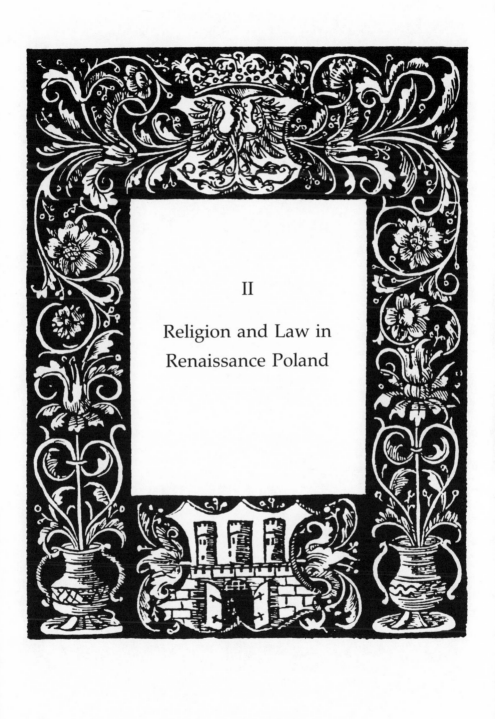

II

Religion and Law in
Renaissance Poland

4

Strains in the Christology of the Emerging Polish Brethren

George H. Williams

I. Introduction

The transaction by which Jesus Christ was understood as a Savior has never been made a conciliar or papal dogma. It is instead referred to generically as a theory of the atonement (*satisfactio*). The stress and metaphor may be incarnational, substitutionary, penal, rectoral, redemptive, death/demon-vanquishing, exemplary, mediatorial. The problem of Christ as soteriological Mediator became prominent in the sixteenth century among Protestants of the second generation.

In antiquity, after the idea of Jesus Christ (Messiah) as a temporal mediator (savior, *soter*) had been largely reconceived by Church Fathers as a postponed eschatological event (with a possible millennial reign), interest shifted to the problem of Christ the cosmological mediator in creation (the concept, if not always the word) and to that of the soteriological mediator between God and man. The Protestant Reformers would take the cosmological mediation of the Logos Son, consubstantial with God the Father, as a credal given in common with Catholics. But they extended the concept of Christ the soteriological mediator in an utterly new theological context in which the doctrine of an intradeical decree of election (in the repristination of Augustine) was the ultimate basis of salvation and in which the inherited sacramental system had been partly undercut. Baptism was no longer the effectual conduit for the merit of Christ in the effacement of original sin, while the Lord's Supper, however differently understood by various Protestants, was for them all primarily a reminder of the once-for-all saving act of Christ in effectuating the decree of predestination for the elect, which was to be experienced in faith.

In the Polish-Lithuanian Commonwealth in the middle third of the Golden Age, eight figures[1] emerged for whom the implications for the Protestant theory of the atonement of the new stress on Christ the Mediator was of considerable interest: Andreas Osiander, Giorgio Biandrata, Francesco Stancaro, Francesco Lismanino, Stanisław Orzechowski, and Andrzej Frycz Modrzewski.[2] In no other state of Europe was there so much troublement about Christ the Mediator (1 Tim. 2:5) as in the Commonwealth.

Apart from the case of the Lutheran Osiander in Ducal Prussia, it would appear that the Reformed in Sarmatia, natives and refugees, raised most of the questions. The answers were mostly formulated in Switzerland, notably by John Calvin. The answers that came from the Reformed cantons of the Confederation were often felt locally to be confusing and possibly heretical. Many of the pastors and patrons remained stubbornly dissatisfied with the authoritarian answers, not always consistent, coming to them from Geneva, Lausanne, Zurich, and Basel. The patrons of the Commonwealth Reformed Church and her pastors, surrounded (as the Confederational Helvetians were not) by other lords and pastors who might be Catholic, Byzantine, Lutheran, or Czech Brethren, and surely with serfs on their land and artisans in the villages and towns which they owned who commonly remained Catholic or Orthodox, felt the full weight of any decision they should make in private or in synod.

In dealing anew with the strains in the Christology of the emerging Polish Brethren, I do not intend to repeat what I myself have elsewhere done and many others about me and before me;[3] but rather I wish to place the emergence of Christian Unitarianism on Commonwealth soil "in its European context," including its ancient European one, as it were, that of the first seven ecumenical councils, 325-787. In the following exposition we set aside the idiosyncracies and provocatively expressed convictions of the Hebraist Francesco Stancaro of Mantua[4] and also the ecclesio-theological intrigues of the perhaps too much maligned physician of the courts of Cracow and of Gyulafehérvár, Giorgio Biandrata of Saluzzo,[5] which usually rivet attention whether in sympathetic or in hostile accounts, in order to deal with John Calvin, as a representative but also as the most influential Helvetian divine for the Commonwealth.

What Calvin wrote up to his death in 1564 to the Polish Reformed about Jesus Christ the Mediator was a body of christological formulation more innovative in relation to scholastic and patristic formularies than he perhaps realized. What he wrote both to those who would remain loyal to him and call themselves, after 1565, the Major (Reformed) Church or Calvinists proper or Evangelicals (the last term not preempted in the Commonwealth by the Lutherans) and to those who would deviate from him as the Minor (Reformed) Church of the Polish Brethren (or, who after their exile in 1660, would eventually be called by their friendly or hostile readers, Socinians) would make of the principal Genevan divine the outstanding formulator and defender of a new christological emphasis, of indeed an almost innovative doctrine. This doctrine of the "Person of the Mediator" would, in fact, become a principal cause for "the conscientious defection of "the main leaders of "the Polish Brethren" (Calvin's name for *all* Reformed in the Commonwealth), lest they be locally dubbed "Arian." It is therefore ironic that in the eventual decrees leading to their banishment, the Polish Brethren of the Minor Church were to be called precisely "Arians" as well as "Anabaptists," charges capitally offensive in Christian antiquity.[6]

If in what follows more is heard about Switzerland than about Sarmatia, it is because of the importance of recognizing precisely in the European context that the principal *theological* contribution of Poles to Protestantism was the questions they raised, along with a number of foreign divines and religious refugees among them, questions that were destined to find their most abiding distillation in the pages of the later editions of the *Institutes*. There were almost no true Arians in Poland, as in contrast, there would be much later, for example, in New England, in the fourth-century senses of the term.

Concerning the century of Arius, patristic scholarship has fairly recently come into some new evidence and especially has it gained fresh perspective on the various kinds of Arians.[7] In the meantime scriptural scholarship has made notable advances in our understanding of the biblical texts adduced by the various ancient Arians and their ultimate vanquishers.[8] Hence, we are in a better position to understand just where the strains were felt in the Christology that eventuated in the schism of the Minor Church of the Polish Brethren, what was old and what was new in the argumentation of Calvin and allied Helvetians, also of Biandrata and Stancaro. The correspondence of the Reformed with the Poles and of Calvin in particular is extensive;[9] but to make the points it is sufficient to deal with Calvin's statements respecting Biandrata and Stancaro, active in the Commonwealth and Transylvania.

Transylvanian (Reformed Christian) Unitarianism, the Minor Church of Polonia, both before and after the engagement in its life and thought by Faustus Socinus (in effect from 1580 to 1604), and the Minor Church of Lithuania under the influence of Simon Budny were three quite different kinds of Unitarian Churches. The first and the last held with Calvin and the classical Protestant Reformers to the view that, as Henry Bullinger of Zurich put it best, there was one covenant in two dispensations, even though the Greek part of the Bible is, in fact, called the New *Covenant*.[10] Transylvanian and Lithuanian Christian Unitarians were not disposed to believers' immersion or to dispensing with the sword. They were Biblical Unitarians. The Polish Brethren in the sense of the Minor Church of Polonia extending after the Union of Lublin of 1569 into fully Byzantine-rite territory (but distinguished from the Minor Church in Lithuania) tended to be New Testament Christians, immersionist pacifists adhering to the Apostles' Creed.

Before the schism of 1565 a factor was operative that is to be associated with the pronounced preference of Jan Łaski, who headed the Helvetian Church in the Commonwealth from 1556 to his death in January 1560:[11] Łaski was a classical Protestant Reformer who remained steadfast to the principle of salvation by faith alone and the one Rule of Faith that prevailed, as he assumed, in the ante-Nicene Church, the Apostles' Creed. He also took an early theological fancy to the idea that he got from Erasmus of the *triplex munus Christi*. This is not as such a scriptural formulation, although the discharge by Christ of the threefold office of Prophet (Teacher), (High) Priest, and King can be found disparately in the New Testament, and the compact formulation was adumbrated by Eusebius of Caesarea and intimated here and there by Thomas Aquinas. Although it would also eventually be given some prominence by Calvin, Łaski got the notion from Erasmus (*Commentary on Psalm 2*), when he was a student resident in the great humanist's house in Basel, soon after Erasmus's work was published.[12]

In any case, the Polish Brethren of the Minor Church would remain loyal to Łaski and ultimately to Erasmus in making of the *triplex munus Christi* the structuring principle of the Racovian Cathechesis of 1574 and the Racovian Catechism of 1605 right up through its various versions to that of Amsterdam 1665. And the Brethren would submit as their Confession of Faith at the Colloquium Charitativum of Toruń, 1644/45, the elaborately annotated Apostles' Creed by Jonas Szlichtyng.[13] They would so long as they were a Church continue to practice believers' immersion despite a temporary and partial minimizing of baptism of any kind under the very special notion of Socinus related to his quasi-gnostic view of Christ's teaching authority authorized at an ascent to heaven *after* his baptism by John.[14]

To the end of their existence as a Church in the Netherlands, Ducal Prussia, and elsewhere, about 1685, the Polish Brethren even in exile took seriously the Apostles' Creed and baptized by immersion in the name of the Father and the Son and the Holy Spirit in accordance with Matt. 28:19. Yet well before Socinus had completed his theological guidance of the Minor Church, though never a member of it because he had declined to validate believers' immersion and fought the practice and any rebaptism, the Polish Brethren were fully Unitarian New Testament Christians with a sense of distance from the Old Testament, a stance not shared by the Transylvanian Unitarians nor by most of the "Lithuanian" Brethren of ethnic Lithuanian, Byelorussian, and Ruthenian inheritance. Indeed, the residual influence of the quite often Orthodox nurture of converts to the Minor Church, especially in the seventeenth century has been little noticed. On Byzantine-rite territories, notably in Volhynia, converts to the Minor Church of the Polish Brethren, especially noblemen who had been educated in the west and often served as co-moderators with pastors in synod, would have been fully aware of the absence in the Orthodox liturgy of the *Filioque* in the Niceno-Constantinopolitan Creed, the prominence of Jesus Christ pictured as Infant in the arms of Mary (Incarnation), as Teacher (Prophet), and as Christos Pantocrator (as King/Judge), along with the absence of any indigenous iconography of the Holy Trinity so common in the Catholic west, especially westward of Catholic Slavia. On Byzantine-rite territory converts would also have been familiar with Orthodox baptismal immersion. Such were some ways in which once Orthodox converts could have felt drawn to the Minor Church and its simplified Triadology and Christology based on the Apostles'

Creed. Much that has just been rehearsed has taken us beyond the decisive years of the strain in the undivided Helvetian Church in the Commonwealth but necessarily, perhaps, to sharpen the focus.

The key to the strain in the sixteenth-century Reformed Church of Polonia is the prominent use by the Helvetian divines and the Reformed divine of the Palatinate, Zacharias Ursinus, and by the Lutheran divines Phillip Melanchthon and Andreas Osiander, first of Nuremberg, then of Königsberg, of the term "Mediator." It is only a bit of an exaggeration to say that the Reformation problem of Christ the Mediator was a problem engendered on Commonwealth soil, just as in antiquity Arianism arose in Egypt and Donatism in North Africa.[15]

A reason why the problem of Christ the Mediator became prominent in Poland in the course of the Reformation is that almost exclusively there the Latin-Byzantine-rite boundary *cut through* a multiconfessional and multiethnic commonwealth where—as in no other Eastern state, including Transylvania, a Latin-rite peninsula in an Orthodox sea (with almost no intermingling of fresh and salt water, as it were)—some converts to various forms of Protestantism had come from an Orthodox heritage, and still more, though Poles of Catholic heritage, had come from or lived in Orthodox terrain. Moreover, several of the *foreign* leaders of the Reformed were either from Orthodox territory within or without the Commonwealth, for example, Francesco Lismanino from Chios (Corfu) or had made a concerted study of the Orthodox Fathers, for example, Francesco Stancaro from Mantua. Furthermore, from the start, the evolving Reformed Church felt special affinity with the Czech Brethren, prominent notably in Great Poland. Converted lords and their Czech pastors, in contact with the higher authorities in their ancestral homeland, were conscious of efforts in the past to establish not only contact but also even, if possible, communion with the Church of Constantinople.

Thus an evocation of the history of the gradual differentiation between the Latin West and the Orthodox on Triadology and Christology helps to explain how the formulations and counsel of Calvin with respect to Christ the Mediator would be differently assessed in, say, London and La Rochelle, in Lublin and around Lwów.

II. A Historical Sketch of the Concept of
Christ the Mediator

In the New Testament *mediator/mesites* appears in only three places: in Gal. 3:19f., Heb. 8:6, 9:15, 12:24, and 1 Tim. 2:5. In Hebrews it is used of Christ twice and Jesus once as Mediator of the new and better covenant. These places are not decisive, although they come to play a part. Nor is the usage in Galatians decisive, where the word serves twice as "intermediary" between God and man respectively: as Law and, without precision, as Christ or the New Law enunciated by him. Decisive is 1 Tim. 2:5: "For there is one God, and there is one Mediator between God and men, the *man* Christ Jesus, who gave himself as a *ransom* for all." The word *ransom* here and elsewhere provides the common alternate soteriological phrasing: theories of *Redemption* (as well as of Atonement).

Without the term "Mediator" its equivalent occurs in Phil. 2:5f: "Christ Jesus, who though he was in the form of God, did not count equality with God a thing to be grasped, yet emptied himself, taking the form of a servant, being born in the likeness of men, . . . obedient unto death." This is another wording for the soteriological Mediator.

In the New Testament there is also Christ the cosmological Mediator, in the sense of the instrument of creation. Most striking here is deutero-Pauline Col. 1:15-20: "He [the Son/Jesus Christ] is the image of the invisible God, *the firstborn of all creatures* . . .; for in him all things were created, in heaven and on earth, visible and invisible . . . all things were created through him and for him. He is the head of the body the Church." And the passage moves on to the soteriological role of the cosmological Mediator, namely, in "reconciling all things . . . by the blood of the cross." The cosmological relationship between God and the Mediator (the term not used) is differently set forth by Paul in 1 Cor. 8:6: "One God from whom are all things; and one Lord, *through whom* are all things."

Now in Philippians and in Colossians the authors were drawing upon pre-Pauline hymns or formularies, 2:1-11 and 1:11-20 respectively, of the early Church in the tradition of the Jewish Wisdom literature, of which the most important single passage in the canonical Old Testament is the soliloquy of Sophia in Proverbs, especially 8:22: "The Lord created me at the beginning of his work, the first acts of old." Hellenistic Jewish converts to Jesus as the Christ or Gentile Christians, who believed in Yahweh or El or Elohim (plural), both meaning God, or Adonai (Lord), were making the claim in these hymns and confessions of faith, embedded in two epistles, that not merely their master, Joshuah ben Joseph, was the pre-existent Mashiach *in the mind of God*, the righteous ruler foreseen by the prophets in the Spirit of God, but also that their Christ was that Sophia that, perhaps identical with the Spirit of God hovering over the Chaos at the beginning of creation, was in fact the instrument or Mediator of creation. By the beginning of the Common Era Yahweh, God, Lord, Father were sensed both by Jews and by Christian Jews to be so far transcendent that some secondary divine eminence seemed necessary in cosmological and then in soteriological mediation.[16]

For Gentile Christians who had not come to Christianity as former proselytes of Judaism, the greatest thing about the new religion was its explanation of the world and all therein on the basis of having the most ancient revelation and compelling cosmogony, creation *ex nihilo*. Clement, counted as the successor of Peter in Rome, in his Epistle to the church in Corinth in 96 C.E., was half priestly writer (as the Elohist Writer in Genesis) and half Stoic when, with many resonances from the liturgy of the Greek-speaking church in Rome, he lauded the Creator of the heavens and the earth. For Clement of Rome and for Justin Martyr of Samaria and then Rome the significance of the Logos in creation was fully as important as the role of the incarnate Logos or eternally begotten Son in his obedience as Jesus Christ on the cross.

Nevertheless, by the last third of the third century in the struggle against the Dynamic Monarchians, headed by the able Paul of Samosata, bishop of Antioch, condemned by the synod there of 268, catholic/orthodox Christianity required, appealing to Proverbs 8, Philippians, and Colossians *inter alia*, the affirmation of a preexistent Jesus Christ as cosmological, i.e., a Joshuah Mashiach Creator, the image of God the Father. The reason for this was that Paul of Samosata held to a Triadology of Father, Wisdom, and Word of a single *hypostasis* (all three entities *homoousioi* within the Godhead before the birth of Jesus); and in his Christology at the Incarnation the Word rested upon Jesus as one person on another. The relation of the thought of Bishop Paul the Samosatene and St. Lucian, teacher of the distinctive exegetical school of Antioch, is not clear. Lucian established the *textus receptus* of the Septuagint. He left behind the only creed in antiquity to make 1 Tim. 2:5 on Christ the Mediator central to the atoning action. He died a martyr under Maximin in 312.[17]

In the course of the Arian controversy, the subordinationist texts of Proverbs, Philippians, and Colossians constituted a problem for those who would emerge as Catholic/Orthodox. During the innumerable local synods and several ecumenical synods that in the end were not counted as such between Nicaea 325 and Constantinople 381, the concerns of ordinary worshipers, theological bishops, and theologically minded emperors oscillated between a stress on *cosmological* to a stress on *soteriological* mediation, while the emperors like Constantine and not a few bishops like Eusebius of Caesarea, Eusebius of Nicomedia (at the time an eastern capital of the Tetrarchy), Asterius, Eunomius, and many more were also concerned with *political* mediation. In this third sense the emperor was accorded a status in temporal salvation, as temporal mediator, Constantine a kind of Gentile Mashiach (cf. Eusebius of Caesarea), i.e., the *Nomos empsychos* for the *pax Romana*, as embodied Law, comparable to Christ on the cross: the one in respect to world order, the other a savior for the afterlife.[18]

The first seven ecumenical councils progressively clarified the identity of the Second Person of the Trinity and the Person of Jesus Christ, set forth in the Niceno-Constantinopolitan Creed as promulgated by the Council of Chalcedon of 451, which Council further defined Jesus Christ as one person (*prosopon*) and one hypostasis (Latin: *subsistentia*) in (Greek: out of) two natures and, by calling Mary Theotokos, Mother of God (as already at Ephesus, 431), accomplished for Christology what the philosophical term *homoousios* (of the same *substantia*) had assured for Triadology at Nicaea I for the Son and at Constantinople I for the Holy Spirit. The remaining three of the first seven ecumenical councils, notably Constantinople II and III, imparted further precision to the terminology and the conceptualization of the hypostatic union of the God-Man Jesus Christ in affirming that his *hypostasis/persona*, of the eternally begotten

Son of the Triune Godhead was identical with the *prosopon/persona*, also the *hypostasis/subsistentia* of Jesus Christ in what has been called an "asymmetrical" Christology,[19] the divine Person prevailing, the manhood, however, understood as complete in every respect, including the will.

In this development of doctrine, reflected in the Niceno-Constantinopolitan Creed, no particular theory of atonement or precise clarification of the central transaction of salvation was elevated to the status dogma. Although numerous creeds were shaped by synods, particularly in the decisive period between Nicaea I, 325, and Constantinople I, 381, the cosmological, the political, and the soteriological mediatorship of Christ were never fully defined or interrelated; and in only one ephemeral creed was Timothy 2:5 with the term Mediator employed, the so-called II Creed of Antioch of the synod there in 341 (possibly the same as that of Lucian, above at n. 17).

The Orthodox Church would continue to hold to the definitions of the first seven ecumenical councils (and would not reckon the Latin series as ecumenical or binding); but the Latin Church in the era of scholasticism would feel free to reopen some of the problems of the hypostatic union regarded as settled by the Orthodox, while still later a sector of that "Latin" Christendom become Protestant, with a stress on scriptural authority alone, would, at first, be even less heedful of even the first five ecumenical councils than the Catholics (on these points more below).

In the meantime, while the East and West preserved a Creed revered as that of the Apostles, alongside the Niceno-Constantinopolitan Creed (having rejected or anathematized the many ephemeral creeds of the fourth century), the West had also the late fifth-century hymnic *Te Deum laudamus*, ascribed, since the ninth century, to Ambrose and Augustine (much esteemed by Luther among the four *Symbola* he commented on in 1538), and the so-called Athanasian Creed, the early fifth-century *Quincunquevult*.

The *Quincunquevult* (used in the Book of Common Prayer in replacement of the Apostles' Creed thirteen holidays in the liturgical year) further complicated Western triadological and christological language by speaking of the *substantia* of God and the *substantia* of Mary joined in the person of Christ, "who although he be God and man, is nevertheless *non duo, sed unus est Christus*." Except in this originally anti-Nestorian Creed the divine being (*substantia/ousia*) was not expressly identified with the divine *natura/physis* of the incarnate Word. And in Christian antiquity the two Latin terms for Person (*persona* and *subsistentia*) and their Greek counterparts were generally kept apart, although because the creeds were liturgicized it was *persona* in Latin and *hypostasis* in Greek that tended to prevail in describing Christ as one in two natures.

By the end of the age of the first seven councils, ca. 800, the Church of the Frankish Empire except for Rome itself had come to accept the addendum of the *Filioque* to the Niceno-Constantinopolitan Creed added by the III Synod of Toledo in 589, roughly corresponding to Augustine's understanding of the Holy Trinity with "the procession of the Holy Spirit" from the Father *and the*

Son. Several Popes resisted the change until ca. 1000. Orthodox assaults on the *Filioque*, beginning in Jerusalem against Frankish monks in 847, and not ending with the Hesychast Controversy led by Gregory of Palamas (canonized 1368),[20] and Latin assimilation of the *Filioque* in medieval papal councils and in scholastic summae could only sharpen the East-West dialogue and eventually the disputations in the one state in Europe, and that the largest in the Era of the Reformation, where "Latins" (Catholics and Protestants) and the Orthodox coexisted as subjects of a common king, as represented in a common Diet. We take note of some of the salient and especially pertinent developments between Charlemagne and Calvin as to the hypostatic union and Christ the Mediator.

Within the reconstituted Empire (of Charlemagne and his German successors), and beyond it, important triadological/christological *developments* took place, as scholastics worked, first within an Augustinian framework with a limited access to Aristotle, especially as transmitted by Anicius Boethius (d. ca. 524)[21] and with the help of Pseudo-Dionysius. They went on in the twelfth century to have much more of Aristotle and a platonized Aristotle and also John of Damascus (d. 749), who had systematically summarized the achievement of Greek theology in his time—all this, of course, in translation. The consequence of this influx was a plethora of new Latin terms reflecting Greek *philosophical* usage. The Greek term *hypostasis* from Aristotle had two well understood meanings apart from theology, in Latin: *substantia* and *subsistentia*. But there were other Latin terms for *substantia*: *esse*, *essentia*, *existentia*, even *natura*. *Subsistentia*, which in Triadology and Christology could mean Person, acquired a companionable near equivalent, *suppositum*. Many other terms became part of the burgeoning scholastic vocabulary in a moment of fresh creativity. Moreover, there could be differences in usage respecting these new terms as they were used by grammarians, logicians, philosophers, and theologians. Also usage differed in developing schools of philosophical and theological opinion.

As for the specific problem of the hypostatic union (*mentioned at nn. 19, 47*), and in consequence of the Mediator, it had been Gregory I the Great (d. 604) who, in a homily on the words of John the Baptist about the strap of Christ's sandal which he was not worthy to untie (John 1:27), had construed this as indicative of "the ligature of the mystery" of the divine and the human in Christ,[22] and thus legitimated the fresh scholastic inquiries when the time was ripe. The first major systematization of Latin theology was the *Sententiarum libri IV* of Peter Lombard (d. 1160), ending his days as bishop of Paris. Lombard therein surveyed the scene and helpfully explained that there were three *opiniones*,[23] any one of which at the time of the *Sentences* (ca. 1155-58) could be entertained as orthodox, *despite* the progressively decisive formulations of the hypostatic union and the plenary character of the humanity of Christ in a succession of seven ancient ecumenical councils, namely: (1) the *Assumptus* theory that the eternal *Verbum* or *Filius Dei* assumed "a certain *homo*"; (2) the Subsistence theory that at the Incarnation the Second *Persona* subsists no longer as intradeically in a simple mode but henceforth compositely as divine and human, the human involving body and soul, the three being each a *substantia*, and (3) the *Habitus* theory that the eternal Son wore humanity as a garment more or less closely to himself.

In this third view, suggested by Peter Abelard (d. 1142) and Peter of Poitiers (d. 1205), Christ according to his humanity was nothing: as *homo non est aliquid*. The position would come to acquire a name, Nihilianism. Pope Alexander II condemned this view in 1170 and again in 1177 and thereby tended to reinforce the *Assumptus* theory by using its distinctive terminology. However, scholastics had inherited from Boethius the fundamental proposition in his *De duabus naturis et una Persona Christi* against Eutyches: *"Persona est rationalis naturae individua substantia"* (Person is an individual substance of a rational nature), a dictum that created problems for those scholastics who felt that orthodoxy was better safeguarded, not by the *Assumptus* theory, but rather by the Subsistence theory, in which, however, Christ would be Person with at least two substances, subsistences, natures. Quoting I Tim. 2:5, Peter Lombard insisted that Jesus Christ was Mediator exclusively in his human nature (III, *distinctiones* xv-xx, esp. xiv, 6 and 7)[24] and, following the *De fide orthodoxa* of the Damascene, Peter disavowed any premundane flesh or human nature of the *Son* (III, iii, 2).

After his death, Peter Lombard was attacked by Walter of St. Victor for his alleged preference for the third theory, Nihilianism. However, as Abbot Joachim of Fiore (d. 1202) had, in his *Liber de vera et falsa philosophia*, attacked the Trinity (not expressly the Christology) of Peter Lombard as in effect a Quaternity (especially in I, *distinctiones* i-xxxvi), the whole of the *Sentences* was under review at the IV Lateran Council of 1215 under Innocent III (by Latin reckoning the XIIth Ecumenical Council), where Joachim's own fascinating Triadology was the primary focus of scrutiny for heresy. Lombard was vindicated against Joachim and his *Sentences* were pronounced orthodox (chapter 2). Rehabilitated, the *Sentences* became the standard theological textbook into the sixteenth century and a university degree was that of *sententiarius*, one who had mastered Lombard; and thus the fathers of the Reformation would all be acquainted with the three christological *opiniones*, although in the course of the centuries the many distinctions and combinations thereof make the history difficult to disentangle. Martin Luther himself would write marginalia on the *Sentences*, 1510-11, and later expressly agree with Joachim, while Calvin would *nominally* endorse Lombard (cf. n. 35).[25]

Peter Lombard, whatever his personal conviction as to the three possibilities, did not connect these *opiniones* directly with soteriological theories or theories of the atonement, although he did distinguish Christ as High Priest and as Mediator. He regarded the salvific work of Christ as made effectual in the sacrament of baptism and insisted, with most of the ancient Fathers, that Christ mediated in his *human* nature. As with Anselm of Canterbury, Christ was Redeemer/Mediator as *homo*.[26]

Thomas Aquinas in his *Summa Theologiae*, III, Part I, in dealing with Christology clearly distinguished Christ as High Priest in question 22 and as Mediator in question 26, wherein the eventually dominant definition was as follows:

It is . . . . as man that he [Jesus Christ] is, in the truest sense of the word, Mediator . . . . As God, Christ is in all things equal to the Father . . . . [E]ven in his human nature he is superior to other men. For this reason he may as man be Mediator; but not as God . . . . [I]t is as man that he atones for the sins of the human race; and it is on this ground that he is called the Mediator of God and men.[27]

It is against this definition of the Mediator, consonant with that of most *post-Nicene* fathers and the first seven councils (all on Greek terrain), that the innovative emphasis of the second generation of Protestant Reformers is to be assessed. Too frequently both the confessional and the favorably disposed historians of the Unitarian schism in the Reformed Church in the Commonwealth tended to join with the Reformed and even the Lutheran interpreters of the same events in holding that Lismanino was unclear and indecisive, that Biandrata was meddlesome and mendacious,[28] and that Stancaro was vainglorious and vexatious. Even Catholic historians, when they come to grips with the problem in Poland, tend to side with the classical Reformers about the Mediator.[29] It is important, therefore, to give especially Stancaro his due, for he was a Hebraist of the first water, a patrologist and student of the councils, and a scholastic who knew Lombard and Thomas well.

III. Christ the Mediator in the Thought of John Calvin

Roughly eleven centuries after the third ecumenical council, that of Ephesus of 431, some of the classical Reformers, presupposing the cosmological mediation of the eternal Word (the eternally begotten Son) as the instrument of the Father in creation, concentrated almost exclusively on Jesus Christ as soteriological Mediator. For the whole of the Reformation could be said to be a struggle over the Word embodied for salvation by faith alone on the basis of the hearing and the study of Scripture alone through the aid of grace alone, *sola fide, sola scriptura, sola gratia,* which in the end meant eternally predestined election to salvation. Peter Lombard's ready asseveration that the salvation of the Mediator was mediated in turn through baptism succumbed. Baptism was no longer decisive in the Reformation soteriological emphasis of eternal (even supralapsarian) election and experiential faith in Christ *pro nobis,* all in a fresh sense of the divine immediacy less dependent than in Catholicism on the mediation of sacrament and ministrant.

With a return to Scripture alone, the classical Protestant divines of the second wave felt relatively free to use for the soteriological Mediator many texts that the council fathers and the scholastics had long since managed to clarify and interrelate in such a way that the subordinationism of the Wisdom passages of the Old Testament and pre-Pauline Wisdom hymns sung to Christ the firstborn of creation had been obviated. And the Reformed divines felt even less restrained by the councils and the Schoolmen than the Lutherans and the Anglicans.

A Polish scholar in his preface to an important collection of documents of Polish thought in the sixteenth century rightly pointed to the absence of an overall intellectual interpretation of what happened in Poland's religious development as distinct from biographical and chronological accounts.[30] The classical Protestant divines of the second wave of theological reflection and consolidation were groping for a formulation of the once-for-all salvific event of the past (Incarnation/Crucifixion) to correspond to their central doctrine of justification by faith alone that presupposed a Pauline-Augustinian predestination to salvation of a limited number of elect from eternity. But significantly, perhaps of all the *classical* Protestant luminaries of first or second magnitude, Jan Łaski *was the most Erasmian* in mitigating this major thrust of classical Protestantism in his interest in free will.

In any case, what the classical Protestant divines in general were all seeking in various ways was a new formulation of the Atonement different from that of scholasticism. Anselm's solution in *Cur Deus homo*[31] was unsatisfactory in not having been cast primarily in scriptural terms. Hence Lutheran (not Martin Luther himself) and Reformed divines alike fixed upon the scriptural term *Mediator* and the idea of mediation. We have already indicated that they were only vaguely aware of the degree to which the Fathers had taken seriously both the triadological problem of the consubstantiality of the Logos/Wisdom/Son as cosmological Mediator and the christological problem of the plenary humanity of Christ and the unity of this divine-human Person, but these formulations had been complicated and confused by the profusion of terminology in the schools of scholasticism already noted.

A further motivation of the second wave of Reformers was the implicit desire to undercut the mediatorial, i.e., sacerdotal role of the Catholic *sacerdotium* by insisting that only the divine-human High Priest and Mediator could perform the definitive salvific action. Thomas Aquinas, in his section on the Mediator, 26, 1, had indeed declared: "The priests of the new Law may . . . be called *mediatores* of God and men insofar as they are ministers of the true Mediator, administering, in his person, the sacraments of salvation to men."[32] Thus, although seldom expressly stated, another reason pressing the Reformers like John Calvin, some of whom had not been ordained by the medieval sacrament of ordination through the several grades and long remained indifferent to the elaboration of even new forms of ministerial consecration, was to minimize the mediatorial role of priests/ministers in order to stress a God-inspired faith as alone efficacious in the salvific action of baptism and the eucharist (two sacraments preserved by them from the medieval seven).

Affirming the presence and the soteriologically mediatorial action of the Second Person and, as we shall see, of Jesus Christ preincarnate, in the Old Testament, Calvin readily used the Latin equivalents of Yahweh, El, Elohim, and Adonai much more freely than the Fathers for Jesus Christ: in both his pre-mundane and post-ascensional soteriological/mediatorial role than did, for example, the Greek and Latin Fathers of conciliar antiquity.

The Reformed, in contrast to the Lutherans, moreover, envisaged the incarnational body in glory as seated at the right hand of God the Father after the Ascension, the Lutherans holding to the ubiquity of Christ with special reference to the eucharist. As both the Lutherans and the Reformed thought of the elect as preexistent (in the mind of God) by the intradeical decree of predestination to election, so they, and particularly the Reformed, tended to find it theologically easier to envisage the Elect Man, the divine Man Jesus Christ, as present beside the Father also from the beginning of creation (Philippians and Colossians: the pre-Pauline formulations) as well as after the Ascension. And most important of all, this Mediator, *qua* soteriological Mediator, performed his office in both natures, as it were before the assumption of human nature at the Incarnation and *qua* "Person of the Mediator," a turn of phrase not found expressly in antecedent formularies from antiquity through scholasticism, was inferior to the Father pre-incarnationally, post-ascensionally, and judicially at the Second Advent. Peter Lombard, in contrast, had been explicit that there could be no human features, flesh, or nature of the pre-mundane Son.[33]

The Reformed divines felt confident in the prominence they were giving Jesus Christ, the soteriological divine-human Mediator and High Priest, over against the clear distinction between these two roles in the less developed and scripturally, patristically, and scholastically more restrained presentation in, for example, Thomas Aquinas. The *Person* of the Mediator in whom something of the created nature of angels and human beings is taken up into the divine is a *novum* of Reformation Era Christology of the second-generation divines, particularly among the Reformed. This is not to pass judgment on the deviation of this Christology from previous norms or on its achievement. It is simply to observe that it was resisted more in the Commonwealth than apparently elsewhere, for Calvin's extreme formulation of Christ the Mediator rather than how he argued Triadology was a major factor in Poland for the withdrawal of many of the foremost leaders of the Helvetian or Calvinist Church there, gradually ending up as the (unitarian) Polish Brethren of the Minor (Reformed) Church.

The second wave of Reformers, devoted to *sola scriptura*, knew well that they could not defend the received Triadology and Christology of the conciliar creeds without making use of them, although Calvin at first desired to use only the Apostles' Creed as Luther had considered it among the four creeds "the truly finest of them." It should be observed that the Christology set forth even in the definitive Latin edition of the *Institutes* of 1559 (French: 1560) does not reflect so fully the extent of the controversies of Calvin with leaders of the Reformed Church in the Commonwealth as the same three christological chapters do reflect controversies closer about him. In Book II, ii, 12 on "The necessity of Christ becoming Man in order to fulfill the office of Mediator," Calvin was responding polemically with the heretical Lutheran Andreas Osiander (d. 1552) (on him see further at n. 43); in II, ii, 13 on Christ's assumption of real humanity,

under the names of ancient heretics, Calvin was primarily fighting the view
of the Anabaptist Menno Simons (d. 1561), who held to the doctrine of the
celestial flesh of Christ; while in II, ii, 14 on "the union of the two natures
constituting the Person of the Mediator," he polemicized extensively against
Michael Servetus (burned at Calvin's instigation in 1553) and mentioned him
by name four times. The christological chapters reflect, then, controversies
within the Empire or in regions related thereto: the Netherlands, Switzerland,
and Ducal Prussia (though a fief of the Polish king). In any case, the three key
chapters on Christology were markedly polemical and bound up with transient
emphases within the range of his awareness and primary interest. The Commonwealth seemed remote and the Poles both too assiduous and intractable.
Calvin even felt badgered by them.

Yet Calvin was fully aware that his concept of the Mediator represented a
new emphasis with a new definition, indeed, that it was "an error of the
ancients" (veterum: the Church Fathers) that they did not attend sufficiently to
"the Person of the Mediator," II, xiv, 4. The post-Nicene Fathers, in fact, in
most cases would have been largely surprised at the heading of Calvin's chapter
xii: "Christum . . . oportuisse fieri hominem," that "Christ (so: the eternally begotten Son) had to become man" as Jesus Christ, and in his mediatorial person
was subordinate to the Father.

Little wonder that Stancaro would find this phrasing and Calvin's whole
concept of the Mediator a curious departure from patristic and scholastic usage
and conceptualization. Moreover, the most daring formulations in the communications Calvin sent to the Poles, stirred up as much by Stancaro as by
Biandrata, scarcely find their way fully into the Institutes, with the consequence
that some of the formulations that most agitated the Helvetians in the Commonwealth often escape the notice of those who survey the Reformed scene
from this theological Mont Blanc and from the other more familiar eminences
of Calvinist thought.[34]

The mention of Lombard at this juncture is apposite because Calvin was
fully aware of the degree to which he departed from him as well as from most
of "the ancients." Although Calvin was indisposed to give names of individual
scholastics and to distinguish among their various schools, he did mention
Lombard often as "the master of the School," as "their choryphaeus," as "their
Pythagoras."[35]

In contrast to Lombard, Calvin held that Christ was Mediator, not in his
human nature alone, but in both natures, in this respect closer to Osiander,
from whom, however, he significantly differed. Moreover, almost unique was
his view, II, xiii, 4, that at the Incarnation the Second Person was not completely
engaged to the extent of vacating his place in heaven: illud extra Calvinisticum,
as the Lutheran critics would come to call it.

Calvin, indeed, held that the Second Person, the eternal Son, even after the
Incarnation, was, though united to the human nature to form one Person, not
restricted to that flesh.[36] As Calvin had a functional, pastoral rather than an

ontological, "systematic" Christology, and as he fell heir to a mingling of the first two of Lombard's christological *opiniones*, checked against the Chalcedonian formulation, while giving unusual prominence to the Person of the Mediator, he was in danger of being charged with having two Christs and hence of being Nestorian, a common Lutheran charge. Moreover, he acknowledged Christ as cosmological Mediator (Col. 1:15) giving order to the universe, as well as the soteriological Mediator of Bethlehem and Calvary.[37] It was, indeed, to avoid the charge of being a new Nestorius (d. ca. 451), that Calvin entitled his chapter xii (as already quoted): "*Christum . . . oportuisse fieri hominem.*" In other words he called both the pre-mundane Son of God and the son of Mary, Christ, "the Person of the Mediator."

That Calvin was dependent at some points on Lombard (and in the instance below, also on John of Damascus) is evident in his taking up into his Christology the idea that during the three days between death on the cross and the resurrection Christ, with respect to his *Persona/Hypostasis*, was *totus* (whole, masculine to Jesus Christ) in heaven, *totus* in hell (for Lombard, Hades; for Calvin, intense suffering), and *totus* everywhere, and yet not *totum* in his divine *aliquid* (something).[38] Although modern ecumenical Catholic scholarship is disposed to find Calvin an orthodox Chalcedonian in Christology,[39] one should also be able to see how "the Polish Reformed" with Stancaro and Biandrata among them would have been confused as to whether their Helvetian mentors, particularly Calvin, were not leading them into the most dreaded of heresies, Arianism, since Calvin unabashedly subordinated the Person of the Mediator to God the Father between creation and the consummation of the world.

In his own commentary on Col. 1:15, wherein Christ is firstborn of creatures, Calvin was aware that in antiquity "stupidly the Arians" tried thereby to make of the Son a creature, but he argued simply that the fact that what follows, "for *in him* all things were created," showed that as Son he was firstborn from the Father intradeically (not Calvin's term), and as a distinct Hypostasis was one essence (substance) with the Father and the Holy Spirit, the *fundamentum omnium*, not a creature.[40] Of interest is the fact that in his fifteenth sermon in French on 1 Tim.2:5 and 6, he simply avoided a direct discussion of "the man Jesus Christ."[41] In the *Institutes*, II, xii, 1 he said of 1 Timothy 2:5: "He [Paul] could have said 'God'; or he could at least have omitted the word 'man' just as he did the word 'God.' " Against the exact words of inspired Scripture at a crucial point, against the traditional interpretation of the *Sentences* (above at n. 24), Calvin was undaunted in his mediatorial theory.

Compressing into a few lines what he had or will have said to the Poles (Part IV), Calvin, making a distinction between the Kingdom of the Son, "which shall have no end" (Niceno-Constantinopolitan Creed—against Marcellus of Ancyra) and the Kingdom of Christ, which will be delivered to "his God and Father" (1 Cor. 15:24),[42] Calvin made his most succinct and most Calvinian definition of the Mediator, right after he already cited reproof of "the ancients": "[T]hose things which apply to the office of the mediator are not spoken simply

BIBLIOTHECA
Fratrum Polonorum qui
UNITARII
Appellantur

Continens

OPERA OMNIA,

JOHANNIS CRELLII FRANCII,

— LUDOVICI WOLSOGENII,

— FAUSTI SOCINI SENENSIS

& Exegetica

—JONÆ SCHLICHTINGII a BUCOWIEC.

Contenta fingulis voluminibus funt præfixa.

IRENOPOLI
Poft annum Domini 1656.

17. *Bibliotheca Fratrum Polonorum*, Irenopoli, 1665-1668. Title page of the first volume (Biblioteka Uniwersytecka, Warszawa). Photo Andrzej Bodytko.

ET RESPONSA. 139

furgeret,quàm improbè homini innoxio maledicebat. Et tamen non aliud poftulo , nifi vt mihi permittas eius contumelias leniter ferre. Quanta fide & integritate Chrifto feruieris, quàm cordatè functus fis tuo officio, quàm conftanter & labores , & certamina quib' te exercuit Dominus,fuftinueris, ego tibi teftis fumac te in pofterum perpetuò tui fimilem fore confido. Itaque nihil magis cupio,quàm faluam inter nos beneuolentiam manere,quò alacrius,& fynceriore ftudio nos vltrò citróque iuuare pergamus. Vale eximie vir, & colende frater. Dominus tibi femper adfit,te gubernet ac tuos labores benedicat. Collegæ mei te plurimùm falutant.Geneuæ xv. Octob. m. d. liiii.

Ioannes Caluinus tuus.

CAL. SERENISS. REGI POLONIAE S. D.

Tfi ego ante annos quinque,Sereniffimè Rex,quandam librorum meorum partem veftræ Maieftati publicè dedicaueram , vt pietatis femen,quod iam tune cordi veftro diuinitus initium audieram , magis ac magis excitarem: nunc tamen minimè auderem homo ignobilis,priuatas tam inclyto Regi literas offerre, nifi venerandus frater nofter cui hoc debeo, & , cuius vt fidelis erga M. V. obferuantia mihi nota eft, ita non dubito , quin fenfus veftros probè compertos habeat, me fuo confilio & hortatu animaffet. Quia ergo fpopondit non ingratum, M. V. fore hoc meum officium : temeritatis culpam non fum amplius veritus. Iam verò quia abfurdum foret, ab Euangelij Miniftro in confpectum tanti Regis vacuas literas venire : illud idem argumentum,quod continet publica mea in Epiftolam ad Hebræos præfatio,quia nullum vel melius, vel Regia perfona dignius, vel tempori aptius occurrit,mihi fumendum putaui. Sic enim perfuafus fum, pro ea, quam Filio Dei communi magiftro deferuis,reuerentia, ab eius feruo moneri,vobis non fore graue, aut moleftum. Et certè hæc modeftia decet omnes Chrifti difcipulos , à fummo vfque ad infimum , à Regibus ipfis ad plebem vfque,cœlefti eius doctrinæ libenter ,& placida animi manfuetudine fe fubmittere. Nam & hoc modo fecundum Dauidis præceptum ofculantur regnorum omnium Principem & caput terreni Reges, dum per homines, quibus docendi munus iniunxit, loquentem audire non refpuunt. Cæterum , quòd mearum partium viciffim effe arbitror,operam dare ftudebo , ne vobis faftidio fit mea prolixitas. Ac primùm horribiles tenebras, quæ paffim graffantur : errorum colluuiem , qua obruitur totus ferè mundus : abufus & corruptelas, quibus fœdata eft religio , non attingam, ne in fuperuacua rei cognitæ tractatione M. Veftram fruftra occupem. Neque enim ad rudem quempiam ,& fynceræ pietatis ignarum mihi habendus eft fermo: fed apud Regem puriotis doctrinæ luce præditum,vt nõ modò à craffis vulgi fuperftitionibus fit ipfe liber , fed etiam quàm exitialis fit labyrinthus ille,quo maior pars generis humani tenetur implicita, rectè iudicet. Nam quum gregarios quoque difcipulos lucernis fimiles effe velit Chriftus,quæ in fublimi pofitæ fulgorem fuum longè emittunt : quid à Rege exiget, quem in fummo dignitatis faftigio locauit , vt aliis omnibus præluceat? Nam quò magis honorifica eft folij cui præeftis ,altitudo , eò difficilius eft, parem gerere animum, vt locus hominis virtute ornetur : & de reddenda apud Deum ratione magis folicitè cogitandum. Quòd fi obfcuris hominibus timendum eft,ne hoc viuificum femen torpore fuffocatum degeneret, vel prorfus intereat, quid. M. Veftræ agendum eft , cui non fatis eft, vberem ex fe fructum proferre , nifi eandem fementem ad multa hominum millia propagare ftudeat. Memineritis ergo, præftantiffime Rex ,in perfona veftra lucem toti Poloniæ diuinitus effe accenfam,quæ fine graui culpa diutius latere nequit. Itaque hæc prima fit cura,& hoc primum ftudium , fubiectas vobis ditiones ex fœda Papatus diffipatione ad Chrifti obfequium colligere. Erumpat tandem heroica ifta,quæ nimis diu intus fopita iacuit virtus, & in re tam præclara,memorabile fui documentum præbeat. Neque verò me fugit,aut quàm arduæ fit molis opus, aut quàm multiplices & magnæ difficultates inftent, quas fuo more ingeret Satan. Sed quum hîc pro gloria Dei de Chrifti regno, pro facrorum puritate, pro humani generis falute pugnetur, ea eft caufæ excellentia, quæ & moleftias omnes abforbeat fua laude ,& obftacula facilè fuperet. Imò quid agendum fit,ipfi veritatis hoftes fuo exemplo præfcribant. Nam quò acrius ad eam opprimendam eniti eos videt.M. Veftra, eò turpius effet, infanum eorum ardorem non faltem cordata ftrenuitate æquare. Ruant igitur,quàm maximo poterunt impetu, machinas

M.iiij.

18. Jean Calvin, *Joannes Calvini, Epistolae et responsa,* Genevae, 1575. The first page of one of Calvin's letters to King Sigismund II August from 1554 in which he tried to exhort the Polish monarch to convert to his church (Indiana University Lilly Library, Bloomington).

19. The Nieśwież Bible. *Biblia to jest Księga Starego y Nowego Przymierza*, Nieśwież, 1572. Title page of the Arian (Polish Brethren) Bible translated by Szymon Budny (Biblioteka Czartoryskich, Kraków). Reprinted from *Polska i jej dorobek dziejowy*, (London: Orbis, 1956).

either of the divine nature or of the human. Until he comes forth as judge of
the world Christ will . . . . reign . . . . Christ having then discharged the office
of Mediator, . . . will be satisfied with that glory which he enjoyed before the
creation of the world. And the name 'Lord' exclusively belongs to the Person
of Christ [the Mediator, before and after the Incarnation] only in so far as it
represents a degree midway (*Medius gradus*) between God and us," II, xiv, 3.

IV. The Problem of the Mediator in the Commonwealth: Stancaro and Biandrata

It is commonly overlooked that the Reformed Church in the Commonwealth,
primarily in Little Poland, was organized by Francesco Stancaro who supplied
it with its first canons. It is better known that he enflamed the controversy
(1549-66) over the Mediator among Lutherans in Königsberg, which ended
with the condemnation to death of three of the followers of Andreas Osiander,
already deceased (d. 1552). This controversy we pass over in the present context,[43] except to observe that its repercussions were felt in the Polish-speaking
Church, the more so for the reason that Philipp Melanchthon (d. 1560), whom
the Polish Reformed also admired, was involved in the controversy. All the
classical Protestant divines, whether Lutheran or Reformed, who moved with
the new thrust towards a premundane divine-human Mediator, thought he
had managed to avoid the intrusion into his Triadology or Christology of any
unintended *tertium quid*[44] like the created Logos or the Son-after-an-interval of
the ancient Arians. They all agreed with Stancaro that Osiander had fallen into
heresy with *his* attempt (closely joined to a rewording of Luther's doctrines of
justification and sanctification).

In Poland many of his best educated and closest readers thought that Calvin,
too, might have become perilously close to heresy: to Arianism in his subordination of the *Person* of the Mediator to the Father, and to Nestorianism in
his seeming to have two Second Persons or rather such a division within the
economy of the Second Person that during the interval between creation and
consummation, the Person of the Mediator, if not his divine essence (substance), was subordinate to the Father. The Polish Reformed, however, were
for the most part content to leave it to the Lutherans to hurl the charge of
Nestorianism at the Reformed, as they in turn retaliated by calling the Lutherans Eutychians (in not sufficiently distinguishing the two natures of Christ
after the Incarnation in the doctrine of the ubiquity).

The Polish Reformed were primarily interested in not falling, through misunderstanding Calvin or in following exactly what he seemed to be saying,
into the generic heresy, as it were, of Arius, "the archheretic" of the ancient
Church. One bears in mind, too, that because of growing dislike of the Poles,
as well as of their Italian spokesmen (Stancaro), Calvin wrote less carefully to
them than in his final revision of the *Institutes* of 1559, dealt with in our Part
III, and, moreover, that because of the late date of the three communications

sent to the Poles we actually overhear Calvin on the Mediator after he has laid down his pen for the last time on his *"Summa"* or "Sentences."

In what follows with quotations it will be seen that Calvin in particular in counseling his Polish followers, disturbed as they were by questions raised whether sincerely or subversively by Giorgio Biandrata and Francesco Stancaro precisely in the years 1557 to 1561, compounded the christological strain in the Helvetian Church in the Polish-Lithuanian Commonwealth during the head-ship of it by Jan Łaski, 1556-60; also that, quite apart from foreign and domestic sympathizers with Antitrinitarianism and Anabaptism working within the Re-formed Church in the Commonwealth, the unsatisfactory character of Calvin in his pastoral care and theological guidance of the Poles and the Lithuanians, with his obsession with "the Person of the Mediator," was perhaps even the major factor in the schism of the Major and Minor (Reformed) Church, 1565, one year after his death.[45]

To make the point, one may sample, amid the abundant correspondence with the Poles, Calvin's three replies, one with respect to Biandrata, 1557, and two with respect to Stancaro (I, 9 June 1560 and II, February 1561).[46]

In general it can be said that in replying to the Polish Reformed before the schism Calvin did not use conciliar and scholastic terminology with precision, at least not to the satisfaction of baffled Stancaro. Calvin opted, moreover, for the scholastic *essentia* instead of the credal *substantia* and used *substantia* in the sense of *subsistentia* for *Persona*, since as already noted in Part II, in Aristotle and hence in scholastic Latin philosophy *hypostasis* had two meanings, as in-deed the Church Fathers well knew; but they did settle for one meaning in their conciliar creeds.

Wrote Calvin to Biandrata: "On the word *substantia* we have to hold that it is not properly *essentia* but *hypostasis* . . . . [S]ince the Word itself is true God, it designates the *essentia*."[47] Calvin seems here to have confused in the Chal-cedonian formula, where Christ, to limit ourselves to the Latin text, is defined as "one *persona* and one *subsistentia* (Greek: *hypostasis*) in two natures/two *phy-sesis*—the etymologically and visually similar terms: *substantia* and *subsistentia* being confused. But on such terms turned the whole controversy over Tria-dology and then Christology from 325 to 787: And indeed from Charlemagne's Council of Frankfurt of 794 to the IV Lateran of 1215, which vindicated Lom-bard.

To be sure, Calvin at this very point acknowledged that the technical words "can be understood in different ways," but Stancaro, if not Biandrata, would have known at once how in one line Calvin departed from credal usage and in the other line clearly confused the decisive words; and yet Calvin felt con-fident in rebuking them: "Those who shamefully misrepresent the orthodox faith by the pretense that speculation on the one *essentia* and the three *personae* is useless [this: to Biandrata], advance a malicious subterfuge; for we do not speculate beyond what Scripture offers us, but we give its simple and genuine meaning."[48]

Calvin's overweening confidence in conflating scriptural, conciliar, and remnants of scholastic terminology allowed him to say incorrectly: "The Council of Nicaea [-Constantinople] . . . asserted that Christ is God from God," where it carefully asserted, rather, that the eternally begotten Son (Logos) is "true God from true God, . . . consubstantialem Patri." In the next paragraph Calvin said correctly, though he did not use the credal term, that "Athanasius and the other ancients said that the Son was coessentialem Patri."[49] Just as the philosophically tutored Fathers said "eternally begotten Son" and had in mind the Stoic distinction between the Logos endiathetos and prophorikos and had on their own gone on to distinguish within the first the prospectively orthodox one-stage and the eventually suppressed two-stage intradeical Logos, all scripturally sanctioned for them by John's simple use of Logos in chapter 1, so in the fullness of time, Calvin could say "Jesus Christ" and mean "the Person of the Mediator" the eternal Son of the Father but at the Incarnation also the son of Mary as God-Man, Calvin evidently felt no theological need to work with the one prosopon/persona and the one hypostasis/subsistentia of the eternally begotten Son incarnate as Jesus Christ in the careful formula of Chalcedon. More expressly to the Poles than in the Institutes of 1559, Calvin subordinated precisely the "Person of the Mediator" to God the Father.

Calvin, acquainted with the Hebrew text, unlike most of the Fathers depending upon the Septuagint and all the Schoolmen depending on the Vulgate, was at his theological ease in using all the Hebrew names of God, Latinized, in reference to the Triune God or, as occasion required, to any of the Three Persons, but especially to the First and to the Second, understood by him also as the preexistent Jesus Christ in his role of Mediator: "Yahweh is certainly one, and this name is common to the Son as well as to the Father."[50] In an extraordinary paragraph Calvin, quoting from the very chapter in which Paul described his having been caught up to the third heaven wherein the Lord was revealed to him, wrote: "That the name of Yahweh used indeterminately suits Christ is . . . clear from Paul's word, 'three times I besought the Lord,' because shortly thereafter he adds "that the power of Christ may rest upon me' (2 Cor. 12:8f.)."[51] In this passage the request of Paul had been the relatively minor appeal concerning assuagement of the never explained "thorn" in his flesh. Yet out of the threefold appeal Calvin made Paul's address to the triune Yahweh more specifically an appeal to the exalted Jesus Christ, understood by him as also the pre-incarnational Jesus Christ of the pre-Pauline, i.e., primitive formulas in Philippians and Colossians. But Calvin made the same point with Paul's own direct formulation: "To restrict the word 'Lord' to the Person of the Mediator is trifling and silly because the apostles indiscriminately use the word Lord of Yahweh. . . . [I]n no other way did Paul pray to the Lord [cf. 2 Cor. 12:18f.] than the way in which Joel [2:32] is quoted by Peter, 'Whoever calls on the name of the Lord [Yahweh] shall be saved' (Acts 2:21)."[52]

It is to be observed that Calvin here went beyond the Fathers and the Schoolmen: he wrote of "the Person of the Mediator" and it is this Person, not clearly

identified with, or distinguished from, the Second Person of the Trinity, that
Calvin equivocally subordinated to the Triune God and caused problems for
his Polish followers:

> The word "Person," when used of Christ, may be taken *in two ways.*
> As the Word (*sermo*) *born* of the Father before the creation of the world,
> the Person is in the *aeterna essentia* of God; as Christ, God made
> manifest in the flesh, he is constituted one Person by the union of
> two natures. Hence it is one thing to speak about the eternal *sapientia*
> [cf. Proverbs 8:22; elsewhere Calvin says also *Logos*] of God before he
> took on flesh, and another to speak about the [Person of the] Mediator
> by whom he [God] was revealed in the flesh.[53]

Since Calvin took for granted what the earliest Gentile converts to Christianity, with its account of God as creator *ex nihilo*, long continued to marvel at,
he was able to use the term "Jesus Christ as Mediator" without any theological
discomfort for the role of Wisdom, sanctioned, to be sure, by Colossians 1:15,
as the firstborn of creation, although he did not acknowledge creatureliness
except for the human nature and yet did not explain how the pre-existent Jesus
Christ could have a creaturely nature. In any case, he expressly subordinated
the Person of the Mediator:

> The name of "Lord" especially befits the Person of the Mediator
> inasmuch as he has maintained a *medius gradus* (degree midway) be-
> tween God and us. It is to this that Paul's saying refers: "One God
> from whom are all things, and one Lord [*Dominus*] through whom
> are all things" (1 Cor. 8:6).[54]

The Greek text has *Kurios Iesous Christos.* Calvin was using the MS Geneva
Bible at this point. That the *Lord* Jesus Christ was he through whom all things
were made conforms to the pre-Pauline formulas of Philippians and Colossians,
but there Jesus and Jesus Christ, substituted for *Sapientia/Sophia* of Prov. 8:22,
was in this primitive Christology a creature, which texts the ancient anti-Arians
had had to circumvent by their theological terms derived from philosophy. In
the Latin version of the Niceno-Constantinopolitan Creed the *per quem omnia*
of 1 Cor. 8:6 (cf. the *omnia per ipsum* of the *Logos* of John 1:3[55] was used of the
eternally begotten *consubstantialis* Son as cosmological Mediator, i.e., not inferior to the Father, while God the Father therein is *factor coeli et terrae*, the *ex
quo* of the same Pauline line having been eschewed, lest creatures would be
said to issue from the *substantia/essentia/ousia* of the Godhead. Calvin did notice
in writing to the vexed Poles how the Creed had successfully neutralized the
seeming and actual subordination of the Mediator in difficult Pauline passages
(1 Cor. 8:6; Col. and Phil.).

Calvin persevered in his soteriological use of the cosmological mediatorship
of Wisdom/Logos/Son of the very early Church and he did not feel any need,
as did the anti-Arian Fathers of Nicaea and Constantinople I, to qualify the
sense of the preexistent Christ as creature (*prototkos pases ktiseos*):

[T]he eternal *Logos* was already Mediator from the beginning, before Adam's fall and the alienation and separation of the human race from God. In this sense . . . he is also called by Paul [Col. 1:15] the first born of all creatures . . . . Therefore, since Christ was head of angels and men in the still innocent state of things, he is rightly considered the Mediator whom the elect angels even now see . . . .[56]

Calvin thus felt no problem in subordinating the Person of the Mediator (*Logos*, *Sapientia*, Jesus Christ, Jesus "before whom every knee shall bow") to God (the Father), whether in his cosmological (not expressly noted) or soteriological role:

[T]he *Logos* and the eternal Son of God is equal to the Father and . . . the Mediator is less than the Father . . .; the Logos by itself and separately is a divine Person . . .; the one Person Christ the Mediator is constituted by two natures . . . . If he [the sacrificed Son of Rom. 8:32, John 3:16] be Son in *both* natures, *it is not by reason of his humanity*.[57]

But surely Calvin would know that Stancaro would know well the last point. Thus Calvin here again came close to having almost two Persons: the Person of the eternal Logos-Filius and that of the Mediator whose career extended from creation to the Last Judgment. He went on to quote Col. 1:20 to show that the Mediator of 1 Tim. 2:5 and the High Priest was able "to reconcile to himself all things, whether on earth or in heaven, making peace by the blood of the cross,"[58] all in the same paragraph of Colossians which describes the same as "the first born of all *creation*." Calvin, as so often, chose not to deal with this problem of inferiority, except as he here turned to Phil. 2:5-7, and, *converting* the textual "Christ Jesus" into "the only begotten Son," he said therefore partially in terms of the ancient councils that, "equal to the Father, [this eternal Son] emptied himself: . . . a Mediator *in both* his natures . . . ."[59]

This phrasing stood in contrast, as Stancaro would have pointed out, to that of most anti-Arian Fathers, of Lombard and Aquinas, all of whom were careful to protect the equality of Word/Wisdom/Son as consubstantial with the Father as cosmological Mediator, though they did not use the term "Mediator" for this role; and they were emphatic and usually consistent in ascribing (1) the functioning of the soteriological Mediator and High Priest in sacrifice on the cross to the *human nature* of the mundane Jesus Christ, and (2) the validating of this work to the universal and infinite *divine nature*, not expressly, as with Calvin, to the *Person* of the Mediator. Thus Stancaro could easily convince many in Poland that Calvin was both cavalier and careless, indifferent to the centuries of patristic and scholastic clarification and refinement in his dogmatic scripturalism which was not always biblical literalism, as in his construing of "man" in 1 Tim. 2:5 (above at n. 41). We look at another passage of Calvin to the puzzled Poles on the Second Person and the Person of the Mediator:

[W]e maintain . . . that the name of the "Mediator" suits Christ, not only by the fact that he put on flesh [a vestige of the third theory of

Lombard, of the *Habitus*], or that he took on the office of reconciling
the human race to God, but from the beginning of creation he already
truly was the Mediator, for he always was the head of the Church,
had primacy over the angels, and was the first born of every *creature*
[Eph. 1:22; Col. 1:15, 2:10]. Therefore we conclude that not only after
Adam's fall did he begin to exercise his office of Mediator, but since
he is the eternal Word of God, both [unfallen] angels as well as [*elect*]
men were united to God by his grace so that they would remain
uncorrupted . . . . [F]rom the title of Mediator he [Stancaro] unskill-
fully deduces that Christ [in his divinity] is less than the Father [unless
the mediatorial role is limited to his humanity as with Lom-
bard] . . . . [But] the only begotten Son was the same God of the
same *essentia* with the Father, and nevertheless he was the *medius*
[midpoint; elsewhere, degree midway] between God and the creatures . . . . It . . . becomes clear that whoever denies that Christ is
Mediator, *with regard to his divinity* [like Stancaro, also Aquinas], takes
the angels away from under his command, and detracts from his
supreme majesty, before which [in the name of Jesus] every knee
should bow in heaven and on earth (Phil. 2:10). Even if that sublime
name [actually two names: Joshua and Mashiach] had been given him
in that flesh in which he had emptied himself, there is no doubt but
that Paul means the whole Person . . . . [60]

Calvin simply saw no need, in contrast to the conciliar Fathers, Lombard,
Aquinas, and Stancaro, to distinguish clearly between Creator Wisdom/Logos/
Son and that same Second Person incarnate as Jesus Christ; for, far more than
the Fathers and the Schoolmen, Calvin, scripturalist first and credalist second,
was at pains to ascribe as much of the function of the Mediator (1) before the
Incarnation, (2) after the Ascension, and (3) up through the Last Judgment, to
the *Person* of the Mediator and when, as with the death on the cross, he of
course ascribed the function to the human nature but even then the intention
thereof to the Person:

If we are to believe in Christ the Mediator (and surely this office
includes [and also at creation possessed] both natures at the same
time), then, since Christ the Mediator possesses supreme power in
heaven and on earth, . . . the name of Mediator is properly attributed
only to the complete Person (Rom. 14:11 [which is a quotation from
Is. 45:23: "As I live, says the Lord (Hebrew, El): "To me every knee
shall bow." ']). [61]

Calvin assumed familiarity with this passage in Romans which is about the
judgment seat of God (El) and continued: "All who stand before his tribunal
(. . . 'to me all knees shall bow'), certainly do not fall down before the human
nature, and nonetheless Paul applies this [same passage about the judgment
of El in Isaiah] to the Person of the Mediator (Phil. 2:9-11)." Calvin here gave

only 2:10 but the whole passage suggests a clear distinction between God (El),— and Paul, once a Pharisee of the Pharisees, knew the Hebrew text, even though in this instance he was quoting from an early formulary of the Christian community: "Therefore God (*ho Theos*) has highly exalted him [Jesus Christ] and bestowed on him the name which is above every name, that at the name of Jesus every knee should bow, in heaven and on earth and under the earth, and every tongue confess that Jesus Christ is Lord (*Kurios*), to the glory of God the Father."

Mentioning the objection that the Mediator had bestowed upon him a kingdom (implied in Phil. 2:9, and frequent enough elsewhere) by God the Father, Calvin wrote that "though nothing new can be conferred on divinity (*in divinitatem*), there is nothing absurd in saying that Christ can increase in reference to his complete Person." Alluding to the same passage in Isaiah where *El* "denies that he will give glory to another," Calvin answered in orthodox trinitarian terms in the rhetorical question: "To whom does he [Paul] say that the supreme name [Jesus] is given, unless to the Son of God who, though equal to the Father, emptied himself taking the form of a servant [Phil. 2:6-8]? Paul places before our eyes a complete Person composed of two natures," already in the time of Isaiah.[62]

But the modern interpreter of Calvin's counsel to the distraught Reformed Poles, shortly before their schism, cannot stress too much the degree to which Calvin by the christological principle of *communicatio idiomatum* (*antidosis ton idiomaton*) of Cyril of Alexandria (d. 444), went much *further* than this anti-Arian and christologically decisive divine in insisting as much as possible upon the Person of the Mediator and the High Priest in the soteriological role:

[T]here are certain characteristics in the Mediator, so proper to the divinity, that they should not be transferred to the human nature except by the communication of idioms . . . . Christ says: "I lay down my life by myself" (John 10:18), and he speaks as Mediator not as man, since no man has of himself the decision over life and death except the one God . . . . Stancaro is greatly mistaken in Paul's words: "There is one God, and there is one Mediator between God and men, the man Christ Jesus" (1 Tim. 2:5) . . . . [T]he entire Deity, the [Triune] God of one *essentia* is understood in the word Father . . . . A union of both natures is required for the office of Mediator, but whatever pertains to the Mediator's role should not be indiscriminately ascribed to either nature.[63]

Calvin did not offer an explanation here where it would be most appropriate as to why Paul himself in fact ascribed the mediatorial role to the Man, not to the God-Man (cf. above at n. 41).

As we have seen, Calvin sensed no difficulty in placing the God-Man, the very Person of the Mediator, below the Father: "[B]ecause God's eternal Son, taking account of our weakness, appeared in the role of Mediator to be intermediary (*medius*) between God and us, he [the eternal Son, for the duration between creation and Judgment] is said with fitting reverence and following the rule of piety to be inferior to the Father."[64]

As we have already anticipated, Calvin in defining a *mediator* as divine-human deprived ordinary priests or ministers of the mediatorial role that Aquinas ascribed to them:[65]

> Christ . . . would not be in a position to fulfill the role of Mediator unless he were God's only begotten Son. Furthermore, the apostle uses this testimony to prove [also] his priesthood: "Thou art my Son, today I have begotten thee" (Heb. 1:5): from this it rightly follows that if the dignity of the Son is inseparable from that of the Priesthood, then no mediator is in any way suitable except one born of God . . . . Hence the divine nature is included in the order of the Priesthood . . . . [W]ho holds to the mind of Christ will free himself from all entanglements since he will see that expressions common to both natures are not to be separately ascribed to one. We do not [,to be sure,] make all that is joined to the office of Mediator or its duties common to both natures.[66]

That Calvin may have had priests even consciously in mind is suggested by the term *nemo*, which would be used of a human being, but scarcely of God:

> The same [dependence on the conjoining of the divine and the human] applies to the Priesthood, which Christ could not undertake without entering into the heavenly sanctuary [at the Ascension]. Wherefore, the apostle, to prove that he is a lawful Priest, adduces the testimony of Psalm 2:7, quoted in Hebrews 1:5, 5:5: Thou art my Son, today I have begotten thee," by which he clearly shows that no one (*neminem*) is equal or suitable for the office without divinity . . . . [I]t is outside of controversy that Christ is the Son of God in respect to both natures, and hence it follows that he is a Mediator no less by reason of his divinity than by his human nature.[67]

Calvin wrote further:

> Christ sits at the Father's right hand, insofar as he is God revealed in the flesh and this is affirmed of the whole Person. But the prophet [David] intimately joins these two together (Ps. 110:1-[4]), that the Lord (*Adon*) who sits at the Father's [actually Yahweh's] right hand is [1] made King [verse 2] and [2] appointed Priest [forever after the order of Melchizedek, verse 4] over the Church.[68]

In Acts 1:4 and 13:33, Heb. 1:5, 5:5, Jesus Christ is reported as having ascended and been begotten at the Ascension as High Priest and hence also as soteriological Mediator. Calvin did not feel obliged to take note of the apparent discrepancy between Acts and Hebrews over against the preexistent Jesus Christ of Philippians and Colossians and did not offer to harmonize these passages which Stancaro kept separate.

Calvin did take up rather casually and not wholly accurately some of Stancaro's patristic citations, none of his scholastic references. He touched upon Cyril of Alexandria, (Pseudo-)Ambrose, John Chrysostom, and Augustine in *Confessiones* and *Civitas Dei*.[69]

Strangely, at one point Calvin indirectly expressed partial agreement with Stancaro in reference to mediation with the Father, to be sure, and not with the entire Triune Godhead, as Stancaro averred; but even for Calvin the Father could stand for the whole Godhead: "[T]he God of one *essentia* in Three Persons was appeased" by the Mediator.[70]

V. The Formation of the Polish [Minor] Reformed Church:

Conclusion

Many of the Polish Brethren recoiled in angered frustration at a series of what seemed equivocal replies to them of Calvin and other Swiss divines: a salvation based upon the intradeical decrees of predestination by Three co-essential Persons implemented by the Person of a pre-mundane Mediator of two natures even before the Incarnation and inferior *qua* Person to God the Father, of a *medius gradus* much like the *tertium quid* of ancient Arius, who at least believed in free will:[71] an atonement of that Mediator on the cross that merely confirmed for an elect few the decrees made for them from eternity regardless of human freedom or striving. This was, of course, a caricature of the whole integrated system of Calvin. But they had much more than the *Institutes* and the three communications we have chosen for close examination sent to them to solve their problems. Some of the Polish Brethren reacted to what appeared to be inconsistencies in replies from 1559 to 1561 and irreversibly moved between 1563 and 1565 as a separate synod of the Minor [Reformed] Church.

Afraid of Stancaro's increasingly vexatious disposition to collaborate with Polish Catholics,[72] afraid of what seemed to be Calvin's Arianizing subordinationism with respect to the Person of Christ the Mediator, the major leaders of the Reformed Church in the Commonwealth, patrons and pastors, finally moved to the scriptural simplicity of the Apostles' Creed, which is silent about the Persons of the Trinity and about the consubstantiality of the Son and about the pre-existence of Jesus Christ in whatever role; and with enhanced satisfaction they also appreciated the summary of Christ's work as formulated in lapidary clarity in the *triplex munus Christi*, the use of both the Creed and the formulary having been prominent in Łaski's thought.

They slowly set their feet upon a path that would lead them to a doctrine of the simple unity of the Godhead, the perpetual High Priesthood of Jesus Christ in the heavenly tabernacle after the Ascension, there seated at the right hand of God the Father, vicegerent of God for the cosmos and the nations,

King of his Church on earth of true believers in every Christian fold; but they did this to avoid being called Arians. The Polish Brethren came to settle for the simple Triadology without consubstantiality of Matt. 28:19 and of the Apostles' Creed and to settle for the soteriological Mediator of 1 Tim. 2:5, the man Jesus Christ, just like their Catholic neighbors following Lombard and Aquinas. Therewith they had God the Father as Creator in Gen. 1, Jesus Christ, the Virgin-born Mediator, and the Holy Spirit as his promised Comforter and gift.

In the names of these Three they presently came to be baptized or even rebaptized by immersion, committed to following the precepts and the counsels of the one Mediator, the man Christ Jesus, prophet or Teacher on earth and in heaven exalted King of the universe and of the Church, seated at the right hand of the Father as also High Priest, sanctioning from above their commemorations of his Last Supper. Although the Apostles' Creed remained for them the primitive Rule of Faith and binding, even as of 1574, less than a decade after the schism in the Reformed Church, the Polish Brethren had a Latin Catechesis structured around the *triplex munus Christi*, a convenient substitute triadology of offices rather than of divine persons. Though worshiping in the Spirit, they adored and interceded in prayer with both God the Father and the Ascended Christ, and awaited him imminently as the Vindicator of his own.

The unwitting father, or, perhaps better, stepfather of Polish Unitarianism was John Calvin.

The Polish Brethren, now in the more restricted sense, having heeded the authentic or prevailing stress of the New Testament and of most of the Fathers apart from Augustine, stressed free will and obedience to Jesus Christ and his precepts and counsels. It is even possible that an Erasmian input by way of Łaski and indeed a traditional aristocratic sense of Sarmatian liberty were contributing factors; possibly even the preservation on the Orthodox marches of Polonia of the Greek patristic view of the freedom of the Christian for Christ and in Christ played a role. Ancient Arians but also Greek patristic anti-Arians were alike fervid in their defense of the freedom of man and also the God-Man, however defined.

When between 1580 until his death in 1604, Fausto Sozzini (Socinus) took over the theological leadership of the Polish Brethren of the Minor Church, they could be properly labeled Samosatenes (rather than Arians), as Socinus acknowledged in his *Defensio animadversionum in Assertiones theologicas Collegii Posnaniensis*, comissioned by the synod of the Minor Church in 1583, but published posthumously (Raków, 1618). The *Confessio Augustana*, 1530, had already condemned Neo-Samosatenes; and subsequently Melanchthon clarified whom he therein intended: the followers of Michael Servetus. But the schism of the Reformed Church in the two parts of the Commonwealth by 1583 into Samosatenes and authentic Calvinists, a score of years after the breach we have been concentrating on, should not be allowed to distort the history of that decade, 1553-63. That the Minor Church *under Socinus* could be plausibly labeled Samosatene by 1583 is valid; but we should avoid the generalization that before and after Socinus "the left wing" of the followers in Poland of Calvin up to 1563 were Arians. That generalization makes too much of the role of Peter of Goniądz and of Biandrata's recoil at the punishment meted out by Calvin to Servetus and obscures the problem created by Calvin among the more learned pastoral and patronal leaders of Calvinism in the Commonwealth in his two uses of Christ the Mediator, cosmological and soteriological, as subordinated to the Father. The Jesuits of Poznań first identified the "Polish" Brethren as Samosatene in a book published in 1581 against the Lithuanian Brother, Simon Budny, a work upheld further by a canon of Poznań in 1583. But the charge and the defense do not establish a primarily Servetian origin of the Minor Church.[73] The Triadology and Christology of Bishop Paul of Antioch from Samosata,[74] under whom St. Lucian[75] conducted his school, is, in any case, difficult to reconstruct.

The Polish Brethren of 1563-73, satisfied with the simplicity of the formulary "Father, Son, and Holy Spirit" of Matthew (28:19), voluntarily died symbolically in trine immersion and rose with Christ to become members of the New Israel, the Church of the freely reborn. And they found what they thought was an Apostolic summary of the role of the Three, without elaboration of their relationship in confusing non-scriptural terms, eminently satisfactory. In any case, they refused to separate soteriology in Calvin's sense of predestined election within the intradeical mystery before even the fall of Adam from their own simple Christology based more on the Gospels than the Epistles. Theirs was a soteriology based on obedience, *imitatio Christi*, and with the theological counsel of Faustus Socinus, they began to expound his distinctive theory of the atonement, namely, that of the Father's *acceptilatio* of the obedience of Jesus for the race of Adam. The Polish Brethren would come to consider a passage of Paul himself decisive just after his quotation of the ancient hymn (adduced above at n. 62), namely Phil. 2:12: "[W]ork out your salvation with fear and trembling."

The Polish Brethren would indeed gradually remove the strain in Reformed Christology and relocate that strain in their own personal and corporate efforts as the Minor (Reformed) Church, seeking to live up to the commands of Christ on the basis not of election but in the confidence that "God" was at work in them, "both to will and work for his good pleasure" (Phil. 12:13). They reinterpreted the historic work of Christ. For them he was soteriological Mediator in three modalities: as Prophet up through his crucifixion, the Man of 1 Tim. 2:5; as High Priest at his Ascension, Heb. 8:6 ff., seated at the right hand of God the Father/Yahweh/Elohim, the Creator of heaven; and as King.

Many of them, too, knew Hebrew, as did Calvin. They adored the glorified Christ as also King of the cosmos, vicegerent of his Father, and also as King of the Church. The Polish Brother and Sister, like every member of the *szlachta*, regarded themselves as free under Christ the King and under the Polish constitutional ruler, elective after 1572. Like Modrzewski, who ended days with the Minor Church and who had earlier written on Christ the Mediator, the schismatic Polish Brethren often carried quite far their view that the lord and the peasant should be held to the same precepts of Jesus Christ, Prophet, High Priest, and King, as also to the same laws and compacts of their elected King.

Notes

1. The best account of this development from a "confessional" point of view is that of Earl Morse Wilbur, *A History of Unitarianism: Socinianism and its Antecedents* (Cambridge: Harvard University Press, 1945); *A History of Unitarianism: In Transylvania, England and America*, ibid., 1952. Much more recent and abreast of the new Polish literature with the Minor Church placed in confessional context is the work of Ambroise Jobert, *De Luther à Mohila: La Pologne dans la crise de la Chrétienté 1517-1648* (Paris: Institut des Études Slaves, 1974).

2. The great publicist wrote three treatises *De Mediatore* between September 1560 and September 1561, printed together as Libri III, *Opera omnia*, IV (Warsaw: PAN, 1958), ed. by Kazimierz Kumaniecki, pp. 11-76.

3. George H. Williams, "The Polish-Lithuanian Calvin during the Superintendency of John Łaski, 1556-60," in *Reformatio Perennis: Essays on Calvin . . . in Honor of Ford Lewis Battles*, ed. by B.A. Gerrish (Pittsburgh: Pickwick Press, 1981), pp. 129-58; idem, "Francis Stancaro's Schismatic Reformed Church, . . . 1559/61-1570," *Harvard Ukrainian Studies in honor of Omeljan Pritsak*, 3/4 (1979-80), pp. 931-57; Jill Raitt, "The Person of the Mediator: Calvin's Christology and Beza's Fidelity," *Occasional Papers of the American Society for Reformation Research*, I (1977), pp. 53-80.

4. Besides the specialized piece in n. 3, see Lorenz Hein, *Italienische Protestanten und ihr Einfluss auf die Reformation in Polen. . . vor 1570* (Leiden: Brill, 1974), ch. 3.

5. Antonio Rotondò, "Biandrata, Giovanni Giorgio," *Dizionario Biografico degli Italiani*, X (Rome, 1968), pp. 257-64.

6. All the decrees are given as documents in my collection and interpretation, *The Polish Brethren, 1601-1685*, Harvard Theological Study, 30 (Chico, California: Scholars Press, 1980). Be sure that copy has printed errata slip that was not in the original subscription mailings.

7. See especially Rudolf Lorenz, *Arius Judaizans? Untersuchung zur dogmengeschichtlichen Einordnung des Arius* (Göttingen: Vandenhoeck & Ruprecht, 1979); Robert C. Gregg and Dennis E. Groh, *Early Arianism—A View of Salvation* (Philadelphia: Fortress Press, 1981); and Thomas A. Kopecek, *A History of Neo-Arianism*, 2 vols. (Cambridge: The Philadelphia Patristic Foundation, 1979).

8. For two decisive New Testament texts, see Eduard Lohse, *Die Briefe an die Kolosser und an Philemon* (Göttingen: Vanderhoeck & Ruprecht, 1968); Dieter Georgi, "Der vorpaulinische Hymnus Phil 2, 6-11," *Zeit und Geschichte: Dankesgabe an Rudolf Bultmann*, ed. by Erich Dinkler (Tübingen: Mohr, 1964), pp. 263-93.

9. Theodor Wotschke, *Der Briefwechsel der Schweizer mit den Polen* (Leipzig, 1908).

10. For the unity of the covenant in Calvin, see Hans Heinrich Wolff, *Die Einheit des Bundes bei Calvin* (Neukirch: Moers, 1958) and in the more seminal Zurich colleague and another correspondent with the Poles, Wayne Baker, *Heinrich Bullinger and the Covenant* (Athens, Ohio: Ohio University Press, 1980).

11. Halina Kowalska, *Działalność Reformatorska Jana Łaskiego w Polsce 1556-1560* (The Reformatory activity of Jan Łaski in Poland, 1556-1560) (Wrocław: Ossolineum, 1969).

12. George H. Williams, "Erasmianism in Poland 1518-1605," *Polish Review*, 22 (1977), pp. 3-50.

13. See the scripturally embroidered Apostles' Creed, the *Confessio fidei* of Jonas Szlichtyng, printed among the many documents in *The Polish Brethren*, n. 6 above, comprehensively interpreted by me in the West-East context, "The Place of the *Confessio fidei* of Jonas Schlichting in the Life and Thought of the Minor Church," *Socinianism and its Role in the Culture of Sixteenth to Eighteenth Centuries*, ed. by Lech Szczucki in cooperation with Zbigniew Ogonowski, and Janusz Tazbir, (Warsaw-Łódz: PAN/PWN, 1983), pp. 103-14.

14. On the speculation of Faustus Socinus on the pre-Ascension ascension of Jesus after his baptism by John, see *Polish Brethren*, topical index, and n. 73 below.

15. Cf. my "Stancaro's Schismatic Church," n. 3 above.

16. See n. 8 above. Angels were also mediators and especially messengers in rabbinical theology.

17. The fact that Paul the Samosatene was condemned for using "consubstantial" (in *his* sense) made the term suspect long into the fourth century, even though used at Nicaea I. See further, nn. 74 and 75. I deal with the creed of Lucian, also perhaps the same as the II Creed of Antioch of 341, and with the related literature in the context of the struggle as to whether will or being should be regarded as most decisive in scriptural/conciliar theology, and this in the still larger context of a current ecclesiastical event, "The World Council of Churches and its Vancouver Theme: 'Jesus Christ the Life of the World' in Historical Perspective," *Harvard Theological Review* 76:1 (1983), pp. 1-51, esp. 28-36 and n. 49.

18. I adduce here an article I would today wish to modify slightly, which had the merit of pointing to the political-soteriological context of the Arian controversy, "Christology and Church-State Relations in the Fourth Century," *Church History*, 20 (1951), September, pp. 3-33; December, pp. 3-26. Per Beskow dealt extensively with my thesis in *Rex Gloriae: The Kingship of Christ in the Early Church* (Stockholm: Almquist, 1962).

19. By Georges Florovsky the phrase is meant to suggest that in the post-Chalcedonian christological debate, Constantinople II and III and Nicaea II brought closer together the Second Hypostasis and the one hypostasis in two natures. Nicaea II, in fact, allowed to slip, away "the one person and one hypostasis" in reference to Christ, saying that "whoever adores the image, adores in it the hypostasis of the Depicted." I have dealt with this in the larger context of his thought, "Georges Vasilievich Florovsky," *Greek Orthodox Theological Review*, 11 (1965), pp. 7-107.

20. This controversy, inflamed by a Calabrian monk, was essentially an intra-Hellenic development of the thought of Gregory Palamas (d. 1359), archbishop of Thessalonica, who distinguished between the divine essence (*ousia*) and the divine (uncreated) energies, and who held open the possibility for a Hesychast (a monk in mystical silence) to have the Beatific Vision of the divine essence. John Meyendorff, an authority on Hesychasm, most recently has shown its religio-political influence in his *Byzantium and the Rise of Russia: A Study of Byzantino-Russian relations in the Fourteenth Century* (Cambridge, London: Cambridge University Press, 1981), with some significance for the background of the piety of monks and lay brotherhoods on the Byzantine-rite soil of the Commonwealth in the sixteenth century.

21. Henry Chadwick, *Boethius* (Oxford: Clarendon Press, 1981).

22. *Humilia in Evangelium Joannis 1.7*; *Patrologia Latina* (henceforth *PL*), 76, cols. 1101B-1102A.

23. III, *distinctio* vi; *PL*, 192, cols, 767A-71B. For the extensive secondary literature, see the third critical edition, *Sententiae in IV libris distinctae*, 2 vols. (Grottaferrata: Collegium S. Bonaventurae, 1971; 1981) 2, pp. 49-59. Especially useful for the problem of the three *opiniones* although not concentrating on Lombard, is Walter Henry Principe, four volumes dealing with *The Theology of the Hypostatic Union* in four thirteenth-century theologians, in the Pontifical Institute of Toronto, Studies and Texts, 7 (Toronto, 1963) on William of Auxerre; 12 (Toronto, 1967) on Alexander of Hales; 19 (Toronto, 1970) on Hugh of Saint Chér; and 32 (Toronto, 1975) on Philip the Chancellor. It is in the first part of the volume on William that one is brought abreast of the inheritance from Lombard. A brief account of the theories and the state of the research is that by Horacio Santiago-Otero, "El 'Nihilanismo' cristologico y las tres opiniones," *Burgense: Collectanes scientifica*, 10 (1969), pp. 431-43, which starts out with the four major alleged or actual Nihilianists: Peter Abelard, Gilbert de Poirée, Peter Lombard, and Peter of Poitiers.

24. *PL*, 192 cols. 785A-800B; for the expressed difference between Luther and Calvin on the IV Lateran decree *Firmiter*, upholding Lombard, cf. Hein, op. cit., p. 172, n. 245.

25. *Werke*, Weimar Edition, vol. 9, pp. 29-84, for the expressed difference between Luther and Calvin on the IV Latheran decree *Firmiter*, upholding Lombard, cf. Hein, *Italienische Protestanten*, p. 172, n. 245.

26. Cf. George H. Williams, *Anselm: Communion and Atonement* (St. Louis: Concordia, 1960).

27. *Summa Theologiae*, Blackfriars Latin text and English translation (New York/London, 1965), 50, pp. 212-13.

28. "Confessional" Unitarian historiography has always dealt harshly with Biandrata because he is credited with having compassed the imprisonment of Francis Dávid.

29. It is with a great debt of appreciation that I here refer to Joseph N. Tylenda, S.J. Although he ecumenically takes the side of Calvin against Biandrata and Stancaro, his delineation of the course of the controversies and his analysis are of interest; and it is his translations in the appendices of his three articles that I use, with only slight changes, especially where I wish to bring out the original Latin, and I do capitalize Mediator and make as vivid as possible the Hebraic words for God that Calvin was aware of in his renderings of the Old Testament in Latin, even though he limited himself to the one: Yahweh (*Iehova*). Tylenda's three articles are "The Warning that Went Unheeded: John Calvin on Giorgio Biandrata," *Calvin Theological Journal*, 12 (1977), pp. 24-62, with Calvin's *Responsio* to Biandrata, pp. 54-62, this being printed in *Opera omnia* of John Calvin (henceforth *OC*), 9 (Braunschweig, 1870), cols. 325-32; "Christ the Mediator: Calvin versus Stancaro," ibid. 8 (1973), pp. 5-16, with Calvin's first letter to the Poles about Stancaro, pp. 11-16 (this being printed in *OC*, 9, cols. 337-41); and "The Controversy on Christ the Mediator: Calvin's Second Reply to Stancaro," ibid., 8 (1973), pp. 131-57, with Calvin's Response to the Polish Nobles and to Francesco Stancaro of Mantua, pp. 146-57 (this being printed in *OC*, 9, cols. 146-57).

30. Lech Szczucki, ed., *Filozofia i myśl społeczna XVI wieku* (Philosophy and social thought in the sixteenth century) (Warsaw: PWN, 1978), pp. 9-29.

31. I have myself worked on the liturgical as distinguished from the philosophical and the feudal context of this work in *Anselm: Communion and Atonement* (St. Louis: Concordia, 1960). In *Cur Deus homo* Anselm used only nineteen passages from the

Bible, only a few of them connected with the later discussions of atonement. He does not use 1 Tim. 2:5.

32. Blackfriars edition, n. 21 above, pp. 208-09.

33. *Sentences*, III, iii, 2. In this Lombard expressly followed John of Damascus, *Fount of Wisdom*, III, *De fide orthodoxa*; but in I, *Dialectica*, lxvi Damascene had *en passant* succumbed to the visualization of the simple faithful. It is true, Calvin did not adduce *Dialectica* to support his position.

34. The major book devoted to Christ the Mediator in Calvin is the doctoral thesis of Hendrik Schroten, *Christus de Middelaar, bij Calvijn: Bijdrage tot de leer van de zekerheid des geloofs* (Utrecht: P. den Boer, 1948). It holds that the theology of Calvin must be understood as pastoral and conforting; that it cannot be understood in terms of the *Institutes alone*, the commentaries being indispensable; and that in II, xv we should recognize in the Calvinian formulation of the *triplex munus Christi* the reemergence of the Recapitulation theory of Irenaeus (d. ca. 200). This is another of the theories of the Atonement in which Christ takes into himself humanity, in this case, in all his ages of life and conduct. The *triplex munus Christi* was not present in the edition of 1536. As important as it is, I hold that John Laski derived it not from Calvin but from Erasmus (see above at n. 12). Schroten did not take note of the *Extra Calvinisticum*, on which see below at n. 36.

35. The best summary of what Calvin knew of scholasticism and particularly of Peter Lombard and John Gratian, since he had studied canon law at Orléans and Bourges, is that of Heribert Schützeichel, *Die Glaubenstheologie Calvins* (Munich: Max Hueber, 1972), pp. 68-73.

36. The history of the concept and its theological implications are admirably traced by Edward David Willis, *Calvin's Catholic Christology: The Function of the So-Called Extra Calvinisticum* (Leiden: Brill, 1966). The *Extra Calvinisticum* appears in the *Institutes* at II, xiii, 4 for the first time in the edition of 1559; but the idea had been expressed in earlier editions in the eucharistic context (a major concern of Calvin) and it is found in its final form in this context in IV, xvii, 30. Willis construes Calvin's double use of Mediator, in "the ordering of the universe" and in redemption, in a section, pp. 67-73.

37. Willis makes this especially clear, p. 71.

38. *Sentences*, III, xxii, 3: *PL*, col. 804.

39. Hans Scholl, *Calvinus Catholicus: Die katholische Calvinforschung im 20. Jahrhundert* (Freiburg/Basel/Vienna: Herder, 1974).

40. *OC*, 52, col. 85.

41. *OC*, 52, cols. 171-84, based on verses 5 and 6. See also Commentary on the Epistles to Timothy, 1548, *OC*, 51.

42. Because of the hazard to the Nicene dogma of the eternal hypostasis of the Son/Mediator and because this passage on the delivery of the Kingdom by Christ was clung to by an embarrassing ally of Athanasius, Marcellus of Ancyra, with its sequel "that God may be all in all," the Niceno-Constantinopolitan Creed says expressly: "and his [Christ's] Kingdom shall have no end."

43. G. Seebass, *Das reformatorische Werk des Andreas Osiander* (Munich, 1967). I deal with him also and with Orzechowski in my "Stancaro's Reformed Church," n. 3 above.

44. The ancient Arians of all groupings did not accept 1 Tim. 2:5 literally, any more than did Calvin, but in their case they held that the cosmological and soteriological Mediator, the Logos, and the premundane Son of God, was begotten at

creation as instrument of creation, and that as incarnate the resultant Jesus Christ was a *tertium quid* in a *medius gradus*, as it were, being less than God (the Father), more than a man.

45. This is overall the view of Nancy Conradt in her unpublished dissertation, "John Calvin, Theodore Beza and the Reformation in Poland," (Madison, Wisconsin, 1974).

46. See n. 29 above.

47. *OC*, 9, col. 330.

48. *OC*, 9, col. 331.

49. *OC*, 9, col. 331. For a single- and two-stage Logos, see Harry A. Wolfson, *The Philosophy of the Church Fathers*, third revised edition (Cambridge: Harvard University Press, 1970), pp. 192-231. The two-stage theory was never formally anathematized, but the single stage or eternally hypostatic Logos became the accepted orthodox view. The intrinsic and extrinsic of Calvin with respect to economies or dispensations in Calvin, Stancaro II, col. 354, do not directly relate to the distinction Wolfson described in the ante-Nicene Fathers, for his distinctions refer to the intradeical Logos (*endiathetos*) and the instrumental Logos (*prophorikos*), the cosmological Mediator.

50. *OC*, 9, col. 325.

51. *OC*, 9, col. 326.

52. *OC*, 9, col. 329.

53. *OC*, 9, col. 326. For the second sense, see also ibid., col. 328: "What concerns the words, "I am ascending to my Father' (John 20:17), confirms . . . what I have said about Christ speaking *in the Person* of the Mediator."

54. *OC*, 9, col. 326.

55. See above, pp. 10-12.

56. Stancaro II; *OC*, 9, col. 350.

57. Stancaro II; *OC*, 9, col. 355, bottom.

58. Stancaro II; *OC*, 9, col. 356.

59. Stancaro II; *OC*, 9, col. 356.

60. Stancaro II; *OC*, 9, col. 338.

61. Stancaro II; *OC*, 9, col. 351.

62. Stancaro II; *OC*, 9, col. 351.

63. Stancaro II; *OC*, 9, col. 352f. The *Responsio* then refers in the third person to Calvin's *Institutes*, II, 14, in which the idea is developed further. All the pastors of Geneva signed the letter but there can be no doubt about who was the principal author.

64. Stancaro II; *OC*, 9, col. 353.

65. For Aquinas on priests as lesser *mediatores*, see n. 32 above.

66. Stancaro II; *OC*, 9, col. 352.

67. Stancaro I; *OC*, 9, col. 339.

68. Stancaro I; *OC*, 9, cols. 339f. It would be too much to go into the High Priesthood of Christ in relation to his Mediatorship, but we note in passing that Aquinas, in *Summa Theologiae*, III: I, question 22, said: "The characteristic function of a priest is to act as Mediator between God and his people . . . . While it is true that Christ was a priest, not as God, but as man, it is also true that it was one and the same Person who was Priest and God. . . . As for the daily sacrifice offered in the Church, it is not a distinct sacrifice from that offered by Christ himself; it is its commemoration." Blackfriars edition, pp. 136-37, 144-45, 146-47. As with the Me-

diator, so with the Priest, Aquinas allows an effectual role for the sacerdotal *mediatores*, since the Sacrifice and the Mediation was accomplished by Jesus Christ also in his human nature. Calvin, by insisting on assigning these actions to the Person of the Mediator and Priest and partly to the divine nature in him, undercuts the intermediary role of priest and minister.

69. Stancaro II; *OC*, 9, col. 353.

70. Stancaro II; *OC*, 9, col. 355.

71. See above at n. 44.

72. Cf. Williams, "Stancaro's Church," p. 943.

73. About the books mentioned in the paragraph, see Alodia Kawecka Gryczowa, *Ariańskie oficyny wydawnicze Rodeckiego i Sternackiego* (The Arian printing houses of Rodecki and Sternacki) (Wrocław: Ossolineum, 1974), pp.178f., 308. For the fundamentally idiosyncratic Christology of Socinus, which should be kept separate from what the Polish Brethren held up to 1580 and also from that of the Lithuanian Brethren and the Transylvanian Unitarians, see my "The christological issues between Francis Dávid and Faustus Socinus during the Disputation on the invocation of Christ, 1578-1579," *Antitrinitarianism in the Second Half of the 16th Century*, ed. by Robert Dań and Antal Pirnat, Studia Humanitatis, 5 (Budapest: Hungarian Academy of Sciences; Leiden: Brill, 1982), pp. 287-321.

74. Gustave Bardy, *Paul de Samosate: Étude historique*, second edition, completely redone (Louvain, 1929); Henri de Riedmatten, *Les Actes du procès de Paul de Samosate* (Fribourg, 1952); Robert L. Sample, "The Christology of the Council of Antioch (268 C.E.) Reconsidered," *Church History*, 68 (1979), pp. 18-26. Bardy in his first edition of 1923 had a useful concluding chapter on echoes of the Samosatene Christology carried into the seventeenth century, which, being but a sketch, he chose to drop in the second edition. See above at n. 17.

75. Gustave Bardy, *Recherche sur saint Lucien d'Antioche et son école* (Paris: Beauchesne, 1936); for the Lucianic Creed, see Philip Schaff, *Creeds of Christendom*, 3 vols., third revised and enlarged edition (New York: Harper, 1890), 2, pp. 25-28; also accessible in Greek and another translation with updated interpretation of the conciliar situation *as of 341*, J.N.D. Kelly, *Early Christian Creeds*, third edition, (Singapore: Longman, 1972), pp. 268-70. See above at n. 17.

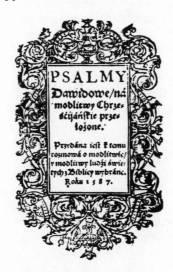

5

Some Remarks on the Social and Religious History
of Sixteenth-Century Poland

Jerzy Kłoczowski

ixteenth-century Poland was a rapidly developing, great European federated state united with the Grand Duchy of Lithuania (formalized in the Union of Lublin, 1569). In 1634 about eleven million subjects lived on 990,000 square kilometers. Apart from Poles and Lithuanians, the Polish-Lithuanian state was also comprised of millions of Ruthenians, ancestors of today's Ukrainians and Belorussians, tens of thousands of Germans in towns (primarily in Gdańsk, but also in other Baltic towns), and also a growing number of Jews who enjoyed broad autonomy under the king's protection. Thus, from the fourteenth century onwards, Catholic Poles and Lithuanians had to live together with Orthodox Ruthenians and it can be claimed that their mutual relations, albeit not without tensions, were on the whole good and peaceful. Almost all branches of European Protestantism came to Poland in the sixteenth century, rendering the already existent national mosaic even more colorful.[1]

Historians have long been interested in the stories of particular denominations and their mutual relationships within the borders of the Polish-Lithuanian state. But critical, international study is needed of the various historiographical schools within various denominational and national traditions: Catholics, Protestants, Jews, agnostics and atheists on the one hand, and Poles, Germans, Lithuanians, Ukrainians, Jews, and Russians on the other. Such research would critically assess the existing studies and develop new perspectives. Particularly important would be the recognition of the extent to which confessional and national perspectives have obscured many aspects of problems and to what extent they have put limitations on research and proposed only superficial understanding of the changes. Current historiography tries to see these changes in a comparative perspective and within the broad context of global history, in order to understand better a variety of religious phenomena. Gaps in research of this kind are enormous; a fully satisfactory history of religious communities living in sixteenth-century Poland still awaits its author.

In the past, the custom has been to isolate the entire century from what preceded it, but greater emphasis should be put on the necessity of linking sixteenth-century transformations with prior evolution, in particular, with what had taken place in the fifteenth century. A perspective of what is called "*la longue durée*" is essential. Today, we assume that the fourteenth and fifteenth centuries brought a deepening Christianization of large social groups, including vlllages, and simultaneously a crystallization of certain features which comprise a typical religious attitude, a Christianity concentrated upon Christ as man with a developed cult of the Blessed Mother. The ideal pattern for this attitude is based on the Holy Family and stresses love and mutual help beginning with one's own family. This is a Christianity constituted less by fear, coercion, and the power of ecclesiastical institutions than by a sort of assimilation by local cultures of values propagated by the long-term pastoral efforts of mendicant friars and later of parishes. Anticlerical currents were strong, particularly among a large and dynamic strata of nobility which increasingly would fight for privileges and power.[2]

Generally speaking, throughout the sixteenth century there are a variety of strong Reformation tendencies evident from the very beginning of the century, but becoming increasingly powerful from its midpoint onward. It is not always possible to confine the entire movement to certain particular denominations which then take definite shape only at midcentury. German townsmen began to identify themselves with the teachings of Martin Luther, while the influence of Calvin was stronger in some circles of the aristocracy and rich nobility. During the first half of the century, Polish elites were particularly attracted to Erasmus; his humanism was congenial to the irenic tendencies typical for a number of distinguished personalities, and also to those who remained within the Catholic church.[3]

The rapid triumph of Protestantism, particularly Lutheranism, in Prussia, Pomerania, and in Silesia (that is, basically beyond the frontiers of the Polish state) appeared to be a prelude to an actual Protestant Reformation in Poland. Significantly enough, already in 1524-25 Albrecht Hohenzollern, the last Grand Master of the Teutonic Knights, secularized his order, submitting it simultaneously to the sovereignty of the Polish king. This, in turn, gave rise to the first state Lutheran church in Poland. Ten years later, a similar church was founded in Pomerania. The Protestant reform achieved a strikingly broad and rapid success in Silesia, which nevertheless remained under the rule of Catholic Habsburgs. Some decades later, the overwhelming majority of parishes from the diocese of Wrocław became Protestant.

Meanwhile, an old and deeply rooted anticlericalism of the nobility acquired a new impetus in Poland, this time in the context of a broader movement aiming at Poland's reform and supported by the masses of gentry. Research has lacked an adequate multireferential analysis of this anticlericalism and its primary as well as secondary sources. Both economic factors, such as tithes or Church lands, and jurisdictional ones, i.e., laymen's dependence on Church courts, played a noticeable role in this anticlericalism. Yet the question arises how deep this anticlericalism really went and to what new proposals and solutions it really led. A considerable expansion of the reform movement came in the fifties and sixties of the sixteenth century, that is, during the reign of Sigismund Augustus (Zygmunt August) 1548-72.[4]

The abolition in 1552 and definitely in 1563-65 of state execution of sentences passed by Church courts appeared to be an important success. Possibly, however, this success weakened further development of the whole movement. The Polish nobility became particularly attached to Calvinism, which precisely then, in the second half of the century, was stabilizing itself in Geneva and gaining a strong position in European Protestantism.[5] Perhaps it was the organizational character of the Calvinist church with an important role played by laymen and synods that the nobility found especially appealing. At this time however, one of the most important issues appeared to be the establishment of the Polish state church, an issue which found supporters both among Protestants and Catholics. An old conciliatory tradition, so strong among the Polish elites of the first half of the fifteenth century, and harmonizing so well with the ambitions of gentry democracy, revived in the teachings of, for instance, a leading Polish intellectual of that time Andrzej Frycz Modrzewski (Andreas Fricius Modrevius). One of the most outstanding Polish representatives of the Protestant Reformation, Jan Łaski (Jonannes a Lasco, d. 1560), devoted the last years of his life to the cause of a national church in Poland.[6] Moreover, this cause had the occasional support of the Polish bishops, particularly of Jakub Uchański (primate from 1562; d. 1581) and of King Sigismund Augustus, who after the 1555 session of parliament sent a special formal letter to the pope with a number of specific demands.

From the very beginning the great weakness of Polish Protestantism was its division. Lutheran parishes within the state gained a particular stronghold in Pomeranian towns led by Gdańsk, and in the province of Great Poland, in both cases chiefly among the German population. From 1548 on, the Czech Brethren, the successors to a moderate Hussite faction, also began to appear in Great Poland after their banishment from Bohemia.[7] Calvinism, particularly strong in the province of Little Poland but also taking root in Lithuania, already by 1562-65 split into a minor, Arian order, and a major one—Calvinist proper. The Calvinist church, with about five hundred congregations at the end of the sixteenth century and with about two hundred fifty in the middle of the seventeenth century, was the largest Protestant community of the time. Arians were considerably fewer in number, with several dozen communities of usually a hundred or two hundred members primarily in Little Poland and in Volhynia until their banishment in 1658. The Arians managed, however, to win over especially interesting people: great doctrinal and, at the beginning, social radicals, sometimes outstanding intellectuals and writers of Polish and foreign origin. Their teachings somehow paved the way for the future ideas of the Enlightenment. Anti-Trinitarianism—the questioning of the basic dogma of Christianity—exposed the Arians (also called the Polish Brethren) to persecution everywhere. In Poland they were completely ostracized and for obvious reasons they did not participate in the famous agreement reached in Sandomierz in 1570 by the Lutherans, Calvinists, and Czech Brethren, which was an attempt to establish some common basis for cooperation with the maintenance of full independence of each of the groups. On the other hand, however, the principles of religious freedom, solemnly proclaimed during the parliament of 1573 as the so-called Warsaw Confederation, were fully applicable to the anti-Trinitarian Polish Brethren just as to all the other denominations.[8]

Both the strength and undoubtedly the weakness of Polish Protestant churches was the fact that their adherents were for the most part nobles. The patronage of magnates and support of the nobility and gentry were decisive for the development and persistence of the Reformation communities; the privileged position held by the nobility in the state and society ensured tolerance, the possibility for action and, at the same time, protection against enemies. On the other hand, however, the nobility's dominance was so great that, as the evidence shows, it left its strong and individual stamp on the life and mentality (including religious attitudes) of particular communities and whole churches. The strict observance prevailing in Calvinism, so many manifestations of which can be found in the sixteenth and later centuries not only in Europe but also in North America, does not seem to have appealed to the mentality of the Polish nobility. This problem, basic for the understanding of the Polish Reformation, urgently requires comparative study concerning European communities of more or less Calvinist provenance. It would be quite proper for Polish historians to participate in the great debate alive even today and carried on by Western historians over Max Weber's argument linking Calvinism with capitalism. This controversial argument, although it has already been revised, contains this important problem of the relationship between religious mentality and general social processes. The nobility's traditional anticlericalism also commonly found expression in arbitrary and erroneous attitudes of particular Protestant communities toward the clergy, who were often of plebeian origin. Worthy of special attention and thorough historical analysis is the evolution of the Polish Brethren, their divergence from all kinds of radicalism, and above all the everyday life of the communities which, it seems, basically adapted themselves to the ordinary way of life and thinking of the nobility.[9]

Yet the old Catholic church, despite its losses and the vehement criticism directed against it, retained great strength. Its material foundations both in Poland and Lithuania basically remained intact and, what is still more interesting and even exceptional in the European context, contemporary debates never centered on the divesting of the Church of its property. The Polish plebeian masses, both in the country and in towns, remained loyal to the old order, a fact which had repercussions in their resistance to new beliefs imposed on them by the lords of parishes. In the course of time, anti-Protestant riots run through towns and supported above all by the Polish populace even became a great menace to Polish tolerance. Yet not only anti-Protestantism—a so-called Counter Reformation in the traditional terminology of nineteenth-century German historiography—characterized Catholics; they were also involved in reform activities aimed at the improvement of the existing situation. In the middle of the sixteenth century cathedral chapters were particularly important circles of people who, on the one hand, severely criticized the existing situation in the Church and the laxity of the bishops, and, on the other hand, undertook various actions either to maintain the order or to support reform. Among the monastic orders which suffered heavy losses in membership, the Dominicans and Bernardines fared the best. Stanisław Hozjusz (Stanislaus Hosius, d. 1579), from 1549 bishop and author of writings widely known in the whole Catholic world, and the only Pole to play some role during the last phases of the Council of Trent in 1562-63, gradually became the head of the most uncompromising Catholics. From the fifties and, particularly the sixties, special representatives of the pope (nuncios) played an increasingly significant role in Poland. In 1564 the first Jesuits appeared in Poland in the province of Varmia, and in 1565 King Sigismund Augustus solemnly accepted the resolutions of the Council of Trent. From then on, the old Church slowly regained ground in Poland.[10]

The importance of the first generations of Jesuits seems to have been especially great. They often managed to win over eminent persons, sometimes even former Protestants, and to propagate their comprehensive and sophisticated teachings with much energy and organizational skill both among the elites and the masses of the society. A new form of Jesuit school immediately gained immense popularity, significantly not only among Catholics but also among Protestants; towards the end of the sixteenth century, at least several thousand young people attended these schools. Missions, sermons, retreats at the courts or among the masses of people in Poland, Lithuania, or Ruthenia increased in popularity and did their part in the conversion of some Protestants to Catholicism. The question remains, however, to what degree the character of Christianity itself as represented by a new monastic order, optimistic and humanistic sofar as it concerns faith in human nature and human abilities, ensured the success of the Jesuits above all among the nobility—the class which was crucial in deciding the religious situation in the country.

A psychological factor is also important for an understanding of the generation of the seventies and eighties of the sixteenth century, the generation returning to Catholicism. Jan Błoński shows this process excellently in his study of Mikołaj Sęp Szarzyński, perhaps the best Polish poet of the generation after Jan Kochanowski. During the sharp denominational struggles and religious wars the churches closed their ranks and cut themselves off from others; there was a collapse of irenical hopes for finding a common solution. The vision of life was a gloomy spectacle full of sin and tragedy. There was an increased need for inner truth, for a mystical and personal contact with God. The writings of the great Spanish mystics, Ignatius of Loyola and Louis of Granada, proved to be particularly important. Louis was frequently translated into Polish after the sixties and he became a sort of patron saint of a quite strong mystical branch in the Polish Catholic revival (particularly among women). Mysticism and inner religious life in general certainly had much in common with Protestant experience. We know that Luther and Calvin used sources similar to those of Ignatius. Catholic mysticism evolved under the strong impact of Christian humanism. It aimed at the formation of strong characters, ready to fulfill all the duties of life. Sęp Szarzyński treats life as a task. Religious commitment played an enormous role also in the individual's personal life and in his duties as a citizen. Such a program mixing mysticism and humanism was well-adapted to the needs of the rising generations of the second half of the sixteenth century and influenced their return to Catholicism.[11]

Towards the close of the century, when the victory of the Catholics was already evident, Catholic reform received considerable impetus. It was undertaken on a large scale by a new generation of bishops who radically reorganized their dioceses and reinforced the entire system of supervision and inspection in order to increase discipline and moral virtue among the clergy. This generation sometimes severely criticized the position of the Church and religion in Poland, as it happened, for instance, in the province of Mazovia (Mazowsze) which in the sixteenth century was almost a political stronghold of Polish Catholicism; yet such criticism was connected with a certain reformatory zeal which, in turn, stimulated comprehensive activities in the field of what is generally understood as socio-religious education. At the same time, some of the monastic orders became very active. New candidates flowed into the monasteries in the hundreds and new houses were built. This movement became really widespread only in the first half of the seventeenth century. Internal reforms got under way and everywhere the number of monastic preachers, missionaries, chaplains, confessors, priests overseeing shrines, organizers of sodalities, etc., increased rapidly. The social foundation of the whole movement was very extensive, and geographically it soon encompassed the whole territory of Poland, together with its Lithuanian and Ruthenian lands. The patronage of magnates and noblemen considerably facilitated the development of monasteries and sacral buildings in general. Magnates even began to remove Protestant ministers from their courts because for various reasons it seems these were less attractive than their successors, the monastic chaplains. However, the monastic chaplains were also not very difficult to remove from court and a new one could be found either in the same or in a competitive order. On the whole, both diocesan and monastic clergy were of plebeian origin, that is, coming primarily from the middle class, but also included noblemen and, particularly, members of the petty gentry. Unlike Protestant communities, the plebeian clergy had the better protection of relatively strong structures—monasteries and dioceses—against the arbitrary measures taken by their lay patrons. Such protection was all the more effective since the post-Tridentine Church put special emphasis on the dignity and prestige of its priests.[12]

20. The Leopolita Bible. *Biblia to jest Księgi Starego y Nowego Zakonu*, w Krakowie, 1577. Title page. The first edition of this first printed Catholic Bible in Polish prepared by Jan Nicz called Leopolita was published in 1561. (Indiana University Lilly Library, Bloomington).

TESTA

MENTV NOVVEGO

CZESC PIERVVSZA

Czterzei Euangeliſtowie ſwieci,
MATTHEVSZ, MAREK:
LVKASZ, I IAN,
Z Greckiego iezyka na Polski prze
lozeni, i wykladem krotkiem
obiasnieni.

Wczym wſzyſtkiem dokſadáno ſie/ Łaciń⸗
ſkiego/ i nakilka inſzych iezykow przeſoſe⸗
miá/t ktemu Starych i Nowych piſma
ſwietego Doctorow.

Przytem przydáná ieſt nauka czytaniá i piſaniá iezyka
polſkiego/ ku tym kſiegám i inſem poſytecsna/
J Regeſtr na wykſad ktory przy ſ. Mat⸗
theuſu/ i na Ewangeljé niedzieł⸗
ne i dniow ſwietych.

W Krolewcu Pruskiem
M D L I.
Menſe Octob:

I. Timo: II.

Vnus eſt mediator Dei & hominum
Ieſus Chriſtus.

21. The Seclucian New Testament. *Testamentu Nowego część pierwsza*, w Królewcu, 1551. Title page of the first part of the Lutheran New Testament translated by Stanisław Murzynowski (Biblioteka Ossolińskich, Wrocław). Reprinted from Maria Kossakowska, *Biblia w języku polskim* vol. 1, (Poznań: Księgarnia Św. Wojciecha, 1968).

Towards the close of the sixteenth century the reform movement also spread to the Eastern church in Poland. The union of the Orthodox and the Roman Catholic churches agreed upon in Brześć in 1596 induced the Orthodox church of Poland to recognize the primacy of Rome without, however, relinquishing its autonomy and individual character. But, in fact, in the eyes of the Orthodox bishops and their supporters, this constituted an attempt to reform relations existing in their church, the bad state of which seemed obvious to contemporaries. Ultimately, the union of 1596 led to a permanent split within the Eastern church into two off shoots, the Uniate and Orthodox churches, and had profound consequences for this territory and the Polish state during the following centuries. Although supported by Rome, the Jesuits, and King Sigismund III, the union was not, however, accepted by the Roman Catholic church with particular enthusiasm and understanding. Latin bishops, for instance, were rather reluctant to admit their colleagues from the Uniate church to the Senate, which certainly would have added to the prestige of this church. The Orthodox hierarchy, initially not recognized by the state, managed, however, to obtain this recognition under propitious circumstances which came in the first years of King Ladislaus IV's reign (Władysław IV Waza), that is, in 1633. Among the factors which made the Orthodox church, with its primary intellectual base in Kiev, particularly strong was its close relationship with the Cossacks, who were rapidly gaining importance. The strong expansion of the Roman Catholic church in the Ruthenian territories of the Kingdom of Poland and of the Grand Duchy of Lithuania also played a very significant role in the whole religious and cultural situation. Masses of noblemen and sometimes of Ruthenian townspeople who had adopted Protestantism now became Catholics; they were followed by many members of the Orthodox and the Uniate churches as well. It is clear that this dissent of the elites, frequently connected with polonization, was detrimental to the position held by both Ruthenian churches. At the same time, however, the daily confrontation of the three churches (disregarding the Protestant communities which retained their strength in some places) led not only to mutual tension and conflict, but also stimulated reform actions based on the experience and accomplishments of others. An excellent example are the reforms undertaken by Peter Mohyła (1596-1647), Orthodox metropolitan of Kiev from 1633, which then became a significant element in the reform of Orthodox churches in the Russian empire, persisting until the middle of the eighteenth century.[13]

Despite great achievements and a concomitant tendency to dominate, Polish Catholicism also managed in the first half of the seventeenth century to retain its individual traits, distinguishing it, as well as the whole Polish situation, from what was happening in other absolutist, Catholic, or non-Catholic countries. Those traits were particularly striking and even shocking to zealous Catholic observers coming from Italy or Spain. Catholic noblemen did not overcome their traditional anticlericalism at all. For fear "that Poland might turn into a kingdom of priests," the 1635 parliament basically prohibited any donation of real estate to churches; even if later the land passed, more or less legally, into the hands of various Church institutions, legal restraints and active resistance always remained significant. As the evidence shows, noblemen of various religious persuasions met together in regional councils, at court, and otherwise maintained social contacts without any difficulties. A Spanish Dominican friar, Damian Fonseca, who in 1617-19 made a thorough inspection of the monasteries belonging to his order, was extremely amazed to find Catholic, Orthodox, and Arian noblemen staying in perfect harmony at the court of Prince Jerzy Czartoryski at Sarny in Volhynia, where Fonseca came at Christmas of 1617 to baptize a son of the prince; moreover, during a sumptuous feast, the prince asked the friar to discuss the divinity of Jesus Christ with an Arian guest. This scene seems to have been characteristic and typical. Only in such an atmosphere was it possible to engage in serious attempts at talks between various denominations; even if the situation worsened from day to day, it never became the intolerance wide-spread in contemporary Europe. Such talks were strongly supported by King Ladislaus IV and his close advisors, such as Chancellor Jerzy Ossoliński, or the Capuchin, Walerian Magni. Although comprehensive negotiations with both the members of the Orthodox church (particularly with Peter Mohyła as their leader) and with Protestants (such as during a famous colloquium at Toruń in 1645 which had wide repercussions in Europe) did not yield any direct results, these negotiations are evidence of the specific situation and unique atmosphere in Poland as well as of the basic affairs of the state at the time of the great religious wars on the continent. The question of the uniqueness of Polish Catholicism requires complex studies which so far have been almost completely neglected. To what degree, for instance, did the peculiar tradition and mentality of the nobility, so important for the history of Polish Protestantism, influence Polish Catholicism after the Council of Trent? Such influence is unquestionable, yet there remain the masses of plebeian and middle class origin whose culture and mentality we find so difficult to grasp. A strict observance in Christian practice did not take root in Catholicism; it somehow dissolved in the sea of Polish customs, social life, and constant debates. This phenomenon is particularly noticeable in the case of monastic orders which, after all, were established to maintain this observance. Even the particularly strong Jesuits tended, consciously or still more significantly, unconsciously, to adjust themselves to new generations, to the requirements, to the needs and points of view held by local society at the beginning of the seventeenth century. From the turn of the sixteenth century not only did some supporters of the Catholic reform (also Jesuits) abandon their plans to strengthen royal power, but their whole mentality underwent a substantial evolution which, although difficult to pinpoint, may be traced, for instance, in some manifestations of the decline of the once excellent educational system. The picture of the Polish Dominican community in 1617-19 which emerges from the remarks given by Fonseca, the Spanish visitor and strict observant mentioned above, resembles a well-known stereotype of Polish faults. While observing the friars he was struck by the lack of discipline, disrespect for the authorities, factional conflict, relentlessness in litigations, and drunkenness. A monastery often resembled a nobleman's regional council, even though the monks were usually of middle class origin. Of course, this was only one side of the community which, in those times, was developing rapidly. Yet this side was tangible proof that the Polish Catholic reform, apart from its successes, also had its rather conspicuous weak points. As in the case of the Protestant reform, here also a thorough analysis is needed which would shed some light on the essence of Polish national history, culture, and economy not only within the context of the elites, but within the context of all Polish society.[14]

Apart from Christian churches, we should also notice the dynamic development of Jewish communities. The number of Jews grew rapidly at that time because of immigration from other European countries, in particular from Germany. With great caution it can be estimated at about 150,000 living mostly in towns (Cracow, Poznań, Lwów, Przemyśl, Jarosław). Jewish communities, the so-called "*kahały*," had substantial autonomy and were under the protection of the king. In the sixteenth century the so-called "*waady*," a sort of Jewish diet representing Jewish interests throughout Poland, began to take shape. The significance of this flourishing period for the culture and religious life of the Jews is an open question. We know of a few particularly famous Jewish scholars, i.e., Luria Salomon ben Jechiel (1510-1573), a rabbi, writer, and after 1555 the rector of "*jeszyba*," the famous Talmud high school in Lublin. He wrote some 20 books, 18 of which were printed, and also worked on a critical edition of the Talmud and its new exegesis. Another famous scholar and rector of the jeszyba high school in Cracow was Moses Isserles (1523-72), who studied mysticism and cabala. From Troki, an important center of Karaites, came a very interesting book, *Faith Strengthened* (translated into English by Moses Mocatt, New York, 1971). It contains an apology for Judaism and polemics with Christianity. The growth of interest in Hebrew resulted in the establishment of a special chair of Hebrew at Cracow University. This chair was given to Lionardus David, a Christianized Jew from Warsaw. Christianized Jews received all the privileges of nobility, hence such cases were not infrequent in the sixteenth century. There were also cases of ennoblement of Jews who remained faithful to Judaism. In 1525, during the ceremony at the market place in Cracow, while Albrecht Hohenzollern of Prussia, head of the first Lutheran state in Europe, was swearing allegiance to King Sigismund the Old of Poland, a Jew, Michael Esefowicz, was ennobled in recognition for his economic activities on behalf of the Jagiellonian dynasty.[15] All these various communities had to live side by side on the same territory. Hence, on the one hand, a great deal could be said about friction, tension, and struggle, but also about peaceful cooperation on the other. It is evident that the Polish situation is quite different in this respect from what occurred in other European, Catholic, Protestant or Orthodox countries. One should look for analogies in some neighboring states: in the then Hungarian Transylvania, which, although under Ottoman rule, was quite independent, or among Habsburgian Czechs, both situations representing typical Catholic absolutism. We can expect a better understanding of the roots of the sixteenth-century social and religious situation from research conducted along the lines suggested at the outset of this essay. The transformations of each particular church must be seen in a global, comparative perspective. Only then would we be able to see the particularity of Polish culture which was so striking to those zealous Catholics who came as visitors from Italy or Spain. On the whole, we see better than before the importance of the sixteenth century changes for a deepening of religious life in the Polish-Lithuanian-Ruthenian community of nations. However, much remains to be done; hence, this essay closes with an appeal for international cooperation in this field, so important for so many nations.

Notes

1. For general background, see: *History of Poland* (Warsaw: PWN, 1969) (16th and 17th century compiled by Janusz Tazbir); *The Cambridge History of Poland* (Cambridge: The University Press, 1950/1); Norman Davies, *Poland. Past and Present. A Select Bibliography of Works in English* (Newtonville: Oriental Research Partners, 1977); Norman Davies, *God's Playground. A History of Poland*, vol. 1, *Origins to 1795* (New York: Columbia University Press, 1981); Claude Backvis, "Les thèmes majeurs de la pensée politique polonaise au XVI s.," *L'Annuaire de l'Institut de Philologie et d'Histoire Orientales et Slaves* (Brussels) 14 (1975): 307-355; Janusz Tazbir, "Die polnische Kultur des XVI. Jahrhunderts," in *Fragen der Polnischen Kultur im 16. Jahrhundert*, ed. R. Olesch und H. Rothe (Giessen: Wilhelm Schmitz Verlag, 1980), pp. 379-390; George H. Williams, "Erasmianism in Poland," *The Polish Review* 22 (1977): 3-50.

2. For medieval Poland, see: Jerzy Kłoczowski, *L'essor de l'Europe Centrale-Orientales aux 14-15 s.*, Peuples et Civilisations (Paris: Presses universitaires de France; 1983); Jerzy Kłoczowski, ed., *The Christian Community of Medieval Poland. Anthologies* (Wrocław: Ossolineum, 1981); Jerzy Kłoczowski, "Les grandes lignes d'histoire de l'Église en Pologne medievale," in *Istituzioni, Cultura e Società in Italia e in Polonia*, ed. Cosimo Damiano Fonseca (Galatina Congedo Editore, 1979), pp. 105-127. For particularly extensive background in world history, including religious and cultural history, see: Jerzy Kłoczowski, *Europa słowiańska w XIV-XV w* (Slavonic Europe in the 14th-15th centuries) (Warsaw: PIW, 1984).

3. Of the vast historical literature on socio-religious changes in the Polish Republic in the 16th and first half of the 17th century only basic works with special reference to books available in Western languages are noted here. A recent general view of religious changes in 16th-17th centuries is given by the following: Stanisław Litak, "L'epoca della svolta (1525-1648)," in *Storia del Cristianesimo in Polonia*, ed. Jerzy Kłoczowski (Bologna: Centro Studi Europa Orientale, 1980), pp. 175-218; Ambroise Jobert, *De Luther à Mohila. La Pologne dans la crise de la Chretienté 1517-1648* (Paris: Institut d'Études Slaves, 1974); Jerzy Kłoczowski, *Dzieje chrześcijaństwa polskiego* (History of Polish Christianity), 2 vols. (Paris: Nasza Rodzina, 1987-88), an attempt at a synthesis from the 10th to 20th centuries, richly illustrated, including maps which together make up an atlas of Polish Christianity; Wiesław Müller,

Stanisław Litak, Jerzy Kłoczowski, and Ludomir Bieńkowski, *Kościół w Polsce* (The Church in Poland), vol. 2 (Cracow: Znak, 1970) provides an extensive description of dioceses, parishes, monasteries of the Latin Church and the Eastern Church (Bieńkowski's basic work on this subject). Includes maps. Various, sometimes denominational interpretations of the works of several authors are presented by *Historia Kościoła w Polsce* (The history of the Church in Poland), vol. 1, pt. 2, edited by Bolesław Kumor and Zdzisław Obertyński (Poznań-Warsaw: Pallotinum, 1979); for 16th and the first half of the 17th century, see the authors: Bolesław Kumor, Tadeusz Glemma, Marian Banaszak, Tadeusz Śliwa. See also Waldemar Gastpary, *Historia Kościoła w Polsce* (The history of the Church in Poland), (Warsaw: Chrześcijańska Akademia Teologiczna [Protestant], 1979).

Marian Rechowicz, ed., *Millenaire du catholicisme en Pologne* (Lublin: Wydawn. Towarzystwa Naukowego Katolickiego Uniwersytetu Lubelskiego, 1969); *Colloque de Varsovie 27-29 Octobre 1971 sur la cartographie et l'histoire socio-religieuse de l'Europe jusqu' à la fin du XVIIe siecle*, Miscelanea Historiae Ecclesiasticae 5, (Louvain: Publications Universitaires de Louvain, 1974); Ludomir Bieńkowski, Jerzy Flaga and Zygmunt Sułowski, *Cartographie historique de la Pologne. Bibliographie des cartes concernant les rapports religieux parues dans les années 1851-1968. Bibliographie de cartographie ecclesiastique 2*, (Leiden: E.J. Brill, 1971).

4. Walerian Krasiński, *Historical Sketch of the Rise,Progress and Decline of the Influence which the Scriptural Doctrines Have Exercised on the Country of Literary, Moral and Political Respects*, 2 vols. (London, 1838-1840). Krasiński's book was "for long the only available study of Polish religious history in England, and the source of many partisan opinions," according to Norman Davies, *God's Playground*, 1, p. 553. A basic reference book is Paul Fox, *The Reformation in Poland. Some Social and Economic Aspects* (Baltimore, 1934); Teodor Wotschke, *Geschichte der Reformation in Polen* (Leipzig, 1911); Karl Völker *Kirchengeschichte Polens* (Berlin und Leipzig, 1930); Zenonas Ivinskis, "Die Entwicklung der Reformation in Litauen bis zum Erscheinen der Jesuiten (1569)," *Forschungen zur osteuropäischen Geschichte* 12 (1967): 7-45; Stanisław Kot, "La Reforme dans le Grand Duché de Lithuanie, facteur occidentalisation culturelle," *Annuaire de l'Institut de Philologie et d'Histoire Orientales et Slaves* (Brussels) 12 (1953), p. 201-261; George H. Williams, "Protestants in the Ukraine during the Period of the Polish-Lithuanian Commonwealth," *Harvard Ukrainian Studies* 2 (1978): 41-72, 184-210; Paweł Skwarczyński, *Szkice z dziejów Reformacji w Europie środkowowschodniej* (Sketches on the history of the Reformation in East Central Europe), (London: Odnowa, 1967). Nicholas Hans, "Polish Protestants and their Connections with England and Holland in the 17th and 18th centuries," *The Slavic and East European Review* 37 (1958): 196-220.

5. Ernst Walter Zeeden, *Calvins Einwirken auf die Reformation in Polen-Litauen, eine Studie über den Reformator Calvin in Spiegel seiner polnischen Korrespondenzen* (Lindau-Konstanz: Syntagma Friburgense, 1956), pp. 323-59; Henryk Barycz, "Voyageurs et étudiants polonais à Genève à l'époque de Calvin et de Théodore de Bèze," in *Échanges entre la Pologne et la Suisse, du XIV au XIX s.* (Genève: Droz, 1964), pp. 67-137; George H. Williams, "The Polish Lithuanian Calvin," *Festschrift for Ford Lewis Battles*, ed. Brian A. Gerrish (Pittsburgh, 1979).

6. See Halina Kowalska, "Jan Łaski" in *Polski Słownik Biograficzny* vol. 18, pp. 237-244; *idem*, *Działalność reformatorska Jana Łaskiego w Polsce 1556-1560* (The reformatory work of Jan Łaski in Poland, 1556-1560), (Wrocław: Ossolineum, 1969.

7. Peter Brock, *The Political and Social Doctrines of the Unity of Czech Brethren in the Fifteenth and Early Sixteenth Centuries*, Slavistic Printings and Reprintings, vol. 9 (The Hague: Mouton, 1957); Joseph Müller, *Geschichte der Böhmischen Brüder*, 3 vols. (Herrnhut 1922-31).

8. George H. Williams, *The Radical Reformation* (Philadelphia: Westminster Press, 1962); and *The Polish Brethren*, 2 vols. (Chico, California: Scholars Press, 1980). Stanisław Kot, *Socinianism in Poland, the Social and Political Ideas of the Polish Antitrinitarians* (Boston; Starr King Press, 1957); Earl Morse Wilbur, *The History of Unitarianism: Socinianism and its Antecedents* (Cambridge: Harvard University Press, 1945).

9. Gottfried Schramm, *Der polnische Adel und die Reformation 1548-1607* (Wiesbaden: F. Steiner, 1965).

10. Damian Wojtyska, *Papiestwo—Polska 1548-1563* (The Papacy and Poland 1548-1563) (Lublin: Towarzystwo Naukowe Katolickiego Uniwersytetu Lubelskiego, 1977), *Cardinal Hosius Legate to the Council of Trent* (Rome: Institute of Ecclesiastical Studies, 1967); "Quarrel Concerning the Cardinalate of Hosius," *Sacrum Poloniae Millenium* (Rome) 8-9 (1962): 207-248; "Stanisław Hozjusz w oczach swoich współczesnych" (Stanislaus Hosius as viewed by his contemporaries), *Studia Warmińskie* (Olsztyn, Warmińskie Wydawn. Diecezjalne) 16 (1979): 103-162; Stanisław Kot, "Opposition to the Pope by the Polish Bishops 1557-1560. Three Unique Polish Reformation Pamphlets," *Oxford Slavonic Papers* 4 (1953): 38-70; Bronisław Natoński, "Początki Towarzystwa Jezusowego w Polsce" (The beginnings of the Society of Jesus in Poland), in W. J. Brodrick, *Powstanie i rozwój Towarzystwa Jezusowego*, 1 (Cracow, 1969), pp. 414-476; George H. Williams, "Stanislas Hosius," in *Shapers of Religious Traditions in Germany, Switzerland and Poland 1560-1600*, Ed. by Jill Raitt (New Haven: Yale University Press, 1981) p. 151-174, and "Peter Skarga," ibidem, pp. 175-194; *Unicus universae Societatis Iesu Vocationum Liber Autobiograficus Poloniae Provinciae proprius (1574-1580)*, ed. Joseph Warszawski (Romae, 1966); A. Berga, *Un Prédicateur de la Cour de Pologne sous Sigismond III. Pierre Skarga (1536-1612). Étude sur la Pologne du XVIe siécle et le protestantisme polonais*, (Paris, 1916); Tadeusz Glemma, "Le Catholicisme en Pologne à l'epoque d'Etienne Batory," in *Etienne Batory* (Cracow, 1935), pp. 335-374.

11. Karol Górski, "Problematyka religijności w epoce potrydenckiej" (Problems of religiousness in the post-Tridentine period), in Karol Górski, *Studia i materiały z dziejów duchowości* (Studies in the history of spirituality) (Warsaw: Akademia Teologii Katolickiej, 1980), pp. 240-256, and "Histoire de la spiritualité polonaise" in *Millenaire du catholicisme en Pologne*, ed. M. Rechowicz (Lublin, 1969), pp. 279-354. Karol Górski studied the spirituality and mysticism of the 16th-17th centuries in a systematic way and tried to revise the views of the well-known historian and sociologist, Stefan Czarnowski, "La reaction catholique en Pologne à la fin du XVIe et au début du XVII s.," in *La Pologne au VIIe Congres International des Sciences Historiques*, 2 (Warsaw, 1933), pp. 287-310. Important for the development of religious mentality is Jan Błoński, *Mikołaj Sęp Szarzyński a początki polskiego baroku* (Mikołaj Sęp Szarzyński and the beginnings of the Polish baroque), (Cracow: Wydawnictwo Literackie, 1967); Czesław Hernas, *Barok* (The Baroque), *Historia literatury polskiej* (History of Polish literature), (Warsaw: PWN, 1973).

12. A valuable edition of bishops' reports to Rome: *Relationes Status Dioecesium in Magno Ducatu Lituaniae*, 1 *Dioceses Vilnensis et Samogitiae*, ed. Paulus Rabikauskas, Sectio Historica Academiae Lituanae Catholicae Scientiarum (Rome, 1971). *Relacje*

o stanie diecezji krakowskiej 1615-1765 (Reports on the state of Cracow diocese 1615-1765), ed. Wiesław Müller (Lublin: Towarzystwo Naukowe Katolickiego Uniwersytetu Lubelskiego, 1978); Teofil Długosz, *Relacje arcybiskupów lwowskich 1595-1794* (Reports of the archbishops of Lwów 1595-1794), (Lwów, 1937). Wiesław Müller, "Diecezja płocka od drugiej połowy XVI wieku do rozbiorów" (Płock Diocese from the second half of the 16th century to the partitions), in *Kościół płocki XI-XX wieku* (The Płock Church from the 11th to the 20th century), ed. Jerzy Kłoczowski, *Studia Płockie* (Płock Studies) (Płock, Płockie Wydawn. Diecezjalne) 3 (1975): 153-226; *Studia nad historią dominikanów w Polsce* 1-2 (Studies in the history of the Dominicans in Poland), ed. Jerzy Kłoczowski (Warsaw: Wydawn. Polskiej Prowincji Dominikanów, 1975); *Dzieje teologii katolickiej w Polsce*, 2 (History of Catholic theology in Poland), ed. Marian Rechowicz (Lublin: Towarzystwo Naukowe Katolickiego Uniwersytetu Lubelskiego, 1975).

13. Oskar Halecki, "From Florence to Brest (1439-1596)," vol. 5, *Sacrum Poloniae Millenium* (Rome, 1958) 444 pp. Julian Pelesz, *Geschichte der Union der ruthenischen Kirche mit Rom*, 1-2 (Vienna, 1878-81); Eugenij Smurlo, *Le Saint Siège et l'orient orthodoxe russe 1609-1654* (Prague, 1928); Albert Maria Amman, *Abriss der ostslavischen Kirchengeschichte* (Vienna: Thomas Morus Presse, 1950). Gunnar Hering, *Ökumenisches Patriarchat und Europäische Politik (1620-1638)* (Wiesbaden: F. Steiner, 1968); Halina Kowalska, Piotr Mohyła, *Polski Słownik Biograficzny*, v. 21 (1976), pp. 568-572; Hugh F. Graham, "Peter Mogila, Metropolitan of Kiev," *Russian Review* 14, no. 4 (October 1955): 345-56; M. Malvay and M. Viller, *La Confession orthodoxe de Pierre Moghila métropolite de Kiev (1633-1646) approuvée par les patriarches grecs du XVIIe siècle*, Orientalia Christiana Analecta, 10 (Rome, 1927).

14. For the history of tolerance, see Joseph Lecler, *Histoire de la tolérance au siècle de la Réforme*, 1-2 (Paris, 1955); Janusz Tazbir, *A State Without Stakes. Polish Religious Toleration in the Sixteenth and Seventeenth Centuries* (The Kościuszko Foundation), Warsaw: PIW, 1973); Wiktor Weintraub, "Tolerance and Intolerance in Old Poland," *Canadian Slavonic Papers* 13 (1971): 21-43; Kai Eduard Jordt Jörgensen, *Ökumenische Bestrebungen unter den polnischen Protestanten bis zum Jahre 1645* (Copenhagen, 1942). The visits of the Fonseca are described by Jerzy Kłoczowski, "Wielki zakon XVII wiecznej Rzeczypospolitej u progu swego rozwoju—Dominikanie polscy w świetle wizytacji generalnej z lat 1617-1619" (The Great Order of the 17th-century Republic in the early stages of its development. The Polish Dominicans in the light of the general visitation of 1617-1619), *Nasza Przeszłość*; 39 (Cracow, 1973): 103-180.

15. For the best introduction to Jewish history in Poland, see *Encyclopaedia Judaica* (Jerusalem, 1971-); Gershon Hundert, "Recent Studies relating to the Jews in Poland from the Earliest Times to the Partition Period," *Polish Review* 18, No. 4 (1973): 34-51. Bernard D. Weinryb, *The Jews of Poland. A Social and Economic History of the Jewish Community in Poland from 1100 to 1800* (Philadelphia: Jewish Publication Society of America, 1976); Marek Wajsblum, "Isaac of Troki and Christian Controversy in the 16th Century," *The Journal of Jewish Studies* 3, No. 2 (1952): 62-77. Szymon Szyszman, "Die Karäer in Mitteleuropa," *Zeitschrift für Ostforschung*, Marburg, 1 (1957): 25-54. Leon Bohdanowicz, "The Muslims in Poland. Their Origin, History and Cultural Life," *Journal of the Royal Asiatic Society*, London (Oct. 1942): 163-180.

6

The Polish Reformation as an Intellectual Movement

Janusz Tazbir

T he movement for the renewal of Christianity (or, more precisely, Catholicism) that is termed the Reformation has already been investigated from many angles. For some time it was seen as a primarily religious current. Since the mid-nineteenth century, under the influence of Marxist historiography, the dogmatic quarrels began to be perceived as an exclusively historical guise for class struggles as they occurred in the fifteenth and sixteenth centuries. After the second Vatican Council, it became fashionable to minimize the doctrinal differences dividing the fifteenth-century Jan Hus or the sixteenth-century Martin Luther from Rome. From some contemporary publications one might conclude that only the obstinacy of both sides, or the short-sightedness of the popes of the time was responsible for the great heretics not becoming pillars of or even saints in the Catholic church. The renascence of theological interests in both the United States and many West European countries has recently caused scholars to take more interest in the doctrinal content of the Reformation than was shown by their predecessors in the nineteenth century or the first half of the twentieth. Studies of the religious life of both mass populations and elites have recently come extraordinarily into vogue.

Polish scholars have also followed the example of the West.[1] Although thanks to the studies of successive generations of Polish historians we can say a great deal about the social (and even the economic) genesis of the first successes of the Reformation in the Polish-Lithuanian Commonwealth, the religious roots of the movement continue to remain rather unclear. Already some years ago, Jan Fijałek lamented that Polish religious life at the close of the Middle Ages is, strictiy speaking, unknown.[2] Although scholarship in this area has progressed somewhat since his time, we are still unable to answer many questions, as, for example, such a fundamental one as that concerning the ripeness of the organism of Polish Christianity for the acceptance of Reformation renewal. It probably can be accepted that the Church structure and its corresponding doctrine had not reached a level of development that would match the corresponding Italian, French, or even German organization which had existed a good many centuries longer than the Polish. Proof of this can be found even in such phenomena as Polish demonology, which in comparison with that of Western Europe, appears rather meager. On the other hand, one increasingly encounters the notion that the process of Christianization, especially in the eastern lands of the Commonwealth, was completed only in the mid-seventeenth century.[3] In connection with this, it could be assumed that the Polish church and Catholicism particularly because of its relative "youth" did not undergo a slackening, deformation, or degenerative process on such a scale as took place, for example, in Germany. If we accept this premise then it must be acknowledged that in Poland, the Reformation represented to some extent a remedy for a disease which in Polish religious life was not yet a very serious one.[4]

It should be emphasized, first of all, that the Reformation movement was far more significant in the development of Polish social and political thought than it was in the field of theology; it contributed more to the intensification of cultural change than to the blossoming of religious life. It was more "a great intellectual adventure" than a search for the "genuine word of God"—that truth about things eternal, untainted by human accretions.

There is no doubt today about the connection of Protestantism with the political life of the gentry.[5] Long before part of the gentry set about building a new church, the entire estate undertook the struggle for the creation of a new type of state. In both these undertakings the gentry stratum desired to play a leading role, and moreover, at least in the sixteenth century, the gentry was to a considerable degree successful. In creating new forms of religious life the gentry made abundant use of its experience gained in the *sejmiki* (dietines) and in the *Sejm* (the Polish Parliament or Diet) and of the forms perfected in the course of sharp polemical struggle with the secular magnateria. An attack upon the bishops was to a great degree a simple extension of the secular struggle to an ecclesiastical "magnateria." The gentry, in the nature of things, did not take part in the synods of the Catholic church; hence, it was rather in organizing Calvinist synods or assemblies of the Polish Brethren that the gentry utilized its familiar experience in debate. Religious debates were often organized in the course of parliamentary sessions in order to allow participation by the deputies and senators from the church hierarchy seated in the parliament. The latter displayed, to the indignation of the plebeian clerics, the pride and superiority ordinarily characteristic of the magnates who did not tolerate opposition.[6]

The goal of the struggle waged (with much success) for freedom of speech, public assembly and press was considered to be of importance in itself regardless of how it might be used in religious or political life.[7] No one could deny the gentry having the right to elect deputies, and, after 1573, the king as well, a similar right to the free choice of its faith, not to mention the school which they would like to attend or to which they would send their offspring. As a result, in the religious propaganda of the time it is sometimes impossible to differentiate stipulations connected with the "execution-of laws" movement from demands put forth by adherents of "religious novelties." This was already expressed in the famous resolutions of the *sejmik* of Środa Wielkopolska (in 1534), requiring in the same breath both the execution of the laws and freedom to print not only the sacred Scripture but secular works in Polish: "that the priests would not prohibit us from printing histories, chronicles, our laws . . . and particularly the Bible in Polish."[8] The struggle for freedom of religion was at the same time a battle for the extension of rights belonging to the gentry.

Politics penetrated everything: even religious controversies were entwined with politics. As religious conflict grew, there ensued a *sui generis* laicization of the arguments employed. The condemnation by the entire camp of the Polish Reformation of the Great Peasant War (1525) or the Münster Commune (1534) became a debate over whether Protestantism really leads to an undermining of the existing state and social-political structures. The entire gentry was interested in their preservation: the work *Gospodarstwo* (Property) (1588), the author of which, Anzelm Gostomski, possessed a considerable fortune and was also a zealous champion of Calvinism, found its way into the hands of adherents of various faiths. It did not end up on the Index, simply because it contained no doctrinal declaration or any traces of Reformation propaganda.

To an even greater degree than it was a political movement, the Reformation was an intellectual current that unquestionably imparted dynamism to sixteenth-century Polish cultural life. Passing over the now customarily quoted statistics concerning the increase in the number of schools, printing houses, printings of books,[9] or travels abroad, a new theory of translation is also worth noting. In contrast to the free adaptation of *belles-lettres* such as Łukasz Górnicki's *Dworzanin polski* (an adaptation of Baldassare Castiglioni's *Il Cortegiano* and printed in Cracow in 1566), translations of theological texts, most of all the Bible, had to be exact, especially as each successive translation gave rise to new dogmatic quarrels. The Reformation also contributed to the dissemination of catechisms, prayerbooks, confessions of faith, as well as previously less widely known dialogues, religious dramas, and finally works of a lampoon-satirical quality. It should not be forgotten, however, that many of these literary genres had appeared in Poland long before the broad-scale development of the Reformation movement. Lampoons or satiric dialogues had constantly accompanied the debates over the programs for the execution of laws and holdings, the anti-monarchical unrest during the rule of Sigismund (Zygmunt) I (the so-called "Hen's War" "(*Wojna kokosza*)" or nobles' rebellion of 1537), or, finally, the heated debate over the marriage of the son of Sigismund I to Barbara Radziwiłłówna. New religious content was simply inserted into literary forms already tested and having their faithful readership. However, interest in them was to some extent derivative in the context of the passion inspired among the gentry by the political struggle over power in the nation.

The Reformation movement promoted the development of national cultures, particularly literature in national languages, music, and learning, but that same development occurred as well in those countries where the Reformation did not take more lasting root. We meet many of its representatives actually among the outstanding leaders of sixteenth and seventeenth-century Polish culture, just as later during the Enlightenment many clerics would contribute to the development of Polish culture and education. It seems, however, that in both cases not only religious motives were involved. For the Enlightenment they played a clearly secondary role; in the epoch of the Renaissance, the Reformation stimulus constituted only one of the impulses shaping the evolution of Polish culture and literature. The influences of humanism and the Renaissance should be placed on at least equal footing with Protestantism. Among the indigenous factors, on the other hand, was the position of the Commonwealth as a great power and the social and political advance of the gentry class. One of its signs was precisely the particularly active participation of that estate in the creation and the consumption of the fruits of culture. Culture would have blossomed even without the nation having undergone the turbulence of the Reformation, although it probably would have taken a different form. Who would presume to say, however, that if the Commonwealth had remained a purely Catholic country in the sixteenth century, that a network of printers, numerous collections of books, and whole throngs of students would not have hastened abroad for knowledge, attending German, Italian, French, Swiss and Dutch universities? Who today would agree without reservation with the words of Aleksander Brückner:

> What would Rej have been without the Reformation? He would have written humorous-didactic poems . . . anecdotes, epitaphs, and inscriptions on spoons and fireplaces, verses in albums and compliments, and in the end he might have even given up scribbling.[10]

The sixteenth century is the century of great cultural confrontations: Western Europe discovered Poland as a great power worthy of note, even though located somewhere in the outer limits of the continent. In turn, the inhabitants of the Polish Commonwealth began to appreciate the wealth of the culture of antiquity, as well as record the riches of her own language and the manifestations of what in today's terminology would be called folklore. Precisely for this reason the first Polish-Latin dictionary appears in 1564, a work which we owe to Jan Mączyński,[11] the second half of the century brings the works of Jan Łasicki on Old Lithuanian rites and customs, and not long after Salomon Rysiński lays the groundwork for Polish paroemiography. That Mączyński was an anti-Trinitarian and that Rysiński and Łasicki were Calvinists is, after all, not the most essential fact. Equally nonessential is the religious affiliation of Piotr Statorius (who later took the surname Stojeński). Statorius-Stojeński, born near the French town of Thionville, studied in Lausanne and Geneva. Having been invited to Poland in 1556 by the Calvinist community, he later wrote the first Polish grammar (*Polonicae grammatices institutio*, printed in Cracow in 1568). He did not write it because he was a Calvinist. It was simply that in most countries the first grammars were written by foreigners who, not having been taught the language in childhood, had to learn a tongue foreign to them from books. A co-religionist of Statorius, Andrzej Trzecieski (Trzycieski; Trecesius), composed the first national anthem to originate in Poland, namely, *Modlitwa za Rzecz Pospolitą naszą i za króla* (Prayer for our Republic and for the king). This is not peculiar or startling, however, if we recall that during just this time the development of national consciousness was taking place as well as the solidification of the sense of community of the entire gentry estate. Trzecieski himself, however, belonged to the political elite of Poland, which to a great degree was composed of dissenters. They did not formulate their own concept of the "gentry nation," but were only its co-authors together with the Catholic leaders of the "execution of laws" movement.

The Calvinist Andrzej Wolan conflicted sharply with Piotr Skarga, defender of the Church against "heresy." However, when we compare Wolan's treatise, *O wolności Rzeczypospolitej albo szlacheckiej* (On the freedom of the Republic or nobles' freedom) (published in Latin in 1572) with Skarga's *Kazania Sejmowe* (Sermons to the Diet) (1597), we are struck by the far-reaching coincidence of their views concerning "temporal affairs." Both Skarga and Wolan in equally sharp terms condemned manifestations of gentry anarchy and spoke out on behalf of strengthening of royal power. It was not they, however, who found a sympathetic ear among the gentry, but rather the publicists who wrote about the gentry as descendants of the courageous Sarmatians, whom God had called to defend the "bulwark of Christianity" against the infidels. One of the originators of the Sarmatian theory was the Calvinist pastor and historian, Stanisław Sarnicki, and the notion of the "bulwark of Christianity" found echoes in the work of Wacław Potocki and Zbigniew Morsztyn—both, as is known, belonging to the congregation of Polish Brethren.

One of the keystones in the governmental program of the gentry was the right to refuse obedience to a king who departed from agreements negotiated with gentry society. The so-called "*de non praestanda oboedientia*" article appeared in statutes limiting the power of the elected kings. This article recalls both the theories of the French "monarchomachs," who attributed to the king's subjects the possibility of coming out against a "tyrant" wishing to impose his own faith upon them by force, and the fact that the gentry had secured from successive kings confirmation of its privilege of free choice of faith (the act of the Confederation of Warsaw in 1573). One would be mistaken, however, to link the gentry position in this matter with influences from the Reformation movement or with knowledge of the doctrines of the Huguenot "monarchomachs." Just the opposite—it was precisely the political practice of the gentry state that inspired the French Calvinists with the courage to formulate their demands.[12]

In many countries of northern and Western Europe the victory of the Reformation brought in its wake the emergence, deepening with time, of the differences between the Catholics and the Protestants in the areas of culture, mentality, art, and, finally, way of life. Some of these differences persisted for quite a long time; the so-called "Huguenot formation" remained in French culture even up to the end of the nineteenth century. In Poland, on the other hand, there was no similar phenomenon. One may speak of the Protestant contribution to Polish culture, but it is a very long road from participation in civilization to creation of a distinct cultural or literary life. Polish Protestants did not embark upon such a road; what is more, they participated in the creation of a common Christian culture that arose in sixteenth-century Poland. Among its founders and consumers we find representatives of all confessions and churches.[13] Entire sections of the Calvinist Mikołaj Rej's *Żywot człowieka poczciwego* (The life of an honest man) were included by the arch-Catholic Józef Wereszczyński in his work, *Reguła, to jest nauka albo postępek dobrego życia króla chrześcijańskiego* (The principle, that is the teaching or the good acts of the life of a christian king) (1587) and Jakub Wujek extracted scattered parts of Rej's *Postylla* (Postilla). Sometimes this produced a peculiar string of interdenominational borrowings, as, for example, when the Jesuit Mikołaj Kazimierz Sarbiewski, referred to Mikołaj Rej's literary portraits of different nations (*Icon nationum*), in his *Descriptio gentium* and in turn the latter was translated into Polish by the Calvinist Daniel Naborowski.[14]

From Wiktor Weintraub's fine essay on Kochanowski, it is clearly evident that the greatest poet of Poland prior to the late eighteenth-century partitions perfectly fits this model of a supra-confessional, all-Christian culture and, from another perspective, was perhaps even its foremost exponent. Jan Kochanowski exemplifies a heterodox attitude "not fitting within the dogmatic confines of any Christian denomination. . . . " "Kochanowski's religious poetry is a dialogue of man with God, and with God alone. . . . " "In vain would we look there for a reference to the Blessed Virgin, and the saints appear sometimes in the nonreligious poetry, always mentioned ironically or with tones of derision." Even banter about the "specialization" existing on Olympus, each inhabitant of which ruled a certain aspect of life, "become a pseudonymous representation of the cult of the saints and is directed against it." One has to agree with Weintraub,who writes: "the constant element of all Kochanowski's religious poetry is a concept of God that is beyond denominations and is strongly rationalized. . . . " Thus, it is not strange that Catholics and Protestants spoke about the poet in similar superlatives, and that the Calvinist historiographer Andrzej Węgierski considered Kochanowski to be a co-religionist.[15]

Weintraub sees the tolerance of Sigismundian times and the high literary culture of sixteenth-century Poland as the reasons why "religious heterodoxy did not hamper Kochanowski's rapid and universal recognition as a great poet by his contemporaries." Pride at having such a great poet dictated looking the other way on the thorny issue of his religious views.[16] To this apt assessment one further consideration should be added, which Weintraub himself points out in passing: namely, the conviction contained in Kochanowski's religious views that Christian ethics is more important than doctrinal differences. This was a view shared by representatives of the intellectual elite of the sixteenth century.

Books about the anxiety that constantly accompanied the history of humanity, which at certain times took the form of paroxysms of collective fear, have recently been popular in Western European historiography. Equally absorbing would be a study of the great hopes and still greater disappointments experienced by successive generations of intellectuals. Just as in the eighteenth century this hope was connected with progress in education, in the nineteenth century with the development of technology, and in the twentieth century with the introduction of a new social system, so in the time of the Renaissance it was associated with, among other things, the possibilites of human thought, which without the aid of Divine Revelation could find the key to truth: scientific, political, or—as the radical Reformation desired—even religious truth. Kochanowski's literary output constitutes an expression of disillusionment in just this respect. For despite the laity's having taken up the teaching of the truths of faith, their effort had not in the least led to a better understanding of God or to a knowledge of last things. "*Więc wszyscy teraz każą, a żaden nie słucha*" ("Thus all now preach and no one listens"), as we read in Kochanowski's *Zgoda* (Harmony) (1564). The poem was a commendation of a division of competence both in society generally, and among intellectuals themselves, who should leave dogmatic debates to the specialists.

Zgoda is a testimony to a double disillusionment: the humanist had to admit that objective and fruitful discussion on the subjects of literature, art, or ethical models were overpowered in the current of intellectually sterile quarrels about theology. The disillusionment of the nobleman-citizen stemmed from the conviction that obstinacy in the religious sphere could lead to disintegration of the political community of his estate, simultaneously harming the interests of the entire Republic. Let us recall that Kochanowski's ideological patron, Piotr Myszkowski, came forth at the Sejm of 1565 with a famous appeal, quoted by all scholars of the history of the Polish Reformation: "*Rozumienie różne Pisma [świętego] niech miłości nie targa między nami.*" ("Let not the different understanding of [Sacred] Scripture shatter the love between us."). The disillusionment of the author of *Odprawa posłów greckich* (The Dismissal of the Greek Envoys) must have been shared by many representatives of the intellectual elite of the time, since in 1580 the Calvinist polemicist and gentry politician, Jakub Niemojewski, asserted bitterly that "*teologija wszytka . . . ludziom ledwo nie obrzydła*" ("people are sick of theology of any kind").[17]

Many intellectuals perceived an opportunity for intellectual renewal precisely in the Reformation. People in the sixteenth century who would later become pillars of the Counter Reformation mingled with the adherents of the new trends, who were searching for their own roads to truth. This occurred not only among those in the famous "Cracow circle," where in the 1540's Stanisław Hozjusz (Hosius) conversed amicably with Andrzej Frycz Modrzewski (Andreas Fricius Modrevius), but also at many magnate courts (not excluding those of the bishops) in the closest circles around the king, and finally during university studies. Gradually, however, a marked falling away of intellectuals from the ranks of Reformation adherents occurred. With some delay, due to the later evolution of this movement in Poland, they retraced the road traveled by Erasmus of Rotterdam or François Rabelais, who, in spite of everything, remained faithful to the old Church and to their former faith.

There were numerous reasons for this. Persecution of the followers of the radical Reformation, conducted not only by Catholics but also by the Calvinists and Lutherans, elicited a shock in Protestant intellectual circles as well, as exemplified by their reaction to the burning of Miguel Servetus.[18] It soon turned out that not only the old Church, but also the new ones, born of revolt against the tyranny of Rome, were trying by means of the stake to check the creative investigation of human thought. The statements of the anti-Trinitarians in particular express a regard for mens' convictions as well as respect for man as a value in and of himself. These sentiments were intimately connected with the ideology of humanism, opposing both Calvinist and Catholic fanaticism. The humanitarianism emanating from such sentiments was something more than the perfunctory love of neighbor exhorted by too orthodox preachers. The anti-Trinitarians saw the "heretic" as an erring man, an unhappy being wandering in forlorn uncertainty about salvation. Why, then, add to his pain and suffering, persecuting him by torture or even death? Not only Christian love forbade this, but the human intellect as well, dictating that forcible means could not produce any positive results in matters of faith.

Intellectuals were also embittered by tendencies of the Reformation that limited free discussion within their own churches. Catholic censorship and its introduction of the Index of forbidden books now had its counterpart in the increasingly severe Calvinist and Lutheran censorship. Even the Anti-Trinitarians were unable to resist this trend, connecting the reprimand against the radicalism in dogma of some of their members with fears of a provocation of attacks by the various orthodoxies, whether of Rome, of Geneva, or of Wittenberg. The consequences of this censorship were felt by, among others, Szymon Budny. Excluded in 1582 (only finally in 1584) from the Minor Church (Zbór Mniejszy), he was accepted into the number of the Polish Brethren only at the price of renouncing those views which so much upset them.[19]

Reformation discussions only partially concerned purely religious matters. To a great degree, they constituted a continuation of the debates conducted for centuries on the question of human nature, man's responsibility for his own fate and that of others, his obligations to society, and, finally, influence of Divine Providence in the events of the world. From this point of view as well, the last quarter of the sixteenth century brings a growing intellectual sterility in Polish Protestantism; it can easily by adduced from the synodical records, the edition of which we owe to Maria Sipayłło. While the first two volumes of that edition, up to the year 1570, are impressive in their rich doc-

22. The Brześć or Radziwiłł Bible. *Biblia Święta to jest Księgi Starego y Nowego Zakonu*, w Brześciu, 1563. Title page of the Calvin Bible, translated by a large Committee (Biblioteka Ossolińskich, Wrocław).

trinal content, the third volume is sadly disappointing in its provinciality strewn upon synodical problems.[20] In place of the former intellectual-religious debate, difficulties with the clergy of one's own faith and complaints about the reprehensible behavior of their wives now appear. According to the reviewer of this edition of the synodical records, the subject-matter of the synods "becomes impoverished; increasingly it is confined to matters internal to the life of the Protestant community, and it is more and more difficult to find traces of involvement of the members of the church in political, state affairs,"[21] and, we might add, in the great intellectual problems of the era.

If only in place of growing intolerance had a coherent vision of the world and man's obligations in it been given! Olbracht Łaski, reproaching his, until recently, co-religionists (and particularly the Protestant ministers) for their constant quarrels, their "varieties of sects" (*"rozmaitość sekt"*) and "the numerous differences among their writers" (*"liczne różnice między pisarzami"*),[22] expressed his disappointment in this area as well. In his last will and testament, Jerzy Szoman encouraged his sons that should they find some more perfect church they should join it, forsaking the community of the Polish Brethren. What for adherents of religious heterodoxy was an obvious fact must have inspired the anxiety of intellectuals searching for stable and ultimate truths.

While the Reformation ceased at a certain point to be sufficiently attractive for the intellectual elite, precisely this intellectual character constituted a barrier for the lower social strata, preventing effective expansion of the new faith. Its emergence quite soon after the invention of the art of printing, which had begun to overshadow other verbal forms of propaganda, contributed to its dynamic development. It relied primarily upon the printed word. Hence the opinion of some scholars that countries with a higher level of literacy turned out to be more susceptible to the slogans of Protestantism. This neglect of traditional, oral forms of persuasion did not always bring the desired results.[23] Furthermore, the intellectual content of the new faith often became a barrier which the inhabitants of small towns (not to mention the peasants) were not in a position to overcome. The anti-Trinitarians especially became convinced of this when after one of the visitations conducted in the sub-Carpathian region in 1612 they had to state with clear resignation: *"Najdowali się też tacy i takie, którzy zgoła o tym nic się nie wiedzieć zdali, jaka by była różność inszych wyznań od naszego o Bogu jedynym."* ("There also can be found those who seemed to know nothing at all about what the difference of other faiths from ours was about the one and only God.").[24]

The Protestant churches were not "less expensive" than the Catholic, nor were their doctrines easier to accept than the "papist" ones. They were not less expensive because the confiscation of church land holdings resulted in the necessity of maintaining schools, printing houses, or education of the clergy by means of offerings from the faithful. Their doctrines were not easier to accept because for doctrinal reasons they had to do without the elaborate ritual surrounding the word of God as it was preached by the Catholic priests. The new form of Christianity, having given up devotion to the saints as well as the belief in the protection of the Mother of God and intentionally cutting its ties with folklore, became a dry lecture of dogmatic content preached in a setting of the barewalls of the Protestant churches. Attempts were made to deal with this problem via greater or lesser compromises: for a period of time, at least, statues and paintings were allowed to remain in the churches adapted for Protestant use; devotion to the saints was winked at; veneration of the Blessed Virgin was tolerated. The Lutherans went the furthest in this direction; the Calvinists and anti-Trinitarians were the least amenable to compromise. All these half-measures did not produce much, and after a period of time they were given up due, moreover, to the pressure of circles concerned about orthodoxy. The Catholic church, on the other hand, possessed means of reaching the population, perfected over the centuries, that the young Protestant church organizations were not in a position to effectively rival.

It would seem that the ruling authorities of Polish Protestantism did not fully realize that this domination of doctrinal content over ritual, print over painting, and reasoning over appeals to emotion and imagination, all hampered contact with the faithful. In any case, although the seventeenth-century Protestant writings known to us indicate numerous reasons why the Reformation did not take deeper root in society (and particularly among the Polish peasantry), nevertheless, one cause is absent, namely that Protestantism was simply too difficult a religion. The peasants were held to their old faith by the richly elaborated forms of ritual that spoke so powerfully to their imagination. However in the sixteenth or seventeenth centuries we find writings about the strong Roman "superstitions" which—with the aid of the devil and the anti-Christ enthroned in Rome—control the souls of many Christians.

The victory of Catholicism among the gentry was, in turn, attributed to the activity of Jesuit colleges, to which the Protestants also sent their offspring. Their program, at least in the first phase of their activity, took advantage of the achievements of humanist pedagogy. Dissident schools could not effectively compete with the Jesuit colleges in this field, since aside from a few exceptions such as Raków or Leszno (or the region of Royal Prussia), Calvinist gymnasiums in Little Poland struggled with lack of funds and with maintaining teachers on an adequate level. Their lower-level education network was also poorly developed and was similar to Catholic parish schools. The seventeenth century brought further change to the disadvantage of the Protestants in this area. In contrast to the sixteenth century when Protestants also could be found among the eminent chroniclers, Protestant historiography in the seventeenth century bears a primarily confessional quality. It is limited in general to the defense of the good name of one's own sect, whether Calvinist (Wojciech and Andrzej Węgierski), Lutheran (Krzysztof Hartknoch), or even Socinian (Andrzej and Stanisław Lubieniecki). Only Joachim Pastorius became famous with his successful outline of the history of Poland (*Florus Polonicus*, 1641), but he then concluded his religious searching with conversion to Catholicism.

It is true that in the baroque period Protestant schooling outshone Catholic in the fields of mathematics, physics, and astronomy. Lively interest in the real achievements of these disciplines appeared particularly in the milieu of the Polish Brethren. Already at the close of the seventeenth century the Copernican theory entered the teaching program of the Lutheran gymnasia in Royal Prussia. The new philosophy (*Philosophia recentiorum*) represented by Bacon, Spinoza, and Locke, among others, found a certain response among them, and the Socinians were quite intensely interested in Cartesianism.[25] None of these, however, were topics that could more closely or deeply interest the gentry, who were happily satisfied by the study of elocution, Latin, law, and certain aspects of history—subjects essential to their political life. All these needs were met by the Jesuit gymnasia rather than those of the Protestants.

To the disadvantage of the Reformation was also the fact that her antagonism with Rome took on in Poland, as it had in Germany and France, a strong national coloration that appeared on both sides of the religious barricades. The Protestants, playing upon public feelings of italophobia began to use the attribute "Roman" in place of "Catholic" so as to emphasize the Italian origins of the papacy. Catholics, in turn, terming Lutheranism the German faith, appealed to germanophobia. And here again the advantage was on the side of the Counter Reformation, since there were few Italians in Poland, while Germans were met at every turn and had been there for centuries. Thus Fausto Sozzini (Faustus Socinus) did not become a synonym for every newcomer from faraway Italy, whereas Luther was seen as the personification of a German.

Although Lutheranism in its Polish form made an essential contribution to the development of the Polish language and literature, at the same time through preaching and printing in German, it retarded the processes of assimilation in Royal Prussia. The strengthening of ethnic ties through religious communities as well meant that residents of Toruń, Gdańsk, or Elbląg could attend en masse the universities of Królewiec, Lipsk, Tübingen, and most of all, Wittenberg. Recently some scholars have questioned the accepted thesis in Polish historiography concerning the exclusively positive influence of the Reformation upon the evolution of Lithuanian national culture.[26] In their opinion, in the seventeenth century in particular, Protestantism aided rather the polonization of the Grand Duchy of Lithuania where in Polish, among other languages, there appeared a considerable portion of dissenters' publications. Let us add that a similar situation presents itself in Ruthenia as well: although already at the close of the sixteenth century Reformation propaganda produces printing in the language of its population, nevertheless, acceptance of Calvinism or the doctrines of the Polish Brethren by the orthodox gentry most often signified the assimilation of that class if not in this generation, then in the next. The history of anti-Trinitarianism in Volhynia in the seventeenth century eloquently testifies to this fact. Thus, the matter of the influence of the Reformation upon the development of national cultures existing in the Commonwealth does not present a uniform picture.

Just as humanism had stimulated interest in antiquity, so the Reformation, in Poland as well, intensified the influence of the Old Testament in various spheres of culture. Poland was far, of course, from the puritanism of England, Scotland, or the Netherlands, where one reached for the first part of Sacred Scripture for direction and inspiration for everything from names to how to treat the Indians in the colonies. The gentry nation also saw numerous analogies between the history of the Polish state and the history of the Jews as recounted in the Old Testament, analogies which would be difficult to detect in the account of the beginnings of Christianity contained in the New Testament.

It is notable that the frequent references to the prophecies, the fate of David, and the wisdom of Solomon did not result in deeper interest in contemporary Jewish culture. Although advocates of the radical Reformation debated with some of the representatives of Judaism (as in the famous dispute between Marcin Czechowic and Jakub of Bełżyce), Protestants also were indifferent or even hostile to Jewish communities. And if they treated with skepticism complaints about profanation of the Blessed Sacrament by certain Jews, it was because, on the one hand, Protestants denied the teaching about transubstantiation, and, on the other, they themselves were saddled with similar accusations. It also should not be forgotten that Polish Protestantism found strong support in the bourgeois milieu of Royal Prussia, which had for generations looked askance at the Jews, seeing them as dangerous competitors in the field of economic activity.[27]

From the time of the Enlightenment the contribution of the Reformation to national culture was recognized as an unquestioned service. It was also seen as justifying the presence of this movement in Polish historical tradition. Today, as well, one has to agree with this point of view, since there is much to support the thesis that in Poland the Reformation was more a cultural than a religious phenomenon—more an "intellectual current that interested people on a certain level of culture, not kindling their emotions or revolutionizing their normal life . . . . A relation to religion was part of the Renaissance attitude toward life, and it was an attitude that could be defined as open."[28]

Several further questions should be added to these valid statements of Andrzej Wyczański. Did not the weak response in Poland to the Reformation (though in its Slavic variant, as was Hussitism) also result from the fact that it happened to occur at a time when neither intellectual life nor political life were such vital forces as they had been in the sixteenth century? Further, to what extent did the rather indifferent attitude of sixteenth-century Poles to doctrinal quarrels influence the transformation of the Reformation movement into a primarily intellectual trend? Did the theological current of the Reformation exceed the perceptive capabilities of society at that time, or did it simply not suit their interests and needs? Which of the Reformation's cultural achievements should be ascribed to the sum total of the flowering of civilization of the Renaissance period, and which should be recognized as an exclusive contribution of the Reformation movement?

Finally, there is a question which I am not sure that anyone would be in a position to answer. Even in the nineteenth century some historians pondered what the fate of the Polish state might have been had the last of the Jagiellons, with the support of part of the magnates and gentry, introduced one of the reformed confessions into the state. The answers have been various, often dependent upon the political views or religious sympathies of the author. One might also ask what the balance sheet of sixteenth-century Polish culture would have been like had the Republic, following the example of both the peninsulas of Iberia and the Apennines, remained indifferent to the Reformation movement. In other words, in such a case would Mikołaj Rej truly have written only "anecdotes, epitaphs, and inscriptions on spoons and fireplaces"? I must admit that such a statement seems to me to be at least debatable.

It might equally well be maintained that remnants of a medieval world view that some scholars discern in the works of Mikołaj Rej arose in great part from his interests in religious controversies. In this respect, the Reformation was a direct continuation of the *"kłótnie o dogmaty"* ("arguments about dogma") that had occurred in the Middle Ages. If we agree with the thesis of Goleniščev-Kutuzov that Hussitism was to some extent a detrimental influence on the development of fifteenth and sixteenth-century Czech culture,[29] the same certainly cannot be said about the Polish Reformation. Thanks to the fact that it was an intellectual and social-political movement and only in further turn a religious one, things did not come to such a bitter conflict on Polish soil as they did in other European countries of the time.

It is time for a few words of summation. In the long run, the intellectual merits of the Reformation did not materialize in the eyes of the Polish intellectual elite; instead they became a barrier preventing the acceptance of Protestantism by the lower levels of society. Because the Reformation also did not win over the support of the ruling Polish dynasty, it could not count upon the introduction of the new faith from above, as happened in the British Isles, the Scandinavian countries, or even in many German states. It remained an activity from below; those who responded in favor of Luther—in great measure on the basis of ethnic solidarity—were most of all Germans living primarily in Royal Prussia. They preserved not only religious but also scholarly ties with the Protestant West which resulted in, among other things, an earlier development of the Enlightenment in Royal Prussia than occurred in other areas of the Polish state.

In its turn, the Counter Reformation did not owe its victory to the intellectual values of that movement. Rather, its ability to adapt to the requirements and needs of the gentry nation, the flexible lowering of its level in accordance with the deepening decline of culture, and its appeal not to the scholarly achievements of the sixteenth century but to the traditions contained in folklore and customs ensured the success of the Counter Reformation. Under the conditions of a blossoming of intellectual life such as occurred in Poland in the sixteenth century, anti-Trinitarianism or Calvinism gained adherents due to the wave of interest in all kinds of intellectual novelty. The subsequent decline of this wave effectively preserved Catholicism in Poland from the influence of Jansenism or libertinism, currents which became so troublesome in the French Church. In the sixteenth century the land on the Vistula attracted intellectuals from various nations, convinced that they would find there the possibility to freely express and publish their views. In the middle of the next century members of sects that were on the highest intellectual level among all the Reformation groups had to emigrate from Poland. The expulsion of the Polish Brethren in 1658, at the same time, constitutes the real closing date in the history of the Polish Reformation as an intellectual movement.

Notes

1. See *Kultura elitarna a kultura masowa w Polsce późnego średniowiecza* (Culture of the elite and mass culture in Poland of the late Middle Ages), ed. Bronisław Geremek (Wrocław: Ossolineum, 1978), passim.
2. Jan Fijałek, "Moderniści katoliccy Kościoła lwowskiego w wieku XVI" (Catholic modernists in the Lwów church in the sixteenth century), *Pamiętnik literacki*, VII (1908): 8-56; 295-430.
3. See *Kościół w Polsce, wieki XVI-XVIII* (The Church in Poland, 16th-18th centuries), ed. Jerzy Kłoczowski (Cracow: Znak, 1970), passim.
4. Janusz Tazbir, "Die Stellung der polnischen Gesellschaft zur Reformation," *Jahrbuch für Geschichte* 23 (1981): 125.
5. According to fairly approximate calculations, barely 16 to 20 percent of the gentry came over to the side of the Reformation; it is another matter, however, that this was the best educated and most politically active segment of that estate.
6. We find complaints about this in the synodical records. See Konrad Górski, *Grzegorz Paweł z Brzezin. Monografia z dziejów polskiej literatury ariańskiej XVI wieku* (Gregory Paul of Brzeziny. A monograph on the history of Polish Arian literature of the 16th century) (Cracow: Polska Akademia Umiejętności, 1929), pp. 136-137.
7. Janusz Tazbir, *Geschichte der polnischen Toleranz* (Warsaw: Interpress, 1977), pp. 194-195.
8. Władysław Pociecha, "Walka sejmowa o przywileje Kościoła w Polsce w latach 1520-1537" (Parliamentary struggle over the privileges of the Church in Poland in the years 1520-1537), *Reformacja w Polsce*, 2 (1922): 165.
9. Polish printing houses, half of which remained in the hands of Protestants in the sixteenth century, produced a total of about two million copies of books. The average edition of a scholarly work at that time was about 500 copies.
10. Aleksander Brückner "Reformacja" (The Reformation) in *Kultura staropolska* (Old Polish culture) (Cracow, 1932), p. 260.
11. A photo-offset reprint of the dictionary appeared in Cologne in 1973.
12. See Stanisław Kot, *Rzeczpospolita Polska w literaturze politycznej Zachodu* (The Polish Commonwealth in political literature of the West) (Cracow: Nakł. Krakowskiej Spółki Wydawniczej, 1919), p. 43.
13. See Janusz Tazbir, *Tradycje tolerancji religijnej w Polsce* (Traditions of religious tolerance in Poland) (Warsaw: Książka i Wiedza, 1980), p. 108ff.
14. Stefan Nieznanowski, "Recepcja Reja w literaturze staropolskiej" (The reception of Rej in old Polish literature) in *Mikołaj Rej. W czterechsetlecie śmierci* (Mikołaj

Rej. On the 400th anniversary of his death), ed. Tadeusz Bieńkowski, Janusz Pelc, and Krystyna Pisarkowa (Wrocław: Ossolineum, 1971), pp. 237 and 241.

15. Andrzej Węgierski (Andreae Wengerscii), *Libri quattuor Slavoniae reformatae* (Varsoviae, 1973), p. 454.

16. Wiktor Weintraub, *Rzecz czarnoleska* (On Czarnolas) (Cracow: Wydawnictwo Literackie, 1977), p. 236ff.

17. Janusz Tazbir, *A State Without Stakes, Polish Religious Toleration in the Sixteenth and Seventeenth Centuries* (The Kościuszko Foundation), (Warsaw: PIW, 1973), pp. 125-126.

18. See Janusz Tazbir, "Les échos de la persécution des hérétiques occidentaux dans les polémiques religieuses en Pologne," *Bibliotheque d'Humanisme et Renaissanse*, vol. 34 (1972), pp. 125ff.

19. Stanisław Kot, "Szymon Budny. Der grösste Häretiker Litauens im 16. Jahrhundert," *Wiener Archiv für Geschichte des Slaventums und Osteuropas* II (1956): 106ff.

20. *Akta synodów różnowierczych w Polsce* (Records of the Protestant synods in Poland), vol. 3 (Małopolska (Little Poland), 1571-1632), ed. Maria Sipayłło (Warsaw: Wyd. Uniwersytetu Warszawskiego, 1983).

21. Halina Kowalska, "Akta synodów różnowierczych w Polsce, tom 3" (Review) *Odrodzenie i Reformacja w Polsce* 29 (1984): 224.

22. Aleksander Brückner, *Dzieje kultury polskiej* (History of Polish culture), vol. 2 (Cracow: Nakł. Krakowskiej Spółki Wydawniczej, 1931), p. 149.

23. See Janusz Tazbir, "Le role de la parole dans la propagande religieuse polonaise," *Revue d'Histoire Moderne et Contemporaine* 30 (January-March, 1983): 16ff.

24. "Księga wizytacji zborów podgórskich" (Book of Visitations of the sub-Carpathian congregations), ed. Lech Szczucki and Janusz Tazbir, *Archiwum Historii Filozofii i Myśli Społecznej* 3 (1958): 129.

25. Janusz Tazbir, "The Fate of Polish Protestantism in the Seventeenth Century," in *A Republic of Nobles: Studies in Polish History to 1864*, ed. and trans. by J.K. Fedorowicz (Cambridge: Cambridge University Press, 1982), pp. 210-211.

26. Henryk Wisner "Reformacja a kultura narodowa: Litwa" (Reformation and national culture: Lithuania), *Odrodzenie i Reformacja w Polsce* 20 (1975): 69-79.

27. Janusz Tazbir, "Die Reformation in Polen und das Judentum," *Jahrbücher für Geschichte Osteuropas* 31, no. 3 (1983).

28. Andrzej Wyczański, "Intelektualny walor reformacji" (The intellectual quality of the Reformation) in *Zarys historii Polski* (An outline of Polish history), ed. by Janusz Tazbir (Warsaw: PIW, 1979), pp. 218-219.

29. Il'ia Nikolaevich Goleniščev-Kutuzov, *Odrodzenie włoskie i literatury słowiańskie wieku XV i XVI* (The Italian Renaissance and Slavic literatures of the 15th and 16th centuries) (Warsaw: PWN, 1970) pp. 228-229.

7

Justice For All: Polish Democracy in the Renaissance Period in Historical Perspective

Wenceslas J. Wagner

An examination of any period in a nation's history would not be complete without investigating its law. One of the basic relationships between individuals among themselves and within the community is the system of legal norms which binds them. It is as old as humanity. Originating from primitive customs, developed by various tribes around the globe, the law has reached a high degree of refinement and sophistication in many countries. At a given moment, the legal rules embody the norms of behavior towards others at the time they are in force, but they are not born suddenly—they reflect a long development and experience accumulated over centuries.[1] It is difficult therefore to discuss a legal system without historical references. The proper understanding of many rules of law depends upon knowledge of their origin.

In the eighteenth century Montesquieu remarked that the law was the product of a nation's soul: it grows from its traditions, beliefs, way of thinking, religion, and moral foundations. This is true to a large extent. Indeed, the law must regulate social phenomena as soon as they arise, and in general, in its broad outlines, it represents the feeling of the population about the propriety of a definite kind of behavior. According to a penetrating analysis of the essence of the law, the foundation of its binding character was found to have roots in the psychology of a nation—an idea elaborated by Leon Petrażycki and his school.[2] Von Savigny and his followers in the historical school of law emphasized the connection between the development of a nation throughout the course of ages and its legal institutions.[3] John H. Wigmore observed that the text of a law may be incomprehensible or even misleading to a person not familiar with the whole background of a nation. To fully understand its working, it is necessary to place it in its "natural habitat."[4] Rudolf B. Schlesinger added that one of the main hazards in comparative law is the difference between

127

the printed word and the actual practice, which is often unknown to a super-ficial researcher. This will be revealed only after a thorough investigation, sometimes painstaking, of the economic, sociological and political foundations of the society in question. To some extent, this discrepancy exists in all legal systems, but in some of them it is so blatant that only naive or ignorant persons may believe in the literal application of the written texts of a constitution or statute.[5]

Whether the law is enacted by a democratic representation of the people or by an absolutist king or arbitrary dictatorship, some fields of the law usually incarnate the tradition and customs of the group of people in which it is in force. Such is the case, in particular, of family law. Marriage, separation, di-vorce, the relationship between husband and wife and between parents and children are problems which are strictly connected with the very foundations of the given society. The same may be said about the decedents' estates law. Constitutional law should reflect the political ideas of the population of a country.

On the other hand, some other legal rules are readily applicable to groups having a very different background. Maritime law has an international char-acter, and some parts of commercial law, and in particular the law of negotiable instruments, grew out of transactions between citizens of various countries. The merchant law had a kind of unifying effect on the dealings between trades-men of southern Europe and those of the north, and between the east and west. It was developed by businessmen from various parts of the globe. In the period of national codifications, commercial law solutions to some problems became different in the several jurisdictions; but these variations did not show any deep dichotomy in the underlying considerations of policy. On many occasions, attempts to re-uniformize the law proved successful. Thus, by in-ternational conventions, the same laws of checks and bills of exchange have been adopted in most of the civilized countries. Usually, the whole field of commercial law became uniform in many federal states before other fields. This happened in Germany, with the Commercial Code, in Switzerland, which enacted a federal code of obligations, and in the United States, where all states except one recently accepted the Uniform Commercial Code.

The transplantation of legal rules from one system to another is the easiest with respect to problems which are readily applicable to relations between any kind of individuals, regardless of their nationality. Sometimes foreign examples were endeavored to be imposed on a nation. Many of these attempts failed. For instance, the introduction of English common law to the province of Quebec after France lost this territory as a result of the Seven Years' War (1756-1763) encountered so much resistance that it was repealed. In other cases, the official law is simply ignored by the population, which applies their own rules. How-ever, there are famous examples of foreign law becoming a part of national law and staying there for good. This could be a result of a domination by one country over another (in this way, important fields of English law found their way to India), or of a determined effort to improve or modernize the national legal system by the ruler (e.g., this happened in Turkey where Kemal Atatürk integrated the Swiss civil law and the German commercial law into the Turkish legal system). Such steps are sometimes taken with respect to other phenomena than legal. Peter the Great reformed Russia on the Western pattern against the strong opposition of the conservative segment of his nation. Recently, a similar attempt of the Shah of Iran resulted in failure and his downfall.

The development of the law is a slow process. Sometimes it may be speeded up by the acceptance of some solutions which have proved to be good in other nations. As Petrażycki rightfully observed, in some instances the law may even precede progress in the prevailing social thinking. Thus, the abolition of the quasi-feudal relationship between the landed gentry and the peasant class in Russia was not readily accepted by a large segment of the nation. More often, however, because of the usual conservatism of the law, some legal rules become obsolete and are ever more disregarded before they are officially abrogated. Popular sentiment changes and paves the way for new legal rules.

In many situations, the development of the legal systems went through similar stages, e.g., in primitive law, legal rules were mixed with those of religion, ethics, and convention. Sanctions against law violators were severe; they appear cruel by our standards. Law reform influenced by examples of more advanced legal systems may not be contrary to the trends of development, but may just tend to bypass some stages which otherwise the law would have to go through.

Having the above considerations in mind, let us examine the background of Polish law and its evolution down to the Renaissance period.

Along with most other nations, Poland developed its legal system around local customs which were its main source of law.[6] It was supplemented by rules in force in the whole country and by foreign influences. Slavic tribes which were to unite and establish the kingdom developed their own ways of regulating the relations among the members of their groups, and when Poland emerged as a well-organized entity from a legendary state in the tenth century, her component parts greatly differed from each other in many essential aspects. For the following nearly two centuries, the country moved in the direction of a more centralized organization. But when Boleslaus the Wry-mouthed (Bolesław Krzywousty) divided the country among his sons,[7] Poland became split into provinces which favored the particularity of their legal developments. Ladislaus the Short (Władysław Łokietek) reunited the country, but final integration was slow to come. The most important, central part of Poland, the province of Mazovia, became an integral part of the kingdom only in 1525, after the death of its last two princes, but retained some autonomy. Polish law did not achieve codification and uniformity before the partitions and the loss of independence at the end of the eighteenth century. In many important respects, private law continued to be local and differed from each other, irrespective of more fundamental differences between the law of the territories which united with Poland. Further, some ethnic groups permitted to settle freely in Poland were allowed to be governed by their own legal rules.

The most important foreign influence was exerted by Roman law. The Renaissance movement reached Poland very early, and the nation became Latinized quite rapidly. This process was facilitated by the establishment of the University of Cracow in 1364. The grip of Latin culture on Poland was stronger than on most other countries. The upper classes spoke Latin; documents, royal decrees, and privileges were drafted in Latin. Literature was written in Latin as late as the seventeenth century, with some poets, such as Maciej Kazimierz Sarbiewski or Casimire—the "Christian Horace"—becoming famous all over the civilized world. During the Golden Age of Polish literature in the sixteenth century, initiated by Mikołaj Rej, Polish writers begin to use their own language to express themselves. The study of Roman law was introduced early into the kingdom, and some Roman legal terminology and approaches found their way into the flexible canvas of local legal structures. The logic of the rules embodied in the Code of Justinian—a result of twelve centuries of development, the refinement of some of its approaches, the elegance of the style of many of its formulas, did not fail to impress the Polish legal minds, along with those of other European countries.[8] The general effect tended towards more uniformity.

On a much more limited scale, elements of German law were brought to Poland in connection with the settlement of the Germans in the kingdom. One of the most important reasons for this colonization was destruction in some Polish territories by invaders from the East—Tartars, and later on, Turks. Some settlements were chartered on the basis of the law of Magdeburg.

French law was introduced much later. While French culture and language became widely known in Poland in the eighteenth century, and particularly under the reign of the last king, Stanisław August Poniatowski, an important transplantation of a part of French law on Polish soil did not occur until Napoleon, whose Civil Code became the law of the central part of Poland and continued to be in force, with some substantial changes, for nearly a century and a half to come.

The most original legal solutions which characterized the outstanding features of Polish law were developed in public rather than private law. Their origin was purely national. In many ways, the approach to constitutional and international law which originated in Poland as early as the fourteenth century and was well established during the Golden Age of the sixteenth century occurred in a direction opposite to that which most other European countries took. Noteworthy is the fact that there was no discrepancy between writings by theorists and scholars, the feelings of the population, the official decisions and the manner in which the country conducted its affairs, as frequently happened in the history of other nations.

The classical Polish school of international law was represented by a bevy of thinkers whose ideas frequently were ahead of their times. Stanisław ze Skarbimierza (Stanisław of Skarbimierz; Stanislaus of Scarbimiria), Rector of the University of Cracow from 1400 to 1413, preached a "just war" one century before Hugo Grotius and advanced the idea that coooperation with pagans is possible. Similarly, Paweł Włodkowic (Paulus Vladimiri), the next Rector of the University of Cracow, advanced the concept of religious tolerance on the internal and international scene. Both theorists objected not only to waging wars which did not have a just cause, but also to improper methods of conducting warfare. Stanislaus of Scarbimiria pioneered a few ideas in international law: self-defense, legality of pagan states, reparation for war damages, and refusal to obey a command if the war is obviously unjust; Włodkowic developed the idea of national self-determination. Jan Ostroróg described the concept of state sovereignty in 1475—one hundred years before Jean Bodin. In 1548, Jakub Przyłuski dealt in his works with diplomatic privileges and the necessity of keeping promises even with respect to enemies. In 1558, Jan Tarnowski discussed the humanitarian aspect of war and condemned aggression. Krzysztof Warszewicki (Varsevicius) described the mechanics of diplomatic relations in 1595.[9]

Thus, the general feature of the Polish school was a deeply humanistic approach to international law and relations, respect for human life and freedom of nations, and application of the principles of "democracy" on the international scene. Implementing those ideas, Cardinal Mikołaj Trąba, Primate of Poland, took a firm stand at the Council of Constance (1414-1418), forcefully speaking, along with Włodkowic, against the use of force in international relations and converting pagan nations against their wishes.

In the period of the Renaissance, the Polish-Lithuanian Commonwealth became the foremost European country in every respect, its power, culture, and vast area stretching from the Baltic to the Black Sea. The gradual territorial expansion of the kingdom was not due to military conquest, which Poland abhorred; it was brought about by voluntary unions with the neighboring nations, such as the major part of Prussia, Livonia (*Inflanty*), Ruthenia, and particularly, Lithuania. The union with the latter country became the first example of an accomplished federation in the history of international law. Established as a loose personal union when the Lithuanian Duke Władysław Jagiełło married the Polish Oueen Jadwiga and became the king of Poland by the union of Krewo in 1386, reinforced after the crushing defeat of the Teutonic Order by the Polish forces aided by the Lithuanians at Grunwald (Tannenberg, 1410), and in the union of Horodło (1413), it became a closely knit federal state in the celebrated union of Lublin of 1569. The spirit in which it was conceived, and which according to the Polish approach should be the basis of international law and relations, was eloquently stated in the preamble to the Union of Horodło in the following phraseology:[10]

It is known to all that the grace of redemption will not be bestowed on those who are not moved by the secrets of love—love which does not act haphazardly, but emanates rays of charity, settles controversies, unites adversaries, abolishes hatred, cancels anger, and gives peace to all; it assembles that which is scattered, comforts the dis- couraged, evens the bumpy, straightens out what is slanted, supports all virtues and does not harm anyone; it cherishes everything, and if someone takes refuge under its wings, will find security and will not fear any attack from anywhere. Owing to it, laws are established, kingdoms governed, towns organized, and the Polish Common- wealth achieves her highest goals: it excellently inspires all virtues, and he who should repudiate it, will lose everything.

From the thirteenth century on, Poland did not wage any aggressive wars, in accordance with the theories of international law and relations laid down by her scholars and statesmen. In case of necessity, she knew how to defend herself and more than once chased away invaders deep into their own terri- tories; but general military service was unknown in her law, and the bulk of her armed forces consisted of noblemen mobilized when need arose. It is worthwhile mentioning that from 1496 on, the right to call the army into being could be exercised by the parliament (Sejm) alone, and beginning in 1573, all kings, before assuming their functions, had to take an oath affirming that they would abstain from waging wars and calling up the army without the per- mission of the parliament. Thus, these vital decisions, involving the lives of human beings, were taken away early from the monarch and placed in the hands of the representatives of the nation, preventing possible speedy action by the ruler. In exercising its right, the parliament examined the situation by a commission in order to find out whether there were not alternatives and whether the Polish interests which were at stake could be supported in equity.[11] In contrast to many other nations which bestowed the nickname of "Great" upon those rulers who showed military achievements, in Poland the only king who merited this title was Casimir the Great (Kazimierz Wielki) who preferred to lose some of the country's territories rather than to let his nation engage in warfare, established the first university (Cracow, in 1364), replaced frame con- struction by stone, and was known to have an outstanding sense of justice. His sobriquet was "King of the Peasants."

Polish legal thinking was no less humanistic and democratic in constitutional law. It developed early ideas which were nothing less than revolutionary con- sidered against the background of the prevailing European attitudes of those times. The era of Jan Kochanowski marked the peak of Polish politico-legal ideas. Thus, in 1551-1554, Andrzej Frycz Modrzewski (Andreas Fricius Mod- revius) advanced the idea of abolishing serfdom and granting equal rights to all citizens irrespective of class origin, in a period when the very structure of nations consisted in a division into social classes. Wawrzyniec Goślicki (Lau- rentius Grimalius Goslicius), writing in 1568, established the theoretical foun- dations of the parliamentary system of government. Some of his ideas circulated widely in England and helped the parliament in its struggle against the ab- solutism of the king, and a few of his formulations, passing through England to America, may have influenced the framers of the American Declaration of

Independence. One such example in particular is his statement that "in the private happiness of the subjects consists the general and public happiness of the commonwealth."[12]

Stanisław Orzechowski (Orichovius) was less liberal and required respect for the concept of authority in his books published in 1563 and 1564. Cardinal Hosius (Stanisław Hozjusz, 1504-1579), a learned jurist, connected the idea of justice with that of love and emphasized the necessity of legal stability in the country. Andrzej Wolan (1530-1610) advanced equality of rights of the citizens. A strict correlation between liberty and equality was found by Stanisław Sokołowski (1536-1593). Łukasz Górnicki criticized extreme forms of civil liberties and exhorted the nation to be just and united in 1588. Other noteworthy contributions to constitutional law were published by many other authors, such as Marcin Kromer, Jan Dantyszek (Dantiscus), Jan Dymitr Solikowski, Jakub Górski, Stanisław Karnkowski, and Fabian Birkowski.

While all around Poland, with insignificant exceptions, developments went in the direction of an absolute and arbitrary power of the monarch, the foundations of the Polish constitutional system became even more solidly based on the premises of human rights and participation of the nation in the running of public affairs. Far from extending the prerogatives of the king, Poland established a constitutional system and parliamentary government as early as the fifteenth century. The framework of the state became for the Poles "a tool to serve the happiness of the living society,"[13] rather than an organization subservient to a ruler entitled to treat it as his own property, using its resources for his own purposes and not hesitating to engage his nation in the scourge of devastating wars for real or imaginary interests of his prestige, ambition, and dynastic planning.

Some of the most important stages in this development were the following. By a law of 1367, Jews who were persecuted in other European countries were granted freedom to settle in Poland, to enjoy the protection of the law and to establish their own organizations and even tribunals. They had a well-developed autonomy. In 1374, the king promulgated the Privilege of Košice by virtue of which the consent of the nobles was a prerequisite to the imposition of taxes. In 1422, the Privilege of Czerwień prohibited the king from confiscating private property without judicial authorization. An unbelievable achievement was reached in 1430. In this period of the Middle Ages, when personal liberties were at the mercy of the monarch, in Poland the Privilege of Jedlna guaranteed personal independence of the nobles from the arbitrariness of the king by proclaiming: *Neminem captivabimus nisi iure victum*—we will not imprison anyone except if convicted by law. This Polish Privilege, which preceded the English Habeas Corpus Act by two and a half centuries, and those of most other countries by a longer period of time, provided that a nobleman could be put in jail only by virtue of a judicial decision, except if caught *in flagranti* while committing murder, arson, larceny, or rape. Later, the application of the Privilege was extended to townsmen, and in 1588, searches of a nobleman's house were prohibited even if he was suspected of harboring an outlaw.

The Privilege of Nieszawa, 1454, marked a significant step in the establishment of the parliamentary system. Provincial assemblies of the nobles (*sejmiki*), which had begun to be called in order to discuss public matters, were given the power to authorize the king to promulgate new laws and to wage wars. The king consented not to act without such an authorization. The local assemblies were soon supplemented by a national gathering of provincial representatives, known as the *Izba poselska* (House of Representatives), which took its final form in 1493. Thus, the Polish parliament or *Sejm* came into being. Officially, it consisted of three chambers: the King, the Senate, and the House. The concurrence of all three chambers was necessary to enact any law and to make any decision. A comprehensive constitutional principle was expressed in the famous Act of 1505, known as the Constitution "Nihil Novi" because of its introductory words: *Nihil novi constitui debeat per nos sine communi consensu conciliariorum et nuntiorum terrestrium*—we will not enact anything new without the common consent of the council and the territorial representatives. The council, or the Senate, consisted of important officials, both secular and ecclesiastical, and the representatives were elected at the sejmiki.

From then on, the life of the country was subjected to the guidance and wisdom of the *Sejm*. Its most important functions consisted of the elaboration and enactment of statutes, imposition of taxes, supervision of the activities of the king, his government and the administration, establishment of the directives for foreign policy, decisions with respect to war and peace. The deliberations of the *Sejm* were open to the public, and after the parliamentary sessions the representatives had to submit reports on how they had fulfilled their duties to the *sejmiki*.

The idea that nothing should be decided about the nation without its own consent went to an extreme in another constitutional principle by virtue of which the highest rank, that of the king, had to be confirmed by the *Sejm*, beginning with Jan Olbracht (1492) and would become elective upon the end of the Jagiellonian dynasty in 1572. This unique approach reflected the belief that the qualities of an individual rather than his birth should be the primary consideration in bestowing upon him the duties of such an importance. However, as long as there was a sufficiently good candidate from the ruling dynasty, the custom was established not to look elsewhere. Thus, one after another, seven kings from the Jagiellonian dynasty succeeded, and then three from among the Vasas and two from the Saxon dynasty of the Wettins. Nevertheless, every nobleman could aspire to become the monarch, and indeed, four times persons not belonging to any royal family were called by the nation to the highest post in the country. For good reasons, while the rulers of other countries enjoyed their title as having been granted to them "by the grace of God," in Poland, just before the partitions, the formula was supplemented by the additional words: "and by the will of the nation." Early, the country began to be known as a "nobles' commonwealth" rather than a kingdom. It is not surprising that in this arrangement broad masses of the Poles participated and were interested in the public life of the nation.

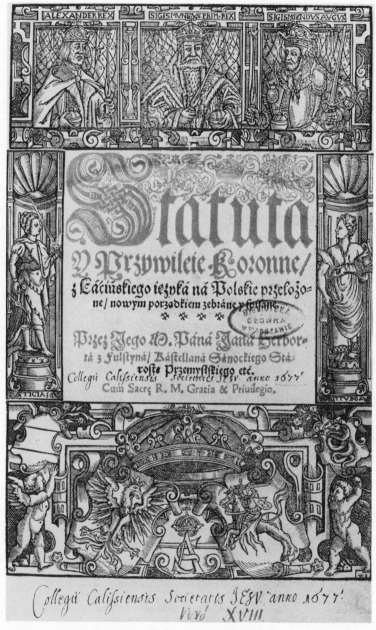

23. Jan Herburt z Fulsztyna, *Statuta i przywileje koronne*, w Krakowie, 1570. Title page of Jan Herburt's Crown Statutes and Priviliges which constitutes a codification of Polish Law and is Herburt's own Polish Version of his *Statuta Regni Poloniae in ordinem alphabeti digesta*, Cracoviae, 1563 (Biblioteka Uniwersytecka, Warszawa). Photo Andrzej Bodytko.

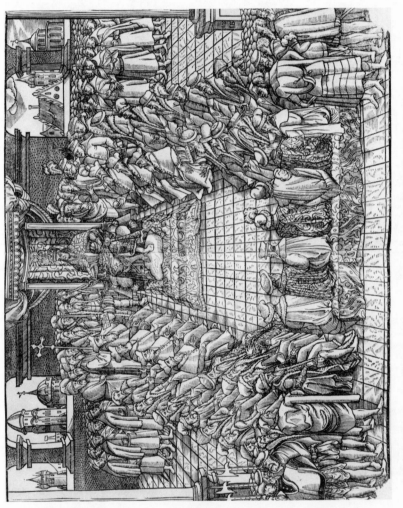

24. The Polish *Sejm* with the King Sigismund II August. Woodcut in Herburt's *Statuta i przywileje koronne*, w Krakowie, 1570. (Biblioteka Uniwersytecka, Warszawa). Photo Andrzej Bodytko.

Furthermore, beginning with the Renaissance period (from 1573 on), before assuming his duties, the king had to take an oath promising to respect the established constitutional system and to accept the conditions upon which he was elected. This oath was not a mere formality. The king had to abide by his promise under the threat that the nation could be relieved from loyalty to the ruler. A statute of 1609, *de non praestanda oboedientia*, provided for a detailed procedure (which included three warnings by the Senate) to be observed before such a step could be taken. However, it did not happen at any time.

Together with these unusual and progressive constitutional principles, there were a few features of the Polish system which lend themselves to criticism. Such was, first of all, that of *liberum veto*, which permitted every member of the *Sejm* to veto any of its resolutions. The rationale of this principle was that the structure, elaborated by former generations, should not be changed lightly and that the majority should not impose its will on the minority. Nevertheless, the minority regularly yielded and the veto was used with extraordinary restraint, being employed for the first time in the middle of the seventeenth century.[14]

Another shortcoming of the constitutional system was the fact that for long periods of Polish history, full civic and political rights were extended only to the class of the nobility. A few points should be made in this connection. The significance of constitutional provisions and their evaluation must be measured by standards applicable to the period in question rather than by the thinking of our times. Nobody denies the greatness of the American Constitution and its first ten amendments, the "Bill of Rights." Yet, that famous document did not abolish slavery. Thousands of human beings continued to be treated not as underprivileged classes, but simply as chattels, subjected to property laws, being sold, purchased, and treated as cattle. It must be mentioned that while in most other countries, where the percentage of nobles was very low, frequently under one percent, in Poland the nobility constituted from one-tenth to one-eighth of the population. In past centuries, the society was divided into classes according to a well-established pattern in all nations. Undoubtedly, the nobility was privileged compared to other classes (except the ecclesiastical class), but it had also to bear some burdens unshared by other groups, in particular, participation in the military effort of the nation in cases of necessity. Tens of thousands of the poorest layers of the noble class cultivated their modest farms with their own hands, in the manner of the peasants, the only difference being that they had the right to carry a sword at all times. Irrespective of wealth, all noblemen were legally absolutely equal to each other, and in order to reinforce this principle, at the end of the sixteenth century the *Sejm* prohibited the bestowing of any aristocratic title on Polish citizens. In 1673, a statute provided for the imposition of the penalty of infamy for life on anyone who would accept a title from a foreign ruler. The principle of equality also found its expression in a steadfast refusal of the Parliament to permit the king to establish decorations.

While the nobility was the predominant class, the lower classes were not deprived of rights. In particular, the townsmen actively participated in public life, assumed many important state positions, and sent delegates to the legislative body. The larger towns were represented at the vital function of the election of the king. Many townsmen amassed great wealth (the fabulous Wierzynek in fourteenth-century Cracow, or Fukier in seventeenth-century Warsaw) and became well-known university professors or writers. The foremost poet of the fifteenth century, Klemens Janicki (Janicius), was the son of a simple peasant. Again, contrary to the law of most other countries, the residents of a few of the larger Polish towns had the right to acquire landed estates.

An important feature of the Polish Commonwealth's constitutional system was the legal and even judicial autonomy of its component parts, both with respect to the territory and to the population.

The Polish-Prussian union was brought about in 1466; the Prussians kept their own law, judicial organization, and German language. Mazovia joined Poland less than a century later, and its own customary law, codified under the name of "Mazovian Excepts," continued to be applicable. Livonia joined the Commonwealth in 1560. Its judicial system was not affected, but little by little, without any pressure, the German language gave way to Polish. Again, the most important union, that with Lithuania, did not result in a unification of the law and the judiciary. A separate "Lithuanian Statute" embodied the bulk of the law of that country, and Lithuanian tribunals, organized according to the Polish pattern, were subject only to the highest court of Lithuania and used Bielorussian rather than the Polish language even after most Lithuanians accepted Polish as their adopted tongue.

Likewise, some important national groups which settled in Poland were permitted to enjoy a broad autonomy which included their own law and administration of justice. In particular, this was the case with the Armenians and the Jews.[15]

Another amazing characteristic of Polish law was freedom of belief and religious tolerance which developed very early, in times of bloody religious wars in most European countries, of international and fratricidal struggles which devastated the continent. There was never any religious persecution in Poland. At the Council of Constance, Włodkowic defended the followers of Hus and declared that membership in a denomination should be left to the conscience of the citizens. While religious fanaticism and the rule *cuius regio, eius religio* were the accepted European approach, Poland proclaimed complete religious freedom in the parliamentary act *De pace inter dissidentes* of 1573.[16] During the Reformation, so many outstanding Polish families espoused Protestantism that for some time the majority of the senators were not Catholic.[17] Some limitations on the rights of the "dissidents" were imposed later, in the period preceding the partitions, but these were very mild compared to the discrimination against and oppression of religious minorities which became a well-established way of approaching the problem in most of Europe. Not until the great French revolution was freedom of belief, "even" religious, solemnly proclaimed. The maturity of the Polish institutions and principles of human rights impressed the famous eighteenth-century French philosopher and state theorist Jean-Jacques Rousseau so much that he called them excellent and stated that the Polish constitutional system was better than the English one. In particular, he attached much importance to the sejmiki or provincial legislatures, and he favored the retention of the unanimity rule (*liberum veto*) in the Sejm, with some reservations.[18]

As appears from the foregoing observations, one of the most outstanding features of the Polish spirit was abhorrence of any kind of compulsion in internal and international life. This feeling markedly influenced the Polish ideas about the law, public and private. Theories similar to the Austinian way of thinking, that legal rules are imposed on the nation by the ruler under the threat of sanctions, were thoroughly repudiated by the Poles. There was a deep feeling that the legal order emanates from, and must be consented to by, the people. A significant example of the predominance of the law over the governmental power was the right of the Chancellor to refuse to affix the seal to a document which was contrary to the spirit of the legal rules in force. "Private wars" and taking upon oneself the administration of justice, bypassing judicial process, so frequent in other countries, were rarely resorted to, and if they were, they usually took the form of "forays": self-execution of judgments when the state machinery acted too slowly.[19] Judicial procedure, which in other countries could resort to ordeals, held in secret (except in England), based on written documents and permitting frequent application of torture, developed modern rules in Poland early. The trials were oral and open to the public, and the accused was entitled to be defended. Those lawfully convicted who did not appear to serve their term in prison became outlaws and could be killed by anyone.[20]

What usually struck foreign visitors was the personal security of the travelers on public roads and streets. According to the testimony of the French historian Rulhière, Cambridge University Professor Coxe, the German writers Biester and Schulz and others, there was no danger in moving around Poland, either to the person or property of the traveler. The tourist could safely leave his belongings on a buggy overnight without any supervision, and tremendous sums of the state treasury's money were transported from the provinces to the capital with one, or at most two, guardians[21]—a striking contrast to the situation prevailing in some countries of the modern world where the citizens feel unsafe on the streets both at night and in the daytime.

The attachment to and protection of private property was striking. Very early, landed estates, which in most countries were only "held" by their possessors by the grace of the ruler, were recognized as belonging allodially to them in Poland, along with chattels. By joining Poland in union, a few other nations secured for their citizens not only personal liberties previously unknown by them, but full property rights. Indeed, even though each member of the union was permitted to keep its own legal system, the strong influence of the progressive Polish ideas brought about rather rapid changes in the politico-legal structure of all territories of the Commonwealth.

The pinnacle of the development of constitutional law ideas of old Poland was reached in the famous Constitution of May 3, 1791, which, however, had a short life because of the forthcoming partitions and loss of independence in 1795. It affirmed the preexisting Polish politico-legal achievements but went further in a few directions. The king, heretofore treated as one of the parliamentary chambers, lost his previous prerogatives: he was deprived of the right to veto decisions taken by the House and the Senate—a rule more advanced than that in most democratic parliamentary systems of today. Again, the *Sejm* was granted the exclusive right to ratify international treaties, and the state of diplomatic negotiations was to be reported by the executive branch of the government to the legislature. The House, being an elective body, received a preeminent position: should the Senate reject a resolution of the House, it could be reenacted during the next session of the House, and then it entered into force without the concurrence of the Senate. The king became the President of the Senate, having one vote along with other senators, but he ceased to be elected. The position of the monarch became inherited.

Marking an important social reform, the Constitution of May 3, 1791, abolished most privileges of the nobility while opening wide the door to people from other classes to be granted the status of a nobleman.

During the long and dark period of partitions, there was no possibility for the Polish law to freely develop on the territories which had been annexed by Austria, Prussia, and Russia.[22] As mentioned above, in the central part of the country, organized at the Congress of Vienna in 1815 as the "Congress Kingdom" under Russian rule, French law was adopted to a large extent, with purely Polish elements soon replacing some parts of the Napoleonic Code, particularly in the field of marriage law and real estate transactions. Being controlled by foreign invaders, the nation was unable to elaborate its own comprehensive legal system. However, historical legal studies flourished and produced many outstanding scholars, particularly at the Universities of Cracow and Lwów.

After World War I, with the recovery of independence on a greatly diminished territory, Poland faced the problem of unifying its law. The country did not return to the monarchical form of government, but was established as a democratic republic by the Constitution of 1921. Extensive work on codification resulted in the elaboration of codes of civil and criminal procedure, a commercial code, and a criminal code. The work on a civil code was not finished before the German invasion of Poland started World War II, but the rules of the most important parts of civil law, contracts and torts, were laid down in the "Code of Obligations," which was hailed as an excellent piece of legislation.[23] When preparing the legal enactments, the drafters engaged in extensive historical and comparative law research. They reverted to some old Polish solutions whenever practicable, retained many Roman law formulations and classifications, and accepted those French and German rules which seemed best. On many points, they devised new approaches, particularly when technological advances and social progress did not permit a return to old Polish law and foreign concepts did not seem perfect. Such was, in particular, the idea of absolute liability for damages occasioned in connection with the use of the "forces of nature," and the famous provision of the Code of Obligations permitting the judge to reform the contracts or even relieve a party from the obligation to perform in the case of unforeseeable calamities like floods which would render the carrying out of the contract particularly burdensome.

Some other very progressive public and private law enactments were adopted in the twenties and thirties. Land reform, voluntarily begun in the eighteenth century by many enlightened magnates, became one of the primary goals of the government. A special ministry of land reform was established, directing and supervising the division of large estates among the peasants. Noteworthy was the effort to protect labor. Legal provisions aiming at giving to the working people job security, adequate compensation, proper work hours, vacations and medical care, were among the most progressive in the world.[24]

With the advent of communism after World War II, many imported elements foreign to the Polish spirit were incorporated in the politico-legal system of Poland. Political and economic ideas devised elsewhere became the basis on which the nation had to build its legal "superstructure." The country was compelled to imitate the pattern set by its eastern neighbor, one which it had shunned previously. In many instances, formulas and solutions applied in the Soviet system were imposed on Poland. Repeatedly, now, the written texts radically differed from the actual practice.

It is unnecessary to linger on the replacement of the former constitutional law rules by the new organization of Poland. But the new ideology, imposed on the nation, penetrated deeply into its legal system. Some of the overriding principles, known as "general clauses," found their way into the constitution itself. One such principle is the idea that no legal relationship will be recognized and enforced by the state if it is contrary to the "principles of community life in the Polish Peoples' Republic"—a formula strictly following the Soviet pattern, repeated in other communist countries, and frequently arbitrarily applied by the tribunals. Besides the constitution, it is found in many Polish statutory enactments, particularly in the Civil Code.[25] A similar formula is the one requiring legal relationship to be in conformity with the "socio-economic purposes" of the law.

Some new kinds of transactions in the new system called for special regulation which did not exist in pre-war Poland. Again, the Soviet system furnished a ready pattern. All business of any importance has been nationalized. State enterprises have to produce goods, to sell and buy them, to distribute them to other state units or to the consumers. The traditional freedom of contracting had to be replaced by an obligation to enter into contracts. The traditional rule that in order to mature into a contract, an offer must be accepted, gave way to another one which provides that in such cases silence of the offeree will have the effect of accepting the terms of the other party.[26]

It is not surprising that whenever the interests of the state are at stake, it tries to regulate them in a way it finds most convenient. But the communist ideology also permeates many relationships which exist among private individuals. In accordance with the basic tenets of Marxism-Leninism, in the stage of socialism the distribution of wealth should be determined by the amount of work. This principle will be replaced, in the stage of communism, by the criterion of the actual needs of the citizens. In accordance with this approach, recovery for mental suffering alone, not coupled with financial losses, is in general not compensated. This rule applies in many situations, such as the death of a close relative and divorce.

Again, in relations between the citizens and the public administration, the latter is especially protected by the law. Lawful decisions of the government officials, who did not act negligently so as to incur responsibility in legal or disciplinary proceedings, do not result in liability in case a citizen suffers damage of any kind. On the other hand, if the official acted in violation of the law and incurred sanctions, the aggrieved citizen recovers. The courts were willing to develop a broad scope of liability of the State Treasury in such cases.[27]

Even though the upheaval brought about by the imposition of a new political system on Poland had to result in many fundamental changes in her law, the restructuring of her institutions was less abrupt and the adjustment process more gradual and restrained than in many other countries, such as China, where the preexisting legal system was abrogated overnight by the communist regime before the new rules were enacted, so that in theory the nation was deprived of all legal rules for some time. While scores of new provisions replaced the old ones in Poland, some of the previous law has been retained. Polish elements and formulations have been blended with foreign ones which the country was bound to follow. In general, its legal system remains less revolutionary than that of some countries which suffered a similar experience. Thus, for example, the Polish Civil Code, repeating dozens of provisions of the former Code of Obligations, is much more traditional than, for example, the Czechoslovak Code.

Legal literature is flourishing. Frequently, behind the Marxist jargon and obligatory references to the official dogmas and statements by communist theorists and activists, there lies an excellent analysis of legal problems. In many of them, the authors show a keen evaluation of questions facing a modern society and a deep desire to answer them to the best advantage of the country, coupled with a thorough knowledge of the underlying legal rules, both in Poland and in other countries. After the many excesses of the Stalinist era, when the law was subservient to politics and promoted the goals of the party, the courts now frequently try to adjudicate controversies in accordance with the dictates of justice.[28]

Notes

The author extends thanks to Mrs. Anne-Marie Findeisen, Esq., of the New York Bar, for help in the preparation of these remarks.

1. *Omnis definitio periculosa est*, and every generalized statement is not accurate in all instances.

2. For a comprehensive study of Leon Petrażycki's work and a bibliography, see Georges S. Langrod and Michalina Vaughan, "The Polish Psychological School of Law," in Wenceslas Wagner, ed., *Polish Law Throughout the Ages*, (Stanford: Hoover Institution Pr., 1970), p. 299. Most of the main ideas of Petrażycki are expressed in an English translation, *Law and Morality* (Cambridge: Harvard University Press, 1955).

3. For a summary of Friedrich Carl Von Savigny's theories, see Roscoe Pound, "Sources and Forms of Law," *Notre Dame Law* 22 (1) (1946): 73-76.

4. John H. Wigmore, "More Jottings on Comparative Legal Ideas and Institutions," *Tulane Law Review* 6 (244) (1932): 263-264.

5. Rudolf B. Schlesinger, *Comparative Law, Cases-Text-Materials*, 4th ed. (Mineola, NY: Foundation Press, 1980), pp. 827-836.

6. Wacław W. Soroka, "Historical Studies of Polish Law," in Wagner, pp. 9, 25.

7. For details, see Wojciech Wasiutyński, "Origins of the Polish Law, Tenth to Fifteenth Centuries," in Wagner, pp. 39, 43.

8. See Juliusz Bardach, "La réception dans l'histoire de L'état et du droit" in *Le droit romain et sa réception en Europe* (Varsovie, Université de Varsovie, 1978); Witold Wołodkiewicz, "The Romanist Tradition of Civil Liability in Contemporary Poland," in William E. Butler, ed., *Anglo-Polish Legal Essays* (Dobbs Ferry, NY: Transnational Publishers, 1982), p. 75.

9. For details, see Wacław Szyszkowski, "The Law of Nations in Poland from the Middle Ages to Modern Times," in Wagner, p. 63.

10. Translated by Wagner, in "Introduction" of Wagner, p. 7.

11. Antoni Chołoniewski, *Duch dziejów Polski* (*The spirit of the history of Poland*), (Rome: Nakł. Biura Prasowego Biskupa Polowego, 1946) p. 70.

12. For details, see Wenceslas J. Wagner, Arthur P. Coleman, and Charles S. Haight, "Laurentius Grimaldus Goslicius and His Age—Modern Constitutional Law Ideas in the Sixteenth Century," in Wagner, p. 97, and *Polish Review* 3, no. 1-2 (Winter-Spring 1958): 37.

13. Chołoniewski, pp. 17-18.

14. For more comments and comparisons, see "Introduction" of Wagner, n. 1, p. 6.

15. For more details on historical features of Polish constitutional law, see Ludwik Kos-Rabcewicz-Zubkowski, "Polish Constitutional Law," in Wagner, p. 215.

16. A passage of the Act of "Warsaw Confederation" of 1573 reads as follows: "in order to prevent the possibility of internal troubles, which we see in other Kingdoms, we promise to each other, in our name and that of our successors, under an oath of our faith, honor and conscience, being of different religious beliefs, to permanently keep peace among ourselves and not to shed blood because of our various denominations . . . and not to impose sanctions of confiscation of the

estates, infamy, imprisonment and exile." Translated from Manfred Kridl, Józef Wittlin, and Bronisław Malinowski, *Polska myśl demokratyczna w ciągu wieków* (Polish democratic thought through the centuries) (New York: Polish Labor Group, 1945), p. 7.

17. However, most of these families returned to Catholicism in later years, so that Poland was predominantly Catholic.

18. Rousseau, *The Government of Poland* (1771).

19. Chołoniewski, p. 61.

20. Chołoniewski, p. 62.

21. For details, see Chołoniewski, pp. 63-64. With the above described characteristics of the Polish approach to the law, it is not surprising that the founder of the psychological school of law was a Pole, Leon Petrażycki (see n. 1). He eliminated the state's power to enforce its orders as the primary element of the law and replaced it by a deep conviction of the population that an orderly society has to abide by the rules organizing the relations between private individuals among themselves and with the state. The very essence of the law was found to consist of mental attitudes of the citizens.

22. For details, see Soroka, "The Law in the Polish Lands During the Partition Period," in Wagner, p. 119.

23. Other fields of the civil law were still under consideration at the outbreak of World War II. Thus, family law, and in particular the question of divorce, was a problem which was the subject of many discussions and on which agreement proved to be difficult to reach.

24. For details, see Bronisław Helczyński, "The Law in the Reborn State," in Wagner, pp. 139, 171.

25. For details, see Wenceslas Wagner, "Obligations in Polish Law," vol. 2, in the series, *Polish Civil Law* Dominik Lasok, ed. (Leiden: Sijthoff, 1974).

26. See, e.g., Wenceslas Wagner, "The Interplay of Planned Economy and Traditional Contract Rules in Poland," *American Journal of Comparative Law* 11 (1962): 348.

27. Wenceslas Wagner, "Recent Developments in State Tort Liability in Poland," *American Journal of Comparative Law* 20 (1972): 247.

28. This text was written before the political upheaval in Poland caused by the suppression of "Solidarity" by the government, introduction of the "State of War," and pressures exerted on all agencies and institutions to abide by the directives of the authorities.

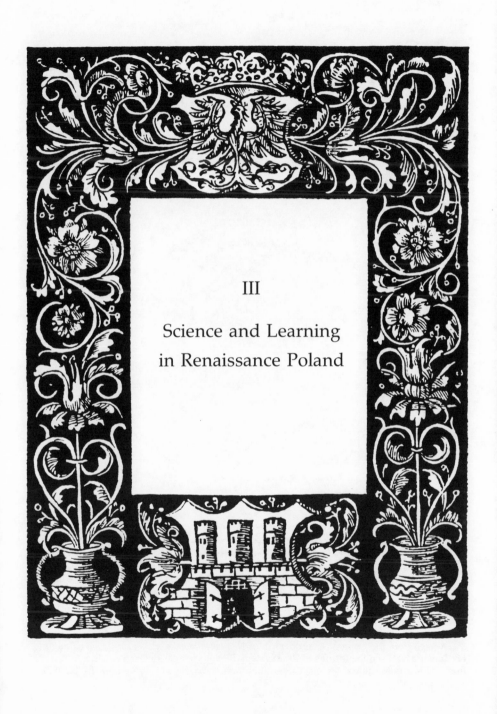

III

Science and Learning
in Renaissance Poland

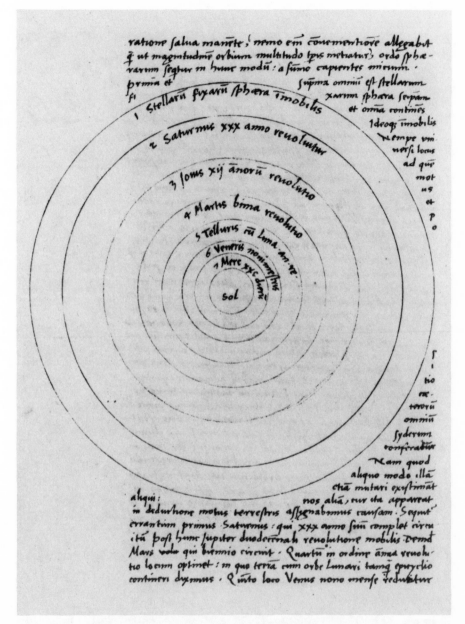

25. A page from the Copernicus autograph of *De Revolutionibus orbium coelestium* containing his drawing representing the heliocentric system (Biblioteka Jagiellońska, Kraków). Reprinted from the facsimile edition, Mikołaj Kopernik, *Dzieła Wszystkie*, vol. 1 (Kraków: PWN, 1972).

8

The Cracovian Background of Nicholas Copernicus

Andrzej Wróblewski

cience during the period of the Polish Renaissance was centered almost entirely at the University of Cracow. The University, founded in 1364 by the Polish king, Casimir the Great (Kazimierz Wielki), was initially organized according to the model of the University of Bologna. It had faculties of law, medicine, and philosophy, but did not have theology. During the first years of its existence the University did not do well and, in fact, collapsed completely in 1370. But Polish intellectuals and scholars soon persuaded Queen Jadwiga and her husband, King Władysław Jagiełło, to restore the University. In 1400 the University of Cracow was re-established with a new structure, one patterned, this time, after the University of Paris. It had all the faculties, including theology and arts, and soon became the most important university in central Europe.

We shall be interested in the activity of the Faculty of Arts or artium, because it was there that physics, mathematics, and astronomy were taught and developed.[1] According to the rule from 1404-1406, studies at the Faculty of Arts comprised two steps: the lower one was concluded with the degree of bachelor, the higher with the degree of master (magister) of arts. During the lower course, the longest period (nine months) was assigned to lectures on Aristotle's *Physics*. These lectures were always reserved for the Dean of the Faculty. Other treatises of Aristotle, such as *De anima*, *Analytica priora*, and his smaller writings on nature, were given much less time. The higher course, for bachelors, reserved the most time (nine months) for Aristotle's *Ethics*. *Metaphysics* was taught for six months, *Politics* for five months; other writings of Aristotle were alloted less time.

Aristotle's *Physics* was taught mainly on the basis of the commentary of Jean Buridan,[2] *Subtilissimae quaestiones super octo Physicorum libros Aristotelis*. This treatise itself served as a source for commentaries by Cracow scholars and its influence was very great until the last quarter of the fifteenth century. Teaching of problems in *De caelo et mundo* was based on *Quaestiones super quattuor libros*

De caelo et mundo Aristotelis by Albert of Saxony; again Cracow commentaries were influenced by this treatise. *De generatione et corruptione* was taught according to the commentaries by Buridan and Marsilius of Inghen; *Meteora* according to the commentary by Nicole d'Oresme, and later by Pierre d'Ailly, Albertus Magnus, and Jean de Tourner. *De anima* was taught according to *Quaestiones super De anima* by Buridan and also the *Summa theologiae* of Thomas Aquinas.

Thus, although teaching was traditionally based on the writings of Aristotle, Cracow scholars and students had an opportunity to learn and assimilate the new ideas of Jean Buridan, Nicole d'Oresme, Albert of Saxony, and other great medieval thinkers. We have proof in the writings of Cracow scholars which began to appear about 1415 that Buridanism in particular found a fertile soil there in which it could flourish almost to the end of the fifteenth century.

In the first half of the fifteenth century the dominating personality at the University of Cracow was Benedykt Hesse (died 1456). This distinguished philosopher wrote many commentaries on Aristotle's treatises, among them *Quaestiones super octo libros Physicorum Aristotelis* (about 1421), a commentary on Aristotle's *Physics*, which was subsequently used by Cracow teachers for almost three decades. In his book Hesse considered, among other things, the problem of forced motion, and, after presenting all its known explanations, he came to agree with that of Buridan, namely that the motion takes place because of the mover (moving factor), which imparts "impetus" to the moving body.

In addition, the ideas of Buridan were discussed and transmitted to the students in many other commentaries written by Cracow scholars. The first Polish commentary to Aristotle's *Physics*, *Quaestiones disputatae super octo libros "Physicorum" Aristotelis* was written in the beginning of the fifteenth century by Andrzej Wężyk, one of the first magisters that Cracow University had produced. Andrzej of Kokorzyn's *Punkta super octo libros Physicorum* and the anonymous *Exercitium super octo libros Physicorum Aristotelis* (1449), and numerous important commentaries written by Jan Schelling of Głogów (see below) all discuss ideas of Buridan's physics in its purest form. Only much later were there attempts to modify the solution of the problem of forced motion, as, for example, in *Epitoma figurarum in libros Physicorum et De anima Aristotelis in Gymnasio Cracoviensi elaboratum* by Michał Falkener of Wrocław (printed in 1518). This distinguished philosopher came very close to the discovery that in a vacuum all bodies fall equally fast. But since he was discussing the influence of the medium on the moving body, he drew false conclusions from his reasoning.

In other Cracow commentaries the ideas of Buridan were also discussed and preserved. In the oldest Polish commentary to Aristotle's *De caelo et mundo*, *Quaestiones Cracoviensis super quattuor libros De caelo et mundo Aristotelis*, written by Jan of Słupcza (1433), the author considered the question whether celestial bodies are made of the same matter as the earth. In answering this question, Jan of Słupcza agreed with Buridan that there is only one kind of matter, which is governed by one set of laws.

The ideas of another great thinker, Nicole d'Oresme, were transmitted to Cracow students through the writings of other masters, as, for example, Piotr of Sienno, who in 1420 wrote a commentary to Aristotle's *Meteora*, entitled *Disputata super quattuor libros Meteorum*. Because of the above-mentioned commentary by Albert of Saxony to Aristotle's *De caelo et mundo* students in Cracow were able to learn arguments for the probable diurnal and annual motions of the earth.

The theory of impetus applied to celestial bodies had far-reaching consequences in astronomy. It eliminated the need for an "intelligence" to move planets and reduced the mechanics of motion of celestial bodies to earthly problems. The activity of God was restricted to imparting to these bodies an initial impetus, which then remained forever, since the motion did not take place in any material medium.

Let us turn to astronomy and mathematics, because it is due to them that the University of Cracow achieved its international reputation in the fifteenth century. About 1410 a rich citizen of Cracow, Jan Stobner, provided funds to form a special chair of astronomy and mathematics, the first of its kind in central Europe. A second chair of astrology was founded later by Marcin Król of Zórawica. This department also enriched the achievements of the Cracow school of astronomy.

Professors who had normal university chairs founded by the king were assigned teaching duties each semester by the drawing of lots; this "honest" rule was designed to provide for every master an equal opportunity to obtain a good income, but made it impossible for anyone to specialize in one field. The only exception to this rule was—as we have seen—the course on Aristotle's *Physics*, which was always given by the Dean of the Faculty of Arts. However, the special chairs founded by private persons, like the two chairs founded by Stobner and Król, had different rules; the professors were allowed to teach the same course for several years, which enabled them to really achieve a high level of specialization.

In the early years of the University of Cracow the teaching of mathematics and astronomy was based on the treatises *Algorismus vulgaris* and *De Sphaera* by John of Holywood (Sacrobosco), on the textbook of arithmetic by Jean de Meurs, and the astronomical tables *Tabulae Alphonsinae*. But soon Cracow masters developed enough skill to do their own calculations, as, for example, for the partial eclipse of the sun in 1406. In 1425 *Tabulae Alphonsinae* were replaced by tables calculated for the Cracow meridian: *Tabulae resolutae de mediis et veris motibus planetarum super meridianum Cracoviensem*. This proves that prior to this date there existed in Cracow a powerful group of astronomers capable of performing observations and calculations on the level of sophistication current in Europe at that time. In 1430 Sędziwój (Sendivogius) of Czechel wrote an important treatise, *Algorismus proportionum*, or tables of proportions which facilitated computations of positions of celestial bodies. One may say that at this time a Cracow school of astronomy already existed, which soon became famous throughout Europe. Cracow scholars produced their own textbooks and developed their own approach to astronomy, which they regarded as an observational and mathematical science, detached from philosophy. Undoubtedly under the influence of Buridan, Cracow scholars stressed the importance of experience and observation.

The greatest Cracow astronomers and scholars, who deserve a place in every account of Renaissance science, were Marcin Król, Marcin Bylica, Jan Schelling of Głogów and Wojciech of Brudzewo.

Marcin Król (Martin Rex) of Żórawica (ca. 1422-1453), after finishing his studies in Cracow, was accorded Stobner's chair of astronomy. In 1445 he began his travels, visiting Prague, Leipzig, Padua, and Bologna, where he taught astronomy(1448-1449) and simultaneously studied medicine. He then spent some time at the Royal Court of Hungary and in 1450 returned to Cracow.

Marcin Król found that the observed positions of celestial bodies and those calculated using the *Tabulae Alphonsinae* often differed. He decided to provide new, improved tables which he prepared using not only Greek but also Arabic sources. These tables, *Summa super Tabulas Alphonsi* (1450-1451), were then used in teaching astronomy in Cracow and were still being quoted many years later, for example, by Wojciech of Brudzewo in his commentary to Peuerbach.

Another well-known treatise by Marcin Król, *Opus de geometria* (about 1450), was the first original text on geometry written by a Polish scholar. An attempt to present geometry as a practical science, *Opus de geometria* contains a very detailed description of measuring instruments and methods. The text was very popular and useful in teaching. The third treatise by Król, *Algorismus minutiarum* (1445), replaced an older textbook by John of Holywood (Sacrobosco). In his testament Marcin Król provided for the founding of a second chair of astronomy at Cracow University.

Due to the work of Marcin Król, the study of mathematics and astronomy became extremely popular in Cracow. In the second half of the fifteenth century the University of Cracow became an important center of astronomy that was recognized throughout Europe. We have evidence for this not only in the number of students arriving from abroad, many of whom were attracted by the fame of the Cracovian astronomy (more than 660 during the period of 1451-1460, about 1600 in the last decade of the fifteenth century, and more than 1700 in the period 1501-1510), but also in the number of masters from other countries drawn by the fame of Cracow University. It is enough to mention Konrad Celtis (Conradus Celtes), Stefan Rosslein of Augsburg (later professor of astronomy in Wittenberg), Erasmus of Horitz (later professor of astronomy in Vienna), and Johannes Virdung of Hassfurt (later professor at Heidelberg), all of whom were students in Cracow.

After the death of Marcin Król, his disciples and successors cultivated and developed his achievements. Among the well-known Cracow astronomers were Andrzej Grzymała of Poznań, who in 1445 was already a professor holding Stobner's chair of astronomy, and later was twice the rector of the University,

Wojciech of Opatów, who taught astronomy and astrology in Bologna (1454-56), Mikołaj Wodka of Kwidzyń, who also taught astronomy and astrology in Bologna (1479-1480), Jakub of Zalesie, who taught in Bologna (1469-1470), Grzegorz of Nowa Wieś, Jan Stercze, Szymon of Sierpc, Marcin Biem of Olkusz, and Piotr Gaszowiec of Łoźmierz, who was three times rector of the University. Nevertheless, the greatest names of the Cracow school of astronomy remained Marcin Bylica of Olkusz, Wojciech of Brudzewo, and Jan Schelling of Głogów.

Marcin Bylica of Olkusz (ca. 1433-1493) was an alumnus and professor of the University of Cracow. During the period 1461-1466 he was in Italy, teaching astronomy in Padua (1463) and Bologna (1463-1464). In 1464 he came to Rome and became an astrologer to Pope Pius II. In 1466 he was invited to Hungary and became professor at the University at Pozsony, founded by King Matthias Corvinus.

During his stay in Italy, Bylica met Regiomontanus and became his friend and collaborator. Together they prepared the well-known astronomic tables, *Tabulae directionum*. Their collaboration also resulted in another treatise, *Dialogus inter Viennensem et Cracoviensem super Cremonensia in Planetarum Theoricas deliramenta* (1474), written as a dialogue between these two scientists. The dialogue presented the views of the Cracow and Vienna schools. Bylica and Regiomontanus concluded that many data in the *Theoricas* by Gerard of Cremona were not correct and that the criticism of that book by Georg Peuerbach was well justified.

Bylica maintained close contact with Cracow and bequeathed to the University of Cracow his collection of books and astronomical instruments, among them the famous celestial globe made in Vienna on Bylica's request in 1486, one of the oldest Arabic astrolabes of 1054, and a torquetrum built according to the description by Franko of Poland in 1284. Bylica's instruments were exhibited at the University of Cracow in 1494, and the rector encouraged masters and students to visit the exhibition. It is possible that young Copernicus was among the visitors.

Jan Schelling of Głogów (ca. 1445-1507) was one of the most erudite scholars in Cracow. He was born about 1445 in Silesia, entered the University of Cracow in 1462, and in 1468 obtained a degree of master of philosophy. In the same year he began teaching at the Faculty of Philosophy, where he continued for 40 years until his death. He taught philosophy and arts (mathematics, geometry, and astronomy), and was also interested in alchemy. He wrote many books, among them numerous commentaries to Aristotle's writings, the first Polish treatise on cosmography, a catalogue of stars (the first in Poland and one of the first in Europe), astronomical tables for the Cracow meridian, and commentaries to other astronomical treatises. His most important and best known works include *Expositio in Aristotelis libros Physicorum* (1499-15001, *Interpretatio Tabularum resolutarum ad meridianum Cracoviensem* (ca. 1488), *Tractatus de 48 imaginibus Caelestibus* (1492), and *Introductorium compendiosum in Tractatum sphaerae materialis Johannis de Sacrobosco* (Cracoviae 1506).

It is generally accepted that Jan of Głogów taught Copernicus in Cracow. In his works, Jan of Głogów discusses the position of the sun, considering it the most dignified of the planets, not only as the source of light, but also as the one which in some way may control the motion of the other planets. Copernicus must have been aware of this opinion. Earlier, Jan of Głogów was the teacher of Wojciech of Brudzewo.

Wojciech of Brudzewo, also known as Albertus of Brudzewo (1445-1497), was an astronomer and teacher of international fame. He wrote several books, among them the Cracow astronomical tables *Tabulae resolutae astronomicae* and his most famous commentary to the treatise of Georg Peuerbach, *Commentaria utilissima in theoricis planetarum*, a textbook of theoretical astronomy well-known in Europe, written in 1482 and published in Milan in 1495. By replacing the obsolete theory of planetary motions of Gerard of Cremona with the new theory elaborated by Peuerbach, Wojciech of Brudzewo significantly reformed the teaching of astronomy. When Copernicus entered the University of Cracow in 1491, Wojciech of Brudzewo was no longer teaching astronomy because in 1490 he had taken another chair and lectured only on Aristotle's writings. However, most biographers of Copernicus agree that Copernicus received instruction in astronomy from Wojciech of Brudzewo in the form of private lessons, which at that time were given outside the university curriculum by many masters. Moreover, professors who taught astronomy in Cracow after 1490 were disciples of Wojciech of Brudzewo, so that his influence on teaching was still present.

In his *Commentaria* Wojciech of Brudzewo accepted the Ptolemaic system, but did not hesitate to criticize the theory of epicycles and equants (such criticism was already present in the commentaries by Averroës to Aristotle's *Physics* and *Metaphysics*) and also Ptolemy's theory of the motion of the moon. He wrote that equants are to be regarded as fictitious circles, which only facilitate the calculation of planetary tables, and remarked that eccentrics and epicycles are to be regarded as a product of the imagination of mathematicians. As Dreyer remarks, "it is quite possible that he may have pointed out to the pupil the extraordinary role played by the sun in the planetary theories, which may have set the great mind of the young student thinking whether this would not eventually furnish the key to the riddles of the planets."[3] As we have seen above, Copernicus obtained a similar hint from Jan of Głogów.

Copernicus entered the University of Cracow in 1491 and was a student there for three years. Unfortunately, to quote Alexandre Koyré:

> We have no information about the course of studies followed by Copernicus in Cracow. Though it is certain that he made a thorough study of astronomy, we have no reason to think that he did not follow the usual curriculum of the Faculty of Arts, based on dialectics and philosophy.[4]

Indeed, we have no firm evidence about the course of studies followed by Copernicus in Cracow; that is, we have no documents such as his lecture notes,

26. Copernicus' name in the *Album Studiosorum* of the Cracow University for the half-year 1491-92. *"Nicolaus Nicolai de Thuronia solvit totum"* (Biblioteka Jagiellońska, Kraków).

grades, etc. However, we do have detailed information about courses in astronomy and mathematics which were taught at the University of Cracow during the period 1491-1495. The list of those courses which Copernicus must have taken and the teachers who taught them is as follows:

1491, winter semester: Wojciech of Pniewy *De Sphaera* according to Sacrobosco, or an introduction to astronomy

1492, winter semester: Bartłomiej of Lipnica—*Geometria* of Euclid

1493, summer semester: Szymon of Sierpc—*Theoricae* planetarum according to the commentary of Wojciech of Brudzewo; Bernard of Biskupie—*Tabulae eclipsium*

1493, winter semester: Michał of Wrocław—*Tabulae resolutae*, or astronomical tables calculated at the meridian of Cracow; Marcin Biem of Olkusz—*Calendarium* of Regiomontanus

1494, summer semester: Wojciech of Szamotuły—*Astrologia*

1494, winter semester: Wojciech of Szamotuły—*Tetrabiblos* of Ptolemy

As Koyré says, Copernicus also must have taken courses in dialectics and philosophy; therefore, he heard the lectures of Jan of Głogów and Wojciech of Brudzewo. Copernicus was ". . . not a narrow specialist, an 'astronomico'—technician, but a man deeply imbued with the entire, rich culture of his period, an artist, savant, scholar, man of action: a humanist in the best sense of the word".[5]

There is enough evidence to claim that it was during his studies in Cracow in the unusual atmosphere of the highest standards of teaching accompanied by criticism of old concepts that Copernicus must have begun his contemplation about a new and better order of the universe. Concerning the probable importance of Copernicus' Cracovian background Angus Armitage has written:

> During his years at Cracow, Copernicus began to make a collection of books on mathematics and astronomy, some of which he kept as long as he lived. Many of these books have been preserved to our own day. Some of them contain jottings and calculations in the handwriting of Copernicus which date right back to the days when he was a student at Cracow. Some of these calculations give us the impression that he had begun to take the first steps in the construction of his new system of astronomy even at that early stage in his career.[6]

Further, we know that Copernicus had made calculations concerning the occultation by the moon of the bright star Aldebaran which occurred on 9 March 1497, and which he had observed in Bologna. This was only several months after his arrival in Italy, and he could not possibly have learned the techniques required for such complicated calculations there. His next calculations concerned the eclipse of the moon, which he observed on 6 November 1500 in Rome.

During his stay in Rome Copernicus gave a series of lectures which, according to George Joachim Rheticus, not only attracted many students but also caused interest among masters of mathematics and astronomy. This is what Koyré says about Copernicus' stay in Italy: "Whilst there, he no doubt continued his studies in astronomy, though he seems to have been sufficiently advanced in his subject."[7] According to Copernicus' disciple, Rheticus, his master (Copernicus) was for the well-known astronomer Domenico Maria da Novara "non tam discipulus quam adjutor et testis observationum".[8]

There can be, therefore, no doubt that it was from the Cracow school of astronomy that Copernicus acquired his technical mastery in astronomical calculations. Moreover, in the very style of his approach to astronomy we can easily recognize the guiding idea of the Cracow school: that astronomy is a mathematical science based on observations.[9]

But there was more than technical mastery in calculations that Copernicus had in all probability acquired from Cracow. We cannot neglect the influence upon a young student of the humanist circles in Cracow led by Phillipo Buonaccorsi, called Callimachus, who organized there the scientific society, "Sodalitas Litteraria," which was reorganized about 1490 by Celtes into "Sodalitas Vistulana." Callimachus, an eager adherent of Italian Neoplatonism, was a friend of the Bishop Lucas Watzelrode, the uncle and protector of Copernicus. No doubt Copernicus knew Callimachus personally, since the latter possessed houses in Toruń (the birthplace of Copernicus) which he often visited.

It is known that the eminent Renaissance philosopher, Marsilio Ficino of Florence, was a close friend of Callimachus. After the publication of his book,

27. Nicolaus Copernicus, *Commentariolus*. The first page of the copy of the first sketch of Copernicus' astronomical system. (Nationalbibliothek, Wien). Reprinted from Aleksander Ludwik Birkenmajer, *Mikołaj Kopernik* (Warszawa, Sztuka, 1953).

De sole: De lumine (published in Florence about 1490), he immediately sent a few copies to Callimachus in Cracow, and it is very probable that Copernicus read it at the beginning of his studies. Ficino praised the sun as the most wonderful light in the sky, as the symbol of God which directs the harmonious course of the world; he also added that the sun was created first and that it is in the center of the heavens.

During his studies at the University of Cracow Copernicus must have heard from his teachers—as we have seen above—similar, although less poetic, statements about the privileged role of the sun.

We know also that during his studies in Cracow Copernicus must have become acquainted with Cicero's text *Somnium Scipionis*, which was commented on during the University lectures. There he could have found sentences on the motion of Mercury and Venus around the sun.

But there is still more to it. Let me quote Eugeniusz Rybka:

> An indirect proof of the great influence of the Cracow intellectual environment on Copernicus may be found in his strong connections with Cracow University. He always referred his observations made in Frombork to the Cracow meridian, and maintained a correspondence with Cracow friends, like Marcin Biem and Bernard Wapowski. Albertus Caprinus of Buk gave the following opinion on Copernicus in 1542: "Nicholas Copernicus, the Canon of Varmia,... derived the beginnings of his admirable mathematical works, of those he has written, and of those he is going to publish in a still larger number, at this University of ours, which not only does he not deny....but on the contrary admits that everything he has become he owes to our Academy."
>
> These words were written still in Copernicus' lifetime and were obviously founded upon some statements which he made himself. We know that the idea of the real structure of the world took a complete and lifelong hold of his mind. And one always remembers best the place at which the idea was first conceived. Thus, the astronomer's statement, that he owed everything he became to the Academy of Cracow, may justly lead to the conclusion that he owed to it his new conception of the structure of the world, since this first came to him in Cracow, within and under the influence of the town's intellectual climate."[10]

It should be noted that the importance of Copernicus' Cracow studies for the origin of his revolutionary ideas is, for many historians of science, a fact unknown or underestimated in comparison with his studies in Italy.

Let me quote several examples. Charles Singer in his well-known textbook[11] says "Copernicus, a Pole . . . studied at several Italian universities." Herbert Butterfield in his highly influential book[12] writes about Copernicus that "he had passed a number of years in Italy at one of the most brilliant periods of the Renaissance." S.F. Mason says in his widely used textbook[13] that "Copernicus . . . born in Thorn, a Hansa town . . . studied in Italy 1496-1506." William Dampier[14] maintains that Copernicus was " . . . a mathematician and astronomer with a Polish father and a German mother" and then he adds: "Copernicus spent six years in Italy and became the pupil of Novara."

In the four books mentioned above there is not a single word about Kraków! Abraham Wolf in his prestigious treatise[15] writes that Copernicus

> spent three years at the University of Cracow. Here, his interest in mathematics and astronomy was awakened under the teaching of Albert Brudzewski, and he became accustomed to the use of astronomical instruments and to the observations of the heavens.

But after this, Wolf adds:

> There is little doubt that it was during his residence in Italy that Copernicus received the initial impulse towards the reform of astronomy, which he achieved in his later, more secluded years.

To the aforementioned opinion of Angus Armitage concerning Copernicus' Cracovian years and the suggestion of their importance for his great discovery, other arguments have been added supporting this point of view. According to Dreyer, who implied that Copernicus' ideas had probably taken shape prior to his stay in Italy

> however useful the acquaintance with Novara may have been to Copernicus, we may take it for granted that neither he nor any other Italian savant sowed the seed which eventually produced the fruit known as the Copernican system.[16]

According to Jerome R. Ravetz:

> we can be farily certain that Copernicus conceived of and worked out his profound innovation while he was still at Cracow. It was very much a young man's stroke of genius, which then took a lifetime to consolidate."[17]

This statement is based on an analysis of the first sketch of Copernius' cosmology *Commentariolus* (unpublished by him) which lead Ravetz to the conclusion that its "numerical data are all taken from the Alfonsine table," that *Commentariolus* shows no trace of acquaintance with the *Epitome* of Ptolemy's *Almagest* published in 1496, the year when Copernicus went to Italy.

A broad overview of the social and intellectual changes which occured in fifteenth century Poland permitted Paul W. Knoll to formulate the supposition

> that in a time of change, when the social foundations of one world view were being profoundly altered; that at a university where the technical level of science and the subtelty of philosophical debate was abreast of that of any *studium* in Europe; that at an institution where

the new critical attitude of humanism had deeply penetrated the curriculum: that in this time and place, the still-unformed youth whose *De revolutionibus* was to be a revolution spent years which were as fundamental to his development as were the later experiences in Italy. This was the context from which he came."[18]

What all these opinions have in common is the recognition of the importance of Cracow University for Copernicus' training in astronomy, philosophy, and in the ideas of humanism, is the acknowledgement that Cracow was then the seat of one of the leading univerrsities in Europe.

The place of the University of Cracow relative to other Renaissance centers of learning has been properly evaluated by Gale Christianson:

> While the University of Cracow has received far less attention from contemporary scholars than many of Europe's other leading universities, the distinguished institution attracted eminent humanists and students from throughout Europe, including many from as far away as Sweden, Italy, and France.... Cracow...certainly was deserving of its reputation as one of the main centers of European commerce and science.[19]

The above points of view marked a return to high regard for the University of Cracow that was expressed by Copernicus' foreign contemporaries.

Hartmann Schedel of Nuremberg, the author of the well-known chronicle *Liber cronicarum*, 1493, wrote that the Cracow University was glorious, it was "filled with many famous, learned men who teach the liberal arts, rhetoric, poetics, philosophy and physics. Astronomy is the most highly developed science. In the whole of Germany (and I know this from more than one source) one can not find a more famous school".[20]

The English humanist Leonard Coxe praised "the most famous Academy" of Cracow, and among its most distinguished and best-known professors he listed Marcin Król, Andrzej Grzymała, Wojciech of Brudzewo, Jan of Głogów, Maciej of Miechów, Marcin Bylica of Olkusz, and Michał Falkener of Wrocław.[21]

Finally, still another a recurring problem in scholarly discussions is the question of Copernicus' nationality. As Edward Rosen pointed out during the International Conference "Copernicus and Modern Cosmology" (Rome, 1975)

> Actually, there is no problem. There is a fictitious or pseudo-problem in this matter, and the whole controversy has revolved around the failure to recognize the shift in the meaning of the word nation. If we look at the matter in its own context, there is not the slightest doubt that throughout the seventy years of his life Nicholas Copernicus was born, lived, and died a subject of the King of Poland.... I would like to call your attention to the fact that in the statutes of the German Nation of the University of Bologna, in which Copernicus was inscribed as a member, it is stated that the membership shall include Bohemians, Moravians, Lithuanians, and Danes.

These four groups are mentioned by name, and it is therefore obvious that the concept of nation, when these statutes were written, was a very different thing from the concept of nation that we have underlying the United Nations today or the League of Nations a generation or so ago. . . . Philipp Melanchthon referred to Copernicus as a Sarmatian astronomer, by which he undoubtedly meant a Polish astronomer,... There is not the slightest doubt that when Melanchthon wrote contemptuously and antagonistically about Copernicus in that famous letter to Mithobius, wherein Melanchthon called Copernicus "that Sarmatian astronomer," he undoubtedly meant that Polish astronomer.[22]

In his remarks, Edward Rosen emphasized that Copernicus' national affiliation became completely obscured after the partitions of Poland in the late eighteenth century when the land where he was born was incorporated into the Prussian Empire. Reliance upon nineteenth-century texts, in large part penned by German historians who had no reason to praise the scientific achievements of the citizens of a country which no longer existed, has perpetuated the "problem" of Copernicus' nationality. In the history of science the texts written a hundred years ago are still being used as reference material; in a similar manner they provided the information which found its way into some contemporary encyclopedias and biographic dictionaries.[23]

Notes

1. *Historia nauki polskiej* (History of Polish Science), ed. by Bogdan Suchodolski, vol. 1 (Wrocław: Ossolineum, 1970) and also on the book by Ryszard Palacz, *Filozofia polska wieków średnich* (Polish Philosophy of the Middle Ages) (Warsaw: Wiedza Powszechna, 1980).
2. See Mieczysław Markowski, *Burydanizm w Polsce w okresie przedkopernikańskim* (Buridanism in Poland before Copernicus) (Wrocław: Ossolineum, 1971).
3. Johan Ludwig Emil Dreyer, *A History of Astronomy from Thales to Kepler* (New a0.25York: Dover Publications, 1953), chapter 13.
4. Alexandre Koyré, *The Astronomical Revolution: Copernicus, Kepler, Borelli*, trans. by E.W. Maddison (Ithaca: Cornell University Press, 1973), p. 20.
5. Koyré, p. 20ff.
6. Angus Armitage, *The World of Copernicus* (New York: The New American Library, 1951), p. 59.
7. Koyré, p. 21.
8. Nicolai Copernici Torinensis, *De revolutionibus orbium   coelestium...* item narratio prima per M. Georgium Ioachimum Rheticum..., Basileae, 1565, p. 197.
9. Grażyna Rosińska, "L'École astronomique de Cracovie et la révolution Copernicienne," in *Avant, Avec, Aprés Copernic* (Paris: Albert Blanchard, 1975), p. 89.
10. Eugeniusz Rybka, "The Influence of the Cracow Intellectual Climate at the End of the Fifteenth Century upon the Origin of the Heliocentric System," *Vistas in Astronomy*, vol. 9, ed. Arthur Beer (Oxford: Pergamon Press, 1967), p. 16a.

11. Charles Singer, *A Short History of Scientific Ideas to 1900* (Oxford: Oxford University Press, 1972), p. 212.

12. Herbert Butterfield, *The Origins of Modern Science 1300-1800* (New York: The Free Press, 1965), p. 38.

13. Stephen F. Mason, *A History of the Sciences* (New York: Collier Books, 1962), p. 127.

14. William Cecil Dampier, *A History of Science* (New York: Macmillan, 1932), pp. 121, 122.

15. Abraham Wolf, *A History of Science, Technology, and Philosophy in the 16th and 17th Centuries* (New York: Macmillan, 1935), p. 11.

16. Dreyer, p. 307.

17. Jerome R. Ravetz "The Origins of the Copernican Revolution," *Scientific American* 215 (October, 1966: 88-89; see also idem *Astronomy and Cosmology in the Achievement of Nicolaus Copernicus* (Wrocław: Ossolineum, 1965), pp. 69-70.

18. Paul W. Knoll "The World of Young Copernicus: Society, Science, and the University," in *Science and Society, Past, Present, and Future* ed. Nicholas H. Steneck (Ann Arbor: The University of Michigan Press, 1975), pp. 19-44.

19. Gale E. Christianson, *This Wild Abyss*: The Story of the Men who made Modern Astronomy (New York: The Free Press, 1978), p. 116.

20. *Sarmatia the Early Polish Kingdom from the original Nuremberg Chronicle by Hartmann Schedel... 1493*, tr. Bogdan Dereszewicz (Los Angeles: Planton Press, 1976), p. 30.

21. Palacz, op. cit., p. 251.

22. Edward Rosen, "Copernicus and His relation to Italian Science," in Accademia nazionale dei Lincei, Q.N. 216, Problemi attuali di scienza e di cultura, Convegno internazionale sul tema: *Copernico e la cosmologia moderna* (Rome, 1975), pp. 66-68.

23. See for example the information about Copernicus in Chambers' Biographical Dictionary (New York: St. Martin's Press, 1961) repeated in the revised 1969 edition.

9

What Copernicus Owed to the West, And What We Owe to Copernicus

Edward Rosen

hat we owe to Nicholas Copernicus (1473-1543) is the first effective statement that our earth is a planet, revolving around the sun in a year, while rotating around its own axis once a day. Before Copernicus, these statements about the earth had been propounded, either separately or in combination. But they had either been ignored or combatted for a variety of reasons which still operated in Copernicus' time and thereafter to impede the spread of his ideas. He succeeded in modifying the thinking of mankind, however, where his predecessors had failed, because his was the first completely developed and carefully reasoned presentation of geokineticism, the doctrine of the moving earth.[1]

Exactly how Copernicus became the world's first successful geokineticist has not yet been fully clarified. He himself shed a little light on this interesting question, but he did not undertake to answer it in full detail. Historians of science are quite familiar with the type of thinker who takes delight in retracing his missteps, correcting his errors, and gloating over his achievements. Copernicus, however, did not belong to that loquacious fraternity. He was rather the tight-lipped recluse who, instead of preserving his preliminary notes to satisfy the curiosity of posterity, discarded them with a view to leaving only the finished product, the consummation of a long and intense effort. In his case, fortunately, the finished product was not quite finished, for he was in no hurry to publish. As a lifelong canon of Varmia, a wealthy diocese, he felt no insecurity about his financial future. This would not be assured by the publication of an admittedly controversial book that challenged traditional dogma hallowed by the acceptance of centuries, if not millenia. Instead of increasing his income or advancing him in his chosen career, that book might have brought down on his prudent head the disapproval of his peers and superiors. No

161

wonder that Copernicus kept his volume hidden among his private papers for decades, and in the end consented to release his manuscript to the printer only in response to the pressure of close friends, led by the bishop of Chełmno, Tiedemann Giese. The covering letter of this printed book bore the signature of Cardinal Nicolaus Schonberg and the dedication was directed to Pope Paul III. These ecclesiastical outer wrappings were designed to provide substantial insurance against a possible charge of heresy, a fate forestalled by the death of Copernicus and of the Master of the Sacred and Apostolic Palace, Bartholomeo Spina of Pisa,[2] but reserved for a loyal admirer of Copernicus and gifted amplifier of his doctrine, Galileo Galilei.

Copernicus' decision to publish his book meant that a fair copy had to be prepared for the printer, for Copernicus had previously composed without the help of a secretary, amanuensis, or copyist. Without any such scribal aid, he wrote his manuscript, 212 folios long, forty-odd lines to a page, with his own hand. His autograph contained numerous corrections between the lines and in the margins. Whole pages were crossed out and replaced. Some sections were out of their proper order, which had to be indicated by special handwritten signs. A manuscript in such a state of disarray could not possibly be dispatched to a publisher in a distant land with any prospect of procuring a satisfactory printed product. After the fair copy was finished, it was taken to the printer by Copernicus' only disciple, George Joachim Rheticus, who was to be its editor. But the autograph itself remained behind with the author and by a phenomenal stroke of good luck has been preserved to our times.[3] A painstaking analysis of the changes made by Copernicus in his autograph permits us, as it were, to compare his first thoughts and second thoughts, and sometimes even his third thoughts, in order thereby to gain some understanding of how he arrived at his epoch-making result.

This could not have been attained without first-hand knowledge of the great masters. These were ancient Greek thinkers, whose works for the most part had not yet been translated into Latin—the international scholarly language of Copernicus' time—or into any modern language. If Copernicus was to acquaint himself with the most advanced thought available to his generation in his field of specialization he would have to learn classical Greek. The humanist movement had swept eastward to the University of Cracow, where he enrolled in the winter semester of 1491.[4] During the three or more years he spent there, however, no instruction in Greek was offered. But when Copernicus went west in 1496 to enroll in the University of Bologna, ostensibly for the purpose of studying law, he encountered Antonio Codro Urceo, a professor of Greek who was friendly with the foremost publisher of classical Greek texts, Aldo Manuzio. A collection of several dozen Greek letter-writers was dedicated by Manuzio to Urceo.[5] From this collection Copernicus chose one epistolographer. With the help of a Greek-Latin dictionary recently published not far from Bologna,[6] Copernicus translated Theophylactus Simocatta's eighty-five letters into Latin. His slender volume was printed in Cracow in 1509,[7] constituting the first published translation from Greek to originate in Poland. His modest contribution to the advancement of humanism in his native country repaid the West in some measure for making the Greek language accessible to him.

Even more important for Copernicus' intellectual development than his contact with Urceo at Bologna was his association with the local professor of astronomy, Domenico Maria da Novara, a childless bachelor who employed no servants. Copernicus lived in his house and "mastered his thinking thoroughly."[8] Copernicus' earliest recorded observation occurred on 9 March 1497 after sunset in Bologna.[9] More than four decades later he told his disciple that "at Bologna . . . he was not so much the pupil as the assistant and witness of observations"[10] of his unconventional professor of astronomy. In a published work he had maintained that the latitudes of Mediterranean cities were more than one degree greater than those recorded in Ptolemy's *Geography*. This increase was to be explained by a (supposed) shift in the direction of the earth's axis.[11] Ptolemy, however, who was also the greatest Greek astronomer and the leading authority in that field in Copernicus' student days, had insisted that the earth was absolutely motionless. But if the earth was not completely deprived of motion, then Ptolemy's astronomy might be just as vulnerable as his *Geography*.

A more easily demonstrable defect in Ptolemy's astronomy had been detected long before by an Islamic scientist.[12] But Copernicus first learned about this serious weakness in Ptolemy's lunar theory from the *Epitome* of Ptolemy's *Syntaxis* (then miscalled the "Almagest") that was published in Venice in 1496,[13] the year of Copernicus' arrival in Italy. Besides epitomizing Ptolemy's *Syntaxis*, the *Epitome* summarized the results achieved by astronomers later than Ptolemy, some of them critical of him. The *Epitome*'s exposure of the flaw in Ptolemy's theory of the moon was repeated by Copernicus in his first brief presentation of his geokinetic alternative to the geostatic Ptolemaic astronomy,[14] an alternative never proposed by any earlier critic of Ptolemy. Withholding his name as author, and declining to give this presentation any title, Copernicus circulated a few copies among trusted friends. The historian and geographer Maciej z Miechowa (Maciej of Miechów), Professor at the Cracow University, listed it among his books and manuscripts in an inventory which he completed on 1 May 1514.[15] Subsequently this untitled presentation acquired the title "*Commentariolus*," by which it is now commonly known. Domenico Maria da Novara and the Venetian *Epitome* of Ptolemy undoubtedly played a certain indeterminable part in stimulating Copernicus to accept the role of open challenger to Ptolemy's tight grip on astronomical thinking.

That grip not only kept the earth motionless, but fastened it forever in the center of the universe. Any loose heavy object, such as a rock sliding down the side of a mountain, moved as close as it could to the center of the universe, which was identified by Ptolemy with the center of the stationary earth. When Copernicus set the earth in motion, rocks continued to slide down the sides of terrestrial mountains. But now they approached the center of the Copernican earth, which was in constant motion at a considerable distance from the center of the Copernican universe. Then what about loose rocks on the moon? They did not fly off into space, seeking the center of the Copernican universe, which was in or near the center of the sun. Instead of whirling around in space, loose lunar rocks slid down toward the center of the moon. Loose heavy objects on Mars similarly sought the center of that planet. The same was true for all the other planets. In other words, there was no longer a single center of gravity, as in Ptolemy's geocentric universe. Instead, in Copernicus' heliocentric universe every heavenly body had its own center of gravity. The earth, with its own center of gravity, was a planet, and like other planets, it revolved around the sun. Like the other planets, the Copernican earth was a heavenly body racing through space, whereas the pre-Copernican earth had been too gross to bestir itself. This drastic change of the earth's status in the cosmos is a part of what we owe to Copernicus.

Here, however, he had to tread very cautiously. He avoided stating explicitly what obviously followed from the planetary status he conferred on the earth.

But he did not close his eyes to the possibility that the Bible might be quoted against him. In his dedication to Pope Paul III he warned:

> Perhaps there will be babblers who claim to be judges of astronomy although completely ignorant of the subject and, badly distorting some passage of Scripture to their purpose, will dare to find fault with my undertaking and censure it. I disregard them even to the extent of despising their criticism as unfounded. For it is not unknown that Lactantius, otherwise an illustrious writer, but hardly an astronomer, speaks quite childishly about the earth's shape when he mocks those who declared that the earth has a form of a globe. Hence, scholars need not be surprised if any such persons will likewise ridicule me. Astronomy is written for astronomers,[16]

not for theologians who meddle in a discipline in which they have not been trained. The authority of the early Christian writers carries no weight in a scientific discipline like astronomy, as the lamentable example of Lactantius shows beyond all cavil. Who will dispute the roundness of the earth simply because Lactantius made fun of those who so described it? A sharp line must be drawn between disciplines dominated by the harsh voice of authority and those which hearken to the dulcet tones of sweet reasonableness. In the west, the slow undermining of authoritarianism and the growing resort to rational discussion in scientific inquiries were furthered by Copernicus' denunciation of distortions of the Bible for non-biblical ends.

Copernicus lived in the epoch of the great voyages of discovery and exploration that radically altered the course of human history. He was a student at Cracow when Columbus discovered the New World, and at Bologna when Da Gama rounded the Cape of Good Hope. He knew about

> the islands discovered in our time under the rulers of Spain and Portugal, and especially America, named after the ship's captain who

Theophilacti scolasti-
ci Simocati eple morales:rurales
et amatorie interpretatione latina:

28. Theophylaktos Simokattes, *Epistolae morales, rurales et amatoriae*, Cracoviae, 1509. The title page of Copernicus' translation from Greek into Latin (Biblioteka Jagiellońska, Kraków).

NICOLAI CO'
PERNICI TORINENSIS
DE REVOLVTIONIBVS ORBI=
um cœleftium, Libri VI.

Habes in hoc opere iam recens nato, & ædito,
ftudiofe lector, Motus ftellarum, tam fixarum,
quàm erraticarum, cum ex ueteribus, tum etiam
ex recentibus obferuationibus reftitutos:& no=
uis infuper ac admirabilibus hypothefibus or=
natos. Habes etiam Tabulas expeditifsimas, ex
quibus eofdem ad quoduis tempus quàm facilli
me calculare poteris. Igitur eme, lege, fruere.

Ἀγεωμέτρητος ὐδεὶς ἐισίτω.

Norimbergæ apud Ioh. Petreium,
Anno M. D. XLIII.

29. Nicolai Copernici Torinensis, *De Revolutionibus orbium coelestium*, *Libri VI*, Norimbergae,
1543. The title page of the first edition of Copernicus' work (Indiana University Lilly Library,
Bloomington).

NICOLAI COPERNICI

net, in quo terram cum orbe lunari tanquam epicyclo contineri
diximus. Quinto loco Venus nono menfe reducitur. Sextum
deniq̃ locum Mercurius tenet, octuaginta dierum fpacio circū
currens. In medio uero omnium refidet Sol. Quis enim in hoc

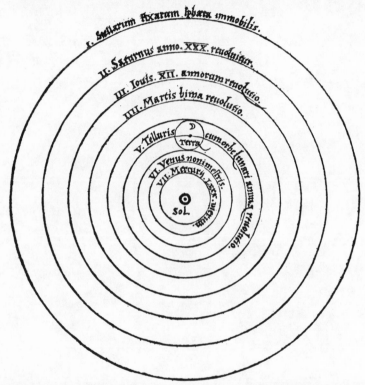

pulcherimo templo lampadem hanc in alio uel meliori loco po
neret, quàm unde totum fimul pofsit illuminare? Siquidem non
inepte quidam lucernam mundi, alij mentem, alij rectorem uo-
cant. Trimegiftus uifibilem Deum, Sophoclis Electra intuentē
omnia. Ita profecto tanquam in folio regali Sol refidens circum
agentem gubernat Aftrorum familiam. Tellus quoq̃ minime
fraudatur lunari minifterio, fed ut Ariftoteles de animalibus
ait, maximā Luna cū terra cognationē habet. Concipit interea à
Sole terra, & impregnatur annuo partu. Inuenimus igitur fub
hac

30. Nicolai Copernici Torinensis, *De Revolutionibus orbium coelestium, Libri VI*, Norimbergae, 1543. Verso of folio 9 with the drawing representing the heliocentric system (Indiana University Lilly Library, Bloomington).

31. Galilaeo Galilaei, *Dialogus de systemate mundi*, Londini 1663. The title page of the London reprint of the Latin edition 1635 of Galileo's Dialog about the Ptolemaic and Copernican Systems of the Universe, showing Artistoteles, Ptolomeus, and Copernicus (Indiana University Lilly Library, Bloomington).

found it. On account of its still undisclosed size it is thought to be a second group of inhabited countries (*orbem terrarum*). There are also many other islands, heretofore unknown. So little reason have we to marvel at the existence of antipodes or antichthones. Indeed, geometrical reasoning about the location of America compels us to believe that it is diametrically opposite to the Ganges district of India.

Ptolemy, whose authority in geography matched his eminence in astronomy, had categorically rejected the view that the entire earth is completely surrounded by water. Yet Copernicus dared to ask "For what are the inhabited countries and the mainland itself but an island larger than the others?"[17] That question was uttered by a free mind alert to fresh movements of men and ideas.

It is well known that Johannes Kepler (1571-1630) was the great continuator and ardent defender of Copernicus' ideas and the following statement of his is well known:

> Because I am absolutely convinced of the Copernican theory, a solemn awe prevents me from teaching anything else, be it for the glory of my mind or for the pleasure of those people who are annoyed at the strangeness of this theory. I am satisfied to use my discovery to guard the gate of the temple in which Copernicus celebrates at the high altar.[18]

In 1589 Kepler was admitted to that leading Lutheran center of higher learning, Tübingen University. There he had the good fortune to study astronomy with Michael Mästlin (1550-1631). Kepler owed a lifetime debt to Mästlin for introducing him to the ideas of Copernicus. Already when he was a student at Tübingen he wrote in 1593 a dissertation which dealt with the following question: how would the phenomena occurring in the heavens appear to an observer stationed on the moon? Kepler had hit upon this ingenious device in an effort to overcome the deeprooted hostility to the Copernican astronomy. According to Copernicus, the earth moves very swiftly. But the people who live on the earth do not see or hear or feel this movement. Yet they can watch the moon perform various motions. These lunar motions, however, would escape detection by an observer located on the moon, for the simple reason that he would be participating in those motions. Since the lunar motions would not be apparent to an observer there, by the same token the terrestrial motions are not noticed by observers here. This seems to have been the basic theme of Kepler's 1593 dissertation.

Kepler expressed his greatest praise of Copernicus on the title page of his first major work, the *Mysterium Cosmographicum*, published in 1596 and based numerically on the Copernicus System of the relative distances of planets from the sun:

> Addita est erudita Narratio M. Georgii Ioachimi Rhetici, de Libris Revolutionum, atque admirandis de numero, ordine, et distantiis

Sphaerarum Mundi hypothesibus, excellentissimi Mathematici, toti-
usque Astronomiae Restauratoris D. Nicolai Copernici.[19]

Kepler was both a sincere Christian and a convinced Copernican, as he demonstrated in Chapter 5 of the *Cosmographic Mystery* devoted to a reconciliation
between the Bible and Copernicanism, omitted by Kepler on the advice of the
Tübingen faculty but later incorporated into the Introduction to his *Astronomia
nova* published in 1609. This is only one example of Kepler's persistent struggle
to persuade his fellow Lutherans, and all others who were willing to listen, to
accept Copernicus' new and revolutionary cosmology, to convince them that
the Copernican astronomy was a giant stride forward in a direction that men-
aced no true believer.

In the years 1618-1621 Kepler's great work, *Epitome Astronomiae Copernicanae*,
was printed. In inserting "Copernican" in the title Kepler emphasized his open
espousal of the new cosmology, and in Book I he stated with delight: "In our
days all the most outstanding philosophers and astronomers agree with Copernicus."[20]   At the end of his life Kepler finished his *Somnium seu Opus Pos-
thumum de Astronomia Lunari*, as it was finally entitled, in which he returned
to the device of his student dissertation. In the *Notes on the Astronomical Dream*
Kepler wrote: "The purpose of my *Dream* is to use the example of the moon
to build up an argument in favor of the motion of the earth."[21] Kepler's astronomical purpose in writing *The Dream* was to adduce a novel argument in favor
of Copernicanism by transferring the observer from the earth to the moon.

Copernicus said twice that "the moon has the closest kinship with the earth."[22]
For Aristotle and Ptolemy, there could be no degree of kinship between these
two bodies. For the two Greek thinkers, the Moon was a celestial body in
unceasing motion, whereas the Earth abided in unceasing rest, being incapable
of the motion which is the distinguishing mark of a heavenly body. Copernicus'
twice asserted kinship impressed Kepler, who reasoned that:

> the clearest proof of this kinship is in the ebb and flow of the tide,
> concerning which see the Introduction to my *Commentaries on the
> Motions of the Planet Mars*. When the moon is located directly above
> the Atlantic Ocean, the so-called Southern Ocean, the Eastern Ocean,
> or the Indian Ocean, it attracts the waters clinging to the sphere of
> the earth. The effect of this attraction is that from all sides the waters
> rush to the huge area which is directly below the moon and is not
> closed off by the continents, so that the shores are exposed. But in
> the meantime, while the waters are in motion, the moon moves away
> from its position directly above an ocean. The mass of water beating
> against the western shore is no longer affected by the attractive force,
> flows back, and in turn pounds against the eastern shore[23]

In the Introduction to his book on Mars, Kepler had declared:

> If the earth ceased to attract its own waters to itself, all the water in
> its seas would be lifted up and would flow into the body of the moon.

The sphere of the attractive power which is in the moon extends as far as the earth.[24]

In Kepler's view, the moon exerts an attraction not only on the flowing waters of the earth but on the entire planet earth itself. This attraction is mutual, since the earth attracts the moon. If these two bodies were not restrained

each in its own orbit, the earth would move toward the moon . . . and the moon would come down toward the earth . . . and they would be joined together there.[25]

Such a joining would exemplify Kepler's novel definition of gravity as a mutual corporeal tendency of kindred bodies to unite or join together.[26] Kepler's novel definition of gravity was an extension of Copernicus, earlier and equally novel definition:

Gravity is nothing but a certain natural desire . . . implanted in parts, to gather as a unity and a whole by combining in the form of a globe.[27]

Whereas Copernicus confined his desire to parts of the same unity, Kepler extended it to kindred bodies (*cognata corpora*), his prime example consisting of the earth and the moon, the very bodies which Copernicus had singled out as having the closest kinship with each other. Later on, Kepler dropped the requirement of kindred bodies from his definition of gravity when he said:

I define "gravity" as a force of mutual attraction, similar to magnetic attraction.[28]

He dropped the requirement of kindred bodies when he learned from experienced sailors that the ocean tides are higher when the sun and moon are found on the same straight line through the earth:

The causes of the ocean tides seem to be the bodies of the sun and moon attracting the ocean waters by a certain force similar to magnetism. Of course, the body of the earth likewise attracts its own waters, an attraction which we call gravity.[29]

Kepler took this small additional step in the direction which led toward universal gravitation. This regards all bodies in the universe as attracting one another, so that they are all kindred bodies, the ultimate generalization of Copernicus' special kinship of earth and moon. In the three editions of his *Mathematical Foundations of Natural Philosophy*, Isaac Newton (1643-1727) spoke of Kepler half a dozen times; in addition, his handwritten note in his personal copy of the second edition referring to Kepler twice more failed to be included in the third edition.[30] A golden chain stretches from the rejection of a unique center of gravitation to the promulgation of universal gravitation, with Copernicus supplying the first link.

Copernicus' assertion of the special kinship between earth and moon led, through Kepler, to Newton's universal gravitation. Our recognition that the earth is a planet in motion is likewise due to Copernicus.

With dogged perseverence, Copernicus reexamined every aspect of astronomy that was known in his time. In each case he asked himself how the earth's motion altered previous ideas. In some instances he found the required correction with amazing clarity, but in others he failed to free his mind from old misconceptions. These his gifted followers later discarded.

Thus Kepler rejected the hoary belief that heavenly bodies, being perfect, had to move in perfect orbits, that is, circles or combinations of circles. Recalling that the circle is mathematically only a special kind of ellipse, Kepler demonstrated the ellipticity of the planetary orbits. Then, perfecting a thought of Copernicus that was extended by Kepler, Newton proved that the elliptical orbit resulted from a combination of two actions — the planet's inertial tendency to fly off at a tangent to its curved path, and the sun's gravitational attraction, pulling it toward a point inside its orbit.

What Copernicus did was to institute an authentic revolution in astronomy. By assigning the earth its true place in the cosmos, he made an imperishable contribution to cosmological thought. He thereby laid the foundations of that splendid edifice within which is housed modern astronomy. In this way he recompensed the West for making classical Greek available to him, and undermining his faith in Ptolemy.

Notes

1. Nicolaus Copernicus, *De revolutionibus orbium coelestum* (Nuremberg, 1543); English translation and commentary by Edward Rosen, in *Nicholas Copernicus: Complete Works*, cited hereafter as "NCCW," 2 (Baltimore: Johns Hopkins University Press, 1978).

2. Edward Rosen, "Was Copernicus' Revolutions Approved by the Pope?", *Journal of the History of Ideas* 36 (1975): 531-542.

3. Facsimile in *NCCW*, 1 (Warsaw, London: Macmillan, 1972).

4. *Album studiosorum universitatis Cracoviensis*, 2, 12; ed. Adam Chmiel (Cracow, 1892).

5. *Epistolae diversorum philosophorum, oratorum, rhetorum* (Venetiis: Aldo Pio Manuzio, 1499).

6. Johannes Crestonus, *Dictionarium graecum cum interpretatione latina* (Modena: Dionisius Bertochiis, 1499-1500). See Paweł Czartoryski, "The Library of Copernicus," p. 366, no. 3, in *Science and History: Studies in Honor of Edward Rosen* (*Studia Copernicana*, 16; Wrocław: Ossolineum, 1978).

7. Facsimile reprint, in *Teofilakt Symokatta, Listy* (Theophylactus Simocatta— Letters), ed. Ryszard Gansiniec (Wrocław: Ossolineum, 1953).

8. Edward Rosen, "Copernicus and His Relation to Italian Science," in *Accademia nazionale dei Lincei*, Q.N. 216, Problemi attuali di scienza e di cultura, Convegno internazionale sul tema: *Copernico e la cosmologia moderna* (Rome, 1975), p. 36.

9. *NCCW*, 2, 218/9.

10. Edward Rosen, *Three Copernican Treatises*, 3rd ed. (New York: Octagon Books, 1971) (cited hereafter as "TCT"), p. 111.

11. P. 323 in the work cited in n. 8 above.

12. For the emergence in Islam of a critical attitude   toward the Ptolemaic astronomy, see A. I. Sabra, "An Eleventh-Century Refutation of Ptolemy's Planetary Theory," at pp. 117-131, in *Science and History*, cited in n. 6, above.

13. Reprinted in *Joannis Regiomontani Opera collectanea*, ed. Felix Schmeidler (Osnabrück, 1972), pp. 145/10-13.

14. *TCT*, p. 72.

15. Leszek Hajdukiewicz, *Biblioteka Macieja z Miechowa* (The Library of Maciej of Miechów) (Wrocław: Ossolineum, 1960), p. 218, n. 189.

16. *NCCW*, 2, 5/37-45.

17. *NCCW*, 2, 10/7-13,9/24-25.

18. Quoted after Max Caspar, *Kepler*, tr. and ed. C. Doris Hellman (London: Abelard-Schuman, 1959), p. 89.

19. Johannes Kepler, *Gesammelte Werke* (Munich, 1937-1983; cited hereafter as "*GW*"), 1 and 8.

20. *Kepler's "Somnium," The Dream, or Posthumous Work on Lunar Astronomy*, translated with a commentary by Edward Rosen (Madison: University of Wisconsin Press, 1967), p. 335. *GW*, 7: 100.

21. *Kepler's "Somnium,"* p. 36.

22. *NCCW*, 2, 22/11-12: *maximam Luna cum terra cognationem habet; (Luna) sit . . . terrae cognata maxime (NCCW*, 2, 173/11).

23. *Kepler's "Somnium"*, pp. 67-70.

24. Ibid., p. 69, n. 142.

25. *GW*, 3: 25/38-4O.

26. *GW*, 3: 25/21-22.

27. *NCCW*, 2, 18/6-8.

28. *Kepler's "Somnium"*, p. 71, n. 66.

29. Ibid., p. 123, n.202/4-7.

30. Isaac Newton's *Philosophiae naturalis principia matematica*; the third edition (1726) with variant readings, ed. Alexandre Koyré and I. Bernard Cohen (Cambridge: Harvard University Press, 1972), pp. 40 on 2/9; 562/6, 10, 21; 569/16; 579/10; 691/18; 743/11; 758/15; facsimile of the insertion at 2/9 in Plate 4 of I. Bernard Cohen, *Introduction to Newton's 'Principia'* (Harvard University Press, 1971).

10

Polish Renaissance Political Theory: Andrzej Frycz Modrzewski

Waldemar Voisé

ndrzej Frycz Modrzewski (Andreas Fricius Modrevius, 1503-1572), humanist, political and religious reformer, spent his early childhood and old age in Wolborz,[1] his family's native place, then a crowded and busy little town in central Poland. After completing his studies at the Cracow University Modrzewski entered in 1523 the services of the primate Jan Łaski. Later the primate's nephew Jan Łaski (Johannes a Lasco) the future religious reformer became his protector. This protection of the powerful Łaski family, very active and prominent in political life, in diplomacy and in the Reformation movement, determined the further course of his career and promoted his travel abroad. He studied at the University of Wittenberg, served as an emissary between Łaski and protestant circles in Germany. Around 1547 Modrzewski became secretary of King Sigismund August and took part in various diplomatic missions.

Like his predecessors (Jan Ostroróg, Filippo Buonaccorsi, Callimachus, and Walenty Eck) in the same field, Frycz Modrzewski grounded his diagnosis of diseases ravaging the State and society in a penetrating observation of life in his own time. In the very same year 1543 in which Copernicus had established the new astronomy Frycz Modrzewski published his two treatises in Cracow. The first *Lascius sive de poena homicidii*, is against the criminal law according to which a murder, if committed by a nobleman is less severly punished than if committed by a burgher or peasant. The second, *Oratio Philaletis Peripatetici*, stands in defense of townspeople threatened with the loss of their meager estates coveted by noblemen.

Frycz Modrzewski composed his works with a definite purpose in mind. All his books, and primarily his work concerning the reform or "amendment" of the state, are directed towards the modernization of two institutions closely connected with man's life: the State and the Church. Afterwards, when he retired to Wolborz to fulfill the hereditary duty of head of this borough, his political and theological works display a number of common ends: while virtually accepting the existing state of affairs, he postulates a well-advanced democratization of many institutions.

Frycz Modrzewski's critical remarks connected with the past and present state of Poland and propositions directed to assure a better future of his country are combined and universally presented in his comments on the reform of government and society. So, despite the abundance of theological works which he produced, in the mind of posterity he remains the author of one fundamental work, *Commentariorum de Republica emendanda libri quinque*.[2] The first, incomplete (as a result of the opposition of the Polish clergy) edition of the first three books appeared in Cracow in 1551; the next two editions were issued in Basel by the printer Oporinus in 1554 and 1559. The work presents a program for a radical reform of customs (*Liber Primus de Moribus*), laws (*Secundus de Legibus*), of matters connected with the waging of war (*Tertius de Bello*), of the church (*Quartus de Ecclesia*), and of schools (*Quintus de Schola*). It should be pointed out, therefore, that the principal reforms or emendations proposed by Frycz Modrzewski were intended to embrace the entire system of the state. Thus, peasants were to be protected by humanitarian penal law and as tillers of the soil were to be considered tenant farmers; trade and handicraft industries were to be concentrated in the hands of the townsmen, and a code of laws was to be binding on all citizens of the State. The Church, reformed and cooperating with the State, was to devote itself chiefly to the improvement of the morals of the citizens while education was to be entrusted wholly to the schools, where the course of studies was to prepare youth for civil service. The State's foreign policy, made sound on the principle of good neighborly relations, was to exclude the waging of wars of conquest. Finally, Frycz Modrzewski saw that the modernization of the state system lay in the neutralization of the growing power of the oligarchy of magnates by investing the king with a power which, while fully safeguarding the sovereign rights of the State, would enable him to regulate relations between the estates.

Apart from the generalized theoretical program for a radical reform of the State (*sui generis* a minimum program of a sort capable of being realized in the prevailing circumstances), *De Republica emendanda* also contained a maximum program—a vision of an ideal State marked by certain utopian traits.[3] The two concepts, the reform of the system on the one hand and the construction of an ideal republic on the other, were often interrelated. This was because Frycz Modrzewski had constantly before his eyes the vision of the reform of the existing and the construction of an ideal Polish State, and not of a State in the general sense.

Beginning in the mid-fifteenth century against the background of the struggle between the gentry and the magnates tendencies toward modernization of the government had begun in Poland. Although still sketchy in character, the fullest program of this kind was put forth by Jan Ostroróg (1436-1501), a diplomat, voivode of Poznań, and one of the first outstanding secular lawyers. His small memorial, rich in ideas about the reform of the republic (*Monumentum pro Reipublicae ordinatione*), was written with the knowledge of those advisers to the king referred to as "the party of the young." At the forefront of his program Ostroróg put two problems: the strengthening of royal authority and the centralization of the state.

When the enlightened circles of the gentry began to increase their ranks in the first half of the sixteenth century, Frycz Modrzewski became one of its active members. The fundamental difference between this group and the rest of the gentry (more and more effectively manipulated by the magnates) stemmed from their different visions of the "ideal Republic." The conservative camp did not see a need for fundamental reform and recommended imitating the old form of government, which they were convinced was capable of ensuring that Poland would overcome her internal problems and maintain her particularly strong position in Europe at that time. The reform camp, on the other hand, despite all its diversity, was united at least on one point: in its view, the gentry form of government needed not minor improvements, but fundamental modernization so that it might be more similar to those modern states then taking shape in Europe. They were primarily concerned with the strengthening of state power (particularly the authority of the king) and with its centralization. There was nothing unusual in this, since as late as the second half of the sixteenth century the French thinker Michel de Montaigne stated that his country was really a conglomeration of separate duchies.[4] Precisely in France, however, the unification of the state and the strengthening of central authority occurred rapidly, while in Poland the opposite tendencies showed up: the middle gentry and the bourgeoisie did not ally against the magnate oligarchy.

It should be emphasized that Frycz Modrzewski's vision of the ideal state contains specific requirements. Frycz Modrzewski, who was always sensitive to signs of social injustice, postulated a moral perfectionism, that is, a submission of oneself to the highest ethical values. Thus, his Book on the Church (the largest book in the whole work) not only linked political reform with reform of the Church but also contained a detailed program for the reform of human morality.

The role of the Church in Frycz Modrzewski's conception was based in great part upon what humanistic morality and political theory recognized to be proper. In his understanding, the Church was to be an institution which ought to establish "social morality" for the citizens of the State, that is, for all the inhabitants of the Commonwealth, regardless of their estate.

Frycz Modrzewski wanted to achieve a fundamental political reform by two means: by changing the law and by changing customs. This was in line with his conviction that at the basis of a well-governed State are good customs (*mores*) and good will (*benevolentia*). Human beings, however, are so weak that the slightest provocation loosens the bonds of their mutual good will. In order to avert this, laws should be enacted in society which have as their goal the restraint of human passions and the punishment of those who succumb to those passions. In Frycz Modrzewski's conception, the role of law thus leads to the return of that equilibrium in the State and in society that exists in an atmosphere of good will and good customs which constitutes the basis of every political system.

Though attached to tradition in many fields, Frycz Modrzewski nevertheless assailed traditional views wherever they served as a screen to hide the pernicious effects of institutions and the inanity of inherited and long out-dated views. Thus, paraphrasing an ancient poet, he wrote: "the gentry has as many enemies as subjects." He stated that it was harmful to identify the concept of the people with the concept of the estate of the gentry: "For in truth the Republic cannot flourish thanks to the gentry alone." Frycz Modrzewski wrote with biting sarcasm about the system of the ancestors (*mos maiorum*) as an allegedly incomparable model of behavior so highly prized by a large conservative section of the nobles and magnates. In contrast to those who lauded the past, he demonstrated that, although the institutions and views inherited from our ancestors deserve our respect, they are now a hindrance in those instances where changes have inevitably occurred. He wrote, for example, that many statutes, though just when they had been enacted, now deserve to be discarded for they are obsolete.

Frycz Modrzewski not only had an accurate idea about the evolution of social institutions, he also recognized the phenomenon of the continuous improvement of human culture. This is what he had in mind when he wrote that skills increase with time and exercise (*tempore et exercitatione artes crescunt*). He also pointed out that the succeeding generation always overcomes the errors committed by the preceding one, although it often benefits from the latter's experience. This led him to conclude that creative continuation is inconceivable without criticism of past achievement. With this conclusion, Frycz Modrzewski countered a deeply rooted conservative pattern of thought with an evolutionary, historically oriented method of reasoning. This enabled him to point to the mutability of all that is human and upon this assertion to found a plan for social and political reconstruction.

We may well ask how Modrzewski was able to think as he did. The greatest influence in this respect was Erasmus of Rotterdam, whose library, purchased by Jan Łaski, was personally brought to Poland from Basel by Frycz Modrzewski. Erasmus' critical mind, attacking the greatest authorities of the time, did not produce any concrete program of reform; his indecision and disinclination to join one of the opposing camps stemmed both from scepticism and from a tendency toward compromise. Although both these elements can be found to a lesser degree in the works of Frycz Modrzewski as well, they were combined with what might be termed a social-political realism that demanded taking the concrete situation into account as the starting point for reform. For this reason, Frycz Modrzewski, even in comparison with the most influential writer of the epoch, managed to maintain his own individuality.

Frycz Modrzewski was also strongly influenced by the work of Juan Luis Vives, the great Spanish philosopher who lived in the Netherlands, as well as by Melanchthon, in whose home he lived for a period. If we add to this the powerful impression made on him by ancient thought, chiefly that of Aristotle and Cicero, we shall have the full intellectual accoutrement of this writer of the age of humanism who had ties with the vigorous center of Cracow. Accepting the Aristotelian and Ciceronian definition of the State, Frycz Modrzewski asserted that all the inhabitants of the State ought to be citizens regardless of the estate to which they belonged, that royal power should be strengthened while the influence of the oligarchy should be weakened, and that appointments to office should be based on an evaluation of individual qualities rather than on the "splendors of one's ancestors." Consequently, ancient ideas served him solely as a point of departure to introduce into the socio-political reality of his time those elements which guaranteed the desired transformation. He postulated reforms aimed at the modernization of the State, and put forth by what was called the camp of the "intellectual gentry," to whom, as was already mentioned, he was ideologically close. Thus, an analysis of the behavior of Frycz Modrzewski the active politician sheds light on many motives behind the development of Frycz Modrzewski the theorist. While indicating ways of transforming the reality around him, Frycz Modrzewski also realized that this would not be possible without a solid and thorough explanation of that reality. Hence, his work is not only a socio-political treatise, but is also a scholarly work offering a profound analysis of relations that prevailed in his time.

The yardstick he applied to the whole gamut of relations he observed with minute attention was reason (ratio), and it is from this standpoint that he judged them to be just and good or foolish and absurd. Experience and reason dictated the need for man's energetic intervention in the reality around him. In his first works Frycz Modrzewski already appealed to "the tribunal of reason" (tribunal rationis) and called experience "the master of all things" (experientia rerum magistra). He considered practice an important criterion of correct thinking and believed that only that knowledge was useful which served action. He often remarked that he was writing in order to "assist the Republic," placing an especially strong emphasis on the ineffectuality of fruitless reflection. In a letter to a friend he asked: "Why is so much zeal spent on learning? Why in sleeplessness and in the sweat of one's brow does one put so much effort into valuable studies if one cannot gain from them anything useful for others?" He believed, too, that the writer's most important duty is to combat false views, especially those which persist in certain circles due to intellectual inertia. So, it was no accident that at the beginning of his career, Frycz Modrzewski adopted the name of Philaletis, or "lover of truth," which we find in the title of his oration: Oratio Philaletis Peripatetici.

As a lover of truth he could not be indifferent to the postulate of freedom of conscience that had been long advanced in Poland. In the Sejm of 1570 the dissident deputies had demanded that "each person be free to believe according to his conscience" ("*wolno było każdemu wierzyć wedle swego sumienia*"). The Arians, called the Polish Brethren, preached the same concept. In proclaiming the watchword of tolerance mainly in his last work, *Silvae*, Frycz Modrzewski called upon the highest authority that he recognized—reason, which was for him (as for Jan Ostroróg) the standard by which he measured all human affairs. In this way, reason became for him an instrument of social struggle, and hence an element dictating involvement in the sphere of human activity, that is, in the private and public life of every man.

Observing what took place around him and drawing correct conclusions, Frycz Modrzewski rightfully considered that the gentry was becoming increasingly closed, and, although it was slowly evolving into a class of landholders, it continued to think of itself as a knightly class. He pointed out that the appellation "knight" belonged only to those who were able to creditably fulfill their duties to the nation; it is a title which cannot be inherited and which must be earned by each man independently. In this way, Frycz Modrzewski challenged the principle which had been the basis for the privileges of those who supposedly inherited the virtues of their forebears by the simple fact of their noble birth. By questioning the inborn natural superiority and inherited "virtuousness" of the gentry, Frycz Modrzewski hoped to reestablish the rights of the nobility upon individual abilities and services. This appeared most forcibly where he insisted that state offices be entrusted not to those of noble birth, but to educated men who had distinguished themselves by meritorious activity and virtue. Like Erasmus, Frycz Modrzewski even scoffed at the hereditary succession of royal authority.

Frycz Modrzewski further reasoned that since the State should be governed first of all by educated men, and that the schools would educate them, it is necessary for the State to take into its own hands all those matters connected with education. The linking of the question of education with that of governing is one of the many proofs that despite the strong influence of the ideas of Erasmus and Vives upon Frycz Modrzewski, he himself conceived his own plan for the ideal school, putting it in the context of his criticism of the current state of affairs and enriching it with elements of a vision of an entire society of educated men. Whereas the majority of humanists thought that man perfected himself through education, Frycz Modrzewski outlined a model of the educated citizen.

His views on the matter of child-rearing were a development of his general principles of schooling about the morality and goals of the State. Here as well, Frycz Modrzewski had in mind primarily the problem of raising the moral level of all citizens, which in his conception was an indispensable condition for the reconstitution of the social and political institutions of the gentry republic. In addition, Frycz Modrzewski was one of the first humanist thinkers to introduce secular elements into education at a time when matters of upbringing and schooling were still in the hands of the clergy.

His *Book on Schools* was also an extraordinary tribute to the goals and responsibilities of those who teach. We may cite the following passage as an
example:

> Thus we understand how very beautiful and useful for men is the
> occupation of the teacher, from whom come so many masters of the
> best arts and from whom all other estates are accustomed to derive
> so many advantages. For this reason do I speak at such length about
> its excellence and dignity so that we might remember that it should
> be defended by every means and preserved from perfidious opinions
> and impertinence.

As Pierre Mesnard correctly observed, Frycz Modrzewski's *Book on Schools* is
"the most beautiful encomium to the school and to teachers ever delivered by
a statesman."[5]

The third part of *De Republica* is entitled the *Book on War*, but actually this is
a book on both war and peace, the best proof being its significant opening
words:

> And so that wars need never be waged, utmost concern should be
> shown for the preservation of peace with the neighboring nations,
> which should never be given any reason for concocting hostile plans
> against us. And if by chance some harm is done on this or the other
> side of the frontier, everything possible should be done to remove it
> either by law or by a judgment of honest people.

These are the words put by Frycz Modrzewski at the beginning of his reflections
in *Liber de Bello*. Frycz Modrzewski emphasized particularly strongly that those
who are bent on starting a war should realize that every war brings misery,
violence, murders and other crimes in its wake. That is why a ruler, instead
of resorting to war, should do everything in his power and show utmost
vigilance in order to save his subjects from harm. His entire effort should be
concentrated on the prevention of war and preservation of peace. In the outline
of Chapter I of his *Book on War* he wrote the significant words: *Bellum modis
omnibus ut avertatur, studendum* (All possible means should be used to avert
war). Thus, at the very outset of his reflections he strongly condemned war
from the moral and political points of view.

Frycz Modrzewski was not a specialist in military matters, but when he wrote
about war he used the experience he had gained during his long service as the
king's secretary and diplomat often sent abroad to discuss Poland's relations
with foreign courts. Being a moralist and a reformer of customs, he regarded
war as an evil which should be avoided.

Following the custom of the age, he quoted many ancient writers who discussed war and related problems. Humanist writers, who as a rule were not
experts in military affairs, usually based their studies on *Veteres de re militari
scriptores*, a work containing treatises on war by Roman writers.

Frycz Modrzewski was not the first writer in Poland to deal with the problem of war and peace in a comprehensive way. A discussion on war and especially on the attitude to non-Christian states (alliances, cooperation, defenses and possible attack) had been conducted in Poland from the beginning of the fifteenth century.

The problem was briefly presented for the first time by Stanisław ze Skarbimierza (Stanisław of Skarbimierz, Stanislaus of Scarbimiria) in *De bellis iustis*, written probably in 1410.

Stanisław's doctrine was for practical reasons widely developed by Paweł Włodkowic (Paulus Vladimiri).[6] On the basis of a very extensive literature (from Aristotle through Roman and canon law up to fourteenth-century West European writers) he adapted theoretical arguments to Poland's wars and conflicts with the Teutonic Order. Until the end of the sixteenth century no equally comprehensive work on the law of war had been written in Europe.

In his speech at the Council of Constance (1415) Paweł Włodkowic exposed the groundlessness of the Teutonic Knights' claims, rejected the arguments they used to justify their attacks and seizure of non-Christian property, denied that the German emperor had the right to rule over the whole world, and insisted that every state, whether Christian or heathen, had the right to exist. Włodkowic, who regarded defensive wars as just and aggressive wars as criminal, applied the same principles to all, including pagans, who, as he emphasized, may not be converted by sword. Włodkowic's opinions, formed under the influence of the political conditions of those times (the struggle against the Teutonic Order), were of great importance for the development of political and moral principles.

These two writers, who were both rectors of Cracow University at the beginning of the fifteenth century, created "the Polish school of the law of nations." Thanks to Paweł Włodkowic the doctrine of that school was presented at a great European congress—the Council of Constance.

As Ludwik Ehrlich writes in his study of the genealogy of law of nations,[7] the theological lectures by the Spanish Dominican Francis de Vittoria, the book by the Spanish-Dutch writer Balthazar Ayala, the work by the Italian professor of Oxford Alberico Gentili on the law of war (1588-1598), and Hugo Grotius' work *De iure belli ac pacis* (1625), based on the three works mentioned above and preceded by a youthful treatise, have been traditionally regarded as the most important of the early works on the law of war. Frycz Modrzewski's *Book on War*, though published earlier, is far superior to all these books, for it devotes much more space to advice on how to prevent war and gives not primarily theological arguments (as did Vittoria and Grotius) but also a rationalistic justification.

The noble desire to preserve peace in relations between states can be seen in practically everything Frycz Modrzewski says on the coexistence of nations. In his introduction to the *Book on War* he writes that when good customs reigned supreme people did not wage wars. This statement is not surprising if one

ANDREAE FRICII
Modreuij Commentariorum
de Republica emendan-
da Libri quinque:
Quorum

PRIMVS, DE MORIBVS.
SECVNDVS, DE LEGIBVS.
TERTIVS, DE BELLO.
QVARTVS, DE ECCLESIA.
QVINTVS, DE SCHOLA.

AD REGEM, SENATVM, PONTIFICES,
Presbyteros, Equites, populumq́; Poloniæ,
ac reliquæ Sarmatiæ.

Cum gratia & priuilegio ad quin-
quennium.

BASILAE, PER IOAN-
nem Oporin.

32. Andrzej Frycz Modrzewski *Commentariorum de Republica emendanda, Libri quinque*, Basileae,
1554. The title page of the first edition of Andrzej Frycz Modrzewski's work (Biblioteka
Uniwersytecka, Warszawa). Photo Andrzej Bodytko.

33. *Von Verbesserung des Gemeinen Nütz*. Fünf Bücher Andree Fricii Modrevij Königlicher Maiestet zu Polen Secretarij .... , Basel, 1557. The title page of Wolfgang Wissenburg's translation of Andrzej Frycz Modrzewski's work *De Republica emendanda* (Książnica Miejska im. Mikołaja Kopernika, Toruń). Reprinted from Waldemar Voisé, "400-lecie tłumaczenia *De Republica emendanda* przez Wolfganga Wissenburga," *Odrodzenie i reformacja w Polsce*, vol. 3. (Warszawa: PWN, 1958).

considers the importance attached by the author of the *De Republica emenanda* to "good customs," which, in his opinion, were the best guarantee of good government and the prosperity of the State. However, when the original conditions could no longer be preserved and more effective means had to be used to prevent wrong-doing, laws were adopted to force people to do what they would have been reluctant to do of their own free will.

One should not allow relations with neighboring states to become tense. If there is some misunderstanding between two states, everything possible should be done to remove it, either "by law or by a judgment of honest people." Referring to ancient authors Frycz Modrzewski writes that wise people should always try to solve conflicts by all peaceful means, this being the best proof of the will to preserve peace. By striving for peace and showing the will to preserve it, one can derive many benefits and gain friends.

Frycz Modrzewski mentions two ways of solving conflicts; he writes, as we have seen, that conflicts should be settled either by law or by a judgment of honest people. But he does not develop his conception of how two states can use law to reach an understanding (he probably had in mind alliances, agreements, and state treaties). However, he deals at length with the settlement of conflicts by means of specially selected mediators whom he calls judges. The judges are selected by the rulers of the two neighboring states "out of their own good will;" they can be either foreign subjects or subjects of the countries involved in the dispute. In the latter case they should be relieved of the oath of loyalty to their king for the duration of the trial to be able to settle the dispute better and more justly.

Frycz Modrzewski emphasizes, and this is particularly important, that "agreements of this kind are permissible not only with nations professing the same faith but also with those of different religions." One should "strive for peace with all people;" examples of such peace can be found in the Bible, which Frycz Modrzewski invokes to strengthen his arguments. His views were much more advanced than those held by many contemporary writers, especially his insistence that the international community should embrace not only Christian states but also those professing other religions. In this way there would be one difference less between states, a difference of major importance, and one that was often the cause of tensions and misunderstandings. Frycz Modrzewski had no doubt that collective security was impossible as long as any state or group of states was excluded from the international community only because its inhabitants professed a different religion. There is no doubt that he had Turkey in mind, for he wrote about that country several lines later.

In the outline of Chapter II of the *Book on War* Frycz Modrzewski writes: "It is explained here what makes a war just and honest; to be just and felicitous, it must have a just cause" (*Belli iusticia et honestas explicatur; quod ut justum sit et foelix, causam iustum habere debet*). As we know, Frycz Modrzewski considered a war to be just if it was declared to avenge the wrongs that could not be redressed in any other way. He regarded the starting of a just war as an act designed to administer justice in international relations.

The state conducting a just war can be sure of victory. But a state conducting an unjust war cannot expect to be victorious; even if it wins, victory will in time turn into a great defeat, "a final defeat and great misery." A similar opinion was expressed by Grotius.

This similarity was not accidental; as Stanisław Kot pointed out, Grotius knew Frycz Modrzewski's works and used similar arguments to justify similar opinions. Writing half a century after Frycz Modrzewski's death and trying to put an end to the cruelty of wars, he made use of Frycz Modrzewski's works. Looking for the ways of solving conflicts dating back to the Reformation, Grotius in his *Via ad pacem ecclesiasticam* (1642) used Frycz Modrzewski's arguments and frequently cited him.[8]

As far as the science of war and peace is concerned, particularly worthy of notice are not only Grotius' plans for preventing wars and preserving peace, which were almost identical with those of Frycz Modrzewski, but also his opinions on the just causes of wars, a literal repetition of what Frycz Modrzewski wrote on the subject. Frycz Modrzewski can be therefore regarded as a forerunner of the "father of the law of nations," even though he did not produce a full presentation of the science of war and peace.

In Chapter XIV of the *Book on War*, entitled *Parta victoria quid agendum* (What should be done after victory), Frycz Modrzewski describes the proper behavior after war, or after a victorious war, for, in his opinion, a just war cannot end in defeat, his tacit conviction being that what is ethical is at the same time profitable, and that unethical conduct does not pay in the long run.[9]

The theoretical and practical merits (both national and supranational) of the *Book on War* did not escape the attention of the intellectuals of the day. One of them, Giovanni Giustiniano, a humanist of Padua, wrote an enthusiastic letter to Frycz Modrzewski in May 1555, in which he said that he had such a high opinion of his work that he would like "to see it translated into all the languages of the world." Giustiniano partly kept his word: he translated the *Book on War* into Spanish and sent the manuscript to Maximilian Habsburg, the King of Bohemia and later Emperor of Germany; he also sent a copy of the translation to the king of England. Both copies have survived until this very day; one is in the Österreichische National Bibliothek in Vienna and the other in the Archiepiscopal Library in Lambeth.[10]

Several years later, in 1557, Wolfgang Wissenburg of Basel, a theologian and three times the rector of Basel University, published in Basel a German translation of Frycz Modrzewski's entire work under the title *Von Verbesserung des Gemeinen Nütz fünf Bücher*. It is not by accident that he used here the unusual expression *"gemeine Nütz,"* the counterpart of which is precisely the Polish concept of Commonwealth (Rzeczpospolita). Wissenburg fully realized that after becoming familiar with the contents of the work there would appear in the minds of the readers the Republica Polonorum envisioned by the author— the model state, the highest goal of which should be the mutual good of all its inhabitants.[11]

As the years passed Frycz Modrzewski became more and more fascinated by theological trends. There is a strong similarity in the conception of important problems concerning the church between *De Republica emenanda* and a number of his theological works. Although we know that he devoted much attention to doctrinal questions, he nevertheless steadily proclaimed that not the latter are to be the subject of principle dispute on the reform of the Church. Rather, improving the morals of the faithful should be its chief aim of reform. He considered that, as in the case of the State, the Church also should have a collegial body, fulfilling the role of an organ deciding ecclesiastical matters. It is therefore not at all strange that for the necessary structure of authority in the Church, Frycz Modrzewski favors entrusting the highest power to a council, which should be the only means of restoring unity to the Church. The guarantee of a democratic system in the Church would be the principle of eligibility for office of all the priesthood, with all the faithful voting, regardless of the estate to which they belonged. Initially he held a position very near to Calvin's creed; later he became disaffected with the Helvetian church, and leaned towards the thesis of Francesco Stancaro (the disagreement here concerned the role of Christ, said to be only a human mediator between God and men); finally, towards the end of his life, he grew closer to the views of the Polish Brethren. In the main center in Raków the posthumous edition of Frycz Modrzewski's *Silvae* was printed in 1590.

The above mentioned translations of *De Republica emenanda*, are proof that Frycz Modrzewski's chief work won renown soon after its publication. The circle of humanists connected with the two Basel editions of *De Republica* (1554 and 1559) that included Curione, Oporinus, Amerbach, and Giustiniano considered Frycz Modrzewski to be one of the most eminent writers of this period. His fame soon, however faded; only later did Frycz Modrzewski again win high esteem. Bayle praised him in his *Dictionnaire* (1669), de Réal appreciated him in his *La Science du Gouvernment* (1751), an unknown author translated *De Republica* into Russian in the seventeenth century, and a reprint of the Polish translation, edited by Cyprian Bazylik in 1577, appeared in Wilno in 1770. The Enlightenment period was slowly approaching, and with it a number of Frycz Modrzewski's proposals began to be realized in fact.

Now, more than 400 years after his death, history has entered upon the stage as the verifier of his views. It compels us to take note both of Frycz Modrzewski's allies and of his opponents. Among the latter was the great French author Jean Bodin, who, in his *Six Books of the Republic*, issued for the first time in Paris in 1576, only a short time after Frycz Modrzewski's death, wrote as follows: "The Polish writer Andreas Fricius even writes that it is an allegedly great mistake not to apply the same punishment to patricians and plebeians, the rich and poor, citizens and foreigners; nothing more absurd could have been written by anyone who, like him, wishes to shape the laws and customs of his Republic." A comparison of the opinions of the two writers is important, for it discloses the criteria used in the evaluation of social progress by two outstanding representatives of sixteenth century European political and social thought.[12]

Like the work of Frycz Modrzewski, another masterpiece of the age, Copernicus' *De Revolutionibus orbium coelestium*, was declared absurd, for in the minds of many it propounded principles which contradicted long accepted notions. Many years had to elapse before the validity of the Copernican vision of the universe was recognized. The ideas of Frycz Modrzewski were destined to wait an even longer time. It appears that it was easier "to stop the Sun and to move the Earth" than to convince many people that human matters must be measured by the same yardstick for everyone.

Notes

1. Stanisław Kot, *Andrzej Frycz Modrzewski, Studium z dziejów kultury polskiej XVI w.* (Andrzej Frycz Modrzewski. A study concerning the history of sixteenth-century Polish culture), 2nd ed., rev. (Cracow: Nakł. Krakowskiej Spółki Wydaw., 1923). This work still remains the basic source of biographical and bibliographical intormation.

2. *Andreae Fricii Modrevii Opera omnia edidit Casimirus Kumaniecki*, 3 vols. (Warsaw: PIW, 1953-55) and *Dzieła wszystkie Andrzeja Frycza Modrzewskiego* (Complete works of Andrzej Frycz Modrzewski), 5 vols. (Warsaw, 1953-1960). See vol. 1 for complete Polish text of *De Republica emendanda*.

3. Claude Backvis, "Le Courant utopique dans la Pologne de la Renaissance," in *Les Utopies à la Renaissance: colloque internationale, avril, 1961* (Brussels-Paris: Presses universitaires de Bruxelles, 1963), pp. 163-208.

4. Pierre Mesnard has written about Frycz Modrzewski's views in the context of European political thought. See his *L'Essor de la philosophie politique au XVIe siècle* (Paris: Librairie philosophique J. Vrin, 1969). On the same subject, see also Tadeusz Wyrwa, *La Pensée politique polonaise à l'époque de l'humanisme et de la Renaissance: un apport à la connaissance de l'Europe moderne* (Paris: Librairie polonaise, 1978).

5. Pierre Mesnard, "La Republique de Modrzewski comme philosophie de l'histoire des institutions polonaises," *Review historique de droit français et étranger* (Paris, 1966).

6. Paweł Włodkowic, *Pisma wybrane* (Selected works) ed. Ludwik Ehrlich, vols. 1 and 3 (Warsaw: PAX, 1966-69). Stanisław F. Belch, *Paulus Vladimiri and His Doctrine Concerning International Law and Politics*, vols. 1 and 2 (The Hague, Mouton, 1965).

7. Ludwik Ehrlich, "Zarys historii nauki prawa narodów w Polsce" (An outline of the history of the science of law of nations in Poland), in Ludwik Ehrlich and Jerzy Stefan Langrod, *Zarys historii nauki prawa narodów, politycznego i administracyjnego w Polsce* (Cracow: PAU, 1949), pp. 7-10.

8. Stanisław Kot, "Hugo Grotius a Polska" (Hugo Grotius and Poland) in *Reformacja w Polsce* (Cracow: 1926), no. 13/16.

9. Valdemar Voisé "Andrzej Frycz Modrzewski (1503-1572) and his Book on War and Peace," in *Europolonica: La circulation de quelques thèmes Polonais à travers L'Europe du XIVe au XVIIIe siècle* (Wrocław: Ossolineum, 1981), pp. 125-36.

10. Voisé,¨"Giovanni Giustiniano—traduttore del libro *Sulla guerra* di Frycz Modrzewski," ibid., pp. 112-117.

11. Voisé, "Wolfgang Wissenburgs Übersetzung des Werkes *De Republica emendanda* von Fricius Modrevius," ibid., pp. 72-90.

12. Voisé, "Deux républiques opposées—Fricius et Bodin," ibid. pp. 22-29.

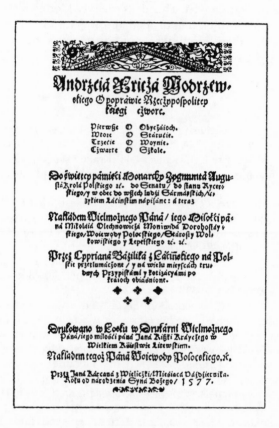

11

The University Context of Kochanowski's Era:
Humanism and the Academic Culture of
the Early Renaissance in Poland

Paul W. Knoll

hen Jan Kochanowski matriculated at the University of Cracow in
the summer semester of 1544, he entered a university whose scholastic character had, in the course of the generations before him,
been transformed by the pedagogical program and literary tastes
of the traditions of Renaissance humanism. The school where he spent some
time in study—though he took no degree—had become, in short, a Renaissance
university. Though not much is known how the formal education of the *studium
Cracoviense* may have had influenced Kochanowski, it was nevertheless of major
importance in the spectrum of intellectual and cultural tastes which characterized early and mid- sixteenth-century Poland.

How the university had come to be a center of humanistic influence is the
subject of this paper. The study emphasizes the background of the Kochanowski era and concentrates upon the fifteenth and early sixteenth centuries.
It was during that period that the foundations of the house of humanist learning
were laid. The process may, for convenience, be divided roughly into three
chronologically unequal periods. The first extends to the death of Professor
Jan of Dąbrówka in 1472; the second covers the next two decades until the visit
of Conrad Celtis in the early 1490's; and the third takes the story into the next
century. Each period is described with reference to particular individuals.

One of the major thrusts of the Polish historiographical tradition has been
that humanism and humanistic interests at Cracow, both outside the curriculum
and within the *studium*, date from early in the fifteenth century.[1] This paper
suggests a more cautious evaluation of the data which others have interpreted
so positively and optimistically. The study makes two fundamental distinctions.
One is between, on the one hand, general humanistic interests as manifested

in the larger spectrum of intellectual concerns among the faculty and students, and, on the other hand, humanism *per se* as a primary cultural orientation on the part of a particular individual who may be termed, therefore, a humanist. It is clear, for example, that many individuals in the fifteenth century manifested humanistic interests; few, in the early part of the century were humanists. Not until the end of the fifteenth and early part of the sixteenth century were there such individuals associated with the university corps in Cracow. The second fundamental distinction is between, on the one hand, activity among the university's personnel outside the formal curriculum and program of the *studium* and, on the other hand, the actual penetration of the institutional structure by humanism and humanistic interests. It is the argument of this paper that extracurricular interests can be observed far earlier than the actual integration of these into the program of the university.

Though this more cautious evaluation may modify the traditional view, it is nevertheless clear that by the end of the fifteenth century, both humanistic interests and the incorporation of some of the humanist pedagogical program had been responsible for altering the tenor and the structure of academic life. The University of Cracow was, therefore, by the early sixteenth century, well on the way to becoming the school which the English humanist Leonard Coxe praised in 1518 as being the equal of Athens in its devotion to literature and poetry.[2]

Humanistic interests came to Poland and its university in three different ways. Sometimes native Poles who traveled abroad, especially to Italy, returned to their homeland with a taste for the *studia humaniora;*[3] in some instances Italian influences penetrated the country directly; finally, the cultural concerns of Italian humanism were mediated to Poland through such neighboring countries as Hungary and Germany. A good example of the first process was Polish participation in the great ecumenical councils of the fifteenth century.[4]

At the Council of Constance, for example, the Polish delegation, which was largely composed of academics and university trained men, would have been aware of the humanist movement. The news of Poggio Bracciolini's sensational discoveries and some knowledge of the tastes of the numerous Italian humanists who attended this gathering would have been available to them. In addition, we know that at least some academic members of the Polish delegation had contact with noted humanists. The famed educational theorist Pietro Paolo Vergerio, who had studied at Padua with Francesco Cardinal Zabarella, later commented in a letter that all the cardinal's students (which of course included himself and rector Paweł Włodkovic (Paulus Viadimiri) of the University of Cracow) had gathered there "from all the lands of the globe."[5] In these meetings, it is reasonable to expect that Vergerio and the Poles would have discussed issues which touched the concerns of the humanists.

At least one member of the Polish delegation would have found humanistic interests congenial with his own. Piotr Wolfram of Lwów, a professor of law and diplomat whose role at the Council of Constance was important, was an avowed enthusiast for the eloquence of antiquity. While at the council, he wrote several letters to Poland, including a long, informative one to the Bishop of Cracow. These provided opportunities for him to reveal his learning, and he cited a variety of antique authors, including Cicero, Quintilian, Ovid, and Epicurus. He recommended the study of the historians of classical civilization, and held up Socrates as a model of wisdom. But his most extravagant prose was reserved for Petrarch, whom he quoted often and whom he in one place termed *laureatissimus poetarum*. In this instance, he made a graceful play on the name of his hero, identifying him as *Patriarcha*.[6] That Piotr Wolfram of Lwów was a proponent of the Latinity of antiquity and the ideals of the early Italian humanistic movement is clear.[7] After his return to Poland, however, there is no direct evidence that he furthered these within the university. His teaching in the law faculty did not provide opportunity for this, and his careerist ambitions soon removed him from academic circles.

Despite this scattered evidence of contact and isolated instances of humanistic tastes, one should not overestimate either the degree or depth of appreciation for Italian humanism at this point among the Poles. The faculty who were at Constance were still fundamentally oriented toward the scholastic traditions of the university. Thus in the early years of the fifteenth century, the growth of humanistic interests in university circles was slow.

If the influence of Constance is to be minimized, that of Basel should be emphasized. There Polish contact with humanistic currents deepened the interests of the masters in, and enriched the base of knowledge about, humanistic concerns.[8] While at Basel, for example, several Poles had close contact with the Koyer scriptorium, which produced fine manuscripts of classical and Christian authors. These were purchased and taken back to Poland, where they were added to professorial libraries. One particularly fine manuscript was a copy of Petrarch's *Epistolarum familiarum*, which was purchased by Mikołaj Kozłowski. Eventually, many of these volumes came into the common possession of the library of the university. The experience of the Poles at Basel attests to the sure penetration into academic Poland of some elements of the humanistic tradition.[9]

These elements were to become even stronger by about 1470, the end of the first period defined above. Several individuals reflect different aspects of the phenomenon of growing humanistic interests among the professoriate. Let us discuss in turn three figures of especial importance: Gregory of Sanok (Grzegorz z Sanoka; Gregorius Sanocensis), Jan of Ludzisko (Jan z Ludziska), and Jan of Dąbrówka (Jan z Dąbrówki).

Gregory of Sanok, whose archiepiscopal court at Lwów after 1451 was to become one of the leading centers of Renaissance letters in east central Europe, was born about 1407. He left home as a youth and wandered from city to city. About the age of fourteen, he arrived in Cracow, where (according to his later biographer Callimachus) "he spent some time in study."[10] Attracted by the possibility of an eventual career in the affairs of the city, but hampered by his lack of knowledge of German, he left the city and went "beyond the Elbe" (*ultra Albim*) into Germany. After five years of further wandering, he returned, having pursued both formal and informal education. In the meantime, he had achieved such a mastery of the language there that it was difficult to know whether German or Polish was his original tongue. One of the fruits of this stay in Germany may have been an interest in rhetoric and literature, for when he enrolled at the university in 1428, he was, according to Callimachus, "naturally drawn to rhetoric and poetry."[11] In contrast to his earlier plans, he now decided to pursue a career, first in medicine, eventually in the church. He earned his B.A. in 1433, then was named as tutor to the children of one of the important civil officials of rural Poland. Residence in the country did not agree with him, for "with difficulty he endured being without the company of learned men."[12] He brought his charges back to Cracow, where he continued his study at the university.

During this time he obtained a copy of the satires of Juvenal. This provided the basis for him to dispute an interpretation given by Jan of Dąbrówka, one of his teachers, in the latter's commentary upon the Polish historian Wincenty Kadłubek.[13] Next, Gregory went to Italy and the papal court of Eugenius IV, where he spent about a year and a half, before returning to Cracow in 1439. It was in these years that his enthusiasm for the humanistic movement matured and his mastery of eloquent Latin was perfected.[14]

Two things are evidence of this. One was the manuscripts he brought back from Italy with him. The most important of these was a copy of Giovanni Boccaccio's *Genealogia deorum gentilium*, which was well-known as a work which had given impetus and depth to the classicism of the trecento. This particular manuscript had previously been the property of the French humanist Gontier Col.[15] There can be little doubt that this work, particularly chapters fourteen and fifteen, exercised considerable influence upon Gregory of Sanok's conception of the importance of poetry. The second item of evidence is an event which took place near the end of the year. He began a series of lectures upon the *Bucolics* of Virgil, "the title of which and whose author," according to Caliimachus' erroneous statement, "had until those days been completely unknown in the region."[16] These lectures, which his biographer insisted were the first to bring the practice and the splendor of antique oratory to Cracow, created a sensation in learned circles. As a result, Callimachus asserts, "against not only his expectation but his hope," Gregory was awarded the degree Master in Arts, "even though in truth he had not yet finished the work by which one gets such a title."[17]

After this, Gregory of Sanok began to prepare lectures on the *Georgics*, but other things intervened. Eventually he went to Hungary, where he became close friends with Pietro Paolo Vergerio, the poet Philippo Podacatharo, and the members of the humanist circle which was gathered around the court of Bishop Janos Vitéz of Varad.[18] After his return to Poland in 1451, Gregory was named Archbishop of Lwów. His relations with the University of Cracow were, however, nonexistent, except when he sent the exiled Italian humanist Callimachus to the school and the capital in 1472. His importance for the topic of this paper ends after his Virgil lectures.

What is one to make of the evidence regarding Gregory of Sanok at Cracow that is derived from Callimachus? Some have seen it as one of the most significant events of early Polish humanism, a phenomenon reflecting the vitality of humanistic interests within the university.[19] Upon examination, however, these events appear to be considerably less significant. They are relevant more to Gregory of Sanok's life and career than to the history of the university.

In the first place, there is no evidence that the lectures were given within the university framework. There is, of course, the possibility that they could have been given in conjunction with extraordinary lectures in rhetoric. But Gregory of Sanok was not yet a master, and even though it was not unknown for advanced bachelors to teach, it is unlikely he would have been formally appointed to give ordinary lectures. Moreover, these lectures did not really fit within the curricular framework of the university at this time. They bore neither upon the substance of grammar and rhetoric nor did they constitute an acceptable set of substitutes for books which were required to be lectured. It is probable, therefore, that these were extra-curricular lectures which Gregory of Sanok chose to give on his own initiative. It is also important to recognize that it is extremely improbable he received an M.A. because of these lectures. He did obtain that degree,[20] but in order to do so, he would have had to fulfill the formal academic requirements provided for in the statutes and enforced by the corporation (*universitas*) of masters who would have examined him. Thus, Callimachus' narrative is undoubtedly an exaggerated record of Gregory of Sanok's involvement at the university.

One is left therefore with the conclusion that Gregory of Sanok's presence and activity at Cracow represent merely an incident which cannot be used to support an interpretation that there were strong humanistic influences at work within the university at this time. Gregory of Sanok found other individuals whose tastes were similar to his, but he seldom met the adherents of scholastic philosophy which he considers to contain nothing more than nonsense.[21] Although Gregory of Sanok's role was largely outside the university, one of his contemporaries was the first to bring a more developed humanistic career within the *studium*.

Jan of Ludzisko was born in social obscurity, probably of peasant background, in Kujavia about 1400. He matriculated at the University of Cracow in 1418, earning a B.A. within a year and an M.A. in 1422. Following this, he lectured in the arts faculty for some years beyond the required two and may have begun the study of medicine, for he went eventually to Padua to complete his education in that field. On 9 March 1433 he received there the doctor's degree in medicine.[22] For the next few years there is no trace of his activity, though it is probable he remained in Italy for some time. No later than the fall of 1440 he returned to Poland and received an appointment as a member of the medical faculty. The last mention of his activity there comes in mid-1449. By 1460, he was dead.[23]

As a professor in medicine, Jan of Ludzisko apparently made little impact upon the university community, but he returned to Poland from Italy having learned more than medical matters. He had also come under humanist literary influences. It is probable that he had personal contact with such individuals as the rhetorician Barzizza and the educator Guarino.[24] It is even possible that it was he who sent a copy of Guarino's translation of Plutarch's *De assentatoris et amici differentia* as a gift to the Polish king Władysław III (Warneńczyk).[25] Moreover, he delved deeply enough into the rhetorical traditions of *quattrocento* Italy to become completely familiar with and sympathetic to them. He made an especial effort to gather as many examples as possible of Renaissance rhetoric, including them in a notebook upon which he drew heavily after his return to Poland.

There he applied his newly developed interests in a series of orations prepared between the years 1440 and probably 1447.[26] An analysis of these addresses enables us to evaluate the contribution which he made to the humanistic tradition at Cracow. Sometime during the summer semester of 1440 Jan of Ludzisko prepared his *Oratio de laudibus et dignitate eloquentiae et oratoriae scientiae*. At about the same time, he was responsible for writing two speeches *Ad concilii Basiliensis delegatos Cracoviam advenientes*. A fourth oration, *Pro susceptione regis Wladislai de Ungaria venire volentis*, was intended to welcome Władysław back from the crusade he had led in mid-decade against the Turks. Three speeches date from 1447. One is addressed to Grand Duke Casimir of Lithuania upon his arrival in Cracow to be crowned his brother's successor as King of Poland (Kazimierz IV Jagiellończyk); a second was addressed to Archbishop Wincenty Kot of Gniezno, who was in Cracow for the coronation; and the third honored the Bishop of Płock, who was there for the same reason. Only an eighth speech, *Oratio de laudibus et dignitate philosophiae*, can not be dated with certainty, though it probably falls within the period defined above. All of these speeches are suffused with an admiration for the literature of antiquity and follow the rhetorical patterns current in Italy. Particularly in the first and eighth orations noted above and in the first Basel-delegate oration are the references to ancient and Renaissance authorities common.[27] Two of Jan of Ludzisko's speeches are, however, of a slightly different character. The second Basel address, which has been shown to be a reworked, expanded version of the first,[28] emphasizes less of the *studia humaniora* and concentrates more upon the immediate issues of church reform which confronted the council. The speech for Casimir IV the Jagiellonian also is concerned less with the humanities; instead it focuses upon humanity, particularly the plight of the peasantry in Poland and the responsibility of the king to rule justly for the benefit of all his subjects.[29] Even these speeches, however, are constructed according to the standards current in Italy and reflect therefore the humanistic tenor of Jan of Ludzisko's rhetoric.

It is thus clear that Jan of Ludzisko may be regarded as a representative of Italian Renaissance humanism. But there must be asked the further questions of how original he was (i.e., did he make any contribution of his own) and what influence he had in university circles. The first of these is answered in part by comparing the materials Jan of Ludzisko gathered, undoubtedly in Italy, with his orations themselves. This shows that in many instances he simply took large sections of speeches by and to such authors as Guarino da Verona, Poggio Bracciolini, and others, changing words and phrases where appropriate and necessary.[30] While this heavy dependence upon his models reduces the degree of originality in Jan of Ludzisko's work, it should not be allowed to obscure the reality that each of his orations is in fact tied to a concrete situation in the life of Poland and the university. They represent a celebration of, or statement about, that situation in terms which reflect new cultural currents.

Evaluating the influence of Jan of Ludzisko's orations and his attitudes is more difficult. Some of the speeches, which are noted only as *collecta* and not *pronunciata*, may not actually have been declaimed, but only circulated in written form. Certainly the one addressed to a monarch upon the occasion of his return from a crusade, from which he did not in fact return, cannot have been delivered. Similarly, the *oratio* to Casimir may not have been given in the presence of the king, but rather only within the community of the university, if indeed it was given at all. The speeches praising eloquence, oratory, and philosophy would have fit more conventionally into the routine of university life, and internal evidence suggests actual delivery. In these, Jan of Ludzisko's views would have been clear to all and the contrast with older styles sharp indeed. But these were not part of the formal instructional program and cannot therefore be said to have played a role in giving a humanistic cast to the curriculum of the school (though he may have been arguing in some of these speeches for the inclusion of more literary interests in the content of university instruction). Nevertheless, in contrast to the outsider Gregory of Sanok, Jan of Ludzisko was a member of the faculty, and one may see in his activity the first unambiguous evidence of an attempt to introduce the traditions of humanistic rhetoric inside the walls of the *studium*.[31]

With the person and career of the poly-math Jan of Dąbrówka we come to the end of the first period of humanist activity at the university. His roles as teacher, scholar, and administrator were central to the life of the university for half a century. In our present context, it is crucial to evaluate two aspects of his career with regard to the question of his importance for, and influence on, the humanistic tradition at Cracow. The first of these is the nature and extent of any humanistic tastes and concerns which may be attributed to him; the second is related to the significance of his reorganization of the *studium* in 1449 and the creation of the *Collegium minus*.

Jan of Dąbrówka's library is one of the clearest indications of his intellectual interests. He held several works of classical antiquity and the humanist movement in Italy. Of the former, he had Virgil's *Aeneid*, Plato's *Timaeus*, Valerius Maximus' *Dictorum factorumque memorabilium*, Cicero's *De officiis* and *Tusculanae quaestiones*, and the third book of Quintus Curtius Rufus' *De gestis Alexandrii*

Macedonii. The latter group included Petrarch's *De vita solitaria* and *De remediis utriusque fortunae* and Vergerio's *De ingenuis moribus et liberalibus studiis*.[32] These works are sufficiently differentiated from the kinds of books which characterize earlier libraries that, taken together, they suggest some of the literary interests of the humanist movement. But one should be careful not to attribute too much to Jan of Dąbrówka in this respect, as an analysis of the way he used those materials shows.

The writings noted above, as well as many others deriving from the historiographical tradition of the Polish Middle Ages,[33] were on the whole gathered for and utilized in Jan of Dąbrówka's historical commentary upon Wincenty Kadłubek's *Chronica Polonorum*. These works are not primarily *belles lettres*, and there is little evidence to indicate that he was interested in these classical and Renaissance materials for their literary value. Rather, they served the pragmatic purpose of supporting his historical commentary, and they shaped his approach to the treatment of historical materials. It is true that Jan of Dąbrówka had Vergerio's *De ingenuis*, one of the most important educational treatises from the Renaissance. But the concern he manifested for education in his commentary was a national and patriotic one which—although it emphasized the civic virtues and edifying examples that history can teach—was nevertheless not quite the same kind of instruction in letters which lay at the heart of humanist educational programs.[34] It is also true that Jan of Dąbrówka emphasized some of the values which ancient Rome defended, particularly love of *patria* and a concern for true *nobilitas*. But from a brief examination of his utilization of the antique and humanistic literary materials which he had, it is difficult to attribute to Jan of Dąbrówka a very deep commitment to the newer cultural currents of the Renaissance.

Let us turn now to the second aspect of Jan of Dąbrówka's career mentioned above. His role in the creation of the *Collegium minus* in 1449, his relationship to it in subsequent years, and its significance with regard to humanism is a controversial complex of issues. Some have seen him as primarily responsible for its establishment, have seen the motivation for this stemming from dissatisfaction with the nature of the educational program at the university, and have seen the *Collegium minus* contributing by its innovation in the teaching of grammar, poetry, and rhetoric to a heightened literary and humanistic tradition within the university as a whole.[35] In one sense, Jan of Dąbrówka was responsible for the *Collegium minus*. In 1449, when the faculty of the *Collegium artistarum* erected it, he was their provost. But careful examination of the background of this minor college for eight younger members of the arts faculty who were subsequently given separate housing reveals that it was perhaps also motivated by considerations of space and of administrative order.[36] The division of the arts faculty into junior and senior sections was not uncommon in other central European *studia* at this time. That Jan of Dąbrówka continued to be involved with the *Collegium minus* is not surprising. He was university rector nine times after 1449 and served as university vice-chancellor from 1458

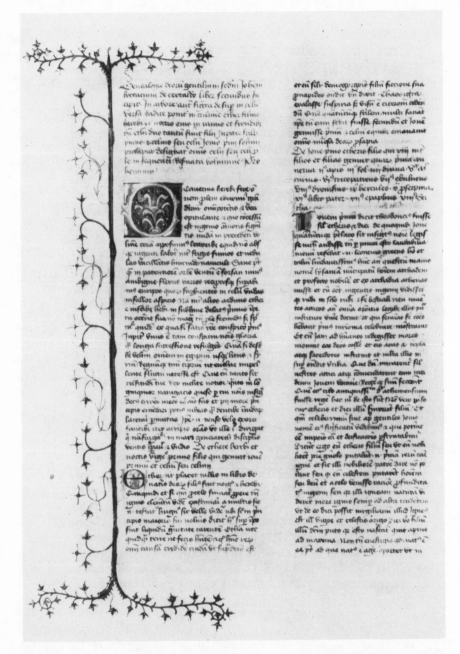

34. Ioannes Boccaccio, *De genealogiis (genealogia) deorum gentilium libri XV.* A page from the manuscript Gregory of Sanok brought back from Italy. The previous owner of the manuscript was the French humanist Gontier Col (Biblioteka Jagiellońska, Kraków). Reprinted from Zofia Amaisenowa, *Rękopisy i pierwodruki iluminowane Biblioteki Jagiellońskiej*, (Wrocław: Ossolineum, 1958).

35. Ioannes Boccaccio, *De casibus virorum illustrium*, Argentinae, ca 1474- 75. The first page of the incunabula which was purchased in Italy by Jan Długosz and donated to the Cracow University in 1479. (Biblioteka Jagiellońska, Kraków). Reprinted from *Dzieje Uniwersytetu Jagiellońskiego w latach 1364-1764*, ed. Kazimierz Lepszy (Kraków: Uniwersytet Jagielloński, 1964).

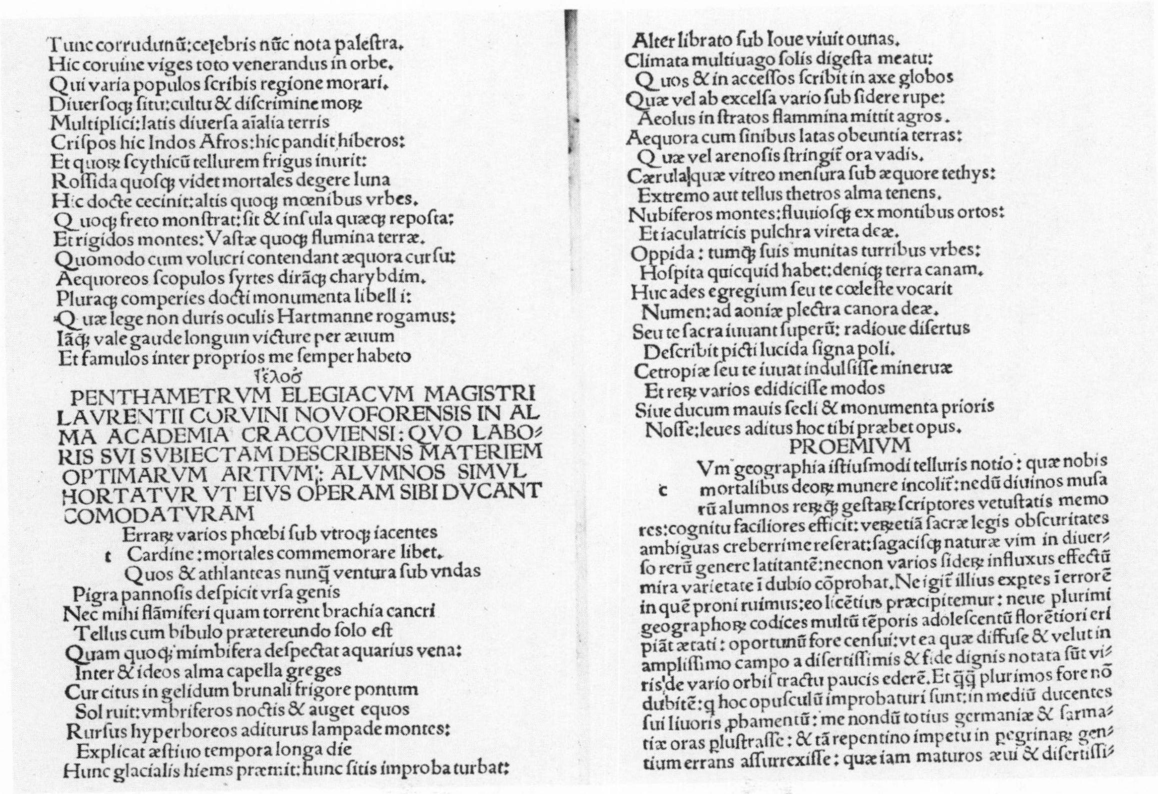

Tunc corrudunũ: celebris nũc nota paleſtra.
Hic coruine viges toto venerandus in orbe.
Qui varia populos ſcribis regione morari.
Diuerſoq; ſitu: cultu & diſcrimine moꝝ
Multiplici: latis diuerſa aīalia terris
Criſpos hic Indos Afros: hic pandit hiberos:
Et quoꝝ ſcythicũ tellurem frigus inurit:
Roſſida quoſq; videt mortales degere luna
Hic docte cecinit: altis quoq; mœnibus vrbes.
Quoq; freto monſtrat: ſit & inſula quæq; repoſta:
Et rigidos montes: Vaſtæ quoq; flumina terræ.
Quomodo cum volucri contendant æquora curſu:
Aequoreos ſcopulos ſyrtes dirãq; charybdim.
Pluraq; comperies docti monumenta libelli:
Quæ lege non duris oculis Hartmanne rogamus:
Iãq; vale gaude longum victure per æuum
Et famulos inter proprios me ſemper habeto
τέλος

PENTHAMETRVM ELEGIACVM MAGISTRI LAVRENTII CORVINI NOVOFORENSIS IN ALMA ACADEMIA CRACOVIENSI: QVO LABORIS SVI SVBIECTAM DESCRIBENS MATERIEM OPTIMARVM ARTIVM: ALVMNOS SIMVL HORTATVR VT EIVS OPERAM SIBI DVCANT COMODATVRAM

Erraꝝ varios phœbi ſub vtroq; iacentes
Cardine: mortales commemorare libet.
Quos & athlanteas nunq̃ ventura ſub vndas
Pigra pannoſis deſpicit vrſa genis
Nec mihi flãmiferi quam torrent brachia cancri
Tellus cum bibulo prætereundo ſolo eſt
Quam quoq; mimbifera deſpectat aquarius vena:
Inter & ideos alma capella greges
Cur citus in gelidum brunali frigore pontum
Sol ruit: vmbriferos noctis & auget equos
Rurſus hyperboreos aditurus lampade montes:
Explicat æſtiuo tempora longa die
Hunc glacialis hiems præmit: hunc ſitis improba turbat:

Alter librato ſub Ioue viuit ounas.
Climata multiuago ſolis digeſta meatu:
Quos & in acceſſos ſcribit in axe globos
Quæ vel ab excelſa vario ſub ſidere rupe:
Aeolus in ſtratos flammina mittit agros.
Aequora cum ſinibus latas obeuntia terras:
Quæ vel arenoſis ſtringiť ora vadis.
Cærula quæ vitreo menſura ſub æquore tethys:
Extremo aut tellus thetros alma tenens.
Nubiferos montes: fluuioſq; ex montibus ortos:
Et iaculatricis pulchra vireta deæ.
Oppida: tumq; ſuis munitas turribus vrbes:
Hoſpita quicquid habet: deniq; terra canam.
Huc ades egregium ſeu te cœleſte vocarit
Numen: ad aoniæ plectra canora deæ.
Seu te ſacra iuuant ſuperũ: radioue diſertus
Deſcribit picti lucida ſigna poli.
Cetropiæ ſeu te iuuat induliſſe mineruæ
Et reꝝ varios edidiciſſe modos
Siue ducum mauis ſecli & monumenta prioris
Noſſe: leues aditus hoc tibi præbet opus.

PROEMIVM

Cum geographia iſtiuſmodi telluris notio: quæ nobis mortalibus deoꝝ munere incoliť: nedũ diuinos muſarũ alumnos reꝝq; geſtaꝝ ſcriptores vetuſtatis memores: cognitu faciliores efficit: verũetiã ſacræ legis obſcuritates ambiguas creberrime reſerat: ſagaciſq; naturæ vim in diuerſo rerũ genere latitantẽ: necnon varios ſideꝝ influxus effectũ mira varietate ĩ dubio cõprobat. Ne igiť illius exptes ĩ errorẽ in quẽ proni ruimus: eo licẽtius præcipitemur: neue plurimi geographoꝝ codices multũ tẽporis adoleſcentũ florẽtiori eripiãt ætati: oportunũ fore cenſui: vt ea quæ diffuſe & velut in ampliſſimo campo a diſertiſſimis & fide dignis notata ſũt viris de vario orbis tractu paucis ederẽ. Et q̃q̃ plurimos fore nõ dubitẽ: q hoc opuſculũ improbaturi ſunt: in mediũ ducentes ſui liuoris pbamentũ: me nondũ totius germaniæ & ſarmatiæ oras pluſtraſſe: & tã repentino impetu in pegrinaꝝ gentium errans aſſurrexiſſe: quæ iam maturos æui & diſertiſſi-

36. "Penthametrum elegiacum Mag. L. Corvini in Alma Academia Cracoviensi,..." in Laurentius Corvinus *Cosmographia dans manuductionem in tabulas Ptholomei*, (Basel, 1496). The book also contains *Ode Saphica ... de Polonia et Cracovia* (Indiana University Lilly Library, Bloomington).

to 1465. He was central to the life of the institution, it was not then surprising that the preserved document containing the new program of instruction in connection with the reform of 1449 is in his handwriting.

In the area of grammar instruction, the reform of 1449 appears to have had a minimal innovative impact. Priscian was specified for lectures, Donatus for recitation exercises, and the second part of Alexander of Villa Dei's *Doctrinale* for either lectures or disputations.[37] Though it is difficult to know what happened between 1449 and 1487, from which latter date the *Liber diligentiarum* provides us with a list of what books were actually taught at the university, it should be noted that after 1487, Priscian was not regularly taught in the remaining years of the century. One may assume that a similar situation obtained before 1487. Donatus and Alexander of Villa Dei were both standard texts for university grammar instruction after about 1200, and both continued to be taught at Cracow, as they were in many other universities, well into the sixteenth century.[38] Their inclusion does not suggest a humanistic thrust in and of itself. More innovative impact could be admitted in the area of poetry, where new names of classical poets were added.

In the area of rhetoric, the impact was, at best, gradual. Some of the works specified marked an addition to, and a theoretical programmatic restructuring of, the rhetorical remnants of the trivium within the university.[39] But one should not overestimate this impact. Grammatical and rhetorical instruction continued after 1449, as it had before, to take up only a small portion (twelve weeks) of the time spent earning a B.A. It should be noted however that there might have been greater attention to the ancient *auctores* and the actual approach to rhetoric was altered. It is known that the full text of Quintilian's *Institutio oratoria* was lectured at Cracow by Leonard Coxe in 1526. The earlier references to Quintilian at Cracow (in 1449 ambiguously, more explicitly in 1475/1476) probably referred to this full text, found by Bracciolini early in the fifteen century. With this full text and the *De oratore* of Cicero (which is included in the new program), students and masters at Cracow could fully appreciate how fragmented the rhetorical tradition of the Middle Ages was in relation to the coherent program of literary education, with its public and civic applications, which lay at the heart of the antique tradition and which formed the basis of the humanistic educational program in Italy. All students in Cracow after midcentury were thus potentially influenced by broadened literary interests, and this eventuaily facilitated the flowering of humanistic activity among the members of the academic community. But the creation of the *Collegium minus* did not bring this about overnight, its contribution was more modest than has traditionally been thought, and the full impact of the reform of 1449 was felt rather closer to the end of the century.[40]

It is one of the coincidences of the past, made sharper by the historian's insistence on interpretation and periodization, that in the year of Jan of Dąbrówka's death there arrived in Cracow an individual whose presence on the Polish scene initiated the second stage in the history of humanism at the university. Filippo Buonaccorsi, called Callimachus Experiens, did much to deepen the humanistic movement, but he and his contemporaries, both inside and outside the *studium*, were able to build upon the tradition whose component parts have been sketched to this point.

The product of the *studia humaniora* in Florence and Venice, Callimachus had led an active scholarly and political life prior to 1468, when he had fled papal disfavor. After a period of wandering, he had found refuge at the residence of Archbishop Gregory of Sanok in Lwów. A year and one-half later, he had left there and come to Cracow, where in the fall of 1472 he matriculated at the university. During the next twenty years Callimachus presided over a humanistic circle whose influence was felt in all areas of Polish intellectual and cultural life. Throughout his career, Callimachus maintained close contact with he university. Although he never obtained the chair he may have been seeking when he originally matriculated, and he never had a formal share in the functioning of the school, his ties were sufficiently close that the faculty marked his passing as if one of their own had died. Callimachus remembered the *studium* in his will with a handsome bequest. The years of his career in Poland coincide almost exactly with the second period of humanism at the university.[41]

This period saw two parallel developments. One was the continued growth of humanistic and literary concerns among those who composed the academic community: these students and faculty pursued these interests outside the formal structure of the university. The other development was the process by which these same tastes were incorporated into the instructional program of the school.

Two measures of the former development should be mentioned here. One was the increasing frequency with which the writings of antique authors, particularly those who had been little appreciated and read during earlier medieval centuries, and the works of Italian humanists were represented in the libraries of the professoriate. A few examples, which are of particular significance, illustrate this. Jan Długosz purchased copies of Boccaccio's *De casibus virorum illustrium* and *De praeclaris mulieribus*, both printed in Strasbourg about 1475, and gave them to the university in 1479.[42] Another manuscript, from an unidentified professor, contains a dialogue between Leonardo Bruni and Vergerio, a Latin translation of the eighth *Philippic* of Demosthenes, and works by Xenophon, Seneca, and Cicero. A third example is a manuscript which has selections from such ancient writers as Xenophon, Seneca, and Cicero, and from such Renaissance authors as Bruni and Guarino.[43] Thus in this period, the *corpus* of literature by which humanist tastes were nourished was greatly augmented. The second measure of the degree of these interests lies in the informal lectures and cultural circles in which those in and around the university were involved. Just as Gregory of Sanok had earlier lectured privately on Vergil, so others in these years presented their praise of antique authors and the values of poetry in similar circumstances.[44] The most important of these came during the visit to Cracow of the German arch-humanist, Conrad Celtis.

Crowned poet laureate in Nürnberg in the spring of 1487, Celtis had soon thereafter begun a decade of restless wandering which took him to many places, none of them for very long. A writer of both good verse and striking prose, and an ardent defender of humanist concerns, he studied first grammar and rhetoric in several Italian centers, then spent some time with Pomponius Laetus in Rome. There he developed an interest in natural science, particularly astronomy and astrology. It may have been in Rome, through Pomponius' knowledge of Callimachus' experiences in Poland, that he learned of the reputation of Cracow in this field.[45] He left suddenly, and by Easter of 1489 he had arrived at the university. There, despite his previous M.A. from Heidelberg, he matriculated as an arts student. Although he was to make an important contribution in humanist circles, it was ironically as a student of the stars that he came to the *studium*.[46]

Celtis spent two years in Cracow, broken only by trips outside the city. It was during this time that he had a vision of his life's work. He later recalled that on one of the prehistoric mounds outside Cracow, while he stood entranced with the panorama of the walls and towers beneath him, Phoebus appeared and commanded him to "rise and let his members seize their ancient vigor so that he might sing of the four corners of his fatherland."[47] Within the university, he apparently tried to obtain a faculty appointment, but was not granted the right to teach, except as an *extraneus non de facultate*. It was in this capacity that in the summer semester 1490 he lectured on the traditional scholastic subject *Parvus philosophiae*.[48]

On at least one occasion he was able to lecture on poetry.[49] On another, in 1489, he announced that on July 23rd *in aula Hungarorum* (i.e., the Hungarian students' hostel), he would lecture on *ars epistolandi*. From the text of this announcement, it is clear that he intended a presentation which was humanistic in character.[50] On the basis of other epigrams which Celtis wrote, it is possibie to conclude that he apparently gave other such lectures while in Cracow. It should be emphasized, however, that this activity stood, by and large, in the tradition of informal and extramural teaching which has been noted above. In this role, Celtis became the focus for a group of like-minded individuals at the university. With them he had close, cordial relations. To many, he eventually dedicated individual poems that he included in his later collection of *Odes*. One went to Callimachus, another to Jan Sommerfeld; Stanisław Selig was honored by one, as was Jan Ursinus.[51] In addition, Celtis was greatly influential upon Wawrzyniec Rabe (Laurentius Corvinus) and Jan Rhagius Aesticampianus,[52] so that his impact upon the humanistic tradition at Cracow continued long after he left. We shall look below at some of the accomplishments of this group.

During this second period, humanistic interests were, in clear degree and for the first time on a continuing basis, manifest within the curriculum as a part of the program of the *studium*. The sustained attention given to literature and to antiquity in formal instruction may be traced in the *Liber diligentiarum* once its extant record is avallable after 1487. One may reasonably assume that this teaching represents the continuation of a tradition whose origin is hidden from us, rather than being something whose inception came only in that year. A few examples must suffice.

In the winter semester of 1487 Jan Sacranus of Oświęcim lectured on Cicero, Jakub of Gostynin on *Poetica*, Stanisław Biel taught Virgil's *Bucolics*, and Jan Sommerfeld Aesticampianus presented the *Volumen maius* of Priscian. (This is the first concrete evidence we have that the Priscian taught after the reform of 1449 was not simply the *Volumen minus* or *ars minor*, i.e., only the seventeenth and eighteenth books of the *Institutionum grammaticae*, which were commonly used in the Middle Ages). In the summer semester of 1488 Stanisław Biel lectured on the *Aeneid*, Jan Thurzo on Ovid, Jakub of Gostynin commented on Statius' *Achilleis* and on Horace's *Odes*, while Stanisław Selig of Cracow taught Vergil's *Georgics*. In the winter semester, Selig lectured on Juvenal, Biel on the *Aeneid*, Jerzy Smeed of Nysa taught Boethius' *De consolatione philosophiae*, and Adam of Wilno presented Horace. The frequency with which Virgil was taught was not atypical, for well into the sixteenth century an average of slightly more than one course per semester was devoted to his writings.[53]

The number of lectures on classical authors increased. For example, in 1492 there were nine given. Jakub of Szadek presented three on Cicero in two semesters, Adam of Łowicz taught Ovid, Erasmus of Cracow lectured on Ovid's letters, Stanisław Selig treated Valerius Maximus and the *Bucolics* of Virgil, Paweł of Zakliczew lectured on the *Aeneid*, and Marcin of Głogów took the *Georgics* for his presentation.[54] In addition to these masters, there were others whose humanistic interests were reflected in their teaching and activity.

Celtis' departure from Cracow and the death, not long after, of Callimachus, marked the end of the second period of humanism at the university. In the third period the school was dominated by those who had been influenced by these two. Let us examine briefly the careers of some of the most important of these.

Jakub of Boksice matriculated at Cracow in 1456 and earned an M.A. in 1462. He went to Italy and earned a doctorate *in medicinis* at Bologna in 1475 or 1476. Eventually he returned to teach at Cracow. That he had developed literary and humanistic interests, perhaps through contacts with Callimachus and certainly as a result of his Italian venture, is reflected in a story told by Callimachus. The two of them, along with others, accepted the hospitality of the Cracow citizen Mirika (Jan Heydecke-Mirica). They would sit in his garden to read the Venetian history of Sabellicus and discuss the histories and affairs of the western nations.[55] Jakub of Boksice was also a participant in the activities connected with Celtis' visit. He died about 1497.[56]

Jan Sacranus of Oświęcim matriculated at Cracow in 1459 and earned an M.A. a decade later. He went to Italy, where, under the influence of Filelfo and perhaps Argyropoulos, he developed humanistic interests. After his return to Cracow, he taught in arts before earning a theology degree and teaching in that faculty. Three things in particular reflect aspects of his humanistic interests.

One was the character of his teaching in arts. One of his students later commented that there was no one else at the university who so successfully developed in those who studied with him a knowledge and appreciation of Cicero and other famous orators.[57] A second humanistic dimension to the interests of Jan Sacranus can be seen in his role as orator. On several occasions he represented the university as official speaker. Another of his students later wrote that he was the "standard bearer and leader of the muses, superior in verse, perfect in prose."[58] The third aspect was Jan Sacranus' interest in epistolography. While the art of dictamen in the Middle Ages had always utilized letter collections as models to depend upon, the humanists' concern for letter writing was a somewhat different matter. Jan Sacranus prepared a treatise entitled *Modus epistolandi* which, while relatively traditional and modest in scope, nevertheless reflected some of the interests he developed in Italy.[59]

Jan Sommerfeld, from the town of the same name in Lower Lusatia, latinized his name to Aesticampianus before his death in 1501 in accordance with the humanistic mode of the day. His very large library contained a broad sampling of classical and Renaissance writers, and one of his own writings was a commentary upon the rhetoric and orations of Libanios in the Latin translation prepared earlier by Francesco Zambeccari and published in Cracow in 1504. Some of his teaching was also in this same vein. In 1492 he lectured on Cicero's *Laelius* and Augustine Dati of Sienna's *De conficiendis epistolis*; in 1493, 1499, and 1501 he lectured on the letters of the Venetian humanist Franciscus Niger; and in 1493 he lectured on the pseudo-Senecan *Epistolae ad Lucilium*. His two most important works were a commentary upon the versified version of Priscian's grammar prepared by Peter Helias in the twelfth century and a collection of twenty model letters, compared and with explanations, entitled *Modus epistolandi*. While the former work, in effect a commentary upon a commentary, is characteristically scholastic, it reflects profound erudition as well as knowledge of the Greek grammarians referred to by Priscian. The latter work shows the influence of Renaissance epistolography. In this respect, it is superior to that by Sacranus.[60]

Another Jan Sommerfeld Aesticampianus, known commonly as Rhagius to distinguish him, was also part of Celtis' circle. In the aftermath of Celtis' visit to Cracow, Rhagius matriculated at the university in 1491. He took no degree and may not even have stayed in Cracow long. While he was there, however, Rhagius became an ardent and zealous defender of the humanistic movement. In this enthusiasm, he is typical of some of the remaining individuals who constitute part of the group in this context.[61]

Stanisław Biel of Nowe Miasto in Ruthenia was known among the humanists as Albinus. His earliest teaching was done in the *Collegium minus*, and he taught chiefly the writings of Virgil and Ovid, noting himself as *magister in poesi*.[62] He became, partly as a result of Celtis' visit, a fervent devotee of humanistic interests. His orations were models of humanist rhetoric. As did other members of this group under discussion, Stanisław Biel wrote a treatise on epistolography, *Exordia epistolarum* (1512), which stands firmly in the Renaissance tradition of this genre.[63]

Jan Ber Ursinus was a slightly younger contemporary of Stanisław Biel, but he died prematurely shortly after 1500. This untimely demise cut short a humanistic career which surpassed all but a very few within the *studium*. Between 1478 and 1488 he had traveled to Italy, where he studied both law and medicine. But these were not his only interests south of the Alps. The muses proved as seductive to him as they had been to countless other students from northern Europe who went to Italy for law or medicine. In Rome he studied with Pomponius Laetus and Johannes Argyropoulos. When he returned to Cracow after 1488, his enthusiasm for the humanist movement was revealed in his speeches and writings. His most important work was his *Modus epistolandi ... cum epistolis exemplaribus et orationibus et annexis*, which he had gathered by about 1493 and which was first printed in Nürnberg in 1496. Unlike the hypothetical and somewhat lifeless letters which, for example, Sommerfeld included in his own collection, these are actual letters which Jan Ursinus had sent to such individuals as Callimachus, King Jan Olbracht, the humanist Maciej Drzewicki, and others. They are full of sparkle and vitality. This book also contained five of Jan Ursinus' orations, together with brief commentary. Throughout, the commitment of the author to the ideals of Renaissance eloquence is clear.[64]

Wawrzyniec Rabe (Laurentius Corvinus) matriculated at Cracow in 1484 and earned an M.A. in 1489. He was early imbued with an enthusiasm for antique literature, and was closely associated with Celtis, with whom he corresponded and whom he regarded as the one who had awakened his humanistic interests. The two most important literary fruits of the interests he developed in Cracow were a comprehensive world geography, *Cosmographia dans manuductionem in tabulas Ptholomei*, and a handbook on Latin versification, *Carminum structura*, which was published in Cracow in 1496 and dedicated to the students of the university. Despite his absence from the Polish capital after 1494, Wawrzyniec always thought fondly of Cracow and of its influences upon him.[65]

These then were some of the more important individuals, who, nurtured in the native tradition of the earlier part of the century, given inspiration by Celtis and support by Callimachus, brought humanistic interests within the university to their highest levels in this third period. The chief thrust of their activity came in the half decade before 1495, when the memory of Celtis' visit was freshest. After that the force of the movement seems to have been somewhat dissipated. Some scholars have seen in the third period a conscious reaction by the traditionalists and scholastics within the university against what they term the "radical humanism" of some of the individuals described above.[66]

It is true that the humanists were less active in the last years of the fifteenth century and the opening years of the new century. For example, the number of lectures in the arts faculty on literary topics declined to fewer than half-a-dozen in some years. Only later in the sixteenth century did it again reach the level of the time of Celtis. In addition, many of those associated with the Arch-

Humanist's circle left the university or died in the late 1490's and the dawning years of the new century. It is not surprising, therefore, that Jan Sommerfeld should write Celtis in 1499 and remark that the University of Cracow ("our school") was no longer flourishing the way it had before.[67]

However it should be remembered that many other humanists continued to be active in Cracow. Within the university, if there was not the spectacular activity of the time of Celtis, humanistic progress, as Henryk Barycz has commented, was gradual and proceeded step by step.[68] Eventually new grammatical and rhetorical textbooks and manuals were introduced as the basis for lectures, new subjects were formally inserted into the required curriculum, Greek became a part of the university's instruction, and the *studia humaniora* became prized by individuals, particularly those among the Polish gentry, as an educational adornment which would enable them to play their proper role in society. This culture is clearly foreshadowed in the interests and activities of the fifteenth century university community, but the culmination did not come in that time. By the time Kochanowski matriculated, however, the seeds of the fifteenth century had germinated and come into full flower. The Renaissance culture to which he contributed so greatly had been nurtured by the academy to which he joined himself.[69]

Notes

1. See especially Kazimierz Morawski, *Historya Uniwersytetu Jagiellońskiego, Średnie wieki i Odrodzenie* (History of the Jagiellonian University, the Middle Ages and the Renaissance), 2 vols. (Cracow: Uniwersytet Jagielloński, 1900), passim; and Ignacy Zarębski, "Okres wczesnego humanizmu" (The period of early humanism), in Kazimierz Lepszy, ed., *Dzieje Uniwersytetu Jagiellońskiego w latach 1364-1764*, vol. 1 (Cracow: Uniwersytet Jagielloński, 1964), pp. 151-187.

2. Leonard Coxe, *De laudibus celeberrimae Cracoviensis Academiae* (Cracoviae, 1518), p. 1. This speech was delivered before the faculty (and probably some distinguished guests) on December 6, 1518.

3. See Jan Fijałek, *Polonia apud Italos scholastica, saeculum XV* (Cracoviae: Typis Universitatis Jagiellonicae, 1900).

4. For this subject, see my study, "The University of Cracow and the Conciliar Movement," in James M. Kittelson, ed., *Rebirth, Reform and Resilience: Universities in Transition 1300-1700* (Columbus, Ohio: University Press, 1984).

5. "Vidit uno tempore tot discipulos suos ex toto orbe terrarum in unum locum congregatos," cited by Nice Contieri, "La fortuna del Petrarca in Polonia nei secoli XIV e XV," *Annali dell'Istituto Universitario Orientale di Napoli: Sezione Slava IV* (1961): 147, n.1.

6. For his letters, *Codex epistolaris saeculi decimi quinti*, A. Sokołowski, J. Szujski, and A. Lewicki, editors, 3 vols. in 4 pts. (Cracow, 1876-1894), II 90-92, 97f., 100f., and 112. His knowledge of Petrarch is discussed by Contieri, "La fortuna del Petrarca," pp. 148-150.

7. Piotr Wolfram of Lwów was an ambitious careerist, whose interests in and appreciation of antique literature and classical Latinity may be traceable to the fact

that he hoped to obtain a position in the papal chancery. Such an appointment would require precisely the skills he was demonstrating in these letters. He brought back several important classical and humanist works from Constance. These manuscripts are discussed by Jerzy Zathey, "Biblioteka Jagiellońska w latach 1364-1492" (The Jagiellonian Library in the years 1364-1492), in Zathey, Anna Lewicka-Kamińska, and Leszek Hajdukiewicz, *Historia Biblioteki Jagiellońskiej 1364-1775* (Cracow: Uniwersytet Jagielloński, 1966), p. 81; see also n. 152.

8. See Zarębski's important study, "Zur Bedeutung des Aufenthaltes von Krakauer Universitätsprofessoren auf dem Basler Konzil für die Geistesgeschichte Polens, *Vierteljahresschrift für Geschichte der Wissenschaft und Technik* V: Sonderheft, 2 (1960): 7-23. A sharp dissent to some of his views may be found in Zathey, "Biblioteka Jagiellońska w latach 1364-1492," p. 74, n. 132 especially.

9. The figure of Mikołaj Lasocki falls technically outside the scope of this paper, but he deserves some mention within the context of a discussion of the importance of Basel. Lasocki was a canon of the cathedral in Cracow and had very close contacts with the university. During the conciliar period he became close friends with Guarino da Verona, with whom he corresponded and to whom he eventually sent his nephew for education. See Henryk Barycz, *Polacy na studiach w Rzymie w epoce Odrodzenia (1440- 1600)* (Poles studying in Rome in the period of the Renaissance) (Cracow: Polska Akademia Umiejętności, 1938), pp. 24ff. The influence of Lasocki's humanist tastes must also be taken into account when considering the growth of humanist currents within the university.

10. *Philippi Callimachi vita et mores Gregorii Sanocei*, Edidit . . . Irmina Lichońska (Varsoviae: PWN, 1963), p. 16: "Ibi aliquamdiu substitit litterisque operam dedit."

11. "Sed circa rhetoricam et poesim, cui naturaliter affectus erat." Ibid., p. 18. Callimachus sets this statement in the context of Gregory's Virgil lectures, which he has him deliver upon his first return to Cracow, i.e. in 1428 or perhaps in 1433. For the problems with this chronology, see Lichońska's notes to p. 18, line 6 and p. 22, line 18.

12. "Cum aegre pateretur abesse a consuetudine doctorum hominum. . ." Ibid., p. 20.

13. "Eodem tempore casu ad manus eius deuenere satyrae Iuuenalis, quas cum studiose legeret. . . . Ex quibus ingeniosus iuuenis illico animaduertit doctorem Dambrowka, qui tunc in Polonorum historias commentaria scribebat, statim in prooemio ipso, ubi de Codro mentio est, errasse." Ibid., pp. 20, 22.

14. On the importance of this stay, see Tadeusz Sinko, "De Gregorii Sanocei studiis humanioribus," *Eos* 6 (1900): 248: "amorem renascentium litterarum hausisse."

15. This codex is described and discussed by Zarębski, "Problemy wczesnego odrodzenia w Polsce: Grzegorz z Sanoka, Boccaccio, Długosz" (Problems of the early Renaissance in Poland: Gregory of Sanok, Boccaccio, Długosz), *Odrodzenie i Reformacja w Polsce* II (1957): 33-39, and "Kodeks BJ Nr 413: Giovanni Boccaccio, *Genealogia deorum* a Gontier Col, humanista francuski wczesnego odrodzenia" (Genealogia deorum and Gontier Col, French Humanist of the early Renaissance), *Biuletyn Biblioteki Jagiellońskiej* 15, no. 1/2 (1963): 39-48.

16. "Coepit enim Bucolicon carmen Vergilii publicitus interpretari, cuius et nomen et auctor ad eam diem extra omnium notitiam ea in regione fuerat." *Vita Gregorii*, p.18. About the knowledge of Virgil in Poland before Gregory of Sanok,

see Lichońska's comment, ibid., p. 18-19. On the problems of the date of these lectures, see above, n. 11.

17. "Primus itaque sordem ac squalorem, quem recentiores grammatici discentium ingeniis offuderant, detergere orsus cultum ac splendorem antiquae orationis Cracouiam induxit tanto omnium fauore, ut non modo praeter spem, sed etiam praeter uoluntatem suam fuerit mox in disciplinis liberalibus magister declaratus, cum re uera nondum eas artes attigisset, per quas ad id tituli peruenitur..." ibid.

18. See L.S. Domonkos, "Ecclesiastical Patrons as a Factor in the Hungarian Renaissance," *New Review of East-European History* 14 (1974): 102-104, and, in more detail, "Archbishop Vitéz, the Father of Hungarian Humanism (1408-1472)," *The New Hungarian Quarterly* 20, no. 74 (1979): 142- 150.

19. See particularly Zarębski, "Okres wczesnego humanizmu," p. 163.

20. Józef Muczkowski, ed., *Statuta nec non liber promotionum philosophorum Ordinis in Universitate studiorum Jagellonica ab anno 1402 ad annum 1849* (Cracoviae: Typis Universitatis Jagiellonicae, 1849), p. 31.

21. Actually "nihil enim in se continere nisi uigilantium insomnia." *Vita Gregorii*, p. 24. On the use of this phrase, cf. Cicero, *De natura deorum*, 1, 8.

22. Diploma printed in Fijałek, *Polonia apud Italos scholastica*, p. 79f. Jan of Ludzisko appears in other Paduan documents as "Iohannes de Cracovia artium doctor, in medicinis scholaris" on 31 October 1430 (this serves as proof of his presence in Padua by that time), on 5 and 21 June and on 4 July 1432; see Barycz, *Polacy na studiach*, p. 23, n. 2.

23. The analysis of his biography and work given by Jacek Stanisław Bojarski, "Jan z Ludziska i przypisywane mu mowy uniwersyteckie" (Jan of Ludzisko and university speeches attributed to him), *Studia Mediewistyczne* 14 (1973): 3-85, has superceded all older accounts, particularly that of Fijałek, *Mistrz Jakub z Paradyża i Uniwersytet Krakowski w okresie soboru bazylejskiego* (Master Jakub of Paradyż and Cracow University in the period of the Council of Basel) 2 vols. (Cracow: Akademia Umiejętności, 1900), 1, pp. 197-249; and, to a lesser extent, Bronisław Nadolski, "Rola Jana z Ludziska w polskim Odrodzeniu" (The role of Jan of Ludzisko in the Polish Renaissance), *Pamiętnik Literacki* 26 (1929): 198-211.

24. See, for this, Fijałek, *Polonia apud italos scholastica*, p. 83.

25. This is the suggestion made by Nadolski, "Rola Jana z Ludziska," p. 200; see, however, the more cautious approach taken by Bojarski, "Jan z Ludziska i przypisywane mu mowy," p. 26f.

26. *Ioannis de Ludzisko Orationes*, ed. Jacek Stanisław Bojarski (Wrocław: Ossolineum, 1971), now replaces all previous texts for this set of material.

27. The following, for example, are cited in the last oration: Alexander, Aristotle, Augustine, Boethius, Cassiodorus, Chrysostom, Cicero, Hermes, Homer, Martial, Pamphilus, Philo, Plato, Plutarch, Ptolemy, Seneca, Socrates, Virgil, and Varro. Among Italian humanist writers are citations from Vergerio's *De ingenuis moribus et liberalibus studiis*.

28. On this point, see Bojarski, "Jan z Ludziska i przypisywane mu mowy," p. 72f. Since the time of Fijałek, *Mistrz Jakub z Paradyża*, I, pp. 21-225, this "second" Basel delegation address had routinely been attributed to Jakub of Paradyż; see, for example, Krystyna Pieradzka, "Uniwersytet Krakowski w służbie państwa i wobec soborów w Konstancji i Bazylei" (Cracow University in the service of the state and in relation to the Councils of Constance and Basel), in Lepszy, *Dzieje Uniwersytetu Jagiellońskiego*, p. 121f.

29. This speech has been often discussed in Polish historiography. See Feliks Koneczny, "Wiadomość z r. 1447 o stanie ludu wiejskiego w Polsce czy na Litwie" (Information from the year 1447 on the status of the peasantry in Poland and in Lithuania), *Ateneum Wileńskie* 6 (1929): 8-15; Franciszek Bujak, "Mowa Jana z Ludziska do króla Kazimierza Jagiellończyka z r. 1447 i zagadnienie niewoli w Polsce ówczesnej" (Speech of Jan of Ludzisko to Casimir the Jagiellonian in 1447 and the question of slavery in Poland of the time), in *Księga pamiątkowa ku czci Władysława Abrahama* (Lwów, 1931), 2, pp. 217—233; and Kazimierz Tymieniecki, "Zagadnienie niewoli w Polsce u schyłku wieków średnich" (Question of slavery in Poland at the close of the Middle Ages), *Prace Komisji Historii Poznańskiego Towarzystwa Prszyjaciół Nauk* 7 (1933): 497-537.

30. For examples, see Bojarski, "Jan z Ludziska i przypisywane mu mowy," pp. 31-33.

31. Jan of Ludzisko is regarded by Władysław Seńko, *Les tendances préhumanistes dans la philosophie polonaise au XVe siecle* (Wrocław: Ossolineum, 1973), p. 28, "comme premier penseur polonais qui ait pratiqué la lecture de la littérature antique et l'art de la rhétorique: cultum ac [etc.]." This last is the statement made by Callimachus about Gregory of Sanok (see above, n. 17). At the beginning of this century, however, Fijałek, *Polonia apud Italos scholastica* p. 77, argued that it was in fact Jan of Ludzisko about whom Callimachus should have said this: "Hic est enim, ad quem laudes a Philippo Callimacho Gregorio Sanocensi ob cultum ac splendorem antiquae orationis Cracoviam primum inductum ascriptae referentur necesse est." Seńko (and the text above) follows this tradition.

32. These parts of his library are discussed by Wacława Szelińska, *Biblioteki profesorów Uniwersytetu Krakowskiego w XV i początkach XVI wieku* (Libraries of the professors of the University of Cracow in the fifteenth and the beginning of the sixteenth century) (Wrocław; Ossolineum, 1966), p. 65-67.

33. This type of material is discussed by Jacek Wiesiołowski, *Kolekcje historyczne w Polsce średniowiecznej XIV-XV wieku* (Historical collections in medieval Poland of the fourteenth-fifteenth century) (Wrocław; Ossolineum, 1967), pp. 52-55, 66-91; and Marian Zwiercan, *Komentarz Jana z Dąbrówki do Kroniki mistrza Wincentego zwanego Kadłubkiem* (Commentary of Jan of Dąbrówka to the Chronicle of Master Vincent called Kadłubek) (Wrocław; Ossolineum, 1969), pp. 114-157.

34. For example, Jan of Dąbrówka although he quoted Petrach many times, he cites Vergerio only one time in his commentary; see Zwiercan, *Komentarz Jana z Dąbrówki*, p. 180.

35. See especially Morawski, *Historya UJ*, 1, pp. 440-443; Antoni Karbowiak, *Dzieje wychowania i szkół w Polsce* (History of education and schools in Poland) (St. Petersburg and Lwów, 1898-1923), 3, p. 306 ff.; and, most explicitly, Zarębski, "Okres wczesnego humanizmu," pp. 173- 177.

36. See Pieradzka, "Uniwersytet Krakowski w służbie państwa," p. 128ff.

37. Printed in Józef Szujski, "Statuta Collegii Minoris Studii Generalis Cracoviensis," *Archiwum do Dziejów Literatury i Oświaty w Polsce* 1 (1878), p. 97.

38. On the survival of the *Doctrinale*, compare Barycz, *Historja Uniwersytetu Jagiellońskiego w epoce humanizmu* (History of the Jagiellonian University in the period of humanism) (Cracow: Nakładem Uniwersytetu Jagiellońskiego, 1935), p. 17f. who emphasized that the *Doctrinale* continued to be taught at Vienna until 1599, at

Wittenberg until 1506, at Fribourg and Cologne until 1522. See also Józef Garbacik, "Ognisko nauki i kultury renesansowej (1470-1520)" (Center of Renaissance learning and culture), in Lepszy, *Dzieje Uniwersytetu Jagiellońskiego*, p. 208.

39. Szujski, "Statuta Collegii Minoris," pp. 97-99.

40. See Barycz, *Historia UJ*, p. 47. See also his comments in this regard, in direct response to Zarębski's interpretation, in "Nowa synteza dziejów Uniwersytetu Jagiellońskiego" (New synthesis of the history of the Jagiellonian University), *Przegląd Historyczno-Oświatowy* 9 (1966): 283ff.

41. The biography of Callimachus is best approached through Józef Garbacik's excellent article in *Polski Słownik Biograficzny*, vol. 11, pp. 493-499, who cites there the contemporary statement that at his death "tutti i dottori della terra in ogni fachulta chol Rettore dello Studio" participated in his funeral.

42. Zarębski, "Problemy wczesnego odrodzenia," p. 42f.

43. Szelińska, *Biblioteki profesorów*, p. 291; see also Contieri, "La fortuna del Petrarca in Polonia," p. 157.

44. Gustav Bauch, *Deutsche Scholaren in Krakau in der Zeit der Renaissance, 1460 bis 1520* (Wrocław, 1901), p. 14, discusses an oration by Jan Ber Ursinus (*De laudibus eloquentiae*) on Sallust's *Coniuratio Catilinae*, which he sets in Cracow in the year 1486. Such a date, however, is impossible, for at this time Ursinus was still in Italy; see below. Whatever the year, this oration would be an example of the type of extramural presentation noted in the text.

45. Suggested by Lewis W. Spitz, *Conrad Celtis, the German Arch- Humanist* (Cambridge, Mass: Harvard University Press, 1957), p. 15.

46. The brief *Vita* which Celtis prefixed to an edition of his *Odes* includes the statement: "Ibique astrorum studio vacauit..." F. Pindter, ed., *Conradus Celtis Protucius, Libri Odarum Quattuor* (Leipzig, 1934), p. 2.

47. See this statement in Pindter, ed., *Conradus Celtis Protucius Quattuor Libri Amorum secundum quattuor latera Germaniae* (Leipzig, 1934), Bk. I, 3, lines 61f. Celtis used four of his love relationships (with Hasilina in Cracow, Elsula in Regensburg, Ursula from the Rhineland, and Barbara, whose symbolic geographical identity is obscure) to symbolize and celebrate the four parts of Germany.

48. *Liber diligentiarum facultatis artisticae Universitatis Cracoviensis (1487-1563)*, edited by W. Wisłocki, in *Archiwum do Dziejów Literatury i Oświaty w Polsce*, 4 (1886), p. 13.

49. This is inferred from one of his epigrams. See Konrad Celtes, *Fünf Bücher Epigramme*, Karl Hartfelder, ed. (Berlin, 1881, reprinted Hildesheim: G. Olms, 1963), p. 21: "Ad gymnasium Cracoviense, dum orare vellet," (Epigram I, 90), which includes the lines: "Cum dicturus ero Cracovina forte palaestra,/Cuius fama omni docta sub orbe volat,... "

50. This announcement was discovered in one of Celtis' poems by Fijałek, *Studya do dziejów Uniwersytetu Krakowskiego i jego Wydziału Teologicznego w XV w.* (Studies for the history of Cracow University and its faculty of theology in the fifteenth century) (Cracow, 1899), p. 24.

51. See the following *Odes*: I,7; I,17; I,23; I,8.

52. Bauch, *Deutsche Scholaren*, p. 39.

53. See Kazimierz Kumaniecki, "De studiis Vergilianis in Universitate Jagellonica priore sec. XVI parte florentibus," in *Commentationes Vergilianae* (Cracoviae, 1930), pp. 193-205.

54. *Liber diligentiarum, sub annis* 1487, 1488, 1492. The presentation in Garbacik, "Ognisko nauki i kultury renesansowej," p. 204, is confused.

55. "Apud Ioannem Miricam in horto una cum Nicolae Mergo Nissensi ac Bascziza Iacobo, quorum utrius doctrina et eloquentia insignior sit an admirabilior, non facile quis dixerit, mirati sumus inter legendum res gestas Venetorum de Persis propemodum dissimulanter, de Tartaris uero nullam esse omnino in historiis Sabellici expressam mentionem." *Philippi Callimachi De his quae a Venetis tentata sunt Persis ac Tartaris contra turcos movendis*, Andreas Kempfi, ed. (Varsoviae: PWN, 1962), p. 22.

56. For his biography, see the comments in Morawski, *Historya UJ*, vol. 2, pp. 112-114; and, more systematically, *Polski Słownik Biograficzny*, vol. 2, pp. 244f.

57. See Barycz, *Historia UJ*, p. 177, n. 3, citing a document in an article by Aleksander Brückner in *Prace filologiczne* IV: 38f., which I have been unable to consult directly. Andrzej Krzycki (or Cricius), a humanist at the court of King Sigismund I of Poland, once wrote the following about Sacranus:

Rhetorices studium confert hanc primus in urbem
Et teneram pubem non sine laude docet.
Non adeo Phoebum Satyri, nec tam Orphea silvae
Quam sequiturque colitque hunc studiosa cohors.
Illius ori inerat dulcis facundia, per quam
Ad summum evasit conspicuumque decus.

Andreae Cricii Carmina, ed. Casimirus Morawski (Cracoviae, 1881), p. 184.

58. Quoted by Barycz, *Historia UJ*, p. 178, from Stanisław of Łowicz's *De arte componendi et resolvendi epistolas libellus*... Sacranus' speeches are printed and discussed by Fijałek, *Studya*, pp. 42-52.

59. This book is analyzed by Lidia Winniczuk, *Epistolografia. Łacińskie podręczniki epistolograficzne w Polsce w XV-XVI wieku* (Epistolography. Latin epistolographic textbooks in Poland in the fifteenth-sixteenth century) (Warsaw: Biblioteka Meandra, 1952). Morawski, *Historya UJ*, 2, p. 80, is probably too harsh in his negative evaluation of the quality of this work.

60. For this work, see Winniczuk, *Epistolografia*; Jan Sommerfeld's biography is best treated by Bauch, *Deutsche Scholaren*, pp. 26-28; and more briefly, in *Nowy Korbut. Bibliografia Literatury Polskiej* (Warsaw, PIW, 1965) vol. 3, p. 277.

61. On Rhagius Aesticampianus, see the biographical treatment by Bauch, "Johannes Rhagius Aesticampianus in Krakau, seine erste Reise nach Italien und sein Aufenthalt in Mainz," *Archiv für Literatur-Geschichte* 12 (1884): 321-370, and more briefly, in Deutsche Scholaren, pp. 41-43.

62. *Acta rectoralia almae Universitatis Studii Cracoviensis* (Cracow, 1893-1909), no. 1381.

63. This work is discussed by Winniczuk, *Epistolografia*. Stanisław Biel's biography is treated in *Polski Słownik Biograficzny*, vol. 2, p. 32.

64. Lidia Winniczuk, ed. and trans., *Johannes Ursinus Modus epistolandi* (Wrocław: Ossolineum, 1957).

65. For his biography, see Bauch, "Laurentius Corvinus, der Breslauer Stadtschreiber und Humanist. Sein Leben und seine Schriften," *Zeitschrift des Vereins für Geschichte und Althertum Schlesiens* 17 (1883): 230-302. There is also a brief biography in *Polski Słownik Biograficzny*, vol. 4, pp. 96-98.

66. Morawski, *Historya UJ*, 2, p. 192, and after him, many other scholars, particularly Garbacik, "Ognisko nauki i kultury renesansowej," p. 207.

67. Hans Rupprich, ed., *Der Briefwechsel des Konrad Celtis* (Munich, 1934), p. 355, no. 213: "Vereor, non in tanto stat flore gymnasium ut olim tu ipse aderas."

68. Barycz, *Historya UJ*, p. 16.

69. A recognition of the way the old and the new were combined at Cracow is given by Bauch, *Deutsche Scholaren*, p. 6: "Sie (the University of Cracow) kam, ohne den scholastischen Traditionen der mittelalterlichen Universitäten untreu zu werden, den wissenschaftlichen Neigungen der Zeit wie keine andere entgegen und pflegte sie mit Bewusstsein und Ausdauer und entging so der Einseitigkeit, die ihre deutschen Schwestern, die zäher am Alten festhingen und sich nur schwer und langsam entschlossen, dem Zeitgeist Concessionen zu machen, ihr gegenüber als zurückbleibend, wohl gar als Hochburgen des Rückschrittes erscheinen liess; sie war eine wirkliche Universitas studiorum im Zeitsinne."

IV

Renaissance Poland
and Other Cultures

12

Polish Humanism and its Italian Sources:
Beginnings and Historical Development

Tadeusz Ulewicz

$\mathcal{A}$t the outset, our terminology and the sequence of events and phenomena relating to it require definition. First, the subject of this essay is Renaissance humanism, which historically reached Poland—as it reached the other parts of Europe under the predominant influence of Latin civilization, for all the diversity of local traditions and circumstances—as an intellectual, spiritual, and cultural influx from Italy. Secondly, as in Western Europe, so too in Poland, the constituent elements of humanism arrived and settled, to progress by means of traditional and continually fundamental route of Western civilization, the *Iter Romanum*; though this was not necessarily a simple or mechanical process, and places such as Padua, Bologna, or Florence also lay on this northward route of cultural advancement. Thirdly, the civilization "time-gap," quite understandable in the circumstances, was no greater for Renaissance humanism north of the Alps in Cracow than, say, in Buda, Prague, Vienna or Nürenberg, as can be easily verified. In other words, the cultural barrier between civilizations of totally different mentalities was determined by the Alps, and not by economic, social, political, or even obvious linguistic differences (regarding local vernaculars), important though all of these factors might have otherwise been, not to mention the host of other divisions—dynastic, political, and administrative, ecclesiastical and denominational, the relevance of which is not to be denied either.

This Alpine barrier provides an explanation for the basic chronology of the subject of our study. There was no one individual—whether in Poland or in any of the Slavic lands, or indeed anywhere in Central Europe—whose career, and cultural, philosophical, and intellectual impact may even remotely be compared to Petrarch's in Italy, and the influence he exerted through contemporaries and, posthumously, through such followers as Boccaccio and later Luigi

Marsigli, Giovanni Malpaghini, and Coluccio Salutati. Apparent points of co-incidence, such as the rather unfortunate Prague episode of Cola di Rienzo in 1350, and even more so, Petrarch's memorable epistle in 1351 to the Emperor Charles IV, inviting him well-nigh officially to Italy and establishing the personal "literary" relations between the poet and the Imperial court (through Chancellor Johannes von Neumarkt, Archbishop Ernest of Pardubice, etc.) that were to continue intermittently for the next dozen or so years, only go to show the mutual political and ideological incomprehensibility, and the incongruity of two different ages and two different ways of thinking.

Thus, the facts we shall be considering begin in the period of the great fifteenth-century Councils, from Constance (1414-18) to Ferrara and Florence (with Florentine Graeco—Roman Union, 1439), when Poland, along with the rest of Transalpine Europe, was for the first time confronted with Italian humanism, its personalities, as represented by some of its foremost exponents. In these crucial negotiations, especially at the Council of Constance, which at last ended the Western Schism and which proved a bitter experience for the Bohemians (the burning of Huss, 1415), but brought Poland an honorable though arduous legal victory over the Teutonic Knights, there emerged in the key positions of the Polish delegation a handful of brilliant men educated in Italian universities: Paweł Włodkowic (Paulus Vladimiri) of Brudzewo, Rector of the University in Cracow, and Andrzej Łaskarz (Laskary) of Gosławice, Bishop of Poznań, both pupils of the famous Francesco Zabarella at Padua (present at the Council as Cardinal and Papal Representative), and others graduated from Bologna, such as Piotr Wolfram, who had read law there, and Bishop Jakub of Korzkiew (Kurdwanowski), *Doctor Decretorum*, a man "distinguished in letters." In its spiritual and political conflict with the Teutonic Order the Polish delegation not only received a sympathetic response from Zabarella himself, but was also supported by several other gifted Italian lawyers, though while all the Polish men belonged to the country's scholastic élite, their Italian colleagues' cultural and literary orientation was undoubtedly humanism—the new, Christian humanism. For an insight into the atmosphere at the Council, it might be well to mention the following detail. In his famous treatise issued at the Council, *De potestate papae et imperatoris respectu infidelium* (1415), in which he denied the emperor any right to convert pagans by the sword, Paweł Włodkowic, the Polish expert on canon law, incidentally mentioned Dante, refuting his contention (in *De monarchia*) that the emperor was not subject to the pope's authority ("*Dantes ... quia fuit Gibellinus nititur ostendere, quod imperium in nullo dependet a papa*"), regarding the poet's attitude as heretical ("*... et propter illum tractatum fuit prope combustionem (?) tamquam haereticus*"), and quoting Zabarella to support his own statement.[1]

In Poland this was spiritually and intellectually still a deeply medieval period, but it saw the first Italian humanists welcomed as guests in Cracow. In 1412, for example, the philosopher and professor at Padua, Paolo Veneto, an Augustinian Friar, arrived on an embassy from Venice, and in the Jagiellonian library a manuscript copy of a funerary speech for him, *Oratio de obitu illustris philosophi Pauli*, by Cristoforo Barzizza, has survived down to our times. At the turn of 1423/1424, Giuliano Cesarini, another Paduan and then only a young doctor beginning his diplomatic career, appeared at King Jagiełło's Court in the name of Cardinal Branda Castiglioni, Papal Legate for Hungary and the Empire. But the most memorable of these diplomatic occasions took place in February, 1424, during the festivities for the coronation of Jagiełło's last wife, Queen Zofia, where the Emperor, Sigismund of Luxemburg, and his Empress, Barbara of Cilli, Cardinal Branda Castiglioni (Pope Martin V's representative), King Eric of Denmark, and a host of other princes and celebrities were present. At one of the many banquets following the young queen's coronation there was even a "wedding oration" delivered in the presence of King Jagiełło, the Emperor and other guests by the representative of Emperor John II Palaeologus of Constantinople, the mellifluous Francesco Filelfo, "one of the Renaissance's greatest snobs," as Stanisław Łempicki has called him. At this time Italians began to appear in the Polish diplomatic service (e.g., Jagiełło's ambassador in Rome from 1419 onwards, Jacopo de Paravesino). Then there was the very exceptional case of prince Alexander, Jagiełło's nephew and son to the Piast Duke of Mazovia, who became Bishop of Trent, patriarch of Aquileia and Cardinal (prematurely deceased in 1444). He is a fairly forgotten figure nowadays, though historically he is interesting in many respects, to mention only the oldest Latin-Polish vocabulary list which we know of today (dated before 1424) and which once belonged to him.[2]

It was in the 1430's and 40's that the new literary culture gradually began to make its first local appearances in Cracow, and the Polish intellectual élite began to show an interest in humanism. The instances of Italian humanist works (in Latin, of course) purchased abroad or copied from other manuscripts and brought into Poland now increased rapidly, and the same was true of the classics, as can be seen from the fifteenth-century endowments (now housed in the Jagiellonian Library's old collection) to the University by its professors.[3] Among the earlier, most outstanding authors in these old collections were Petrarch (with his *De remediis utriusque fortunae*, *De vita solitaria*, and several letters including the *Rerum familiarium libri*) and his junior colleague, Boccaccio, with *De casibus virorum illustrium*, *De montibus*, and more especially with an exquisite copy of *Genealogia deorum gentilium*.[4] An unexpected coincidence involving Petrarch has survived through the Jagiellonian collection—a valuable parchment codex containing the Third Decade of Livy's *Ab urbe condita*, once handled by Petrarch himself (though he did not own it) and bears notes in his handwriting. It later became the property of Lorenzo Valla, before finally being purchased for Poland's famous fifteenth-century historian, Jan Długosz, and finding its way into the Jagiellonian Library's early collection.[5]

Besides such manuscripts of earlier masters, there were also works in this library by contemporary Latin humanists. One of these latter writers was the highly esteemed educator, Guarino de' Guarini of Verona, who had a special affection for his Polish pupils, and whose letters and speeches, as well as his *Dictionarius*, occurred in the early Cracovian collections. His contemporary, the Venetian from Istria, Pier Paolo Vergerio the Elder, was to be found there as well, with his book *De ingenuis moribus et liberalibus studiis*, and so was another contemporary, the Florentine Chancellor, writer and scholar, Leonardo Bruni of Arezzo, with his letters, speeches, dialogues,[6] and the Latin comedy, *Poliscena*. Then there was the eminent Greek scholar, translator of Aristotle and professor of Creek at Florence and Rome, Joannes Argyropoulos, who coined the historical maxim, *"Graecia transvolavit in Italiam,"* whose works survive in Cracow both in manuscripts and incunabula editions. Another was Poggio Bracciolini, an ardent searcher of classical texts who became a Papal secretary and subsequently Chancellor of Florence. A number of his works existed in fifteenth-century Cracow, including *De miseria conditionis humanae* and his translation of Xenophon's *Cyropaedia*. But of special importance were the works of Enea Silvio Piccolomini, who sometimes held rather unfavorable opinions about Slavs (notably about Czechs).[7] Nevertheless, at one time he was on fairly close terms with the royal Cardinal, Alexander of Mazovia, and he also kept up an extremely polite and complimentary correspondence with the Cracovian Cardinal Zbigniew Oleśnicki whose humanist culture he deeply admired.

It would not be difficult to continue the list of texts similar to those enumerated (though not always correctly ascribed in the Polish manuscripts to their real authors, e.g., *Contra versutos Ypocritas* and *De nobilitate* were marked as by Leonardo Bruni instead of Poggio), adding to it many more names and titles of university textbooks and other scholarly works on a range of subjects from Roman law (Bartolus de Saxoferrato) and philosophy to astronomy and medicine. Acquired by Cracovian churchmen and university teachers (who were also members of the clergy), their number increased rapidly from the 1450's onwards, in the wake of the new, post-conciliar intellectual contacts with Italy. First and foremost, these links were religious and, understandably, ecclesiastical, including monastic ties, such as those connected with the fruitful work of St. John of Capistrano, who came to Poland at the invitation of the King and Oleśnicki, bringing the new Order of the Strict Observance whose members soon began to distinguish themselves in the field of the new national literature. But there were also political and generally cultural contacts, such as, for example, Italian records of the defeat and death of King Władysław III (Warneńczyk) at Varna in 1444. The literary vestiges of this fateful battle were to reecho throughout Europe for several generations, but the man who initiated them was Filelfo, with the premature compliments (*"Christianae reipublicae propugnaculum,"* *"Christi cultor et lumen,"* etc.) in his famous letter addressed to the young monarch, *Vladislao Hungariae Regi*.[8]

At the same time the first signs of native humanism and humanists began to appear in Poland, the most important one being a series of lectures (as later recorded by Callimachus) on Virgil's *Bucolics* delivered in Cracow in 1433 (or, at the latest, 1439) by the young Gregory of Sanok (Grzegorz z Sanoka; Gregorius Sanocensis)—later Archbishop of Lwów. This was not surprising, in view of Zbigniew Oleśnicki's initial plans, around 1435, for modernizing studies at the University in the "Artium" Faculty. These changes he brought about in the well-known reform of the University's syllabus in 1449, when the Faculty of Arts became "virtually the chief object of the attention" of its reformer,[9] who set it ambitious, novel and far-reaching tasks to fulfill in the advancement of the new culture and learning.

As regards the people of the early Polish Renaissance—and among them a group of some very interesting individuals—one finds that virtually all of them were in one way or another connected with the great humanist personality, Zbigniew Oleśnicki. There was the well-known theologian, Mikołaj of Kozłów (Kozłowski, d. 1443) who represented Oleśnicki at the Council of Basel. Mikołaj of Kozłów was a preacher and orator of international repute, well versed both in the classics and in early humanist writings, and he owned a valuable collection of manuscript codices (including the works of Petrarch) which he bequeathed to the University. Then there was his junior by some ten years, Mikołaj Lasocki, a relative of Włodkowic's and Dean of the Chapter at the Cathedral in Cracow. Lasocki received a nomination to the See of Cujavia, but died in 1450 of the plague at Termi near Camerino before he could return to Poland to take up his appointment. During his frequent journeys to Italy, this distinguished lawyer and orator, who had acquired his political experience in the Royal Chancellor's Office in Cracow became so deeply imbued with Italian Renaissance thought and culture that not only the Roman Curia and Pope Nicholas V himself, but also the culturally and politically important personalities in Italy, France, and Hungary (where he declined an offer of the primacy) all had the utmost respect for him as an intently humanist figure, for well-nigh a quarter-century in the employ of Polish diplomacy.[10] Lasocki had also been present at the Battle of Varna and had become a close acquaintance of Cardinal Cesarini. But for Polish-Italian Renaissance contacts it was his personal relations with such humanists as Giovanni Aurispa, Poggio Braccio-lini, Pier Paolo Vergerio, and Enea Silvio Piccolomini that were important. In particular, his personal association with Guarino de' Guarini of Verona, whom he entrusted with the education of his nephews, is documented in a collection of Latin correspondence between Poles and Italians which has survived as a remarkably vivid piece of literary evidence, not only about the Roman cultural environment which Lasocki entered, but also for the "fairly numerous Polish colony" of students in Rome in the years 1447-1450.[11]

Leaving aside other contemporary luminaries of the early Polish Renaissance (such as Jan Elgot, Jan of Ludzisko, Jan of Inowrocław the Elder, and Jan Dąbrówka), we turn to the chief inspirer and patron himself, the Chancellor of Poland, Cardinal Zbigniew Oleśnicki (1389- 1455). Though he never personally studied in Italy, he did visite Rome and in his style, followed the classics, (especially Cicero) and the humanists. But his role was, above all, in the generous patronage which he afforded culture and which proved to be a decisive and long-lasting influence. He was a major benefactor of the Cracovian University, looking after its interests and founding the "Bursa Hierusalem" students' hall. He was the *spiritus movens* of the historians. He inspired the spread of the new humanist ideas on scholarship, and he sponsored their advocates, such as the learned Greek, Demetrio's (in 1439), providing for them within his immediate environment. He received humanist letters from Enea Silvio, and even posthumously he was commemorated in various epitaphs and in the already conspicuously humanist trend that flowed from the pens of late fifteenth-century Cracovian Latin poets. A good illustration of this is to be had in a 375-verse hexameter *Dialogue on the Death of Zbigniew Oleśnicki*, maintained in the Virgilian spirit, "its origins in the early Renaissance literary tradition of the Italian bucolic epitaph";[12]

But this diffusion of the elements of humanism into Poland was by no means simple and straightforward. Jan of Ludzisko (ca. 1400-before 1460), who spent several years studying in Cracow and in Italy, where he obtained a doctorate in medicine (Padua, 1433), and who was subsequently appointed to the Chair of Rhetoric in his home university, whose representative orator he was for several years, serves as an enlightening example of this process. As the University's official orator he made a brilliant debut with an exquisitely humanist speech, *De laudibus et dignitate eloquentiae et oratoriae scientiae*, and subsequently, in the same year, l440, joined Jakub of Paradyż in welcoming the embassy from the Council of Basel. He commended the value of learning and philosophy, and finally, in 1447, delivered the memorable address to King Casimir IV the Jagiellonian (Kazimierz Jagiellończyk), welcoming him in the University's name with the (though frequently oversimplified) stress on the social responsibilities of kingship, a concept familiar from the *speculum regis* tradition. Owing his rhetorical education to Italy and possessing his own manuscript copies of contemporary Italian models of rhetoric (of which some 50 have survived), Jan of Ludzisko imitated them so closely that "very often he would copy out whole extracts"[13] from these treatises, incorporating them into his own orations. When, for example, his *De laudibus et dignitate eloquentiae* of 1440, considered the "first (official) appearance of Cracovian humanism,"[14] he said:

> Neque dubito multos esse, qui haec humanitatis
> officia negligunt, immo, quod turpius est,
> vituperant; quod hac forte de causa accidit, ut
> quoniam ipsi ea tarditate sunt ingenii, ut nihil
> altum neque egregium valeant intueri et, cum etiam
> ad nullam eloquentiae minimam partem ascendere
> possint, nec alios quidem ad id ascendisse
> vellent. Sed hos cum eorum ignorantia
> relinquamus, vilipendamus, parvipendamus, quorum
> puerilem opinionem ... etc.[15]

it was, in fact, a mechanical repetition of the well-known statement by Leonardo Bruni from the prologue to St. Basil's Homily to the Youth,[16] a key patristic text important in the Renaissance, on the need for a knowledge of classical pagan literature from which healthy fruit may be culled.

To close the early stage of Polish-Italian humanist relations, in Oleśnicki's times, a word must be said about the change of the academic syllabus in the 1449 reform which he sponsored. A host of classical authors were thus introduced into the University's curriculum: Virgil, Ovid, Horace, Terence, Statius, and probably others, too, such as Propertius, Tibullus, Martial, etc., while prose writers were now represented primarily by Cicero's *Rhetoric*, Quintilian's *De institutione oratoria* (available *in toto* since its discovery by Poggio, though Petrarch had used an incomplete version), Valerius Maximus' *Factorum dictorumque memorabilium libri IX*, and several others. But before we turn to later events, a brief pause must be made to consider Jan Długosz (1415-1480), the most important historian in the whole of the Slavic lands up to the nineteenth century, and his individual attitude toward this phenomenon of humanism.

Długosz was a brilliant academic continuator of his master Oleśnicki's policies, and as a historian he gave them a permanent place in his written work. But he was clearly distrustful of the humanists, though superficially he appeared to be attracted by their intellectual creed. For the old medieval philosophy of scholasticism had never held much of a grip over him, while at the same time he was also busy on his master's behalf with letters to Enea Silvio (whom he had occasion to meet personally). He was a close friend of Mikołaj Lasocki too. He was in constant touch with Italian humanists both in Cracow and during his diplomatic missions abroad, and he admired their intelligence and their Latinity—even when he could not trust them as individuals (such as, for example, Callimachus, who was well-nigh petulant in his compliments to Długosz), even when he had misgivings about the rapidly spreading temptation of humanism as the fashion of the times. He knew Italy well and had visited the tomb of Dante in Ravenna, recalling the poet's name so warmly in his *Annals* for the year 1321. He was a diligent reader of the Latin classics and humanists, especially all the historical works: ancient, medieval, and contemporary. His knowledge of historical works was perhaps unrivalled in his times. But at this point his contact with humanism stopped, for it is not so much a scholar's method or bibliography, but rather his own attitude and mentality that decide as to which intellectual ideology he espouses.

And here there can no longer be any doubts as to Długosz: he was steadfast in his traditionally medieval attitude. Even his Latin was unmistakably medieval in style, although it was certainly fine and efficient as a historian's tool, and though he set himself Livy as his guiding example, bringing into Poland the first of the Livian manuscripts that ever reached the country. But all in all, Długosz provides us with a most interesting image of a man of transition. As a figure he is to be associated with the general climate of Polish fifteenth-century religious piety, alongside such churchmen as the University professor, St. Jan Kanty, the prematurely deceased prince, St. Casimir (Długosz's pupil), Blessed Izajasz Boner, Szymon of Lipnica, Jan of Dukla, Michał Giedrojć and others. He was a pious man who managed to be culturally a creative individual and full of initiative, while remaining in attitude firmly rooted in the Middle Ages (when this was surely no longer easy), yet in practice using a historio-graphical method far superior to that of many of his followers in the sixteenth to eighteenth centuries whose works could only come into being thanks to his research.

Thus, the date of the Polish "threshold of humanism," 1470-72, precedes by almost a decade the conclusion of Długosz's *opus vitae*, his *Annales seu Cronicae incliti Regni Poloniae*. This threshold is dated from the arrival in Poland of Filippo Buonaccorsi (Callimachus) (about the beginning of 1470), and his rapid and brilliant career in Jagiellonian Cracow. For Callimachus was a literary celebrity, but moreover—and fortunately for himself—he came to Poland at a time that was ideally ripe to receive him.

In that year the tranquillity of Dunajów (near Lwów), the country home of Gregory of Sanok, now Archbishop of Lwów and patron of the humanists, was to provide a peaceful refuge for the runaway Italian humanist poet, who had disgraced himself politically by his part in a plot against Pope Paul II and was forced to flee from justice. Callimachus, who boasted about his "perse-cution" and "bitter experience" at the hands of Fate (and hence added the epithet of *"Experiens"* to his *nom de plume*) was a brilliant Latinist, an excellent individual specimen of what the pinnacle of the Renaissance could offer, and with his composite Tuscan, Venetian, and Roman selection of its culture, es-pecially with his experience of the famous Roman Academy of Pomponio Leto, he at once began to shine as a literary star on the Polish firmament. Settling down to the composition of elegant Latin verse, he paid his literary respects first to his protector, Gregory of Sanok, but especially . . . to the ladies, pro-ducing the well- known *Fannietum* cycle of love elegies and epigrams to "Fan-nia" Świętochna. This was all the more effective, as along with the poems the affair itself progressed turning into something of a scandal in society. For the girl was high-born and the poet ventured too far . . . But luck was on the side of the fugitive penman whose highly suspicious part in the Chios episode had not helped his reputation either.[17] At that moment, the Polish King, Casimir the Jagiellonian was not on particularly good terms with the Roman Curia, whilst in the meantime Paul II died in 1471, and the political amnesty granted the conspirators by his successor enabled Callimachus to launch seriously into his new, Polish career. In the spring of 1472 he moved to Cracow, arousing the excited interest of its intellectuals, especially in the University, and winning the support of its politicians and writers. Armed with the recommendations of Gregory of Sanok and the Vice-Chancellor, Zbigniew Oleśnicki the Younger, he was soon at Court, appointed tutor (*"consiliarus et praeceptor"*) to the royal princes, and by about 1474 even King's secretary. By 1476 he was making his way as a politician and diplomat, sent on his first, and very important, mission to Rome and Venice.

Callimachus' adventure and success show that the climate in Cracow was ready for the flourishing of humanism. At the University he could not have been a complete novelty, for prior to his arrival, in 1469/70, another Italian humanist, the Florentine Jacopo Publicio, a Petrarchan Latinist, had lectured there as a visiting professor. But the reverse process had also been taking place. For twenty years already Polish scholars from the Cracovian University school of Astronomy, famous then throughout Europe, had been lecturing in their field at Bologna and occasionally Padua, and the names of several such Polish astronomers at Bologna are known, beginning with Marcin of Żórawica (d. 1453).[18] But it was Callimachus' humanist fame and faculty, and his wide-ranging personal contacts and friendships with the topmost Italian humanists of the time that were of crucial importance for their prestige value in the Jagiellonian capital. Besides his reminiscences of Pomponio's literary circle and his Roman acquaintance with Cardinal Bessarion (commemorated in his epigram, *In hortum Bessarionis*) his correspondence (with Angelo Poliziano, Giovanni Pico della Mirandola, Marsilio Ficino, and even with Lorenzo de' Medici and many others) equipped this new "Tuscoscytha" and "Conplatonicus" with a golden key to opportunity and preferment in Poland, of which he certainly made very good use.

In the light of these new vistas it is not surprising that Callimachus exerted such an enticing influence on the culture of Cracow. There now appeared a couple of learned clubs and societies connected with his person, such as the Sodalitas Vistulana (1489-1491), which usually tends to be linked with a much younger itinerant humanist, Konrad Celtis, but also the earlier but long-lived debating society chaired by an eminent City Council lawyer, Jan Heydecke-Mirica, who somewhat later distinguished himself by his work in his parish of St. Mary's. This debating society nowadays tends to be forgotten, but unjustly so, for among its members it counted the humanists Maciej Drzewicki, Mikołaj Mergus, Mikołaj Wodka, Jakub of Boksice, and even Piotr of Bnin, and probably Bernardinus Gallus of Zara, as well as its star, Callimachus, who used to meet in the hospitable Mirica's garden to continue the memorable tradition of the Dunajów debates.[19]

They must have certainly had a wide variety of subjects, from literature and generally cultural questions, philosophy (a hint of which is given by Callimachus' minor philosophical writings, addressed to Ficino and Pico della Mirandola)[20] and, of course, theology, to politics and current affairs. Callimachus' colleagues and associates must have quickly realized the historical significance of his arrival in Poland, for the newcomer was already celebrated in Cantalicio's witty epigram *De Callimacho Geminianensi*, that it was a barbarian (Pietro Barbo, Paul II) who had put Callimachus to flight, while the refugee was turning barbarians into Romans

Callimachus Barbos fugiens ex Urbe furores,
Barbara quae fuerant regna, Latina facit.[21]

But Callimachus' posthumous triumph as a humanist created a still greater stir. His funeral (November, 1496), which turned out to be well-nigh a public

37. A page from the parchment codex Titus Livius, *Ab urbe condita*, containing marginal notes by Petrarch and Długosz. (Biblioteka Jagiellońska, Kraków). Photo Jan E. Sajder.

EPIST. LIB. IIII.   137

ANDREAE PATRICIO,
Patauium.

N AE tu rationem tui indicandi per commodam
inijsti. ego enim, non cuiates homines sint, quibus ue terris ac regionibus profecti, sed quibus
moribus , quo ingenio, qua doctrina præditi;
soleo quærere: &, ut olim Annibal , qui ho-
stem feriret, Carthaginiensem sibi fore dicě-
bat; sic ego totum in una uirtute constituo.
Epistola tua ita loquitur, ut nullam in te pa-
tiatur aut humanitatis, aut doctrinæ partem
desiderari. itaque ne te posthac Sarmatam po
tius, quàm Romanum, dixeris. tametsi Sarmatia iam ita feritatem, si qua olim fuit , &
quæcunque fuit, abiecit, ut ex transalpinis na
tionibus nulla neque ad litteras , neque ad beni
gnitatem, mutuaq; officia dicatur esse propen
sior. Italia uero, in qua uigebant olim artes bo
næ, in qua summis ornata præmijs eloquentia
primas aliquando partes obtinuit, ita neterem
illam quasi formam uidetur amisisse, uix iam
ut agnoscatur. simulacrum duntaxat aliquod
in libris relictum est; cuius excellentem pulchri
tudinem animo intuentes admiramur, & stu-
demus imitari: præsentem effigiem oculis frustra quærimus. Tu autem, doctissime Patrici,
T   si

PAVLI MANVTII
si qui nunc antiqua Italia digni reperiuntur,
qui quàm pauci sint, quaq; id accidat culpa,
non dubito quin intelligas, his te ut adiunge-
res, præstantiumq; uirorum numerum auge-
res, plane mihi, cum tua scripta lego, & cum
eos, qui tecum uiuunt, de te loquentes audio,
uideris esse consecutus. quo nomine tibi gratu-
lor plurimum, & patriæ tuæ, in quam refe-
res gloriam, omnibus thesauris, omnibusq; o-
mnium Regum triumphis præferendam. Ego
autem, cuius amicitiam in tuis litteris blanda
quadam mearum laudum commemoratione ui
deris aucupari, cum tua merita, quæ ego sen-
tio esse maxima, modeste nimis dissimulas, &
extenuas, mea uero nimis liberaliter amplifi-
cas, atque extollis, nisi te tam nostri amantem
redamem, nisi multis ornatum uirtutibus omni studio colam, quis me sit inhumanior? quis
iudicij magis, aut etiam rationis expers? equidem, quid de te sentiam, quantiq; apud me sis,
officijs conabor ostendere: sin, ut mea tenuitas
est, hoc præstare non potero; tu tamen, ut spe
ro, de mea uoluntate tibi persuadebis id, quod
cupere uideris, te mihi esse, ac semper fore ca-
rissimum. in quo profecto, nisi ego meam in a-
micitijs diligentissime tuendis consuetudinem
dediscam, tua te nunquam fallet opinio. Vale.

Eidem,

38. The pages with a letter of Paolo Manuzio to the philologist and humanist Andrzej Petrycy Nidecki in *Epistolarum Pauli Manutii, libri VI ...* Venetiis, 1560. The publication also contains letters to the Bishop of Cracow Andrzej Zebrzydowski and the the the Royal Vice-Chancellor Bishop Piotr Myszkowski. (Indiana University Lilly Library, Bloomington).

manifestation, was attended by King Jan Olbracht himself,[22] the bishops and friends of the deceased, the entire University, the nobility and gentry—"*post hoc erat turba magna di tutti li scolari*"—and a crowd of many thousands of townsmen taking him to his last resting-place within the walls of the Dominican Basilica in Cracow. As the presumed author of the so-called *Consilia Callimachi*, and often referred to nowadays as the "most direct antecedent and precursor of Macchiavelli" (who most certainly knew about him), Callimachus may be said to have opened a new chapter in the history of Polish-Italian cultural relations—the Poles' contacts with Florence. Although this occurred fairly late in comparison with the already well-established contacts with Rome, Bologna, Padua, Venice, Milan, Naples, etc., the Florentine link was critical in the Renaissance transformation of the Royal Castle on Wawel Hill. Beginning with the monument on King Jan Olbracht's tomb (1502-1505) in the Cathedral, the great artistic enterprises in the Florentine style continued for the next thirty years to change gradually the entire structure and face of the Castle, including the impressive arcaded courtyard and the Golden Sigismundian Chapel (1519-33), the creators of which were Francesco "the Florentine" (at one time mistakenly believed to have been Francesco della Lora) and, after Francesco's death in 1516, Bartolomeo Berreci (d. 1537).

Returning to the history of literature and ideas in the final three decades of the fifteenth century, it should be stressed that, among the factors contributing most to cultural relations—besides the ever-important ecclesiastical, and growing Court contacts (such as, for example, the career of the Dalmatian-born Venetian, Bernardino Gallo, author of an epitaph on Callimachus, who settled in Poland about 1489, became secretary to Cardinal Fryderyk the Jagiellonian, and was a friend of subsequent bishops of Cracow),[23] and besides the artistic contacts—a vital constituent was, as before, the role of the Cracovian University. Within the half-century from 1470 to 1520, which was perhaps the period of her greatest flourishing ever, the University witnessed the "most intense humanist conglomeration within her walls . . . occurring from about 1487 to 1494."[24] This was the time of Jan of Oświęcim (Sacranus, 1443-1525), first a student and later Rector of the University and chaplain to three Polish kings, who after a five-year sojourn at Italian places of learning (under Filelfo and, no doubt, Argyropoulos as well) began lecturing in 1475 and lived to hear himself praised in the poetry of Andrzej Krzycki (Andreas Cricius, 1482-1537). There were two more famous astronomers: Wojciech of Brudzewo (1445-1497), whose *Commentaria . . . in theoricis planetarum . . .* were published in Milan in 1495, and Jan of Głogów (ca. 1445-1507), philosopher, geographer, and astrologer. It was here, from the autumn of 1491 to 1495, that the young Copernicus obtained his university introduction to the science of astronomy, before setting off, significantly, for further studies in Italy.

A separate question important as a contributory factor, was the setting up in Cracow in 1473 of the first printing press in the whole of the Slavic lands. The fact itself we shall leave aside, although the date is notable for its early chronology, preceding the printing presses of Caxton at Westminster (1476), London (1480), and printing in Prague (about 1477), Vienna (l480), etc., for on the Continent most of them were the mobile workshops of wandering German printers whose chief output were devotional books and traditional works—all publications guaranteed to sell. But the wave of itinerant German printers also swept along a few Polish craftsmen. In 1478 we find a printer called Ioannes Adam de Polonia working in Naples, while at the turn of the century (1491-1504) Stanislaus Polonus flourished as a printer in Spain,[25] where he went after his apprenticeship at the Neapolitan workshop of Matthias of Moravia. We shall also leave aside the question of the various Polish writers in incunabula editions (in Latin), printed in Italy and elsewhere in Western Europe,[26] and likewise the liturgical books printed to order abroad for Polish dioceses, such as the very first of the ten Polish incunabula breviaries known today, *Breviarium secundum usum ecclesiae Cracoviensis*, printed in Venice in 1483. Instead we shall turn to some further aspects of early printing relevant here but which often tend to be glossed over.

One is the question of dedications to Poles in early Italian printed books. These *epistolae dedicatoriae* to Poles begin, according to our present-day knowledge of them, with the letters of Filippo Beroaldo the Elder (d. 1505), philologist and professor at Bologna, a familiar figure in the Western Slavic lands and Hungary, who from the 1490's onwards used to address his printed books to former pupils of his, including the Polish aristocrats Paweł Szydłowiecki in 1497 and prior to 1500, and Stanisław Ostroróg in 1499,[27] and also to eminent humanists, such as Erazm Ciołek (1505). Soon the master printers copied his custom, notably Aldo Manuzio (Manutius), who added an elegant letter of dedication to the distinguished Bishop of Poznań, Jan Lubrański, to his *editio princeps* of Valerius Maximus' *Dictorum et factorum memorabilium libri novem* (1503/4). Subsequently there followed dozens of other Polish dedications throughout the sixteenth and seventeenth centuries.

The second point is the intriguing field of reports of private travel and official missions (such as those by Venetian envoys—Giosafat Barbaro, Ambrogio Contarini, etc.) to Poland and the East, some of them published in the sixteenth century (in Giambattista Ramusio's collection, *Navigationi et viaggi*). These accounts contain historical and cultural information which is sometimes unexpected and valuable, but which has not yet been studied in detail by Polish scholars. There were, for instance, the voyages of Pomponio Leto who, in 1472, accompanied Zoë Palaeologina on her journey from Rome to Moscow to be married to the Grand Duke, Ivan III. Subsequently, in 1479/80, Pomponio went to the Ukraine as far as the shores of the Black Sea and nearby Tartary. In other words, he must have also seen the lands stretching from Cracow to the mouth of the Dnieper. He left a description of his travels in his *Commentariolus*,[28] unfortunately long since lost.

Thirdly cultural relations between the two lands now gave rise to an increasing number of strictly literary links, especially in the epistolary exchanges, but also in certain prose fictional themes which merit the attention of research. In the multifarious correspondence which passed between Poles and Italians one sometimes comes across facetiae, such as Vergerio's anecdote on linguistic misunderstandings between Poles and Czechs,[29] or there may occur moralizing passages, such as in the letters of Filelfo, which served Jan Leopolita the Elder as passages for commentary in his university lectures, or the epistles might be official and ceremonial in tone, such as Lorenzo de' Medici's letter in 1489 to King Casimir the Jagiellonian. At the same time, against the background of historical and political fact with the tragic figure of King Vladislaus of Varna, there flourished, from the mid-century onward, a spate of sensational fictional plots such as Andrea da Barberino's about the mighty King Marcabruno di Polonia and about the exploits of Buovo d'Antona in Poland (in his *I Reali di Francia*), or the story of *"el re di Polana"* and his *"trentamila di valentissimi Polani"* in *Storia di Ajolfo del Barbicone*. . . . Similarly, in the popular *Novellino* by Masuccio of Salerno (*editio princeps*, Naples, 1476) we find the fantastic story of an evil *"regina de Polonia,"* born a Bosnian and sister to the *"franco re de Bosnea."* The murderous lady *"manda a morire suo figliolo, o da uno suo cavaliero se ingravida e parturisce femena."* But, of course, the son survives and, exposing *"la verita del fatto, fa morire la regina sua matre, e lui, re rimasto, piglia la figlia del re de Ungaria e regna nel suo stato."*

So much for the fifteenth-century equivalent of romance and detective stories, a rather lightweight side of our subject. Of the more interesting literary links, there was the satirical verse, *Responsio cuiusdam Italici*,[30] a reply to the rather tactless, and, possibly, deliberately arrogant address to Pope Paul II in 1467 by the King of Poland's Ambassador, Jan Ostroróg, himself a Doctor of Canon and Civil Law from Bologna. This and other individual events go to form a kaleidoscopic medley of facts—a further contribution to which was the frequent criss-cross pattern of the custom of mutual exchange of poetry between friends. Initialiy, the key sender and recipient in Poland was Callimachus. He received the *Rusticus* of his friend, Angelo Poliziano, as a token for a gift,[31] and also a book of epigrams and the *Carlias* from Ugolino Verino, delivered personally by the poet's son. In exchange, the young courier was pleased to accept a collection of Callimachus'"epigrams and hendecasyllabic verses" for his father.[32] But literary contacts had to wait another generation before there could be any practical, working influence by contemporary Italian Latin poets on the verse of their Polish counterparts. It was not until the early sixteenth century, in the times of Andrzej Krzycki (Cricius), and somewhat later of the keen young student at Padua, Klemens Janicki (Janicius, 1516-1543),[33] that poets like the Venetian Hermolaus Barbarus (d. 1493), or Antonius Codrus Urceus (d. 1500) received this kind of attention from Polish writers.

This remark has brought us rather hastily to the advent of the firmly established Renaissance in sixteenth-century Poland. The new century found all the main aspects of Polish culture already set on the humanist course of development. Firstly, it was now that the University in Cracow, ever- sensitive to

Italian stimuli, introduced Greek into its teaching syllabus, employing Italian masters, Joannes Silvius Amatus of Sicily and Costanzo Claretti de' Cancellieri, and using largely Italian textbooks. Secondly, this was the time when publishers' and booksellers' contacts with Venice were reinforced and developed steadily, both through orders from Poland and by the efforts of Aldo Manuzio with his already mentioned dedication to Bishop Lubrański, his permanent representative (perhaps the young Wietor?) in Cracow,[34] and his extensive correspondence with Poles.[35] Thirdly, following the Italian example, the humanist bishops of Poland— Konarski, the Primate Jan Łaski, Lubrański, Drzewicki, Tomicki, Maciejowski, Padniewski, Myszkowski and others—maintained an extensive patronage of learning and the arts. But this was no idiosyncrasy of the sixteenth century; they were merely continuing the custom of their fifteenth-century predecessors (Oleśnicki, Gregory of Sanok, Piotr of Bnin, and Cardinal Fryderyk the Jagiellonian), bringing it into the "Golden Sigismundian Age." It was a custom which, in Poland, antedated by far patronage by aristocratic laymen.

At the beginning of the sixteenth century the thirty-year rebuilding program of Wawel Castle which attracted many Italian—especially Florentine and Tuscan—craftsmen (about 25 percent of the workforce)[36] and which made it a most magnificent royal residence, graced by the largest arcaded courtyard in Europe, and similarly, many other important achievements of the Polish Renaissance now reached their fruition. It was now that humanist literature (mainly Latin) by native Polish writers flourished and attained a universal level. In the prose there was both elegant oratory and occasional writings; there was, for example, a paraenetic and educational treatise, *De institutione regii pueri* (1502), and Maciej Drzewicki's dedicatory epistles to Lorenzo de' Medici and Marcantonio Mauroceno. But, above all, there were the various works on history—Miechowita, Decius, Wapowski and their successors—and especially the scientific revelations, first in Miechowita's *Tractatus de duabus Sarmatiis* (*editio princeps*, 1517), overthrowing Ptolemey's hitherto unchallenged authority as to the geography of Eastern Europe, and subsequently and most importantly in the work of Copernicus (1543). The non-fiction was accompanied by an abundance of mature Latin verse by Polish humanist poets who sought to satisfy local demand by applying elegant admixtures of classical and contemporary Italian Latinist patterns to their works. Meanwhile, in 1518 a new Queen arrived in Poland from Italy to be married to King Sigismund I. She was Bona, the sole surviving child of Gian Galeazzo Sforza, Duke of Milan, and Isabella d'Aragona. The marriage and coronation in Cracow of this highly educated princess (who *"Latinaeque linguae ita assuevit ab annis teneris, ut ... in colloquiis cum Rege marito Regnique primoribus sibi familiarissimis, lingua illa potissimum uteretur"*)[37] was attended by the patron of Ariosto, Cardinal Ippolito d'Este, who came to Poland specially for these festivities. Surrounded by an Italian and Latinist retinue (including Polish humanists), the young Queen quickly learned Polish and would readily consent to marriage arrangements between her ladies-in-waiting and Polish gentlemen; whilst for native Polish writers she soon proved a gracious patroness.

We shall not probe into the details of Polish humanist Latinity in the reign of Sigismund I (1506-1548). But it was in this period, the "Golden Age" of the Polish Renaissance, that Latin humanism became so thoroughly intermingled with, and welded to other, especially native, aspects of Polish cultural life, that it gave rise to a composite, rich, and complex phenomenon that truly merits its "golden" epithet. To this the classical Latin of humanism lent its intellectual and ideological form, while indigenous elements—linguistic (in the Polish language literature), political and constitutional (in the new social aspirations of the intermediate gentry), and eventually also religious (in the early Reformation)—began to build a new body work of national culture on this humanist frame. The great depth and variety of the Polish latter sixteenth-century Renaissance is really a matter beyond the scope of this essay, and we shall return to the one aspect of it treated here more or less as an introduction to the general question, a brief synopsis of Latin humanist poetry in the reign of Sigismund I, a reign which saw a veritable eruption of talented poets.

The showpieces of early sixteenth-century Polish Latin poetry were written by the pen of Paweł of Krosno (Crosnensis, d. 1517), founder of the University school of poetry, whose works are clearly marked by the influence of the Italian Latinists Poliziano, Pontano, and Mantuano, and by the scholarship of Guarino and Beroaldo; by the prematurely deceased Jan of Wiślica (Vislicensis, d. 1516 or 1517), author of a fairly modest composition, *Bellum Prutenum*, about the wars with the Teutonic Knights, incidentally drawing comparisons between Jagiellonian Cracow, ancient Athens, and contemporary Italy. There followed greater talents. About the time of Queen Bona's arrival, a former student at Bologna and pupil of Codrus Urceus and Beroaldo, Andrzej Krzycki, a Canon in Poznań and subsequently Bishop and Primate, came to the fore as a gifted court poet. His excellent *Epithalamium Divi Sigismundi Primi Regis et Inclitae Bonae reginae Poloniae* on the occasion of the royal wedding (Cracow, 1518) was highly commended by the Italian writers present at the festivities, and Celio Calcagnini immediately had a copy sent to Rome, where it also won the admiration of other writers.[38] There was no dearth of praise for the poems of Krzycki who could keep up a conversation in Latin distichs even at table and whose other admirers included Thomas Niger, and Joannes Silvius Amatus, and even Erasmus himself, as evidenced by his letters to Krzycki and a complimentary mention in the *Ciceronianus*. It was not an easy matter to compliment Krzycki on his not infrequently sharp-tongued poetry, for side by side with his courtly verse and polite bows to the Queen (such as the epigram, *Lepus captus in venatione per reginam Bonam de fato suo*) there were also cutting attacks on her, such as *In serpentem Bonae reginae Poloniae* on the Sforza coat of arms, which he issued at moments when her gynecocratic meddlesomeness became too much for him. But in the long run such poetic sallies did him no harm.

Another gifted poet was Mikołaj Hussowczyk (Hussovianus or Ussovius) who wrote a long composition on bison hunting. Hussowczyk was a courtier of the humanist parvenu diplomat, Bishop Erazm Ciołek (d. 1522, in Rome) who was highly esteemed by Popes Alexander VI and Julius II, and was also a friend of Leo X. Hussowczyk was in his master's retinue in Rome in 1521 when the Pope asked Ciołek for a . . . stuffed bison (' . . . *ut effigies bisontis, quem nos* zubrum *vocamus, impleta feno pelle Romae repraesentaretur''*). The Bishop promised to satisfy the Pontiff's wish as soon as possible. Meanwhile he commissioned Hussowczyk to describe the beast and the hunting thereof in verse, *"volens eius speciem tam re quam verbis Pontifici exhibere."* Unfortunately, the vivid, 1,072 verse poem in elegiac distichs, entitled *Carmen de statura, feritate ac venatione bisontis*, was not completed before the deaths of the Pope and Bishop Ciołek. It was published in Cracow in 1523 with a humanist dedication to Queen Bona as well as epigrams on her coat of arms and addressed to her secretary, Ludovico d'Alifio. In spite of this, it did not bring its author fame or success, though it was of high quality artistically (an eminent twentieth-century poet, Jan Kasprowicz, ranked it along with Mickiewicz's *Pan Tadeusz!*). Marked by the links with classical and contemporary Latin poetry in praise of hunting that are only to be expected in a work of this kind, it concluded with an appeal for unity in Christendom against the Turks.

Of the further Polish early sixteenth-century Latin poets, at least two more deserve a mention. The first, Jan Dantyszek (Dantiscus, 1485-1548), distinguished himself in the Polish diplomatic service and as an ambassador, especially at the Imperial Court of Maximilian I and Charles V where he was made a Laureate in 1516 and acclaimed as the *"primus Sarmata"* in poetry. Dantyszek's personal acquaintances, friendships, and correspondence with the foremost European personalities, such as Erasmus of Rotterdam, the Imperial Chancellor, Mercurino Gattinara, Joannes Campensis, Riccardo Bartolino, and even the conquistador, Hernán Cortés, especially enhanced the fame of his poetry, which was well-known, and read throughout Europe and widely published, (*De nostrorum temporum calamitatibus silva*, for example, was issued four times in 1530 alone: in Bologna, Cracow, Cologne, and Antwerp). Finally, the most talented, the prematurely deceased Klemens Janicki (Janicius)—who in 1540 gained a doctorate in philosophy at the University of Padua—was made the Pope's Laureate. His earliest Polish patrons had been Krzycki and the aristocrat, Piotr Kmita. An excellent lyric poet, during a two-and-a-half year scholarship in Padua Janicius built up an impressive artistic achievement, reaching the very forefront of the select circle of poets at the court of Sigismund I. Among his works there are moving personal elegies to his friends and patrons in Poland, to posterity (for the young poet sensed his imminent death), to his much-admired Professor, Lazzaro Bonamico, and to Pietro Bembo who was full of affection for him, to his Italian literary friends, Daniele Barbaro and Lodovico Dolce, and to the learned physician, Giovanni Battista Montano, and several others. His works are marked by a maturity unusual in such a young man. In them the Italian reflections of the poet whose health had always been frail are firmly entwined by fast strands of humanism, Christianity, and pa-

Tadeusz Ulewicz

triotism, of which a particularly moving sign is to be found in the memorable lines of his Seventh Elegy, to Voivode Stanisław Sprowski:

Italiam miror, patriam venerorque coloque,
Afficit illius me stupor, huius amor.
Altera blanditiis animum tenet, altera magno
Iure, haec hospitium dat mihi, at illa larem.[39]

On this note, reminiscent of the similar humanist lines (*"Cultius Ausonio nil sol vagus aspicit orbe,/ Oceano surgens, oceanumque petens,"* *Eleg.* III 4, 9-10) that Jan Kochanowski was to create twenty years later, this essay closes. If it was replete with facts and names (though only in a much reduced selection),[40] it is because this was its aim and ambition: instead of generalizing, to show a panorama of people—at least the more important people—phenomena, and events. As regards the scanning of the problem's extensive range, the author feels that he has done what his faculties have permitted him: *"fecit quod potuit,"* hoping that perhaps *"faciant meliora potentes."*

Notes

. *Starodawne prawa polskiego pomniki* (Ancient monuments of Polish law), vol. 5, pt. 1: *Rerum publicarum scientiae quae saeculo XV in Polonia viguit monumenta litteraria*, ed. Michał Bobrzyński (Cracow: Akademia Umiejętności, 1879), p. 170; Paweł Włodkowic, *Pisma wybrane* (with an additional title in English, *Works of Paul Wladimiri, A Selection*) ed. Ludwik Ehrlich, vols. 1-3 (Warsaw: Pax, 1966- 1969): see vol. 1, p. 42; vol. 2, pp. 144, 355, and vol. 3, pp. 163-164.

2. Edmundus Winkler, *"Liber disparata antiqua continens" Alexandro Masoviensi episcopo Tridentino dicatus*, Elementa ad Fontium Editiones, vol. 2 (Roma, 1960), p. 7 and tables 6-17 idem, "Il piu antico dizionario latino-polacco (del 1424)," *Ricerche Slavistiche*, vol. 8 (Roma, 1961) pp. 96-111.

3. Władysław Wisłocki, *Katalog rękopisów Biblioteki Uniwersytetu Jagiellońskiego (Catalogus codicum manuscriptorum Bibliothecae Universitatis Jagellonicae Cracoviensis)*, pts. 1-2 (Cracow: Polska Akademia Umiejętności, 1877-1881), passim.

4. Titles are quoted according to the manuscripts in the Jagiellonian Library (See Wisłocki, *Katalog rękopisów*, passim).

5. Giuseppe Billanovich, "Nuovi autografi (autentici) e vecchi autografi (falsi) del Petrarca," *Italia Medievale e Umanistica*, vol. 22 (Padova, 1979), pp. 223 ff.

6. There is a discussion of ms. 519 (of the Jagiellonian Library's collection) in Hans Baron, *Humanistic and Political Literature in Florence and Venice at the Beginning of the Quattrocento. Studies in Criticism and Chronology . . .* (Cambridge: Harvard University Press, 1955), pp. 138-139, 152.

7. See also Ignacy Zarębski, "Stosunki Eneasza Sylwiusza z Polską i Polakami" (The relations of Enea Sylvio with Poland and with Poles), *Rozprawy Wydziału Historyczno-Filozoficznego PAU* (Cracow, 1939), vol. 70, no. 4.

8. This letter was plagiarized by Joannes Ursinus (cf. Ryszard Gansinienc, "Listownik Jana Ursinusa" (The letter writer of Jan Ursinus), *Sprawozdania Polskiej Akademii Umiejętności*, vol. 53 (Cracow, 1952-1954), pp. 18-231. For European echoes of the Battle of Varna, see Karol Estreicher, *Bibliografia polska*, vol. 33 (Cracow, 1939),

p. 149; and Arturo Cronia, *La conoscenza del mondo slavo in Italia. Bilancio storico-bibliografico di un millenio*. (Padova: Stedir, 1958), passim.

9. Ignacy Zarębski, "Okres wczesnego humanizmu" (The period of early humanism), in *Dzieje Uniwersytetu Jagiellońskiego w latach 1364-1764*, ed. Kazimierz Lepszy, vol. 1 (Cracow: Uniwersytet Jagielloński, 1964), p. 173.

10. Zygmunt Lasocki, *Un diplomate polonais au Congrès d'Arras an 1435* (Paris, 1928); Tadeusz Witczak, "Lasocki Mikołaj h. Dołęga," in *Polski Słownik Biograficzny*, vol. 16 (1971), pp. 542-544; Janina Kozicka, "Mikołaj Lasocki," *Materiały do Historii Filozofii Średniowiecznej w Polsce*, vol. 4 (15) (Wrocław: Ossolineum, 1971), pp. 41-71.

11. Henryk Barycz, *Polacy na studiach w Rzymie w epoce Odrodzenia (1440-1600)* (Poles studying in Rome during the period of the Renaissance) (Cracow: Polska Akademia Umiejętności, 1938), pp. 24-35 (with a list of the earlier bibliography).

12. Stefan Zabłocki, *Od prerenesansu do oświecenia. Z dziejów inspiracji klasycznych w literaturze polskiej* (From the pre- Renaissance to the Enlightenment. The history of classical inspiration in Polish literature) (Warsaw: PWN, 1976), p. 78. The original text in Latin has been published from the manuscript by Ludwik Piotrowicz, "Dialog o Zbigniewie Oleśnickim" (Dialogue about Zbigniew Oleśnicki), *Archiwum do Dziejów Literatury i Oświaty w Polsce*, vol. 2 (Cracow: Polska Akademia Umiejętności, 1882), pp. 325-362.

13. Bronisław Nadolski, "Jan z Ludziska" in *Polski Słownik Biograficzny*, vol. 10 p. 461; idem, *Jan z Ludziska, pionier Odrodzenia w Polsce* (Jan of Ludzisko, pioneer of the Renaissance in Poland), (Inowrocław-Strzelno, 1977), passim.

14. Jan Fijałek, *Mistrz Jakub z Paradyża i Uniwersytet Krakowski w okresie soboru bazylejskiego* (Master Jakub of Paradyż and Cracow University in the period of the Council of Basel), vol. 1 (Cracoviae: Polska Akademia Umiejętności, 1900), p. 231 ff.; idem, *Polonia apud Italos scholastica, saeculum XV*, fasc. 1 (Cracoviae: Polska Akademia Umiejętności, 1900), pp. 78, 83.

15. Quoted after Fijałek, *Mistrz Jakub z Paradyża*, vol. 1, p. 239. The full text has recently been published in: Ioannis de Ludzisko, *Orationes*, ed. Helena S. Bojarska, Bibliotheca Latina Medii et Recentioris Aevi, vol. 19 (Wrocław: Ossolineum, 1971), pp. 31-47; see p. 42.

16. Bronisław Biliński, *Tradizioni italiane all'Università Jagellonica di Cracovia* (Wrocław: Ossolineum, 1967), p. 35.

17. Józef Garbacik, *Kallimach jako dyplomata i polityk* (Callimachus as a diplomat and politician) (Cracow: Polska Akademia Umiejętności, 1948), pp. 25-29; Gioacchino Paparelli, *Callimaco Esperiente (Filippo Buonaccorsi)*, (Salerno: Beta, 1971), pp. 81ff.

18. See Aleksander Birkenmajer's biographical entries (in *Polski Słownik Biograficzny*) on Marcin Bylica (vol. 3, pp. 166-168), Jakub of Zalesie (vol. 10, pp. 369-371), and Jan de Bossis (vol. 10, pp. 443); idem, "Uniwersytet Krakowski jako międzynarodowy ośrodek studiów astronomicznych . . . " (Cracow University as an international center of astronomical studies) in *Odrodzenie w Polsce. Historia nauki*, vol. 2, pt. 2 (Warsaw: PIW, 1956), pp. 363-377; see also the collective work, *Historia nauki polskiej* (History of Polish science) ed. Bogdan Suchodolski, vol. 1 edited by Paweł Czartoryski (*Middle Ages*), and Paweł Rybicki (*Renaissance*), (Wrocław: Ossolineum, 1970), passim.

19. A remark of Callimachus' in his *De his quae a Venetis tentata sunt* [recently republished by Andrzej Kempfi, et al., Bibliotheca Latina Medii et Recentioris Aevi,

vol. 5 (Warsaw: PWN, 1962), see p. 22] provides the source information for this inference. In the past century the matter has been mentioned by Henrich von Zeissberg and Kazimierz Morawski, and more recently by Józef Garbacik and Leszek Hajdukiewicz (in *Polski Słownik Biograficzny*), vols. 9 and 11.

20. Published by Heinrich von Zeissberg, *Kleinere Geschichtsquellen Polens im Mittelalter*, Archiv für Österreichische Geschichte, vol. 55 (Vienna, 1877), passim.

21. There is a Polish translation of the epigram in Heinrich von Zeissberg, *Dziejopisarstwo polskie wieków średnich* (Polish Historiography of the Middle Ages), vol. 2 (Warsaw, 1877), p. 270. The Latin is after J. Gruter, *Delitiae CC. Italorum poetarum huius superiorisque aevi illustrium …* (Francofurti, 1608), p. 567.

22. Józef Garbacik, "Kallimach," in *Polski Słownik Biograficzny*, vol. 11, p. 497; see also Gioacchino Paparelli, *Callimaco Esperiente*, pp. 202ff.

23. Jan Krzemieniecki, *Bernardinus Gallelus de Jadra, vicarius et officialis generalis Cracoviensis* (Cracoviae: 1934), idem, "Bernardino Gallo (Gallus, Gallelus)," in *Polski Słownik Biograficzny*, vol. 1, p. 460f.

24. Józef Garbacik, "Ognisko nauki i kultury renesansowej (1470-1520)" (Center of science and Renaissance culture, 1470-1520), in *Dzieje Uniwersytetu Jagiellońskiego w latach 1364-1764*, vol. 1, p. 200.

25. See the monograph by Alois Ruppel, *Stanislaus Polonus, polski drukarz i wydawca wczesnej doby w Hiszpanii . . .* (Stanislaus Polonus, Polish printer and publisher of the early period in Spain . . .), expanded Polish edition, ed. Tadeusz Zapiór (Cracow: PWN, 1970).

26. Cf. Tadeusz Ulewicz, "Die lateinischen Schriftsteller des polnischen Mittelalters in westeuropäischen Wiegendrucken," *Wiener Slavistisches Jahrbuch* 21 (1975), pp. 257-274; idem, "L'edizione veneziana del'Breviarium Cracoviense' del 1483," in *Studi slavistici in ricordo di Carlo Verdiani*, ed. Angelo Maria Raffo (Pisa, 1979), pp. 327-333.

27. Karol Estreicher, *Bibliografia polska*, vol. 8, (1882), pp. 3 and 4 and vol. 12 (1891), p. 509f.; also Bohumil Ryba, *Filip Beroaldus a čeští humanisté* (Českě Budejovice, 1934); Jerzy Axer, "Dedykowana Polakowi XV-wieczna edycja mów Cycerona," (A fifteenth century edition of Cicero's speeches dedicated to a Pole) *Meander* 32 (Warsaw, 1977), pp.167- 171.

28. Vladimiro Zabughin, *Giulio Pomponio Leto. Saggio critico*, vols. 1-2 (Rome-Grottaferrata, 1909-1910), passim; Henryk Barycz, *Polacy na studiach w Rzymie*, pp. 56-58; Tadeusz Ulewicz, *Sarmacja. Studium z problematyki słowiańskiej XV i XVI w.* (Sarmatia. Study on the Slavic problem of the fifteenth and sixteenth centuries) (Cracow: Wydawn. Uniwersytetu Jagiellońskiego, 1950), pp. 36-39, 158-159; Arturo Cronia, *La conoscenza del mondo slavo in Italia*, p. 95f.

29. Pier Paulo Vergerio, *Epistolario*, ed. L. Smith, *Fonti per la Storia d'Italia*, (Roma, 1934), p. 384; Cronia, *La conoscenza del mondo slavo in Italia*, p. 96ff.

30. The text has been published by Ignacy Chrzanowski and Stanisław Kot, in *Humanizm i reformacja w Polsce. Wybór źródeł* (Humanism and Reformation in Poland. A selection of sources) (Lwów-Warsaw-Cracow: Gebethner i Wolf, 1927), pp. 58-60.

31. Von Zeissberg, *Dziejopisarstwo polskie wieków średnich* 2, p. 269.

32. Ibid., 2, 269f.

33. Janina Mosdorf, "O wpływie humanistów polskich i obcych na Janickiego" (On the influence of Polish and foreign humanists on Janicki), in Klemens Janicki, *Carmina. Dzieła wszystkie* (Carmina. Complete works), ed. Jerzy Krókowski and

Janina Mosdorf, *Biblioteka Pisarzów Polskich*, Series B, 15 (Wrocław: Ossolineum, 1966), p. xxxvi.

34. Stanisław Łempicki, "Polskie koneksje dynastii Manucjuszów" (The Polish connections of the Manutius dynasty) in *Renesans i humanizm w Polsce* (Cracow: Czytelnik, 1952), pp.53-54, 89; Tadeusz Ulewicz, *Wśród impresorów krakowskich doby Renesansu* (Among the Cracovian printers of the Renaissance) (Cracow: Wydawnictwo Literackie, 1977), pp. 38 and 122.

35. Ester Pastorello, *L'Epistolario Manuziano. Inventario cronologico-analitico, 1483-1597* (Venice-Rome: Fondazione J. Cini, 1957), passim.

36. See Henryk Barycz's "Posłowie" (Afterword) to the Polish version of the collective volume *W renesansowej Florencji, panorama społeczności* (In Renaissance Florence; a panorama of the community) (Wrocław: Ossolineum, 1973), p. 289.

37. *Janociana sive clarorum atque illustrium Poloniae auctorum maecenatumque memoriae miscellae*, vol. 2 (Varsaviae & Lipsiae, 1779), p. 25; see also Jerzy Krókowski, "Język i piśmiennictwo łacińskie w Polsce XVI wieku" (Latin language and literature in sixteenth-century Poland) in *Kultura staropolska* (Cracow, 1932), p. 395f.

38. In a letter (reproduced in *Opera aliquot*, Basileae, 1544), Calcagnini wrote to a friend in November, 1518, " . . . Clarissimum praeterea fortunis et honoribus Andream Critium, sed sapientia et litteratura multo clariorem, poetam plane absolutum: cuius doctissimum et lepidissimum *Epithalamium* legi non sine admiratione. Italia certe atque *ipsa Roma*, ad quam illud dedi, tam *qratanter accepit*, tam ex animo *laudavit*, ut non quasi Germanicum aut Sarmaticum foetum, sed tanquam nativas et genuinas delicias agnoverit, ut multos ingenue suppuderit, Musas Romanas multo apud vos (for Calcagnini was addressing a Pole) magis quam in Latio latine loqui . . . " [quoted after Władysław Pociecha, *Królowa Bona (1494-1557). Czasy i ludzie Odrodzenia* (Queen Bona (1494-1557). Times and people of the Renaissance), vol. I, (Poznań: Poznańskie Towarzystwo Naukowe, 1949), p. 276; italics mine].

39. Janicki, *Carmina. Dzieła wszystkie*, p. 118.

40. For further general information and bibliography, see Ilja N. Goleniščev-Kutuzov, *Il Rinascimento italiano e le letterature slave del secolo XV e XVI*, ed. Sante Graciotti and Jitka Křesálková, vol. 1 (Milan: Univ. Cattolica S.C., 1973), pp. 269-335; and the extensive bibliography in vol. 2.

Ne mirer e simul iuctos anguem a qlam cp
Hos g cūctapotest iungere, iunxit amor

13

The Significance of the Polish Renaissance and Baroque for Eastern Slavic Nations

Samuel Fiszman

In the context of Poland's sixteenth and seventeenth century cultural relations with other countries, those with the East Slavic nations stand apart as exceptional; hence, we speak here not so much about relations, but rather about the role of Polish culture in the cultural development of three East Slavic nations. The road this influence traveled led through the Ukraine and Byelorussia to Muscovy, and therefore, certain aspects of this subject are interconnected, constituting part of the larger question of the penetration of West European and Central European civilization Into Eastern Europe. At the same time, however, the problem of the influence of Polish culture upon the East Slavic countries can be divided into at least two parts, both in terms of the chronology and the nature of that influence. Because of the Polish-Lithuanian union, Byelorussian and Ukrainian lands entered the orbit of direct Polish cultural impact at the end of the fourteenth century. Western European influences reached Muscovy in considerable, primarily, though not exclusively measure, by means of an intermediary road, in a form already partially adapted, and at a point later in time.

Before, however, Muscovy had both an opportunity and need to avail herself, whether by direct or indirect contact, of the achievements of Polish culture and West European culture already assimilated by Poland, Muscovy was influenced by her Western neighbor in two areas of primary importance. First of all, Poland introduced Muscovy to Western Europe, by supplying Western Europe with reliable information about the whole of the area of Eastern Europe. Jan Długosz was the first to act in this capacity. He was the first Polish historian to use Old Rus' chronicles, including the information they contained in his *Annales seu Cronicae inclyti Regni Poloniae*.

Although the *Annals*, written over a twenty-five year period up until the author's death in 1480, were printed later (the first six volumes in 1615 and in their entirety finally in 1712), they were known in numerous partially preserved copies,[1] some of which even turned up abroad; historians both in Poland and elsewhere in Europe utilized them frequently.[2] They used them directly as well as indirectly through the works of Polish historians which were based upon Długosz; among these latter *Tractatus de duabus Sarmatiis* (1517) and *Chronica Polonorum* (1519) of Maciej of Miechów should be mentioned above all.

Długosz was the first among European historians to use not only Polish, German, Hungarian, and Czech sources, but to go back to the old chronicles of Kievan Rus', as well as to the chronicles of Halicz and Volhynia and others for the early period up to the thirteenth century, and to Bielorussian-Lithuanian chronicles for the fourteenth and fifteenth centuries. Precisely which chronicle or chronicles he used remains an open question and on that subject various hypotheses have arisen. What is essential is that the information in the *Annals* has its counterparts in chronicle sources, and some of the information itself already has the character of source material, since some of the chronicles that Długosz used have not survived. Most importantly, Długosz's work bestowed upon Old Ruś chronicles their citizenship in European historiography of the time."[3] Whether in shortened form or referred to, not infrequently very close to the original, written in Latin and hence accessible to Humanist Europe, the *Annals* introduced into European historiography a considerable number of passages from the Old Rus' chronicles, information from the history of lands then subject to Lithuania, at that time joined by union to Poland. In this way, from Długosz or from the works of his Polish successors came the legends about the founding of Kiev and its first rulers, about Vladimir's choice of religion and the introduction of Christianity, about the battles with the Polovetzians and the fratricidal struggle between the princes of Rus', about the wars and alliances with Poland, about Tatar raids, and in the last volumes of the *Annals* in connection with presentation of the history of Lithuania, information about the Grand Duchy of Muscovy.[4] Długosz opened his historical *Annals* with very detailed information on the subject of the geography of the Polish lands and those of the Grand Duchy of Lithuania that included the river basins of seven rivers: the Vistula, Odra, Warta, Dniestr, Bug, Niemen, and Dniepr—information known under the title *Chorographia Regni Poloniae*. In addition to the names of the rivers and their tributaries, lakes, and mountains, Długosz gives a huge number of place-names. The chances are that during his visit to Rome in 1449 or 1450, Długosz met Cardinal Nicholas of Cusa and the future author of the *Chorographia* delivered much geographical information, particularly the names of places, to Nicholas of Cusa the author of the well known map of Germany and neighboring countries as far as the Sea of Azov, Riazań, and Reval. Thus, many Polish place names, including that of the little town of Brzeźnica, Długosz's birthplace, as well as places in Lithuania and southern Rus', found themselves for the first time on the geographical map to be later repeated in subsequent sixteenth-century maps.[5]

Thanks to its many manuscript copies, Długosz's great work was known to European historians, but an astounding popularity, greeted as a revelation by the European reading public, was attained by a small text: Maciej of Miechów's treatise, *Tractatus de duabus Sarmatiis Asiana et Europiana et de contentis in eis,* printed in Cracow in 1517.[6] Although its title recalled the Ptolemaic tradition of dividing Sarmatia into European and Asiatic parts, the content of the treatise was fundamentally a polemic with the accepted notions about these lands based on the ancient authorities and upon contemporary historians. In his description of the territories between the Vistula and the Don (termed European Sarmatia) and between the Don and the Caspian Sea (described as Asiatic Sarmatia), Maciej of Miechów relied upon Długosz's *Annals,* and thus indirectly upon the chronicles, but also directly upon some copy of a south Rus' chronicle; most importantly, and what at that time was new from the point of view of scholarly method, he tried to collect faithful botanical, ethnographical, geographical, and practical information from persons who knew from their own experience the eastern terrain of the Jagiellon state, the lands of Rus' and Lithuania and the territory extending to the north, subject to the Grand Duchy of Muscovy. In the dedication to Stanisław Turzon, Bishop of Ołomuniec, Maciej of Miechów opposed the improbable tales recounted by ancient writers and their followers about the Elysian Fields on the shores of the Northern Ocean, about the legendary Hyperboreans living there, the ambrosia growing there, the quantities of gold found there and guarded by griffins, about the moon, stars, and sun that never sets. He wrote: *"Quod in toto confictum est et in rei veritate illic aut alibi nequaquam repertum."*

He contradicted the views of contemporary authors (including even Eneas Silvius Piccolomini) who maintained that the Tatars on the steppes of Asiatic Sarmatia were of native origin, when in reality they had come from the Far East and previously had been unknown there. He thence proceeded to the statement that evoked the most amazement and achieved the greatest fame, namely that contrary to the opinion of both ancient and contemporary authors who accepted the existence of the Alanian, Hyperborean, and Riphean Mountains in the north from which presumably flowed the rivers Tanais (Don), the Greater Borystenes (Dniepr), the lesser Borystenes (Boh), and the Volga, these mountains did not exist at all, a statement striking a blow simultaneously at the traditional theory of the mountain origins of the rivers. He rejected all these opinions on the basis of experience:

> Quod cum alienum sit a vero, non abs re, experientia docente, quae est magistra dicibilium, confutandum et reiciendum est, tanquam prophanum inexperteque promulgatum.... Montes autem Hiperboreos, Ripheos et Alanos nuncupatos illic non existere certo certius scimus et videmus et iam praedictos fluvios ex terra plana consurrexisse ac emersisse conspicimus.

Maciej of Miechów returns to this same important matter in the text of the treatise, again addressing Turzon:

> Accipiat itaque Reverentia Tua et contra omnes adversantes tueatur et dicat, quod praelibata flumina non de montibus nec de radicibus montium, quoniam ibi montes sunt nulli, oriuntur et fluunt.

Accipiat secundo, quod montes Hyperborei et Riphei, de quibus emanasse ista flumina ab aliquibus fabulose scripta sunt, nec in Moskouia neque in aliis partibus septemtrionis sunt. Recteque dicetur confictos fore et nusquam existere, nisi forte in libro scripti aut picti et non in terra reperiri affirmarentur.[7]

The appearence of Maciej of Miechów's treatise at the end of 1517 was a celebrated event in the European scholarly world. In the age of great geographical discoveries this treatise—small, but containing so much unknown information about the east of Europe—was treated as yet another important discovery. Its contradictions of the stories of ancient authors, including those of the prince of geographers, Ptolemy, provoked a real shock in humanist Europe, so enthralled with the world of antiquity. Less than a year after the appearance of the *editio princeps* a reprint was published in Augsburg; in that same year a German translatlon by Johann Eck was printed[8] again in that same year the well-known epistle of 25 September of Ulrich von Hutten to Wilibald Pircheimer appeared, in the conclusion of which he wrote that he was so perturbed by the revelations in Maciej of Miechów's treatise that he sought information and its corroboration from Sigmund von Herberstein who in 1517 had travelled as an envoy of Maximilian I to Basil III. Herberstein corrected Miechowita's error about the Volga flowing into the Black Sea, but fully confirmed the non-existence of the mountains...

Idem Segimundus mirae in illius Sarmatae libello rei fidem mihi fecit, et iuxta persuasit, non esse Rypheos, non esse Hyperboreos montes.

Von Hutten was shocked.

...omnes enim illas regiones esse planas, neque usquam montes occurrere, quantumcunque late in septentrionem quis expacietur: nisi quos ipse quoque vidit, humiles quosdam colliculos in montium numero ponere quis velit. Quod me audientem attonitum prope reddidit: rem adeo hominum opinioni infixam, adeo praeclarissimorum virorum literis decantatam, in fabulas abire, in nugas, et nullam penitus esse, aut si fuerit, esse desiisse.

After a short enumeration of other information surprising to people of the time, the conclusion of the letter contains the oft-cited exclamation: "*O seculum! o literae! Iuvat vivere, etsi quiescere nondum iuvat, Bilibalde. Vigent studia, florent ingenia. Heus tu, accipe laqueum, barbaries, exilium prospice.*"[9]

In 1525 in Rome Paolo Giovio printed a brief description of Muscovy based partly upon the information of the Muscovite envoy to the pope, Dymitr Gierasimov, and also upon Miechowita's treatise; already in his title Paolo Giovio did not fail to include the revelation about the non-existence of the hitherto famous mountains.[10]

Today we are inclined to consider Miechowita's proud words closing his dedication to Turzon as exaggerated:

Utque, sicut plaga meridionalis cum gentibus adiacentibus oceano
usque ad Indiam per regem Portugaliae patefacta est, sic plaga sep-
temtrionalis cum gentibus oceano septemtrionis imminentibus et versus orientem spectantibus, per militiam et bella regis Poloniae aperta,
mundo pateat et clarescat.

But Miechowita's contemporaries looked at this matter differently. Based on
material collected by Johann Huttich, Simon Gryneus in 1537 in Basel printed
an anthology[11] of descriptions of eighteen famous discoveries including those
of Columbus, the Pinzoni brothers, Vespucci, Cortez, Cadamosto and others
and among them was *Mathiae a Michou de Sarmatia Asiana atque Europea lib II.*
The anthology appeared in the same year in Paris and later in an expanded
edition in Basel in 1537, 1555 and 1587. In 1534 Gryneus' anthology was published in a Strassburg German translation by Michel Herr under the title *Die
New Welt* and this edition also contained *Zwey büchlin Mathis Von Michaw, von
beden Sarmatiis in Asia und Europa gelegen.* The German translation was next
printed in Antwerp in a Dutch translation by Cornelis Ablijn (Ablyen) under
the title *Die nieuvve vveerelt* 1563, and again Miechowita's treatise was included:
*Twee boecxkens Mathijs van Michauw van beide die Sarmatien in Asia eũ Europa
gelegen.* In the sixteenth century and sometimes even later the treatise as a
whole or in part became an obligatory element in various collections of descriptions of discoveries or of editions of materials on the history of Poland or
Muscovy.[12] Miechowita's treatise enjoyed particular popularity in Italy; Albert
Pighius Campensis used it in his information about Moscow in the form of a
letter written about 1523 to Pope Clement VII that encouraged such deluded
endeavors of the Vatican as the attempt to convince Muscovy to agree to unite
with the Catholic Church. The text appeared in Venice in 1543 after the death
of both the pope and Campensis; its Italian translation was included in the
famous publication of Gian Battista Ramusio in 1558[13] and was repeated in all
subsequent editions. Thus it came to be considered an original work both in
the sixteenth century and in later centuries; only relatively recently was Campensis' total dependence upon Miechowita's treatise confirmed, as regards the
repetition of both a considerable quantity of information and errors as well,
with the addition of some of his own.[14] The Italian translation of Miechowita's
treatise by Annibale Maggi appeared in 1561,[15] with subsequent editions in
1562 and 1584. Maggi's translation was included in the second volume of the
next Venice edition: the 1583 publication of Ramusio.

The first data about Eastern Europe contained in Miechowita's work, particularly that about the Tatars and Muscovy, its scope as well as the method
of gathering it from eyewitnesses, became the foundation and guide for the
collection of further information about these areas. It considerably affected the
already mentioned Herberstein, who travelled twice (in 1517 and 1526) as an
imperial envoy to Basil III in order to negotiate a peace between Muscovy and
Poland and to persuade Basil III to join Poland against Turkey. In 1549 Herberstein published his famous work, *Rerum Moscoviticarum commentarii*, based

upon material collected during his journeys and, thanks to that work, Herberstein became the second discoverer of this part of Europe after Miechowita. Already in 1526 in a letter from Moscow to the Archduke Ferdinand, Herberstein communicated as something very important:

In Polonia reperi Cronicam noviter impressam authore quodam Canonico Cracoviensi, narrat originem modernorum? regum.[16]

This of course refers to Maciej of Miechów's *Chronica Polonorum*, probably the edition of 1521. In the dedication of his work to Ferdinand, Herberstein lists Mattheus Mechovita among the authors whose works he used, having in mind, as a reading of the *Rerum Moscoviticarum commentarii* indicates, both of Miechowita's works: *Tractatus de duabus Sarmatiis* and *Chronica Polonorum*. Among the authors he noted in the dedication, Herberstein most frequently used the treatise of Miechowita (moreover, not always mentioning his name), as if he had the treatise always at his side while writing his own work. It should be further added that Herberstein counted among his sources of information Campensis (in considerable measure based upon Miechowita), and also Giovio; thus, the amount of information taken from Miechowita by this indirect method increases even more. Herberstein more than once corrects errors contained in Miechowita's treatise or does not agree with Miechowita's judgments, but he repeats a considerable amount of information, such as the description of the river Don, data about the Tatar rulers, about the expansion of the Slavic languages, about the origins of Hungary, about the crushing defeat of Novgorod by Ivan III, about the custom of forced resettlement of the Muscovite population, about the golden stone figure ("*Slata baba*"), venerated by the people in Viatka, a tale later repeated by many writers in the sixteenth and seventeenth centuries[17] and which also turned up on maps of Muscovy beginning with the map appended to Herberstein's work. Herberstein based his information about Kievan Rus' and Muscovy to a considerable degree upon chronicles, but there is no doubt that the *Chronica Polonorum*, in which the history of the early period of these areas is based mainly upon Długosz and for the end of the fifteenth century upon chronicles and documents, as well as the *Tractatus de Duabus Sarmatiis*, played the role of an important source, a fact pointed out by Herberstein in his dedication to Ferdinand.

The next noteworthy utilization of information from Miechowita is the work of Sebastian Münster, *Cosmographia universalis libri VI*, Basileae, 1550 (previously printed in German in 1544 reprinted later and many times translated). Among the scholars' works that he used, Münster mentions (Johannes) Jodocus Lodovicus Decius de Polonia, as well as Mathias Mechovensis de Sarmatia. Like Herberstein, Münster took information about Poland from Miechowita; he also relied primarily on Miechowita for his description of south-west Rus' and Muscovy.[18]

The significance of Maciej of Miechów's work for the introduction of Eastern Europe to Western Europe was most accurately and succinctly described by

Heinrich Michow in the title to his article, "*Das Bekanntwerden Russlands in for-Herbsteinischen Zeit. Ein Kampf zwischen Autorität und Warheit.*"[19] As Tadeusz Ulewicz wrote: "The growing influence of humanism appeared in the field of Polish geography and cartography in the characteristic phenomenon of Poles taking the initiative into their own hands and—as a result—their appearance in the new and hitherto unknown role of those informing Europe about their own lands and about the countries of the Ukraine-Scythia and Muscovy lying further to the East, so exotic for the world at that time."[20] As S. A. Anninskii, the translator into Russian and commentator on the *Tractatus de duabus Sarmatiis* stated: "The treatise really opens for the first time a new page in the book of 'great discoveries' for the European reader, and is not only the first published work but the first work in general specially devoted to the description of countries and nations of north-east Europe."[21] Bolesław Olszewicz thus described the role of Miechowita's treatise: "Of course there is no lack of historical errors in Miechowita, nor are geographical errors lacking ... but despite this, one may state without hesitation that the work properly discovered eastern Europe, refuting erroneous and hitherto widespread ideas of the ancients about eastern Europe."[22] Based on the previous research concerning this problem Erich Donnert came to the conclusion that Miechowita:

> hat mit seinem Traktat in der damaligen Gelehrtenwelt, vor allem in Humanistenkreisen, geradezu eine geistige Revolution hervorgerufen. Der Krakauer Gelehrte wandte sich in seiner Abhandlung gegen die herrschende aristotelische und ptolemäische Lehre im Bereiche der Orographie und Hydrographie Osteuropas und leugnete die Existenz der Rhipäischen Gebirge.
>
> Das Erscheinen von Miechows Werk stellte die Geburtsstunde der neuzeitlichen Geographie Osteuropas dar.[23]

In the field of cartography, Bernard Wapowski played a pioneering role similar to that of Maciej of Miechów in the field of East European geography. In 1506, Bernard Wapowski assisted in drawing the map, *Tabula Moderna Polonie, Ungarie, Boemie, Germanie, Russie, Lithuanie* that was included in the 1506-1508 Rome edition of Ptolemy's Geography published by Marco Beneventano. Wapowski accomplished his great cartographic work later, however, when in Cracow in 1526 he published two maps which also included areas of Muscovy. While original editions of these maps have not survived, there is reason to believe that they influenced the drawing of later maps of East Europe done by Gerard Mercator, Caspar Vopelius, or the Scandinavian, Claus Magnus.[24]

The works of later Polish historians also served in Western Europe as a source of information about Eastern Europe and about Muscovy as well. In this connection, first of all should be mentioned Marcin Kromer's *De origine et rebus gestis Polonorum libri XXX*, Basileae, 1555, reprinted in 1558, 1568, and in a German translation in Basel in 1562. This work, intended for the foreign reader, became one of the primary sources of information about the Polish Common-

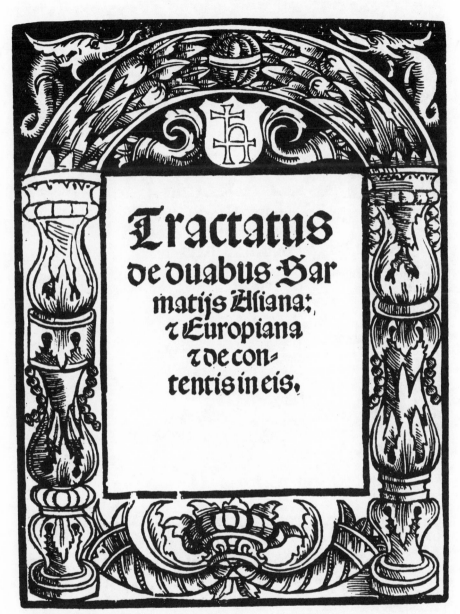

Tractatus
de duabus Sar
matijs Asiana:
z Europiana
z de con-
tentis in eis.

39. Maciej z Miechowa, *Tractatus de duabus Sarmatiis* ... Cracoviae, 1517. The title page (Biblioteka Uniwersytecka, Warszawa). Photo Andrzej Bodytko.

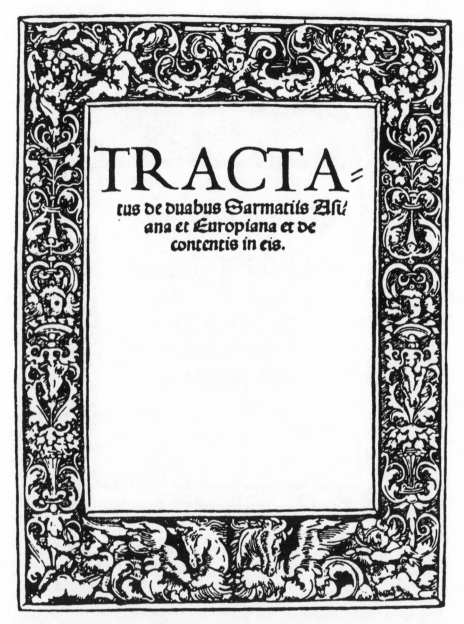

40. Maciej z Miechowa, *Tractatus de duabus Sarmatiis* … Vindelicorum, 1518. The title page of the second edition published in Augsburg (Biblioteka Czartoryskich, Kraków).

DELLE DVE SARMA-
TIE DI MATTHEO
DI MICHEOVO,

DOTTOR FISICO, ET CANONICO
CRACOVIESE,

TRADOTTA PER IL SIGNORE
ANNIBAL MAGGI.
CON LA TAVOLA DELLE COSE NOTABILI,

CON PRIVILEGIO.

IN VINEGIA APPRESSO GABRIEL
GIOLITO DE' FERRARI.
M D LXI.

41. Maciej z Miechowa, *Historia delle due Sarmatie* … Vinegia, 1561. The title page of the Italian translation (Biblioteka Czartoryskich, Kraków).

wealth and about Muscovy. Kromer relied upon Długosz and Miechowita, and in addition, upon Herberstein, but also independently of them used old Rus' chronicles, continuing the work of his predecessors[25] in expanding knowledge about them in the west. A good example of the popularity of Kromer's work is the utilization of much of his information by Giles Fletcher in his famous book, *Of the Russe Common Wealth*, London, 1591. In the course of his nearly one-year stay in Moscow in 1588-89 as the ambassador of Queen Elizabeth, Fletcher noted down his penetrating observations in a diary; after his return to England, while preparing a report based upon his impressions, he set to work reading the known works on the topic of Muscovy that he mentions in his own text and which included "the Polonian Storie." As was long ago confirmed, this refers to Marcin Kromer's *De origine et rebus gestis Polonorum*. In his introduction to a contemporary facsimile edition of the first printing of *Of the Russe Common Wealth*, Richard Pipes gives a list of the probable sources for particular questions in Fletcher's work; Pipes lists as taken from Kromer: the origin of Slavs and Russian, the origin of the Russian language and the name "Slavs," the origin of the name "Poles" and "Laches," and the conversion of Russia. He attributes the story of "*Slata Baba*" to Herberstein, but as it has been noted, Herberstein took this from Miechowita.[26] To this list should be added certain stories taken from Kromer about the Tatars, including the degrading homage of the Great Princes of Muscovy to the Tatar Khan.

The next example of the role of Polish historiography in supplying Western Europe with authoritative information about Muscovy is Reinhold Heidenstein's *De bello Moscovitico commentariorum libri sex*, Cracoviae, 1584, reprinted in Basel, 1588, and translated into German. Heidenstein frequently emphasizes that he bases his information about Muscovy on chronicles. Among Polish historians, Heidenstein was the one who took the most material from the chronicles, but from another set than that used by Długosz, and he transmitted the information contained in them in a language comprehensible to the West. From the comparisons of Jurii A. Limonov it appears that Heidenstein's presentation of the history of Kievan Rus' and later of Muscovy up to the time of Ivan the Terrible, the history of Pskov from the time of her independent existence up to her later subjugation by Muscovy as well as the various changes in the history of Polock and the wars fought over that city are based to a considerable degree upon the Pskov and Novgorod 'latopisy.' Heidenstein's work was used by many historians in the West and it is particularly evident in Jacques Auguste de Thou's large and highly valued work, *Historiarum sui temporis...* , printed for the first time in Paris in 1604-1608 and later published many times in Latin and in French. De Thou knew the works of many Polish historians, such as Kromer, Heidenstein, Gwagnin, and others, but an analysis of the author's sources of information about Muscovy indicates that he took a particularly large amount from Heidenstein both as concerns Kievan Rus', the Tatar invasion, and the history of Muscovy in the fifteenth and sixteenth centuries, about the throwing off of the Tatar yoke, about the constant conquest of new lands, about Ivan the Terrible and his despotic form of rule, about Polock, and about the victorious campaign of Stefan Batory against Muscovy in the years 1579-1581. These and many other details that Heidenstein alone gives or are in his distinctive interpretation appear on the pages of de Thou's work. De Thou also did not overlook information about Muscovy, particularly about the organization of the army under Ivan the Terrible and about his subjects' servile attitude toward him from *Sarmatiae Europeae descriptio. . .* Cracoviae, 1578 by Alexandro Gwagnini,[27] a polonized Veronese and participant in wars such as those between Poland and Muscovy. Gwagnini based his text upon matierial collected by Maciej Stryjkowski, then his subordinate, or perhaps he reworked a text written by Stryjkowski, the subsequent author of, among others, a work so important for the historiography of Eastern Europe: *Kronika polska, litewska, żmodzska i wszystkiej Rusi*, Królewiec, 1582. (A Chronicle of Poland, Lithuania, Samogitia, and all Rus'). *Sarmatiae Europeae descriptio* was reprinted many times, and translated into Italian, German, Czech, and Polish. The Italian translation was included in the second volume of Ramusio's 1583 Venice edition, together with the treatise of Maciej of Miechów.

The above examples, limited to significant works in European historiography (and there is no doubt that future study will increase their number), eloquently testify to the broad range of the rich and various information about Eastern Europe, including Muscovy, that Polish historiographers were the first to provide for Western Europe. One example which vividly illustrates the significance that West European historiography attached to information about Muscovy in the works of Polish historians of the Renaissance period is the volume: *Rerum moscoviticarum auctores varii unum in corpus nunc primum congesti*; Francofurti, 1600. Chapters from Gwagnin are included in it, along with two chapters of Miechowita's treatise entitled, "*De Moscovia*," as well as Heidenstein's *De bello Moscovito*. As the above discussion indicates, the road by which information about Eastern Europe in the works of Polish historians reached the west was often circuitous and indirect. An interesting illustration of this is a small anonymous text entitled, *Magni Moscouiae ducis genealogiae brevis epitome ex ipsorum manuscriptis annalibus excerpta*, and printed in the publication *Edictum Serenissimi Poloniae regis ad milites, ex quo causae suscepti in Magnum Moscoviae Ducem belli cognoscuntur...* apud Maternum Cholinum, Coloniae, 1580. The text was then reprinted at the beginning of *Rerum Moscoviticarum auctores varii* as is stated in the information in the table of contents, "edita Coloniae apud Maternum, Cholinum." At the same time, this text with some changes and omissions, was included in English translation together with many other accounts and information about Muscovy in the first volume of the second edition of Richard Hakluyt's famous work, *The Principal Navigations, Voyages, traffiques and discoveries of the English nation. . .*, London, 1598-1600. This text bears there the title: *A Brief Treatise of the Great Duke of Moscouia, his genealogie, being taken out of the Moscouites manuscript Chronicles written by a Polacke.*[28] In the introduction to the reader the author explains the reasons for including this information:

Finally that nothing should be wanting which might adde any grace
or shew of perfection unto this discourse of Russia i have prefixed
before the beginning thereof, the petigree and genealogie of the Russian Emperors and Dukes, gathered out of their owne chronicles by
a Polonian, containing in briefe many notable antiquities and much
knowlegde of those partes.

This anonymous text as it could be assumed was attributed to a Pole because
it was taken from the above mentioned publication *Edictum Serenissimi Poloniae
Regis*, containing Polish matierial. In *Rerum Moscoviticarum*... after the anonymous *Magni Moscouiae ducis genealogiae* its continuation appears entitled, *Na-
ruratiuncula de successione Moscouiae princpatus subiicienda Genealogiae quae huic
operi prefixa est*. This time the author is revealed: Daniele Printz a Buchau J.
C. M. Consiliario et olim Legato ad magnum Ducem Moscouiae. A comparison
of the anonymous *Genealogy* with the publication of Printz's *Moscouiae ortus et
progressus* (already mentioned in note 2, in connection with the spread of manuscript copies of Długosz's *Annals*) shows irrefutably that both these texts are
by the same author,[29] that the *Genealogy* is a condensation of the first twenty
pages of the first chapter of *Moscouiae ortus et progressus*. As was already indicated, in this first part Printz quotes Długosz; in the *Genealogy*, however, he
quotes the work of a later Polish historian, Herburtus Fulstinus' *Historiae Polonicae*. This means he quotes Jan Herburt from Fulsztyn *Chronica sive Historiae
Polonicae compendiosa . . . descriptio*, Basileae, 1571, a work reprinted several
times later and twice translated into French, Paris 1573. The history of Kievan
Rus' and the Tatar invasions of Rus', Poland, and Hungary presented in Printz's
Genealogy are based primarily upon Długosz, Miechowita, and Herburt and
information about the later period probably also upon Herberstein and Heidenstein.

This *Genealogy* "written by a Polacke" had yet its own continuation. In 1682
in London a book entitled, *A Brief History of Moscovia . . .* by John Milton
appeared. This small work by the renowned poet, printed posthumously, contains a Chapter IV, entitled "The Succession of Moscovia Dukes end Emperours
taken out of their Chronicles by a Polack with some later additions." Both the
title and the contents are based on Printz's *Genealogy* as found in Hakluyt and
they repeat, among other things, details from the history of Kievan Rus' and
the Tatar onslaughts which had their ultimate source in Długosz. Data about
Eastern Europe introduced to West European historiography by Polish historians was repeated in various ways throughout the centuries. Noteworthy is
the fact that Hakluyt and Milton quoted an anonymous Pole as a recognized
authority on the affairs of Muscovy, particularly as upon a faithful transmitter
of information contained in Rus' chronicles.

The second area, one of a different kind, in which the Polish culture of the
sixteenth century is notable for its role in the development of culture in Eastern
Europe, is the beautiful art of book printing. This influence began as early as
the end of the fifteenth century. In Cracow, the printer Szwajpolt Fiol[30] financed

Д ѡкончанаѣыͥснакннгаѵкеѧнкоцьградѣоѵ
краковѣпрндержакѣкеѧнкагокоролапоѧскаго
казпцнра · ндоконѣанаѣыцѣщаннноͦкраковь
скыцьшванполтоцьͮ · фѣ°оль , н͛знѣцеϥьне
цецкогородоѵ, франкь · нͨконѣашапокожнеци
народженнецьͥ·дꙇ сꙋть·девѧтьдесⷶ н ꙗ лѣто.

42. *Osmoglasnik*, u Krakowie: Szwaipolt Fiol, 1491. Colophon with the coat of arms of Cracow. Facsimile of a copy previously in the City Library in Wrocław which disappeared during World War II. Reprinted from Szczepan R. Zimmer *The Beginning of Cyrillic Printing Cracow 1491* (New York: Columbia University Press, 1983).

by a Cracow burgher and town councillor, Jan Turzon, opened a printing house which possessed a set of 230 Cyrillic type molds. In the course of the year 1491 (or even beginning several years earlier), Fiol published four liturgical volumes which are the first Cyrillic printings in the world: *Osmoglasnik* and *Chasoslovec* printed in 1491, with a colophon containing the printer's initials and the coat of arms of Cracow as well as *Triod Postnaja* and *Triod Tsvetnaja*, without colophons. Numerous hypotheses have long been proposed concerning the origins of Fiol's printing house, the printing in Cracow of Church Slavic liturgical books for the Orthodox Church, and the origins of the texts upon which these books were based. Among these hypotheses, (for example, that the printings were inspired by the circle of Cracow humanists, who would like to unite the eastern and Catholic churches, or that the printings were intended for Moldavia,) the most probable is that these printings were made for the Orthodox inhabitants of the eastern lands of the Polish Lithuanian Commonwealth.

Zacharii Kopystenskii, archimandrite of the Pecherski Orthodox monastery in Kiev, stated in his polemical work, *Palinodia*, Kiev, 1621, that he had seen many copies of all four of Fiol's printings in numerous places in the Ukraine and in Bielorussia. Of the 79 preserved copies of the printings done by Fiol, 68 are now in the collections of Soviet libraries. But the further hypothesis based upon this fact, that Fiol's printings were either commissioned by Moscow or that Fiol at least counted upon Moscow's patronage[31] is groundless. To begin with, these collections include copies that either are presently or were originally held in the eastern lands which belonged to the Polish-Lithuanian Common-wealth. More importantly, according to such reasoning, the majority of the copies of Fiol's printings should have appeared in Moscow already at the end of the fifteenth century or at the beginning of the sixteenth; in reality, the majority of them turned up there in the seventeenth century or later, un-doubtedly brought to Moscow from the areas for which they had been in-tended.[32] Rather, the fact is that Fiol's printings performed an additional service in Muscovy. A certain number of copies to be sure reached there quite early. They were the first Cyrillic printings there and they were obviously in great demand and were carefully preserved.

Subsebquent Cyrillic printings made in the Polish-Lithuanian Common-wealth in the first half of the sixteenth century are connected with the activity of the founder of Bielorussian printing, Francishak Skoryna, the first translator of the Bible into Bielorussian.[33] Skoryna studied during the years 1504—1506 (and perhaps even longer) at Cracow University where he attained the degree of bachelor. He studied in the city where not much earlier the first Cyrillic printings had been done, where the printing art, begun in 1473, was just flour-ishing and new printing houses were being established, some of them (like Jan Haller) using the king's privilege. He studied at a Faculty, renowned in Europe of the time, that brought together a considerable number of Polish and foreign students, a faculty with which eminent visiting humanists from many countries were associated. All conditions were present to inspire or strengthen in the young Skoryna a love for books and the beautiful art of printing, as well as for scholarship. The memory of the *Artes liberales* studied in Cracow remained in Skoryna's mind and he considered them essential, since, as Petr V. Vladi-mirov emphasizes, "Skoryna recognized these seven liberal arts as indispen-sable for recommendation to his Bielorussian readers in the course of their reading of the books of the Bible"[34] and he mentions them in order according to the then accepted division into the *trivium* and *quadrivium*.

Like many citizens of the Commonwealth, Skoryna traveled to Padua where he attained the degree of doctor of medicine. He began his pioneering trans-lation and printing activity in Prague where, in the years 1517 to 1519 his magnificent *Biblia Ruska* appeared (Beloruthenian—Bielorussian Bible ...) in twenty-two separate books, with the support of Bogdan Onkov, the son of the Wilno councillor. Skoryna's next printing venture took place in Wilno where, in the home of the mayor of the city, Jakub Babicz and with his help, he established a printing house and printed the volume *Apostol (Apostle)* and a prayer-book, *Malaja Podorozhnaja Knizhica* (A Traveler's Small Prayer-book.) As Vladimirov points out, from the point of view of typography, Skoryna's vol-umes "are most closely related with the Cracow printings of Fiol," thus con-stituting in several of their features a continuation of the first Cyrillic printings. At the same time, they also represent a great advance, for due to "their beauty, they sufficiently stand out among all the Church Slavic printings of the first half of the sixteenth century, they provoked imitations not only in southwest Rus', but in Germany as well."[35]

The next stage in Poland's role in the beginnings of printing in Muscovy, as well as in the Ukraine, is connected with the person and activity of Ivan Fedorov.[36] Evgenii L. Nemirovskii's supposition that an entry in Liber Promotionum of Cracow University refers to Ivan Fedorov is not universally accepted. This entry states that in the year 1532 one Johannes Teodorus Moscus received the title of Bachelor. Nemirowski's general supposition goes without question: Ivan Fedorov's evident sound education, his familiarity with ancient languages, his knowledgeability as a typographer and editor of liturgical texts could not have been obtained in Muscovy of that time.[37] There exists the greater possibility that he was educated in the brilliant center of scholarship and printing which then flourished in Cracow.

These suppositions concerning Fedorov's ties with Polish printing already during the earliest stage of his activity are in a way confirmed by information provided by Giles Fletcher in the above mentioned book, about the fate of Fedorov's first printing house in Moscow. Speaking about the Muscovite clergy Fletcher wrote:

As themselues are voyde of all maner of learning, so are they warie to keepe out all meanes that might bring any in: as fearing to haue their ignorance, and ungodlinesse discouered. To that purpose they haue perswaded the Emperours, that it would breed innouation, and so danger to their state, to haue anie noueltie of learning come within the Realme. Wherein they say but trueth, for that a man of spirit and understanding, helped by learning and liberal education, can hardly indure a tyrannicall gouernment. Some yeres past in the other Emperors time, there came a Presse and Letters out of *Polonia*, to the citie of *Mosko*, where a printing house was set up, with great liking & allowance of the Emperour himselfe. But not long after, the house was set on fire in the night time, and the presse and letters quite burnt up, as was thought by the procurement of the Cleargy men.[38]

The Moscow printing house of Ivan Fedorov and Petr Mstislavec that Fletcher describes did not last long. After the publication of *Apostol* (1564) and *Chasoslov* (1565), the printing house was destroyed as a work of the devil. Ivan Fedorov was forced to flee Moscow and return to the Polish Commonwealth where he produced the crowning achievement of his life, the renowned Ostróg Bible. Ivan Fedorov's connections with Polish printing are not based solely upon the fact that his major activity occurred in the territory of the Polish Commonwealth; his Polish connections are reflected in the very printings themselves. Research in this area is not yet far advanced, but what has been possible to ascertain so far confirms Fedorov's Polish connections. For example, his letters and arrangement of the printings are known to reflect those of Fiol; certain ornaments and illustrations used in Fedorov's printings are similar or even identical to those in the printings of such Cracow printers as Ungler and Szarffenberg.[39] Further, it has been observed that the printer's sign used by Fedorov in his Lwów and Ostróg printings is almost identical with the coat-of-arms of Śreniawa, the bearings of the Voivode of Cracow, Piotr Kmita, patron of scholars and writers and himself a bibliophile.[40] Fedorov undoubtedly maintained close contacts with Cracow during the time of his printing activities in Lwów and Ostróg.

Despite their notably early occurrence, their invaluable introduction of Eastern Europe, including Muscovy, to Western Europe and disproving of old ideas with new information, as well as their connection with printing, an art essential to the development of every culture—these phenomena are nevertheless of initial significance in the role which Polish culture played in the development of the Eastern European Slavic nations, of the culture of Muscovy, and later of Russia. The route by which these phenomena reached Moscow were in part direct, but primarily they went indirectly via the Ukraine and Bielorussia since, as part of the Commonwealth, these areas were within the range of direct influence of Polish culture. Translations from Polish which appeared in Muscovy at the end of the fifteenth and in the sixteenth, as yet not numerous, have an initial significance as well. These translations include Polish and Lithuanian codes of law, certain legends and apocrypha (such as the Legend of the Three Kings), *Skazanie o smerti nekoevo mistra velikovo sirech filosofa*, a prose rendering of one of the most valuable works of medieval Polish literature *Rozmowa Mistrza Polikarpa ze Śmiercią* (Conversation of Master Polikarp with Death), an original adaptation of the Latin *Colloquium inter Mortem et Magistrum Policarpum*. The translation contains many Ukrainianisms and Polonisms.[41] *Kronika sveta* is a Bielorussian translation done at the request of King Sigismund Augustus of Marcin Bielski's *Kronika wszystkiego świata* (*Chronicle of the Whole World*) printed in Cracow in 1550, and then later in 1554 and 1564. In 1584 a Russian rendering, was made from this Bielorussian translation and later a second Russian rendering was made directly from the Polish. Bielski's *Chronicle* played an important role in the development of historiography of Muscovy.[42]

Lechebnik (A book of home cures) is a translation of Hieronim Spiczyński's work, *O ziołach tutecznych y zamorskich y o moczy ich* (On herbs, local and from beyond the seas, and about their healing powers) Cracow 1542. The translation contains many Bielorussianisms and Polonisms.[43] A translation of the New Testament done in the Ukraine in 1581, together with notes written in the Arian spirit was made from the translation published in Raków in 1577 by one of the outstanding leaders of the Polish Brethren in the sixteenth century, Marcin Czechowic;[44] the translation is one of the examples of the role of the powerful Reformation movement in the Polish—Lithuanian Commonwealth, a movement which had repercussions in the territories subject to Moscow at that time. This is a problem which would require separate study.

From the end of the sixteenth century date Bielorussian translations of several chivalric-picaresque romances, an example of which is *Historya o Atyli koroli ugorskom* (History of Attila, the Hungarian king) translated from the 1574 Cracow printing of *Historia spraw Atyle krola węgierskiego z łacińskiego języka na polski przełożona przez Cypriana Bazylika* (History of the deeds of Attila, the Hungarian king, from the Latin language rendered into Polish by Cyprian Bazylik).[45]

It was confirmed recently that the sixteenth century manuscript known from its incipit as *Kniga glagolemaia naziratel sirech uriad domovnych detel* (A book of counsel that is on household affairs) and long since recognized as a translation from Latin, is a translation of four of the twelve chapters of Piotr de Crescentis, *Księgi o gospodarstwie* (Books on agriculture) Cracow, 1549 and 1571, itself a translation probably of the edition of Petrus Crescentiis, *De Agricultura*, Basileae, 1538. *Naziratel* contains many Polonisms and Ukrainianisms.[46]

The above list is not only not complete, rather it represents a part of what Poland or through Poland was adopted already in the sixteenth century by Eastern Slavs. Many of these translations have not survived; some of the titles mentioned above, for example, have been preserved in a single copy. Others have been recognized as translations from Latin, but the case of *Naziratel* (which is not unique) indicates that closer analysis of the translation leads to the conclusion that the basis for the rendering was a Polish text. Other translations await discovery in the manuscript collections of libraries.

The influence of Renaissance Poland notwithstanding, the period of Polish culture's transforming role in the development and change of the culture of Muscovy, (at the time of her turning point and transformation into Russian culture) the period in which Polish culture constituted the major factor in that process, is the seventeenth century.[47] Along with direct connections, the Ukraine played a significant role of intermediary, most important the Kiew Collegium, founded in 1632 and modeled on the other *collegia* of the Commonwealth and later transformed into an Academy. The Academy constituted an important intermediate road by which Polish literature and customs reached Moscow and extended over all Russia.[48] Having assimilated achievements of Polish Renaissance and Baroque culture and of Western European culture of previous centuries through Poland as an intermediary, Moscow could, by the seventeenth century, break out of her medieval isolation and establish contact with Western European culture. The only comparable transforming influence had occurred in the earlier history of Kievan Rus' and Muscovy in the form of Byzantine cultural influence, the so-called first and second South Slavic influence. In Russia's later history, neither the period of Peter the Great nor the latter half of the eighteenth century constitutes such a turning point. The number of arguments is now sufficiently convincing to shift the beginning of modern Russian literature forward from the era of Peter the Great to the latter half of the seventeenth century. Whereas during Peter's reign no new phenomena appeared in literary development or in dramaturgy, and new works continue seventeenth-century traditions, latter seventeenth-century literature possesses all the signs of a new age. Only then in Russia, on the basis of knowledge brought from Poland, could poetry, theater, and the first attempts at dramaturgy emerge; novels translated from Polish gained wide popularity, novels which actively influenced then developing native prose. New literary genres appeared, new concepts, new works and new attitudes toward them as well. The writer's profession appears, and the first literary trend in the history of Russian literature, Russia's first artistic style, the baroque, takes hold. The baroque then proceeds to regulate the development of both literature and the arts. The process of the emancipation of culture is set in motion; culture becomes secularized, broadened to encompass new, hitherto excluded fields now represented by works translated primarily from Polish, and so on, to mention only the most important changes. Not only literature and science were involved here, however; this great wave of change stimulated by Polish cultural influence affected all areas of intellectual and artistic life—music, painting, architecture, education, etc.

Despite many outstanding individual achievements, research in this field has been fragmentary until now, confined primarily to specific disciplines. Only a total integrated view of this period in its beginning and final phases of transformations occurring under the influence of Polish culture will convey an accurate impression of Polish culture's extraordinary role.

Russia did not have her own Renaissance and entered the baroque period, "by-passing the Renaissance, directly from the Middle Ages, because of the grafting on to her own soil of the knowledge of neighboring Polish literature."[49] This fact explains not so much the differences between Polish and Russian baroque, though these are not inconsiderable, but rather the different role of the baroque in Russian culture. "Here, the baroque had another significance than it did in Western and Central Europe. The baroque played the role of the Renaissance in seventeenth century Russia, fostering the emancipation of the human personality and the secularization of literature; it promoted faith in human intelligence, in science, and for the first time since the Middle Ages, created in Russia conceptions about social progress and encouraged hope for reforms in social and governmental life."[50] This turning point was of incalculable significance for culture and human thought. Nowhere in Western Europe or in Poland did the baroque play this role; hence all the greater is the significance of those values the baroque carried from Poland to Russian soil in the seventeenth century. In older scholarship, this period in Russian history is termed "the Polish period." I think that we should return to this term, recalling it not only because of its relevance to the past, but for its relevance to the present as well.

Notes

1. Henryk Barycz. "Dwie syntezy dziejów narodowych przed sądem potomności," (Two syntheses of national history before the court of posterity), *Pamiętnik Literacki* 43, 1/2 (1952): 194-251; Wanda Semkowicz-Zarembina, Przedmowa do Jana Długosza *Roczniki czyli Kroniki sławnego Królestwa Polskiego* (Preface to Jan Długosz's Annals or Chronicles of the illustrious Kingdom of Poland) vols. 1-2, (Warsaw: PWN, 1961), pp. 9-60.

2. An example that these copies were known in the sixteenth century is the testimony of Daniel Printz contained in the posthumously published small volume *Moscouiae ortus et progressus*, Nissae, 1668, pp. 4-5: Dlugossus Polonicorum annalium scriptor, cuius opera manuscripta solummodo in quibusdam familiis extant...." Born in Lwów (1546-1628), Printz traveled on behalf of the emperor as ambassador extraordinary to Moscow in 1576 and 1578 and the small volume is a report of these missions.

3. Iuri A. Limonov, "Russkie letopisi i polskaja historiografia XV-XVI v." (Russian Chronicles and Polish historiography in the fifteenth and sixteenth centuries) in *Kulturnye sviazi narodov vostochnoi Evropy v XVI v*, (Moscow: Nauka, 1976), p. 161.

4. Aleksander Semkowicz, *Krytyczny rozbiór "Dziejów polskich" Jana Długosza* (A critical analysis of Jan Długosz's "Polish History") (Cracow, 1887); Eugene Perfeckij, *Historia Polonica Jana Długosza a ruske letopisectvi* (The Polish history of Jan Długosz and Rus'chronicles) (Prague, 1932); Franciszek Sielicki "Kroniki staroruskie w dawnej Polsce" (Old Russian chronicles in ancient Poland), *Slavia Orientalis* no. 2 (1964): 133-157; Jurii A. Limonov, *Kulturnye sviazi Rossii s evropeiskimi stranami v XV-XVII v.* (Cultural Relations of Russia with European Countries in the fifteenth to seventeenth centuries) (Leningrad: Nauka, 1978), pp. 6-96. Hereafter Limonov.

5. Karol Buczek, *The History of Polish Cartography* (Wrocław: Ossolineum, 1966), p. 26.

6. Aleksander Borzemski, "Kronika Miechowity. Rozbiór krytyczny," (The Chronicle of Miechowita. A critical analysis) in *Rozprawy Akademii Umiejętności, Wydział Filozoficzno-Historyczny*, seria 11 (1891); Karol Buczek, "Maciej Miechowita jako geograf Europy wschodniej" (Maciej Miechowita as a geographer of Eastern Europe), in *Maciej z Miechowa, 1457- 1523, Historyk, geograf, lekarz, organizator nauki* (Wrocław: Ossolineum, 1960), pp. 76-164; Waldemar Voisé, "The first intellectual exploration of Eastern Europe," *Janus* 64 (1977): 41-49; Matvej Mechovskii, *Traktat o dvuch Sarmatiiakh* vvedenie perevod i komentarii S. A. Anninskogo (Treatise on the two Sarmatias—introduction, translation, and commentary by S.A. Anninskii) (Moscow: Izd. A.N. SSSR, 1936)—referred to hereafter as Anninskii; Limonov, pp. 97-109.

7. I am quoting after the first printing, *Tractatus de duabus Sarmatiis Asiana et Europiana et de contentis in eis* (Cracoviae, 1517).

8. *Tractat von beiden Sarmatien und anderen anstossenden landen, in Asia und Europa von sitten und gepräuchen der völcker so darinnen wonen . . .* (Augspurg, 1518).

9. "Ulrichi de Hutten equitis ad Bilibaldum Pirckheymer patricium norimbergensem Epistola vitae suae rationem exponens" in Ulrichs von Hutten, *Schriften*, ed. Eduard Böcking (Leipzig, 1859), vol. 1, pp. 214-217.

10. *Pauli Iovii Nouocomensis libellus de legatione Basilii magni Principis Moschouiae ad Clementem VII Pont. Max. in quo situs Regionis antiquis incognitus, Religio gentis, mores et causae legationis fidelissime referuntur. Caeterum ostenditur error Strabonis, Ptolemaei, aliorumque Geographiae scriptorum, ubi de Rypheis montibus meminere, quos hac aetate nusquam esse, plane compertum est.* (Roma, 1525).

11. *Novus orbis regionum ac insularum veteribus incognitarum...* (Basileae, 1532). The text differs in some places from the first Cracow publications of 1817 and 1821. The dedication to Turzon was changed into a preface and stylistic changes were made both in it and in the *Treatise*.

256   Samuel Fiszman

12. *Epitome orbis terrarum*, (Venetiis, 1542); Pistorius, *Polonicae Historiae Corpus . . .* (Basileae, 1582),vol.l; *Rerum moscoviticarum auctores varii*, (Francofurti, 1600).
13. *De Moscovia ad Clementum VII Pont. Max.* (Venetiis, 1543); "Lettera d'Alberto Campense intorno le cose di Moscovia..." in Gian Battista Ramussio *Navigatione et Viaggi*, (Venice, 1558), vol. 2.
14. In his commentary Anninskii compares both texts and points out those places in Campensis which are taken from Miechowita's *Treatise*.
15. *Historia delle due Sarmatie di Mattheo Dic, Micheovo dottor fisico et canonico Cracoviense*, (Venegia, 1561).
16. Joseph Fiedler, "Siegmund's Freihern von Herberstein zweiter Mission nach Russland," in *Slavische Bibliothek*, vol. 2 (1858), p. 91.
17. In his commentary Anninskii points out those places in Herberstein which are taken from Miechowita.
18. A comparison of Miechowita's *Treatise* and Münster's *Cosmographia* was done by E. Zamyslovskii, "Opisanie Litwy, Samogitii, Russii i Moskovii Sebastiana Münstera" (The description of Lithuania, Samogitia, Rus', and Muscovy of Sebastian Münster), in *Zhurnal Minist. Nar. Prosv.* (St. Petersburg, 1880): 114-121.
19. *Verhandlungen des Fünften Deutschen Geographentages in Hamburg* (Berlin, 1885) pp. 119-130.
20. Tadeusz Ulewicz, *Sarmacja, Studium z problematyki słowiańskiej XV i XVI w.* (Sarmatia. A study on the Slavic problem of the fifteenth and sixteenth centuries) (Cracow: Wydawn. Uniwersytetu Jagiellońskiego, 1950), p. 13.
21. Anninskii, p. 1.
22. "Geografia polska w okresie Odrodzenia" (Polish geography in the period of the Renaissance), in *Odrodzenie w Polsce*, vol. 2, pt. 2 (Warsaw: PIW, 1956), p. 343.
23. *Russland an der Schwelle der Neuzeit* (Berlin: Akademie Verlag, 1972), p. 467.
24. Karol Buczek, *The History of Polish Cartography*, pp. 32-33.
25. Ludwik Finkel, "Marcin Kromer historyk polski XVI wieku. Rozbór krytyczny" (Marcin Kromer, sixteenth-century Polish historian. A critical analysis), *Rozprawy Wydziału Historyczno-Filologicznego Akademii Umiejętności* (Cracow, 1883) p. 357ff.
26. Giles Fletcher, *Of the Russe Commonwealth*, 1591. Facsimile edition with an introduction by Richard Pipes (Cambridge, Mass: Harvard Univ. Press, 1966), pp. 20-21.
27. Limonov, pp. 168-230.
28. D.B. Quinn, *The Hakluyt Handbook*, vol. 2 (London: The Hakluyt Society, 1974), pp. 163-164; Limonov, p. 250.
29. A comparison of the two texts is given in Limonov, pp. 231-251.
30. Karol Heintsch, *Ze studiów nad Szwajpoltem Fiolem* (Studies on Szwajpolt Fiol), pt. 1 (Wrocław: Ossolineum, 1957); Szczepan R. Zimmer, *The Beginning of Cyrillic Printing, Cracow, 1491* (New York: Columbia Univ. Press, 1983).
31. Evgenii L. Nemirovskii, *Nachalo slavianskogo knigopechatania* (The beginning of Slavic book-printing) (Moscow: Kniga, 1971), pp. 206-219.
32. Zimmer arrives at similar conclusions in chapter 4 of his book.
33. Petr. V. Vladimirov, *Doktor Francisk Skorina* (St. Petersburg, 1888), hereafter cited as Vladimirov; "Skoryna, Franciszek" in *Drukarze dawnej Polski od XV do XVIII wieku. Zeszyt 5: Wielkie Księstwo Litewskie* (Printers of Old Poland from the fifteenth to the eighteenth century. Issue no. 5: The Grand Duchy of Lithuania), ed. by

Alodia Kawecka-Gryczowa with Krystyna Korotajowa and Wojciech Krajewski (Wrocław: Ossolineum, 1959), pp. 224-230.

34. Vladimirov, p. 53.

35. Vladimirov, pp. 81; 201.

36. *Ivan Fedorov pervopechatnik* (Ivan Fedorov, first printer) (Moscow: Akademia Nauk SSSR, 1935); "Ivan Fedorov," in *Drukarze dawnej Polski od XV do XVIII Wieku. Zeszyt 6: Małopolska, Ziemie Ruskie* (Printers of Old Poland from the fifteenth to the eighteenth century. Issue no. 6: Little Poland, Rus' lands) (Wrocław: Ossolineum, 1960), pp. 82-98.

37. Evgenii L. Nemirovskii, "Pervopechatnik Ivan Fedorov v Krakovskom Universitete" (The first printer Ivan Fedorov at Cracow University), in *Sovetskoe Slavianovedenie*, no. 1 (1969): 49-56.

38. Giles Fletcher, *Of the Russe Common Wealth or Maner of Gouernement by the Russe Emperour* (London, 1591), pp. 85-85v.

39. Aleksander Birkenmaier, *Studia bibliologiczne* (Bibliological studies) (Wrocław: Ossolineum 1975), pp. 332-334.

40. Evgenii L. Nemirovskii,*Pervopechatnik*, pp. 54-55.

41. Aleksej I. Sobolevskii, *Perevodnaia literatura moskovskoj Rusi XV-XVII vekov* (Translated literature of Muscovite Rus' fifteenth to seventeenth centuries) (St. Petersburg, 1903), p. 234. Hereafter cited as Sobolevskii; R.P. Dmitreva, "Russkii perevod polskogo socinenia 15 veka" (Russian translation of a Polish work of the fifteenth century), *TODRL* 19 (1963): 303-317.

42. Sobolevskii, pp. 41; 55.

43. Sobolevskii, p. 42.

44. Vladimirov, p. 78.

45. Julian Krzyżanowski, *Romans polski wieku XVI* (The Polish novel of the sixteenth century) (Lublin: Dom Książki Polskiej, 1934), pp. 40-67.

46. *Naziratel. . .* (A book of counsel . . .), ed. by V.S. Golysenko, et al. (Moscow: Nauka, 1973).

47. Samuel Fiszman, "Nowe aspekty badań nad rolą polskiej kultury w rozwoju kultury rosyjskiej w wieku XVII," (New aspects of research on the role of Polish culture in the development of Russian culture in the seventeenth century) in *For Wiktor Weintraub* (The Hague: Mouton, 1975), pp. 113-133.

48. Ryszard Łużny, *Pisarze kręgu Akademii Kijowsko-Mohylańskiej a literatura polska* (Writers connected with the Mohylanian Academy at Kiev and their associations with Polish literature) (Cracow: Uniwersytet Jagielloński, 1966).

49. Igor P. Eremin, *Sbornik otvetov na voprosy po literaturovedeniju* (Collection of responses to questions on the history of literature.) (Moscow: Akademia Nauk SSSR, 1958), p. 84.

50. Dimitrii S. Lichachev, "Semnadcatyj vek v russkoj literature" (The seventeenth century in Russian literature), in *XVII vek v mirovom literaturnom razvitii* (Moscow: Akademia Nauk SSSR, 1969), p. 322.

14

The Senator of Wawrzyniec Goślicki and The Elizabethan Counsellor

Teresa Bałuk-Ulewiczowa

The subject of this study is the book *De Optimo Senatore* by Wawrzyniec Goślicki (Goslicius; Laurentius Grimallius), first published in Latin in 1568 in Venice,[1] and its first printed translation into English, *The Counsellor*, London, 1598. *De Optimo Senatore* belongs to a class of literary works known generally as the *speculum* or "mirror," popular throughout the Middle Ages and during the Renaissance, especially in sixteenth-century Poland.[2] Basically, a *speculum* presented instruction and advice in the form of a "mirror image" or model of behavior to be emulated by, and addressed to, various persons. Originally *specula* were written for kings and princes (the *speculum regis* or *de regimine principum*, but during the Renaissance mirrors for counsellors, ambassadors, courtiers, etc. developed as literary offshoots from the *speculum regis*. Goślicki's mirror of the Ideal Senator appears to have enjoyed a considerable popularity as one of these secondary *specula*, not only in its author's own country, but also in Shakespeare's England.

The fact that Goślicki's book was written and first published in Italy must have been of crucial importance to its reaching England. In Italy it could well have gained the attention of Englishmen, influential personalities like Sir Philip Sidney (resident in Venice, 1573),[3] who, in spite of the recently imposed restrictions on travel to Italy for their countrymen, maintained the well-established humanist channel of cultural flow. But if the book's Italian origins were so decisive in its eventual career in England, they were no less so in the author's native land, and it was undeniably with a deep consciousness of the Italian stamp so clearly impressed on the book's message that its first Polish readers must have approached it.

Like the countless other European mirrors, *De Optimo Senatore* was not written merely as a work of aesthetic erudition and abstraction, but with a very definite, down-to-earth purpose. To understand the book—its author's intentions and its readers' potential reactions—we must look at it against the background of the historical events which spurred the author on to set down his political dialectic, as artistically constructed and yet as purposefully as a spider's web, spun across the supportive frame of humanist rhetorical prose.

The first clue to the topical content of *De Optimo Senatore* lies in its date and letter of dedication to King Sigismund Augustus, written in the turbulent year preceding the finalization of the long constitutional process that made the Kingdom of Poland and the Grand Duchy of Lithuania a united commonwealth, by the Lublin Act of Union (28 June 1569) in which the King played the decisive part. Indeed, the book was published, distributed, and probably also presented to the King[4] at the time when the long-drawn-out campaign for political, economic, and social reform waged since the early 1500's by the rising gentry class against the more privileged aristocrats and high officers of the state was rapidly reaching its boisterous climax in a series of Diets throughout the 1560's in which the protagonists of reform endeavored to press their proposals through the legislative process, courting—and eventually winning—the support of the King as the alliance indispensable for victory. The emergence in 1568 of this book from a Venetian printing press was no random event: it is the Polish sixteenth-century constitutional controversy that forms the real subject-matter of Goślicki's Senator—the pith of substance beneath the platitudes of the *speculum*.

Goślicki's book of the Ideal Senator is thus the product of a twofold intention: to create a book of literary and academic excellence, and to put forward the political wisdom and creed of a particular group of individuals actively involved at the time in Polish affairs of state. It was, in fact, a group whose views there could be no other way of expounding except through the mouthpiece of ancient philosophy and Renaissance scholarship; a group which Goślicki, like many of his promising and ambitious compatriots then studying in Italy, wished to enter, to become a servant of the state under the patronage of the Master of the Royal Chancellor's Office in Cracow, Vice-Chancellor Piotr Myszkowski, to whose virtues he left a permanent tribute in *De Optimo Senatore*. For a book full of references to historical examples, praise of certain figures and criticism of others, *De Optimo Senatore* is remarkable for its reticence on contemporary Polish personalities. Apart from the eulogy of the King, his forebears and the ancient Polish monarchs and saints, it contains expressly laudatory mentions of only two names: Jan Zamoyski and Piotr Myszkowski, both intimately connected with Italy and Italian culture and both destined to leave deep imprints on their nation's political and cultural history. Even Goślicki's letter to the king is not merely a string of complimentary clichés; not hesitating to mention and regret the sad demise of the Jagiellonians in the neighboring countries which subsequently fell to the Turk, Goślicki hints at his practical intention of setting out a policy whereby such a catastrophe might be avoided in the dynasty's Polish kingdom. And whilst his opening pages begin with a flourish of humanist references to ancient letters and learning on political science, with the next stroke of his pen Goślicki dissociates himself from the all too theoretical and idealistic images portrayed in Cicero's *Orator*, Plato's *Republic*, and Xenophon's *Cyropaedia*, beloved of an earlier generation of Polish humanists trained by Callimachus.[5] Goślicki's desire is to be practical.

His choice, then, of the Senator as the figure singled out for apotheosis in the traditional *speculum* fashion immediately identifies his position on the contemporary controversy between the Polish Senate and the rising mass of *szlachta* (gentry). But to say that he speaks for the Senate and against the challenge to its established powers by the Deputies of the *szlachta* would be to simplify the issue. The real question is not merely why does he side with the Senate, but what sort of Senator does he envisage? The "why" is answered within the very first pages, even in the dedicatory letter, where he says openly to the King that the Senate is the body which has always aided the Polish king with its advice, and in Book One where he expresses the opinion that the Senate is the institution best qualified to govern and assist the monarch in his rule (ff. 10A, 16A, 14A, 36B-37A). It is the second part of the question—what should the Senate be like?—that forms the subject of the rest of the work; and Goślicki's portrait of the Ideal Senator in no way suggests that he was a whole-hearted supporter of *all* the men who sat at the time in the Polish Senate, of the means by which they got there, or of all the deeds for which they were responsible. Briefly, his Ideal Senator is highly educated and well acquainted with a wide spectrum of public matters, both at home and abroad (ff. 23B-29A). He is rich enough to afford the financial burdens of senatorial rank, but does not live in luxury nor is he the slave of avarice or materialism (ff. 61A-B, 62A, 78A-80A). His senatorial office should not be merely hereditary, but rather should depend on his personal merit (ff. 33A-35B, 36A). And, above all, he must be endowed with all the traditional moral virtues, marks of the highest dignity in the classic *speculum*: he should always show political prudence and wisdom (ff. 37B, 38A, 39A-B, 43B, 47B, 49A), in other words he should be well-versed both in the theory and practice of politics; he should be just, honest and truthful (ff. 36B-41A, 55B-60B),always putting the public welfare before his own interests; he should be courageous (ff. 65B-70B), able to eschew cowardice and back up word with unflinching deed in the service of the state; and he should be temperate (ff. 71B-74B), living an exemplary life of self-control yet remaining the sociably disposed man of action. All these, together with their "ancillary" virtues, Goślicki describes, in traditional *speculum* manner, in Book Two of *De Optimo Senatore*—but not before he has defined, in Book One, the political predominance he ascribes to his Senator (ff. 10A, 16A-B, 33A) and the education and vocational training he stipulates as the indispensable condition for this position of power and honor (ff. 17B-28B).

Goślicki is an exponent of the theory of the "mixed" state consisting of a combination of the three classical forms of monarchy, aristocracy and democracy as the most just political condition (ff. 10A, 6A). This concept was to become a traditional element of pre-partition Polish political theory; but in

Goślicki's version there is a distinctive preponderance of the intermediary senatorial constituent—a preponderance clearly indicating contemporary Venetian
influence (ff. 9B-10A, 13B, 15A, 17B, 35A) coexisting with the classical, Poly-
bian, root of the tradition. In this Venetian "infatuation" (as it was later called
by its critic, Piotr Skarga),[6] Goślicki was not alone. Many of the young Polish
intellectuals who went out to Italy, and especially to the University of Padua,
to complete their education before seeking employment in the Royal Chancellor's Office in Cracow, hoping eventually to become dignitaries, came under
the spell of the Venetian constitutional arrangement, saw parallels between
Venice and Poland, and wanted to introduce further innovations at home along
the Venetian model. The most striking example of this is Łukasz Górnicki, also
a protégé of a culturally-oriented, earlier, Vice-Chancellor and Bishop of Cracow, Samuel Maciejowski. Venice and Padua play a prominent part in Górnicki's writings—from the Paduan student "club of Polish men" in his version
of Castiglione which is set in the Bishop of Cracow's country house (could this
club's members have shared a common *political* enthusiasm for Venice?)[7] to the
Italian critic who vanquishes his Polish disputant in a debate on the inade-
quacies of the Polish constitutional system [*Rozmowa Polaka z Włochem . . .* (A
Discourse between a Pole and an Italian)]. The ideal which Goślicki sets up for
his Senator has the polish of an international, Italian-inspired, education and
the political sophistication of a Venetian patrician, yet at the same time he is
not a cosmopolitan completely bereft of the national traditions, that should
mark him out as a Senator of Poland. For all his admiration of foreign, particularly Italian, institutions, Goślicki strives to preserve what is good and healthy
in the indigenous tradition, believing that its indiscriminate removal must
inevitably lead to the collapse of the state (ff. 15B, 26B-27A). In this respect
Goślicki's book was an early exposition of Polish patriotism put on the international book market (cf. ff. 25B, 30A, 36B, 68B, 69A-B, 73A).

Probably the best illustration of Goślicki's combination of a humanistically
patriotic piety for the traditional Polish political institutions with a comprehensive inspection and consideration of the corresponding arrangements in
other countries is afforded by what he says about selection for senatorial office—
a subject drawn out from the very core of the furnace of the constitutional
controversy then consuming his countrymen's political skills and passions, and
placed at the crescendoed culmination of Book One of his *Ideal Senator* (ff. 33A-
37A). After a detailed and critical account of the electoral practices of other
countries, including the most distinguished states of classical and biblical antiquity and certain contemporary ones (but with most emphasis on Venice),
he leads logically up to his point, which is that the Senators of his theoretical
"mixed" state (though the implied meaning is Poland) ought to be *elected*—not
appointed according to an automatic hereditary principle—by the monarch,
and by the monarch alone; chosen for their outstanding moral, political and
intellectual virtues. Such a procedure, though not observed in his favorite
example, Venice (which has no permanent monarchy) has nevertheless been

traditional in many of the best constituted states, including his own, and thus further hallowed by the authority of ancient (national) custom. By means of rhetorically refined and learned argument, yet with forceful clarity, Goślicki states his position on the dispute about the Senate plainly enough: his Polish readers of 1568-9 could have had no doubt, by the end of Book One, that he stood on the side of the Senators—those of them, that is, who looked to the classical tradition of the educated, beneficent (and sometimes liberal) philosopher-statesman whose image was being consciously revived, in theory at least, in particular Italian humanist-inspired states, for guidance in the awesome task of governing the vast territories of Poland-Lithuania.

By the same method of dialectic survey leading up to the final statement, he tackles the other subject of popular contention: religion (ff. 12A-13A, 42A-47B, 53A-55B, 59A-60A). Though there can certainly be no question of any accusation against Goślicki of religious pragmatism of the sort which might be levied against various later princes of the Church or doubt that the piety and religious feeling reflected in his book are anything but genuine, one nevertheless senses that his concern with religion in the treatise is primarily the relationship between Church and State. His position is that no state can exist for long without a healthy established religion and that it cannot flourish without the class of priests actively participating in its government. This in itself is an ancient notion, and Goślicki duly quotes his classical and biblical references. However, the established religion that he means—and this is where the medieval sincerity of his Christianity cannot be denied—is not any arbitrarily accepted state creed, but the one that is established universally, not merely in the geographical sense or through unbroken apostolic succession, but fundamentally through its universal authority and validity regarding the human soul with its faculty of choice between good and evil, in the Augustinian meaning of the City of God and the Old Testament meaning of Zion. And yet it is the medieval notion of the linking of the spiritual with the temporal that absorbs Goślicki's attention here, for he notes the practical, *worldly* and political results of the rupture of this bond. "What happens to a state which allows Religion to be attacked by heresy, either standing idly by or embracing the unauthorized innovations?" he asks, and, looking out from his Tridentine vantage-point, cannot fail to see the recent "deplorable examples of France and Germany still smouldering in the aftermath of civil war" (cf. ff. 42A-B). It is against this *political* danger that he warns other countries, undoubtedly thinking first and foremost of his own, where the Reformation was challenging not only the spiritual authority of the Catholic priesthood, but also, through the vociferous Protestant wing of the *szlachta* reform movement, the political power exercised by the Catholic Church in Polish affairs of state thanks to the superior position of the bishops in the Polish Senate. Here again we have evidence that Goślicki is speaking on behalf of the men grouped around Piotr Myszkowski, a senator and high-ranking churchman, and perhaps too the ordained professors of the University in Cracow, corporately loyal to Rome.

Intimately involved in the details of Polish internal affairs, Goślicki's book could not have failed to make some sort of impact on a politically avid national readership. Unfortunately, today—apart from the King's note about receiving a copy and sending it to his library and Krzysztof Warszewicki's (Varsevicius) later comment[8]—we have no written records as to its immediate reception, perhaps because Goślicki had chosen to support the minority opinion. But what of its fortunes in England? Just how popular was the *speculum* type of literature in Elizabethan England? Ruth Kelso attempts to answer the question in her book, *The Doctrine of the English Gentleman in the Sixteenth Century*,[9] supporting her answer by an extensive bibliographical supplement of nearly a thousand titles listing "treatises on the gentleman and related subjects published in Europe to 1605." Stressing the general popularity of such works in England, she adds the significant remark that there were not many *native* English treatises with special information on offices such as that of the ambassador, counsellor, or secretary, but that works in foreign tongues and translations of them seem to have supplied the demand.[10]

There was thus a general literary trend, a constituent part of which was the appearance in 1598 of a translation of Goślicki, entitled *The Counsellor, Exactly Pourtraited in Two Bookes, Wherein the Offices of Magistrates, the Happie Life of Subjectes, and the Felicitie of Common-weales is pleasantly and Pithilie Discoursed, A Golden Worke, Replenished with the chiefe learning of the most excellent Philosophers and Lawgiuers, and not onely profitable, but verie necessarie for all those that be admitted to the administration of a well-gouerned Common-weale, Written in Latin by Laurentius Grimaldus, and Consecrated to the honour of the Polonian Empire, Newlie translated into English*. London, Imprinted by Richard Bardocke, Anno Salutis Humanae MDXCVIII. We shall go into the details concerning this particular publication—why it appeared and in what circumstances, who was responsible for its translation and publication, who indeed could have wanted it translated and publisned—although Ruth Kelso has already supplied the basis of our answer. Simply, in the England of Elizabeth there was a literary fashion and need for this kind of literature.

Leaving aside all the other matters connected with Goślicki and his *speculum* (including its other, earlier and later, English translation),[11] we shall concentrate chiefly on the relation between the Latin original of *De Optimo Senatore* and the English text of *The Counsellor*. . . .

At the outset, before the facts of the two texts themselves can be approached, some of the deadwood of errors and mistaken notions about the 1598 edition that have accrued as a result of generalizations and various misunderstandings must be removed. The first such notion is that there was a separate edition of Goślicki in translation in 1607, distinct from the 1598 one.[12] A brief inspection immediately reveals that there was only one edition of the work, the 1598 and 1607 copies differing only in the title page and letter dedicatory, of which a second printing, dated 1607, was presumably attached later to copies of the original edition still at the bookseller's. The next erroneous piece of information

on the 1598 edition has done more damage, bandied about so readily as a
sensational "fact" until it has become accepted and unquestioned, though
entirely unfounded, while documentary evidence implies rather the opposite.
Since the 1930's, when it was most probably first presented, the story has
circulated about the alleged "confiscation" and even "burning" of the Goślicki
translation in England.[13] But there is an entry in the name of the stationer,
William Blackman, for ownership of, and permission to publish, "a book entitled The Counsellor" into the Stationers' Register (March 6th, 1598) "under the
hands of My Lord the Bishop of London and Master Man."[14] Since the officers
of the Stationers' Company virtually controlled the whole of the legal book
trade in England and, as partners of the ecclesiastical authorities, had a say in
matters of censorship, this registration hardly suggests that confiscation of the
published book ensued—the more so, as (in spite of the possibility of records
being incomplete) numerous adjacent documents in the Register for the same
period, proscribing various publications, go into meticulous and repetitive detail to make sure that the titles of banned books should be known to the
booksellers. There is not a hint of The Counsellor... in these lists; indeed, after
the single entry, neither it nor its owner, Blackman, are ever mentioned in the
Register again. The conclusion, strengthened by Kelso's account of the general
popularity in England of Continental works similar to Goślicki's, none of which
were ever, as far as I am aware, believed to have been confiscated, is that the
alleged confiscation of Goślicki in England is at the very least an entirely
groundless supposition.[15]

The exact relation between the stationer and the printer behind The Counsellor... is somewhat puzzling. As already mentioned above, the stationer in
whose name the book was entered in the Register was a certain William Blackman, most probably a young man who had finished his apprenticeship only
two years previously (26 July 1596),[16] and had the entry of only one other book
to his credit[17] before his disappearance from the Register after this final record
of 6 March 1598. But on the title page of The Counsellor... there is no sign of
Blackman's name; a stationer's device, noted in the catalogues as used by others
as well as Blackman,[18] appears together with a note that the book was printed
by Richard Bradocke. The "1607" title page, however, bearing a new title (A
Common-wealth of Good Counsaile, or Policie's chief Counseller...), mentions another
stationer: "Printed by R.B. for N. Lyng," this time with Nicholas Lyng's device.
The question arises how a book entered in the name of one stationer became
the property of another, with no written records of the exchange.

Much more information about Bradocke and Lyng may be gleaned from the
Stationers' records reproduced in Arber's Transcripts. In contrast to Blackman,
both appear by 1598 to have already acquired a certain reputation and status
as fairly senior members of the Company—Bradocke as a printer (his first entry
for ownership of a book was as late as 1598, and the book's title was The
Hunting of the Romish Fox—hardly suggesting a predilection for works likely to
be confiscated on religious grounds!), Lyng as a stationer and bookseller with

a taste for what was then popular literature, including the first two quarto editions of Shakespeare's *Hamlet*.[19] Some of Lyng's books of satirical verse earned him a censure in 1599, when a list of nine condemned books of satirical and erotic literature, including his own *Shadow of Truth in Epigrams and Satires* and *Caltha Poetarum*, was brought to the notice of the Stationers' Company by the ecclesiastical censorship authorities.[20] The absence of Goślicki's work on this particular censor's list is noteworthy. But the 1599 incident seems to be the only serious misdemeanor in Lyng's long career. Both he and Bradocke had been promoted to the Company's livery the previous year—an unlikely distinction for a man who had *just* printed an allegedly "condemned" book.[21]

The "1607" copies of Goślicki in translation were never entered in the Register, as distinct from the 1598 edition; nowhere apart from the new title page, is Lyng referred to as the stationer responsible for *A Commonwealth of Good Counsel*. Some writers believed that an entry of 2nd September, 1607, for a book called *A Court of Good Counsel*, in the name of R.B., was a registration. Again, simple inspection of the title page of the book in question reveals its true essence: *The Court of Good Counsel Wherein Is Set Down the True Rules How a Man Should Choose a Good Wife from a Bad and a Woman a Good Husband from a Bad. . . .*[22] With no re-entry into the records, it seems that Lyng simply took over Blackman's property, after the latter had ceased to be a member of the Company (perhaps he had died in the interval between 6 March 1598 and 1607).

Another strange point about both the 1598 and 1607 copies is that both title pages inform their readers that the book is "consecrated to the honour of the Polonian Empire," and that—instead of dedications to some English person of rank—they reproduce the original Venetian letter of dedication "to the most excellent Prince Augustus King of Polonia etc.," who had been dead for well over 30 years by then. Could it be that, for some reason, a person or persons in England in 1598 had a special motive to have this translation dedicated, if not to its original addressee, then to his successor on the Polish throne—reimbursing, perhaps, the stationers' loss of revenue as a result of not dedicating the work to a less inaccessible patron?

The quality of the translation itself and its relation to the Latin of the Venetian edition have never been examined seriously, if at all.[23] A detailed juxtaposition of original and translation reveals the translation's inadequacy. On purely technical grounds, the English text is littered with numerous errors of translation due to carelessness and insufficient knowledge of Latin. In its rendering of the first 20 leaves of the Venetian text, for instance, serious mistranslations occur at an average of over one a leaf, and the rest of the translation is hardly any better, though what one might call the "error density" fluctuates and virtually mistake-free pages are interspersed with others which, if they had occurred in a schoolboy's notebook, would have been red with the Latin master's corrections. This rather suggests that several persons might have been engaged in the translation, each covering a small section of the work. At any rate, there does not seem to have been much co-ordination or checking of the translation before it went to the printer's; indeed, the large number of mistakes even suggests that the assignment might have been carried out in great haste. Some examples of these errors might be instructive:

In a discussion of how to react to ingratitude, especially on the part of one's own country, Goślicki refers to Plato.

Plato ... interrogatus, quomodo erga patriam ingratam se gerere oporteat ...

(Ven.f.17B)

This should have been, "When asked how one should behave with respect to one's own country when it is ungrateful to one, Plato said ..." But the unfortunate translator renders it as

Plato asked ... in what sort a man should be ungrateful to his country ...

(L1598, p. 32)

About a page later, on the subject of naturalization and the granting of citizenship in ancient Rome, Goślicki's

Fiebant autem cives, vel pleno iure, hoc est cum suffragio ...

(Ven.f.18B)

which means that "some became citizens with full rights, that is with full political rights", becomes in the translation:

some were made citizens *pleno iure*, which was by consent of voices . . .

(L1598, p. 34)

A few sentences further on, Goślicki's

quadam imitatione et similitudine

(Ven.f.18B)

becomes

by imitation and courtesy

(L1598, p. 35)

instead of "by imitation and similarity." When Goślicki considers the subject of nobility, and writes

Qui claribus sunt orti parentibus, laudandi merito sunt . . . si maiorum virtutes . . . superare aut . . . exaequare contendunt.

(Ven.f.19A),

which means, "those who are born of noble stock are worthy of praise if they try either to surpass or to equal their ancestors' virtue,"—but the 1598 translator has it as

who so is descended from noble parents, doth deserve to be commended . . . so that he endeavour himself to equal, . . . or excel the
glorious acts . . . of his ancestors . . .

(L1598, p. 35).

Page 36 of the translation begins with two more errors of the same type,
and a third of a different kind. The majority of Goślicki's "examples" were
drawn from the history, customs, and practices of the ancients. However, the
translator does little or nothing to render some of these details into accurate
English, sometimes not even bothering to translate them into English at all (no
translations are given for the numerous quotations from classical poetry, despite the availability of good contemporary English verse translations, and
proper nouns or special terms tend to be copied down chaotically in their Latin
or Greek versions, regardless even of the oblique cases in which some of them
happened to occur in the original). In this part of the discourse on nobility,
Goślicki mentions the old Roman custom of displaying a deceased citizen's
death-mask at the funeral and later adding it to the collection of family death-
masks hanging in the atrium of the house. The word used for death-mask is
imago. But the 1598 hack duly mistranslates it, and for *"atrium plenum fumosis
imaginibus"* we have "hall painted full of proud arms or badges." Elsewhere
in the book he does not take any greater pains over similar antiquarian's detail,
so for the story of how Aristides was asked by an Athenian ignoramus to put
his own name down for ostracism (Ven.f.9A), in the English version the poor
wretch comes "bearing a scroll of paper" (L1598, p. 16-17) instead of a potsherd
(for *"testula oblata"*). In view of his carelessness with other classical details, it
seems unlikely that these anachronisms were deliberately introduced for the
sake of comprehensibility.

And so the translation continues, riddled with mistakes which occasionally
evoke a grin, as, for example, in the place where the translator evidently
misread *coniungi* ("to be joined") as *coniugi* (dative singular of *coniunx*, "wife").
Thus the sober sentence

Summum igitur bonum in amicitiis sentiunt Respublicae, haec enim
si adsit, nulla civilis dissensio nasci potest, desiderabunt omnes propter vehementem amorem velut amantes coniungi, et ex multis, ut
Pithagoras dicit, unum efficere, ea enim est vis amicitiae, ut unum
ex pluribus efficiat animum.

(Ven.f.63A)

which means, "Thus commonwealths attain great good through friendship,
for where there is friendship, there no civil dissension can arise, and because
of their great mutual love, all desire to be united, just like lovers [viz. friends],
for all to be joined into one, as Pythagoras says, so powerful is the force of
friendship that it unites many, making them unanimous." But in the translation
it becomes

Therefore commonweals receive great good by friendship, for where
it is, no civil dissension can arise, and all men with one assent (as it

were one particular man loving his wife) will (as Pythagoras saith) join in love, and become as it were one man: for so much is the force of friendship, as of many it maketh one only man.

(L1598, pp.113-114)

On discovery of the liberal sprinkling of such errors, it is not hard to assess the 1598 English version of Goślicki, as far as the technicalities of translation go, as something of a non-entity. As noted above, none of the English translations of Goślicki, to my knowledge, have ever been studied in any depth from this aspect before, yet this straightforward procedure of philological comparison yields basic results.

But there is far more to the question than just the simple mechanics of translation, treated in the 1598 edition as something of minor importance only, over which not much trouble need be taken. On the other hand, and in striking contrast to this apparent negligence, large passages of it have been carefully edited and whole sentences or phrases likely to be controversial or arouse official disapproval have been removed or skillfully paraphrased by a writer who was infinitely more painstaking than the lackadaisical hack-translators who dealt with the "harmless" fragments. The two subjects which, judging by their treatment in the 1598 translation required careful edition were first kingship and whether it should be hereditary or elective, and secondly the contemporary religious controversy.

The first of these, though crucial to Goślicki's book, was relatively simple to handle, as it occupied only a small amount of space in the original Latin. Loyal to his country's political theory and practice, and also under a strong Venetian influence, Goślicki expressly preferred elective monarchy to hereditary succession, and said so outright in one of his sentences (*"Qui haereditarios reges praeficere caeperunt imperiis . . . "*—Ven. f.8B): "those who would set up hereditary kings as their masters, copied the customs either of subversive citizens, or else of barbarians; and we observe how in their countries everything is ruled by tyranny and autocracy." This was, of course, totally incompatible with contemporary Tudor home policy and propaganda, and the only reasonable course for a would-be English publisher was to omit the whole sentence—which the 1598 editor did in fact do. As elsewhere in his comments on kings and kingship Goślicki was full of respect and admiration for monarchy in general, though with a slight emphasis on the elective form, all that was necessary for the English translator to make these remarks not only acceptable but, indeed, positively orthodox with respect to the established Elizabethan political canon, were a few clever paraphrases in a limited number of expressions. When, for instance, in the sentence preceding the omitted one, Goślicki brought up the traditional notion of God's favor of the good monarch, using a phrase drawn from the elective theory that God elevated the best man up to the throne (*"Omnium optimos . . . in solium regale evehit,"* f.8B), the English editor adapted this to:

LAVRENTII
Grimalii Goslicii

DE OPTIMO SENATORE
LIBRI DVO.

In quibus Magiftratuum officia, Ciuium uita
beata,Rerumpub. fœlicitas
explicantur.

Opvs planè aureum,fummorum Philofophorum & Legifla
torum doctrina refertum,omnibus Refpu. ritè adminiftra-
re cupientibus, non modò utile, fed apprime neceffarium.

Acceßit locuples rerum toto Opere memorabilium Index.

CVM PRIVILEGIO,

*V*ENETIIS, *Apud Iordanum Zilettum,*

M D LXVIII.

43. Laurenty Grzymała Goślicki, *De optimo senatore libri duo*, Venetiis, 1568. The title page of
the first Latin edition of Goślicki's work. (The Department of Rare Books and Special Collections, The University of Michigan Library, Ann Arbor).

THE COVNSELLOR.

Exactly pourtraited in two Bookes.

VV HEREIN THE OFFICES OF

Magiſtrates, The happie life of Subiectes, and the felicitie of
Common-weales is pleaſantly and pithilie diſcourſed.

A GOLDEN WORKE, REPLENISHED

with the chiefe learning of the moſt excellent Philoſophers and
Lawgiuers, and not onely profitable, but verie neceſſarie for
all thoſe that be admitted to the adminiſtration of a
well-gouerned Common-weale.

Written in Latin by, LAVRENTIVS GRIMALDVS, and
conſecrated to the honour of the ·Polonian Empyre.

Newlie tranſlated into Engliſh.

LONDON

Imprinted by RICHARD BRADOCKE.
Anno Salutis Humanæ M.D.XC.VIII.

44. Laurenty Grzymała Goślicki, *The Counsellor*, London, 1598. The title page of the first
edition of the English translation of Wawrzyniec Grzymała Goślicki's work *De optimo senatore*,
Venetiis, 1568 (The Folger Shakespeare Library, Washington, D.C.).

God ... doth allow, or rather commend the government of one
(L1598, p. 16)

But these were relatively minor alterations compared to those necessary for passages dealing with the second troublesome topic, religion, quantitatively amounting to some ten pages of text in the Venetian edition, the equivalents of which in the 1598 English are barely recognizable as their translation.

Not much needed editing in the first passage on religion (Ven.f.12A-13A), on the necessity of high offices in secular government for clergymen, as the argument rested on universally accepted examples, mostly drawn from biblical, ancient and classical history and was in no way contradictory to Elizabethan policy or practice. It was only towards the end, when the finale of a sentence of Goślicki's described the priesthood as God's *"vicarios suae divinitatis"* that the censor's scissors felt obliged to intervene and remove the offending words, preferring to mutilate the classical period rather than risk the damage to which any word-associations, let alone meanings in the phrase might expose his English readers. For it was the monarch who stood at the head of the Church of England, nominating all its prelates. The following sentence, with the implication that a spiritual leader's authority should be respected and his counsel treated as coming from an equal, or sometimes even as from a superior, by the secular ruler, and that the king should not only accept this state of affairs, but even consider it just, useful and necessary, also had to take a paraphrase for the word *"principes"* qualifying the *"sacerdotes"* of the original:

It was therefore thought expedient, profitable and necessary that the princes of every commonweal shall be accompanied and counselled with spiritual ministers . . .

(L1598, p. 24)

Far more has been visibly altered of Goślicki's passage on divine justice (Ven.f.53A-55B). Its six pages of Latin have been fitted into just over one of English (pp. 99-100), and of its fifty sentences twenty-eight have been omitted completely and one partially. What remains are the platitudes on religion in general, again the classical references and the assertion how important religion is in the running of a state. What has disappeared is a lengthy exposition of the role of the priesthood as a "divine magistracy" with an inalienable monopoly in all matters of religion, and on the superiority of Church over State, with a defense of the established faith on the grounds that any change thereof inevitably brings about the downfall of the State. Hence the deplorable results of the Reformation, Goślicki argues, not hesitating to name the countries he considers worst stricken. All of this, of course, is also absent in the translation.

To sum up, the degree of editing in these two paramount matters of religion and kingship is such in the 1598 English version as to disqualify the book from any claim to being a reasonable translation. But at the same time the editorial censor's therapy conducted in it with respect to the original shows the groundlessness of the theory of its confiscation. With all the trouble the editor must have gone to over these alterations, the book produced was not likely to fall foul of official criticism but, on the contrary, could well have been an orthodox and approved manual, even intended to act as a smoke-screen to discourage would-be readers from reaching for the unabridged Latin original.

For the sake of comparison, it might be well to glance at the rather similar fate of two other Continental mirrors, translated into English and published by prominent London stationers about the same time as Goślicki's. The first, Bartolome Felippe's *Tractado del conseio y de los consejeros de los Principes* (first edition, Coimbra, 1584)—mentioned along with Goślicki's as the standard portrait of the Senator in Gabriel Harvey's *Pierces Supererogation* (1593)[24]—became the property of the publisher-cum-fishmonger, John Wolfe, whose rather devious way into the Stationers' Company had caused a ripple of scandal somewhat earlier.[25] Having secured the registration of the Spaniard's book in the Stationers' records, and presumably with the Company's blessing,[26] Wolfe set about issuing the work . . . first in a Spanish version, with a publisher's inscription *Segunda Impression Turino . . . 1589.* One of the existing copies of this pirate edition bears an enlightening handwritten note on its title page: *Johannes Thorius hunc librum possid[it] a se lectum correct[um] et versum in Anglicanum sermonem die 19 Augusti 1589.* Impressio Segunda. It is full of marginal remarks and notes in the same hand, obviously referring to Thorius' translation, which came out in the same year under the title *The Counsellor. A Treatise of Counsels and Counsellors of Princes. Written in Spanish by Bartholomew Phillip, Doctor of the Civil and Canon Law, Englished by J.T.,Graduate in Oxford.* London, Printed by John Wolfe, 1589; and with a dedication to John Fortescue instead of the original to Albert, Archduke of Austria. A brief comparison immediately discloses various textual discrepancies between the Coimbra original and Wolfe's versions, including notorious omissions and revisions of passages on such subjects as the Portuguese succession (where Phillip II is presented in the original as the rightful heir), criticism of Henry VIII's putting away of Catherine of Aragon, the naming of Luther and other reformers in passages denouncing heresy, and general, numerous, and fairly elaborate panegyrics to Phillip II.[27] How fortunate for us that Thorius' copy of the pirated "Spanish Counsellor,"[28] with its marginal notes actually marking the omitted fragments, has survived to allow us a glimpse of the backstage activities behind the facade for this curious production. But there remains a tantalizing question: why was the fishmonger Wolfe ever attracted by the idea of giving an ineradicably Spanish publication such a face-lift in the year after the vanquishing of the Armada, when anti-Spanish feelings must still have been running high?

In the same year that Goślicki's work emerged from the press in its English habiliment, there also appeared an English translation of a French *Miroir Politique*: Guillaume de la Perrière's work published by Adam Islip under the title *The Mirror of Policy . . .* Instead of its original dedication to a French Notable, it carried only an address from the printer to the reader and, like the earlier reproduction of Felippe with its references to Spain carefully edited, it too had most of its original panegyrics of France and French institutions removed or at least heavily retouched. In this respect both translations were so unlike the curious 1598 English Goślicki—on sale to would-be readers complete with a meticulous reproduction of the original dedication to the King of Poland and with all the laudatory (though relatively modest) glosses on Poland, its princes and its polity, and issued within months of a major diplomatic fracas between England and Poland.

In the summer of 1597 diplomatic relations between these two countries had undergone a considerable strain.[29] There was a state of war between England and Spain, and a danger that the King of Poland, related by marriage to Phillip II, might become Spain's military ally. Polish sea exports to Spain of food and building materials were being intercepted by English pirates and confiscated. After previous apprisals and protests to Elizabeth had failed, Ambassador Paweł Działyński was sent by the King of Poland and demanded outright that the acts of piracy should cease and restitution be made for the confiscated property of his master's subjects. The impulsive Elizabeth had not expected such a direct address and was outraged. In an improvised reply in Latin, she ticked off the Ambassador for what she regarded as "insolence," with the following digression on his conduct:

> Quod ad te attinet, tu mihi videris libros multos perlegisse, libros tamen Principum ne attigisse, sed prorsus ignorare quod inter Reger conveniat . . . [30]

> I perceive you have read many books to fortify your arguments in this case, yet I am apt to believe that you have not lighted upon the chapter that prescribeth the form to be used between Kings and Princes ...[31]

This is how the fragment was rendered in English by Robert Cecil, one of Elizabeth's highest-ranking political servants and son of her most renowned counsellor, Lord Burghley. Elizabeth instructed the younger Cecil to write an account of the incident to her favorite (but his political rival), the Earl of Essex, then absent from Court.

The expression "libros Principum," in Cecil's report "the chapter that prescribeth the form to be used between Kings and Princes," might perhaps be a reference to the mirrors of princes, the literary genre from which Goślicki's mirror of the Ideal Senator is descended. And would not the sarcasm in this have been all the more venomous if the bystanders, the Queen's courtiers, could have immediately associated it with the treatise by Ambassador Działyński's countryman—a treatise, indeed not on kings and princes, but on the humbler subject of senators?

But, like all records of the past in which innuendo is suspected but not proved beyond doubt, this sentence of Elizabeth's obviously meant to be scathingly sarcastic, must remain as only a hint that she might have heard of Goślicki's book and, perhaps, might even have known it fairly well. A direct assertion of the book's popularity in England occurs in a 1599 collection of works by Krzysztof Warszewicki, a Polish political writer closely connected with both the Habsburgs and the Jesuits. Perhaps it was from English Jesuits that he obtained the following information:

> . . . I am told that there is no other work which in England is handled more readily than yours . . .[32]

It seems more probable that Warszewicki meant the popularity of the original Latin version of Goślicki, rather than the hack translator's English. The fact remains, however, that it was only a few months after the diplomatic incident of 1597 that Goślicki's book was published in a hurried but edited English rendering, apparently with the approval of the authorities but without a trace of local sponsorship and "dedicated to the honour of the Polonian Empire." Perhaps the junior stationer who published it had been encouraged and supported financially in his enterprise by powerful but anonymous men interested in preventing a potential public outburst of xenophobia which might have been triggered by the unfortunate episode with the Polish Ambassador and might have further aggravated the already critical situation: Men such as Lord Burghley, Elizabeth's most senior politician? But if there was, indeed, a political force behind the book's publication, then it seems unlikely that we shall ever know for certain, unless documentary evidence turns up. As for the 1598 translation itself—apart from the information which may be obtained by sheer textual analysis—it seems unlikely we shall ever *know* much about the background to its appearance, though guesswork might yield interesting attempts at explanation.

Notes

1. The present paper is based on my Ph.D. thesis, *"De optimo Senatore" Wawrzyńca Goślickiego i jego oddziaływanie w Anglii ("De optimo Senatore"* of Wawrzyniec Goślicki and his influence in England) defended in the Jagiellonian University on 29 June 1979). For a bibliography of previous work on Goślicki, see Karol Estreicher, *Bibliografia polska* (Polish bibliography), vol. 17 (Cracow, 1899), pp. 276-278; and *Bibliografia literatury polskiej "Nowy Korbut"* (Bibliography of Polish literature, "Nowy Korbut"), vol. 2, *Piśmiennictwo staropolskie* (Old Polish literature), ed. Roman Pollak (Warsaw, 1964), pp. 214-216. A photographic facsimile exists of the 1598 English translation (*The Counsellor*): see Witold Chwalewik, *Anglo-Polish Renaissance Texts* (Warsaw, PWN, 1968), pp. 45-203.

2. The subject still awaits its synthesis, but for one writer, Mikołaj Rej see Aleksander Brückner, *Mikołaj Rej* (Cracow, 1905), pp.283-351; and Wilhelm Bruchnalski, *Studia nad literaturą polską w epoce Odrodzenia. I. Rozwój twórczości pisarskiej Mikołaja Reja* (Studies on Polish literature in the period of the Renaissance. I. Development of the literary output of Mikołaj Rej) "Rozprawy Wydziału Filologicznego Akademii Umiejętności w Krakowie," vol. 44, (1908), pp. 112-196.

3. Sidney was also intimately interested in Polish affairs, particularly in the royal elections. The country was a frequent subject in his correspondence. In 1574

he traveled to Poland. A contemporary rumor (recorded in several books) describes Sidney as a candidate to the Polish throne. See Henryk Zins, *Polska w oczach Anglików, XIV-XVI w.* (Poland in the eyes of Englishmen, fourteenth to sixteenth centuries), (Warsaw: PIW, 1974), pp. 89-95.

4. See Stanisław Bodniak, "Kartka bibliotekarskich i starościńskich zajęć Górnickiego" (A page from the library and "starost" activites of Górnicki), *Silva Rerum* 4 (1928), Cracow, pp. 72-76.

5. Ven.f.14B; cf. the laudatory references to Callimachus and particularly to Xenophon in the so-called *Polish Queen's Letters to Her Son* (otherwise known as *De Institutione Regii Pueri*, ed. Heinrich von Zeissberg, in *Kleinere Geschichtsquellen Polens im Mittelalter* (Vienna, 1877), pp. 99-136.

6. See the "Szóste kazanie sejmowe" (Sixth sermon to the Diet) in Piotr Skarga, *Kazania na niedziele i święta całego roku*, (Cracow, 1597) ed. Stanisław Kot, Biblioteka Narodowa I, vol. 70 (Lwów: Ossolineum, 1939) (2nd edition), p. 126-146). Cf. also Tadeusz Grabowski, *Piotr Skarga na tle katolickiej literatury religijnej w Polsce wieku XVI 1536-1612* (Piotr Skarga in the context of Catholic religious literature in Poland of the sixteenth century, 1536-1612), (Cracow: Akademia Umiejętności, 1913), p. 429.

7. For Łukasz Górnicki's remarks about this "Polish club" in Padua, see Łukasz Górnicki, *Dworzanin Polski* (The Polish courtier), in *Pisma*, vol. 1, ed. Roman Pollak (Warsaw: PIW, 1961), p. 66-68, and Pollak's comments (ibid.).

8. Krzysztof Warszewicki, *Opera Omnia*, (Cracoviae, 1599/1600), f.202-203.

9. Ruth Kelso, *The Doctrine of the English Gentleman in the Sixteenth Century*, University of Illinois Studies in Language and Literature, vol. 14 (Urbana: University of Illinois Press, 1929).

10. Ibid., pp. 53-54.

11. These included an earlier manuscript translation of Book One of *De Optimo Senatore*, by a Robert Chester (*The first booke of Lawrentius Grimalius Goslicius of the best Senator*, British Library, Ms. Add. 18613), translated before 1585; a 1660 plagiarism in à Royalist pamphlet, based on the 1598 translation, (J.G., *The Sage Senator Delineated; Or, A discourse of the Qualifications, Endowments, Parts, external and internal, Office, Duty and Dignity of a Perfect Politician. With a Discourse of Kingdoms, Republiques, and States-Popular. As Also of Kings and Princes: To which is annexed, The New Models of Modern Policy* ... London, printed by Ja. Cottrel for Sam. Speed, at the signe of the Printing-Press in St. Paul's Church-yard. 1660); and finally William Oldisworth's translation, *The Accomplished Senator. In Two Books. Written originally in Latin, by Laurence Grimald Gozliski, Senator and Chancellor of Poland, and Bishop of Posna or Pozen. Done into English, from the Edition Printed in Venice, in the Year 1568. By Mr. Oldisworth* . . . London: Printed for the Author, in the Year 1733.

12. Arthur P. Coleman, Charles S. Haight, *The Miracle of the Good Senator. A Study of Goslicius' "De Optimo Senatore"* ... New York, 3 May 1941, p. 2, 17; and its revision, A. P. Coleman, C. S. Haight and Wenceslas J. Wagner, "Laurentius Grimaldus Goslicius and His Age—Modern Constitutional Law Ideas in the Sixteenth Century," in *Polish Law Throughout the Ages*, ed. W. J. Wagner (Stanford, Cal.: Hoover Institution Press, 1970), p. 103-104; H. Zins, p. 170; however, Joseph A. Teslar "Shakespeare's Worthy Counsellor", *Sacrum Poloniae Millenium*, vol. 7 (Rome, 1960), p. 103) recognizes the 1607 copies as identical (save for title page and dedication) with the 1598 ones.

13. See Tytus Filipowicz, "The Accomplished Senator," *Proceedings of the American Society of International Law*, Washington, D.C., 1932, p. 239; idem. "Goślickiego *De optimo senatore* a myśl polityczna w krajach anglosaskich" (Goślicki's *De optimo senatore* and political thought in Anglo-Saxon countries), *Przegląd Współczesny*, no. 13, vol. 98 (Cracow, 1934): 70; Coleman and Haight, p. 17; Coleman, Haight and Wagner, pp. 108-109; W.J. Stankiewicz, *The Accomplished Senator of Laurentius Goslicius*, Oficyna Warszawska Abroad, 1946, p. 11; Teslar, pp. 55-60; Zins, p. 172.

14. Edward Arber, *Transcripts of the Registers of the Company of Stationers of London*, vol. 3 (London, 1876), p. 105.

15. About the theory that Goślicki's book influenced and inspired the American founding fathers, see Filipowicz, *The Accomplished Senator*, pp. 234-241; idem, *Goślickiego "De optimo senatore"*, pp. 68-79; Haight and Coleman, pp. 3-5; 19; Haight, Coleman and Wagner, p. 104; see also a reply to this theory: Teresa J. Bałukówna, "Z zagadnień kariery anglosaskiej Wawrzyńca Goślickiego" (On the problems of the Anglo-Saxon career of Wawrzyniec Goślicki), *Silva Rerum* Series Nova, vol. 1 (Cracow, 1981), pp. 63-80.

16. Arber, vol. 3, p. 159.

17. Ibid., vol. 3, pp. 29-30, 79.

18. R. M. McKerrow, *Printers' and Publishers' Devices in England and Scotland 1485-1640* (London, 1913), p. 108, no. 280.

19. Arber, vol. 3, pp. 29-30, and 365.

20. Ibid., vol. 2, p. 316.

21. Ibid., vol. 2, pp. 872-873.

22. Ibid., vol. 3, p. 358.

23. Teslar, pp. 117-121 quotes a few extracts of the various translations of Goślicki together with the relevant passages of the Venetian original but makes no attempt to analyze them critically.

24. Gabriel Harvey, *Pierces Supererogation, or a New Praise of the Old Ass* (London, 1593), p. 114.

25. For information on John Wolfe, see M. Plant, *The English Book Trade* (London, 1939), pp. 105-108, 123; Colin Clair, *A History of Printing in Britain* (London: Cassell, 1965), p. 100.

26. See Kelso, p. 268; and Arber, vol. 2, p. 517.

27. Cf: (A) Bartolome Felippe, *Tractado del conseio y de los conseieros de los principes* . . . (Coimbra, 1584); (B) *Tractado del conseio y de los conseieros de los principes compuesto por el Doctor Bartolome Felippe* . . . , Segunda Impression (Turino, 1589) (in fact J. Wolfe's pirate, London, 1589), (C) *The Counsellor. A Treatise of Counsels and Counsellors of Princes* . . ., Englished by J.T., Graduate in Oxford, London, Printed by John Wolfe, 1589. In the above, cf. Chapter 3, 2 (on the Portugese succession): f.10b-11a (A); f.13a-11a (B-nb. wrong pagination); f.12b (C); also at the very end of (A) - passage missing in (B) and (C); - Chapter 3, 5 (Henry VIII's divorce from Catherine of Aragon): f.14b (A); f.15b-13a (wrong pagination - B); f.14b (C); etc.

28. The emulation of foreign statesmen by English gentlemen provoked a series of satirical poems on "Italianate" Englishmen; cf. Gabriel Harvey's *Speculum Tusculanismi* (in *Elizabethan Critical Essays*, ed. G.G. Smith (Oxford, 1904), vol. 1, pp. 353-354); also Thomas Nashe's remarks on Harvey and his foreign manners in *Have With You to Saffron Walden* (in *Works of Thomas Nashe*, ed. R.B. McKerrow (London, 1904), vol. 3, p. 50), and on "foreign counsellors" and "counterfeit statesmen" in *Pierce Penniless His Supplication to the Devil* (ibid., vol. 1, pp. 162, 166-167).

29. For the English documents on the incident, see *Acts of the Privy Council of England*, New Series vol. 26. AD. 1597, ed. J. R. Dasent (London, 1903), pp. 302, 307-308; *Calendar of State Papers. Domestic Series, Elizabeth, 1593-97*, ed. M.A. Everett Green (London, 1869), pp. 473, 476, 481; W. Camden, *Annales Rerum Anglicarum et Hibernicarum Regnate Elizabetha* ... (London, 1717), pp. 746-750. In the Polish archives, see *Mercurius Sarmaticus ex Belgio et Anglia* ... , 1597, preserved in many libraries in ms. form (eg. Biblioteka Czartoryskich—"Teki Naruszewicza," ms. no. 97), and published in a Polish translation (by Irena Horbowy), *Merkuriusz sarmacki z Niderlandów i Anglii*, ed. Ryszard Marciniak (Wrocław: Ossolineum, 1978).

30. Camden, pp. 746-750.

31. Sir Robert Cecil to the Earl of Essex, Landsdowne ms. no. 85 art. 19 (British Library); published in *Original Letters Illustrative of English History*, ed. Henry Ellis, First Series, vol. 3 (London: Dawsons of Pall Mall, 1969), letter 234, pp. 41-46.

32. Warszewicki, f. 202. 203.

THE

Accomplifhed Senator.

In T W O   B O O K S.

Written Originally in LATIN,

By LAURENCE GRIMALD GOZLISKI,
Senator and Chancellor of P O L A N D, and
Bifhop of POSNA or POZEN.

Done into E N G L I S H, from the Edition Printed
at V E N I C E, in the Year 1568.

By Mr. OLDISWORTH.

Omnis in Hoc Uno variis Difcordia effet
Ordinibus.——   Claudian.

L O N D O N:
Printed for the AUTHOR, in the Year 1733.

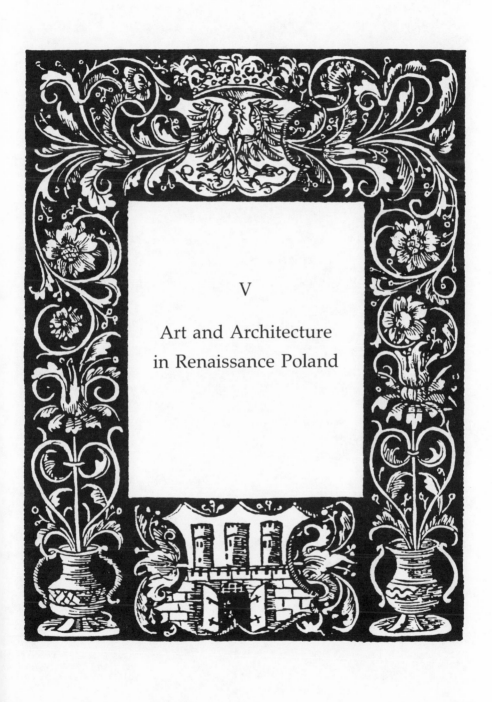

V

Art and Architecture
in Renaissance Poland

15

Renaissance Sculpture in Poland in its European
Context: Some Selected Problems

Jan Białostocki

nterestingly enough it was not in Western Europe that Italian Renaissance art was first assimilated. France, Spain, Germany, and the Netherlands adopted the new Italian style which was based on the imitation of classical antiquity only during the sixteenth century. Much earlier the first Italian artists were invited to work in East Central Europe, namely in Hungary, which was at that time a prominent cultural center under the reign of Matthias Corvinus. From there the italinate style and the Italian artists spread out to the then powerful Kingdom of Poland, united to the Grand Duchy of Lithuania, and it was in the first years of the sixteenth century that mature Italian Renaissance forms appeared in the works erected on the Wawel hill in Cracow. Both in architecture and sculpture the new models and ideals quickly became accepted. They emanated from the royal court towards smaller centers, supported both by the fairly early acceptance of humanism and by the frequent travels of young Polish nobles to Italy.[1]

The achievements of the Renaissance style in Poland were fairly advanced both in time and in quality. Principles and models of the Renaissance were adopted relatively quickly and, at least, some of the general principles were applied in a reasonably faithful way. They were introduced into Poland by Italian masters coming—sometimes through Hungary—from Tuscany and bringing the new style in a rather pure version.

However, the adoption of the Renaissance in Poland was limited both in its functions and by the social base of the patronage. In the early period it was mainly an art of the court; it had to fulfill both secular and sacred functions: on the one hand castles, and on the other chapels and tombs were its main objectives. Polish patrons relied on German masters in painting, as they did also in the field of decorative arts. The most magnificent result of the Polish royal patronage in the second half of the sixteenth century remains the set of

Flemish tapestries, partly commissioned, partly bought in Brussels for King Sigismund II Augustus (Zygmunt II August).[2]

One might well ask what was the situation of sculpture in sixteenth century Poland? In its first phase, sculpture was either produced by Italian masters or imported from the outside: from Hungary, where Italian workshops were active, or from the famous Nuremberg studio of the Vischer. The Italians working in Poland included prominent masters, such as Bartolomeo Berrecci, the master of the royal sepulchral chapel; Giovanni Cini, specializing in decoration; Bernardino Zanobi de Gianottis, author of some tomb effigies; the Northern Italian artist, Gian Maria Padovano, from Padua, unlike the majority of the other Italians, who were from Florence; Santi Gucci Fiorentino, who brought to Poland the tendencies of Florentine mannerism; and Girolamo Canavesi, who popularized the average types of Italian sepulchral sculpture. Rather late a distinguished master of local origin gained prominence against this background. He was Jan Michałowicz z Urzędowa (Jan Michałowicz of Urzędów), who was active in the 1560s-1570s.[3]

In Poland the adoption of Italian Renaissance solutions was very selective. In sculpture, which was primarily tomb sculpture, niche wall tombs with an arch encompassing the reclining figure of the deceased situated on the sarcophagus were accepted first and foremost. In late medieval art in Poland that type was nonexistent; its origins were in Italy where it often appeared in the fourteenth century.[4] In Poland the type of freestanding sarcophagus with the figure of the deceased recumbent on its lid was used for all the medieval royal tombs in Cracow. Less prominent people received stone slabs, more or less three-dimensional, inserted either horizontally or vertically into the walls. There was also a type called a "lectern tomb" with an obliquely inclined slab placed on the tomb. This last type continued to appear in the Renaissance as well, for instance in the tomb of Archbishop Jan Konarski in Cracow or that of the last two dukes of Mazovia, to which we shall return.

In Renaissance Poland the *prime object* (to use George Kubler's terminology[5]) of the type of niche tomb is the magnificent triumphal arch decorated with symbols of military glory, which Franciscus Florentinus erected in 1502-05 in the Cracow Wawel Cathedral. It encompassed the stone carved figure of the King Jan Olbracht, done not much earlier by a late Gothic sculptor, most probably Jörg Huber.[6] There is no evidence whether or not this was the source for the startling monument of Barbara Tarnowska from Rożnów in the Tarnów Cathedral, made about 1520.[7] The form of that work, by an artist unsure of himself, inexperienced in Renaissance forms, but attempting their application, may have been suggested by other models, like portal architecture or prints. Nevertheless, the niche tomb type gained wide popularity in Poland, far more so than in other European countries, especially after it had been used by Bartolommeo Berrecci in his royal tomb erected from 1529 to 1531.[8]

Work on remodeling the tomb began before the death of Sigismund II Augustus, and in 1575 it was modified in order to accomodate the sarcophagus and the effigy of the successor to Sigismund I. The sarcophagus of the older king was raised and that of his son was placed below.[9] The resulting composition which took the form of the double-decker niche tomb had already appeared earlier in Poland, for instance in the tomb of the two representatives of the Kościelecki family in Kościelec (1559) and in that of Jan and Jan Krzysztof Tarnowski (1570) in the Tarnów Cathedral.[10] But the royal tomb must have imparted to that type of composition an exceptional authority: throughout the following decades of the latter sixteenth century and the early seventeenth century countless double-decker niche tombs appeared in Poland. Although that type cannot be claimed to be exclusively Polish, it certainly occurs in Poland much more often than anywhere else in the world. Seen in a European context, Polish tomb sculpture excels in that field.[11]

Continuing in the field of tomb sculpture, attention should be drawn to four very original solutions, sometimes connected with old iconographic traditions, strangely enough revived in sixteenth century Poland. The first example is the otherwise undistinguished tomb of the Cracow nobleman Piotr Boratyński (1558) in the Wawel Cathedral.[12] In the very shallow niche, encompassed by two Ionic pilasters and the entablature which they support, is situated a rather flat, slightly inclined relief representing the deceased clad in armor, reclining, his legs crossed, his right hand stretched and holding his commander's staff which rests against his armor, his left hand, bent at the elbow, supporting the head. The upper part of Boratyński's body reposes on a pillow, but that pillow and the rest of the body repose on a ground formed by round stones which look like plaster pavement. The sword of the deceased knight lies close to his side resting on those stones.

Such treatment of the ground seems unique among Polish tombs, but it had striking parallels among the earlier English tombs of the fourteenth century, those famous tombs of the so-called "fighting knights" represented recumbent in their armor and drawing out their swords as if to fight against the invisible enemy—supposedly death or the devil.[13] What is still more interesting is that in some classical representations of people reclining the ground upon which they repose is characterized as stony.[14]

In the *Concordantia caritatis* the stone which brings life to the roots of the fruitless tree is compared to the miracle of Christ's resurrection.[15] We can suppose Boratyński is shown on the stony ground because he was considered a Christian soldier, unafraid of any discomfort in his strong belief in the salvation, represented at the top of his tomb by the figure of the resurrected Christ. Or are the stones an allusion to his first name, Piotr, meaning *Petrus*: rock? He seems to be half asleep yet partially awake; with his staff in his hand, and sword and helmet at his side, he awaits the moment of resurrection.

My second example of the originality of Polish Renaissance sculpture is an enigmatic relief which adorns the tombs of one of the most powerful men in Poland of the first quarter of the sixteenth century, that of chancellor Krzysztof Szydłowiecki, who died in 1532.[16] His tomb in the collegiate church in Opatów

45. The royal mausoleum known as the Sigismund Chapel in the Wawel Cathedral in Cracow. Reprinted from Helena and Stefan Kozakiewiczowie, *The Renaissance in Poland* (Warsaw: Arkady, 1976).

is a rather awkward composition in which several elements have been combined, one of them being the rather stiff effigy of the chancellor, another the plaque commemorating his young son, and finally the intriguing long relief in bronze, the so-called Opatów lamentation, the object of various interpretations by Polish art historians.[17] From the iconographic point of view, it is probably the most interesting bronze relief of this period in Poland, although its artistic form shows some incongruities, and it does not represent the highest standard of design. A very long rectangular shape is filled out by three groups of figures, the central one seated at the table, the two at the sides standing; all figures either show strong symptoms of despair or are lamenting. It has been always supposed that the relief shows the distress of the members of Szydłowiecki's court as the news of his death is being brought. Indeed the man to the left of the table approaching the seated figures seems to bring some terrifying news, to which the others are reacting in a dramatic way, throwing up their arms or abandoning their musical instruments (as do those who are on the right).

It seems that some classical inspiration could have contributed to the formation of that *conclamatio*, and there exist Italian examples of reviving such classical composition, as in the Sassetti tomb in Florence, in the reliefs representing the death of Francesca Tornabuoni made by the workshop of Verrocchio, and in the reliefs of the della Torre tomb by Andrea Riccio once in San Fermo, Verona, now at the Louvre.[18] On the other hand, one may point out that the falcons and hunting dogs, shown at the bottom of the relief, are related to local tradition. Very similar birds and dogs adorn the base of the splendid tomb of Władysław Jagiełło, the founder of the Jagiellonian dynasty, in the Wawel Cathedral, usually dated to the 1430s.[19] The patterns of the representation of birds and dogs at the tomb of Jagiełło seem to originate from the North Italian drawings of the International style.[20] Here in the so-called Opatów Lamentation there is no visible formal connection to that artistic style, but the iconographic link seems to be evident. Both this and the uneven artistic quality indicate the local origin of the relief, although there are some similarities to the design and handling in the Vischer workshop bronze plaques.[21]

My third example of an exceptional solution in the field of tomb sculpture extends beyond the field of sculpture alone because it forms the whole conception of the tomb. This example is the monumental sepulchral composition made for the Cracow bishop, Filip Padniewski (about 1575), by the first outstanding sculptor of Polish extraction working in the period of late Renaissance in Poland, the above-mentioned Jan Michałowicz of Urzędów.[22]

The sarcophagus on which the deceased reclines is encompassed by a double arch and supported by three terms. Today its architectural surrounding bears the imprint of neo-classical remodeling of 1832-40. Fortunately, the outstanding architect of the period, Francesco Lanci, executed a drawing recording the composition of the tomb wall before it was remodeled. From that drawing, discovered in 1970, we see that the central term was moved to its present location after the drawing was executed and that originally there were four

terms, two at each side, but none in the middle.[23] Instead, below the sarcophagus two doors were visible only one of which was actually functional: it
led to the sacristy (and later to the staircase). The tomb originally had much
more decoration and it had immobile lateral wings connected to the central
part by volutes. Small angels appeared on the top of the wings and at the
corners of the entablature to the left and right of the scrolls buttressing the
central inscription tablet. How much more brilliant and rich it is, not in artistic
form but in the specific symbolism, which seems to distinguish the original
composition of the Padniewski tomb. This tomb constitutes one of several
examples of doors appearing in sepulchral compositions and is expressive of
the symbolism of the borderline between the two modes of existence, life and
death.[24]

The best known Renaissance example of such symbolism is found in Padua,
a town in which hundreds of young Polish nobles studied at the university,
and therefore especially well-known in Cracow. In front of Santo Antonio
basilica stands a monument to Gattamelata made in bronze by Donatello. It
stands on a tall base, the side walls of which have doors, one of them ajar,
the other closed.[25] It is not possible to see in the Lanci drawing whether there
was any difference between these two doors which are below the sarcophagus
and the figure of bishop Padniewski, and we cannot, of course, be sure of their
symbolism. As an argument for its existence however, we may adduce the fact
that some tradition for it has persisted in the Cracow Cathedral and may have
found its expression in the composition of two eighteenth century royal tombs
conceived as a pair, each including a door, one with an open door, the other
with a closed door.[26]

My fourth example of specific tomb conception in Renaissance Poland, though
escaping total destruction, survived World War II, but only in a very damaged
state. It is the double tomb of the two last dukes of Mazovia, Stanisław and
Janusz (who died in 1524 and 1526, respectively), in Warsaw in St. John's
cathedral which is attributed to Bernardino Zanobi de Gianottis, Bartolommeo
Berrecci's main collaborator.[27] The ornamental border of the tomb was lost a
long time ago, and in the last war the heads and figures also were very seriously
damaged. In its present state the tomb is considerably restored. Nevertheless,
the idea itself of the two men reclining in armor close to each other, a shaft of
the flag between them, their arms embracing each other, demonstrates an
emotional mood quite unusual in Renaissance sepulchral sculpture. The idea
of combining two figures of men instead of those of man and wife in one tomb,
is rare although not unique.

It should be stressed that free-standing tombs are not represented in Renaissance art in Poland; statuary is an extreme rarity, and outside of the mar-
velous marble statues of saints in the Sigismund Chapel (1529-30), where one
sometimes almost perceives distant reflexions of Michelangelo's art, there is
scarcely any, even on the most elaborated tombs like those by Canavesi.

This brief analysis should not conclude, however, by only indicating the
refusals of Western types and solutions, forms and functions, but rather it

should indicate the creation of specific artistic phenomena which remain distinctive for Polish artistic heritage, i.e., sculpture of the trend formerly termed "vernacular" by Polish art historians. This includes neither statues nor narrative reliefs, but find instead a dynamic and imaginative architectural decoration, sometimes so developed that there is no doubt that it should be considered as sculpture and not just decoration.

Refined or sometimes awkward, but always attractive, early seventeenth century decorative patterns adorning the vaults of churches, even if they are protruding and possess often an almost three-dimensional plasticity (such as, for instance, the stucco patterns in the Firlej chapel at the Dominican church in Lublin, of the early 1630's, or the decoration of the interior of the dome of Holy Trinity Chapel at the collegiate church in Środa, of about 1610-1615) are usually not classified as works of sculpture but rather as architectural decoration; they are actually developed ornaments.[28] It is different with the buoyant decorative works which adorn parapets or walls of burgher houses in Kazimierz, or the interior of the Firlej chapel at Bejsce. These are usually fully or almost fully three-dimensional; they are to a great extent figurative and capture attention by their dynamic and expressive intricacies—as well as by their fantastic inspiration—sometimes almost demanding comparisons with exotic art, as the small caryatids in the Uchański tomb at Uchanie certainly do.[29]

In comparing the quality of central and provincial works it is rewarding to compare the full marble sculpture of one of the saints of the Sigismund Chapel with the huge stucco relief of St. Christopher decorating the front of one of the houses of the Przybyła family in Kazimierz Dolny (1615).[30] Obviously the refinement and perfection of design and execution typical of Italian masters working in Cracow in the royal chapel has disappeared. In St. Christopher, we note vernacular expression on an almost folk-art level.

In the same town, however, there is some architectural sculpture of an astonishingly inventive richness. It is dated to an only slightly later time and is connected with the late stage of development of the workshop originally directed by Santi Gucci Fiorentino at Pińczów. The cresting of the high parapet of the Celejowski house in Kazimierz Dolny (done about or before 1635) is enlivened by fantastic animals, gargoyles, dragons, and birds of prey which seem to constitute an apotropaic program, expressive of perhaps primitive, but powerful and creative feelings. Those monsters surround the figures of Christ and the Virgin in the central part of the cresting, and those of saints Bartholomew and John, patron saints of the founder of the house and of his son, at the sides.[31]

Similar motifs frequently appear as decoration of portals and tombs, and this function seems to confirm the apotropaic roots of that kind of imagery, applied for instance in the portals of the Baranów castle, in tombs such as those of the Uchańskis at Uchanie (two tombs, one about 1590, another in the early seventeenth century), of the Opalińskis at Kościan (about 1590), and most importantly in the Firlej chapel at Bejsce (1593-1601, done by the workshop of Samuel Świątkowicz).[32]

In this last work the fantastic imagination characteristic of this trend has achieved its climax. The two reliefs of the deceased kneeling in adoration before the crucified Christ are dominated by the intricate and powerful play of decorative motifs. It is dated about 1600, at the time when the severe Tridentine style inspired by the Counter Reformation made its appearance in Poland. It is indicative for the stylistic borderlines, in that extremely complicated time when Renaissance, mannerism, and the early baroque coexist and produce their specific vernacular versions.

If we compare the Bejsce chapel with the noble and restrained composition of the Opaliński tomb at Radlin, erected at the same time (Andrzej Opaliński died in 1593; his wife Katarzyna in 1601), we can measure the immense differences between two strictly speaking contemporary works in Poland.[33] The Opaliński tomb is harmonious; it is classical in its decorative elements, correct in design and execution, restrained in expression. The Bejsce chapel is disharmonious, unclassical, incorrect, and unrestrained. But if the Radlin tomb possesses several analogies both in Poland and all over Europe dominated by italianate style, the Bejsce monument has a quality rarely achieved in that type of work: it is unique and wholly individual. It condenses and expresses in the best way the specific tendencies born from the combination of manneristic attitudes with vernacular imagination.

Notes

1. See my *The Art of the Renaissance in Eastern Europe: Hungary, Bohemia, Poland,* Wrightsman Lectures, Metropolitan Museum of Art. (Oxford: Phaidon, 1976), and "Renesans polski i renesans europejski" (The Polish Renaissance and the European Renaissance), in *Renesans. Materiały sesji naukowych Komitetu Nauk o Sztuce PAN i Stowarzyszenia Historyków Sztuki* (Warsaw: PWN, 1975), pp. 179-193, and "Rinascimento polacco e Rinascimento europeo" in *Polonia-Italia, Relazioni artistiche dal medioevo al XVIII secolo.* Alli del Convegno tenutesi a Roma, 1975. Bronisław Biliński, ed. (Wrocław: Ossolineum, 1979), pp. 21-58.

2. Jerzy Szablowski, ed., *The Flemish Tapestries at Wawel Castle in Cracow* (Antwerp: Mercator, 1972).

3. To the extensive bibliography in my *Art of the Renaissance* should now be added Helena and Stefan Kozakiewicz, *Renaissance in Poland* (Warsaw: Arkady, 1976), a richly illustrated book.

4. For a general survey of tomb art see Erwin Panofsky, *Tomb Sculpture* (New York: H.N. Abrams, 1964).

5. George Kubler, *The Shape of Time* (New Haven: Yale University Press, 1962).

6. Białostocki, *Art of the Renaissance,* fig. 16.

7. Ibid., fig. 23.

8. Ibid., figs. 104-105.

9. Ibid., figs. 174, 200.

10. Ibid., figs. 196, 199.

11. On this type of tomb see: Helena Kozakiewiczowa, "Renesansowe nagrobki piętrowe w Polsce" (Renaissance double-decker tombs in Poland), *Biuletyn Historii Sztuki* 18 (1955): 3-47.

12. Białostocki, *Art of the Renaissance*, p. 54, fig. 195.

13. See Sten Lundwall, "The Knights with the Crossed Legs," in *Formae. Journal of Art History and Criticism (Tidskrift för konstvetenskap)* 36 (1960): 94-102. An English example of this type, the tomb of Sir Roger de Kerdeston, 1337, St. Mary's Church, Reepham, Norfolk, is reproduced in Białostocki, *Art of the Renaissance*, fig. 184.

14. For example, a sepulchral sculpture in the Museo Chiaramonti, Vatican, nr. 8.

15. See Alfred A. Schmidt, "Concordantia Caritatis," in *Reallexikon zur deutschen Kunstgeschichte* (Stuttgart, 3, 1954), sp. 851-2, nr. 155. Stones and rocks may also stand for "steadiness" (*constantia*) or "faithfulness" (*fides*), see Fritz Graf, "Fels," *Reallexikon* 7 (1980), pp. 1210-1226.

16. See Jerzy Kieszkowski, *Kanclerz Krzysztof Szydłowiecki, Z dziejów kultury i sztuki Zygmuntowskich czasów* (Chancellor Krzysztof Szydłowiecki. A study in culture and art of Sigismundian times), (Poznań, 1912).

17. Jan Bołoz Antoniewicz, "Lament Opatowski i jego twórca" (The Opatów Lamentation and its creator), *Prace Komisji Historii Sztuki Polskiej Akademii Umiejętności* vol. 2, no.2 (1922) pp. 123-158. Władysław Tomkiewicz, "Lament Opatowski, Próba interpretacji treści" (The Opatów Lamentation. An attempt to interpret its content), *Biuletyn Historii Sztuki* 22 (1960): 351-364.

18. See Białostocki, *Art of the Renaissance*, p. 52 and n. 59, p. 97 with detailed references.

19. See Piotr Skubiszewski in Białostocki, ed., *Spätmittelalter und beginnende Neuzeit* (West Berlin: Propyläen Kunstgeschichte, 1972), n. 229, p. 286f.

20. See Pietro Toesca, *La pittura e la miniatura nella Lombardia* new ed., Torino: Einaudi, 1966), figs. 242, 249, 250, 381, 382, 361.

21. See some reliefs of the *Sebaldusgrab*, in St. Sebald's Church in Nüremberg.

22. Białostocki, *Art of the Renaissance*, p. 56.

23. Andrzej Rottermund, "Nowe przekazy ikonograficzne do kaplicy Potockich (dawniej Padniewskiego) w kaplicy na Wawelu" [New iconographic evidence concerning the Potocki Chapel (originally Padniewski Chapel) in the Wawel Cathedral], *Biuletyn Historii Sztuki* 32 (1970): 199-201.

24. Jan Białostocki, "The Door of Death," *Jahrbuch der Hamburger Kunstsammlungen* 18 (1973), pp. 7-32.

25. Panofsky, *Tomb Sculpture*, p. 85.

26. The tombs of the two kings, Jan III Sobieski and Michał Korybut Wiśniowiecki, discussed in my "Door of Death," 1973.

27. Romana Zdziarska, "Nagrobek książąt Mazowieckich w katedrze warszawskiej" (Tomb of the Mazovian dukes in the Warsaw Cathedral), *Biuletyn Historii Sztuki* 16 (1952), no. 4: 180-185. Helena Kozakiewiczowa, "Spółka architektoniczno-rzeźbiarska Bernardina de Gianotis i Jana Cini" (Architectural-sculptural firm of Bernardino de Gianotis and Jan Cini), *Biuletyn Historii Sztuki* 21 (1959): 151-174.

28. Białostocki, *Art of the Renaissance* p. 86; nn. 69-71.

29. On this "vernacular" type of decorative sculpture see among others my "'Mannerism' and 'Vernacular' in Polish Art," in *Walter Friedländer zum 90 Geburtstag. Eine Festgabe seiner europäischen Schüller, Freunde und Vereher* (West Berlin, 1965), pp. 47-57.

30. Białostocki, *Art of the Renaissance*, compare fig. 350 with statues shown in figs. 102-105.

31. Białostocki, *Art of the Renaissance*, fig. 351 and illustrations in the article quoted in n. 29.

32. See illustrations in Białostocki, *Art of the Renaissance*, figs. 341, 343-346.

33. Helena and Stefan Kozakiewiczowie, *Renaissance in Poland*, fig. 188.

16

Architecture under the Last Jagiellons in its Political and Social Context

Adam Miłobędzki

ure Renaissance architecture in its Tuscan version was adopted by only two European countries: Hungary and then Poland.[1] In Poland where this new art was patronized by Sigismund I (Zygmunt I) even before his accession to the throne in 1506. Late quattrocento forms had already been imported to Cracow about 1500 by Franciscus Florentinus and his successor, Bartolommeo Berrecci, the architect of the magnificent arcaded courtyard added to the still traditionally shaped castle (1516?-49) and, above all, of the Sigismund Chapel (1517-33), the most splendid monument of Renaissance architecture north of the Alps.[2] This royal oratory and mausoleum, in its own ideally central form, was also rich in an intricate iconography of decoration, reflecting the sepulchral traditions of antiquity as well as the cosmological symbolism of the dome rediscovered by humanists.

Many examples of Sigismund I's interference in his architects' activities have been recorded, and the fact that Italian architectural drawings were obtained through him indicates that he was a conscientious patron of the arts.[3] On the other hand, the magnitude and splendour of his architectural monuments undoubtedly served more as conventional political propaganda assuring him eternal glory. His heraldic symbols, inscriptions, and decorations manifested the traditional ideals of the Jagiellonian dynasty, as well as the intellectual acumen of its court, particularly in these symbols' humanistic allegories and astrological themes so typical of contemporary university circles of Cracow.[4]

Although Sigismund I was familiar with humanistic literary and artistic culture it does not seem that he fully understood the principles of Italian art. His preference for derivative Renaissance forms, still fettered by the Gothic tradition of local workshops of Augsburg, Nürnberg, Prague, or Wrocław is proof of this assumption. In architecture side by side with pure Tuscan forms, he long supported the latest italianized *modus* of the late Gothic which, as evidenced by his castles, had a far greater reception in Poland than the much more accomplished if sporadic works of the Tuscans. Outside of Cracow, where works in the Tuscan *modus* were concentrated on the Wawel castle, they were an exceptional phenomenon, almost entirely limited to sculpture and mini-architecture.[5]

In investigating the origins of the artistic revolution as exemplified by the most spectacular examples funded by Sigismund I in pure Renaissance forms, it is necessary to turn to the earliest works of the new style in Cracow: the tomb of Jan Olbracht (1502-5) and the decoration of the Queen's palace (1502-07). It has been proven that the Queen Mother Elizabeth and Sigismund used their imperial aspirations in their heraldic program.[6] Most probably they similarly used rich classical forms "full of allusions to Roman triumphal glory,"[7] which were appropriate for imperial iconography. The idea that the Jagiellons were legal inheritors of the imperial crown of the Luxemburgs and the main line of the Hapsburgs was also manifested in political tendencies to equate the status of the Polish monarchy with the Holy Roman Empire.[8] It is worth noting that the substantiation of these claims fell coincidentaly with that part of Sigismund I's reign in which the main monuments of his glory were erected and adorned, in what was perceived at that time as Roman style—later such pure classical forms were not used.

Research on the architecture of the period of the last Jagiellons has until now favored Renaissance works valued all the more, the closer they were to the Italian model. In this way, these excellent, if sporadic Tuscan imports, foreign to local culture and artistic traditions, obscured the picture of the architectural output of the age as a whole, rendering it inapplicable to the colorful background of social and political life. In reality, this picture was more Gothic than Renaissance,[9] and one must add that buildings of stone and brick were extremely few as compared with those of wood: around the year 1500, only about 0.4 percent of city and village construction was in masonry.[10] During the sixteenth century this great disproportion—much greater in Poland than in neighboring Silesia, Bohemia, Hungary, and both Prussias—changed, slowly, although increasing prosperity and demographic growth influenced a considerable intensification of construction.

The entire construction of wood and masonry had originally been a product of the universal culture of Central Europe, crossing national and ethnic barriers, and to some extent social ones. This culture may be called late Gothic,[11] although its intellectual center, whether at the royal court or in the circle of Cracow university, assimilated the ideas of humanism quite early.[12] This universal cultural phenomenon met with opposition, however, even in the realm of architecture, since it emerged from within the social elite[13] and in isolation, to a degree, from those social classes whose influence began to grow at that time.

In Poland, this process was closely connected with a sudden increase in the political power of the gentry, combined with their stimulating economic growth;[14]

towards the close of the Middle Ages, this was common throughout Europe. As the standard of living rose and the formal feudal fiefs disappeared, gentry economic activity protected their proportion of income, permitting them to satisfy consumption and cultural demands in line with their class status.[15]

If in the fifteenth century the abode of the average knight differed little from that of a well-off peasant, by the middle of the sixteenth century the status of the average gentry demanded a comfortable and ornate "lordly manor" towering amid a courtly complex, in accord with to the ideal model of an agricultural center as was described by economic literature (Petrus de Crescentiis' *De Agricultura*, translated into Polish in 1549).[16] In Poland, the greatest landlords and clergy who, though legally equal with other gentry—in fact, functioned as a separate estate—also adapted their castles to the new economic situation. Castles became distributing centers in the middle of the estate complexes. To satisfy increased needs of comfort and design, they added residential wings within ever-more regular foundations.[17]

The change in the values of the feudal system brought idealized traditions of chivalry (more than once additionally heroized through humanism)—a phenomenon which compensated for the decline of the ancient knighthood as an armed force and its integration into the productive structures.[18] This rebirth of a chivalrous *ethos* inspired towers and other medieval military forms as decoration of the castles of big landlords—despite decline of their actual ability to defend—becoming, therefore, a new class symbol.[19] A radical version of such a sign, a "symbol castle" is the seat of the Boners. It was probably not accidental that the non-noble banking geneology of the owners was masked by ostentatious pseudo-feudal picturesque silhouettes.[20] Among the middle gentry, this semiotic aspect of architecture appeared in the return of the fashion of residential towers, carried on beyond 1550, when, after a rejection of transplantation of the Italian *villa rustica*, this rising class actively sought the new ideal for a residence.[21]

The new castles of the Jagiellons did not display military attributes either in symbols or even concrete defense installations. Characteristically, the Jagiellons did not build huge castles with modern fortifications, which were more frequent throughout Europe as a statement of the Renaissance absolutism of princes and tyrants.[22] An exception was the great castle at Kamieniec Podolski begun in 1505, built, however, not in support of the internal politics of the king, but rather as a major fortress against the Turks. The strategic value of this castle was appreciated throughout Europe, as evidenced by the fact that its construction was financed even by the Pope.[23] Only in the eastern part of Poland, threatened by the Tatars and the Turks—and where the greatest fortunes were made due to the general changes in the upper class—did mid-sixteenth century private castles appear which were more like a fortress than a representative residence.[24]

The continual growth in the political significance of the gentry did not halt the development of cities even temporarily. Burghers could be treated as a fully worthy co-creative force in the intellectual and religious culture of the age.[25] This is evidenced in the further improvement of city construction and— particularly from about 1550—in a series of communal constructions, whose rich form and symbolic content reflected the new humanistic attitudes of the patriciate which idealized public institutions in the spirit of the ancient *civitas* (as clearly shown by the decoration of the city hall in Poznań, 1550-60).[26]

The most general tendencies of Polish architecture were the same in the fifteenth and sixteenth centuries. These consisted of introducing regularity into planes, in stressing axes and symmetry in composition, in rejecting the Gothic skeleton structure and in stressing cubic masses. In elevations the tendency was to discard vertical articulations in favor of horizontal ones. None of this conflicted with the principles of Renaissance architecture, as both came from a common source, namely the International Gothic of the 1400's. Thanks to the prolongation of this tradition in Poland, interaction of Renaissance with Gothic progressed more harmoniously than in the other countries north of the Alps, which in this period underwent an opposing artistic course, deeply rooted in the expressive trends of late Gothic.[27]

Gothic building shapes and ornamentation prevailed the longest in church architecture.[28] Through the first half of the sixteenth century, church architecture experienced a great blossoming, especially in central Poland, until the culmination of the Reformation after 1550 brought it to a standstill. In this period the still universal wooden churches were also built. The most exquisite examples of this type of architecture which blossomed in Poland were erected at this time.[29]

In the southern and central districts of Poland, in the early years of the sixteenth century a regular version of a grand castle was developed. It included palatial buildings with ornamental architecture that increasingly resorted to Renaissance motifs, and which still applied the mood of late Gothic *modi*. They are headed by royal castles built by the workshop of Master Benedykt, an architect of German extraction and include Piotrków, 1511-22; Sandomierz extension, 1520-26; Wawel, at least the main eastern wing, 1521-29;[30] as well as several castles of the magnates.[31] A very unusual version of their stone-masonry, mixing gothic and italianate forms was evolved after 1510 by the royal workshop and soon became very popular in southern Poland. These "Wawel-type" portals constituted the most characteristic Polish addendum to contemporary European art.[32]

All these manifestations or modifications of the Gothic traditions, as well as the simultaneous reception of Italianism, progressed somewhat independently from the general cultural changes. The intellectual environment, whether at the court or at the university, could at most be a transmitter of certain architectural ideas of humanism such as, for example, the symbolism of central temple. Humanist aspirations to fame, according to Aristotle, eternally within reach through patronage of construction,[33] could awaken patronal activity, but did not determine the form of its materialization. Even into the mid-sixteenth

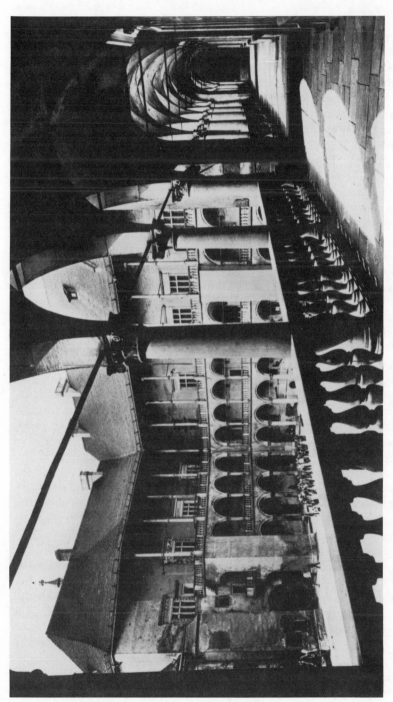

46. The three-storey arcaded galleries on the courtyard of the Royal Wawel Castle in Cracow. Reprinted from Helena and Stefan Kozakiewiczowie, *The Renaissance in Poland* (Warsaw: Arkady, 1976).

century, many patrons founded buildings either in Gothic forms or in forms which alternated Gothic with Renaissance.[34]

The new style did not become widespread until the middle of the sixteenth century, when the increased prosperity of 1550-60 stimulated investment in the majority of Polish provinces. Sigismund I's Poland functioned, in essence, as part of the greater European economic and cultural community. Poland in the times of Sigismund II Augustus (Zygmunt II August) isolated itself, concerned rather with its own internal matters and tilted its geopolitical balance towards the east. The slower development—in comparison with other European countries of this second phase of the Renaissance in Poland was, on the one hand, caused by the small number of great patrons, and, on the other hand, by their rather diffuse efforts. As an architectural patron, Sigismund II Augustus was rather passive, and in light of preserved relics,[35] not very effective, as if reflecting his approach as a king who was one among equals with the magnates and the gentry.

New architecture developed significantly under the influence of builders immigrating in large numbers from the Lombard Lake District, and who—just like local masters—freely simplified Renaissance forms. They were not in any sense an elite, like the Tuscans, yet their skills were brought from the construction lodges of Lombardy or Veneto, where the majority had been thrust into the role of workmen.[36] This more artisan than artistic immigration was weakest in Cracow, where the Tuscan tradition still persisted and was able even to direct itself towards mannerism (Jan Michałowicz, Santi Gucci). *Comaschi* came in mainly through Silesia, where they added local Czech-Saxon Renaissance forms to their repertoire, just as later, traveling throughout Poland, they adapted neo-Romanesque *modus* forms brought here from the Netherlands through Gdańsk.[37] Designs were also brought to their attention through prints of Renaissance ornamentation, as well as through pattern books with Serlio's treatise in the foremost position.[38]

Thus, not many buildings were erected that were inspired directly by the Renaissance theory of art, or by particular Italian examples, whether through a "perspective" conception of space (such as the churches of Giambattista of Venice), through the humanistic symbolism of a central building (such as the dome chapels), through the designs of theoretical/conventional plans (such as the royal castle in Niepołomice), through the venture of Italian military engineers (such as *beluardo* in Rożnów), through specific model fortresses (such as the castle in Brzeżany), or, lastly, through rules of architectural orders changing vacant elevations for spectacular facades (such as the city hall in Poznań). All of these works were still connected with quattrocento models as well as with the formal language of the Lombardy-Venetian provenances.

Elsewhere, on the whole, only the decoration of buildings changed into italianate and became richer. Traditional layouts of castles, manors, town halls, and burghers' houses were only expanded and standardized. The attraction of the patrons was not so much to Renaissance art as to italianism, accepted by the gentry, clergy, and burghers along with Italian fashion, customs, and language.[39] The shallowness of its reception is best exemplified in the architectural painting of the Noskowski Chapel in Pułtusk (after 1554), which proves that for Central European patrons, painted columns or arcades meant as much as stone at this time.[40]

The degree to which the intellectual attitudes of the educated served as an integrating factor for manifestations of Italianism in architecture in various classes should be considered. Its interests were directed now particularly towards nonpersonal social structures: the state political system and law, estates, and religions, matters which from the 1540's were the subject of nationwide rhetoric and polemics.[41] In architecture, actual political-social or religious-moral ideas were sometimes presented in maxims on buildings or in masked allegorical decoration. More infrequently symbols of these notions found expression in architectural motifs and, very exceptionally, in a comprehensive architectural structure, i.e., in domed mausoleums.

The complexity of these non-artistic mechanisms accepted in various forms appears in the examples of the so-called Polish parapet raised with the development and decoration of the rich north Italian crenelles.[42] Parapets in castles, towers, or manor homes, even if they did not serve defense purposes, displayed a military attribute of construction for the nobility and reflected the idealized chivalrous tradition. But from the mid-sixteenth century parapets started to dominate in cities as well, which, other than for fire-control purposes, reflected the idea of communal buildings in the role of a paramilitary *corona muralis*, a symbol reborn through humanism, the notion of *civitas*.[43]

Renaissance architecture was thus accepted as a fashionable novelty, or sometimes for the sake of the symbolic meaning of its forms, but the artistic values of the new style seem to have been rather insignificant for Polish society. Average architecture could be called upon through the conative function (using a linguistic notion), for the aim of glory, commemorative or devotional, but in reality its function was often only phatic, resulting from passive acceptance and repetition of circulating patterns.[44] None of the contemporary architects were able to appeal, as Berrecci had, with a more improved and more conscious artistic language. In its conventional applied typology, in simple planning conceptions, as well as in freely interpreted classical forms, architecture of the reign of Sigismund Augustus delivered itself from the orthodox Renaissance of the great humanist-architects. It tended towards the colorful post-Renaissance which in the seventeenth century blossomed again, displaying its richness, colorfulness, and immanent artistic values independent of the canons of Western art.

Notes

1. Jan Białostocki, *The Art of the Renaissance in Eastern Europe: Hungary, Bohemia, Poland* (Oxford: Phaidon, 1976); Helena and Stefan Kozakiewicz, *Renesans w Polsce* (The Renaissance in Poland) (Warsaw: Arkady, 1976); Adam Miłobędzki, *Zarys*

dziejów architektury w Polsce (An Outline history of the architecture in Poland), 3rd ed. (Warsaw: Wiedza Powszechna, 1976), pp. 90-133.

2. Białostocki, *Art of the Renaissance*, pp. 18-25, 35-43.

3. Stanisław Wiliński, "O renesansie wawelskim" (The Wawel Renaissance), in *Renesans: Sztuka i ideologia* (Warsaw: PWN, 1976), pp. 216- 217; Hereafter cited as *Renesans*; Adolf Pawiński, *Młode lata Zygmunta Starego* (Early years of Sigismund the Old), (Warsaw: Gebethner i Wolff, 1893), pp. 39, 251.

4. Stanisław Mossakowski, "Treści dekoracji renesansowego pałacu na Wawelu" (The content of the Renaissance decorations of the Wawel palace), in *Renesans*, pp. 349-380.

5. Miłobędzki, *Zarys*, p. 124.

6. Jerzy Kowalczyk, "Triumf i sława wojenna 'all'antica' w Polsce XVI w." (Triumph and military glory *all'Antica* in sixteenth-century Poland), in *Renesans*, p. 295; Mossakowski, p. 359.

7. Białostocki, *Art of the Renaissance* p. 10.

8. Aleksander Gieysztor, " 'Non habemus caesarem nisi regem.' Korona zamknięta królów polskich w końcu XV wieku i wieku XVI" (The closed crown of the Polish kings at the end of the fifteenth and sixteenth century), in *Muzeum i twórca. Studia z historii sztuki i kultury ku czci Prof. Dr. Stanisława Lorentza*, ed. Kazimierz Michałowski (Warsaw: PWN, 1969), pp. 282-291; Barbara Miodońska, "Władca i państwo w krakowskim drzeworycie książkowym XVI w." (The ruler and the state in Cracow woodcut book illustration of the sixteenth century) in *Renesans*, pp. 50-61.

9. Adam Miłobędzki, "Architektura i społeczeństwo" (Architecture and society), in *Polska w epoce Odrodzenia. Państwo, społeczeństwo, kultura*, ed. Andrzej Wyczański (Warsaw: Wiedza Powszechna 1971), pp. 227-228. Hereafter sited as *Polska*

10. Adam Miłobędzki, "Architektura Królestwa Polski w XV wieku" (Architecture of the Polish kingdom of the fifteenth century), in *Sztuka i ideologia XV wieku*, ed. Piotr Skubiszewski (Warsaw: PWN, 1978), pp. 464-465.

11. Jerzy Kłoczowski "Rozwój środkowo-wschodniej Europy w XV wieku," (The development of East-Central Europe in the fifteenth century) in *Sztuka i ideologia XV wieku*, pp. 41-43; Vaclav Mencl, *Lidová architektura v Československu* (Folk architecture in Czechoslovakia) (Prague: Academia, 1980), p. 559.

12. Paweł Czartoryski, "Rodzime źródła kultury umysłowej polskiego Odrodzenia" (Native sources in the intellectual culture of the Polish Renaissance), in *Polska*, pp. 266-282.

13. Andrzej Wyczański, "Społeczeństwo polskie" (Polish society) in *Polska* pp. 126-161.

14. Stanisław Herbst, "Ekonomika a kultura renesansu" (Economics and Renaissance culture), in *Renesans* pp. 21-23; Kłoczowski, "Rozwój," pp. 25-30; Wyczański, "Społeczeństwo," pp. 149-150.

15. Jerzy Topolski, "Ekonomiczne podstawy przemian w kulturze materialnej szlachty polskiej w XVI wieku" (Economic bases for changes in the material culture of the Polish nobility in the sixteenth century), *Kwartalnik Architektury i Urbanistyki* 24, no. 4 (1979), pp. 306-8.

16. Teresa Jakimowicz, *Dwór murowany w Polsce w wieku XVI* (The Manorhouse in masonry in Poland of the sixteenth century); (Warsaw: PWN, 1979), pp. 33-43.

17. Miłobędzki, in *Polska*, pp. 252-254.

Architecture under the Last Jagiellons 299

18. Herbst, "Ekonomika," p. 21; Dobraslava Menclova, *České hrady* (Czech castles) (Prague: Odeon, 1952), II, pp. 359-361.

19. Adam Miłobędzki, "Pałac i zamek 'renesansowy' " (The 'Renaissance' palace and castle), in *Renesans*, p. 415.

20. Miłobędzki, "Pałac," p. 415.

21. Jakimowicz, *Dwór*, passim.

22. Miłobędzki, "Pałac" p. 413.

23. Miłobędzki, in *Polska* p. 256.

24. Bohdan Guerquin, "Zamek w Jazłowcu" (The Jazłowiec castle), *Studia i materiały do teorii i historii architektury i urbanistyki*, vol. 2 (Warsaw: PWN, 1960), pp. 133-149.

25. Miłobędzki, in *Polska* pp. 246-251.

26. Miłobędzki, in *Polska*, pp. 248-249.

27. Miłobędzki, in *Polska*, pp. 228-229.

28. Miłobędzki, in *Polska* pp. 226-227.

29. Marian Kornecki, "Małopolskie kościoły drewniane w XVI i XVII wieku" (Little Poland churches in wood of the sixteenth and seventeenth centuries), *Teka Komisji Urbanistyki i Architektury* 10 (1976), pp. 129-145.

30. Teresa Jakimowicz, " 'Turris Pyothrkoviensis'-pałac Zygmunta I" (Palace of Sigismund I), *Kwartalnik Architektury i Urbanistyki* 17, no. 1 (1972): 21-40; Adam Miłobędzki, "Zamek sandomierski" (Sandomierz castle), in *Studia Sandomierskie*, ed. Jan Pazdur and Teresa Wąsowicz (Sandomierz: Ludowa Spółdzielnia Wydawnicza, 1967), pp. 258-259; Białostocki, *Art of the Renaissance*, pp. 19, 23.

31. Castles in Ćmielów (1519-31), Drzewica (about 1535), Ogrodzieniec (1530-45), Szydłowiec (1510-26), Wiśnicz (1516?-53).

32. Białostocki, *Art Of the Renaissance*, pp. 22-23.

33. Concerning this idea, see Witold Krassowski, "Przesłanki gospodarcze programów architektonicznych w Polsce około roku 1600" (Economic grounds for architectural programs in Poland about 1600), in *Sztuka około roku 1600* (Warsaw: PWN, 1974), pp. 129-136.

34. i.e., Archbishop Jan Łaski: See Helena Kozakiewiczowa, "Mecenat Jana Łaskiego. Z zagadnień sztuki renesansu w Polsce" (Jan Łaski's patronage. Problems of Renaissance art in Poland), *Biuletyn Historii Sztuki* 23, no. 1 (1961): 3-17.

35. The Low Castle (before 1550) with St. Anna and Barbara Churches (1551-72) in Wilno, the Niepołomice castle (1550-71), and the extension of Sandomierz (about 1554) and Warsaw castle (1569-72).

36. Miłobędzki, in *Polska*, pp. 232-233, 243.

37. Miłobędzki, in *Polska*, pp. 231-232.

38. Jerzy Kowalczyk, *Sebastiano Serlio a sztuka polska: o roli włoskich traktatów architektonicznych w dobie nowożytnej* (Sebastiano Serlio and Polish art; on the role of Italian architectural treatises in the modern period), (Wrocław: Ossolineum, 1973).

39. Miłobędzki, in *Polska*, pp. 264-265.

40. Jerzy Z. Łoziński, *Grobowe kaplice kopułowe w Polsce, 1520-1620* (Centralized domed sepulchral chapels in Poland: 1520-1620) (Warsaw: PWN, 19731, pp. 63-77.

41. Julian Lewański, "Polskie piśmiennictwo renesansowe wobec Europy—nowe narzędzia i nowe cele" (Polish Renaissance literature against a background of European literature—new instruments and new goals) in *Renesans*, pp. 143-144.

42. Miłobędzki, in *Polska*, pp. 262-263.

43. Miłobędzki, *Zarys*, p. 130.

44. Lech Kalinowski, "Model funkcjonalny przekazu wizualnego na przykładzie renesansowego dzieła sztuki" (A functional model of visual communication exemplified by the Renaissance work of art), in *Renesans*, pp. 170-173.

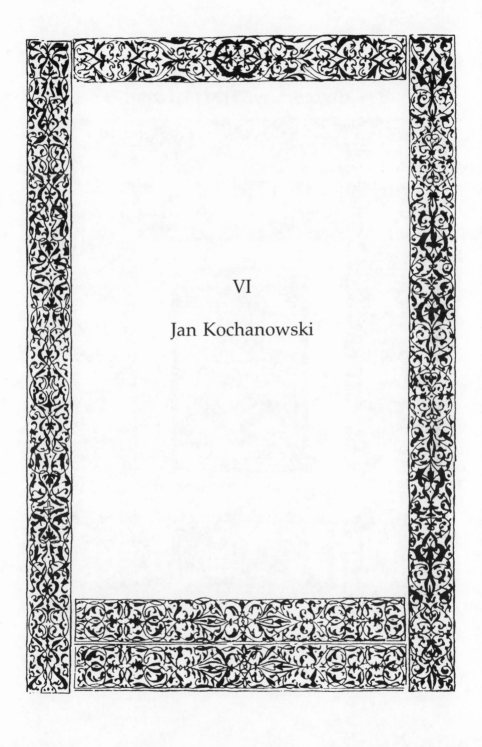

VI

Jan Kochanowski

Jan Kochánowski/ którego własnie możemy zwáć
Oycem: ięzyká POLskiego.

47. The supposed likeness of Jan Kochanowski surrounded by the Muses with the inscription "Jan Kochanowski whom we can indeed name the Father of the Polish Language," in Bartłomiej (Bartosz) Paprocki, *Gniazdo cnoty*, w Krakowie, 1578 (Biblioteka Uniwersytecka, Warszawa).

17

Kochanowski's Fame

Wiktor Weintraub

ochanowski is a great poet above all as a writer of lyric poetry and as an author of a dramatic composition, *Odprawa posłów greckich* (*The Dismissal of the Greek Envoys*). Both his lyrics and his drama appeared in print late. The first volume of his lyrical poetry, *Psałterz Dawidów* (*David's Psalter*), was published in 1579 when the poet was almost fifty years old; *The Dismissal* was printed one year earlier. Before that date the poet's bibliography is meagre: eight short works alone, and most of them of marginal value from our point of view. Only two of his lyrical poems were available in print before 1578: the hymn *"Czego chcesz od nas Panie, za Twe hojne dary"* ("What do you wish o Lord in return for your bounteous gift") and the so-called *Pieśń o potopie* (*Song about the Deluge*).

Kochanowski's fame as a great poet, however, did not follow the publication of his major works, the *David's Psalter*, the *Treny* (*Laments*), *Fraszki* (*Trifles*), *Pieśni* (*Songs*), and *The Dismissal*, but rather preceded them by at least fifteen years. It looks as if for a number of years he was famous on credit. How was this possible?

First of all, we should keep in mind that in the sixteenth, and even in the first half of the seventeenth century (as the reception of John Donne's poetry proves) manuscript copies could secure a poet's recognition among his contemporaries. We know that some of Kochanowski's poems, especially his lyrics, circulated in such copies before their publication. They must have contributed to his renown. But that is not the whole story— far from it.

A late tradition, recorded for the first time in the second decade of the seventeenth century, alleges that the poet sent home from France, i.e., in 1558 or 1559, his above-mentioned hymn, that the poem was read at a gathering of the gentry where Mikołaj Rej was present, and that the older writer, enraptured by it, recognized the superiority of the young poet in a distich:

Temu w nauce dank przed sobą dawam
I pieśń bogini słowieńskiej oddawam.

I recognize his priority in learning
And I hand over to him the song of the Slavic goddess.

In other words, I hand over to him the position of the leading Polish poet.[1]
The story gives the impression of an *ex post* created legend, of a later imagining of how an exemplary apostolic succession in the literature of the Golden Age should have been: having heard Kochanowski's one poem recited, the leading writer of the older generation recognizes Kochanowski's superiority and acknowledges that thenceforth not he but Kochanowski should be acclaimed the leading writer. Too good to be true.

Such a legend could have originated the more easily since the earliest printed eulogy of Kochanowski came precisely from the pen of Rej. It is to be found in Rej's *Żwierzyniec* (*The Zodiac of Life*), printed late in 1561. In an eight line poem Rej praises Kochanowski as a nobleman who unites inborn talent with learning (*"poczciwe ćwiczenie"*) as shown by his "numerous writings." He is a better writer than Tibullus because his poetry is virtuous.[2]

When Rej was publishing his *The Zodiac of Life*, Kochanowski was the author of only one printed item, a funeral poem in honor of Jan Tarnowski (*O śmierci Jana Tarnowskiego*). At that time, however, a number of the poet's Latin elegies which he had begun to write in his student years in Padua already circulated in manuscript copies (and one such copy has been preserved). Both in structure and language these poems imitated classical Latin elegies, above all Tibullus and Propertius. Rej who, like Shakespeare, knew "little Latin and less Greek" and whose familiarity with classical Latin poetry was rather modest, must have heard that people were comparing Kochanowski's elegies to their Roman models and, most probably, in his laudatory poem he echoed current opinion. Thus, Rej's testimony proves that as early as 1561 Kochanowski distinguished himself as an author of Latin poetry.

Kochanowski, however, owes his renown as a great poet not to those Latin compositions which, *nota bene*, strike us today as rather derivative and conventional, but to an undated poem in the vernacular, published about two years later (around 1563 or 1564) and entitled *Satyr albo Dziki Mąż* (*The Satyr or the Wild Man*). The appearance of *The Satyr* . . . was greeted with an enthusiasm which strikes us initially as rather strange. Although the poem is written with gusto and humor, one cannot but consider it to be conventional and narrow-minded in its satirical thrust. We read in the poem that formerly, Poles led a modest, virtuous life and were full of knightly spirit. They despised any endeavors at enrichment, they did not send their sons to foreign universities (the poet himself owed his solid literary background to a large extent to his studies in Italy), they shunned religious reforms and left theological disputes to the professionals, the clergy.

Such conservative, backward-looking criticism was in demand at that time. Sixteenth-century Poland owed her prosperity to the discovery of America. Transport of gold from Peru and Mexico made the export of grain and wool to the West, primarily to Holland and England, a highly profitable business.

The English word "spruce," deriving from the Polish "z *Prus*," meaning "from Prussia," is a relic of those trade relations. The export trade made the gentry affluent and revolutionized their life, enabling them to travel abroad and to send their sons to the best European universities, mostly to Italy. Owing to their new affluence, the old simple style of life was quickly disappearing. Such radical changes were the despair of moralists. How often we read in the sermons, pamphlets, and satires of the period that a terrible calamity has befallen society: it has become rich.

Thus could the poet have answered a critic: I have included in my poem the type of censure expected of me, one that would strike a sympathetic chord in a large number of readers. But the poet could resort to another line of defense as well: it is not I who exhibit this narrow-minded, conservative spirit, but the speaker in my satire, the "wild man." What else could you expect from such an uncouth simpleton?

A wild man who, naked, roams the forests appears primarily in Italian medieval folklore tradition, where he is called *l'uomo selvaggio*, and in old German tradition, where he appears as *der wilde Mensch*.[3] No stories about wild men have been preserved in medieval Polish texts, but they must have existed in Poland, since in the Polish gloss to a Latin manuscript from 1447, we find the notation *"vir bestiarius—dziky mąsz,"*[4] and such a creature was mentioned before Kochanowski by two sixteenth-century writers, Biernat of Lublin and Mikołaj Rej.[5] Such a familiar savage promoted to a critic of contemporary society must have been seen as something unexpected and amusing by Kochanowski's first readers.

Kochanowski identified the wild man from the native tradition with the classical satyr, a fertility spirit distinguished by his lust and irrepressible sexual appetite. In his honor contemporary medicine classifies *"satyriasis"* as an excessive sexual drive in men. Kochanowski's Satyr, however, criticizes not only political matters. He advises how a decent Christian should live, and scoffs at the Protestant gentry and at home-bred theologians. Any deity from classical mythology sermonizing about Christian duties must look queer, and a satyr is doubly inappropriate for such a part. Kochanowski was not only well aware of that absurdity but even ironically emphasized it. His Satyr, just after having finished preaching about proper Christian behavior, reminisces fondly about old times and his part in the story of Bacchus and Ariadne:

> Bachus był na mię łaskaw i żadnej biesiady
>   Nigdy nie miał beze mnie, mogę rzec, i rady.
> Kiedy niósł Aryjadnę, jam tuż przed nim siedział;
>   Com też sobie pomyślał Bache, byś był wiedział![6]

> Bacchus was fond of me, kept no revel
> Without me and, I may say, no council.
> I was in front of him when he was carrying off Ariadne.
> I wonder whether you know, Bacchus, what I was thinking there!

Ovid's frivolous *Ars amatoria* was the best known Latin work telling the story of Bacchus and Ariadne (I, 525-564), and although the poem did not figure in school curricula, it was widely read. Thus, Kochanowski reminds his reader quite emphatically what part his moralist and guardian of Christian orthodoxy had played in ancient tradition.

The game does not end there, however. In the final part of the poem, Kochanowski's Satyr quotes at length the centaur Chiron lecturing Achilles about the qualities expected in a perfect ruler. The then reigning king, Sigismund August (Zygmunt August), had scandalized his subjects first by his marriage to Barbara Gasztołd, née Radziwiłł (reputedly dissolute and syphilitic), then by his notoriously bad conjugal life with his second wife, an Austrian princess, as well as by his love affairs. Thus, when Chiron says that the first duty of a ruler is to live an exemplary life, a contemporary reader knew whom the poet had in mind. In political matters, the king was widely criticized for his policy of détente with the Ottoman empire. Against such a background, Chiron's statement that a martial spirit was the prime virtue of a good ruler sounds like indirect criticism of royal pacifism. Renaissance decorum would not allow direct criticism of a ruling monarch; such indirect hints became all the more titillating. The reader could not miss the point since the poem was dedicated to the king.

Should we conclude then that the poem is a sort of parody of conservative clichés which the poet only pretends to share? No, it is not as simple as that. In other poems in which he speaks in his own name, Kochanowski both repeats some of the Satyr's complaints and yet occasionally makes fun of his Satyr too. Thus, in a later Latin elegy opening with the words *"Patria rura colo,"* in which he celebrates his settling down in his country house, he could announce that he would trade in grain, cut trees and build a barge even though his "angry Satyr might gnash his teeth (*"Iratus Satyrus frendeat ore,"* El. III, 15, line 42).[7]

The point is that the text becomes ambiguous; the poet is obviously playing with the medium and exploring its possibilities. A simple-minded, old-fashioned squire would read the poem as an expression of his own misgivings, identifying himself with the Satyr. Some literary historians read it that way also. A more sophisticated reader would not fail to notice that Kochanowski wrote his poem with tongue in cheek, in a playful mood; not everything uttered by the Satyr should be taken at face value. This was the first time such a sophisticated poem, a text playing hide-and-seek with the reader, had appeared in Polish and this is precisely why its first readers were so elated. They realized that this short poem was opening a new chapter in the history of Polish poetry.

A second edition quickly followed, as well as imitations even containing homages to Kochanowski. The first imitators saw the source of the poem's success in the invention of an unexpected and amusing spokesman and tried to rival Kochanowski in similar inventiveness. Such is the case with an anonymous satire whose title alludes to Kochanowski's poem: *Proteus abo Odmieniec* (*Proteus, or the Changing One*). It contains two tributes to Kochanowski, one by Cyprian Bazylik and another especially enthusiastic one by the anonymous author of the satire. Playing on Kochanowski's last name, it calls the poet "the love of our century" ("*kochanie wieku tego*") and proudly announces that henceforth Poles are equal in poetic achievements to the ancient Greeks and Italians.[8] Thus, as early as 1564 the young author of *The Satyr* ... was declared a classic, a writer equal in rank with the great poets of Greece and Rome.

Several years later, in one of his satires, Marcin Bielski introduced as spokesmen two rams from a bas-relief of a house in Cracow's Market Square and stated in the preamble that Kochanowski's poem was his source of inspiration.[9] Instead of trying to invent increasingly peculiar spokesmen, numerous subsequent imitators made *The Satyr* ... their mouthpiece. Thus originated the specifically Polish subgenre of the satire, "the Satyric poem." The best known representative of this subgenre is Samuel Twardowski's *Satyr na twarz Rzeczypospolitej* (*The Satyr on the Visage of the Commonwealth*), published in 1640. The last specimens of that subgenre date from the first decades of the eighteenth century, and in the middle of that century a Croatian poet, Matija Antun Reljković, wrote a satire modeled on Kochanowski's *The Satyr* ....[10]

Thus, *The Satyr* ... not only revealed Kochanowski as a great poet to the Polish reading public, but was also the first of his works to initiate a particular tradition in Polish letters. Of course, the moment the Satyr became a traditional spokesman through whom the poet criticized the society, the chief asset of Kochanowski's invention, the effect of amused surprise was lost. The Satyr in that role became another literary convention. Moreover, Kochanowski's imitators were not able to follow him in establishing their distance from such a spokesman, in treating him with irony. The Satyr simply became the author's alter ego, and it would not matter if he were replaced by the author's "I". Thus, duplication of Kochanowski's model resulted in considerable impoverishment.

Kochanowski's *The Satyr* was published in 1563 or 1564, most probably in 1563. In February of 1564, the poet's patron, Vice Chancellor and Bishop Piotr Myszkowski, turned over to Kochanowski his own Church benefice, the post of parish priest of the Poznań cathedral. The poet (who in fact was never ordained) received an exceptionally well-endowed benefice for the parish priest of the Poznań cathedral received an income from no less than six villages.[11] The convergence of the two dates, that of the publication of the poem and that of the offer of the benefice to the poet, might have been accidental. Possibly, however, the benefice may have been intended as a literary prize, the highest literary prize ever given in Poland. After all, for his Trilogy Sienkiewicz was offered only one village, Oblęgorek. Moreover, two years later, Kochanowski was also given the benefice of another, less lucrative parish, Zwoleń.[12] The pre-Tridentine Church knew how to be generous in rewarding literary merits.

The reception of *The Satyr*, from our point of view a minor and rather marginal poetic contribution, has been discussed at some length because it seems to be the cornerstone of the poet's renown: it revealed to delighted Poles the presence of a great poet among them. Subsequent publications, much more substantial achievements, confirmed the public in their opinion and these were received as the works of a master.

Sixteenth-century Poland lacked strong urban centers and the institutions which only such centers could foster. Consequently, criticism of literature is scarce in that century. Moreover, most literary opinions that have survived are of a rather rudimentary character. However, we have at our disposal other, quite reliable gauges of the popularity of literary works at that time.

One such gauge of popularity is the number of reprints. In the case of Kochanowski's works, however, it is not easy to ascertain the exact number of subsequent editions, because in order not to pay royalties, the poet's publishers sometimes disguised new reprints as parts of previous editions, publishing them under false dates. Only laborious typographical analysis, done half a century ago by a great specialist, Kazimierz Piekarski, revealed that the number of actual editions was much greater than it seemed to be.[13] To cite one instance alone, it turned out that Kochanowski's largest work, his poetic paraphrase of the psalms, *Psałterz Dawidów* (*David's Psalter*), was published between 1579 and 1641 in no less than twenty-five editions, four of them bearing the date 1586, and seven dated 1608.

Further decisive proof is the fact that each work by Kochanowski brought in its wake a number of imitations; most of his works set new fashions in Polish letters. Especially revealing in this respect is the reception of Kochanowski's *Fraszki* (*Trifles*).

That particular collection of poems was first published late, in 1584, the year of Kochanowski's death. But a number of *Fraszki* must have been in circulation through manuscript copies much earlier. Łukasz Górnicki in his paraphrase of Castiglione's *Il Cortegiano*, *Dworzanin polski* (*The Polish Courtier*), mentions them as known and appreciated for their wit.[14] Two years later in his Polish grammar, Piotr Statorius quotes passages from them as models of fortunate formulations.[15] The *Fraszki* belong to the most popular among Kochanowski's works: in the course of fifty years they were published in a separate volume twelve times, and they could be found as well in the volume of Kochanowski's collected poetry, entitled *Jan Kochanowski*, which also had a run of twelve editions.

The genre of short, epigrammatic poems was cultivated in Poland before Kochanowski, mostly in Latin, while in the vernacular Rej wrote a collection of them, entitled *Figliki* (*Little Jokes*). Most probably, it was Kochanowski who coined the name "*Fraszka*" from the Italian *frasca* and having the meaning of Latin *nuga*, "a trifle."[16] It is true that the word *fraszka* was used once by Rej in the title of the introductory poem to the above-mentioned collection, "*Ku temu, co czyść będzie ty fraszki*" ("To the person who will read these trifles").[17] Rej's collection was published posthumously in 1574, five years after his death. Introductory poems are usually written late, after the collection has been completed, and since Kochanowski's *Fraszki* were, as we have seen, in circulation already in the 1560's, it is quite possible that Rej might have borrowed the word from his younger colleague. In any case, after Kochanowski, the word *fraszka* acquired in Polish the value of a technical literary term, the name of a genre.

After Kochanowski, this epigrammatic poetry became the most popular genre in Renaissance and baroque Poland. Poets borrowed topics, formal solutions, and above all, expressions from the master. At the same time they substantially narrowed Kochanowski's idea of that kind of poetry.

Kochanowski's *Fraszki* is a collection of about three hundred poems. Their thematic and emotional range is very broad. Many are jocular poems, funny anecdotes, or sallies. These are, however, interspersed with items of a quite different character: reflective poems, short lyrics, tomb inscriptions, appeals to friends. Most of the love poems included are written in an Anacreontic vein, but some of them are in a grave, elegiac mood. The whole is quite carefully organized, although at first sight it makes the impression of a chaotic conglomeration of disparate poems. The reader is to lose himself in "the labyrinth," to use the poet's expression. A number of autothematic poems, poems about poetry, appear as well. All of these poems have only one feature in common: they must be short. Only a few of them are more than twenty lines long.

When writing the *Fraszki*, Kochanowski used as his model a vast anthology— more than four thousand poems—by different authors of classical Greek and early Byzantine provenance, all of them short, a mixture of serious and jocular poetry, known as *Anthologia greca* or *Anthologia palatina*.[18] Moreover, some fifty of Kochanowski's fraszki are direct adaptations from that anthology.

For a twentieth-century reader the thematically serious *fraszki* are Kochanowski's most easily accessible poems. We establish contact with them without any difficulty. Our response to the jocular poems is not as easy, however. Some of them are quite witty and cleverly done, but in some the humor has evaporated with time. Górnicki, for example, gives in his *Courtier* as the model of apt witticism the six-line poem, *"O koźle,"* II, 16 ("About Mr. Billy-Goat").[19] A man with the name of Billy-Goat (*kozieł* in Polish) becomes so drunk that he cannot find the way to his home and asks a passerby to help him. The other man inquires about his name and when learning that it is Kozieł advises him: *"Idźże spać do chlewa!"* ("Go to sleep in a sty"). Today we read such a versified anecdote with some embarassment; such a lame play on words seems unworthy of the poet. But we should not forget that few things change as radically with time as a sense of humor. For Wacław Potocki, a seventeenth- century baroque poet, for instance, the sight of a bald head was something particularly funny, a source of endless jokes. A contemporary reader, even one endowed with a full crop of hair, when faced with such jocular poems has to admit that he lacks common language with Potocki.

However, sixteenth- and seventeenth-century Polish poets imitated primarily the jocular *fraszki*. For them, Kochanowski's *Fraszki* must have been above all a collection of witty epigrams, versified jokes and biting sallies. If we speak of *"balladomania"* in early Polish romanticism, we can speak as well of *"fraszkomania"* in Renaissance and baroque Poland. There were hundreds and hundreds of poems termed *fraszki*, especially in the poetry that was written for private consumption only and remained in manuscripts. Those *fraszki*, however, are almost exclusively versified jokes, anecdotes, puns, and only exceptionally a later poet takes as his model what in Kochanowski's collection was a miniature lyrical poem. Thus, in spite of the great popularity of Kochanowski's *Fraszki*, his model of a short epigrammatic poem became simplified and vulgarized in its later reception.

The influence of Kochanowski's longer lyrics, the so-called *Pieśni* (*Songs*) on subsequent love, civic or religious poetry cannot be overestimated. To a great extent, Kochanowski created the language of Polish lyrical poetry. Baroque poets, even when adhering to poetics different from those of Kochanowski, studded their works with expressions peculiar to him. Kochanowski became for them a classic upon whose poetry they learned the basic rules of poetic language. Such apprenticeship was natural, since baroque poetics was not opposed in principle to Renaissance poetics, as, for instance, romanticism was to classical poetics. Baroque poets wanted to emulate their Renaissance predecessors, to do the same, but to do it better, in a more sophisticated and striking way. Only Mikołaj Sęp-Szarzyński (ca. 1550-1581), chronologically closest to Kochanowski and the greatest among his successors, remains, with his strikingly original poetic diction, relatively free from the influences of Kochanowski's lyrical poetry.

Sęp-Szarzyński, however, is an exception to the general rule. Elsewhere, the influence of Kochanowski's poetic idiom is obvious, and, in most cases, massive. The influence of deeper structures, involving lyrical attitudes, the character of the poetic "I," and the rules of composition, is much more difficult to determine, and for an obvious reason. Kochanowski's lyrical poetry is modeled primarily on Horace's *carmina*, and several of Kochanowski's so-called "songs" are adaptations of Horace's poems. After Virgil, Horace was the best known Latin poet in old Poland. Every alumnus of a Jesuit school knew by heart several, occasionally even scores, of such poems. Thus, in later Polish poets, it is difficult to differentiate features learned directly from Horace from those modeled specifically on Kochanowski's lyrical poetry.

Kochanowski's *Treny* (*Laments*), a cycle of nineteen poems in which the poet mourns the death of his little daughter, also found numerous imitators. In old Polish literature, the so-called epicedia, poems praising the dead and expressing grief after their death, were quite numerous. In the cultural life of Renaissance and baroque Poland they functioned as obituaries do in our times. The death of an important person prompted such poems, and Kochanowski's first printed Polish poem, *O śmierci Jana Tarnowskiego* (*On the Death of Jan Tarnowski*, 1561), was an epicedium.

In the *Laments* the traditional epicedium was replaced by a cycle of poems, and after Kochanowski such cycles of lyrical poems became fashionable in Polish poetry. Appropriately, the first such cycle, *Żale nagrobne* (*Funeral Lamentations*), mourns the death of the author of the *Laments*; it was written by

¶ Pyesń.

Czego chceſʒ od nas pánie ʒá twe hoyne dáry?
　Cʒego ʒá dobrodʒieyſtwá/ktorich niemáſʒ miáry?
Koſcyoł cie nie ogárnie/ wſʒedy pełno ciebie/
　I w odchłániach/ y w morʒu/ ná ʒyemi/ ná niebie.
Złotá teſʒ/ wiem/ nie prágnieſʒ: bo to wſʒytko twoie/
　Cokolwiek ná thym ſwiecie cʒłowiek mieni ſwoie.
Wdʒyecʒnym cie tedy ſercem pánie wyʒnawamy/
　Bo nád to prʒyſtoynieyſʒey ofiáry nie mamy.
Tyś pan wſʒytkiego ſwiátá/ tyś niebo ʒbudował/
　I ʒłotemi gwiaʒdámi ſlicʒnie uháwtował.
Tyś fundáment ʒáłoʒył nieobeſʒłey ʒyemi/
　I prʒykryłeś iey nágość ʒyoły roʒlicʒnemi.
Zá twoim roſkaʒánim w brʒegach morʒe ſtoi/
　A ʒámierʒonych gránic prʒeſkocʒyć ſie boi.
Rʒeki wod nieprʒebránych wielka hoyność máia/
　Byały dʒyeń/ á noc ciemna ſwoie cʒáſy ʒnáia.
Tobie k woli roʒlicʒne kwiatki Wioſná rodʒi/
　Tobie k woli w kłoſiánym wieńcu Láto chodʒi.
Wino Jeſień/ y iábłká roʒmáite dawá/
　Potym do gotowego gnuśna Zimá wſtawa.
S twey łáſki/ nocna roſá/ ná mdłe ʒyołá pádnie/
　A ʒágorʒáłe ʒboʒa deſʒcʒ oʒywia ſnádnie.
S twoich rák wſʒelkie ʒwierʒe pátrʒa ſwey ʒywnośći/
　A ty káʒdego karmyſʒ ʒ twey ſʒcʒodrobliwośći.
Bádʒ ná wieki pochwalon/ nieſmiertelny pánie/
　Twoiá łáſká/ twa dobroć nigdy nie uſtánie.
Choway nas poki racʒyſʒ ná tey niſkiey ʒyemi/
　Jedno ʒáwʒdy niech bedʒiem pod ſkrʒydłámi twemi.

48. Jan Kochanowski, "*Czego chcesz od nas panie.*" The first publication of the Hymn, the only one surviving copy published together with Jan Kochanowski *Zuzanna*, w Krakowie, ca. 1562 (Biblioteka Ossolińskich, Wrocław) Photo Zbigniew Kapuścik.

49. Jan Kochanowski, *Szachy*, w Krakowie, 1585. The title page of the third edition (Biblioteka Ossolińskich, Wrocław).

SATYR
Albo Dziki Mąż.
Iana Kochanowskiego.

50. Jan Kochanowski, *Satyr albo Dziki Mąż*, w Krakowie, ca. 1564. The title page of the earliest surviving edition (Biblioteka Ossolińskich, Wrocław). Reprinted from the facsimile edition by Paulina Buchwald-Pelcowa (Warszawa: Czytelnik, 1983).

Odpráwá Posłow
Graeckich.

IA'NA KOCHANOVVSKIEGO.

Podáná ná Theátrum przeb Krolem Jeg Mśćia
y Krolową Jey Mśćia/ w Jázbowie nád Wár-
żáwá. Dniá dwunastego Stycżniá/Koku Páń-
stiego. M. D. L X X Viij.
Ná Feśćie v Jeg Mśći Páná podkánclerzego
Koronnego.

W Wárżáwie/ M. D. L X X Viij.

51. Jan Kochanowski, *Odprawa posłów greckich*, w Warszawie, 1578. The title page of one of the only three surviving copies (Biblioteka Narodowa, Warszawa). A facsimile edition was published by Alodia Kawecka-Gryczowa (Warszawa: Czytelnik, 1974). Photo Stanisław Stępniewski.

Sebastian Klonowic and published in 1585. In the same year, Tobiasz Wiś-
niowski published a cycle in which he mourned the death of his mother. The
very title of them, *Laments* (*Treny*), referred to Kochanowski, and the word
treny reappears in titles of later cycles as well.

Later cycles managed to follow Kochanowski only up to a certain point.
Kochanowski's *Laments* are the expression not only of mourning, but also of
a spiritual crisis triggered by his child's death and then overcome. The crisis
theme gives his cycle considerable structural unity. Later epicedial cycles lack
such unity. Rather, they are lyrical variations on the theme of grief and mourning, in which often the sequence of individual poems seems to be arbitrary.
Most of the poetry is repetitive and of little literary value. The popularity,
however, of such a cyclical form confirms the impact of Kochanowski on subsequent poets.

Kochanowski considered his poetic adaptation of the Psalter, *Psałterz Dawidów* (*David's Psalter*), to be his highest achievement. In the dedicatory poem
which opened it he stated:

I wdarłem się na skałę pięknej Kalijopy,
Gdzie dotychczas nie było znaku polskiej stopy.

And I scaled the rock of beautiful Calliope,
Where hitherto there was no trace of a Polish foot.

We would expect Erato rather than Calliope, the Muse of epic poetry, to be
mentioned here. Kochanowski, however, had good reasons for preferring Calliope at this point. According to Renaissance poetics, there existed a hierarchy
of literary genres, with epic poetry ranking highest. Thus, the poet's proud
words should be understood in the sense that he created with his *David's Psalter*
a monumental poetic work, equal in importance to an epic poem, one with no
precedent in Polish letters.

As I have already mentioned, Kochanowski's *Psalter* must have been a best-
seller; in the course of sixty years, a new edition appeared every two or three
years. The music, composed by Mikołaj Gomółka and published in 1580, only
one year after the appearance of the first edition, must have contributed to
that popularity. Individual psalms in Kochanowski's version found their way
into psalm-books, Catholic as well as Protestant, the poet's adaptation shun-
ning any denominational coloring.

In 1605 there appeared another poetic version, *Psalmy Dawidowe* (David's
psalms), by Maciej Rybiński, a Protestant minister. Strictly speaking, it is not
so much a new version as an adaptation of Kochanowski's *Psalter* for use in
church services.[20] Rybiński tried to simplify Kochanowski's diction and to render the psalms better fit for singing.

Kochanowski's *David's Psalter* was popular not only in Poland but also abroad,
and the testimonies to that popularity, translations into other languages, are
quite numerous. Most probably, the Lithuanian translation was the earliest.
Not a single copy of its first edition has been preserved, and we know of its

existence only from a reprint done in 1653 in Kiejdany.[21] Twenty years later, in 1673, Dosoftei, metropolitan of Moldavia, who had fled to Poland two years earlier, in 1671, published his paraphrase of Kochanowski's paraphrase, *Psaltirea a lui David*, which is considered the highest achievement of seventeenth-century Rumanian poetry.[22]

In 1680 *Psaltyr' ryfmotvornaya* by Simeon Polockij appeared in Moscow. From its preface, we learn that Kochanowski's adaptation *"sladkoye i soglasnoye penie polskiya Psaltiri,"* enjoyed tremendous popularity in all East Slavic countries, Moscovy included, where, we read, even people who "know little or no Polish" sing psalms in Kochanowski's version.[23] After Hetman Żółkiewski's reign in this country in 1610, Kochanowski's influence is the second notable Polish triumph in seventeenth-century Moscovy. Despite the warm tribute contained in the preface, some literary historians don't believe that Kochanowski's version was the model for Polockij's rendering.[24] A comparison, however, of the versification of both versions makes the influence obvious. Polockij's rendering is written in syllabic verse form, and as many as sixty-eight psalms were rendered by him in lines of exactly the same length as in Kochanowski's *Psalter*. Such a coincidence could not have been accidental. Moreover, analysis of the text proves that occasionally Polockij deviates from the canonical Orthodox version and follows Kochanowski's.[25] In one of his poems (*Songs* II, 24) Kochanowski boasted: "Moscow and the Tartars will know about me." Most probably, as the inclusion of the Tartars suggests, it was meant as a *sui generis* poetic provocation, as an absurd hyperbole. In retrospect it turned out, however, that the poet was right in prophesying his fame in Moscovy.

Kochanowski's and Rybiński's Polish paraphrases of the Psalter were mentioned by Martin Opitz, a leading German baroque poet, in the preface to his own poetic version, *Die Psalmen Davids*, published in 1637.[26] By the end of the century, twenty psalms from Kochanowski's adaptation were translated into German by Andreas Wedecke.[27] Individual psalms were rendered into Hungarian as well.[28] No other work in Polish Renaissance or baroque literature exerted comparable influence abroad and inspired so many foreign poets.

Only one major work by Kochanowski—major by our standards—passed almost unnoticed by both the poet's contemporaries and later by the seventeenth-century reading public: the drama, *Odprawa posłów greckich* (*The Dismissal of the Greek Envoys*). Initially it might seem that such neglect was due to the fact that *The Dismissal*, alone among Kochanowski's works, was published not in the capital but in then provincial Warsaw. This, however, cannot be sufficient reason, since *The Dismissal* was later reprinted several times in the edition of Kochanowski's collected works and, thus, was as easily available as any work of the bard.

The institution of regular theater was unknown in old Poland and no dramatic text enjoyed great popularity then. It seems, however, that the main reason for the lack of response to Kochanowski's drama is to be found elsewhere, namely in its peculiar poetic diction and versification to which Kochanowski's contemporaries, as well as following generations, were not attuned.

In *The Dismissal* Kochanowski experimented with a new verse form, with blank verse in which enjambement is much more frequent than in any other of his works. In traditional Polish versification, rhyme was the main signal of the end of the line. In *The Dismissal*, the lack of that signal together with the profusion of run-on lines make the passage from one line to another less conspicuous than elsewhere in Kochanowski's poetry. In other words, the verse pattern is more discreet; to people reared on traditional versification it must have sounded like something half-way between prose and poetry. Such an impression must have been reinforced by the language of the dialogues which avoids metaphors and inversions, and uses epithets sparingly.

If Kochanowski's poetic diction is always classical, here we have to deal with an ascetic classicism. *The Dismissal* was staged and printed in 1578, that means at a time when a new baroque poetry with its rich, elaborate poetic language was already in the offing. Such is already the style of the first baroque poet in Poland, Mikołaj Sęp-Szarzynski, who died in 1581, only two years after *The Dismissal* had been printed. Most probably, for the first readers of the drama its idiom seemed to be anaemic, and they failed to recognize its austere beauty. With the exception of Piotr Ciekliński and Jan Smolik, none of Kochanowski's immediate successors explored the potential of blank verse in dramatic dialogues. In the following century, Krzysztof Opaliński wrote his *Satires* in a heavy, clumsy blank verse and his work remained an isolated experiment.

The Dismissal, structured after ancient tragedies, has three choral songs, two written in the stanzaic form of Kochanowski's *Songs*, and the second of these was also included in the collection of those *Songs* (II, 14). The third choral song is a bold metrical experiment. "It follows in the footsteps of Greek choruses," to quote the poet from his preface, and it is written in tonic lines of uneven length. With its elaborate poetic diction and its slow, stately rhythm, it is considered today one of the masterpieces of Polish lyrical poetry. But none of the later Renaissance or baroque poets dared to imitate Kochanowski in this verse form and we had to wait until 1851 for a parallel metrical exploration: Norwid's *"Bema pamięci rapsod żałobny"* ("To the Memory of Bem, A Funeral Rhapsody").

The lack of readers' response to *The Dismissal of the Greek Envoys* is, however, an exception to a remarkable success story which has no parallel in the annals of Polish literature. At the threshold of his literary activity, Kochanowski was acclaimed a great poet, "the love of this century." Quite early, the poet's patrons guaranteed his financial security with an unusually generous bequest. His works were reprinted over and over again. Although his practice went counter to the rules of baroque poetics, the coming of the baroque era did nothing to diminish his stature. In his treatise on poetics, the baroque poet Maciej Kazimierz Sarbiewski asserted that Kochanowski was a greater writer than Dante, Petrarch, or Ronsard.[29] Poets, contemporary as well as succeeding ones, followed, imitated, echoed, and plagiarized him. What more could he expect?

And yet at one moment in his life he complained of lack of recognition and of readers. He did so in the poem *Muza* (*The Muse*), most probably written after he had already published *The Satyr*, which had been so enthusiastically received. The poem opens with the lines:

Sobie śpiewam a Muzom, bo kto jest na ziemi,
Co by serce ucieszyć chciał pieśniami memi?

I sing for myself and for the Muses, since who is there on earth
That would like to gladden his heart with my songs?

The phrase "I sing for myself and the Muses" was a popular Renaissance *topos* of classical provenance.[30] The mere existence, however, of such a traditional *topos* does not explain its appearance and function in Kochanowski's poetry. It proves only that for a poet familiar with the classical heritage such a *topos* was available, if he felt that he needed it. But why should Kochanowski feel so?

The *topos* expresses the feeling, characteristic of any authentic artist, that he creates primarily for himself, following his inner urge. But Kochanowski complains in *The Muse* that he lacks an audience ("*A poeta słuchaczów próżny*"— "But the poet is devoid of listeners") as well, and here we are at a loss for an explanation. Perhaps that particular complaint was prompted by some failure unregistered by us? We might guess perhaps that behind it lies the poet's realization that, as we have seen, the reception of his poetry, although enthusiastic, had its shortcomings, that the readers followed what the poet was doing up to a certain point only? Perhaps the complaint lacks objective reasons and was written in a moment of depression? We simply don't know.

The Muse also registers the poet's proud consciousness of his own worth and the conviction that in the future he will be famous

Jednak mam tę nadzieję, ze przedsię za laty
    Nie będą moje czułe nocy bez zapłaty;
A co mi za żywota ujmie czas dzisiejszy,
    To po śmierci nagrodzi z lichwą wiek późniejszy.
I opatrzył to dawno syn pięknej Latony,
    Że moich kości popiół nie będzie wzgardzony.

lines 13-18

I have the hope, however, that with years
My nightly vigils will not go unrewarded,
And what the present day diminishes in my lifetime,
The future will recompense with usury.
And the son of beautiful Leto provided long ago
That the ashes of my bones will not be scorned.

A correction is in order here. The son of beautiful Leto, Apollo, was kind to our poet both during his lifetime and after his death as well. For such a spectacle of parallel fame, accompanying a poet's first fruits and never abandoning him afterwards, we have to wait in Polish letters until 1822, the year in which Mickiewicz published his first volume of poetry.

Notes

1. The story was told in 1612 by Jan Szczęsny Herburt in his preface to an edition of Kasper Miaskowski's poetry. Quoted after Janusz Pelc, *Jan Kochanowski w tradycjach literatury polskiej (od XVI do XVIII w.)* [Jan Kochanowski in the traditions of Polish literature (from the 16th to the 18th century)], (Warsaw; PIW, 1965), p. 27.

2. Mikołaj Rej, *Źwierzyniec* (The Zodiac of Life), ed. W. Bruchnalski, Biblioteka Pisarzów 30 (Cracow, Akademia Umiejętności 1895), p. 157.

3. A comprehensive discussion of the wild man motif, based primarily on German material, is to be found in Richard Bernheimer, *Wild Men in the Middle Ages. A Study of Art, Sentiment and Demonology* (New York: Octagon, 1970). Tadeusz Ulewicz, "O 'Satyrze' Jana Kochanowskiego" (On *The Satyr* of Jan Kochanowski) [in *Literatura, komparatystyka, folklor. Księga poświęcona Julianowi Krzyżanowskiemu* (Warsaw: PIW, 1968),pp. 132), cites rich Italian matierial. See also Janusz Pelc, *Jan Kochanowski. Szczyt renesansu w literaturz polskiej* (Jan Kochanowski. Zenith of the Renaissance in Polish literature) (Warsaw: PWN, 1980), pp. 185-187.

4. As quoted by Aleksander Brückner, "Średniowieczna poezja łacińska w Polsce" (Medieval Latin poetry in Poland), pt. 2, *Rozprawy Akademii Umiejętności. Wydział Filologiczny*, vol. 22 (1893), p. 41.

5. Ulewicz, "O 'Satyrze' Jana Kochanowskiego," p. 128.

6. Kochanowski's Polish texts are quoted here after Jan Kochanowski, *Dzieła Polskie* (Polish works), ed. Julian Krżyzanowski, 7th ed. (Warsaw: PIW, 1972).

7. J. Cochanovii *Carmina latina. Emondavit, argumentis et notis instruxit* Josephus Przyborowski. (Warsaw, 1884).

8. *Proteus albo Odmieniec* (Proteus, or the Changing One), ed. Władysław Wisłocki, Biblioteka Pisarzów Polskich 8 (Cracow: Akademia Umiejętności, 1890), p. 33.

9. Marcin Bielski, *Satyry* (Satires), Władysław Wisłocki, ed., Biblioteka Pisarzów Polskich 4 (Cracow: Akademia Umiejętności, 1889), p. 21.

10. On the rich progeny of Kochanowski's *Satyr*, see Juliusz Nowak-Dłużewski, *Poemat satyrowy w literaturze polskiej w. XVI-XVIII. Z Dziejów inicjatywy artystycznej Jana Kochanowskiego* (The satiric poem in Polish literature, 16th-17th century. From the history of the artistic initiative of Jan Kochanowski) (Warsaw: Prace Wydziału Filologicznego Uniwersytetu Warszawskiego, 1962), and Pelc, *Kochanowski w tradycjach*, pp. 247-287. On Reljković: Stojan Subotin, "Wokół zagadki wpływu 'Satyra' Jana Kochanowskiego na 'Satyra' M.A. Relkovicia" (On the enigma of the influence of *The Satyr* of Jan Kochanowski on *The Satyr* of M.A. Relković) in *For Wiktor Weintraub* (The Hague: Mouton, 1975), pp. 505-514.

11. Edmund Majkowski, "Jan Kochanowski, proboszcz kapituły katedralnej poznańskiej" (Jan Kochanowski, vicar of the Poznań cathedral chapter) in *Kochanowski. Z dziejów badań i recepcji tworczości*, ed. Mirosław Korolko (Warsaw: PWN, 1980), pp. 103-108, and Pelc, *Jan Kochanowski*, p. 56.

12. Pelc, *Jan Kochanowski*, p. 56.

13. Kazimierz Piekarski, *Biblioqrafia dzieł Jana Kochanowskiego. Wiek XVI-XVII* (Bibliography of the works of Jan Kochanowski. 16th-17th centuries), 2nd ed. (Cracow: Polska Akademia Umiejętności, 1934).

14. Łukasz Górnicki, *Pisma* (Writings), vol. 1, ed. Roman Pollak (Warsaw: PIW, 1961), p. 224.

15. Pelc, *Kochanowski w tradycjach*, pp. 62-63.

16. Sante Graciotti, "'Fraszki' i fraszki" (The *Trifles* and trifles) *Język Polski* 94 (1964): 257-268.

17. Mikołaj Rej, *Figliki* (Little jokes), ed. Maria Bokszczanin (Warsaw: PIW, 1970), p. 40.

18. For a more lengthy discussion, see my *Rzecz czarnoleska* (On Czarnolas) (Cracow: Wydawn. Literackie, 1977), pp. 273-274.

19. Górnicki, *Pisma*, 1, p. 224.

20. Pelc, *Kochanowski w tradycjach*, pp. 149-151.

21. See Jerzy Ziomek's Introduction to his edition of Jan Kochanowski, *Psałterz Dawidów* (David's Psalter), Biblioteka Narodowa I, 174 (Wrocław: Ossolineum, 1960), p. clxi.

22. See Pierre P. Panaitescu, *Influence de la littérature polonaise sur les Roumains au XVIIe siècles* in the collective *Pamiętnik Zjazdu Naukowego im. J. Kochanowskiego* (Cracow: Polska Akademia Umiejętności, 1931), p. 174.

23. Simeon Polockij, *Izbrannye socineniia* ed. Igor P. Eremin, (Moscow- Leningrad, 1953), p. 213.

24. Dmitrij Čiževskij, *History of Russian Literature from the Eleventh Century to the End of the Baroque* (The Hague: Mouton, 1960), p. 354.

25. See Ryszard Łużny, "*Psałterz rymowany* Simeona Połockiego a *Psałterz Dawidów* Jana Kochanowskiego" (*The Psalter in verse* of Simeon Polockij and *David's Psalter* of Jan Kochanowski), *Slavia Orientalis* 15 (1966) : 3-27. See also Paulina Lewin, "Rosyjskie tłumaczenia z Kochanowskiego" (Russian translations of Kochanowski), *Archiwum Literackie* 22 (1972) : 81-85.

26. Marian Szyrocki, *Martin Opitz* (Berlin: Rütten and Loening, 1956), pp. 122-124.

27. Olga Dobijanka-Witczakowa, "Niemiecki przekład Psalmów Kochanowskiego z czasów Jana III" (The German translation of Kochanowski's Psalms from the time of Jan III), *Archiwum Literackie* 23 (1974) : 109-135. See also Anna Wróbel, "Kochanowski a literatura niemiecka" (Kochanowski and German literature) *Pamiętnik Literacki* 93, 1/2 (1952) : 487-501.

28. Géza Papp, "Przyczynki do związków dawnej poezji węgierskiej z polską" (Contributions to the connections of ancient Hungarian poetry with Polish poetry) in *Studia do dziejów polsko-węgierskich stosunków literackich i kulturalnych*, Jan Reychman, ed. (Wrocław: Ossolineum, 1969), pp. 138-143.

29. "Certe illis Ioannes Kochanovius non inferior modo, sed etiam—quantum potui ex lectione Marini, Guidonis Cassonii, Francisci Petrarcae, Dantis Italorum et Ronsardi, Galli lyrici prestantissimi, colligere—urbanitate sermonis Polonici, gravitate sententiarum, inventionis, praecipue obliquae, praestantia, nervo demum quodam superior sit." Maciej Kazimierz Sarbiewski, *Wykłady poetyki* (*Praecepta poetica*), ed. Stanisław Skimina, Biblioteka Pisarzów Polskich, ser. B, 5 (Wrocław: Ossolineum, 1958), p. 38.

30. Julian Krżyzanowski, *Mądrej głowie dość dwie słowie* (The smart man needs only two words), vol. 2, (Warsaw: PIW, 1960), pp. 326-327. See also Pelc, *Jan Kochanowski*, pp. 221-222.

![decorative ornament band]

18

Jan Kochanowski, Creator of Polish National Literature, and the Renaissance in Poland

Janusz Pelc

Was Jan Kochanowski, the author of *Treny* (Laments or Threnodies) and *Fraszki* (Trifles) born in 1530? So one would think on the basis of the inscription beneath his portrait on his tombstone in the church in Zwoleń. According to this inscription, Jan Kochanowski died on August 22, 1584, at the age of fifty-four. Kochanowski's earliest biography, published in 1612 with the second edition of his philological and poetical work (a reconstruction of Cicero's translation of Aratos' *Phaenomena*) and later included in Szymon Starowolski's *Scriptorom Polonicorum* ξκατοντασ *seu centum illustrium Poloniae scriptorum elogia et vitae* (1625, later reprinted), stated that the poet of Czarnolas was born in 1532. This biography was first printed during more or less the same period in which the Zwoleń epitaph was being constructed (the epitaph was unveiled around 1610). One would assume that the poet's family, which commissioned and surely oversaw the construction of the monument, knew the correct date. Was this really the case? Or was Kochanowski's first biography mistaken? Sebastian Fabian Klonowic in *Żale nagrobne na ślachetnie urodzonego i znacznie uczonego męża, nieboszczyka Pana Jana Kochanowskiego* . . . (Laments on the grave of the noble and very learned man, the late Jan Kochanowski . . .) (1585) wrote that the poet died not on the 22nd, but on August 16, 1584.[1] Was he mistaken as well? At least the month and year of Jan Kochanowski's death (August 1584) are not questioned, for this information is confirmed by the records of chroniclers of the time. But concerning the date of his birth it would be safer to say that Jan Kochanowski was born "about 1530" or "probably in or around 1530" or even that he was born "probably in 1530 or perhaps in 1532."[2]

Interest in Kochanowski and his writings leads us to the history of the Renaissance in Poland and to its European context. Jan Kochanowski, the most remarkable Polish and Slavic Renaissance poet, lived and wrote precisely at

321

this time. His writings which set the course for the future development of Polish poetry, are read to this day, and have been translated into different languages of the world. Not without reason is the Renaissance period also called the Golden Age of Polish culture and literature.

The works of Polish writers of the time, not only political writers [the most prominent of whom was Andrzej Frycz Modrzewski (Andreas Fricius Modrevius), respected throughout Europe] but also poets as well, were connected with the larger problems of the period, with the social, political, and philosophical discussions that pervaded Polish society of the time. Jan Kochanowski also participated in these discussions, such as when in one of his earliest works, the poem *Zgoda* (Harmony) printed in 1564—in the spirit of Renaissance neoplatonism and out of concern for the nation and the entire society—he exhorted his compatriots—the gentry deliberating in the *Sejm* (Diet)—to "social harmony." In accordance with traditions of Renaissance poetics the poet put the exhortation in the mouth of a personified daughter of Love, Harmony, who maintained the proper rhythm and harmony so valued by Renaissance artists and audiences of the "contentious planets," the complex mechanism of the entire universe. Here the poet called upon Harmony to come to the descendents of Lech and determine their actions. Kochanowski also expressed the atmosphere of social debate of his day and the uncertainty connected with it in one of his other early works, *Satyr albo Dziki Mąż* (The Satyr or the Wild Man) (three times in ca. 1564). In the dedication of the poem to the king, Sigismund Augustus (Zygmunt August), Jan Kochanowski addressed the monarch thus: " 'Panie mój' (to nawiętszy tytuł u swobodnych)" [" 'My Lord' (This is the highest title among free men)"]. The words contain the pride of a Renaissance Polish nobleman, his feeling of freedom under law binding both the ruler and his subjects and based upon a common respect for that law. In his poetry, Jan Kochanowski also expressed pride in the achievements of Polish toleration that attracted the attention of humanists in various European countries torn by religious debates, struggles, and wars. Kochanowski clearly emphasized this in his Latin poem "*Gallo crocitanti*", in which he polemicizes with the French poet and courtier of Henri de Valois, Philippe Desportes, the author of a libelous verse about Poland. In this polemic Kochanowski pointed out that such events as the St. Bartholomew's Day Massacre would be impossible in Poland, where neither dagger nor sword constitute an argument in religious or political disputes.

Kochanowski's works are the crowning achievement of the Renaissance in Polish literature and they were composed at a time that constitutes the zenith of the Renaissance in Polish literature. We can observe the first signs of humanism and Renaissance in Polish literature in Poland as early as the fifteenth century, particularly its latter half. These are still times described by historians of culture and literature as "the golden autumn of the Polish Middle Ages."[3] This was the time of the historical writings of Jan Długosz, in whose work, style, vision of the past, and relation to the tradition of antiquity, the "new" meets with the "old." This was the time of the activities and writings of Gregory of Sanok (Grzegorz z Sanoka; Gregorius Sanocensis), who at his *Dunajów court* welcomed the refugee from Italy, a poet of the new style, Filippo Buonaccorsi, called from the Greek, Callimachus. As a poet, Callimachus was also active at other centers, first of all in Cracow, where at the court of King Casimir the Jagiellonian (Kazimierz Jagiellończyk), and among the scholars of the University of Cracow he was highly regarded as a poet. Callimachus observed the coexistence of aspects of the old and new styles even in the early writings of Gregory of Sanok, in his poems and primarily in his Latin prose.

At the turn of the fifteenth and sixteenth centuries, during the first quarter of the sixteenth century, Renaissance humanistic poetry written primarily in Latin developed more markedly as did prose writings. Works in the new style gained increasing recognition, as indicated by the poetic contests on the occasion of the wedding of King Sigismund I with Barbara Zápolya in 1512, and then on the occasion of his second marriage to Bona Sforza d'Aragona in 1518. Polish poets, primarily Andrzej Krzycki (Critius) and Jan Dantyszek (Dantiscus), as well as poets from abroad, participated in these contests. The first quarter of the sixteenth century brings the complete victory of the Renaissance style in Latin poetry in Poland. From the pens of Krzycki, Dantyszek, and Mikołaj Hussowski (Hussovianus) flowed Renaissance poetry of high artistic merit highly regarded both in Poland and throughout Europe. In his *Ciceronianus* (printed in 1528), Erasmus of Rotterdam noted Polish poets as well among the outstanding writers of various European countries. He singled out Andrzej Krzycki in particular, who "composes verse with talent" and "has an even better command of prose," and who "with a thorough education" combines ease and artistry in style of expression—the qualities most highly valued among Renaissance humanists.[4]

Krzycki, a poet and epistolographer, corresponding (like Dantyszek) with many European humanists, including Erasmus of Rotterdam, also made a contribution to the history of Polish art that is not always appreciated or even observed. In the years 1520-1527 when the project to build the Sigismund Chapel and remodel the royal castle matured and was realized, Krzycki—a trusted courtier of King Sigismund I and nephew and close collaborator of Piotr Tomicki, vice-chancellor of the crown, bishop of Cracow, and dispenser of royal patronage—maintained important ties with Bartolommeo Berrecci, the primary architect of the Sigismund Chapel.[5] Krzycki's connection with the creation of the Chapel, added on to the cathedral on Wawel Hill, is attested to by his Latin poem inscribed with the royal coat of arms (the Sigismundian eagle) on an outer wall of the building. Krzycki himself later became a famous patron of the arts and literature, as bishop of Płock and then archbishop of Gniezno. In the last years of his life he was the protector and patron of the youthful and talented Polish poet writing in Latin, Klemens Janicki (Janicius), the most outstanding lyric poet in Poland prior to Jan Kochanowski, and unfortunately prematurely deceased in the year 1542 or at the beginning of 1543.

Janicki composed masterful Latin elegies and epigrams, as well as satiric dialogues in which the interlocutors were the deceased King Władysław Jagiełło and the contemporary jester at the court of Sigismund I, Stańczyk, described with the Erasmian formula "morisophus." During his studies in Padua, Janicki earned a doctorate and the title "poeta laureatus"; he was well-regarded by Italian humanists, including Pietro Bembo himself. At the lectures of the famous Lazzaro Bonamico, Janicki came into contact with Filip Padniewski (who witnessed Janicki's doctoral promotion) and Piotr Myszkowski, both of whom in later years were Kochanowski's patrons and protectors and who began their activities in the humanist circle of Piotr Tomicki in Cracow. This is a notable testimony to the continuity of events in the Polish Renaissance in literature and patronage of literature.

Dantyszek, Krzycki, Mikołaj Hussowski and Janicki wrote poetry exclusively in Latin. Contemporaneously with them however, were poets who composed poetry in Polish, among these is Biernat of Lublin, who represents a slightly different type of literary culture. To this group also belongs Stanisław Kleryka (his real name, Gąsiorek), who like Krzycki and Dantyszek composed Renaissance court poetry. Unlike them, however, he wrote not in Latin but in Polish, as is attested by his poetic panegyrics written in 1529-1530 (as well as later works) on the occasion of the naming of the young Sigismund Augustus (during the lifetime of his father Sigismund I) as Grand Duke of Lithuania and King of Poland. Gąsiorek's poetry is wholly Renaissance in style and represents quite a high level of artistic mastery, although he did not equal Krzycki or Janicki and in writing in Polish undertook unquestionably a more difficult task than contemporary Polish Latin poets.

Polish literary historians for a considerable time debated the Renaissance and medieval characteristics of the writings of Biernat of Lublin, translator of the *Fables* and the *Life of Aesop*, as well as the medieval or Renaissance qualities of works by other writers of translations and adaptations of popular romances printed in Poland in the sixteenth century. While often still of medieval provenance, these works nevertheless may bear imprints of humanism in varying degrees. They often reached Poland from Bohemia or other regions of Europe. These were works which "co-created," we may say, the most mass, broad circulation in European literary culture of the time, and combined much of what the Middle Ages retained from antiquity, with what was transmitted by the Renaissance humanist culture of the new age. While this was a very important trend in literary culture of the time, it is one which does not lead directly to the work of Jan Kochanowski, but rather represents a current parallel to him, one of course not separated by an impenetrable barrier. No doubt Kochanowski himself did not disdain this type of literature. He has even left a little epigram in his *Fraszki* in which he commemorated the printing of a Polish version of a popular work of this kind, *Historyja trojańska* (A Trojan history) (1574). But Kochanowski himself did not write works intended for this kind of mass audience. I would like to emphasize, however, that in the sixteenth century the situation in Polish literature in the area of this kind of writing was no different from that in other European countries. Polish literature evidences numerous analogies with what was occurring not only in the central European countries closest to Poland culturally, but also in countries such as France. Even in Italy, where the Renaissance triumphed the earliest, similar phenomena can also be found.[6]

The works of Mikołaj Rej composed primarily about 1543, represent a similar relationship to the inheritance of the Middle Ages and of antiquity. His works reached back to the heritage of antiquity not only directly but also through medieval culture.[7] The year 1543, the year of the printing of Rej's *Krótka rozprawa miedzy trzema osobami: Panem, Wójtem, a Plebanem* (A short conversation among three persons: a Squire, a Bailiff, and a Parson), was a date significant not only in the history of Polish culture as the year of the appearance of Mikołaj Kopernik's (Copernicus) great work, but it was also a date significant in the history of Polish literature for now the poetic achievements of Krzycki and Janicki belonged to the past. Instead, a generation of young writers entered the literary arena—writers born at the beginning of the sixteenth century and contemporaries of Rej (b. 1505) or Andrzej Frycz Modrzewski (b. around 1503), or who were even younger, like Stanisław Orzechowski (Orichovius) (b. 1513) or Marcin Kromer (b. around 1512). The year 1543 was extremely significant in the literary activities of precisely these writers. Not only did Rej's *Krótka rozprawa* . . . appear, but Orzechowski's *Turcica* and Andrzej Frycz Modrzewski's outstanding literary debut in the form of a speech on the enactment of uniform punishment for murder *Lascius sive, de poena homicidii* were published.

This was a literary generation which had to define its attitude toward the Reformation, developing extraordinarily dynamically in those years in Poland, toward the first signs of which Andrzej Krzycki was rather unfavorably disposed (as evidenced by his satiric *Encomia Lutheri*) and Janicki remained completely indifferent. It was a generation which reacted intensely to the widely and enthusiastically discussed problems of reform of customs, of the mechanisms of functioning of the state and church, of the molding of the image of "an honest man" (*człowiek poczciwy*, the counterpart of the Latin formula of the time, *homo honestus*), a man who would be able to live with dignity and justice, a credit to himself, his surroundings, and his society. Questions of "civil life" (*życie obywatelskie*) that occupied the attention of Renaissance thinkers and writers in Italy (*vita civile*) and in other European countries were important for the pioneers of humanism in Poland even in the fifteenth century; questions about finding the most perfect form of religious expression and organization of denominational life were leading topics in the writings of Rej and Frycz Modrzewski, and their contemporary, Stanisław Hozjusz (Hosius), as well as of the already noted, slightly younger Kromer and Orzechowski. The peak of these writers' activity occurs in the 50's and the beginning of the 60's of the sixteenth century.

These were years of domination of prose over poetic literature, although Rej composed many of his works in verse. They were years of polemics and de-

bates. They were also years in which representatives of another new generation
of Polish Renaissance writers matured. Somewhat overshadowed by the writings of Rej, Frycz Modrzewski, Kromer and Orzechowski, these writers absorbed their youthful readings and what is more important, they undertook
their first literary efforts. The work of this generation and its most eminent
representatives Jan Kochanowski and Łukasz Górnicki (nephew of the above-
mentioned Stanisław Gąsiorek) constitutes the apogee of the Polish Renaissance
in literature.

Górnicki, born in 1527, was slightly older than Kochanowski, but their life
and intellectual experience, the extent of reading, taste, and predilections allow
us to treat them as representatives of the same generation. They developed in
the atmosphere of Renaissance Cracow and their sojourns in Italy (especially
Padua) exerted a great influence on their intellectual formation. After traveling
abroad, they found their places at the court of Sigismund Augustus alongside
other former Paduans who were now guiding royal politics, the vice-chancellors
Filip Padniewski and Piotr Myszkowski. The eminent philologist and orator
Andrzej Patrycy Nidecki, the closest companion of Kochanowski and Górnicki,
and Wawrzyniec Goślicki (Goslicius; Laurentius Grimalius), author of *De optimo
senatore libri duo*, both belonged to this generation of Paduans who later became
royal secretaries. Their generation achieved its full maturity in the mid- 60's
of the sixteenth century precisely around 1565.[8]

At that time Rej, Frycz Modrzewski, Orzechowski, and Kromer were still
writing. Rej's *Żywot człowieka poczciwego* (Life of an honest man), part of the
collection entitled *Źwierciadło* ... (The Mirror), appeared only in the years 1567/
1568. In the estimation of comtemporary writers and intellectuals already in
1564-65 Kochanowski and Górnicki had attained universal recognition. They
remain recognized as the most excellent Polish writers of that time. Mikołaj
Rej expressed a flattering opinion of Jan Kochanowski's writing in his *Źwierzyniec* (The Zodiac of Life) at the turn of 1561/62. In the year 1564 an expression
of the *opinio communis* appears in the words of the anonymous author of *Proteus
albo Odmieniec* (*Proteus, or the changing one*) stating that Kochanowski had surpassed Rej and equalled the excellence of the masters of Hellas and Rome. In
the same year (1564), Andrzej Patrycy Nidecki in sending a copy of Kochanowski's *Satyr* ... to Hozjusz (Hosius) stated that the young poet was excellent
in both Polish and Latin verse, and in the latter language had exceeded the
achievements of the highly-regarded Janicki.

By the mid-60's of the sixteenth century Kochanowski, as the author of the
printed works, the hymn "*Czego chcesz od nas, Panie, za Twe hojne dary*" ("What
do you wish, o Lord, in return for your bounteous gifts"), *Zuzanna, Szachy*
(Chess), *Zgoda* (Harmony), *Satyr* ... (The Satyr), the epicedium *O śmierci Jana
Tarnowskiego* ... (On the death of Jan Tarnowski ...), as well as quite widely
known privately circulated handwritten copies of the earlier version of *Elegiarum libri duo*, and a version no longer extant of the *Fraszki*, and Górnicki, as
the author of *Dworzanin polski* (The Polish courtier), (completed by the middle

of 1565 and printed in 1566), together were recognized in Poland as the most excellent writers, whose accomplishments surpassed what the older generation of writers had created and continued to create. They were recognised as writers who equalled the masters of antiquity as well as the contemporary literary attainments of writers in other European nations. In the minds of their contemporaries, the new generation of writers had achieved a dominant position in Polish literature, and with this generation Polish literature of the Renaissance would attain the peak of its development.

Kochanowski and Górnicki themselves were also aware of their own great success. Łukasz Górnicki's preface to *The Polish Courtier*, dated July 18, 1565 and addressed to King Sigismund Augustus, eloquently testifies to this consciousness. It was a characteristic manifesto of the generation of writers centered most strongly during these years (later it would be different) around the patronage of the royal court, who while aware of their success, had no intention of resting on their laurels. In particular, Kochanowski considered his early recognition as an obligation to create still finer works.

In their writings Kochanowski and Górnicki did not in the least deprecate the real problems pervading Polish society in the 1560's, as evidenced by Kochanowski's *Harmony* and *The Satyr* ... and Górnicki's early unpreserved works, as well as even his major work *The Polish Courtier*. For Frycz Modrzewski and Orzechowski, outstanding stylists, experts in the arcana of humanist rhetoric and the application of its achievements in their own writings, the primacy of practicality was especially important. They accepted practicality as the leading imperative of their own writing through the influence of Erasmus of Rotterdam in his *Adagia* and *Enchiridion*. That primacy of practicality was no less emphasized by Mikołaj Rej. But for Kochanowski and Górnicki especially essential was that their writing be not only wise and useful, but to an equal, certainly no lesser degree, that it fulfill the ideals proper to the classicism of the mature Renaissance, ideals determining the perception of beauty: harmony, decorum, and grace (*gratia*).

As a poet the young Kochanowski enjoyed the recognition of Rej, who while viewing the goals and obligations of his work differently, undoubtedly appreciated the generally accepted Renaissance conviction based on Horatian counsels that the writer should both teach and entertain the reader. But how did Kochanowski view Rej's writing? As a young man, Kochanowski, who was immediately acknowledged as a more outstanding poet than Rej, and then even later as he moved toward the peak of his literary maturity, Kochanowski treated Rej's writing with full respect. Precisely as an author already fully aware of his own success, he stressed—*nota bene* in a Latin elegy—that Rej was his eminent predecessor in Polish literature and that he, Kochanowski, now followed in those footsteps to create a great Polish Renaissance poetry.

Was this merely an expression of courtesy? I think that Kochanowski surely realized the distance which separated his Polish literary creation from that of Rej and the acclaim which his work had met among his contemporaries, but perhaps precisely because of this Kochanowski was not concerned with idle flattery of Rej's writing, but wished to stress all Rej's true contributions. For Rej was not only a traditionalist, a writer still linked by many threads to medieval culture. He was first and foremost a writer wishing to adopt everything from the inheritance of the nearer and more distant past (antiquity), and from the wealth of his own time that might be useful in his own work, that might teach and entertain the reader in order more effectively to accomplish moral edification. Rej adopted diligently, even rapaciously absorbing and accumulating the most diverse and heterogeneous material, seeking inspiration for the construction of his own works in numerous and varied ancient, medieval, and contemporary writings. It was Rej who in his *Wizerunk własny żywota człowieka poczciwego* (A faithful image of an honest man) paraphrased the *Zodiacus vitae*, the monumental work of the Italian humanist, Palingenius, an undertaking highly valued by Kochanowski. It was Rej who referred to the fashionable *Emblemata* (Emblems) of Alciatus (Andrea Alciati), a work representing a new genre in European literature, which immediately gained great esteem.[9] Rej freely delved into and utilized ancient and contemporary collections of all kinds of dicta, apothegms, fables, and tales. But it should be remembered that such literature in sixteenth-century Europe was by no means an anachronism. Like the earlier Polish writing of Biernat of Lublin or his European counterparts, such writings represented instead a vigorous current of popular literature circulating among broad masses of readers in the early, mid-, and late Renaissance period. In the writing of the mid-sixteenth-century French author, Gilles Corrozet, translator of Aesop's *Fables* and author of the multi-genre collection of literary miscellany, *Hecatomgraphie...* (1540), we find a strikingly analogous construction to that of Rej's *Źwierzyniec* (The Zodiac of Life) printed "for the year 1562" (i.e., most likely at the end of 1561), and containing emblems, *icones*, dicta, apothegms, fables, tales, and anecdotes. Not accidentally are analogies between the work of Rej and Rabelais pointed out. But those between Rej and Corrozet, highly respected in sixteenth- century France, are even more indicative. One can find many writers who represent this kind of literary culture, authors of similar sixteenth- century works and compendia, in various European countries during Renaissance and Reformation times.

Jan Kochanowski represented another kind of literary culture, however; like Górnicki and his Italian master Castiglione, he was a Renaissance classicist, a student of the University of Padua and its masters, and most likely a listener and reader of the works of Francesco Robortello. Kochanowski wrote after Rej, but had no intention of writing like Rej. Quite the contrary—he intended to write differently. However, he fully appreciated the fact that Rej deliberately wrote in Polish and wanted to adapt for literature in the national language, as much as possible, that which he considered useful and worthwhile from past and present literature. Rej's concept to not only serve his countrymen with his writing but convince the "neighboring nations" that "Poles have a tongue of their own" (*"A niechaj narodowie wżdy postronni znają / Iż Polacy nie gęsi, iż swój język mają"*)[10] and could express themselves on different subjects and create varied works was not an idea foreign to Kochanowski. Kochanowski only understood it more profoundly and more throroughly drew practical conclusions from it.

It is sometimes said that Rej wrote exclusively in Polish because he was a writer connected with the Reformation, and the Reformation particularly demanded the writing in national languages and translation of the Bible into national languages. While this is of course true, it should be remembered that the demands of Reformation denominations were accepted by reform-minded representatives of the Roman church, although they did not at that time agree to a complete introduction of national languages into the liturgy. But during the Renaissance, particularly the high Renaissance, writers completely (or almost completely) unconnected with confessional disputes and polemics demanded writing in the national language. This was an expression of the awakened and increasingly spreading national consciousness. At a certain stage in the maturing of this consciousness it became essential to create a great literature in national languages, a kind of literature once created in their own languages by the great poets and writers of Greece and Rome, a kind of literature like which the sacred books, the Old and New Testaments, became and remain for the Hebrews and then for Christianity. Such a task was undertaken by the eminent Italian humanists and by the poets of the French *Pléiade*. Such a task was also undertaken by Jan Kochanowski and his friend, Łukasz Górnicki.

Like Joachim Du Bellay, the author of the manifesto of *La Pléiade*, Kochanowski remained to be sure a bilingual poet writing in his native tongue and in Latin, but he attached particular significance to his work created in Polish. Writing in Latin, he was aware of belonging to the international Renaissance community of humanist writers; writing in Polish, he was aware of creating a great national Polish literature, a literature as was said then, worthy of Orpheus, the first poet, the arch-poet. Precisely as a poet writing in Polish and creating outstanding works in this language which included the poetic paraphrase of the Psalms, *Psałterz Dawidów* (David's Psalter), Kochanowski proudly declared:

> I wdarłem się na skałę pięknej Kallijopy,
> Gdzie dotychmiast nie było znaku polskiej stopy.[11]

> And I scaled the rock of beautiful Calliope
> Where hitherto no Pole has left his footprint.

This was the "rock" named after the mother of Orpheus and according to men of the Renaissance only the most outstanding writers reached its summit.[12] Jan Kochanowski, conscious of his own great poetic achievements, included himself among these "poets of Calliope."

Jan Kochanowski was a very ambitious writer, aware of the need to create a great national literature and no less aware that he was creating it. In the

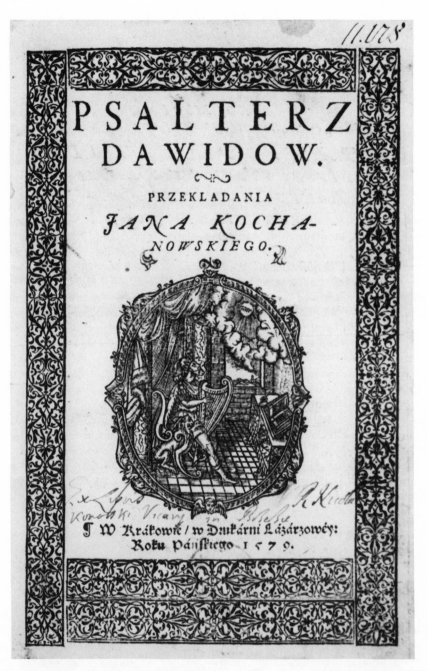

52. Jan Kochanowski, *Psałterz Dawidów*, w Krakowie, 1579. The title page of the first edition (Biblioteka Czartoryskich, Kraków). For the facsimile of the second 1583 edition see Jan Kochanowski, *Dzieła Wszystkie*. Wydanie Sejmowe vol. 1, Part 1, *Psałterz Dawidów*, ed. Jerzy Woronczak (Wrocław: Ossolineum, 1982).

MELODIÆ
Ná Pſalterz Polski, przez Mikoláiá Gomólke vczynioné.

W Krákowie

W Drukárni Lázárzowéy : Roku páńſkiégo

1 5 8 0.

53. *Melodie na Psałterz Polski* przez Mikołaja Gomółkę uczynione, w Krakowie, 1580. The title page of the first edition of Mikołaj Gomółka's Melodies to Jan Kochanowski's translation of the Psalter (Biblioteka Czartoryskich, Kraków). Reprinted from the facsimile edition by Mirosław Perz (Kraków: PWM, 1981), and Jan Kochanowski, *Dzieła Wszystkie*. Wydanie Sejmowe, vol. 1, Part 4 (Wrocław: Ossolineum, 1983).

54. The second page of Kochanowski's letter to Stanisław Fogelweder of October 6, 1571 concerning his work on the translation of *David's Psalter*. Facsimile of the lost autograph in Jan Kochanowski, *Dzieła Wszystkie*. Wydanie Sejmowe. vol. 1, Part 1. *Psałterz Dawidów*, ed. Jerzy Woronczak (Wrocław: Ossolineum, 1982).

earlier version of his Latin *Elegies* (*Elegiarum libri duo*) (in the final, substantially reworked edition there were four books), he states that in following the masters of antiquity he competed with them for precedence, which was in accordance with the principle of imitation already proposed by Petrarch for ambitious writers of his time. For Kochanowski, this would be competition not only, nor primarily, with the Roman elegists, but with their Greek masters, with Callimachus, considered the creator of the elegy (according to, among others, Francesco Robortello). Renaissance humanists voiced the slogan *"ad fontes"* ("to the sources"), desiring to establish a link with the masters of their masters. Hence Kochanowski's fascination with the Greek literature to which writers of ancient Rome once had referred, hence his translation of Book III of the *Iliad*, his undertaking to translate a fragment of Euripides' tragedy about Alcestis, and his numerous translations of Anacreontic poetry, and poetry from the Greek anthology so revelatory for Renaissance writers in Europe. He also translated and imitated the "songs more valuable than gold" (*"Pieśni nad złoto droższe"*) of the Roman lyric master, Horace. He paraphrased the masterpiece of the Hebrew biblical lyric, the Psalter, translated into Greek, Latin, and many other languages. In this way he delved into three great traditions of antiquity, those of Greece, Rome, and the Bible, treating them together, syncretically, as one great tradition of the ancient world.[13] In creating a great national literature, the Master of Czarnolas naturally did not overlook the experience of Renaissance writers of his own day. Nor did he overlook native Polish tradition. He appreciated the works of his Polish predecessors, including Rej, nevertheless fully realizing that he himself accomplished a task far more important and ambitious. He held the heritage of national and folk culture, native customs and habits in high regard as well. Through the words of the first Maiden in *Pieśń świętojańska o Sobótce* (Song of St. John's Eve), the Czarnolas poet very clearly emphasized that the values and customs of a culture survive because they are passed on to ever new successive generations whose duty it is to hand down this valuable inheritance to their offspring. John Bowring, the nineteenth-century English translator of Kochanowski's poetry, rendered it as follows:

... from centuries far away,
Upon St. John's joy-rousing night
Sobótka's festal fire to light.[14]

In his poetry Kochanowski wished to preserve the memory of Midsummer folk rites, songs, and dances and transmit these to the next generations. But their beauty and unique color he sought to meld integrally into the material of his own poetry. Of course, we should necessarily be wary of detecting signs of folklore in *Pieśń świętojańska o Sobótce*. For here elements from antiquity, Polish and folk elements, and as have been pointed out, certain Renaissance analogies with popular Italian literature, are undoubtedly combined and reworked into a unified, cohesive whole. Kochanowski's relationship to tradition, not only in this cycle, but throughout his *ouvre*, is a highly complex question;

he was marked by the syncretism typical for outstanding writers of the high Renaissance in Europe.[15] Renaissance poetics and the statements of writers themselves, most notably Petrarch and Erasmus of Rotterdam, often recalled and attached great significance to a comparison, known from the writings of Plato and Seneca, between the work of the writer, poet, and artist and the work of the bee. Like the bees, writers gather nectar from the gardens of the literature of different times, distant and near, and from these nectars they had to make honey, the works they compose. According to the quality of this "honey" one would recognize the rank of the creators, the artists of words. In the works of the greatest Renaissance writers, the components of the "honey" are often difficult to distinguish, much less clearly to isolate. They have melted inseparably into a new whole. Just such a situation occurs in the poetry of Jan Kochanowski, and this unquestionably testifies eloquently to its artistic value, indicating the highest order.

The epopee, the tragedy, and the hymn occupied a particularly important and high place in the Renaissance hierarchy of literary genres. The most prominent writers of the national literatures of the time attempted to cultivate these especially valued genres. The already famous Ronsard, admired and esteemed by Kochanowski at the beginning of his career, had written many hymns. Known and respected Italian poets and poets of other countries also wrote hymns. The young Kochanowski also created a hymn "*Czego chcesz od nas, Panie, za Twe hojne dary*", (What do you wish, O Lord, in return for your bounteous gift) described by Wiktor Weintraub as the "Renaissance manifesto" of the Polish poet.[16]

Renaissance humanist elites and creators of national literatures attached particular significance to their accomplishments in the realm of the great epic, the epic poem. Petrarch, the precursor of the Renaissance in Italy, had already written a great epic work, the Latin poem entitled *Africa*, considered to be an epic about the ancient history of his nation. Little is remembered about it today; only the lyrics of the "singer of Laura" are still read and admired. Ronsard intended to compose a great epic poem with the significant title, *Franciade*. He even composed the first four songs out of an intended twenty-four. But he went no further. For posterity he remains the poet of great lyrics. It was only the Portugese Renaissance poet, Luis Camões, who managed to create a great epic poem entitled *Os Lusiadas*, a work in ten songs that is admired and translated until today. Camões expressed himself most fully in it, although he was also a writer of lyric poetry. In sixteenth century Italy Lodovico Ariosto and Torquato Tasso created great epic poems. But Italian literature of the time was more dominated by lyric and dramatic genres, and by smaller epic poems including mock-heroic poems. Different kinds of pastoral poetry were also increasingly regarded.

Jan Kochanowski also dreamed of creating a great national epic poem. He even began writing one in the form of a poem about Polish history under the Jagiellon kings, or perhaps it was to have been only about the famous deeds of Władysław III (Warneńczyk), king of Poland and Hungary (killed fighting the Turks at the Battle of Varna in 1444). Today it is difficult to answer even this basic question about the topic of the work, since only small fragments of it have remained.[17] Jan Kochanowski was unable to complete as much of his epic as did Ronsard of his *Franciade*. He wrote, however epic poetry on a smaller scale, such as *Szachy* (Chess), *Pamiątka ... Janowi Baptyście hrabi na Tęczynie ...* (Memorial ... to Jan Baptist, count of Tęczyn), or *Proporzec albo Hołd pruski* (The Banner, or Homage from Prussia). In a later expanded version of the Elegies Kochanowski included a tale about the ancient legendary Polish princess, Wanda (I,15), but none of these constituted the fulfillment of the dream to create a great epic poem. Instead, the dream had to be given up, and the poet bade it farewell on a melancholy, but also a characteristically humorous note, tinged with irony, or more properly, auto-irony, when he wrote in an Anacreontic verse in the *Fraszki* (I,4):

> Lutnia swym zwyczajem g'woli
> O miłości śpiewać woli.
> Bóg was żegnaj, krwawe boje,
> Nie lubią was strony moje.[18]

> The lute as is its custom
> Prefers to sing of love.
> God bid you farewell, bloody battles,
> My voice does not like you.

It was in drama that Kochanowski was more successful, in the field of tragedy that was so highly regarded by theoreticians and writers of Renaissance tragedies. Here the Polish poet truly accomplished a great deal, although less than he demanded of himself in his extraordinarily ambitious plans. *Odprawa posłów greckich* (*The Dismissal of the Greek Envoys*), performed for the first time in January of 1578, was a work which equalled contemporary European achievements. In Poland, the work opens the history of modern tragedy, and its staging begins the history of theater that deals with great moral and moral-political problems, that addresses itself to the conscience of the citizenry and to those "who govern the Republic" ("*którzy Pospolitą Rzeczą władali*"). The poet's famous words, "*mistrz nie po temu*" ("the master is not up to it") in a letter to Jan Zamoyski, dated December 22, 1577, printed as a preface or dedication to the work, were not simply a coquettish disclaimer. These were the words of an artist proud of his accomplishments, and especially of his successful attempt in the construction of the choruses, of which the "third almost equals the Greek choruses" ("*trzeci jakoby chorom greckim przygania*"), that is, equals them in excellence. The chorus in question begins with the words: "*O białoskrzydła, morska pławaczko*" ("O white- winged sea swimmer") written in blank verse with a varied syllabic form imitating the rhythm, metaphors, and sentence order of the choruses of Greek tragedy. And alongside these proud words is an uncertainty typical of the ambitious writer: "I do not know what it will sound like in the Polish

language" (*"Nie wiem, jako to w polskim języku brzmieć będzie"*).[19] Precisely because
of the innovatory character of his writing Kochanowski must have experienced
such doubts frequently and he was not ashamed of them. Like the Italian
Renaissance dramatists, Kochanowski translated Euripides and composed his
The Dismissal of the Greek Envoys in unrhymed blank verse. That itself was an
important artistic achievement, but particular satisfaction as well as artistic
doubt was caused by the third chorus, its skillful metric and stylistic construction lending the requisite tragic pathos. Nevertheless, Kochanowski expected
something more from his tragedy. Thus, the founder of modern Polish tragedy
and creator of Polish drama about the community—so significant for the subsequent history of Polish drama of the romantics, for Wyspiański, and for later
writers as pointed out by Claude Backvis[20]—realized after composing the *The
Dismissal of the Greek Envoys* that tragedy was not the genre in which he could
express himself most fully and most perfectly. Despite his unquestionable
achievements as a dramatist, Kochanowski realized that he was and would
remain first and foremost a lyric poet. Posterity has confirmed this, as it has
continued to seek and find in Petrarch, Ronsard, and Kochanowski great and
living lyric voices.

Kochanowski's lyric output consists not only of hymns, although he expressed himself in this form early and perfectly. His major lyric forms are
songs, written in Polish and in Latin, and lyric epigrams dealing with both the
great and small matters of everyday human affairs, indicating how one should
live to be worthy of the name man, lyric poetry which is a constant companion
in good and bad times, bringing joy and assuaging the "troubled spirit" (*"myśl
utrapiona"*). These lyrics reveal the lures and delusions of fickle Fortune. They
present the thinking and feeling man in various dimensions of time and space
that man himself organizes in a special way, taking on to a degree the role of
a demiurge, or at least of a creator of a literary vision which places the visible
world concentrically around the perceiving subject of the lyric. According to
Renaissance artists (and Kochanowski particularly emphasizes this), man not
only determines the vision of the world around him, but also defines his nature,
his personality. As Giovanni Pico della Mirandola wrote in *De hominis dignitate
oratio*, man is the being to whom God has once said:

> The nature of all other beings is limited and constrained within the
> bounds of laws prescribed by Us. Thou, constrained by no limits, in
> accordance with thine own free will, in whose hand We have placed
> thee, shalt ordain for thyself the limits of thy nature. We have set
> thee at the world's center that thou mayest from thence more easily
> observe whatever is in the world. We have made thee neither of
> heaven nor of earth, neither mortal nor immortal, so that with free-
> dom of choice and with honor, as though the maker and molder of
> thyself, thou mayest fashion thyself in whatever shape thou shalt
> prefer.[21]

But even for Pico, man's greatest power of self-creation had certain limits.
He saw both the splendor and misery of human existence. All the more so for

Kochanowski the freedom of self-creation was not absolute. Freedom is conditioned by the most varied circumstances, but not totally. Man—"composed with a dual nature" (*"ze dwojej natury złożony"*)—chooses as he can and he is *able*, that form for his life and personality that is either worthy of human greatness or fettered by immediate desires and illusory gain. The ability to make that choice distinguishes man from all other creatures; this choice must be worthy of man. This is the guiding thought in Kochanowski's lyric poetry of the *Songs*, *Fraszki*, the Latin *Elegies*, the *Foricoenia*, and the odes in the collection *Lyrica*. We also find it of course in his cyclical poem on the great world view crisis of the Renaissance poet-intellectual when experiencing life's harshest blow, *Treny* (Laments). For the *Laments* express how difficult it is in moments of severe trial to maintain human dignity, and yet how one must do so nevertheless. Attainment of this goal was the highest achievement for the human being.

However, Kochanowski's lyric hero, man, is distinguished from other living creatures not only by his sense of and fulfillment of the requirements of dignity, of dignified behavior. He is also distinguished by the gift of speech, intellectual expression, and besides, by laughter:

> Sam ze wszytkiego stworzenia
> Człowiek ma śmiech z przyrodzenia...

In John Bowring's translation:

> To man—to man alone has Heaven
> The privilege of laughter given.[22]

This idea, known if only from Aristotle, was expressed by many European Renaissance writers; we need mention only Ronsard and Rabelais as examples. In the lyrics of Jan of Czarnolas, a thinking man who chooses a life worthy of humanity is a being who enjoys the beauties of the world and of life, laughing for amusement at others and at himself, criticizing with humor the failures and weaknesses of others and his own, and with both good-natured and biting irony or auto-irony observing their complaints, the great and small affairs of the world, and the behavior of others and of the perceiving subject as well. In this sense of greatness and smallness, intimacy and distance, beauty and misery, good and evil, is expressed a sense of human worth as well.

A virtuous life and poetry that expresses the beauty of such a life worthy of humanity, the beauty of a rational universe occupy the highest places in the value system created in Kochanowski's poetry. And as we have said above, poetry would be the necessary companion for such a worthy human existence, speaking about beauty and fascinating man with the beauty of her own unique order.

As a Renaissance *poeta doctus*, Kochanowski attached great significance to knowledge of and adherence to the poetic rules. Knowledge, the foundation of poetic invention, facilitated proper choice of appropriate rules of composition, selection of the most appropriate construction of genres. Let us take an example. In undertaking the composition of a poetic work which he wished to be the most fitting monument to his beloved Orszula, which would express the pain and shock, the intellectual and world view crisis of a poet-father, Kochanowski could employ more traditional composition, according to the rules of a unified *"epicedium raz mówionego"* (*"epicedium igitur semel tantum dicitur"*) as advocated in Scaliger's *Poetics* (1561), or he could choose a composition more fashionable and highly regarded, but from Greek tradition, the composition of a cycle of laments.

In an earlier work, Kochanowski had selected the first solution when in 1561 he had written in Polish the epicedium, *O śmierci Jana Tarnowskiego ...* (On the death of Jan Tarnowski ...) On the eve of the 1580's, as a fully mature artist setting the highest demands for himself, he chose a solution, as we may say, which was at that time innovative, although Renaissance poets and theoreticians (Robortello's opinion being important here) had found a real or supposedly real antecedent for cyclic compositions in Greek antiquity.

Selection of the rules also applied to elocution, expression, and style. Kochanowski was the master of the generalization, allusion, irony, and epigrammatic conciceness, found not only in the *Fraszki*. Among all the possibilities, Kochanowski chose the suitable word or phrase and this distinguishes his poetry from the prolixity of Rej's poetry and prose. The modern Polish lyric and its poetic styles, familiar and readable today, was born in this selection process.

The practice of subsequent generations of poets and the further development of the Polish literary language, the lyric in particular, has confirmed these choices. Precisely for this reason Kochanowski's poetry is readable and comprehensible today, although this accessibility is sometimes only apparent. This has even caused trouble for many commentators, not to mention less well-prepared readers, pupils and students of Polish literature. Sometimes translators of Polish poetry encounter difficulties. In general, Kochanowski's language is more readable today than, for example, the French of Ronsard and the poets of *La Pléiade*. But changes in language have inevitably occurred, and may create traps during reading and especially for translation. We may take as a relatively simple but illustrative example, the opening of Lament IV, where we read:

Zgwałciłaś, niepobożna Śmierci, oczy moje,
Żem widział umierając miłe dziecię swoje![23]

Unholy death, thou hast brought injury to my eyes,
I have seen dying the kind child of mine.

Were this a contemporary statement, we would think that the poet-father saw his own child at the moment of his own death (*"umierając"*). In the text of the *Laments*, *"umierając"* refers to *"dziecię"*, the child. The poet-father saw *"umierające"* (dying) his beloved child, he saw her precisely when or while she was dying.

Difficulties in reading and especially in translation are of course not only a matter of understanding the peculiarities of the writing of the time in which the work was written. They are also a matter of understanding Renaissance poetics and the individual features of the language of the Master of Czarnolas. Kochanowski himself fully realized the difficulties and all the troubles of translation. In a letter from Czarnolas dated October 6, 1571, Kochanowski writes about this to Stanisław Fogelweder concerning his (Kochanowski's) work on a poetic translation of the Psalms. His friend Fogelweder advised him to follow specific rules in translation, only we don't know today exactly which ones, since Fogelweder's letter to Kochanowski has not survived and Kochanowski's answer does not specify them. But what is ultimately more important for us today is that Kochanowski considered knowledge of the rules (undoubtedly not only the one applicable to the paraphrase of the Psalms and encouraged by Fogelweder but all the rules) insufficient. Knowledge of all the rules could be important in writing, but Kochanowski could not imagine the possibility of producing a worthwhile poetic translation (in this case his *Psalter*) without an attempt to penetrate the ethereal, almost elusive and undefineable essence of the work which infuses it with a unique poetic magic.

In my opinion, for Kochanowski such comments formulated in connection with work on the poetic paraphrase of the Psalms refer more broadly to all poetic creation (*nota bene*, we may find similar thoughts in other Renaissance writers, for examples, as in the case of the manifesto of Du Bellay).[24] In the practice of poetic art an extraordinarily important role was played by *"necessitas"*, the knowledge of the constraints, the rules, but no less important was *"poetika, nescio quid blandum spirans"* ("poetry which breathed with that uncapturable magic").[25] For Kochanowski the translation of poetic texts especially such a masterpiece of lyric poetry as the *Psalter*, as well as less refined, minor and transitory texts, constituted the *creation of poetry*.

At different points in his literary career, Jan Kochanowski endeavored to define the essence of his creative personality, revealing himself although not always completely and not always directly through the construction of the speaking subject. He aptly compared his transformations as a man and artist to those of Proteus, a particularly expressive and noble comparison in Renaissance times.[26] Let us recall, for example, that Erasmus of Rotterdam saw in the transformations of Proteus symbolic representations of Christ. How highly Pico valued the comparison between the thinking man defining his own nature and Proteus! In an earlier version of his Latin *Elegies* known only in manuscript, Kochanowski describes his creative personality as a "singer of Love" (*"piewca Miłości"*) in the broad neoplatonic sense of that word, in the sense of Love which animates the universe. As early as the 1560's Kochanowski revealed yet another attitude of the artist, an attitude which I would term the Socratic-Silenian. This attitude is characterized by irony and auto-irony of a mentor of society and yet its participant, one of many (*"jednego z wiela"*) who is a reflective observer expressing his views about the essence of human nature. At the time when he achieved his artistic maturity, Kochanowski—like many outstanding writers in different European literatures—set himself the goal to equal Orpheus, considered the first poet and the master of poets. Orphic excellence, according to the conviction of men of the Renaissance the zenith of the poet-artist's excellence, was achieved by Kochanowski following the development of his own art and that achievement, confirmed by others, Kochanowski himself testifies to in his own poetic statements.[27]

Utilizing the rich resources of the literature and poetry of antiquity broadly understood including Greek literature, Roman literature, and the Bible, Kochanowski created modern Polish poetry, and lyric poetry above all. He created modern Polish poetic styles, primarily lyric styles. Models of these poetic styles, particularly in the lyric, were adopted by later generations of Polish poets. Kochanowski also shaped the model of modern Polish versification, most importantly in its syllabic form. He also defined the basic fund of Polish stanzas, enriched of course by Polish baroque and later poets. He established the form of Polish poetic genres, again mainly lyric but not only. It is enough to recall, for example, the history of the genre of Old Polish satirical-political and civil poetry which begins with the *Satyr albo Dziki Mąż* (The Satyr or the Wild Man).[28]

Already in his youth, Kochanowski described his hardships as a Renaissance poet-imitator as a struggle peculiar to him (*"certare"*) with the masters of antiquity. As I mentioned, Petrarch had already clearly challenged ambitious poets with this struggle in his letter, *"Ad Thomam Mensenensem,"* stating that imitation of the masters should be based on competition with them for the achievement of excellence. In this sense, *"imitare"* meant the same as *"certare"*.[29] The principle of Renaissance imitation, the work of the poet-bee was understood in just this way by Kochanowski in his writing of Latin poetry and even more clearly in his poetry written in Polish. His efforts and achievements in this field were probably first fully appreciated by Maciej Kazimierz Sarbiewski, himself an outstanding poet and author of treatises on poetry.[30] Subsequent generations of poets accepted the achievements of Jan Kochanowski as a codifier of Polish poetry, its versification and poetic styles.

Toward the close of 1558 or perhaps at the beginning of 1559, Kochanowski—after several long stays in Italy to whose culture and literature he owed so much—appeared briefly, in transit only, in Paris and in France. Here he "saw" Ronsard, admired as a poet, highly esteemed by the king and royal court, by French society, and by foreigners in Paris. Kochanowski's words, *"Ronsardum vidi,"* were a subtle poetic allusion to antiquity (*"Vergilum vidi tantum"*) and an expression of admiration for the achievements of the elder poet universally recognized as the creator of national literature. Kochanowski took on this same role after his return to Poland in mid-1559. It was not just a matter of equalling Ronsard, called the "French Orpheus," or any other master of poetry in Europe of the time. Kochanowski thought not only of his own personal success. Both in his early youthful work that was soon acclaimed, as well as later when as a recognized poet, he undertook his great poetic program, he aimed through his literary success to establish Polish poetry and literature as an equal partner with the leading European literatures of the time and with the great works of antiquity. And Kochanowski's achievements contributed greatly to the hastening of the pace of development of Polish literature. As a result, the first fruits of new directions, new styles, new formations in Polish literature, the beginnings of the baroque were able to appear in Poland at an early date, with no delay, a fact particularly remarkable when considered in the context of Europe north of the Alps.

Notes

1. The dates 20 and 24 August 1584 are given in Andrzej Trzecieski's poems on the occasion of Kochanowski's funeral edited with S.F. Klonowic' *Żale nagrobne* ... (Laments on the grave ...) (Kraków, 1585).

2. See Janusz Pelc, *Jan Kochanowski, Szczyt renesansu w literaturze polskiej* (Jan Kochanowski, Zenith of the Renaissance in Polish literature) (Warsaw: PWN, 1980), p. 15. We remain cautious towards these matters in *Cochanoviana I. Źródła urzędowe do biografii Jana Kochanowskiego* (Cochanoviana I. Official sources for the biography of Jan Kochanowski) by Maria Garbaczowa and Wacław Urban, ed. by Janusz Pelc (Wrocław: Ossolineum, 1985).

3. Henryk Samsonowicz, *Złota jesień polskiego średniowiecza* (Golden autumn of the Polish Middle Ages) (Warsaw: Wiedza Powszechna, 1971), passim. See also Janusz Pelc, "Renesans w literaturze polskiej. Początki i rozwój" (The Renaissance in Polish literature. Beginnings and development) in *Problemy literatury staropolskiej*, Series 1 (Wrocław: Ossolineum, 1972), p. 42.

4. Erasmus Rotherodamus, *De recta Latini Graecique sermonis pronuntiatione ... Dialogus. Eiusdem ... Ciceronianus.* (Lugduni, 1528), pp. 248-249.

5. Karol Estreicher, "Szkice o Berreccim" (Essays on Berrecci), *Rocznik Krakowski* 43 (1972): 92-94; Janusz Pelc, "Renesans w literaturze polskiej" p. 61; Janusz Pelc, "Europejskość i swoistość literatury polskiego renesansu" (The European character and the specificity of Polish Renaissance literature) in *Literatura staropolska i jej związki europejskie. Prace poświęcone VII Międzynarodowemu Kongresowi Slawistów w Warszawie w roku 1973*, ed. Janusz Pelc (Wrocław: Ossolineum, 1973), p. 31; Stanisław Mossakowski, "Tematyka mitologiczna dekoracji Kaplicy Zygmuntowskiej" (The mythological theme in the decoration of the Sigismund chapel, *Biuletyn Historii Sztuki*, 40, 2 (1978): pp. 128- 132.

6. Janusz Pelc, "Europejskość i swoistość literatury polskiego renesansu," pp. 40-41.

7. Ibidem.

8. Janusz Pelc, "Problemy periodyzacji twórczości Jana Kochanowskiego a periodyzacja literatury polskiego renesansu" (Problems in periodization of the work of Jan Kochanowski and the periodization of Polish Renaissance literature), *Odrodzenie i Reformacja w Polsce*, vol. 27 (Warsaw, 1982): pp. 10-16.

9. Janusz Pelc. "Dialog i wizerunek. Dwa dominujące typy konstrukcji wypowiedzi w poetyce Reja" (Dialogue and image. Two dominating types of construction of utterance in Rej's poetics), in *Mikołaj Rej. W czterechsetlecie śmierci*, ed. Tadeusz Bieńkowski, Janusz Pelc, Krystyna Pisarkowa (Wrocław: Ossolineum, 1971), pp. 135-157.

10. Mikołaj Rej, *Figliki* (Little jokes), ed. Maria Bokszczanin (Warsaw: PIW, 1970), p. 160.

11. *Psałterz Dawidów przekładania Jana Kochanowskiego* (David's Psalter in the translation of Jan Kochanowski) (Cracow, 1579), p. 2 (in the dedication to Piotr Myszkowski).

12. Janusz Pelc, "Orfeusz pisarzy renesansowych" (Orpheus of Renaissance writers), *Pamiętnik Literacki* 70, 1 (1979), pp. 87-89.

13. Janusz Pelc, *Jan Kochanowski Szczyt renesansu*, pp. 212-218, 228.

14. John Bowring, *Specimens of the Polish Poets*. With notes and Observations on the Literature of Poland (London, 1827).

15. Janusz Pelc, "Czarnoleska Arkadia Jana Kochanowskiego" (The Czarnolas Arcadia of Jan Kochanowski), in *For Wiktor Weintraub, Essays in Polish Literature, Language and History, presented on the occasion of his 65th birthday.* (The Hague: Mouton, 1975), p. 332.

16. Wiktor Weintraub, *Rzecz Czarnoleska* (On Czarnolas) (Cracow: Wydawnictwo Literackie, 1977), pp. 287-303.

17. Paulina Buchwald-Pelcowa, "Jan Kochanowski: The Poet's Sixteenth Century Editions in the Context of Contemporary Polish and European Printing," in the present publication.

18. Jan Kochanowski, *Fraszki* (Cracow, 1584), p. 5.

19. Jan Kochanowski's letter to Jan Zamoyski dated Czarnolas, 22 December 1577, printed as a foreword to Kochanowski's *Odprawa posłow greckich* (Warsaw, 1578), k. Aij recto.

20. Claude Backvis, *Szkice o kulturze staropolskiej* (Essays on Old Polish culture), selected and ed. Andrzej Biernacki (Warsaw: PIW, 1975), pp. 117-121, 82.

21. Giovanni Pico, della Mirandola, *Opera* (Basilea, 1572), p. 314, as quoted in *Petrarca, Valla, Ficino, Pietro Pomponazzi, Vives; The Renaissance Philosophy of Man, Selections in Translation* ed. Ernst Cassirer, Paul Oskar Kristeller, John Herman Randall, Jr. (Chicago: University of Chicago Press, 1948), p. 224 (Selections from Pico trans. Elizabeth Livermore Forbes).

22. Jan Kochanowski, *Pieśni* (Cracow, 1586), p. 59; Bowring.

23. Jan Kochanowski, *Treny* (Cracow, 1583), p. 5.

24. More fully on this subject in Janusz Pelc, *Jan Kochanowski. Szczyt renesansu*, pp. 229-231 and *Europejskość i polskość literatury naszego renesansu* (The European character and Polish specificity of our Renaissance literature) (Warsaw: Czytelnik, 1984), passim.

25. Compare the copy of the manuscript of this letter reproduced on the end papers of *Jan Kochanowski. Szczyt renesansu*.

26. Janusz Pelc, *Europejskość i polskość literatury naszego renesansu*, p.275.

27. Janusz Pelc, *Jan Kochanowski. Szczyt renesansu*, pp. 488-501 and passim.

28. Ibidem, pp. 502-535; Janusz Pelc, *Jan Kochanowski w tradycjach literatury polskiej* (Jan Kochanowski in the traditions of Polish literature) (Warsaw: PIW, 1965), passim.

29. Francesco Petrarca, *Opera* (Basilea, 1554), vol. 2, pp. 646-648.

30. Maciej Kazimierz Sarbiewski, *Wykłady poetyki (Praecepta poetica)*, trans. and ed. Stanisław Skimina, Biblioteka Pisarzów Polskich, series B, no. 5 (Wrocław: Ossolineum, 1958), pp. 75-78.

19

The Linguistic Form of Jan Kochanowski's Poetry

Maria Renata Mayenowa

The feature of Jan Kochanowski's language which I attempt to outline here is based upon a close reading of only one of the poet's works, namely, *Treny* (*Laments*), a reading supported by material from the *Słownik polszczyzny XVI wieku* (Dictionary of Sixteenth-Century Polish).[1] The essay proposes a tentative reconstruction of those meanings which Kochanowski's contemporaries could extract from his poetic text. The discussion is organized so as to provide answers to two questions. The first is what was the poet's attitude toward lexical and phraseological standards he had inherited? Secondly, what lexical and phraseological traditions combined to give the *Laments* the poetic form they have?

These are old questions posed by Russian formalism and its Czech structuralist version, questions about the meanings (items of information) which Kochanowski's contemporaries could extract from his texts. The meanings which we attempt to discover in the *Laments* do not exhaust the meanings of the expressions employed. The meanings often also result from the relation to the norms of the Polish of Kochanowski's time and to the tradition of poetic language. Here we attempt to comprehend to the extent possible the principles of the poet's choices and the context in which those choices were made.

We must bear in mind that the essential changes in the vocabulary of the Polish language resulting in its modern form had occurred before Kochanowski began writing. Numerous medieval grammatical and lexical forms had fallen into disuse before his time. Kochanowski's works had been preceded by a rich Polish-language literary production consisting of works of Marcin Bielski, Mikołaj Rej, Łukasz Górnicki, and at least two complete translations of the Bible. Kochanowski did not mark the beginning of the emergence of multistyle written Polish. He was active in a period when the very intensive evolution of literary Polish was already far advanced and had yielded many varieties of lay and religious narratives, both ones in sharp opposition to the colloquial language and ones marked by a lesser departure from it.

Let us begin with that property of the linguistic form of Kochanowski's poetry which is interpreted as a departure from the tradition of the spoken language, the tradition which was common also to written texts, a tradition which was, apparently, part of an entirely different cultural formation than that represented by Kochanowski.

Every reader of Old Polish texts is aware of the fairly high frequency of the particle -ć, -ci. This particle also occurs in Kochanowski's prose and poetry, but less frequently than in the works of Rej, although Rej himself is a *sui generis* puzzle in this respect. A comparison of the frequency of the occurence of this particle—disregarding those differences in frequency which are essential, obvious, and connected with literary genres—yields spectacular results when we consider translations (or paraphrases) of a single text, namely the Psalter. The *Dictionary of Sixteenth-Century Polish* offers the following information: the said particle occurs 54 times in Walenty Wróbel's translation of the Psalter (Cracow, 1539), nine times in Rej's (Cracow, 1541-42?), 139 times in Jakub Lubelczyk's (Cracow, 1558), and 20 times in Kochanowski's translation. Let us also look at some other texts: Kochanowski's *Fraszki* (Trifles), with a total of 70,000 letters (as the measure of the length of the text), has 19 occurrences of the particle in question: Rej's *Figliki* (short jocular poems) has 46 occurrences of that particle in a total of 48,000 letters; Górnicki's *Dworzanin polski* (The Polish courtier) (Cracow, 1566), a paraphrase of *Il Cortegiano* by Baldassare Castiglione, has 44 occurrences per 490,000 letters, and Rej's *Źwierciadło* (The Mirror) has 293 occurrences per 920,000 letters.

The sparing use by Górnicki and Kochanowski of the particle -ć, -ci as compared with the use in Rej's text is beyond any doubt.

One further observation should be made before we try to explain this phenomenon. The reader of the *Dictionary of Sixteenth-Century Polish* gradually becomes able to identify the examples drawn from Rej's works even without the reference to Rej at the end of the respective quotations. The reader does so by means of a specific feature: use of the indicative pronoun *ten, ta, to* ("this" differentiated by gender). Examples of such uses of the pronoun are: "*O wszechmogący nasz miły Pánie, gdyż bez twej łáski záwżdy muszą być zaślepione ty nędzne á mizerne oczy násze ...*" ("Our mighty beloved Lord, without thy grace *these* our miserable and poor eyes must always be blind...") *Postylla (Postilla)* 109; "*... co się dzieje á co spráwuje to święte Bóstwo Páná twojego ...*" ("... what happens and what *that* sacred Divinity of thy Lord incessantly does..."), *Postilla* 109. Were we to quote more comprehensive contexts in which these examples occur, we would find reference to eyes in the former case, and to Divinity in the latter. Thus the pronoun in a sense functions as an anaphora, with the proviso that it is superfluous in its anaphoric role because it does not replace the respective substantives, which also occur in the surface structure of the text. It is also to be noted that the substantives preceded by the said pronoun in the examples above refer to objects which are indicated just as singular objects are. Whoever recalls contemporary Polish phrases such as: "*co tam w* tych

Kielcach?" ("What is going on in *that* Kielce?")—*Kielce* being a place name which is grammatically plural although it denotes a town), or: "te oczy *tak patrzą ...*" (*"these eyes* are looking so ..."), must agree that the indicative pronoun under consideration only seemingly plays an anaphoric role, while in fact, like the particle *-ć, -ci*, it carries some sense of emphasis. I would like to explore this emphatic usage further.

Calling *-ć, -ci* an emphatic particle does not tell us much about its meaning. Some dictionaries add the information that it is an emphatic affirmative particle. It seems that the semantic analysis of the particle must be pushed further. Genetically, the particle *-ć, -ci* is treated as derived from the root of the pronoun *ten* ("this'); it is also admitted, following Aleksander Brückner, that it may be derived from the personal pronoun *ty* ("thou") whose dative is *ci*.[2] Whatever its origin, its distribution in the fifteenth- and sixteenth-century texts (and in those from later periods as well) shows the following regularities and tendencies: (1) the particle in question does not occur after verbs in the imperative nor after nouns in the vocative; (2) it tends to occur in the rhematic part of the sentence; and (3) it may be attached to any part of speech (very rarely to prepositions, never to typical interjections). These rules and/or tendencies of its use seem to indicate that in the period with which we are dealing it was understood as part of the dative of *ty*, as an abbreviation of the sentence: *"mówię ci"* ("I tell you", or more archaically, but closer to the Polish, "I say unto thee"), such a sentence performing a phatic role. This explanation of the particle would confirm that its intuitive interpretation would be affirmative in character.[3] Affirmativeness here means as an assurance of truth: *"Jać dałem mu chleb"* = *"Ja (mówię ci) dałem mu chleb"* (cf., "I *did* give him bread.") It introduces the speaker to confirm the fact that it was he, the speaker, who gave bread to the person indicated by the pronoun *mu*. The same may occur in sentences in which the personal pronoun *ja* ("I") does not appear: *"Onci dał mu chleb"* = *"On (mówię ci) dał mu chleb";* (He I tell you gave him bread) *"A toci historia"* = "A to (mówię ci) historia" ["And that, I tell you, was a (funny) story"].

The fact that the particle cannot be used with a verb in the imperative thus becomes explicable because an imperative sentence can neither be confirmed as true nor rejected as false. On the other hand, the fact that it can be used with those parts of speech with which the indicative pronoun cannot form a name suggests that in the minds of the speakers at that time the particle under consideration was associated with the meaning of the personal pronoun *ty* ("thou") as part of a concretion, in a sense, an abbreviation of a sentence.

Upon closer examination, those texts and their fragments in which the said particle occurs prove to be dialogic in character. The particle points to the presence of listeners, addressing the utterances directly to them; moreover, the introduction of the listener necessarily introduces the speaker. This form appears to be one characteristic of colloquial oral statements, and in literature, one designated by the Russian term *skaz*. If we disregard *skaz* as a form of stylization, we find the use of the said particle in genuine folk stories in which the monologue, as a derivative form, has not fully dissociated itself from its dialogic substratum. This form of oral statement, or utterance, is typical of early monologues (with a single speaker each) in Polish literature. In my opinion, in the case of Rej it was already a *sui generis* stylistic operation used in persuasive texts as a means to introduce a language common to the writer and his assumed readers. In the work of Górnicki and Kochanowski, it is used only in "real" dialogues and is not characteristic of either author.

We have referred simultaneously to two specific manifestations of linguistic culture, namely, the frequent use of the particle *-ć, -ci* and the use of an indicative pronoun in a specifically emphatic function. The indicative pronoun, seemingly deictic in nature, here plays the role of a *sui generis* article in a language which has no articles and is always typical of spoken language.

It seems that Kochanowski does not admit such uses of the indicative pronoun, with two exceptions. One of these is to be found in the *Laments*, namely in Lament IV: "*Której równia nie widzę* w tej tu śmiertelności." The relevant words read literally, "*in this mortality here*". But this is the only instance in the *Laments*.

Another choice made by Kochanowski which belongs to the same set of linguistic phenomena should be discussed here: the use of diminutives. It is common knowledge that Polish, with its complex morphology, offers great opportunities for the formation of diminutives. Many occur in Rej. If we disregard those dimunitives which really denote the small size, etc., of the object to which they are applied, then we find in Rej's works a large number of adjectival and adverbial diminutives such as *caluczki, cieniuczki, częściuchny, maluczki, równiuczki, wąziuczki*, etc., and such as *dopiruczko, częściuchno, pomaluśku*, etc. He also has a peculiar type of substantival diminutives such as *pszeniczka*, similar to *masełko*, in present-day Polish used by waiters or when encouraging children to eat (the use is purely affectionate in Polish and in no sense refers to the physical smallness of the objects so named).

The examples of the diminutives quoted above have been drawn from a single text by Rej, namely *The Mirror*. Data is available for all of Kochanowski's works. If we disregard substantival diminutives, small in number and including no case like *pszeniczka*, we find in Kochanowski's texts the adjective *maluczki* twice (once in the *Laments*: *maluczka dusza*) and the adverb *maluczko* once.

Let us consider a word such as *caluczki*. This adjective occurs in Rej's *Wizerunk* ... (137) (A faithful image ...) in the formulation: "*Cáluczką noc słoneczna światłość mu świeciła*" ("sun shone to him the whole night"). The use of the diminutive stresses the credibility of the statement which says that something lasted the whole night, and not only during part of it, as one could think when taking *cała noc* not quite literally. It seems that these diminutives, which sometimes contain the meaning of "very" plus the meaning of the adjective or adverb in question, most often are expressive in character: they speak not so much about the objects described with the given diminutive, as about the values of the speaker and his experiences connected with the objects. This is yet another way, in addition to the use of the particle under consideration and the use of an indicative pronoun, of introducing the speaker and the quasi-dialogic form. It seems that our attitude toward diminutives points to the departure of that literary style which refers to the spoken language and is now certainly felt to be characteristic of folklore.

It appears that Kochanowski represented a different attitude and used a language which was more intellectual, objectified, and in a sense oriented toward an individual emotional softening, toward a pure literary monologue.

It must be emphasized again that the second half of the sixteenth century witnessed that form of the evolution of the Polish language in which written styles began to dissociate themselves from their base of spoken Polish. This applies even to Rej, and not to Górnicki and Kochanowski alone. Yet Rej's idea of literary style differs greatly from Kochanowski's. It suffices to read Rej's dedicatory letters, prefacing *The Mirror* where the forms we are discussing show a diminishing trend, to realize the extent to which the main works are marked by a stylization oriented toward spoken and internally dialogic speech statements that seem to attack the listener or the reader, constantly mixing the author's statements about the external world with his own responses to that world.

In Kochanowski's poetry, departure from the spoken language and from quasi-dialogic forms, from styles which appear to be folklore-based, are accompanied by a deep rooting in the native lexical tradition. This is manifested in his knowledge of earlier tradition enabling him to use it as a source of archaization and of forms of expression which were nonexistent in his times and which he himself needed when writing poetry. We stress *when* writing poetry, because there is usually a marked difference in this respect between his poems and his texts written in prose.

As a poet Kochanowski was not an inventor of neologisms. Those words which in our materials occur only once and only in Kochanowski's texts cannot be considered as words not occurring in the Polish language of that period. Their existence is confirmed either by texts not used for compilation of the *Dictionary of Sixteenth-Century Polish* (such as the word *dziewczyna*) or by words which are derivatives of those *hapax legomena*. Finally it may be claimed that still surviving mechanisms of word formation in Polish at least potentially confirm their existence in our language.

It may also be said that, with the exception of two forms of words known only from the language of the Kochanowski family, his language is not marked dialectally. In any case, Jan Kochanowski used far fewer dialectal forms than did his brother Andrzej, translator of the *Aeneid*. In the *Laments* there are no so-called Sandomierz rhymes, even though the poet often makes use of the admissible parallel nasal and non-nasal forms. Yet the non-nasal forms do not occur in the rhyme position. The one possible exception indicating a dialectal form may be seen in the pair *zdrojem/moim*; in Andrzej Kochanowski we find the rhyme, *zdrojem/twojem*.[4]

These findings confirm the generally accepted thesis that "Jan Kochanowski's phonetic system fully complied with the then universally accepted standard of written Polish."[5] It should be added that the same applies to his vocabulary, which is well-rooted in the Polish language of his times and strives neither for novelty nor for archaisms, with the exception of such genres as the Psalter that assume a certain stylization. The same may be said about other prominent representatives of the world of letters at that time, such as Górnicki, Rej, and Skarga.

Now, what lexical and phraseological traditions combined to give the language of the *Laments* its shape?

Initially, the vocabulary of the *Laments* seems to present an extraordinary amount of expressions drawn from translations of the Bible. But like many modern European languages, Polish had to work out its own lexical and phraseological standards to be used in the translations of the Bible, a comprehensive text, marked by many different styles, including different genres, and carrying an ideological weight not ascribed to any other literary work. For Kochanowski, the tradition of the vocabulary and phraseology found in Polish translations of the Bible was the "received" standard; it also represented that part of the vocabulary and the phraseology currently understood by the broad strata of his contemporaries, including those not equal to him in education.

Translations of the Bible, including the Psalter, formed a long and rich tradition in Polish literature before Kochanowski. They served as a point of departure for the poet and determined what was common to him and his readers and what would render him comprehensible to them. The linguistic stuff of the Bible was a clearly marked object of successive poetic transformations. It also easily absorbed elements of classical phraseology when the world of classical mythology and that of the ideas connected with the Bible resembled one another.

In order to show the extent of Polish Biblical phraseology and the classical images and phraseology being imposed upon it in the language of the *Laments* I shall begin with images of death and the land of the dead. The first instance of the opposition of life to death as the land of the dead occurs in Lament II:

I nie napatrzywszy się jasności słonecznej
Poszła nieboga widzieć krajów nocy wiecznej:

And having not seen enough of the brightness of the sun,
She went, poor soul, to see the lands of eternal night.

As translated by Jan Leopolita,[6] Ps. 48 says about death: *"Wnidzie aż do narodów ojców swoich a na wieki nie ogląda światła"* ("He will go to the nations of his fathers and will not see light for ages"). Not seeing light is a paraphrase for death (in the sense of being dead), and seeing light is a paraphrase for life. Ps. 87, in the same translation, says: *"Wtłoczyli mnie w głębokie jezioro, w ciem-*

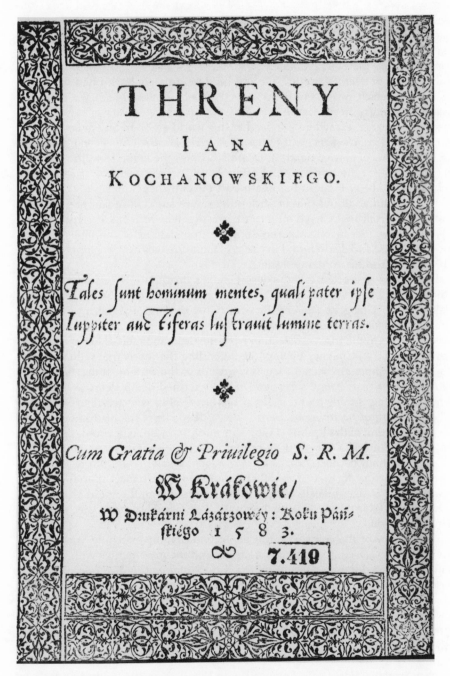

THRENY

I A N A

KOCHANOWSKIEGO.

❖

Tales funt hominum mentes, quali pater ipfe
Iuppiter auc tiferas luftrauit lumine terras.

❖

Cum Gratia & Priuilegio S. R. M.

W Krákowie/

W Drukárni Łázárzowéy: Roku Páń-
fkiégo 1 5 8 3.

7.419

55. Jan Kochanowski, *Treny*, w Krakowie, 1583. The title page of the second edition (Biblioteka Ossolińskich, Wrocław). For the facsimile of this edition see Jan Kochanowski, *Dzieła Wszystkie*. Wydanie Sejmowe. vol. 2 ed. Maria Renata Mayenowa et. al. (Wrocław: Ossolineum, 1982).

nościach w cieniu śmierci" ("They pushed me into a deep lake, into darkness in the shadow of death"). Likewise in Job (3:5 and 3:16) we have: *"Niech go* [the day of his birth] *zaćmią ciemności i cień śmierci ... Abo jako niedoszłe dziecię skryte nie byłbym, abo jako ci, co począwszy się nie oglądali światłości"* ("Let darkness and the shadow of death stain it ... Or as a hidden untimely birth I had not been; as infants which never saw light"). In Wróbel's *Psalter* (142/3) we read: *"A położył się między ciemnościami, tam gdzie są martwi tego świata"* ("And he lay between darknesses, where the dead of this world are"). In *St. Florian's Psalter* (3) we have: *" ... choćbym chodził w cieniu śmierci wiecznej"* (" ... even if I walked in the shadow of eternal death"). Death separates the living from the dead; as in Ruth 1:17 (in the translation of Leopolita): *" ... jeśli nie sama śmierć mnie z tobą rozłączy"* (" ... if aught but death part me and thee").

It is beyond all doubt that in ancient literature sunlight meant life, and the lands of eternal night have an exact correspondent in Seneca: *perpetua nocte oppressa regio.*[7] Because it was rooted in the translations of the Bible, the opposition of life and death found in classical literature was easily comprehensible to the poet and his contemporaries.

Death was also often called sleep. Ursula's death is referred to as "iron", "deep" (in Polish *twardy,* "hard"), "unending" (*nieprzespany*). On death being called sleep, Grzegorz Paweł z Brzezin (Gregory Paul of Brzeziny) in his *O prawdziwej śmierci, zmartwychwstaniu i żywocie wiecznym Jezusa Krystusa Pana naszego ...* ("On the true resurrection from the dead and eternal life of our Lord Jesus Christ ...") Cracow, 1568, p. 38; defending the thesis that the faithful of the Old Testament expected their reward not in the distant future, but soon, cites as proof that *"śmierć snem zwali"* ("they termed death sleep"). The same understanding is to be found in Rej (*The Mirror,* 94v), who refers to Scripture. The formulation *twardy sen* ("hard", i.e., "deep sleep") is also known from Rej's translation of the Psalms (117v). The ancient tradition of comparing death to sleep is not only confirmed by numerous examples, but seems to have led to lexicalization, because *Gradus ad Parnassum Latinum* refers the reader from the entry *somnus* to that of *mors.* The definition of Ursula's mortal sleep as *żelazny* ("iron" sleep) recalls Virgil, but in this case, too, the tradition of translation of the Bible proves that Kochanowski's phraseology was rooted in Polish language habits.

The history of the comparison of death to a dragon snatching young birds from their nest, a comparison in which the ancient *draco* merges with the devil embodied as a dragon known from the New Testament, is also relevant here.[8] Both Rej and Jakub Wujek[9] confirm that the dragon was understood as the devil. In his poem *"Ku temuż to Krześcijańskiemu Rycerzowi napominanie"* ("Admonition Addressed to the Christian Knight") Rej wrote: "The devil, ferocious dragon, also waits for you." When commenting on Rev. 12:7 Wujek says explicitly: *"Smok ten jestci szatan"* ("That dragon is Satan"). These suggestions prompted by the biblical text and modifying and amplifying the traditional ancient image almost begin Lament I with the allusion to be repeated later in Lament XI in the reference to *"nieznajomy wróg"* ("the unknown enemy") who "*miesza ludzkie rzeczy*" ("confuses things human").[10] Such suggestions are also connected with the distich describing Ursula as "*duchem zaraźliwym srogiej śmierci otchniona*"(V) ("upon whom furious death breathed his contagious air"). Death is quite often mentioned in texts that refer to the Bible and occurs in the series *śmierć, grzech, czart* ("death", "sin", "Satan") [cf., Rej's Postilla, 14v].

Lament XIV begins with the words, "*Gdzie te wrota nieszczęsne, którymi przed laty / Puszczał się w ziemię Orfeus ...*" ("Where are those gates of calamity through which Orpheus years ago entered underground"). "The gates of death" in Job 38:17 were translated verbatim by Leopolita as "*wrota śmierci.*"

The passage in Lament XIX "*Ziemia w ziemię się wraca a duch z nieba dany, Miałby zginąć ani na miejsce swe wezwany?*" ("dust returns to dust so why should the spirit from heaven perish without being called to its place?") has parallels in two *loci*. It is found in Cicero's *Tusculanae*,[11] but the whole is a reformulation of a passage in Eccles. (12:7), namely, "Then shall the dust return to the earth as it was; and the spirit shall return unto God who gave it," which is rendered by Leopolita as "*a nawróci się proch do ziemie swej skąd był a duch nawróci się do Boga, któryż dał onego.*" The beginning of the passage under consideration (Eccles. 3:20) "all are of the dust, and all turn to dust again" is rendered by Leopolita as "*z ziemie się stali i w ziemie jednako się obracają.*"

The *Laments*, like the whole poetic production of the period, contain numerous references to biblical phraseology not reformulated by the classical tradition. When in Lament XII we find (with reference to grain) "*znowu cię w smutną ziemię sieję!*" ("I sow thee again into the sad land!"), *smutna ziemia* turns out to be reference to the biblical formulations which function in Polish translations as *żałosna ziemia* (e.g., in Leopolita's translation of Jer. 12:4 "how long shall the land mourn"), etc. This always means the land whose crops have been destroyed and which would not bring forth new crops again. But the final part of the passage: "*nie wznidziesz ... (nie) zakwitniesz*" ("thou wilt not grow ... thou wilt not blossom"), which continues the metaphor of the grain sown to no avail, is a repetition of a biblical phrase, a metaphor known already to Rej: "*zakwitniesz przed oblicznością jego*" ("thou wilt blossom before his face"), Postilla 240/38; "*wznidzie a zakwitnie sprawiedliwość*" ("justice will grow and blossom"), Postilla 211/49, and many other similar cases.

Let us now consider reflections on man. Man is a passing shadow, his life is a like going astray, both he himself and everything around him is vanity. We shall not consider the biblical reference *in fine* of Lament I: *Wszystko prózno!* ("All is vanity!" or "all is in vain!") because its connections are well known.[12] But let us proceed to the ending of Lament X: "*staw się przede mną / Lubo snem, lubo cieniem, lub marą nikczemną!*" ("appear before me as a dream, or as a shadow, or as a bodiless ghost!"). We can easily refer to Greek and Roman poetry and beliefs: Pindar's formulation that man is a dream of a shadow, and passages in the *Aeneid* which mention the ungraspable shadow of Aeneas' wife. It must be remembered that their linguistic form and the accompanying suggestions are known to translations of the Bible, such as Ps. 143/4 from the Radziwiłł

Bible: *"człowiek jest podobny próżności a dni jego jako cień przechodzą"* ("man resembles vanity and his days pass like a shadow").[13] Such phraseological references are even more clearly marked in Lament XIII: *"Omyliłaś mię jako nocny sen znikomy"* ("thou has deceived me like a vanishing dream at night"). The whole biblical phraseology connected with shadow is associated with its being volatile and ungraspable; compare in this connection such phrases *przemijać, uciekać, przechodzić,* and even *zniknąć jako cień* (to "pass," "flee," "vanish like a shadow"). The biblical source of the comparison of the child to the olive has been demonstrated by Wiktor Weintraub[14] all phrases such as *kości suszyć, przejmować do kości, nasycić uszy, krajać serce* (to "dry bones," to "penetrate to the bones," to "fill one's ears," to "cut one's heart") also have a biblical provenance.

To conclude the discussion of biblical relationships, let us consider the word *zgasnąć* (to "become extinct") in the sense of "die", a sense in which it functions to this day. There is no doubt that it is a calque from Latin. Now the material compiled for the preparations of the *Dictionary of Sixteenth-Century Polish* does not record before Kochanowski such a lexicalized use as applied to denote human death. *Gaśnie cnota, gaśnie miłość* ("virtue becomes extinct," "love becomes extinct") means that virtue or love ceases to exist. *Zgasnąć* as referred to human death occurs only once used metaphorically in Marcin Bielski's *Kronika wszystkiego świata* ... (Chronicle of the whole world) (Cracow, 1551), 73v: *"I aby Dawid ... pochodnia albo świeca izraelska nie zgasła"* ("So that David ... the torch or the candle of Israel should not become extinct"). Hence Ursula's *zgaśnięcie* ("extinction") must be interpreted only as a pure calque from Latin. But Leopolita translates Ezek. 32:8 thus: *"zali światło niepobożnego nie będzie zgaszone"* (which is rather remote from the English version: "all the bright lights of heaven will I make dark over thee ..."), where *zgasić światło* ("to extinguish the light") refers to the biblical and classical synonymy *light = life*. The point, however, is not to treat the expression concluding the dedication of the *Laments* as dissociated from the Latin tradition. Rather the point is that those relationships are richer and belong to two traditions which taken together were decisive for the linguistic form of Kochanowski's poetry. Moreover, it is also difficult to claim that *zgasła* cannot be interpreted as "ceased to exist", for just a little further we read *"Nie masz cię, Orszulo moja"* ("Thou art not here [no more], Ursula"), where *nie masz cię* = "thou existeth not".

The most essential element in a description of the language of Polish Renaissance poetry is the intertwining of literary and poetic phraseology (worked out through translations of the Bible) with what had existed in the tradition of Polish literary prose and poetry, and then assimilating certain classical phraseology. This amalgam of poetic, and broadly literary, phraseology from the Bible with what resulted from the far-reaching Renaissance reception of the poetry of Greece and golden-age Rome, as well as deeply rooted native elements, determined the particular force of poetic expression in Kochanowski's works. It proves that he had assimilated both the general European and native cultural tradition. The native Slavic tradition, while difficult to pinpoint, should also not be overlooked. Kazimierz Moszyński wrote that shadow, already mentioned above, was a usual reference to dead persons among northern Slavs (Poles and Ruthenians).[15] It is also common knowledge that the parting song of brides was included in the text of the *Laments*. To this we have to add that *niedoszła jagoda* ("unripe berry") has been frequently recorded by Paweł Shein in the lamentations of the dead sung in the territories of the former Grand Duchy of Lithuania, that is, in the eastern lands of Poland. The green bush mentioned in the *Laments* might have also been taken from native folklore, and native folklore certainly accounts for the final formula in the dedication of the *Laments*, *Nie masz cię, Orszulo moja*, also to be found in Shein.[16] This formula will be discussed below.

We have already mentioned the fact that Polish, like all Slavic languages, has almost unlimited possibilities for the formation of diminutives; those possibilities were fully used in sixteenth-century literature. But we already know that Kochanowski is not a writer who provides much material for a hunter of diminutives. In the *Laments* we find only substantival diminutives, with the sole exception of *maluczka dusza* ("little soul"). Let us examine the substantival diminutives more closely because some are *hapax legomena* in the material upon which the *Dictionary of Sixteenth-Century Polish* is based. Ursula has *ręczynki* ("little hands'): as in Lament III *"... a ty więc z drogimi/Rzuć się ojcu do szyje ręczynkami swymi!"* ("and thou dost embrace your father's neck with your little hands!"). This diminutive has not been recorded in texts which are earlier than Kochanowski's, and in the later period has been recorded only once in Górnicki's *Troas*, a translation and adaptation of Seneca's tragedy, *Troades*. Górnicki seems to have imitated Kochanowski in this respect. But we do find *rączki* ("little hands"). Ursula's *stopeczki* refers to the small footprints of her little feet: *"a stopeczkami twymi Ciebie naśladować"* ("to follow your small footprints"). Such a diminutive would not be used even today, and it occurs as a *hapax legomenon* in our lexicographical data. *Ustka* ("little mouth") is not recorded anywhere else: *"nie zamykając ustek nigdy"* ("never closing thy little mouth") in the sense of *"never ceasing to talk."* *Gardłko* ("little throat") of the nightingale, to which Ursula is compared in the phrase, *"gardłkiem swym ucieszonym"* ("with thy little joyful throat"), has been recorded first in Kochanowski and twice after him, in both senses of the word *after*. *Członeczki* ("little limbs") is found earlier in Baltazar Opeć's *Żywot Pana Jezu Krysta* (The Life of Lord Jesus Christ) (Cracow, 1522), but is not recorded in *The Dictionary of Old Polish*. *Główki* in the phrase, *"W główki włożył"* in Lament VII ("Placed at the head end") is only once recorded in the sense of at the head of a bed, with a possible reference to the coffin; on the other hand, it is fairly often recorded as the name of a part of the human body. *Włoski* ("little hair") is recorded only in the *Laments*, in *"włoski pokręcone"* ("curly little hair") and in Jan Mączyński's *Lexicon Latino-Polonicum* (Królewiec, 1564) primarily in set phrases and idioms.[17] We also find the diminutive *włosek* in the phrase *"włosek z głowy nie spadnie"* ("not a hair shall fall from thy head") in the sense of one's being absolutely safe. It is striking to see that apart from the *Laments* there are no diminutives to denote parts of a child's body, with the exception of *The Life of Lord Jesus Christ*, already mentioned above, where we find quite frequently the word *rączka, nóżka, członeczki, główka* ("little hand', "little foot", "little limbs", "little head", respectively) used to denote parts of the body of the infant Jesus and of the Blessed Mother. It is instructive to trace the occurrences of those forms in *Rozmyślania Dominikańskie* (Dominican Meditations).[18] As is well-known, this is a manuscript on parchment, in which some parts of the text have been erased and a new text written in those places much later, perhaps in the seventeenth century. Where we now have *ręka, głowa, noga*, the erased text often had *rączka, główka, nóżka*, that is, the respective diminutive forms. This change of the old text, dating from the fifteenth century, into a new one is strikingly frequent. The *Dominican Meditations* are not concerned with the infant Jesus, but with Jesus at the time of his passion. It would seem, therefore, that we may interpret this use of diminutives to denote parts of a child's body found in the *Laments* in the following manner: there is no doubt that such diminutives did exist and were used in colloquial Polish, but they did not always mean the smallness of the limbs to which they referred. On the contrary, they most often expressed the affection of the speaker. They came to be eliminated at the time when an opposition between the colloquial and the literary language began to emerge. They are a mark of colloquiality, perhaps of folk origin.

When Kochanowski wrote his *Laments*, the Polish language still did not have a literary vocabulary to express one's tender feelings toward one's child. By resorting to a certain shift, Kochanowski made use of the old vocabulary, deeply rooted in medieval literature but in his own time perhaps merely colloquial, a vocabulary that was the sole instrument available to perform such a role. This is the only set of words which existed in Polish and carried the emotional load imparted to them by earlier texts which referred to the infant Jesus and the Blessed Mother, an emotional load which those words could still have in colloquial Polish at that time. To this we may add that manner of addressing the child, namely, *pociecha moja* ("my consolation" or "my comfort"), known from the *Dominican Meditations* and from Opeć, and also the old verb *tolić*, in the sense of comforting a crying child, which is to be found in Opeć and in the *Laments*, and is later confused with *tulić* ("embrace") and occurs only in that later form. This gives us a fairly complete picture of the functions of that vocabulary which was inherited from apocryphal literature and was perhaps still vivid in the colloquial language of Kochanowski's time.

The diminutives in this group require further comment. Philipe Ariés, author of the study *L'Enfant et la vie familiale sous l'ancien régime* (Paris, 1960), says that sixteenth-century Europe witnessed a turning point in adults' attitude towards children. At this time, childhood was discovered to be a specific age in the development of human beings. The child ceased to be treated as a small adult. The discovery of children's charm and admiration for that charm assumed certain forms of *mignotage* that gradually led to the comprehension of the specific features and needs of childhood. Andrzej Vincenz, who in a brief paper has demonstrated the importance of Ariés's study for the interpretation of the Polish data,[19] shows the beginnings of that *mignotage* in Poland to be present in the works of Rej. But it is also true that in the *Laments* we find whole sections in which Ursula is described precisely as a small adult. What is of interest here, and what I would not call *mignotage*, is the way in which the old medieval tradition was used to express emotion which we can so well understand.

We are able to trace in the *Laments* the four traditions listed above and whose amalgamation determines the linguistic form of those poems. In conclusion, while all Kochanowski's phraseology is rooted in tradition, it is uniquely marked by delicate metaphorical shifts. The resulting metaphorization becomes visible when we recognize the amalgamation of several different traditions that has been described here. In such a brief essay a sole example of this metaphorization must suffice, namely the concluding words of the dedication, *"Nie masz cię, Orszula moja"* ("Thou art not here, Ursula"). If I have correctly identified the origin of that formula, it could have been a child's exclamation, *"Oj, nie masz mojego tatoczka"* ("Oh, my daddy is not here"), or something similar. Kochanowski eliminated both the diminutive and the exclamation and thus uniquely metaphorized it by addressing it to an absent, departed person.

Notes

1. *Słownik polszczyzny XVI wieku* (Dictionary of 16th century Polish), vols. 1-5 (1966-71), ed. Stanisław Bąk, et al.; vols. 6-13 (1972-81), general ed. Maria Renata Mayenowa (Wrocław: Ossolineum, 1966-1981).

2. See Aleksander Brückner, *Słownik etymologiczny języka polskiego* (Etymological dictionary of the Polish language) 3rd ed. (Warsaw: Wiedza Powszechna, 1957), s.v. *ci.*

3. See in particular, Franciszek Pepłowski, "O funkcji partykuły -*ci* w utworach Reja" (On the function of the particle -*ci* in Rej's works), *Pamiętnik Literacki* 60, 4 (1969): 137-167.

4. Henryk Borek, "Język Andrzeja Kochanowskiego na podstawie pierwodruku *Eneidy* z roku 1590" (The language of Andrzej Kochanowski based on the first edition of the *Aeneid*, 1590), *Zeszyty Naukowe*, Opole 1 (1957).

5. Stanisław Rospond, *Język i artyzm językowy Jana Kochanowskiego* (The language and linguistic artistry of Jan Kochanowski) (Wrocław: Prace Wrocławskiego Towarzystwo Naukowego, 1961).

6. *Biblia to jest Księgi Starego i Nowego Zakonu* (The Bible, that is the Books of the Old and of the New Testament), (Cracow, 1561).

7. See Jan Kochanowski, *Dzieła wszystkie Wydanie Sejmowe* (Complete Works. Sejm edition), vol. 2, *Treny* (Laments) edited by Maria Renata Mayenonna and Lucyna Woronczakowa in collaboration with Jerzy Axer and Maria Cytowska (Wrocław: Ossolineum, 1983), commentary 2, p. 118.

8. See Jerzy Axer, "Smok i słowiczki. Wokół wersów 9- 14 Trenu I Jana Kochanowskiego" (Dragon and Nightingales. On lines 9-14 of Lament I of Jan Kochanowski), *Pamiętnik Literacki* 70, 1 (1979), 186-191.

9. *Biblia to jest Księgi Starego i Nowego Testamentu* (The Bible, that is the Books of the Old and of the New Testament), (Cracow, 1599).

10. See Wiktor Weintraub, "'Fraszka' w tragicznej tonacji" ('Fraszka' in a tragic key) in *Rzecz czarnoleska* (Cracow: Wydawnictwo Literackie, 1977), p. 304 ff.

11. See Jan Kochanowski, *Dzieła wszystkie* (Complete Works), vol. 2, *Treny* (Laments) p. 175.

12. See *Treny* (Laments) (Biblioteka Narodowa, 1, Cracow: Ossolineum, 1919), Tadeusz Sinko's commentary to "Tren" 1, lines 15-17.

13. *Biblia Święta to jest Księgi Starego i Nowego Zakonu* (Holy Bible, that is the Books of the Old and of the New Testament) (Brześć, 1583).

14. See Wiktor Weintraub, "Styl Jana Kochanowskiego" (The style of Jan Kochanowski) in *Rzecz czarnoleska*, p. 83.

15. Kazimierz Moszyński, *Kultura ludowa słowian* (Folk culture of the Slavs), 2nd ed., vol. 2, pt. 1 (Warsaw: Książka i Wiedza, 1967-68).

16. See Paweł W. Shein, *Materialy dlia izucheniia byta i jazyka russkogo naseleniia Severo-zapadnogo kraia* (Materials for the study of the life and language of the Russian population of the Northwestern territory), vol. 1, pt. 1 (St. Petersburg, 1890).

17. Reprint by Rheinhold Olesch. *Slavistische Forschungen* (Cologne: Bolen Verlag, 1973). *Wyrazy polskie w słowniku łacińsko-polskim Jana Mączyńskiego* (Polish words in the Latin-Polish dictionary of Jan Mączyński), ed. Władysław Kuraszkiewicz (Wrocław: Ossolineum, 1963).

18. See *Rozmyślania Dominikańskie* (Dominican meditations), Biblioteka pisarzów polskich, series A, no. 3 (Wrocław: Ossolineum, 1965).

19. See Andrzej Vincenz, "Historia dzieciństwa" (History of childhood), *Kultura* 5/199 (May 1964): 131-138.

20

Jan Kochanowski's Versification

Mieczysław Giergielewicz

uring the late period of the medieval epoch individual words of the Polish language acquired paroxytonic stress. This gradual evolution lasted about two centuries, and coincided with the development of subsequent verse-making. By the dawn of the European Renaissance Polish versification followed several independent tracks. Polish melic vernacular sounded in the churches. Chants compiled in modernized Latin were made available in Polish. Melic texts which included cadenzas and anticadenzas were influential in designing lines and determining the syntactic patterns of verses.

Some of the polonized songs were so thoroughly and skillfully assimilated that they were easily accepted by the audiences and treated as an original national product. One of the most successful transfers was a Polish translation of the Latin rhymed song *"Horae Canonicae Salvatoris,"* glorifying the martyrdom of Jesus Christ; the Polish version with its 13- syllable line divided by a caesura was universally assimilated, and before long it became the most popular genre of national versification.[1] Besides religious texts, secular verses were also compiled in increasing amounts.

Following medieval Latin patterns, verses consisted of a definite number of syllables ending with rhymes. The number of syllables involved was often calculated in a liberal way. For example, if the poem contained basically eight syllables, sporadic lines with one or even two were also acceptable. As to rhyming, both oxytona and paroxytona were introduced, and unison accuracies were not required. Such presyllabic versification (often termed relative syllabism) remained acceptable as late as the first half of the sixteenth century, and lines containing from four to sixteen syllables (occasionally even more) were tolerated.

Gradually the influence of the Church in supplying versified writings lost its medieval predominance and some secular writers gained considerable acclaim. Educated people sought contact with modern literature of Western countries, mainly Italy and France. Among the Protestants, Mikołaj Rej (1505-1569), a prolific versifier, belonged to the most influential people of his generation. It should be also assumed that a spontaneous folklore existed as an independent trend, known to the whole population, but as it was not made available in printing or writing, it was not preserved, and only occasional traces of its activity survived.

The innovator and reformer of creative poetry was Jan Kochanowski. He did not leave any literary theories, but rather demonstrated them in his lifetime writings. While his works written in Latin followed the prosody inherited from the ancient Greek and Latin masters, his Polish writings continued the native tradition established by the earlier presyllabic fashion. However, once in his lifetime he ventured an experiment amalgamating the two basic languages of his literary profession. In this daring idea he could have been influenced by the Italian master of macaronic poetry Teofilo Folengo, as well as by the macaronic verse of his friend living in Poland, the Spaniard, Pedro Ruiz de Moros (Piotr Rojzjusz). Following these examples, Kochanowski compiled *Carmen macaronicum de eligendo vitae genere*, mixing Polish and Latin vocabulary and grammar with simplified Latin prosody. This work was conceived as a treatise discussing the advantages and shortcomings of the different professional occupations available to a young nobleman. Its prosody followed the rhythm of the ancient hexameter with, however, all vowels of the text treated as equal. The work was curious as a transitory literary experiment.[2]

Kochanowski's outstanding contribution in the literary field, however, is connected with syllabism. This particular technique of verse-making has flourished in different European countries: Italy, France, the Iberian peninsula, and Wales. Most recently it gained approval among some prominent British and American writers, the English traditional dedication to iambic feet notwithstanding. Among the poets representing the new prosody in Anglo-Saxon communities are Robert Bridges, Elizabeth Daryush, Dylan Thomas, Marianne Moore, W.H. Auden, Kenneth Rexroth, and others. Syllabic verse accepted from Polish poetry was also introduced at the end of the sixteenth century in Russian writings, but in the middle of the eighteenth century this system was supplanted by syllabotonic versification.

For the sake of comparison, a modern definition of syllabism might be instructive. Syllabism can be defined as follows:

> Verse that merely *counts the number of syllables* in the lines, and neither counts the stresses nor distributes them determinately, is known as *syllabic* verse. In the syllabic language—that is, a language in which the stress is weak or nonexistent—is the easiest kind of verse to construct. French verse is traditionally syllabic, as is Italian, although accent is much more prominent in the latter, and Italian verse shows the tendency to fall into a foot pattern.[3]

In his own treatment of syllabism, Kochanowski took into consideration the positive achievements of his Polish predecessors, enriching and consolidating the established national tradition. His most striking reform was connected with the treatment of lines, but he subjected to scrutiny almost all aspects of prosody. On the other hand, he found inspiration and encouragement in his Italian contacts. He realized that modern Italians conserved and cultivated with careful respect the literary heritage of their ancient Roman predecessors, but nevertheless succeeded in creating and developing their modern national language and producing admirable literary masterpieces. Conscious of these magnificent achievements, the Polish author carefully safeguarded his national identity and reconciled it with the creative spirit of the international Renaissance. His modernized poetic craft embraced different aspects of poetic art: lines, caesura, clausula and rhyming, rhythmic problems, and stanzas.

When the poems of Kochanowski were made available, relative syllabism lost its former recognition, but was not quite forgotten. In this respect the young newcomer set a standard from the outset. His lines were pleasantly regular. Never did he produce a poem consisting of lines in which the number of syllables oscillated. Isosyllabism became one of the compulsory rules. Versemaking was submitted to a canonized discipline which was considered unshakable.

The poet did not endeavor to increase the number of lines available in his poetic heritage. He even eliminated the four-syllable lines favored in the past by some of his predecessors (including Rej). Moreover, he did not risk exceeding the upper limit of fourteen syllables. However, if a syllable were added or reduced, a different category of lines would be established. Casual addition or reduction of even one syllable would be treated as a dissonance, unless a different kind of verse was consciously inserted.

The caesura was considered an important structural element of the lines. It was inserted in all longer lines containing at least nine syllables. Occasionally it also could appear in the popular eight-syllable verses, but no systematic regularity in this respect was to be expected. The other shorter lines, containing five syllables, were inserted by the poet mainly among his *Fraszki* (*Trifles*); verses with six syllables were included in his translation of the Psalms.

The stresses accompanying the caesura could oscillate. Usually the initial half of the line preceding the caesura ended with a paroxytonic conclusion consisting of two syllables, of which the first one was stressed, while the second one remained unstressed ($-\ -$). Such a structure was natural, because Polish words became paroxytonic (excepting, of course, words consisting of a single syllable). However, the placement of the stress immediately before the caesura or on the third syllable before it was also tolerated. As a result, an oxytonic or proparoxytonic effect could occasionally be obtained.

Such a manipulation of stresses enriched the rhythmic structure of the lines and stimulated diction. The resulting effect depended on the individual treatment by the author concerned. Later on, it would be more frequently exploited by some romantic poets. As to Kochanowski, he did not seem to abuse the device, which, moreover, could be helpful in avoiding rhythmic monotony.

Creative treatment of the caesura was applicable to all categories of lines containing at least nine syllables [the following examples are taken from *Psałterz Dawidów* (*David's Psalter*), i.e. "Ps." and *Pieśni* (*Songs*)]:

14 syllables (8 + 6)
Imię wielkie, imię groźne i błogosławione.

(Ps. 99, line 6)

Ty nas będziesz żywił, a my wzywać Cię będziemy,

(Ps. 80, line 38)

Okaż swą twarz, a wszytko się nam po myśli stanie!

(Ps. 80, line 16)

14 syllables (7 + 7)
Panu ja ufam, a wy mówicie: między góry

(Ps. 11, line 1)

Prawa zgoła upadły, nie masz sprawiedliwości,

(Ps. 11, line 5)

Człowiek dobry prózno ma ufać swej niewinności.

(Ps. 11, line 6)

13 syllables (8 + 5)
Utwierdziłeś krok mój, a nikt nie był tej siły

(Ps. 18, line 71)

Schylił nieba i spuścił się: ćma nieprzejźrzana,

(Ps. 18, line 19)

13 syllables (7 + 6)
Czego chcesz od nas, Panie, za Twe hojne dary?

(*Songs*, II, 25, line 1)

Chwalcie Boga, który jest Bóg nad insze bogi,

(Ps. 136, line 3)

Chcesz mię uczcić? Dajże mi dobrą wolę w domu,

(*Songs*, I, 18, line 19)

12 syllables (7 + 5)
Świętobliwe Twe drogi, wszechmocny Boże!

(Ps. 77, line 29)

Szczęśliwy, którego Ty uczniem swym liczysz,

(Ps. 94, line 21)

A okrutni będą Twej syci srogości.

(Ps. 94, line 44)

12 syllables (6 + 6)
Panem ja się chlubię, skromni niech słuchają,

(Ps. 34, line 5)

Wszytko zgubi i sam zniszczeje w kłopocie;

(Ps. 34, line 46)

A nie opuszczaj mię w mój dzień nieszczęśliwy;

(Ps. 102, line 6)

11 syllables (5 + 6)
Cnota skarb wieczny, cnota klenot drogi;

(*Songs*, II, 3; line 21)

Cieszy mię ten rym: "Polak mądr po szkodzie":

(*Songs*, II 5; line 45)

Rozpłynąłem się jako woda prawie,

(Ps. 22, line 37)

11 syllables (4 + 7)
Co zginęło, trudno tego wetować;

(*Songs*, I, 22; line 2)

Rozumie mój, próżno się masz frasować:

(*Songs*, I, 22; line 1)

Wyda mię twarz, gdy się serce źle czuje;

(*Songs*, I, 22; line 14)

10 syllables (5 + 5)
Kleszczmy rękoma wszyscy zgodliwie,

(Ps. 47, line 1)

Spadnie jako deszcz nieprzepłacony

(Ps. 72, line 13)

Posadziłeś mię za stół kosztowny,

(Ps. 23, line 13)

10 syllables (4 + 6)
Dziś bądź wesół, dziś użyj biesiady,

(*Songs*, I, 20; line 25)

Nie idzie mu w smak obiad obfity;

(*Songs*, I, 2; line 22)

Nie macie tu oględać się na co.

(*Songs*, I, 20; line 20)

9 syllables (5 + 4)
Cieszy mię, Panie, dobroć Twoja,

(Ps. 130, line 13)

Nawiedź mię na szlak drogi swojej,

(Ps. 86, line 33)

A nie puszczę się prawdy Twojej;

(Ps. 86, line 34)

Among the longer lines the 13-syllable verse line succeeded in maintaining its triumphant successes, both in the stichic texts and in stanzas. The 11-syllable line with the regular caesura after the fifth syllable was adopted in Poland with other Latin writings; it was comparable to similar lines flourishing in Spain, Portugal, Italy, and England. Kochanowski was well aware of its expansion in other languages. He tested it on a relatively larger scale when he assimilated the narrative poem *Scacchia ludus* (written in Latin in 1527 by the Italian Renaissance writer Marco Girolamo Vida). Kochanowski's work, *Szachy* (*Chess*), was paraphrased in the stichic 11-syllable Polish verse, initiating the subsequent brilliant career of that line in Polish poetry.

Despite triumphant successes, the 11-syllable line was not as widespread in Poland as in Italy, where its usage was universal. Italian versifiers inserted it into different stanzas, while among Polish contemporaries its stichic function seemed to prevail. The version established by Kochanowski rather resembled the Spanish type. In manipulating 11-syllable lines the Spaniards distinguished three different alternatives: 1) *endecasillabo*, with stresses on the 6th and 10th syllables (this rather resembling the Polish pattern) and called iambic or heroic; 2) lines with two stresses: on the 4th and 8th syllables, called *sapphico*; 3) lines with three stresses: on the 4th, 7th, and 10th syllables, called *dactylico*. The Spanish 11-syllable verse had penetrated into Spain as a borrowing from Italy, where it remained the most important category of poetic lines. The Polish solution was less complicated than the Spanish varieties, but more disciplined than the Italian model, which was deprived of any caesura.

The habit of underscoring the ends of versified couplets with rhyming seemed to exist in Poland among early versifiers. This device had been unknown to the ancient Greeks and did not appear in the works of Latin classics. (However, it can be traced in Chinese poetry of the 5th century B.C.). It appeared in the versified texts of the Latin Church in North Africa, where it was inserted into hymns and other religious chants. By the 4th century A.D., rhymed sacred poetry became a regular feature of the Christian liturgy. Gradually it reached wandering students, who spread their rhymed songs throughout different European countries. Rhymes appeared in writings in Provence, France, Italy, Spain, German lands, and England. It also penetrated into Slavic lands, and could be found in *Bogurodzica* (*Mother of God*), the earliest Polish prayer, venerated as a national anthem.

Various rules and customs guided rhyming versifiers. Some contradictory regulations were adopted in European countries. In England, for example, the so-called "identical rhymes" have been considered undesirable, while in France *"consonnes d'appui"* were treated with esteem. Naturally, the regulations underwent different changes. In Poland, the early versifiers tolerated rhymed endings with approximate similarity and did not hesitate to mix paroxytonic and oxytonic words.

In contrast with most of his predecessors (including Rej), Kochanowski submitted rhyming to radical reform. He eliminated the oxytonic words from the rhyming positions completely, and admitted exclusively the paroxytonic "feminine rhymes," embracing the penultimate vowel and all succeeding sounds: one or more subsequent consonants, another vowel, plus possible supplementary consonants. The brave decision of the poet extended the habitual rhyme to one syllable and a half. He fixed and canonized the rule reminiscent of Italian rhyming (even though Italian vocabulary contained not only paroxytona and oxytona, but also proparoxytona). The code conceived by him was acknowledged in Poland by respectable versifiers for over two centuries.

Departures by Kochanowski from his own method of rhyming were infrequent and usually appeared accidental. Some of these "inaccuracies" may be quoted: *"dobrze-szczodrze"* [*"Dziewosłąb"* (*"The Matchmaker"*), lines 157-159], *"kąska-Frącka"* [*"Do starosty"* (*"To the Starost"*), *Fraszki*, III, 60], *"zakon-Polakom"* (*Songs*, I, 10; lines 39-40), *"zysku-blisku"* [*"Do starosty Muszyńskiego"* (*"To the Starost of Muszyna"*), *Fraszki* III, 74, 15-16], *"Wszyscy aniołowie Jego, Wszytki wojska, wyznajcie Go"* (mixed paroxytonum with oxytonum, Ps. 148, lines 5-6). Even in the poet's last longer work *Jezda do Moskwy* (*Campaign to Moscow*) only a few mistakes were left, easily noticeable, and one of them may have been conceived in a jocular spirit:

I wojewodę tegoż wojska zaczapili,
Kniazia Obolińskiego. Ruszywszy się z Koło-
mnej, położyłeś wojsko, Sotow zową sioło.

> (lines 356-358).

(Significantly enough, assonances inserted by the author resembled assonances reintroduced by modern Polish versifiers of the "Avant-Garde.")

Occasionally Kochanowski exploited rhyming for sheer amusement. Among his *Fraszki* he inserted one entitled *"Raki"* ("The Crayfishes," I, 14) which could be read normally or backwards without losing the rhyming effect, but acquiring a diametrically contrasting meaning. In another fraszka, entitled *"Na Barbarę,"*("On Barbara," 1, 37) he listed some ugly vices of a hag, but replaced all rhymed words with meaningless phrases, leaving to the reader the doubtful satisfaction of guessing the rhymed uncomely truth. Time and again the writer would inject proper names into the rhymed position, creating an amusing effect. Another humorous touch resulted from the insertion of a funny Ukrainian saying at the end of a rhymed line in the *fraszka "O sobie"* ("About Myself," I, 24).

The poet was well aware of the refreshing fascination resulting from rare words inserted into the prominent rhyming position. He also exploited the connection between the skill of rhyming and the manipulation of syntactic structure. His skill in this respect excelled in masterful distichs, such as in the *fraszka "Do Hanny"* ("To Hannah", II, 66):

Na palcu masz dyjament, w sercu twardy krzemień,
Pierścień mi, Hanno, dajesz, już i serce przemień!

The *Fraszki*, patiently collected by the writer during his lifetime, revealed different aspects of his poetic craft. Kochanowski was probably the first Polish versifier who succeeded in manipulating the rhyme involving the multiconsonantal name of his native country:

Bogdaj w sławie i w dobrym zdrowiu do Polski
Przyjechał, dobrych ojców cnotliwy Wolski!

> "Do Mikołaja Wolskiego"
> ("To Mikołaj Wolski," *Fraszki*, III, 77)

Kochanowski's mastery of rhyming was submitted to a difficult test in his translations. Manipulation of the vocabulary in rendering the majestic content of one hundred and fifty psalms required tremendous ingenuity and skill. His rendition of the Psalter survived in the consciousness of the nation, and some of the psalms may still be heard in churches. Moreover, the Polish text was translated into several other languages.

While stichic verse written by Kochanowski did not appear as often as his stanzas, it was never neglected. It was used, for example, in the early poem *Szachy* (*Chess*), as already mentioned in connection with the 11-syllable line, an adaptation of Marco Girolamo Vida's *Scacchia ludus*. The work underwent a far-reaching transformation in Kochanowski's version. The original poem takes place in the world of the ancient gods; its Polish adaptation is a kind of short story developing at the Danish royal court. Moreover, the Italian wrote his narrative in Latin hexameters, while the Pole chose his native tongue. The Polish paraphrase was composed in the rhymed stichic 11-syllable verse, contributing to its success. In other longer poems, such as *Zgoda* (Harmony), *Proporzec* (The Banner), *"Marszałek"* (*"The Marshal"*), *"Muza"* (*"Muse"*), *Satyr* (The Satyr), *"Dziewosłąb"* (*"The Matchmaker"*), and *Jezda do Moskwy* (Campaign to Moscow), the Polish author preferred stichic 13-syllable lines. Similar in this respect was also *Pamiątka o śmierci Jana Tarnowskiego* (Memorial on the Death of Jan Tarnowski), but the lines of this work were arranged in regular four-line quatrains.

As to stanzas, they still remained less popular in Poland than in other European countries such as England, France, Italy, and Spain. Nevertheless, in this respect the personal contribution of Kochanowski was considerable. Among the 58 categories of stanzas employed by the Polish writers during his lifetime, 39 specimens—a definite majority—were introduced by Kochanowski. His usual pattern was to combine lines in parallel rhymed couplets, but he also tried other patterns, and occasionally inserted enclosing rhyming, as well as alternate combinations. He manipulated several categories of the Sapphic stanza; most of them contained three 11-syllable lines supplemented by one shorter five-syllable line. Only once did he introduce alternate lines.

Being acquainted with different masterpieces of rich Italian versification, Kochanowski adopted some of its most renowned stanzas, even if he decided to reduce his contribution to a small number of samples. Twice he tested the famous Dantean *terza rima*; one of these specimens was inserted among *Fragmenta albo pozostałe pisma* (*Fragments*), and another test can be found among the psalms in his *Psałterz Dawidów* (*David's Psalter*) in Ps. 15. Such specimens of short lyrical poems composed in *terza rima* became fashionable among the Italian literati during the later decades of the Renaissance; some of them may have influenced the Polish poet.

One of Kochanowski's favorite stanzas was a quatrain consisting of two 13- (or 11-) syllable lines divided by a pair of 7-syllable lines, both pairs rhymed (11 + 7 + 7 + 11) and (13 + 7 + 7 + 13). Both of these were recognized as

FRASZKI

IANA

Kochánowſkiégo.

Jan Kochanowski

❖

FRASZKI tym ƙiążƙom dżieią ∴. ƙto
ſye puśći ná nie
Ʊſczypliwym iezyƙiem / za ſráßƙe nie
ſtánie.

❖

W Kráƙowie.
W Druƙárni Łázárzowéy : Roƙu Pánſƙiégo
1 5 8 4.

56. Jan Kochanowski, *Fraszki*, w Krakowie, 1584. The title page of the only surviving copy
of the first edition (Universitätsbibliothek, Marburg). Reprinted from the facsimile edition by
Władysław Florian, (Wrocław: Ossolineum, 1953).

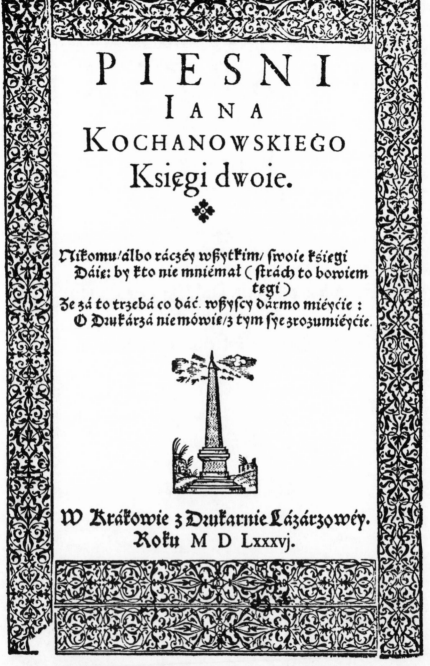

57. Jan Kochanowski, *Pieśni. Księgi dwoie*, w Krakowie, 1586. The title page of the first edition of one of the three surviving copies. (Biblioteka Ossolińskich, Wrocław). Reprinted from the facsimile edition by Władysław Florian (Wrocław: Ossolineum, 1953).

the invention of the poet. Attention should also be paid to his sextains with rhyming patterns *ababcc* and *aabbcc* (Ps. 43, 76, and 95). The translation of Ps. 6 consists of two parts, each containing ten 13-syllable lines. In his rendering of Ps. 92, the poet compiled four 8-line stanzas, in which the 11- and 10-syllable lines have been intermixed (11 + 10 + 11 + 10 + 11 + 10 + 11 + 10). This is the stanza which consists of four pairs of lines differing respectively by one single syllable. In the *Fragments*, Song I he mixes four 11-syllable lines with two 7-syllable lines plus a pair of additional 11-syllable lines (11 + 11 + 11 + 11 + 7 + 7 + 11 + 11). These sporadic experiments illustrate the writer's persistent search for new, refreshing stanzas.

Among 14-line poems inserted in the *Fraszki* were some sonnets. The encouragement for writing them has been usually attributed to Petrarch, but other incentives are not excluded.[4] Even prior to Petrarch, Guittone d'Arezzo (1230-1294) discussed several suggestions which in his opinion deserved to be taken into consideration by eventual sonnet writers. In his view, the initial eight lines should contain the theme and the exposition, whatever subject might be involved. The subsequent sestet should furnish the solution of the suggested problem and the ultimate conclusion. As to rhyming, several patterns were considered tolerable; priority, however, belonged to the pattern *abba-abba-cdc-dcd*. A subdivision between the 11th and 12th lines was also suggested.[5]

Kochanowski's sonnets seem to indicate that their author might have been acquainted with Guittone's instructions or their subsequent transcription. The Polish poet dedicated his sonnets to outstanding personalities deserving public acclaim. The list of honored individuals included a distinguished traveler who died in Italy, *"Do Franciszka"* ("To Franciszek") (II, 105), a gallant soldier and diplomat *"Do St. Wapowskiego"* ("To St. Wapowski"), (III, 24), and a respectable and charming lady, *"Do paniej"* ("To a Lady") (I, 97). It appears that the poet reserved the sonnet for some specific purpose, as an expression of courteous reverence or admiration. On that score his attitude followed the incentive inherited from his two great predecessors—Dante and Petrarch.

Poetic lines, still containing the distant echo of former religious chants (with cadenza and anticadenza), had gained more independent expressiveness through recent structural changes. Reinforced rhyming contributed to the animation of couplets; the effect of multiplied stanzas was similar. Some drive towards more general unity was to be expected.

The incentive for further reform came from Italy. Naturally Kochanowski was well aware that ancient poets of Greece and Rome manipulated the syntactic structure of their verses. In his own works in Latin he followed their example, but a prosody based on the distinction of long and short vowels was not applicable to syllabic versification. Several years spent by the young poet in the Italian environment allowed him to observe similarities existing between Polish and Italian verse and to draw conclusions.

Like Petrarch, Kochanowski was primarily a lyric poet for whom emotional messages were of supreme importance. He understood the enjambements that animated ancient prosody and applied them in his Latin verse. The Italian master provided him with valuable encouragement by running from one line to the next in his sonnets and other poems. By means of such enjambements Petrarch obtained more structural unity and organic fluency. As an illustration of this technique, lines 1-14 of *Canzone CXXVII*, one of his numerous canzoni to Laura, may suffice:

> In quella parte dove Amor mi sprona
> conven ch' io volga le dogliose rime,
> che son seguaci de la menta afflitta.
> Quai fien ultime, lasso, e qua' fien prime?
> Colui che del mio mal meco ragiona
> mi lascia in dubbio, sì confuso ditta.
> Ma pur quanto l'istoria trovo scritta
> in mezzo 'l cor, che sì spesso rincorro,
> co la sua propria man, de' miei martiri,
> dirò, perché i sospiri
> parlando àn triegua et al dolor soccorro.
> Dico che perch' io miri
> mille cose diverse attento e fiso,
> sol una Donna veggio e 'l suo bel viso.[6]

Kochanowski was well aware of this structural innovation, but he applied it mainly when he wished to convey the most violent emotional messages. He struck a patriotic chord when he heard of the disastrous aggression of the Tatar invaders in a rich southeastern province of Poland, and immediately composed a passionate appeal to the nation calling for swift revenge (Song V in *Songs, Book Two*). In the first quatrain of his passionate appeal, every line remained suspended and submitted to an enjambement:

> Wieczna sromota i nienagrodzona
> Szkoda, Polaku! Ziemia spustoszona
> Podolska leży, a pohaniec sprosny,
> Nad Niestrem siedząc, dzieli łup żałosny!

> Eternal shame and unredeemed loss,
> O Pole: the Podolian land lies
> Devastated and the lewd pagan
> Sitting at the Niester river divides lamentable booty!

Another sad incentive for mourning was the passing of the poet's beloved daughter Ursula, to whom the father dedicated his *Treny* (*Laments*). Time and again the poet ruffled regular diction to submit fluent verse to expressive distortions, as in Lament V:

> Przed oczyma rodziców swoich rostąc, mało
> Od ziemie się co wznióswszy, duchem zaraźliwym
> Srogiej Śmierci otchniona, rodzicom troskliwym
> U nóg martwa upadła.

Grown before the eyes of her parents, being
A mere child, she was swept up by the infectious breath
Of cruel Death and fell
At the feet of her parents.

The poet was also successful in adapting his poetic diction for translating. Some of his Psalms excelled in manipulating syntactic alterations and complicated enjambements, as in Psalm 21, lines 1-4:

Panie, za Twoją zawżdy pomocą król bije
Nieprzyjaciela swego, przeto też użyje
Nieśmiertelnej radości; bo jaka być moze
Większa uciecha, jedno łaska Twa, mój Boże?

The king shall joy in thy strength,
O Lord; and in thy salvation
how greatly shall he rejoice!
Thou hast given him his heart's desire,
and has not withholden the request of his lips.

(Ps. 21, lines 1-4, King James version)

Shifting a part of one line and placing it in the subsequent verse was one of the devices which Kochanowski appreciated and used on various occasions. However, he resorted to enjambements in a moderate way. He introduced them for definite emotional reasons, avoiding sheer mannerisms. That is why his diction sounded so effective.

While Kochanowski mastered the Latin language to such perfection that he could use it like an expert, his command of Greek was limited to reading and translating. Included among his *Fraszki* were several miniatures of Anacreon (ca. 570-480) in Polish translation. One *fraszka* was conceived as a tribute to this witty predecessor. Several other verses were defined as "taken from Greek," but the names of the authors were not revealed.[7]

A more ambitious achievement was the translation into Polish of a large fragment of the *Iliad*. The selected episode was limited to the third canto, concentrating on the fight between Alexander and Menelaus. Hector, who arranged their duel, treated it as an attempt to bring the Graeco-Trojan conflict to a speedy conclusion, but his endeavor failed. The poet selected this particular fragment because it contained some valuable information which he planned to exploit in his own prospective drama.

Another effort serving the same purpose was Kochanowski's *Alcestis męża od śmierci zastąpiła*, a translation of the initial passages from Euripides' tragedy *Alcestis*. The selected episode dealt with an attempt of Apollo to convince Thanatos (Death) that he should spare the life of Alcestis, the consort of King Admet; the monarch was mortally ill, and his wife declared that for the salvation of her husband she was prepared to sacrifice her own life. Apollo endeavored to persuade Thanatos that he should not approve of this heroic sacrifice. Apollo and Thanatos quarrel, and the scene closes with a brief song of the worried choir about the fate of Alcestis.

Other stimulating and productive incentives anticipating the playwriting of Kochanowski originated from Italian drama.[8] Primary among these was the work of the Italian scholar and playwright Giangiorgio Trissino (1478-1550). His tragedy *Sofonisba*, based on the conflict between the Roman Republic and Carthage, was written in the year 1515 and published ten years later. It achieved much theatrical success and was often performed and reprinted. Moreover, it was selected in Vicenza to celebrate the solemn opening of the official Palazzo de la Regione; the ceremony took place in the year 1562, anticipating by sixteen years the performance of Kochanowski's play *Odprawa posłów greckich* (*The Dismissal of the Greek Envoys*) in Jazdów (Ujazdów, subsequently a district of Warsaw).[9]

Trissino distinguished himself not only as a revitalizer of ancient theatrical tradition that had flourished in Greece and Italy, but also as a learned linguist. His *Castellae della lingua Italiana* (1529) was a dialogue on the relative merits of different Italian idioms. The author discussed the treatment of vowels and consonants in various Italian provinces, and came to the conclusion that the Etruscan dialect was the most beautiful tongue on the Italian peninsula. Trissino also wrote a treatise on poetics, *Arte Poetica*, the fifth part of which deals with his theories on modern tragedy. He popularized the verse *endecasillabo sciolto*, which became the standard "heroic meter" in Italy. Trissino was basically considered a disciple and admirer of Euripides, whereas closer to Sophocles was Giovanni Rucellai (1475-1525), whose *Rosmunda* was written almost simultaneously with Trissino's *Sofonisba*.[10]

While Trissino accepted different technicalities from the Greek master Euripides, he maintained an independent attitude in his verse. He came to the conclusion that the Greek meter did not fit the modern Italian language. Sometimes he introduced rhyme in his tragedy, but he also used rhymeless blank verse, classified as *endecasillabo sciolto*. As a playwright he owed his master Euripides some structural features and emotional coloring.

Such were some highlights of the theatrical atmosphere in Italy during the period preceding Kochanowski's studies and the publication of *Odprawa posłów greckich*. The poet was solidly equipped for his own theatrical venture. His close acquaintance with the Homeric epic provided him with some valuable information, including the names of characters. Not in vain had he done some enlightening and instructive translating. In this respect his study of *Alcestis* was especially productive: the initial scene of this tragedy anticipated the prospective strife of two human beings in *The Dismissal*, Antenor and Alexander, revealing the traditional "stichomythia." Such was the origin of the most dramatic encounter of the drama—the opening episode preceded only by a monologue.

The appearance of Helen with her companion and their peaceful dialogue provides the audience some respite. As to the debate of the Royal Council, it was reported by a messenger whose narrative was nevertheless so dramatic that it could create suspense, even though its conclusion would be anticipated by the audience. The remainder of the play brings the reaction of both envoys after the failure of their mission, the hasty preparations of the Trojans for the imminent war, Cassandra's anticipation of the Trojan disaster, and the initial clashes of the hostile sides. (It might be observed that if the text spoken by the messenger were replaced by the persons whom he represented, the scene would acquire the grandeur of similar Shakespearean episodes.)

The prosody of the drama (resembling Trissino) resulted from careful deliberation. The initial monologue of Antenor was written in 11-syllable blank verse, tested by the poet in translating *Alcestis*. The same verse appeared in the dialogue between Antenor and Alexander and in the talk of Greek women. For the augury of Cassandra the author chose stichic 12-syllable verse, also unrhymed. Aside from these passages and two songs of the Trojan maidens, the 13-syllable blank verse dominated the play; thus, *The Dismissal* resembled Kochanowski's translation of the *Iliad*, but was unrhymed.

Rhyming in *The Dismissal* was reserved for only two songs, both consisting of quatrains. The third one, however, was composed in blank verse differing from all other stichic passages of the play. It is the longest and most innovative chorus. Kochanowski himself stated "it seems to imitate Greek choruses...." It contains lines with nine (or, in two cases, ten) syllables consisting of dactylic and trochaic feet. Such was the poet's original sample of syllabic-accentual verse. The drama became in reality Kochanowski's display of modernized versification. It comprised 13-, 12-, and 11-syllable blank lines, an unrhymed stichic song, conceived as a specimen of syllabic-accentual prosody, and two rhymed songs consisting of different stanzas. (It should be added that the song in *Alcestis* had contained nine blank 8-syllable lines.)

The final song of Trojan maidens indicated that although strict syllabism definitely dominated the prosody of Kochanowski, he did not feel irrevocably attached to this kind of versification. An earlier deviation in this respect had been his narrative poem *Zuzanna*. Its content was based on the well-known biblical tale. While the dedication of this versified story (addressed to Princess Radziwiłł) was written in the habitual, rhymed 13-syllable syllabic verse, the narrative was set down in 14-syllable rhymed verse maintained in trochaic rhythm ($- - - - - - - - - - - -$) with occasional deviations arranged in amphibrachic feet:

Czas po temu masz i miejsce, drzwi zawarte stoją,
Żywy człowiek nas nie widzi, pomóż łaską swoją.

(lines 77-78)

It is not improbable that some foreign tale served as a model or as an incentive. As *Zuzanna* was the only poem of this kind, it could be considered as a testimony to the author's versatility, whatever was the reason for this deviation from his habitual technique. The last distich of the poem struck a note which sounded frequently in psalms:

Wszyscy wielkim głosem krzykną i cześć Bogu dali,
Że On nigdy nie opuścił, którzy Mu dufali.

(lines 207 - 208)

All cry out in a great voice and gave praise to God,
That He never had forsaken those who trust in Him.

This marginal deviation was a minor episode in Kochanowski's literary output. He eclipsed his predecessors and established the domination of strict, canonized syllabism embracing various aspects of prosody. For over two centuries his authority determined various aspects of national versification.

Notes

1. For discussion of the oldest examples of Polish religious songs, including the Polish version of the medieval Latin hymn "Horae canonicae Salvatoris" ("Jesus Chrystus, Bóg-człowiek, mądrość Oćca swego"), see Jan Łoś, *Początki piśmiennictwa polskiego* (The Beginning of Polish Letters) (Lwów: Ossolineum, 1922), pp. 399-402. Maria Dłuska notes that this song is both the oldest thirteen-syllable line and the oldest verse line with a caesura. While the earliest preserved copy of the translation was done about 1420, she dates the song according to linguistic evidence at about 1400. See Maria Dłuska, *Studia z historii i teorii wersyfikacji polskiej* (Studies on the history and theory of Polish versificationl), vol. 1 (Cracow: Polska Akademia Umiejętności, 1948), pp. 11-13.

2. Marian Pełczyński, *Studia macaronica: Stanisław Orzelski na tle poezji makaronicznej w Polsce* ("Macaronic" studies: Stanisław Orzelski in the context of macaronic poetry in Poland) (Poznań: PWN Poznańskie Towarzystwo Przyjaciół Nauk, 1960), pp. 12-14. Janusz Pelc, *Jan Kochanowski. Szczyt renesansu w literaturze polskiej* (Jan Kochanowski: Zenith of the Renaissance in Polish literature) (Warsaw: PWN, 1980), pp. 208-209.

3. Karl Shapiro and Robert Beum, *A Prosody Handbook* (New York: Harper and Row, 1965), pp. 54-55.

4. See Pelc, *Jan Kochanowski*, pp. 281-283.

5. Guittone d'Arezzo is considered to have established the *abbaabba* octave which then became traditional through its preference by Dante and Petrarch. See *Princeton Encyclopedia of Poetry and Poetics*, enlarged ed., Alex Preminger, ed. (Princeton, N.J.: Princeton University Press, 1974), p. 782; and Ernest Hatch Wilkins, *A History of Italian Literature* (Cambridge: Harvard University Press, 1954), pp. 26-27.

6. Francesco Petrarca, *Rime. Trionfi e Poesie Latine*. A cura di F. Neri, et al. (Milan and Naples: Riccardo Ricciardi Editore, 1951), p. 178.

7. The three categories of fraszki based upon Greek sources are: a) "miniatures" from Anacreon entitled "Z Anacreonta" found in Book I (4, 8, 40, 76), Book II (90), and Book III (4,5); b) a tribute to Anacreon, entitled "Do Anakreonta," Book II, 46; and c) fraszki entitled "Z Greckiego" found in Book II (38, 50, 54, 58), and Book III (25).

8. See Maria Dłuska, *Studia i rozprawy* (Studies and treaties), vol. 2 (Cracow: Wydawnictwo Literackie, 1970), pp. 16-19; and Tadeusz Ulewicz, Introduction to *Odprawa posłów greckich* (The Dismissal of the Greek Envoys), 11th ed., Biblioteka Narodowa I, 3 (Wrocław: Ossolineum, 1969).

9. On the probable form of the first production of Kochanowski's *Dismissal* at the palace in Jazdów, see Ulewicz. Introduction, pp. lx-lxii; and Pelc, *Jan Kochanowski*, pp. 87-91; and Julian Lewański, *Dramat i teatr średniowiecza i renesansu w Polsce* (Drama and theater in the Middle Ages and Renaissance in Poland) (Warsaw: PWN, 1981), pp. 320-323.

10. See Beatrice Corrigan, Introduction to *Two Renaissance Plays* (Manchester: Manchester University Press, 1975), pp. 8-15.

21

Classical Tradition in Kochanowski's Work: Problems of Reception

Jerzy Axer

While I have entitled this essay "The Classical Tradition in Kochanowski's Work," nevertheless I do not claim to propose any synthetic approach. I do not think that a comprehensive determination of the relation between Kochanowski's poetry and the tradition of ancient literature ought yet to be attempted. With so much analysis still to be done, it would be premature. The view that I wish to express concerns only one aspect of the functioning of classical material in Kochanowski's works. I arrived at this view while editing only some of the poet's works, but I am tempted to believe that it applies to his entire output and, in part, more broadly to all Renaissance poetry of whatever quality. I wish to show that appropriate research into the classical tradition in these works can provide important information that may well elucidate certain mechanisms of their perception. It can help us understand the variety of the public intended by the author, some aspects of reception among later generations, and even some scholarly disputes. In my opinion, the potential of such research has not been fully acknowledged.

At the outset, one characteristic of the research conducted until now on Kochanowski's borrowings from ancient works should be stressed. Scholars have not isolated and developed the question of literary allusion, understood as using one literary text in the context of another for the purpose of expressing the latter's own message. Whereas most critics of Enlightenment, romantic, and contemporary poetry take the possible presence of such allusions into account, the approach to Polish Renaissance poetry is usually different. In the last-named case all is still lost in analyses of so-called "influences" or imitations. This is understandable inasmuch as the majority of material has been gathered by classics scholars, in particular by Tadeusz Sinko, and in part by scholars of Polish literature at a time when the problems of literary allusion had not yet been distinguished in research on references to other literary texts in a given work at all.

Interest has concentrated mainly on the origin of the work and the psychology of the author. The influences found were to indicate to what degree an ancient text was the source of a given work by Kochanowski and to what degree the poet's imagination and memory yielded to the thoughts and images suggested by classical tradition. If the effects of the appearance of references to the tradition in a work were considered, this was done in accordance with the post-romantic trend to contrast convention with originality, erudition with spontaneity, and borrowing with innovation. Since the first fully consistent analyses of Renaissance texts in terms of Renaissance poetics, scholars have focused on the phenomenon of imitation. Thus, impressive lists of *similia* are often appended to the poet's works. These *similia* show how, in accordance with the *imitatio* principle, portions of works by classical authors, removed from their original contexts, are placed in new contexts. We have abundant material illustrating how the Polish language fed upon Latin and how the Polish language was formed. But the role of borrowings from classical authors that acted as literary allusions and introduced the context of an ancient work as a background to emphasize the poet's thoughts is still underestimated.[1]

Scholars speak only about the peculiar pleasure that the reader experienced when he recognized the ancient incrustation created by the author in the framework of his "erudite feat."[2] At times the possible use of this incrustation for polemic or satirical purposes has been pointed out.[3] In principle, however, as the practice of poetry using obviously borrowed formulas is no longer opposed by contemporary literary tastes, discussions of how the links between a given text and a classical work affect its impact are even less frequent than before. It seems at times that whenever a scholar recognizes a borrowing in the course of interpretation, he states that there is nothing wrong with that, and that on the contrary the practice is highly humanistic; then he is quite ready to forget about it with relief.

In the course of my research on the link between Kochanowski's poetry and ancient tradition, I was struck by the degree to which the meaning of the text was shaped by the reference to the meanings contained in the texts of classical writers. I was amazed by the disproportion between the attractiveness of the phenomenon observed and the slight attention paid to it in research, between its significance for understanding the author's intentions and the scant information that the contemporary reader is offered in commentaries. In fact, Kochanowski's poetry makes extensive use of the context of ancient texts in order to express its own message. The system of references to the plots, the mosaic of parallel images and situations, and especially the network of phraseological borrowingss (such as quotations, paraphrases, crypto-quotations, etc.) introduce meanings from classical texts into the works in question on a broad scale; only if we are aware of these messages can we fully understand a given work. The *imitatio* technique permits a refined literary interplay on all levels of a work's artistic structure; the context from which the borrowing comes may appear in the reader's consciousness more or less clearly, it may last for a longer or shorter time, it can disappear and reappear. Appropriate sequences of borrowing result in the crossing, blending, and recomposition of the contexts suggested to the reader's memory. At the same time, many borrowings are completely separated from their original contexts so that the reader's memory is either not directed to any concrete text or directed to a number of texts at once.

A more detailed analysis of this method of using classical material has been attempted in my other works.[4] Here it is necessary to point out this under-estimated aspect of the function of the classical tradition in Kochanowski's poetry, in order to discuss a direct and obvious consequence of the acknowl-edgement of its significance. If literary allusion, which reminds the reader of the meanings contained in an ancient text, is an important element of the impact of this poetry, clearly this impact depends on the reader's readiness to recall these meanings. His knowledge of various components of classical tra-dition conditions his reaction to various allusions. The varying degree to which the reader was able to recognize the patterns and follow their modifications led to varying understandings of a work. Accepting this viewpoint, we must agree that by the introduction of an ancient borrowing, the author must have been aware of the variety of possible responses, the variety of which the scholar also must be aware. Hence it is not enough to establish the source of the borrowing by indicating the closest ancient model, taking into account what the author had read; rather, we should ask to which model (or models) was the reader's imagination directed. In this understanding, the classical tradition is no longer unequivocal and easy to describe.

A phraseological borrowing might bring a Ciceronian phrase together with its surrounding context to mind for one reader; another might recognize Cicero but, instead of the original context, his memory suggests a relevant excerpt from St. Augustine where the same expression of Cicero is quoted; in the mind of yet another reader the Senecan mutation of this thought might overshadow all other associations. But there are certainly readers in whose mind no concrete context emerges but only a general sense of contact with a sample of ancient wisdom. Thus, depending on the reader, we have either Cicero, or Seneca, or Augustine, or no one, or all at once. In turn, let us consider an elaborate epic simile. Again, we have the same mechanism of response: associations with Homer or Virgil or Lucan might be evoked or, instead of these, Job, or all of these at once, depending on the reader's knowleage and sensitivity. Hence, depending on the reader's knowledge and sensitivity, the meaning of the classical texts may appear or not. By an appropriate use of elements from the classical tradition, the poet was able to construct layers of meaning intended for different circles of readers.[5]

Yet the dependence of perception upon the reader's familiarity with the classical tradition cannot be confined only to the public of the poet's times.

With the passage of time, a text may undergo an essential change in meaning according to readers' readiness to respond to references to this tradition. This phenomenon can explain many aspects of the reception of Kochanowski's texts by subsequent generations, as well as the very special kind of reception in scholarship. One might easily trace the dependence of certain views of the poet's texts expressed by scholars of various generations upon their response to the classical tradition. The situation has not changed to this day. Scholars' decreasing sensitivity to allusive references to ancient literatures causes many of them to overlook the role of this tradition, both in the construction of the meanings of a given text and as effective means of communication between author and readers—different readers, let us observe. That is why I have considered it necessary to stress this particular function of the classical tradition in Kochanowski's works and illustrate my view with an example of how precise understanding of the text can depend on the ability to recognize elements of this tradition. Since numerous examples cannot be analyzed here, and since I do not intend to refer to Polish quotations, I will concentrate of the reception of Kochanowski's *Treny* (*Threnodies* or *Laments*) as a whole.

The most important discovery concerning classical literary tradition, that research for the commentary to the latest edition of the *Laments*[6] produced, is the ramified system of borrowings from Cicero's texts. They constitute a significant part of the ancient phraseology used in the *Laments*. Some of the borrowings were indicated in earlier research, but we have been able to triple their number. It has turned out that the references are to certain easily distinguishable groups of Ciceronian texts. The selection is particularly noteworthy. The groups are as follows:

1. The scant fragments of Cicero's lost little work entitled "Consolatio," written by the philosopher after his daughter's death—the only known ancient example of self-consolation in the strict sense of the word. Only a few bits, mostly of no more than a few words, have survived. They were collected first by Carolus Sigonius[7] and later by Andreas Patricius Nidecki [Andrzej Patrycy Nidecki].[8] Almost all of them were built into the text of the *Laments*;
2. All of the letters written both by and to Cicero that are thematically linked with his daughter's death;
3. Numerous excerpts from various philosophical works, notably the *Tusculanae disputationes*;
4. Minute fragments of Cicero's poetry: the two verses in the original taken as a motto and further, paraphrases of the short bits of Ciceronian translation from Homer and the Greek tragedians, blended with Kochanowski's text;

Only the basic consequences of this choice will be indicated here. The first three groups evidence Cicero's own mourning. The system of references to these works is such that those aware of them read the *Laments* accompanied

by a vision of a Sage in Mourning. One can go even further; it appears that
these are in principle the same texts that Sigonius used to make up his counterfeit version of the complete text of the Ciceronian "Consolatio."[9] This was
published three years after the *Laments* but previously it had been read in
manuscripts.[10] Whether Kochanowski knew this work or not is less interesting
in this argument. The contents of Sigonius's work and its considerable popularity indicate that Kochanowski's contemporaries believed it to be material
documenting Cicero's perplexity in his despair at his daughter's death. It was
believed that these very thoughts and these or similar expressions appeared
in the work that Cicero had written about his suffering. It seems as if the whole
system of references to Cicero's different works directed the reader of the
Laments to one work only. Though the work had not survived, it appeared
well-outlined in the imagination of the poet's contemporaries. Finally, the
fourth group of references concerns Cicero's poems. First collected by Nidecki,
these poems long fascinated Kochanowski. They supply a meaningful accent
in the *Laments* images of Cicero the Father and Cicero the Sage are complemented with that of Cicero the Poet. Thus, the correspondence with Kochanowski's situation is now complete.

Despair and hope, complaint and comfort, belief and doubt in the *Laments*
are partly the despair, hope, and doubt of Cicero suffering and Cicero seeking
consolation—but only for certain readers, for those conscious of the above
discussed elements of tradition. It must be said that in the *Laments* the borrowings from Cicero created a layer of meaning fully understandable only to
a limited circle of readers, those for whom Nidecki's *Ciceronis fragmenta* and
Aratus by Kochanowski himself had been intended. For the same elitist public
Kochanowski's reference to Cicero's "Consolatio" was an attractive literary
experiment that consisted of reaching for the roots of the consolatory tradition
and of a bold attempt to propose the poet's own solutions. At the same time,
this reference indicated that Kochanowski had entered the path outlined by
his predecessors ranging from the Fathers of the Church to Sigonius. Similarly
Aratus had been an experiment: an attempt to reach to the roots of an important
trend in Roman poetry and continue this trend creatively.[11] Hence, there was
a circle of readers of the *Laments* capable of appreciating a search for a new
form, on the pretext of recreating a lost ancient pattern, a procedure typical of
the foremost Renaissance humanists.

Yet it would be absurd to insist that one who failed to recognize the above
references was not able to understand and appreciate the *Laments*. It is not a
question of a failure to understand the text on the part of such a reader. Those
who did not think of "Consolatio" or had never heard of Cicero's poetry still
remained under the influence of consolatory schemes shaped over the centuries. All of Cicero's texts mentioned above are at the same time elements of
these schemes, in whose framework they occur in various poetic and prose
variants, placed in different contexts and at different points of the consolatory
reasoning. They are quoted, summarized, and paraphrased.[12] They are ele-

ments of the mourning scheme to such a degree that the structure of the *Laments*, a literary experiment on a European scale, parallels the structure of Kochanowski's prose address over his brother's grave.

The reader of the *Laments* could have been more or less aware of the classical background of certain expressions and motifs, his world of literary associations could be richer or poorer. If poor, it limited and simplified but did not hinder his understanding of Kochanowski's writing. More precise references, the interplay of allusions, and special points were lost in favor of a general awareness of the classical dignity of the patterns, and the classic aptness of the formulas. All of these remained within the variety of responses predicted by the author. Yet this mechanism remains unchanged even when the ability to understand the classical references has dropped to a degree not expected by the author. The argument can be extended to embrace the average contemporary reader who is so slightly versed in the classical tradition that he is only generally aware of any contact with a poetic expression of long gone grief and love.

To round off the discussion of the influence of classical tradition on the understanding of the *Laments*, mention must be made of the opposite extreme in contemporary reception of the cycle, namely, scholarly analyses. I shall concentrate on one observation only. The *Laments* increasingly have been treated as a crypto-philosophic work, a record of a worldview drama as experienced both by an individual and a generation, where personal disaster plays only a limited role. The tendency to view the *Laments* as an anti- Ciceronian polemic is also very much alive. It is believed that this anti- Ciceronianism was intended as a method to formulate a new view of the world.[13] Undoubtedly, the radical character of this interpretative trend is directly linked to observation of the references to Cicero's texts in the *Laments* without sufficient awareness of the position that these texts occupy within consolatory schemes. Without this awareness, without distinguishing between precise and broader contexts, and without recognizing the interplay of allusions, the evident role of Roman philosophic prose in the phraseology and imagery of the *Laments* must lead to seeing the philosophic motif as the primary one, largely independent of the consolatory message. Consequently, auto-polemics may be seen as a pure anti-Ciceronianism and a ritual gesture of mourning as blasphemy.

I have limited myself to remarks about the reception of the cycle as a whole, but the dependence relationship between response and degree of understanding of the classical references could be illustrated through an analysis of the text on the level of the individual poems, individual images, and individual expressions. Still, every element of the structure of the work offers convincing evidence. The motto, for instance, a quotation from Homer in Cicero's translation, has a slightly different meaning for the reader who only remembers the context in which the quotation appeared in St. Augustine than for one who also remembers its role in the writing of Sextus Empiricus. The motto acquires a mournful meaning for the reader of the pseudo-Plutarchian consolation, but its direct link with the opening of the first "Lament" is apparent only to those who remember it from the *Vita Heracliti* by Diogenes. Finally, the special effect of Nidecki's conjecture could only be appreciated by a humanist familiar with the latest edition of *Fragmenta Ciceronis*.[14] Let us take the central image of "Lament I", a dragon ravishing a bird's nest. The dragon's devilish nature, revealed through an interplay of ancient and biblical allusions, was probably sensed by most sixteenth-century readers, but as soon as a portion of the allusions was no longer quite clear, the image turned into an overly elaborate, slightly pretentious decorative motif.[15] Let us take the famous line from "Lament VIII", "*Jedną maluczką duszą tak wiele ubyło*," ("So much has gone away with one little soul") that has been regarded as the most "romantic" and "spontaneous" expression of the cycle by commentators ranging from Mickiewicz and Krasiński to contemporary ones. It turns out, however, that it is a faithful quotation from a letter to Cicero, and as such, it is an important element of the mosaic of references to the philosopher's mourning, intended for a certain sphere of readers.[16] Such examples can be easily multiplied.

In conclusion, in Kochanowski's Polish-language poetry the classical matter permits the reader's particularly active participation in building the meanings of the work. By this is meant not simply "understanding" or "not understanding," but rather that understanding varies according to the choice, sequence, and impact of the elements of the ancient tradition appearing in the reader's consciousness influenced by suggestions contained in the text. One can follow exactly the poet's effort to create a harmonious coexistence of various levels of response by means of appropriately formed multilayered references to a classical tradition. One can determine how carefully the author avoids severing his constant link with the reader on every level of response, how, when using a borrowed phrase, image, or motif, he is anxious to shape it so as to make the borrowing an element of any possible reading, although the borrowing might not mean the same thing within the framework of each of the readings. Perhaps this approach to the ancient tradition is one of the reasons for the general and longstanding popularity of Kochanowski's poetry with very different publics. An analysis of different responses resulting from the reader's varying preparation for understanding the classical tradition is not an example of a comparative scholar's over-zealousness, but a task that must be completed because it will permit a more profound understanding of the contents of the texts in question. Failure to carry out these studies may lead to false interpretations of the poet's intentions, the artistic structure of his work, and the information it contains. It may also lead to erroneous editorial decisions.

In research on the poetic craftsmanship of an author who worked in accordance with the *imitatio* principle, one grows accustomed to following the poet's "bee-like" effort, as they said in the Renaissance: the collection and transformation of bits of classical prose and poetry. We become used to identifying borrowings carefully, taking into account the author's education and preferences. We try to consider the thus acquired canon of the text from the standpoint of a man of the Renaissance. However, we must realize to a greater degree than has been done until now that the classical allusions and references in these texts are signs which the poet used fully aware that there were several keys to some of them.

Thus, we must understand the classical tradition in Renaissance poetry as the set of all ancient works whose meanings could have emerged in the reader's mind because of the suggestions contained in the text. The set of references is only potentially present in the poems. The readers' erudition determined which elements of the set affected his response to the poems. Varying familiarity with the classical tradition could thus signify varying response. Or, viewing the problem from a different angle, we may say that different circles of readers found different classical traditions in Kochanowski's poetry.

Notes

1. Analyses such as Wiktor Weintraub's, "*Fraszka* in a Tragic Key: Remarks on Kochanowski's Lament XI and Fraszki I, 3," in *For Roman Jakobson. Essays on the Occasion of his Seventieth Birthday* (The Hague: Mouton, 1967), pp. 2219-2230, appear only exceptionally.

2. Cf. Konrad Górski, "Aluzja literacka; Istota zjawiska i jego typologia" (Literary allusion; essence of the phenomenon and its typology), in *Z historii i teorii literatury. Seria druga* (History and theory of literature, series 2) (Warsaw: PWN, 1964), pp. 7-32.

3. Konrad Górski, "Słowacki jako poeta aluzji literackiej" (Słowacki as a poet of literary allusion) in *Z historii i teorii literatury*, pp. 177-178.

4. See "Rola kryptocytatów z literatury łacińskiej w polsko-języcznej twórczości Kochanowskiego" (Crypto-quotations from Latin literature in Kochanowski's Polish-language works), *Pamiętnik Literacki* LXXIII, 1/2 (1982), pp. 167-177.

5. If we are sufficiently aware of the reader's role as an interpreter of the author's references to ancient works, our view of the contribution of Latin and Greek literature to the classical tradition in Kochanowski's output changes. Regardless of his own readings and ideals, the poet could count on a widespread and detailed knowledge of certain texts of Roman literature,but, in principle, could not count on his readers remembering Greek expressions. If an allusion was meant to bring context in an unchanged verbal shape to the reader's mind, it had to refer almost only to Latin works. On the other hand, regardless of kind of reference to Greek antiquity, the Hellenic model might have easily been overshadowed by a more or less faithful Roman copy for most readers in Poland.

6. Jan Kochanowski, *Dzieła Wszystkie*. Wydanie Sejmowe, (Complete works) vol. 2: *Treny (Treny)*, ed. by Maria Renata Mayenowa and Lucyna Woronczakowa in collaboration with Jerzy Axer and Maria Cytowska (Wrocław: Ossolineum, 1983).

7. *Fragmenta Ciceronis variis in locis dispersa Caroli Sigonii diligentia collecta* (Venetiis, 1559). "Consolatio": f. 104a-108a.

8. *Ciceronis fragmentorum tomus tertius qui philosophica continet. Ex Andr. Patricii Striceconis secunda editione* (Venetiis, 1565). "Consolatio": f. 27v-29.

9. The *editio princeps* entitled *Ciceronis consolatio vel de luctu minuendo* was published in Venice in 1583. Between 1583 and 1585 at least ten editions appeared in Venice, Leyden, Piacenza, Bologna, London, Paris, Nuremberg, Frankurt, and Erfurt.

10. The work had circulated in manuscript from before 1565 (see Maria Cytowska, "Sur la 'Consolatio' de Ciceron. Sigonio-Nidecki-Kumaniecki," *Eos* 68 fasc. 1 (1980); p. 126.

11. See Jerzy Axer, "*Aratus*—miejsce poematu w twórczości Kochanowskiego" [*Aratus*—the position of the poem in Kochanowski's work] in, *Jan Kochanowski i epoka renesansu* (Warsaw: PWN, 1984), pp. 159-167.

12. See, e.g., Peter von Moos, *Consolatio; Studien zur mittellateinischen Trostliteratur über den Tod und zum Problem der christilichen Trauer*, B. I-IV (Munich: W. Fink, 1971) with relevant texts by Cicero according to index; Rudolf Kassel, *Untersuchungen zur griechischen and römischen Konsolationsliteratur* (Munich: 1958), *passim*; Kazimierz Kumaniecki, "Die verlorene 'Consolatio' des Cicero," in *Acta Classica Univ. Scient.*, Debrecen, 4, 1968, pp. 27-47. Cf. Joachim Gruber, *Kommentar zu Boethius De Consolatione Philosphiae* (Berlin-New York: de Gruyter, 1978), pp. 24-27

13. The latest interpretations of the *Laments* Janusz Pelc, "*Treny*" *Jana Kochanowskiego* (Jan Kochanowski's *Laments* (Warsaw: PWN, 1972), and Stanisław Grzeszczuk, *Materiały do studiowania literatury staropolskiej* (Materials for studies of old Polish literature) (Rzeszów: Wydawnictwo Wyższej Szkoły Pedagogicznej, 1977), pt. 2, pp. 31-130; "*Treny*" *Jana Kochanowskiego* (Jan Kochanowski's *Laments*) (Warsaw: Wydawnictwa Szkolne i Pedagogiczne, 1978); "*Treny*" *Jana Kochanowskiego. Próba interpretacji* (Jan Kochanowski's *Laments*. An attempt at interpretation) (Wrocław: Ossolineum, 1979). Cf. survey and summary of research, Janusz Pelc, *Jan Kochanowski. Szczyt Renesansu w literaturze polskiej* (Jan Kochanowski. Zenith of the Renaissance in Polish literature) (Warsaw: PWN, 1980), pp. 434-459.

14. For the link between the motto and Nidecki's edition, see Maria Cytowska, "Nad *Trenami* Jana Kochanowskiego. Od motta do genezy poematu" (On Jan Kochanowski's *Laments*. From the poem's motto to its origin), *Pamiętnik Literacki* LXX, 1 (1979): pp. 181-186.

15. See Jerzy Axer, "Smok i słowiczki. Wokół wersów 1-14 Trenu 1 Jana Kochanowskiego" (Dragon and nightingale nestlings. On lines 1- 14 of Jan Kochanowski's "Lament 1") *Pamiętnik Literacki* LXX, 1 (1979) pp. 187-191.

16. For complete analysis, see Axer, "Rola", *Pamiętnik Literacki*, pp.169-171.

22

Everything is But a Trifle

Jerzy R. Krzyżanowski

Kochanowski wrote at the beginning of "Book One" of his "trifles", *Fraszki*, published at the end of his life in 1584.

> Fraszki to wszytko, cokolwiek myślemy,
> Fraszki to wszytko, cokolwiek czyniemy;
> Nie masz na świecie żadnej pewnej rzeczy,
> Próżno tu człowiek ma co mieć na pieczy.
> Zacność, uroda, moc, pieniądze, sława,
> Wszystko to minie jako polna trawa;
> Naśmiawszy się nam i naszym porządkom,
> Wemkną nas w mieszek, jako czynią łątkom[1]

To quote it in Czesław Miłosz's translation:

> Everything that we think is trifles,
> Everything that we do is trifles,
> There is no certain thing in the world,
> In vain men take so much care.
> Virtue, beauty, power, money, fame
> Will pass like the grasses of the fields.
> We and our order will be laughed at
> And into a sack we will be cast like puppets
> after a show.[2]

Usually we associate the generic term *fraszka* (from the Italian *frasca*, or "little twig") with a rather light-hearted type of poetry, as has been amply documented in numerous studies, monographs, and anthologies. This time, however, we are presented with a phenomenon hardly commensurate with such a tradition. Entitled *"O żywocie ludzkim"* ("On human life"), this *fraszka* fills us with a sad, depressing mood of helplessness, even despair, for there seems to be no way of opposing those mysterious forces identified in Kochanowski's poem only as "they." No matter how hard we try, no matter what we do, "they" will put an end to our activites, actions, and even thoughts, reducing our life to the movements of puppets who have performed their insignificant roles and will disappear in a bag once the show is over. Indeed, this hardly seems to be a poem to open a collection of mostly funny little epigrams, aphorisms, anecdotes, and jokes. And yet it plays a major role both in Kochanowski's personal philosophy and our perception of his poetic art.

In a long and extensive bibliography of studies on Kochanowski the problem of *fraszki* of this unusual, reflexive kind has attracted the attention of scholars whose works enrich our understanding of Kochanowski and his poetry. Particularly noteworthy among them is Wiktor Weintraub's essay "Fraszka in a Tragic Key," a penetrating commentary on Kochanowski's Lament XI and the *fraszka* under consideration. Weintraub calls the latter a product of "quiet but deep human melancholy" and classifies it as "a bitter and sad" epigram, a testimony to the poem's "total pessimism."[3] The critic traces the *topos* of human life seen as a comedy to the sixteenth-century Italian poet, Pier Angelo Manzoli de la Stellata, called Palingenius, with whose works Kochanowski must have been familiar ever since his university years in Padua. The publication of Palingenius' major work *Zodiacus vitae* ... in 1535-36 preceded Kochanowski's arrival in Italy by only sixteen years and must have been known to every humanist as keenly interested in the Rnaissance movement as the Polish visitor was.

Janusz Pelc, on the other hand, in his monograph study on Kochanowski points out that the poet deliberately opened and closed his "Book One" of *fraszki* with two poems entitled "On human life," producing the effect of a particularly important and programmatic role for the thoughts expressed in the two *fraszki*. They reveal a unique interweaving of the themes of the tragedy and comedy of human life. According to Pelc, in the first six lines of *fraszka* 3 "On human life," the lyric subject expresses a pessimistic, even tragic vision of reality and human actions. These are followed, however, by an ironic concluding distich which prepares the way for a vision of this tragic nature of life "more cheerful in tone, although also marked by distance toward the optimistic convictions about the effectualness of human actions, a vision of the tragic nature, or rather the tragicomedy of the fate of man busily scrambling after worldly goods, thus providing a kind of entertainment for the Eternal Thought or divine Essence as is conveyed by the *fraszka* of the same title ("On human life") that closes "Book One . . . "[4] Clearly then, a dilemma emerges here in our considerations: is the opening *fraszka* meant to create a tragic, pessimistic image, or an image of a melancholic, perhaps even stoic acceptance of the facts of life and death conceived as a human comedy performed in the face of some unknown powers? Is this *fraszka* an act of submission to God's will or an expression of fear of the unknown? Should it be taken in or out of context of Kochanowski's philosophy as we know it from his other works? The answer to these questions seems to be in the text itself.

Maciej Kazimierz Sarbiewski in his *Praecepta poetica* at the beginning of the seventeenth century wrote *"finis epigrammatis est anima ipsius."*[5] A modern Polish poet, Tadeusz Polanowski, a successful author of many contemporary *fraszki*, commenting on this particular literary genre, remarked recently that the secret of writing "a *fraszka*—or an epigram—lies in beginning it actually from its end, from the *pointe* which is, as it were, the embryo of the piece. The entire structure of a *fraszka*, its rhythm, its versification, its rhymes are all subject to the most precise formulation of this initial idea that must explode like the last segment of a rocket."[6] If we accept Polanowski's theory, proven many times over in his own practice, we should try to apply it to Kochanowski's poem as well. Furthermore, we can narrow our focus from the last line, containing the conclusion of the poem, to its last key word, *łątki*, for it seems to provide us with answers to the questions asked above.

According to the Dictionary of old Polish, *Słownik staropolski* (IV, 109-110) and also to the *Słownik polszczyzny XVI w.* (Dictionary of sixteenth-century Polish), XII, 540, the term *łątka* referred to a puppet, and the meaning of that word must have been clear and unambiguous to Kochanowski's contemporaries. Thus, the image created in the last line amounted to a rather melancholic and sad vision of life as a show after which the acting puppets were just stowed away by the director of the show, God, who had watched it, smiling benevolently at our conduct and our attempts to introduce some order into our affairs *(naśmiawszy się nam i naszym porządkom)*. This idea of the world as a stage and human beings as actors had its source in the literature of antiquity and can be found in Plato and Plotinus.[7] In addition to this *topos*, Kochanowski adds a Christian context to his *fraszka* with the line, *"Wszystko to minie jako polna trawa"* ("everything will pass like the grasses of the field"). As Weintraub observed, this notion is taken directly from the Bible.[8] A new, Christian logic explains the earlier line, *"Próżno tu człowiek ma co mieć na pieczy"* ("In vain man take so much care"). With this layer of meaning added to the classical *topos*, there is a consolation in faith, and many poems in Kochanowski's entire work, including his cycle of *Treny* (Laments), confirm it beyond any doubt. The last line of the *fraszka*, *"wemkną nas w mieszek,"* should be construed merely as a grammatic usage of the passive voice, and read, as in Miłosz's translation, "into a sack we will be cast." If we accept such a reading we can easily follow Pelc's interpretation of the closing lines of this *fraszka* as a transition to a more cheerful tone of other *fraszki* following in the collection.

The fact remains, however, that Kochanowski's poetry has withstood the pressures of time, and speaks to us today with the same power it conveyed to his contemporaries four hundred years ago. A modern reader, even if not necessarily versed in philology, perceives it with similar emotions and philosophical impact, although his perception most probably results in a different, more profound imagery, thus changing the original character of Kochanowski's poems. The *fraszka* "On Human Life" provides a perfect case in point. The key word, *łątka*, happens to be in modern Polish a "dragonfly," for many a symbol of carefree beauty, charm, grace, and perhaps some short-lived summer happiness; it conveys some notions of freedom doomed to last just one brief moment.

It might be interesting to follow the gradual change of meaning of this particular word in Polish, in order to comprehend a new image emerging for a modern reader of Kochanowski's *fraszka*. As mentioned earlier, *lątka* was listed in the Dictionary of old Polish as a puppet, and the same explanation for the word was given by Samuel Bogumił Linde (1855) and Jan Karłowicz (1900). But a dictionary of modern Polish edited by Witold Doroszewski (1962) gives two meanings, listing dragonfly as the first. Both meanings are also given in an etymological dictionary by Franciszek Sławski (1975) in chronological order, first the puppet or a doll, and next the dragonfly, with the explanation of the latter term as taken from German *Schlankjungfer*, a slender maid with a doll-like look. Polish encyclopedias, however, with the exception of Zygmunt Gloger's Encyclopedia of old Polish, *Encyklopedia staropolska*, explain the meaning of *lątka* exclusively as dragonfly, beginning with Samuel Orgelbrand (1859) and up to the *Wielka Encyklopedia Powszechna PWN* (The Great Universal Encyclopedia) (1962). Clearly, for a contemporary reader the reading of *lątka* as a dragonfly becomes overwhelming. It is quite obvious that while only the specialist will reach for a vocabulary of sixteenth-century Polish, the common reader will comprehend Kochanowski's *fraszka* in the terms he is best familiar with, namely, the contemporary meaning of that word.

The resulting effect is almost opposite to that of the reading presented before. If human beings are depicted as dragonflies, their actions, cares, worries, and ambitions are as short-lived and insignificant as those of the insects which do not perform under a watchful eye of any director laughing at their show. They are not only accidental, they are completely meaningless. Moreover, the last line in this context achieves a new, ominous tone: rather than being perceived as the passive voice suggested before, the third person plural *wemkną nas* becomes indeed threatening as an image of those mysterious and incomprehensible forces, presumably the forces of evil, since this particular grammatical form in modern Polish normally indicates a disassociation of the speaker from the acting forces which he either cannot or refuses to identify. The threatening tone is amplified even further when we consider the verb used in conjunction with the image of dragonflies, *jak to czynią*, "as they do to" some helpless subjects. If we accept this concept, then even the sack mentioned in the context attains some eschatological proportions. Without bringing in here evidence from medical, clinical, and psychological studies of the dying process,[9] let me quote just one passage from "one of the very greatest stories ever written," as an American critic, F.D. Reeve, called Tolstoy's "The Death of Ivan Ilyich," since it is literature that shapes our imagery of certain phenomena of life and death:

> Throughout those three days, which for him were timeless, he struggled in that black sack that some invisible and irresistible force was

pushing him into ... He felt that his torture was caused by his being pushed into that black hole...[10]

It might also be remembered that four years later in 1890 a Polish novelist, Bolesław Prus, used an almost identical image in describing the death of Ignacy Rzecki at the end of his novel *Lalka* (The Doll)—the same Rzecki who earlier in the novel used to play with mechanical dolls, laughing at their meaningless actions. What clearly emerges here is a new implication of unlimited terror before the unknown, a terror clearly perceived by a modern reader when he associates in his mind all those elements of modern imagery with the text of Kochanowski's *fraszka*. Hence, "everything we think, everything we do is nothing but a trifle." Weintraub's interpretation sums it up correctly as a testimony to a poet's "total pessimism."

By presenting these two almost entirely different readings of the *fraszka* in question I have tried to contrast two types of perception as different as the representatives of two different epochs could have been. For it is actually the reader's perception which makes literature a living phenomenon. It stays alive not on the dusty pages of books stocked somewhere in a library, but in the perception and reception of the reading public. It is perpetuated by a continuing interest, of both the academic community which interprets it in new critical studies and the public at large accepting it on its own terms in its own idiom appropriate for a given time. Kochanowski's *fraszki* had been widely circulated long before the poet decided to collect and publish them,[11] and we may safely assume that it was public demand that persuaded him to do so and to preserve them for the enjoyment of the generations to come.

But to sustain such an interest in his work and make it last throughout centuries a poet must achieve a universal character in his poems, a quality which retains its appeal to a society which is constantly changing in the most diversified social, intellectual, and political conditions. He must come as close as humanly possible to the very truth and to a solid set of values common to his own nation and his cultural milieu: if he is successful, he will then surpass the boundaries of time and space and will become the property of a human race motivated by the same or at least similar principles. His philosophical, moral, and humanistic ideas must be expressed in a literary form that speaks directly to his readers no matter where or when they reach for it. *Fraszki*, as a literary genre, are a primary example of such a literary form, thanks to their precision, brevity, and quite often, humor. *"Jeśli nie grzeszysz, jako mi powiadasz/ Czego się, miła, tak często spowiadasz?"* ("If you do not sin, as you say, my dear, why do you go to confession so often?")—asked Kochanowski four hundred years ago, and this question could be asked now, evoking the same smile it must have evoked in 1584. For great poetry, no matter how serious or light-hearted it might be, never grows old and holds every generation in its sway.

The very fact that we enjoy Kochanowski's *fraszki* today as much as they were enjoyed by his contemporaries proves that the total pessimism voiced in the *fraszka* "On human life" was unfounded. Even *sub specie aeternitatis*, or at least in the perspective of almost half of a millenium, Kochanowski's art has prevailed, an achievement which is not a trifle at all.

Notes

1. Jan Kochanowski, "*O żywocie ludzkim*" ("On human life"), *Fraszki* Bk. I, 3, *Dzieła polskie*, vol. I (Warsaw: PIW, 1953), p. 152.

2. Czesław Miłosz, *The History of Polish Literature* (New York: Macmillan, 1969), pp. 64-65.

3. In Wiktor Weintraub, *Rzecz czarnoleska* (On Czarnolas) (Cracow: Wydawnictwo Literackie, 1977), pp. 319-321. In the original English version of his essay Weintraub calls Palingenius' pessimism "more unmitigated." See *To Honor Roman Jakobson. Essays on the Occasion of His Seventieth Birthday* (The Hague: Mouton, 1967), p. 2230.

4. Janusz Pelc, *Jan Kochanowski, Szczyt renesansu w literaturze polskiej* (Jan Kochanowski. Zenith of the Renaissance in Polish literature) (Warsaw: PWN, 1980), p. 290.

5. Maciej Kazimierz Sarbiewski, *Wykłady poetyki* (*Praecepta poetica*) (Wrocław: Ossolineum, 1958), p. 78.

6. Tadeusz Polanowski, "Jeszce fraszka nie zginęła" (The *fraszka* has not yet perished"), *Pămiętnik Literacki*, vol. 3 (London, 1980), pp. 49—50.

7. Pelc, *Jan Kochanowski*, pp. 290-292.

8. Weintraub, *Rzecz czarnoleska*, pp. 319-321.

9. Michael Sabom, *Recollections of Death: A Medical Investigation*, (New York: Harper & Row, 1982). Some of 50 percent of patients who had died clinically and were brought back to life recall the experience of traveling through a dark tunnel toward bright light.

10. *Six Short Masterpieces by Tolstoy*, with introduction by F. D. Reeve (New York: Dell Pub. Co., 1963), pp. 281-282.

11. Janusz Pelc, "Chronologia fraszek Kochanowskiego" (The chronology of Kochanowski's *fraszki*) in *Ze studiów nad literaturą staropolską* (Wrocław: Ossolineum, 1957), pp. 141-204.

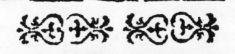

23

To Whom Does the Poet Sing?

Tymoteusz Karpowicz

𝕵n works about Kochanowski, the common opinion emerges that *"Muza"* ("Muse"), written ca. 1567-68, is his poetic manifesto.[1] For Jerzy Ziomek, this manifesto "brings to a close the artist's previous experiences while it at the same time sets forth a new program."[2] Thus, it is a work which is normative, postulative, and directed toward the future. In fact, there cannot be found a second text in the entire output of Kochanowski which contains such a large quantity of the themes, plots, and *topoi-loci communes*—commonplaces typical of manifestos. We encounter here the characteristic invocation to the Muses, the description of the poet's loneliness, the statement of society's insensibility to the poetic achievement, the Horatian pride of one chosen by the Muses, faith in the posthumous victory of the poet, and the efficacy of the power of the creative act that is capable of bestowing immortality on its heroes. The intellectual background of this manifesto is the world of thought of: Homer, Plato, Aristotle, Anacreon, Catullus, Ovid, Propertius, Tibullus, Horace, Lucretius, Seneca, Cicero, and others. It concludes with a powerful picture of the posthumous "resurrection" of the poet, who rises up into heaven through the clouds in the form of a fire-light, though it is not clear whether from the peak of Olympus (the destiny of Prometheus) or from the pagan mountain, Sobótka, locus of the pagan cult of the ancient Slavs.

I know of no other text of Kochanowski which would awaken in me such faith in the themes presented yet at the same time some doubts as "Muse." The first doubt concerns the degree of originality of the arguments in this manifesto. Many scholars who have written about the "Muse," such as Tadeusz Sinko, Henryk Barycz, Julian Krzyżanowski, and Janusz Pelc, have demonstrated clearly the insistent intellectual and textual links between Kochanowski's poem and such authors as Plato, Cicero, Horace, Symmachius, Valerius Maximus, Saint Hieronymus, and others.[3] The most essential part of "Muse," describing—after Plato—the poet as prophet (*vates*) and speaking of the creative power of poetry, a power preserving for eternity events from the lives of individuals and nations, reads:

Nie sama od przyjaciół ni od matki z łona
    W obce kraje Helena morzem uniesiona,
Nie jeden Menelaus o żonę się wadził,
    Nie pierwszy Agamemnon tysiąc naw prowadził,
Nie raz Troja burzona; przed Hektorem siła
    Mężnych było, którym śmierć przy ojczyźnie miła,
Ale wszyscy w milczeniu wiecznym pogrążeni,
    Że poety zacnego rymy przebaczeni.[4]

Not she alone from friends nor mother's womb
Was Helen taken by sea to foreign lands,
Not only Menelaus fought for his wife, nor was,
Agamemnon first to lead a thousand ships,
Not merely once was Troy destroyed; before a Hector,
There were uncounted brave men, for whom to die,
For the fatherland was sweet, but,
All have sunk into eternal silence,
Since overlooked by poet's rhyme.

This passage is an obvious adaptation of the 9th song from Book IV of the *Songs* of Horace. As Pelc observes, the poet actually has simplified Horace's idea[5] nevertheless, the similarities in the two texts are enormous. Of course, one can defend the originality of the ideas and formulations of "Muse" by recourse to the classical theory of imitation, as deriving from Aristotle and embraced by his followers. Bernard Weinberg describes how widespread during the Renaissance was the use of imitation as a standard means of artistic expression.[6] In Kochanowski's time artistic imitation was equal to artistic originality and in this form it entered the poetics of the Enlightenment (above all through translations and adaptations of the *Ars poetica* of Horace). Bernardino Tomitano, author of the most popular poetics of the Italian Renaissance, *Ragionamenti della lingua toscana* (1545) (and in all probability well known to Kochanowski)[7] writes: "Unceasingly do I advise imitation and hold to the opinion that making use of Cicero and Demosthenes is greatly to be praised, imitating them rather than, enamored of self as Narcissus, vainly valuing our own dreams."[8] The Aristotelian principle, formulated in the first chapter of the *Poetics*, that art imitates nature (*mimesis*) ("Epic poetry, tragedy, and also comedy, dithyrambic poetry, and most music on the flute and lyre all fall into the general class of imitation")[9] was later expanded to include imitation of perfect models of art, of the perfect authors.

Concerning Kochanowski's borrowings a modern poet Mieczysław Jastrun writes: "It does not concern us how much and from where the poet borrowed, but why he experienced so deeply this particular, and not some other work of some other author, why he identified so closely with it, why he so merged with the author that he was able to create something new, moving, true ... therefore the discovery of this particular and not some other link with Horace, Catullus, or a Greek Anthology in no way negates either his independence, or the sincerity of the works, which he was always carrying in himself, not knowing yet the appropriate expression to give to them."[10] Nevertheless the conventionalism of "Muse," appearing above all in its borrowings, stands out clearly. We should, however, assume that this insistent patency of conventions was consciously employed by the poet.

The next doubt concerns something other than the problem of "imitation." It has to do with the degrees of authenticity, with the credibility of the basic formulations of this manifesto, which have been accepted by some Kochanowski scholars as a possible reflection of real fact of the poet's life at the time when he wrote the "Muse" when as a royal secretary he lived at the court.

In "Muse" there is the well-known passage of the abandoned poet singing outside the fence, the rival of summer crickets. From the context we infer that it is the indigent poet of whom Kochanowski is speaking here. The image itself of a fence is not associated in Polish with wealth but, with poverty and isolation, as in: "to lie beneath the fence"; "to clutch a picket of a fence like a blind man"; "to die at the foot of the fence." The cricket—the poet's partner—is not identified with power in Polish folk tale tradition. The anonymous author of the poem *Proteus albo Odmieniec* (Proteus or the Changing One), published in 1564 left behind a bitter witness to the poet's situation in Poland.

> To jedno tu przydawam, że w Polszcze, przyjaźni
> Poetowie nie mają i są mało ważni.[11]

> This merely I have to add, that in Poland
> Poets have no friendship and are little valued.

Whatever might have been the situation of the Polish poet in the Renaissance period, it would be difficult to say for certain that Kochanowski suffered penury and isolation. In the same *Proteus* ... the author speaks in the highest praise of Kochanowski and he calls the poet "the love of our century." Everything we know of his situation in Polish society, from his earliest years to the moment of death, is an open contradiction of the portrayal of the poet in "Muse." We encounter here a sudden divergence between the contents of the poem and the poet's biography, which do not bear any resemblance to the portrait of the poet who, outside the fence (walls), competes with the crickets present in "Muse."

Does then the manifesto rest on fabrication? Yes. But then why is this highly conventionalized, "fabricated" work presented as if it were moving, beautiful, and true?

The years during which Kochanowski studied in Padua (1553-1558) are years of an ever increasing influence of Aristotles' *Poetics*. Italy, shortly before Kochanowski's arrival in Padua as well as during his stay in the city, underwent a veritable Aristotelian renaissance, of which Bernard Weinberg writes: "There is no doubt but that the signal event in the history of literary criticism in the Italian Renaissance was the discovery of Aristotle's *Poetics* and its incorporation into the critical tradition."[12] At that time Aristotelian thought fascinated such scholars of poetics as: Francesco Filippi Pedemonte (1546), Claudio Tolomei (1543), Francesco Robortello (1548), Vincenzo Maggi (1550), Giacopo Grifoli (1550), Lilio Gregorio Giraldi (1551), Giason Denores (1553), Francesco Lovisini (1554), Benedetto Varchi (1553-1554), and others. It is worth remembering that according to contemporary opinion, Francesco Robortello, the author of *In librum Aristotelis de Arte poetica explicationes* (1548), was the professor of Jan Kochanowski. Everything points to the fact that like the famous Paduan, the author of the "Muse" was fascinated by Aristotle's theories. But which ones?

In general, Aristotle is spoken of as originating the theory of imitation of nature in art, as originating mimetics. This theory links art quite narrowly with realism, objectivity, and the commonly understood dependency between reality and the portrayal of this reality in artistic work. The excellence of imitation (and the excellence of a work of art as well) has to consist in the very closest approximation of artistic description to the described object. The complete correspondence between both elements would be therefore the peak of creative accomplishment. In Aristotle's mimetic theory, critics often overlooked the strange discrepancy which, within the rigoristic canons of mimetics and the prescriptions of veracity, completely justifies worthy artistic fabrications. In the XXIV chapter of the *Poetics*, the Athenian philosopher writes: "The poet should choose probable impossibilities rather than incredible possibilities."[13] On the other hand, in the next chapter he documents in greater detail his contention, comparing at the same time two types of a poet's errors: in the use of poetics and in the violation of objective laws of reality. "If the poet— writes Aristotle—chooses to imitate something and fails because of a lack of imitative ability, the error is in the poetic art itself. But if he makes a mistake about what he chooses to imitate or writes of impossible things, for example, a horse that moves both its right legs forward at the same time, or the faults that can occur in dealing with every one of the arts, as a mistake about medicine, or something in any other art whatever, then the error is not germane to poetry. ... If he has represented impossible things, he has committed a fault, but he is right if he ... thus makes one part or another more astounding."[14] In the already cited XXIV chapter of *Poetics*, Aristotle uses the very word "lie" and praises Homer in that "Homer has been very influential in teaching the other poets how lies should be told."[15] It is a curious thing that in the seventeenth century Franciszek Ksawery Dmochowski in his *Sztuka rymotwórcza* (The Art of versifying) (1788) adopting, through Boileau's *L'Art Poetique*, the *Poetics* of Aristotle, treats with great restraint this bold acceptance of the artistic "lie" on the part of the Athenian. Dmochowski cautions poets:

> Zmyślenie jest żywiołem i dusza poety,
> Gdy wytkniętej rozumem nie przechodzi mety.
> Czyż mogą w lasach morskie przebywać delfiny?
> Czy mogą pływać dziki wśród morskiej głębiny?[16]

Fabrication is the soul and native element of the poet,
Which guided by reason does not abuse its goal.
Can sea dolphins exist in forests?
Can wild boars swim in the ocean depths?

In Padua, in the circle of Aristotelians like Robortello, Kochanowski must have been in contact with the theory of the artistic "lie." Kochanowski understood it differently than Dmochowski later did. The author of "Muse" does not ascribe the Aristotelian lie to a superficial fantasy, to the narration of fiddle-faddle, but to the acts of the imagination which bestow on man's senses the presumed function of God's senses, which humanize nature and naturalize man. Actually, it was for Kochanowski a matter of the reconstruction, in the imagination-lie, of the divine means of communicating within a pantheistically and animistically understood nature, a means which conferred the possibility of co-partnership between man and universe:

O Piękna nocy nad zwyczaj tych czasów,
Patrz na nas jasno wpośrzód tych tu lasów, ...[17]

O exceptionally beautiful night of these times,
Look on us brightly amidst these forests here, ...

The lie was necessary also to him for penetration of people, for a transformation into their existence, for the Protean metamorphoses, which gave to him an almost fleshly, sensory awareness, whether of what was Ovid's dramatic "I sing to myself and the Muses" or of the loneliness and penury of other poets of the world who had to "play outside the fence and compete with the crickets." This entrance into Proteus' multiformity led the poet to "unceasing lies" that conflicted with the poet's biography, but it was also a gate leading him to the universalization of individual experiences. Only with the greatest caution, as regards the "Aristotelian lie" in the works of Jan of Czarnolas, can one rely upon his works for a reconstruction of his biography (Proteus!), for an interpretation of his poetry of personal experience (as in the *Laments*), of his descriptions of joy and pain, as well as to accept on the greatest faith beautiful "lies" speaking of man in general, expressed for the first time with such artistic power in the Polish Renaissance.

But then, to whom, finally, did the poet sing? He sang, above all, to the greatest of the Muses, the Muse of personal Freedom, which is characterized by the right of unlimited penetrations into all things and all men. In a world which is always—for genuine creative artists—too constricting, always resembling a strait jacket, woven sometimes of gold thread, other times of barbed wire, but a strait jacket nonetheless, in this world Kochanowski counted more on hypotheses (artistic lies) than on reality. For such was the essence of the Renaissance—hypothesizing. Besides the rock of Calliope—here too he took the first Polish step, while the inventions of Biernat of Lublin and the writings of Mikołaj Rej had nothing at all in common with the acts of imagination of

Jan of Czarnolas. As a Renaissance poet, and thus a poet discovering new horizons, Kochanowski for the first time in Polish literature stood before the riddle of which roads he would have to take to discover new truths about man: was it by knowledge of *others* (his entire social and political writings) or by the Pythian *Nosce te ipsum*—knowledge of one's own self (his *Psalms*, *Laments*, *Songs*, and *Fraszki*)? To this end, time, isolation, and the quiet of Czarnolas were necessary. And he sang neither to himself nor to the Muses, but only to this newly awakened Renaissance awareness in himself that it was necessary to acquire a certain universal measure of things, measure deriving neither from knowledge of the organization of society and state, or of culture, but from the very fact that he was himself a man. In Kochanowski's singing, incarnations and metamorphoses became a necessity and began to be expressed not in a language of Aesop but of Proteus. We can now finally imagine to ourselves as it were the final phase of these transformations—in the fullness of Czarnolas. There sits the Athenian with Jan beneath a linden tree; Epicurus is pouring him some Grecian wine into glazed Polish mugs. The shade of the Czarnolas linden becomes the sunny clock of the world. And Jan has the soul-filled face of Prometheus, or rather the slightly clouded countenance of Swarożyc, the fire-god of the ancient Poles.

Notes

1. See such studies as: Stanisław Tarnowski, *Studia do historii literatury polskiej. Wiek XVI: Jan Kochanowski* (Studies on the history of Polish literature. The Sixteenth Century: Jan Kochanowski) (Cracow, 1888); Władysław Nehring, *Jan Kochanowski* (St. Petersburg, 1900); Stanisław Windakiewicz, *Jan Kochanowski* (Cracow, 1930); Zofia Szmydtowa, *Jan Kochanowski* (Warsaw: PWN, 1968); Wiktor Weintraub, *Rzecz czarnoleska* (On Czarnolas) (Cracow: Wydawnictwo Literackie, 1977); and Janusz Pelc, *Jan Kochanowski. Szczyt renesansu w literaturze polskiej* (Jan Kochanowski. Zenith of the Renaissance in Polish literature) (Warsaw: PWN, 1980).

2. Jerzy Ziomek, *Renesans* (The Renaissance) (Warsaw: PWN, 1976), p. 273.

3. Tadeusz Sinko, "Sobie śpiewam a muzom" (I sing for myself and the Muses) in *Echa klasyczne w literaturze polskiej* (Cracow, 1923); Henryk Barycz, "Dwie syntezy dziejów narodowych przed sądem potomności" (Two syntheses of national history before the court of posterity) in *Pamiętnik Literacki* 43, 1/2 (1952), Julian Krzyżanowski, "Sobie śpiewam a muzom" (I sing for myself and the Muses) in *Poezja* 1, 1 (1965); Janusz Pelc, *Jan Kochanowski. Szczyt renesansu w literaturze polskiej*, pp. 221-227.

4. Jan Kochanowski, *Dzieła polskie* (Polish works), ed. Julian Krzyżanowski, 11 ed. (Warsaw: PIW, 1980), p. 121.

5. Janusz Pelc, *Jan Kochanowski. Szczyt renesansu w literaturze polskiej*, p. 225.

6. Bernard Weinberg, *A History of Literary Criticism in the Italian Renaissance*, vols. 1-2 (Chicago: University of Chicago Press, 1961). See the Index, p. 1170.

7. Quoted after Henryk Barycz, *Spojrzenia w przeszłość polsko-włoską* (A look into the Polish-Italian past) (Wrocław: Ossolineum, 1965), pp. 221-240.

8. Quoted after Barycz, *Spojrzenia*, p. 232.

9. The text in: Allan H. Gilbert, *Literary Criticism. Plato to Dryden* (Detroit: Wayne State University Press, 1962), p. 69.

10. Mieczysław Jastrun, *Poeta i dworzanin* (Poet and courtier) (Warsaw: PIW, 1954), pp. 80-81.

11. Quoted after Zofia Szmydtowa, *Jan Kochanowski*, p. 83.

12. Bernard Weinberg, *A History of Literary Criticism in the Italian Renaissance*, vol. 1, p. 349.

13. The text in: Allan H. Gilbert, *Literary Criticism*, p. 107.

14. Ibid., pp. 108-109.

15. Ibid., p. 106.

16. Franciszek Ksawery Dmochowski, *Sztuka rymotwórcza* (The art of versifying) (Wrocław: Ossolineum, 1956), p. 15.

17. Jan Kochanowski, "Pieśń XIII," *Pieśni. Księgi pierwsze* (Song XIII, Songs. Book one), in *Dzieła polskie*, p. 240.

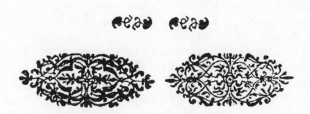

24

Jan Kochanowski: The Poet's Sixteenth-Century Editions in the Context of Contemporary Polish and European Printing

Paulina Buchwald-Pelcowa

Six years after Jan Kochanowski's death, in 1590, there appeared a small book entitled *Fragmenta* (*Fragments*) printed in the famous Cracow printing house, Officina Lazari. The book contained several hitherto unpublished prose works: *"Apoftegmata"* ("Apophtegms"), *"Przy pogrzebie rzecz"*—the funeral oration delivered at the funeral of the poet's brother, Kacper. Works in verse in the book included some of the *Pieśni* (*Songs*), poetic epistles to the archbishop of Gniezno and Mikołaj Firlej, *"Carmen macaronicum de eligendo vitae genere"*, as well as a real fragment of an unfinished epic poem, *"Fragment bitwy z Amuratem u Warny"* ("Fragment of the battle with Amurat at Warna"), and *"Fragment nagrobku"* ("Fragment of the epitaph") for Radziwiłł.

The owner and manager of the printing house, Jan Januszowski, who was the poet's friend and who, like the poet himself and like the chancellor and commander-in-chief of the Polish army, Jan Zamoyski, had worked for some years in the king's chancellery and had acquired, again like the other two, his education in Padua, provided this posthumous edition of the *Fragments* with his own dedication. Januszowski considered this small collection of unpublished works of the great poet who in his opinion was "unique" in Poland, unique in the perfection of his profession, to be a gift more valuable than a gift of gold, silver or precious stones, though it consisted only of "written" and "not painted" pages. Januszowski used the concept that art is more valuable than gold to emphasize the significance of the literary works of the greatest Polish poet.

No less expressive of his high opinion of Kochanowski's poetry was the very fact of his publishing a volume which gathered hitherto unedited, even fragmentary, unfinished pieces and bearing a title usually reserved for books marked by great philological precision, a title indicating admiration for the heritage of antiquity such as *Fragmenta Ciceronis ... Caroli Sigonii diligentia collecta ...*, Venetiis, 1559. A continuation of Sigonius' work was done by a friend of Kochanowski, Andrzej Patrycy Nidecki, who prepared several annotated and enlarged editions of *Fragmenta Ciceronis ...*, beginning with the Venice edition of 1561. In their editions of *Fragments*, humanists, Renaissance philologists, and lovers of antiquity strove to save and bequeath to others every single fragment by their beloved masters that they had found. This practice was, however, rarely applied to contemporary writers. Admittedly, there were several editions of the first four books of Ronsard's *Franciade*, but these constituted the first part of the poem and not a random fragment of the work. In the context of the European practice of the time, Januszowski's decision to print Kochanowski's unedited and fragmentary pieces is all the more conspicuous. He presented the *Fragments*—"the last gem" of the Polish treasure—to a member of the wealthy Firlej family with whom Kochanowski had maintained good relations, and the *Fragments* included a poetic epistle to one of them. Januszowski also found it deplorable that the edition was incomplete and expressed his hope that those who had other unpublished works of Kochanowski would send them to him so that they could be published. These hopes were thwarted. Publication of the *Fragments* in 1590, six years after the poet's death (a span of time equal to that which elapsed between Shakespeare's death and the appearance of the "First folio") completed Januszowski's work of editing collected works of the poet, not in one, but in several volumes, grouped into the so-called series. The list of Kochanowski's published—and thereby known to us today—works was practically closed. Only a few works were to be added to those contained in the editions of Kochanowski's poetic works both in Polish and in Latin, published by Januszowski in the years 1579-1590: Kochanowski's translation of the Psalms, *Psałterz Dawidów* (*David's Psalter*) (1579); *Lyricorum libellus* (1580); *Treny* (*Laments* or *Threnodies*) (1580); *Fraszki* (*Trifles*) and *Elegiarum libri IV — Foricoenia* (1584, the year of the poet's death); the volume entitled *Jan Kochanowski* (1585/6), and *Pieśni* (*Songs*) (1586). The list also includes minor works published, some of them more than once, by Januszowski or other printers starting from 1561, and later on included in larger collections, such as the above-mentioned volume entitled *Jan Kochanowski*, itself enlarged in successive editions. These collections did not include some of Kochanowski's poems originally published with the works of other authors (e.g., with Jan Mączyński's dictionary entitled *Lexicon Latino-Polonicum*, with the works of Stanisław Sokołowski, or those of the poet's friend, Patrycy Nidecki)[1] and not reprinted with his own works throughout the Renaissance and baroque periods. Neither did the collected works of Kochanowski published in the sixteenth century by Januszowski, and in the seventeenth century by Skalski and Piotrkowczyk, include a very interesting project for a new spelling of the Polish language. The abbreviated, probably later version of that work appeared in 1592 in a grammar book edited in Lwów by Jan Ursinus, while Januszowski included the earlier version in 1594 in the book *Nowy karakter polski* (*New Polish Type*), actually printed in new types designed for texts in Polish, hence the title, the "new Polish type," that is, a new type face, fit for the characteristics of the Polish language. In addition to the texts of Kochanowski and Januszowski himself, the book also contained a text by still another former secretary to the king and student of Italian universities, Łukasz Górnicki, who translated into Polish Castiglione's *Il Cortegiano*.

The main canon of Kochanowski's texts, however, had reached the reader by 1590, chiefly in the years 1579-1590. Yet the fact that basic collections of his both Latin and Polish works were disseminated in print only in the year of the poet's death or even later, is rather striking and unusual in Europe at the time, especially when considering that the author's reputation had already been extremely high in Poland for many years; even in his lifetime, Kochanowski was recognized as the greatest poet of his generation. But in 1560 only *"Epitaphium Cretcovii"* had appeared in print—in distant Basel—in Bernardino Scardeonius's enormous volume, *De antiquitate urbis Patavii*, and in 1561, this time in Poland, the poem *O śmierci Jana Tarnowskiego* (*On the Death of Jan Tarnowski*). Nevertheless, shortly after his return from abroad, late in 1561 or at the beginning of 1562, when his works were not published yet, his poetry was already highly praised by Mikołaj Rej, a poet of merit, known from many printed works and called, not quite justly, "the father of Polish literature." Some years later, in 1564, a similar appraisal of Kochanowski's poetry is to be found in the anonymous author of *Proteus*, an imitation of Kochanowski's *Satyr albo Dziki Mąż* (*The Satyr or the Wild Man*), published in the same year.[2]

Thus, it is a phenomenon peculiar to Polish literary life that the works of Jan Kochanowski, the greatest poet not only in Poland but in all the Slavic countries of the time, in spite of being initially published in scarcity, so quickly gained the highest recognition. The process of dissemination of the poetry of the Czarnolas master differs considerably not only from the similar processes in the case of writers in other European countries of the sixteenth century, especially France and Italy, but also from those of his compatriots. It seems that Kochanowski takes his time with publication of his works. For over a decade after the above-mentioned *"Epitaphium Cretcovii"* was published for the first time, his works only seldom appear in print. Those that do appear in print are short ones, either of an occasional character, such as the poem, *O śmierći Jana Tarnowskiego* (*On the Death of Jan Tarnowski'*), *Zgoda* (*Harmony*), *Satyr albo Dziki Mąż* (*The Satyr or the Wild Man*), or *Pamiątka Janowi na Tęczynie* (*Memorial to Jan of Tęczyn*), or of the "diversion" kind like *Szachy* (*Chess*), or the poem *Zuzanna*. Admittedly, such beginnings were not unusual for many prominent European poets of the period, to mention only Ronsard, who also initially published only short works; but whereas both Ronsard and other French and Italian poets soon began to publish larger collections of their poetry or even complete works, Kochanowski did not.

It should be remembered that Ronsard's first separate pieces appeared in 1549, and already in 1560 his collected works were published, to be enlarged and revised in subsequent editions, of which there were six during his lifetime, followed by another eight in the years 1587-1630. Naturally, the publication of Ronsard's collected works did not hinder separate editions of single poems or their collections, e.g., *Élégies* in 1565, or *Franciade* in 1572 and 1573.

In Kochanowski's case the situation is quite different. Larger collections of his works appear only toward the end of his life, and furthermore the process of disseminating his poetry in print is rather irregular, with noticeable gaps.[3] This is true not only of the early period; after his death as well there are periods abounding with editions of his works, alternating with years in which not a single text of his is published. Yet we must be aware that this statement on the irregular, sporadic character of Kochanowski's editions is perhaps exaggerated, since the phenomenon may be a consequence of the fact that a great number of prints in Poland, not only sixteenth-century ones, have been destroyed or lost.[4] Those editions of Kochanowski that have come down to us are for the most part represented by rare copies, and some are extant only as unique specimens, still others are no longer available (eg., *On the Death of Jan Tarnowski* or the first editions of *The Satyr* ... and the *Laments*). Bearing this in mind, we can ascertain, on the basis of the preserved editions or those well testified to, some periods in which Kochanowski's editions were particularly copious: 1561-1565; 1578-1580; 1583-1585/6; 1587-1590; 1611-1612. Characteristically, in these years we see not only publications of the poet's new texts, but also reprints, and this is true even of the first period, in which Kochanowski's works only began to be edited. The first to appear in print were always works of an occasional character, of topical interest. These were also the first to be reprinted and often in a short time. *The Satyr* ... was published three times c. 1564 (by two different printing houses), and *Harmony* three times in the years 1564-65 (all three editions printed by Łazarz Andrysowic).

Early editions of Kochanowski are printed by various Cracow printers: Łazarz Andrysowic, Maciej Wirzbięta, heirs of Marek Szarffenberg, Mateusz Siebeneycher, Stanisław Szarffenberg. The only printing that appeared elsewhere was *Pamiątka Janowi na Tęczynie* (*Memorial to Jan of Tęczyn*) (c. 1570), published in Brześć Litewski. As we see, Kochanowski's texts were of interest both to the most prominent printers of the time (Łazarz Andrysowic and Wirzbięta) and to those less distinguished in the history of Polish printing; yet curiously enough, none of them put his name on the poet's editions of the time. By publishing Kochanowski's works twice or even three times, in some cases even after many years (Wirzbięta reprinted *Zuzanna* about 1585, still anonymously, while his anonymous edition of *Chess* about 1564 was republished by him in 1574 and 1585, this time with his name given), printers monopolized, as it were, their printing rights to those texts.

These early editions, though typographically anonymous, all give the name of the author (except for *Harmony* and *Pieśń o potopie* (*A Song on the deluge*) which in all their editions appear without it). This general practice of not revealing the names of the printers or even the place of publication in the early editions of Kochanowski (later on *Aratus* was also published anonymously by Piotrkowczyk in 1579) is rather odd considering the customs prevailing in Polish printing of the time. There are, to be sure, many typographically anonymous editions among Stanisław Orzechowski's or Jan Dymitr Solikowski's works published in Poland, and anonymous editions are also to be found with Andrzej Frycz Modrzewski and Mikołaj Rej, but none of the major Polish sixteenth-century writers had his works published in a certain period exclusively in that way. Two possible explanations can be offered: either Kochanowski's early prints appeared only on his own (or his protectors' or friends') initiative, or, on the contrary, the printers published those works without the author's consent and therefore chose not to reveal their names. It is true that many of the poet's early prints include his dedications or addresses to definite persons, but these could, after all, have been appended to manuscript copies of the text, not necessarily meant for print.

As late as 1578 Kochanowski's *Odprawa posłów greckich* (*The Dismissal of the Greek Envoys*) is published and only thanks to Jan Zamoyski, who saw the significance of disseminating in print those political and topical messages useful for current state policy which are conveyed by a great poet under the ancient costume of this first Polish humanist tragedy. *The Dismissal* ... was printed in Warsaw, in the so-called "flying printing house," established at the king's order so that proclamations and other official texts needed by the king and his chancellor might be printed as quickly as possible. Indeed, it was Zamoyski who was also responsible for the publication of Kochanowski's other works during the second "boom" of his editions. After *The Dismissal* ... there were two editions of *Pieśni trzy* (*Three Songs*)[5] and one of the *De expugnatione Polottei Ode*, all printed in 1580 in Warsaw, *Dryas Zamchana* and *Pan Zamchanus* were published earlier in 1578 in Lwów. All these publications were printed in the previously mentioned "flying printing house,"[6] sub-office of the Cracow printing house of Mikołaj Szarffenberg that followed the king and his court and was supervised by Zamoyski. The publication of these works was preceded by the sending of special messengers to Czarnolas in December 1577, before the performance and publication of *The Dismissal* ... and twice in the beginning of 1580, probably in connection with the *Three Songs*.

It was the translation of *David's Psalter*, printed in 1579 in Cracow by Jan Januszowski, (who from then on was to be Kochanowski's chief, and for many years sole publisher), which the poet himself recognized as his first "ripe" poetic achievement, "the first sheaf of his harvest." This "sheaf" was one of the many editions of the Psalms that appeared in abundance in the sixteenth century in all European countries, in various language versions, especially in Latin, Greek, and Hebrew, but also frequently in poetic translations into nearly all the modern languages. Obviously, Kochanowski's paraphrase was not the first one to appear in print in Poland; it was preceded and accompanied by numerous other translations, both anonymous and done by outstanding writers. Especially worth mentioning are Jan Leopolita's *Psałterz Dawidów porządkiem*

Kościoła Świętego... według postanowienia S. Concilium Trydeńtskiego ... na każdy dzień ... rozłożony (The Psalter according to the rite of the Holy Church ... as provided for by the Tridentine Council ... for each day ... arranged), edited in the same year and in the same printing house as Kochanowski's translation, and Jakub Wujek's *Psałterz Dawidów teraz znowu z łacińskiego z greckiego y z żydowskiego ... przełożony* (The Psalter, again from Latin, Greek and Hebrew ... translated), published in 1594 with both a woodcut medallion representing David playing the lyre that is to be found in all editions of Kochanowski's *David's Psalter* and with a formula about observing the laws of the Roman Catholic church almost identical to that placed on Kochanowski's *David's Psalter* starting from the second edition of 1583. And yet it was only Kochanowski's version which won immediate general recognition, even before the whole of it was printed—there is evidence of sending the texts of the psalms to some of his neighbors.[7] The first edition of *David's Psalter* was soon followed by many subsequent editions, and in both the sixteenth and seventeenth century particular psalms repeatedly appeared also in popular hymnals designed for use in Roman Catholic churches as well as various reformed churches.[8]

As far as we know, in the sixteenth century, in the years 1579-1600, Kochanowski's *David's Psalter* had fourteen editions[9] (all printed in Januszowski's Officina Lazari run by Januszowski), an unusual occurrence in Poland of the time, especially since there were also single editions of other translations that were not reprinted. Obviously, the number of the sixteenth-century editions of Kochanowski's version is rather low when compared with French editions of the Psalms in Marot and Bèze's translation, the number of which, according to the French bibliographers, Bovet and Douven, ran to 228 in the sixteenth century.[10] On the other hand, we know that other poetic versions of the Psalms, which appeared in Germany, the Netherlands, and Italy, as well as in France and other European countries, were published in single editions (e.g., Flaminius's, 1537; Spinola's, 1562; Jan Major's *In psalmos Davidos paraphrasis heroicis versibus*, Wittenberg, 1574; Bonade's, Paris 1531), and only sometimes twice (eg., *Sesante Salmi di David tradotti in rime volgari italiane*, 1573, 1585; the incomplete French translation by Baïf, 1569, 1573) or more (eg., Campensis's paraphrase, Buchanan's, and that by Hessus).

Kochanowski's translation of the Psalms is thus seen in the context of the great popularity of the book in sixteenth-century Europe, as demonstrated by the great number of its editions. Many contemporary French and German poets (and a lesser number of Italian) attempted to render the poetic value of this text in their own languages or in Latin or Greek paraphrases, often publishing their results in the form of incomplete translations. As an example one should mention the successive editions of Marot's translation (at first only six psalms, then 30, later on 52, and finally 80) or of Desportes's translation, to say nothing of numerous editions of the particularly popular seven penitential psalms.[11]

In Kochanowski's case, too, the publication of the entire collection of psalms was preceded by the edition of *Siedm psalmów pokutnych* (*Seven Penitential Psalms*).

Both carry the same year of publication, but *David's Psalter* certainly appeared late in the year, as can be inferred from King Stefan Batory's privilege issued for this publication, dated November 7, 1579, in which we read that the translation has just gone to press. The *Seven Penitential Psalms* could have been the first to appear. In this edition we find no information that the work is a translation. The absence of such a formula may suggest that the psalms were more personal, that we hear the poet's own voice, as it were, though they do not, except for a few errors and misprintings and one instance of omitting a whole stanza, differ from those to be found in the complete edition of *David's Psalter*. Perhaps they first revealed the pain of the poet severely tried by disease and death in the family, the pain that would find its most powerful expression in the *Laments* published a year later and which expressed Kochanowski's fatherly suffering after the death of his beloved daughter, Orszula. The *Seven Penitential Psalms* could, with their plea for mercy, be the first expression of this suffering and this could have been a reason for publishing them separately.

Other considerations, however, may have led the poet or his publisher to this separate edition. The *Seven Penitential Psalms* could have been conceived as an announcement, an advertisement, of the whole book soon to appear; in this they would have been encouraged by the long European tradition which distinguished those Psalms in separate editions in France, Italy, Germany, and also in Poland. Yet we know that neither the poet nor his publisher followed the example of Marot with his incomplete edition of the Psalms, though Kochanowski worked on them so long that they could have been tempted to publish an incomplete work. We know from Kochanowski's letter to Stanisław Fogelweder, dated 1571[12], the only letter giving us some insight into his poetic labor, that as early as 1571 Kochanowski intended to bring 30 of his paraphrases of the Psalms to the king, so the work must have been advanced by then. And he surely intended to bring them in manuscript and not printed. He treated his translation of the Psalms as a great poetic task, considering it the result of both inspiration and hard work, as he hinted in the letter where we read of two antagonistic forces, embodied by goddesses, Necessity (*"necessitas clavos trabales et cuneos manu gestans ahena"*) and Poetry (*"poetika, nescio quid blandum spirans"*). He did not intend to finish this work hastily and in the letter to Fogelweder he refused to be rushed in his work. When after nine years of labor he decided to publish the complete *David's Psalter*, he conceived a way to still further improve and perfect his work.

In the king's privilege[13] we read that Kochanowski decided to publish only a certain number of copies of *David's Psalter* in order not to make the book widely available, a situation making further improvement impossible. We may assume that Kochanowski feared that were the reading market saturated with a large number of copies, an immediate reprinting (in which possible defects or errors would be eliminated) would become unnecessary. This formulation of the king's privilege is unique not only in Polish practice but European as well, apart from the very fact of providing a poetic work with the king's privilege, which in itself was rare too.

The king's privilege in the printed *David's Psalter* mentioned the consequences which printers or booksellers would suffer if they reprinted or sold the book without the author's (and later his successors') knowledge. In the text of the privilege as reprinted in subsequent editions we find, however, no reference to the considerations which led the poet to seek to obtain such a privilege. These were, as we have seen, mainly of a literary character; their source is to be sought in the literary consciousness of the author, in his belief in the necessity of constantly perfecting his work. But it is not unlikely that this unusual form of the king's privilege was also employed to protect the work against all attacks on any possible error or discrepancy and, above all, against anyone else's intervention in the text, since the privilege ensured the author that no reprinting could be done without his consent.

The privilege forbidding reprints is also to be found at the end of the collection *Jan Kochanowski*, but in both cases it failed to prevent reprints which were in fact unlawful, though in the sixteenth century they were all done exclusively by Jan Januszowski, the first and legitimate publisher of the whole literary output of the poet. We cannot fully explain the phenomenon but it is well documented, thanks to the outstanding Polish bibliographer, Kazimierz Piekarski.[14]

Jan Januszowski published successive editions, especially of *David's Psalter*, but also of the *Fraszki*, *Fragments*, and the collection, *Jan Kochanowski*, several years or even more than a decade later than indicated by the date to be found in a given edition. For instance, there were four editions of *David's Psalter* bearing a 1586 date of publication; the last one appeared in the seventeenth century, c. 1604, and the others mainly in the years 1590-1600, although in all of them we find the date 1586 both on the title page and in the colophon, and despite the appearance in the meantime of editions dated 1601. Similar false dates were given in the editions of the *Fraszki*, *Fragments*, or the collection *Jan Kochanowski*. We may assume that Januszowski wanted to conceal the fact of multiple reprintings of the works which must have been in demand and sold well; his concealment was motivated by financial reasons. Perhaps he thus avoided the necessity of satisfying the claims of Kochanowski's successors with each edition of the poet's works, although author's rights were not so strictly defined at the time. In sixteenth-century Poland pirated editions of official documents such as the texts of the constitutions and other resolutions of the diet, city statutes, or state laws were frequent. But both in Poland and elsewhere pirated editions of poetic texts were rather unusual. Some analogies may be seen here with editions of Shakespeare in England, but there the matter is more complicated, because of the so-called good and bad quartos. In Kochanowski's case the reprints are literal; the publisher clearly wanted them as faithful in every detail to the original as possible, but errors were unavoidable and their number grew with successive reprintings.

Thus, for various reasons, the road of Kochanowski's poetic texts to their readers was not, as based on the example of this "first sheaf of his harvest,"

ZA przywileiem Jeo Królewſkiey Mśći/ nikomu zgołá nie
ieſt wolno pſáłterzá tego/ przekłádá-
nia JAná KOchánowſkiego / bez
dołożenia ſámego autorá / nápotym
drukowáć : áni gdźie indźiey druko-
wánego w páńſtwách Jeo Królewſkiey Mśći do korony náleżacych prze
dáwáć : Ktoby ináczey vczynił / w-
ſzyćki kśiegi tráći / y wine do ſkárbu
Jeo Królewſkiey Mśći w przywile-
iu miánowáng przepada.

Ee   Regeſtr

58. The King's privilege forbidding reprints appended to Kochanowski's *David's Psalter*. Jan Kochanowski, *Psałterz Dawidów*, w Krakowie, 1579 (Biblioteka Czartoryskich, Kraków). Reprinted from the facsimile edition Jan Kochanowski, *Dzieła Wszystkie*, Wydanie Sejmowe. vol. 1, Part 1. *Psałterz Dawidów*, ed. Jerzy Woronczak (Wrocław: Ossolineum, 1982).

59. *Jan Kochanowski*, w Krakowie, 1585. (Edition B. published in 1589 or 1590) (Biblioteka Narodowa, Warszawa). Photo Stanisław Stępniewski.

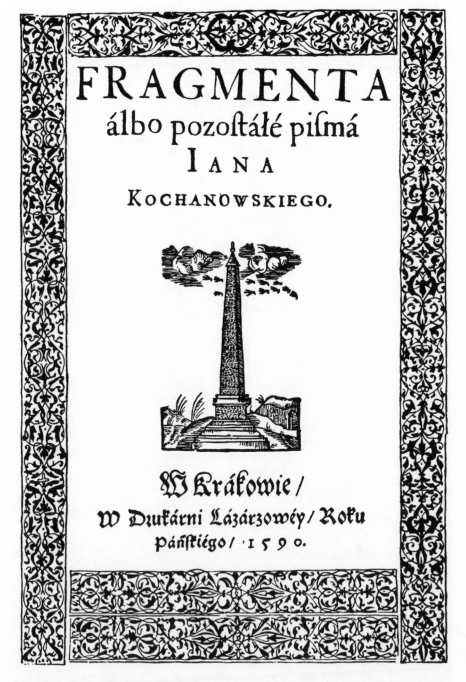

60. Jan Kochanowski, *Fragmenta albo Pozostałe pisma*, w Krakowie, 1590 (Biblioteka Poznań-skiego Towarzystwa Przyjaciół Nauk).

typical. The texts reached their readers not only as a printed matter, but in many cases even prior to printing. This fact is well documented, to mention only Sebastian Klonowic's testimony in his dedication to Paweł and Piotr Czerny of *Żale nagrobne na ślachetnie urodzonego i znacznie uczonego męża, nieboszczyka pana Jana Kochanowskiego* ... (Laments on the grave of a noble and very learned man, the late Jan Kochanowski ...). We read there about Kochanowski's Psalms circulating among the neighboring gentry through the mediation of the Czernys and their servant, Adam. As already mentioned, Kochanowski's first works to appear in print were shorter, occasional ones or those of the "diversion" kind, such as *Chess*. The poet took his time with later works which show his maturity such as those in the larger collections of *Songs*, *Fraszki*, Latin elegies, odes, and *Foricoenia*. His publisher, Jan Januszowski, said in his preface-dedication to the collection entitled *Jan Kochanowski*, that the poet had sought to publish his poetic output only when he had felt his days coming to an end; indeed most of the poet's achievements were published in the year of his death or even later. Yet probably in great part they were prepared for publication by Kochanowski himself because Januszowski says also that the poet discussed with him the edition of the *Fraszki* and explicitly stipulated that nothing should be expurgated, even possible offenses to decency and decorum. The poet's will was not fully respected, however, for in subsequent editions a few *Fraszki* were separated from the main body of the text and published in a supplement at the end of the volume, risking that they might be destroyed, and the *fraszka* "*O księdzu*", I, 54 (About the Priest), was omitted altogether. A still more but only supposedly serious intervention on the part of the publisher could probably be found in "*Carmen macaronicum de eligendo vitae genere*," published in the latest collection in the *Fragments* where even whole verses are omitted, being indicated by dots, which seems to be a unique case in the history of Polish sixteenth-century editions of poetic texts. On the other hand, we do not know for sure whether it is the publisher who is to be blamed for these omissions; could it not have been the poet himself attempting to excite readers' curiousity? Or perhaps the missing verses were not reprinted because of their illegibility or a defect in the manuscript.

Januszowski's violation of the integrity of the *Fraszki* in their later editions and his supposed intervention in the text of "*Carmen macaronicum* ..." (while nevertheless proving his concern for the poet's text by supplementing the volume *Jan Kochanowski* and *Fraszki* with Errata) cannot diminish the significance of the owner and manager of the Officina Lazari in making the whole of Kochanowski's output (at least as we know it) available in print. Undoubtedly, the publication of Kochanowski's works is the most notable enterprise in the history of this leading printing house in Poland, one which both in the opinion of contemporaries and posterity could be compared with the most outstanding printing houses of the time: those of Plantins or Estiennes, to which (like the Manutiuses and Henricpetri) Januszowski himself paid a tribute in *New Polish Type*. And indeed there are many analogies with those dynasties of printers to be found in Januszowski's career, and although his achievements were of necessity often less conspicuous, they were by no means less ambitious.

The son and heir of the distinguished Cracow printer, Łazarz Andrysowic, Januszowski continued the best traditions of the house. A generation earlier, his father had succeeded Hieronim Wietor, the most eminent Cracow printer of the first half of the sixteenth century. The house was distinguished by its boldness and broad-mindedness in publishing ventures, as well as by its careful execution and concern for maintaining the high standard of its publications, in terms of both quality and technology. Januszowski's designing in the 1590's of a new Polish type adapted to the characteristics of his native language, linked, as it were, his achievements with those of Wietor. In the 1520's Wietor had provided Polish printing with a type of his own design using beautiful decorative italics in Latin texts by transferring to Poland Jenson's roman type and Aldine italics. Similar parallels with Wietor can be seen in the choice of printed books, ranging from scientific to polemical and popular works, with literature, poetry, constituting a considerable part of the whole production. The house repeatedly published texts of the most outstanding writers. In the years 1518-1526 Wietor printed 12 editions of Erasmus, and Januszowski's father, Łazarz, may be called Orzechowski's printer (about 15 editions).

In this context it becomes more easily understandable that Januszowski monopolized the publication of Kochanowski's works both when the poet began to gather "the sheaves of his poetic harvest" and then after his death. This was possible mainly due to the king's privileges, which, though given to the poet and then his heirs, explicitly stressed Januszowski's rights to print those works. It is true that Wirzbięta, called Rej's printer, published without any privileges the master of Nagłowice's works from the time of the establishment of his printing house, but in this case relations between the printer and the writer were of a different character: after all, Wirzbięta's printing enterprise was supported financially by Rej. But in both cases the poets' publications were monopolized only later in their careers, when they had a considerable output. We cannot tell, however, whether or to what extent they decided about the form in which their printed works were to be presented to the reader.

All collections of Kochanowski's poetry differ indeed from the form poetic books usually took in France, Italy, or Germany at the time, but all editions of the *Songs, Fraszki,* the collection *Jan Kochanowski,* the *Fragments,* as well as Latin *Lyricorum libellus,* and *Elegiarum libri* are identical. His works were published not in the small handy volumes introduced by Aldo Manutius for editions of the classics, and then generalized by printers' practice in many countries for numerous editions of the poetry of Petrarch, Sannazaro, Marot, Baïf, Tasso, or Ronsard, although the collected works of Ronsard or Petrarch sometimes also had the monumental in folio form. Small volumes, in octavo, duodecimo or sedecimo, or even in a still smaller format were printed in italics, in small but distinct type. These were really "handy" or, as we would say today, "pocket" books. In Poland the poetry of Grzegorz z Sambora-Vigilantius, Pietro Illicinus, or Klemens Janicki (Janicius) also appeared in such formats. Books published in Italy used types frequently differentiated according to the form involved: prose was set in roman type and poetry in italics; it was rather unusual for poetry to be printed in roman type. Volumes of poetry were often adorned with delicate vignettes or illustrations, also of small size and usually simple, though elegant and harmonious in their decorations. Obviously, even then we find examples of excessive ornamentation, especially in Italy in the latter sixteenth century where editions of poetry were affected by mannerism which particularly manifested itself in multiplication of small ornaments.

Volumes of Jan Kochanowski's poetry (except for some "occasional" poems) as well as volumes of his collected prose and verse works appeared in the same format: in quarto, printed in rather large, distinct type. His texts in Polish were usually set in Gothic type (black-letter type), used then and for a long time afterwards for texts in the vernacular; works in Latin were set in roman type and in italics.[15] Titles or headings were usually printed in a different, larger type. If Kochanowski's Polish poetic texts were not printed in italics it was certainly because an appropriate type was not available. It should be remembered, however, that in *The New Polish Type* (containing projects for the new Polish orthography by Kochanowski, Górnicki, and Januszowski himself) Januszowski introduced—taking as a model the printing practice in France and Italy, while at the same time striving for the national character of a Polish book, and breaking away from the German influences heavily weighing on Polish printing since the sixteenth century—a new type of quasi-italics or italics adapted to Polish texts, the so-called Polish sloping type. He did not use this new type in any of his later editions of Kochanowski's poetry, but the very attempt at inventing italics for Polish texts is worth mentioning.

In the editions of Kochanowski's works published in Officina Lazari the text was placed within a simple linear frame. On the title page there was also a simple frame made up of typographical elements, but there were practically no ornaments, except for a few simple initials and ornamental vignettes, also usually made up of small elements, some printing ornaments, and sometimes the printer's imprint. The title pages of *Chess, Harmony, The Satyr ...*, *A Song on the deluge*, and *David's Psalter* show small woodcut scenes connected with the subject matter of the works: for *Chess* the scene of a game of chess; for *Harmony* a picture from Alciati's *Emblems* showing the symbol of harmony (ravens flying to the scepter bearing an appropriate inscription); for *The Satyr* ... the title character against a background of trees hewn down; and for the title page of the *David's Psalter* King David playing the lyre. In no edition of Kochanowski's works can we find the author's portrait, although such portraits had been customary, especially in Italian books, since the fifteenth century. According to Hirsch, the author's portrait was introduced for the first time in a book published in Milan in 1479.[16] Even in Poland there were books edited with portraits of their authors, to mention only the examples of Rej and Marcin Bielski.

In general the sixteenth-century editions of Kochanowski's works are simple but solemn. They are analogous to certain European editions of the classics or they could be compared with Petrarch's works in quarto, even though in the latter the poetic text was printed in italics and the commentary in roman type. Quarto editions of poetry were not unusual in Italy, but in general they were more richly decorated than volumes of Kochanowski, often with pretty illustrations or at least subtle vignettes, especially in the later, mannerist period (e.g., editions of Tasso or Guarini). Mannerist vignettes like those we find in the 1590 edition of J.G. Guarini had already appeared in the mid-century Lyons editions. Kochanowski's poetry in Januszowski's editions lacks ornaments of that type and is rather austere. The poet's word speaks directly to the reader without any additional aid of ornamental or pictorial elements so usual at the time of the emblematic book.[17]

The example of the editions of Petrarch may have influenced the title of the basic collection of our poet's works. The volume was given only the name of the poet instead of a title, just as in the case of some editions of Petrarch and great poets of antiquity, but rarely of modern ones (eg., Dante, Strozzi). Instead of the traditional formula, *opera*, *oeuvres*, "works" or "rime," etc. the title page of the volume reads only Pindar or Suidas, Dante or Petrarch. Presumably such a title was a form of homage paid to the author, for it could be found only on the works of the greatest writers. Among Polish poets only Kochanowski attained this honor. Not many other European writers attained it, both among his contemporaries, and among modern poets in general. We can be sure, however, that this formula was intended as a tribute to the poet who was really the maker of great Polish poetry, to the one who "scaled the rock of beautiful Calliope where no Pole had left his footprint before him."

Notes

1. For a list of Kochanowski's separate prints, his works published together with works of other authors, and those in manuscript form, see Janusz Pelc, *Jan Kochanowski. Szczyt renesansu w literaturze polskiej* (Jan Kochanowski. Zenith of the Renaissance in Polish Literature) (Warsaw: PWN, 1980), pp. 536-541. A complete bibliography of separate editions can be found in Kazimierz Piekarski, *Bibliografia dzieł Jana Kochanowskiego. Wiek XVI i XVII* (Bibliography of Jan Kochanowski's works. The 16th and 17th century) 2nd revised ed. (Cracow: Polska Akademia Umiejętności, 1934).

2. Janusz Pelc, *Jan Kochanowski w tradycjach literatury polskiej (od XVI do połowy XVIII wieku)* (Jan Kochanowski in the tradition of Polish literature. From 16th to mid-18th century) (Warsaw: PIW, 1965), pp. 61-62; Janusz Pelc, *Jan Kochanowski, le poète de la Renaissance* (Paris: UNESCO, 1986).

3. Paulina Buchwald-Pelcowa, *Jan Kochanowski i jego staropolscy wydawcy* (Jan Kochanowski and his old Polish printers) (in press).

4. Alodia Kawecka-Gryczowa, "Rola drukarstwa polskiego w dobie Odrodzenia" (The significance of Polish printings in the Renaissance) in *Z dziejów polskiej książki w okresie Renesansu. Studia i materiały.* (Wrocław: Ossolineum, 1975), pp. 116-

117. In estimating the number of sixteenth-century prints in Poland, Kawecka-Gryczowa says that about 3450 editions appeared in Cracow, and about 750 in other cities. In her opinion, another 50 per cent of lost and unrecorded prints should be added.

5. Paulina Buchwald-Pelcowa, "Nieznane pierwsze wydanie *Pieśni Trzech* Jana Kochanowskiego" (Unknown first printings of Jan Kochanowski's *Three Songs*) in *Studia z dziejów literatury i piśmiennictwa polskiego. Książka poświęcona ku czci Bronisława Nadolskiego* (Toruń: Acta Universitatis Nicolai Copernici, 1979), vol. 100, pp. 101-112.

6. Alodia Kawecka-Gryczowa, "Dzieje drukarni latającej" (History of the flying printing-house), in *Z dziejów polskiej książki*, pp. 189-228.

7. Sebastian Klonowic, *Żale nagrobne na ... Jana Kochanowskiego* (Laments on the grave of ... Jan Kochanowski) (Cracow, 1585). See the verse dedication to Czerny's family.

8. Janusz Pelc, "Teksty Kochanowskiego w kancjonałach staropolskich XVI i XVII wieku" (Kochanowski's texts in old Polish psalm-books of the 16th and 17th centuries, *Odrodzenie i Reformacja w Polsce*, 8 (Warsaw: PWN, 1963): 241—247.

9. Paulina Buchwald-Pelcowa, "Jeszcze jedno nieznane XVI-wieczne wydanie Psałterza Jana Kochanowskiego" (Another unknown 16th-century printing of Jan Kochanowski's *David's Psalter*), *Pamiętnik Literacki*, 70, no. 1 (1979): p. 226.

10. Stanisław Dobrzycki, *Psałterz Kochanowskiego, Jego powstanie, źródła, wzory* (Kochanowski's *David's Psalter*. Its origin, sources, and models) (Cracow: Akademia Umiejętności, 1910), p. 31.

11. Mikołaj Rej, in addition to his *Book of Psalms* and the many editions of single psalms in his translation (chiefly in the so-called miscellaneous psalm books), published the Seven Penetential Psalms, cf. Irena Rostkowska *Bibliografia dzieł Mikołaja Reja. Okres staropolski* (Biobliography of the works of Mikołaj Rej. Old Polish Period), (Wrocław: Ossolineum, 1970), p. 23.

12. The autograph of the letter, dated Czarnolas, Oct. 6, 1571, has not survived. A reprint and facsimile of the text in: Włodzimierz Stanisław Broel-Plater, *Zbiór pamiętników do dziejów polskich* (Collection of documents of Polish history), vol. 1 (Warsaw: Drukarnia Gazety Codziennej, 1859), pp. 230-231.

13. *Materiały do dziejów piśmiennictwa polskiego i biografii pisarzów polskich* (Materials on the history of Polish literature and the biographies of Polish writers) ed. Teodor Wierzbowski, vol. 2: 1526-1830 (Warsaw: Drukarnia Estetyczna, 1904), p. 26.

14. Kazimierz Piekarski, *Bibliografia dzieł*.

15. Ernst Philip Goldschmidt, *The Printed Book of the Renaissance. Three Lectures on Type, Illustration, Ornament* (Amsterdam: G.T. van Heusden, 1969), pp. 16-17. Goldschmidt writes that to Renaissance men roman type—as the "ancient" script of Romans—seemed beautiful, which accounts for its career in Renaissance printing. In Poland the first, still rather awkward, roman type was introduced in 1513 by Ungler, and from 1515 by Haller. But Goldschmidt is wrong when as an example of the use of roman type he gives a page set in this type as printed in Cracow by Haller in 1504; the book was actually printed in Germany. Italian type faces were introduced in Poland by Wietor. Cf. Kazimierz Piekarski, "Książka w Polsce XV i XVI w." (The book in Poland in the 15th and 16th centuries), in *Kultura staropolska* (Cracow: Polska Akademia Umiejętności, 1932), p. 360. But both roman type and italics were used in sixteenth-century Poland only in Latin texts, while texts in Polish were set in Gothic type. Piekarski (pp. 360-361) also points out that in Polish

printing of the time schwabacher type competed with Fraktur (German) type. Except in the northern parts of the country, the former prevailed, so it is only natural that it is the type predominantly found in Kochanowskl's prints.

16. Rudolf Hirsch, *Printing, selling and reading 1450-1550*, (Wiesbaden: Otto Harrassowitz, 1967), p. 49, 60.

17. In Kochanowski the influence of emblematics is considerably less conspicuous than in many European writers, or even in Rej. Cf. Janusz Pelc, *Obraz-słowo-znak. Studium o emblematach w literaturze staropolskiej* (Image-word-sign. A study of emblems in old Polish literature) (Wrocław: Ossolineum, 1973), pp. 104-119, 136-142; Paulina Buchwald-Pelcowa, *Emblematy w drukach polskich i Polski dotyczących XVI-XVIII wieku. Bibliografia* (Emblems in Polish printings and imprintings concerning Poland, 16th-18th centuries. Bibliography) (Wrocław: Ossolineum, 1980); pp. 22-24.

Cum Gratia & Priuilegio S. R. M.

W Krákowie/
W Drukárni Lázárzowéy. Roku páńſkiégo.
I 5 8 3.

25

Jan Kochanowski Through the Eyes of His Earliest Biographer*

Erna Hilfstein

The earliest biography of Jan Kochanowski (1530-1584) appeared in 1612 in the front matter of his Latin work *M.T. Ciceronis Aratus, Ad Graecum exemplar expensus, et locis mancis restitutus.* The anonymous author of this biography informed the readers that Jan Kochanowski, whose coat of arms was Corvin,[1]

was born in 1532 A.D. in his father's village Sycyna. His father Piotr held the office of a so-called land judge in the Sandomierz palatinate; his mother, Anna Odrowąż of Białaczów, was a woman of tested virtue and severe morals.

After the death of his father, whom he lost as a child, he and his five brothers were raised by his mother in the strictest discipline. Once he acquired, with a remarkable success, the rudiments of the liberal arts in his native country, burning with an extraordinary desire to gain knowledge, he went first to Germany, and thereafter to Paris. After about seven years devoted to the study of philosophy, history, languages, and poetry, for which he had a flair, he went from there to Italy, traversed through it, and spent a few years in Rome and Padua, attracted by the possibility of association with learned men, of whom at that time there was a multitude. In fact, he was especially attracted by conversation with Robortello and Manuzio. From there also originates his friendship with the following scholars: Jan Zamoyski, Andrzej Patrycy (Nidecki), Stanisław Fogelweder, and Łukasz Górnicki.[2]

After Kochanowski's return to his native land, Filip Padniewski, Bishop of Cracow, who also performed the duties of chancellor, taking note of Kochanowski's reputation, summoned him to the royal court. Delighted by his charm and fine intellect, coupled with the ability to

write in Latin, which at the time was used not only for public but
also for private matters, Padniewski recommended him to King Sigismund August, and secured for him an entry on the roster of secretaries. In that capacity Kochanowski was traveling to the provincial
assemblies of the gentry and, more frequently, to foreign rulers. Padniewski tried very hard to pressure him into entering the priestly
estate, but to no avail. Kochanowski was a person devoid of vain
ambition, endowed with a free spirit which was perhaps incapable
of withstanding the rigors of the priesthood; and to pretend he believed to be a sin. Since he considered himself to be unfit for the life
of a courtier, he easily put a tranquil life and the literary occupation
above the purple and the miter. This way of life seemed to him to be
more in line with his conscience than an increase of his estate and
the acquisition of high offices. However, Piotr Myszkowski, the successor of Padniewski, incessantly urged Kochanowski to accept a
position of importance; to that end he employed some effective mach-
inations. He ceded to Kochanowski the office of a provost in Poznań,
an office which he acquired for himself, and he obtained for him some
other benefices from the king. Although Kochanowski accepted them
in order to satisfy the wishes of his sponsor, nevertheless, he could
not be persuaded to enter holy orders. Moreover, when Myszkowski,
desiring to lead the quieter life of a bishop, withdrew from the royal
court, even though King Stefan (Batory), desiring to retain him at the
court, offered him a stipend of 1200 florins, Kochanowski decided
that the time was ripe for him to relinquish the advice of someone
else and start following his own calling. Thus he declined the proposal
to assume the sacerdotal duties offered to him against his wishes (for
through the efforts of Jan Zamoyski the monks of Sieciechów tried
to obtain for Kochanowski the king's nomination to their abbacy) and
left for Czarnolas, the estate of his (late) father. There, without delay,
he renounced the ecclesiastical benefices, and took a wife from the
noble family Podlodowski. When Zamoyski learned about it, not
wanting to leave in the obscurity of a private life the man on whom
he bestowed the greatest benevolence, he allegedly offered him the
office of a castellan of Połaniec by sending him a royal diploma obtained from King Stefan. Kochanowski, however, declined, and while
thanking them both for such a great favor, he reiterated his satisfaction
with a minor position by stating that he hesitated to admit into his
father's estate such a sumptuous and thriftless castellan who, consumed by arrogance and ambition, might, without any qualms,
squander all that Kochanowski gathered.

Although these were the reasons he gave, yet the true reason behind such a firm decision was his delight in a quiet life combined
with a literary activity. This is evident from his repudiation of a sen-

atorial office and his acceptance of the office of an equestrian tribune (*wojski* in Polish) in Sandomierz. Exempted from army services, these tribunes stayed at home during military expeditions and took care of the fortresses. Upon the acceptance of this office, he returned to the private life which he so ardently desired and dedicated himself to poetry for which he had an innate inclination.

Kochanowski attained such an excellence in the command of his native language that, from then on, he not only had no peer but also he left others far behind. He said about himself that he reached heights yet untrodden, and declared that the Polish language shows no lack of beauty and elegance of which other cultures are boasting.[3] On the other hand, in his Latin poems he came very close to those ancient writers who attained both fame and a refinement of style.[4]

He led a most pleasant life away from troublesome matters, both public and personal, he fathered six daughters and one son, born posthumously; at the same time he enjoyed friendship of the most eminent men in the Republic.

To the great sorrow of all, at fifty-two years of age, Kochanowski succumbed to apoplexy in Lublin, where in the name of friends, he had attempted to plead before King Stefan the case of Jakub Podlodowski, murdered by the Turks in violation of the law of nations. Kochanowski was buried in his family sepulchre in Zwoleń.[5]

This 1612 biography, in a slightly expanded form, containing also a list of most of Kochanowski's Polish and Latin works, appeared thirteen years later in the Polish polyhistor Szymon Starowolski's (1588-1656) little book entitled *Scriptorum polonicorum* ξκατουτασ *seu centum illustrium Poloniae scriptorum elogia et vitae.*[6] Now, since Starowolski's *Hekatontas*, and especially its revised and enlarged 1627 second edition,[7] enjoyed great popularity, Kochanowski's biography, its numerous errors repeated and new ones introduced, found its way into encyclopedic works of biographical nature put together by well-known seventeenth- and eighteenth-century writers.

For example, Kochanowski's family coat of arms was Corvin. Starowolski, following the 1612 biographer, writes "*Cochanovius, gente Corvinus.*" Girolamo Ghilini (1589-1668), believing that the word *gente* refers to Kochanowski's lineage, in his popular work *Teatro d'huomini letterati*, changed "*gente Corvinus*" into "*Regia stirpe de'Corvini,*" and in this way transformed Kochanowski, a member of the Polish lesser nobility (*szlachta*), into an offspring of the Hungarian royal family.[8] Following Ghilini, Nicolaus C. Papadopoli (1655-1740), that unreliable historian of the University of Padua,[9] states that "*Joannem Cochanovium tradunt e regia Corvinorum stirpe oriundum.*"[10] Furthermore, both the 1612 biography and the 1625 edition of the *Hekatontas* give 1532 as the year of Kochanowski's birth, which rather took place in 1530. Therefore, he did not lose his father (who died in 1547) "as a child" (*quem puer amisit*),[11] as reported by Starowolski after the 1612 biography, nor during his early childhood (*ne'primi anni della fanciullezza*),[12] as in Ghilini, nor during his boyhood (*intra pueritiam*),[13] as Papadopoli has it, but as a young man seventeen years old, who already during the summer semester of 1544 enrolled at the University of Cracow.[14] Through a typographical error, the 1627 edition of *Hekatontas* gives the year of Kochanowski's birth as 1552.[15] This is responsible for a further error in Ghilini who, obviously using the 1627 *Hekatontas*, repeats the above date. In addition, when Ghilini mentions that Kochanowski died at the age of 52 years, he performs the addition: 52 + 1552, and announces that our poet "*passo . . . all'altra vita l'Anno 1604.*"[16] This mistake is made worse by Papadopoli, who repeats, after Ghilini, that Kochanowski died in "*MDCIV, aetatis LII,*" yet, a few lines earlier, he says that "his (Kochanowski's) name is inscribed in the register of the Polish nation" in Padua in the year 1552,[17] thus making him the youngest university student ever. Moreover, while the 1612 anonymous writer merely states that Kochanowski was "attracted" (*illectus*)[18] by conversation with the Paduan professor of philology Francesco Robortello (1516-1567), Papadopoli makes him a "student of Robortello" (*fuisse discipulum Robortelli*)[19], which he most probably was.

Who, however, was the author of Kochanowski's earliest biography? Was it Starowolski, who, as we have seen above, incorporated it into his lives of the hundred most illustrious Polish writers? Or was it perhaps Jan Januszowski (1550-1613), Cracow's "royal archtypographer"[20] and author, who published, among others, the first collected works of our great poet?

Janusz Pelc, supported by the authority of earlier scholars, states that the biography of Kochanowski

> inserted anonymously into the 1612 edition of *Aratus,*... is probably ... a work penned by Szymon Starowolski. This is confirmed by the fact that it was inserted into the work of Starowolski entitled *Scriptorum polonicorum* ξκατουτασ *seu centum illustrium Poloniae scriptorum elogia et vitae* published in 1625.[21]

More recently, in their preface to the Polish translation of *Hekatontas*, Jerzy Starnawski and Franciszek Bielak declared in quite explicit terms that Starowolski is the author of the 1612 biography. In that they went much farther than Pelc, because they not only claim the insertion of the 1612 biography into *Hekatontas* as being tantamount to authorship, but also add that:

> even though Starowolski could indeed incorporate into *Hekatontas* a biography of Kochanowski already in existence and recognized by tradition, yet the incorporation of a text of a contemporary author would incur the risk of being exposed. Moreover, the style, composition, and the entire structure of this biography are in agreement with the biographical manner used by Starowolski and [therefore] the ascription of its authorship to him should not invoke any reservation.[22]

While the possibility that Starowolski was in fact that author of the 1612 biography cannot be ruled out completely, none of the arguments in support of his authorship presented by the above scholars may be regarded as sufficient for its positive identification.

First, "the style, composition, and structure" of Kochanowski's biography reproduced in *Hekatontas* are not typical of most of the other biographies presented in that work; most of them are characterized by scarce biographical data embelllshed by a high-flown language.[23] On the contrary, Kochanowski's biography is very factual, and the only embellishment is the sentence: "these men held Kochanowski to be Christian Apollo, prophetically born in our warlike Sarmatia," typical of Starowolski's style, does not appear in the 1612 biography. Secondly, since the 1612 biography was not signed, Starowolski was not obliged to give any specific reference to its author, even if he knew his name. And finally, Ghilini in his *Teatro d'huomini letterati* produced an almost literal Italian translation of Starowolski's text which, as we saw above, Ghilini undoubtedly used, likewise without disclosing the source of his information.

The question then may be asked whether Starowolski did utilize, in any of his other lives of the famous Polish writers, any printed or manuscript sources without providing a clear identification of their authors. Now, in the first (1625) edition, of *Hekatontas*, Starowolski published a very short and error-ridden life of the celebrated Polish astronomer Nicholas Copernicus (1473-1543). However, in his 1627 edition of this work he printed an enlarged and vastly improved version of Copernicus' biography.[24] For in the meantime Starowolski read the handwritten *Raptularzyk* (*Memoranda*) of Jan Brożek (1585-1652), professor of astronomy at the University of Cracow, which was attached to his copy of the 1617 Amsterdam edition of Copernicus' *De revolutionibus orbium coelestium*. [25] Since parts of Brożek's *Raptularzyk* are reproduced in the improved version of Copernicus' life published in the 1627 edition of *Hekatontas*, it had been argued that Brożek and not Starowolski is its author.[26] However, upon a close scrutiny of the text, it becomes apparent that Starowolski merely incorporated suitable parts of Brożek's *Raptularzyk* into Copernicus' biography.[27] Similarly, in the same biography, Starowolski cites word for word certain information contained in the letter written by Bishop Tiedemann Giese (1480-1550), Copernicus' close friend, to George Joachim Rheticus (1514-1574) Copernicus' only disciple.[28] But while Starowolski admits that this information was gathered from the Giese-Rheticus letter, he is silent on the use he made of Brożek's *Raptularzyk*, although the name of the latter is mentioned in that biography in reference to another matter. Judging from this example it may be assumed that Starowolski failed at times to identify his sources. It must also be added that sometime before 1610 Starowolski accepted the position of tutor to the young princes Konstanty and Janusz Ostrogski, whom he accompanied on their European tour. The exact date of his return from abroad is not known, but he enrolled at the University of Cracow on December 10, 1612[29] and therefore it is entirely possible that he was not in Cracow when the 1612 edition of *Aratus* was being prepared for publication and could not be asked to write a biography of Kochanowski.

On the other hand, it is plausible that Januszowski, who knew both Kochanowski and his wife, was, as Władysław Nehring suggested,[30] the author of the first Kochanowski biography in print. Only the fact that this biography contains certain errors which could not have been made by a person who was personally acquainted with the poet speaks against Januszowski's authorship. For example, we read in the biography that Kochanowski went first to Paris and then to Italy, while it is well known, that just the opposite is the case. Such a mistake, however, becomes understandable if we consider that the biography was most probably written around the year 1611, that is, some 17 years after the poet's death, when the memory of the chronological sequence of his travels became dimmer in the mind of the biographer.

Yet, whoever its author, the biography, with all its shortcomings, gave a correct-picture of Jan Kochanowski, the Renaissance poet who "had no peer" and "left others far behind."[31]

Notes

*I am indebted to the late Professor Edward Rosen of the CUNY Graduate Center and Mgr. Tadeusz Pochopień of Cracow, Poland, for supplying material otherwise unavailable to me.

1. *M.T. Ciceronis Aratus. Ad Graecum exemplar expensus, et locis mancis restitutus a Ioan: Cochanovio* (Cracoviae: Ex officina Andreae Petrocoui ..., 1612), fols. 3b-4b. Strictly speaking, this is not Cicero's *Aratus*, but Cicero's Latin translation of Aratus' (third century B.C.) famous astronomical poem φαινομενα, corrected and completed by Kochanowski on the basis of a Greek MS, edited and published in 1565 by his friend Andrzej Patrycy Nidecki (1522-1587).

2. Szymon Starowolski, *Scriptorum polonicorum* ξκατοντασ *seu centum illustrium Poloniae scriptorum elogia et vitae* (Francoforti, 1625); (hereafter *Hekatontas*), p. 44, and 2nd edition (Venice, 1627), p. 72, after the name of Łukasz Górnicki (1527-1603) have the following addition:

> ...(Łukasz Górnicki) whom he won over by his exceptionally great poetic talent. These men held Kochanowski to be a Christian Apollo, prophetically born in our warlike Sarmatia.

3. In this place, Starowolski's *Hekatontas*, adds:

> He wrote in our language: *Psałterz Dawidów, Fenomeny, Szachy, Apoftegmata, Satyr, Treny, Epigramaty, Pieśni, Wojna Trojańska, Epitalamia, Epitafia, Fraszki*, and other things in this genre (1625 ed., p. 46; 1627 ed., p. 75).

4. In this place, Starowolski's *Hekatontas* adds:

> He left the following works: *M. T. Cic. Aratum, Orphaeum Sarmaticum, Libros Elegiarum, Epithalamiorum, Lyricorum, Foricoeniorum*, et *Carmen de expugnatione Polottei* (1625 ed., p. 46; 1627 ed., p. 75).

5. Starowolski's 1627 *Hekatontas* adds here:

> His brother Mikołaj translated Virgil's *Aeneid* into a Polish verse, and with an equal talent he wrote *Rotuły*, that is, instructions in virtues for his sons. Yet another member of his family, Piotr Kochanowski, wrote *Gottfred abo Jeruzalem wyzwolona*, an imitation of Torquato Tasso (p. 76).

Actually, Mikołaj authored only *Rotuły*; Vergil's *Aeneid* was translated by Andrzej Kochanowski.

6. Cf. note 2, above.

7. Ibid. Janina Hoskins, *Early and Rare Polonica of the 15th-17th Centuries in American Libraries* (Boston: G. K. Hall, 1973), p. 150, no. 1072, gives the following description of the various editions of Starowolski's *Hekatontas*:

This (i.e., 1625 *Hekatontas*) first attempt at a history of Polish literature provides biobibliographical information about its writers. An enlarged edition was published in Venice in 1627 and in Frankfurt in 1644.

Hoskins errs in describing the 1644 Frankfurt edition as enlarged; Jacob de Zetter, the publisher of the 1625 edition, reprinted it unchanged in 1644. Starowolski was undoubtedly not aware of the 1644 edition, otherwise he would have insisted on the reprinting of the enlarged 1627 version; cf. Erna Hilfstein, *Starowolski's Biographies of Copernicus*, series *Studia Copernicana 21* (Wrocław:Ossolineum, 1980; hereafter *Starowolski's Biographies*), p. 9; cf. also *Catalogue Général des Livres Imprimés de la Bibliotheque Nationale*, vol. 177, col. 376.

8. Girolamo Ghilini, *Teatro d'huomini letterati* (Venetia, 1647), p. 123, hereafter *Teatro*.

9. Leopold Prowe, *Nicolaus Copernicus*, 1 (1883-1884 ed., reprinted Osnabrück, 1967), p.297, cites several opinions concerning Papadopoli's work, all of which are highly critical. For example:

Papadopolis ist ein Fälscher erster Klasse. Er citirt Werke, welche gar nicht vorhanden sind; er entnimmt ihnen Belegstellen, die rein erfunden sind. Er geht sogar so weit, Ausgaben von Büchern zu erwähnen, welche niemals erschienen sind.

10. Niccolo C. Papadopolis, *Historia Gymnasii patavini*, 2 (Venetiis, 1726), p. 266; hereafter *Historia*.

11. *Hekatontas*, 1625 ed., p. 44; 1627 ed., p. 72.

12. *Teatro*, p. 123.

13. *Historia*, II, 266.

14. *Album studiosorum Universitatis Cracoviensis*, II, ed. Adam Chmiel (Cracow, 1892), p. 315, has the following entry: "Johannes Kochanowski Petri de Syczynow dioc. Cracoviensis 3 gr. (ossos) s. (olvit)."

15. *Hekatontas*, p. 72.

16. *Teatro*, pp. 123-124.

17. *Historia*, II, p. 267: "Eius nomen inscriptum est albis Polonicis (1) ad An. 1552 . . . "

18. *Hekatontas*, 1625 ed., p.44; 1627 ed., p. 72.

19. *Historia*, 2, p. 267.

20. Alodia Kawecka-Gryczowa, "Rola drukarstwa polskiego w dobie Odrodzenia" (The role of Polish printing in the period of the Renaissance), *Odrodzenie w Polsce*, 4, (Warsaw: PIW, 1956), p. 488.

21. Janusz Pelc, *Jan Kochanowski w tradycjach literatury polskiej, od XVI do połowy XVIII w* (Jan Kochanowski in the traditions of Polish literature, from the sixteenth to the mid eighteenth centuries) (Warsaw: PIW, 1965), p. 68.

22. Szymon Starowolski, *Setnik pisarzów polskich albo pochwały i żywoty stu najznakomitszych pisarzów polskich* (One hundred Polish writers or the eulogies and biographies of one hundred of the most illustrious Polish writers) (Cracow: 1970), p. 30.

23. *Starowolski's Biographies*, pp. 9-10.

24. Ibid., pp. 13-15, 85-87.

25. At present in the Jagiellonian Library in Cracow, BJ 311 204 Stare Druki. The title of this edition of *De revolutionibus* has been changed by its editor to *Astronomia instaurata*.

26. See for example Henryk Barycz, "Dzieło literackie Jana Brożka," *Pamiętnik Literacki*, 14 (1954), 61-90, esp. 78-88.

27. *Starowolski's Biographies*, pp. 64-65.

28. Ibid., pp. 15, 33-35, 89-90.

29. *Album studiosorum Universitatis Cracoviensis*, 4, ed. Jerzy Zathey (Cracow, 1950), 32.

30. Cited after Pelc, *Jan Kochanowski w tradycjach literatury polskiej, od XVI do połowy XVIIIw*, p. 68, who mentions that Nehring ascribed the 1612 biography to Januszowski; Nehring's *Jan Kochanowski* (Petersburg, 1900) was not available to me.

31. For a revaluation of the problem of the authorship of Kochanowski's earliest biography including a new well argued hypothesis that the author was Jan Brożek, see Henryk Barycz "Dookoła najstarszego życiorysu Jana Kochanowskiego" (About the oldest biography of Jan Kochanowski) in *Z zaścianka na Parnas. Drogi kulturalnego rozwoju Jana Kochanowskiego i jego rodu* (Cracow: Wydawnictwo Literackie, 1981), pp. 271- 299.

26

Jan Kochanowski and Croatian Literature

Ante Kadić

uring his student years at Padua University, Jan Kochanowski met and struck up friendships not only with his Polish colleagues, but undoubtedly also with students of other nationalities present there. Andrija Dudić (1533-1589) was the most well known and eminent among them.[1] Although his father was a Croat, but being employed at the court of Ferdinand I, Andrija was born in Buda(pest). At first a Catholic priest, a notable theologian at the Council of Trent and then a bishop, Dudić became an ambassador of Maximilian II of Austria at the court of Sigismund August (Zygmunt August). While in Poland, Dudić fell in love with Regina Straszówna and married her; he was forced thereafter to abandon his bishopric. When Regina died, Dudić married Elizabeth Zborowska, a follower of Faustus Socinus who preached the Arian, anti-Trinitarian doctrine. Dudić thus moved from Catholicism to Lutheranism to Socinianism, and finally to Calvinism. However, thanks to his erudition in various areas and good manners, he did not lose his former friends and protectors. Only in 1575, after trying in vain to secure the Polish throne for his protector Maximilian II, when Stefan Batory, his former colleague from Padua, became the Polish king, did he feel obliged to leave Poland. He settled in Breslau (Wrocław), where he lived in seclusion and died of pestilence.

This extremely versatile man, a translator from Greek, an excellent Latinist, an enthusiastic Ciceronian (about whom it was said that he copied the entire output of Cicero three times), a renowned speaker, an able ambassador, and an attractive personality, was so much distracted by his travels and manifold occupations that he did not leave any outstanding work. He was very popular during his lifetime and corresponded with many writers all over Europe. Among his most devoted friends was Jan Kochanowski. They had met in Padua, perhaps traveled together in France in 1559, and remained on excellent terms during Dudić's prolonged stay in Poland.

Among Kochanowski's *Fraszki* there is one, unusual for him [*"Na świętego ojca"*(I, 44)]—written during his alleged early sympathy with the reformation—in which he mocks "the holy father":

Świętym cię zwać nie mogę, ojcem się nie wstydzę,
Kiedy, wielki kapłanie, syny twoje widzę.[2]

I can not call you holy, but I am not ashamed to call you father,
As, mighty priest, I gaze upon your sons.

This distich for a long time was considered a paraphrase of a poem by Dudić. This opinion was expressed by the editors of Kochanowski's *Complete Works* (1884, II, 347) and repeated, for example, by J. Langlade in his book, *Jean Kochanowski* (Paris, 1932, p. 124) although long before the correct name of its author was revealed. It is now definitely proven and accepted that Kochanowski had followed another Croatian humanist, Janus Pannonius, whose almost identical verses (belonging to a cycle of four epigrams written in 1465 against Pope Paul II) were known in Poland's Protestant circles.[3] They read as follows:

Sanctum non possum, patrem te dicere possum,
cum video natam, Paule Secunde, tuam.[4]

When only twenty years old, Dudić accompanied Reginald Pole, the English cardinal and papal emissary, on his journey through the West European countries (1553-1557). Kochanowski wrote an elegy (I, IV)[5] at that time in which he compared most probably Dudić with himself. While Dudić is abandoning his poor girlfriend Menophile:

Tu tamen, heu misera frustra obtestante puella,
Andrea, longas pergis inire vias.

and going through inaccessible Alps, Kochanowski, on the contrary, prefers the company of Lydia to all the riches of this world:

Sim potius pauper, dum sim, mea Lydia, tecum,
Cum te habeo, cedunt omnia regna mihi.

During this long trip and later, after he continued and finished his studies in Padua (1558-1559), Dudić spent some time in Paris. While in the French capital, he made friends not only with certain members of Catherine de Médici's royal entourage but also among the intellectual elite. Ivan Esih (following Stanisław Kot) assumes that it was Dudić who introduced Kochanowski to Pierre de Ronsard and to the circle of poets of the *Pléiad*.[6]

Kochanowski's first poem addressed by name to Dudić written in all probability during the early years of their friendship in Padua, is the Latin epigram *"In imaginem Andreae Duditii"* (*Foricoenia* 26),[7] written in the genre of *icones*, in which he praised Dudić's honesty and virtue:

Quis te Duditi, novus hic expressit Apelles?
Quae te tam solers est imitata manus?
Cui probitas non est, aut cui tua cognita virtus,
Ex facie mores aestimet ille tuos.

Dudić, who is this new Apelles who has painted you?
What experienced hand has so faithfully rendered you?
He to whom your honesty and virtue are unkown,
shall appraise your character from your face.

After his brief participation at the Council of Trent and a subsequent appointment as a secretary at the royal court and a bishop, Dudić, as mentioned above, went to Poland in 1565 as ambassador of Maximillian II. On this occasion probably, Kochanowski sent him a 32 line poem in the form of a poetic letter "Ad Andream Duditium" (Foricoenia, 63)[8] in which he greeted his old friend from Padua with joy.

Quod superos nunquam coelestia templa colentes
Ausus fuissem poscere,
Id nunc oblatum est ultro mihi sorte benigna,
Duditi amicorum optime,
Ut te tot spatia emensum terraeque marisque
Hoc ultimo orbis angulo ...

Dudić, best of friends!
That which I would not have dared to ask the gods
residing in heavenly realms,
has now by chance become my fortune:
you, who have traversed so many lands and sea,
I see in this corner of the earth ...

He expressed his sorrow that he is deprived from seeing him now because he is forced to stay in Czarnolas to defend his ancestral patrimony. The poet concluded his letter jokingly:

Mitto tibi me ipsum: non quem nunc cura laborque
Noctes diesque conficit,
Sed quem tu aspexti nuper nardoque fluentem,
Dulcique amore saucium.
Utrum horum mavis? —utrumque ais:—hunc age primum
Evolve, dum alter advolat.

I am sending you myself: not the one who
night and day is afflicted by work and cares,
but him whom you recently saw
bathed in fragrant oil and tormented by sweet love
Whom do you prefer? Both you say—take then first
the latter—before the other comes running.

When shortly after, in 1567, Dudić married and became closely associated with the Protestant intellectuals, Kochanowski considered Dudić's apostasy his own affair and remained on good terms with him. Moreover, for Dudić's wedding he composed a Latin elegy (III, XVI)⁹ an Epithalamium in which he depicts Dudić in the most flattering terms as a "man filled with knowledge and experience, equally able with pen and eloquence, the emissary of kings." The poet lauded his friend that above the riches and magnificent mitre he valued higher the riches of love.

We do not know if Kochanowski kept in contact with Dudić after the latter felt he could not stay longer in Poland. The distinguished Polish poet, who was three years older than his gifted, but controversial Croatian colleague, died five years before his friend. Dudić, who died in Breslau (Wrocław) in 1589, was buried in a Reformed church and over his tomb his widow placed an extravagant epitaph.

As Tadeusz Ulewicz stated, Kochanowski's influence on Croatian literature came comparatively late in the history of the reception of his works in other countries.¹⁰

Ignjat Durdević (1675-1737), a prominent Croatian baroque poet, first a Jesuit and then later a Benedictine monk, as a young man before taking holy orders, wrote many love poems ("pjesni ljuvene"). In later years he collected those which he had not destroyed when (supposedly) he was abandoning forever the pleasures of this sinful world.¹¹ Since Durdević was very much influenced by Ovid, he thought it appropriate to devote his introductory poem to the Roman from whom he learned the poetic art. Like many others before and after him, Durdević believed that Ovid, while exiled in Tomi (today Constanza, on the shores of the Black Sea) where he learned "sarmatice loqui," had mastered the Slavic language, the Sarmatians being commonly taken to be the ancestors of the Slavs. Ovid appears to Durdević in a dream. Speaking highly of the Slavic language, he finds that its finest exponents are the Croatian poets from the Dalmatian shores. Among the northern Slavs, he mentions only Kochanowski. In Durdević's opinion, this Pole distinguished himself not only for his astounding knowledge but also for his beautiful poems; unfortunately, however, he did not have successors, since the icy North had stifled the flow of poetry:

Gled' onamo, s kraja od svita
gdi od leške roden krvi
gre pun znanja glasovita
Kokanovski pjesnik prvi;
na njegova pjenja uredna
mrazni sjever tijek ustavi ... ¹²

It is hard to say why Durdević had such a special esteem for Kochanowski. It is clear that he knew Kochanowski's works. But the question arises which particular ones and in which language he read them.

Durđević considered as his own greatest achievement the fact that he translated into Croatian all hundred and fifty psalms of David (*Saltijer slovinski*, Venice 1729). Like Kochanowski before him, he too tried to diminish monotony in his rendition by employing various metrical forms. Tadeusz Ulewicz stated that Kochanowski's *Psałterz Dawidów* was popular among the Bohemians and the South Slavs,[13] it is not surprising then that this erudite Benedictine read and perhaps imitated him. Though not always successfully, Durđević in general created a work which some specialists consider among the better ones in old Croatian literature.

In 1564 Kochanowski published his poem *Satyr albo Dziki Mąż (The Satyr, or the Wild Man)*; this mythological creature, half animal and half man, an inhabitant of the Polish forests, complains that these forests are being destroyed in order to buy foreign luxuries—the Poles are foolishly cutting down timber for export. At the front of this didactic and political work there is a picture of this "wild man," who has horns, big ears, a tail and shaggy legs; in the background, on a hill, someone with a huge ax is cutting a tree. The Satyr immediately states why he is abandoning his ancestral habitat:

Tak jako mię widzicie, choć mam na łbie rogi
    I twarz nieprawie cudną, i kosmate nogi,
Przedsięm uszedł za boga w one dawne czasy,
    A to mój dom był zawżdy, gdzie nagęstsze lasy.
Aleście je tak długo tu, w Polszcze, kopali,
    Żeście z nich ubogiego Satyra wygnali.[14]

(lines 17-22)

Although, as you see, I have horns on my head,
my face is not beautiful and my legs are hairy,
in ancient times I was taken for a deity.
My dwelling was always in the deepest forests.
But you, in Poland, have dug in them so much
that you have chased from them this poor Satyr.

Not only this Satyr but many other "wild men" in medieval literature and art are paragons of virtue, gentle, and enlightened.

Matija Antun Reljković (1732-98), a captain in the Austrian army, participated in the Seven Years' War. He was taken prisoner, and for a time was held at Frankfurt-on-Oder, where he was allowed to use the private library of his host. Though he loved his Slavonia, he realized how primitive it was when compared with the German lands and decided to enjoin his countrymen to improve intellectually, morally, and economically. Since the most popular form of writing among the masses was a decasyllabic verse, Reljković used this meter to please and captivate his readers in his *Satyr, or the Wild Man (Satir iliti divji čovik)*, Dresden 1762; a second and much enlarged edition was published in Osijek, 1779).

As in Kochanowski's poem, so too in the first edition of Reljković's work, there is an explanation that "a Slavonian, cutting wood in the forest, came

upon a Satyr;[15] they became friends and decided to go to various places together. The man invited the Satyr to lunch with him; while the Slavonian was
preparing lunch, the Satyr described to him in verse the beauty of Slavonia.
By indicating its previous and present condition, he convinced the Slavonian
both of its shortcomings and how to correct the same."

Tomo Matić, author of many articles about Reljković and editor of a critical
edition of his works,[16] indicated already in 1911 the possibility that Kochanowski influenced the Croatian poet.[17] Matić held that opinion until the end of
his long life. In his study "The Slavonian village in the works of the Croatian
writers at the end of the eighteenth century" (published in 1961), Matić wrote
that, to judge from Reljković's manuscript kept in Vinkovci, the Croatian author
had introduced the Satyr after the work was completed. He believed that this
innovation, the identity of the title (*The Satyr, or the Wild Man*) and the introductory explanation are reason enough to suspect that Kochanowski was one
of his inspirational sources.[18]

Ivan Esih has also discussed "the parallel" between Kochanowski's and
Reljković's *Satyr or the Wild Man*. Esih was totally unaware that Matić had
treated the same topic before him. After giving a biobibliographic outline on
Kochanowski and the content of his *Satyr ...*, Esih compares the two poetic
works. He stresses not only their identical titles and similar picture of a wild
man, but also their moralistic tendency: while Kochanowski had in mind the
Polish gentry, Reljković spoke to the primitive Slavonian peasants who had
been freed only recently from the centuries-long Turkish yoke. Both authors
wished to see their countrymen less egoistic and not so much prone to follow
foreign customs. Esih also stresses their Slavic patriotism.[19]

In recent surveys or articles, however, Kochanowski's impact upon Reljković
is either not mentioned or dismissed. Thus, Kombol and Bogišić totally ignore
this question. Krešimir Georgijević, in his excellent survey of Croatian literature
in Slavonia, says that the two writers, aside from the title of their respective
works, have nothing in common. He asks: "Did Kochanowski's work, two
hundred years old, come into Reljković's hands? If we accept this possibility,
we do not know yet that he read it."[20] Stojan Subotin has surveyed the critical
literature on the Polish and Croatian *Satyr*.[21] Having reviewed those who saw
the parallel (Matić and Esih), he mentions Georgijević, who has remained very
skeptical. Subotin continues to believe that Reljković, who created an original
work, would have been unable to come to this idea by himself. A careful reading
of Subotin's arguments incline us to an affirmative answer, but there is no
certitude. It may even be possible that both authors had some common medieval German source.

Notes

1. See Pierre Costil, *André Dudith, humaniste hongrois; sa vie, son oeuvre et ses
manuscrits grecs* (Paris, 1935). Janusz Pelc, *Jan Kochanowski. Szczyt renesansu w literaturze polskiej* (Jan Kochanowski. Zenith of Renaissance in Polish Literature) (War-

saw: PWN, 1980), passim. Jan Ślaski, "Jan Kochanowski i Węgrzy" (Jan Kochanowski and the Hungarians) in *Jan Kochanowski i epoka renesansu*, ed. Teresa Michałowska (Warsaw: PWN, 1984), pp. 421-424. See also the articles of Ivan Esih in *Hrvatska Revija* 11 (1932): 706-712, and Vladimir Bazala's in *Enciklopedija Jugoslavije* vol. 2 (1956) s. v. and Bazala, *Pregled hrvatske znanstvene bastine* (Survey of Croatian scholarly heritage) (Zagreb, 1978), 188-189.

2. Jan Kochanowski, *Dzieła polskie* (Polish works) ed. Julian Krzyżanowski. 11th ed. (Warsaw: PIW, 1980) p. 144.

3. See Jan Ślaski, "Janus Pannonius i Polacy" (Janus Pannonius and the Poles) in *Literatura staropolska i jej związki europejskie*, ed. Janusz Pelc, (Wrocław: Ossolineum, 1973) pp. 165-168.

4. Jan Pannoonius, *Poemata quae uspiam reperiri potuerunt omnia*, ed. S. Teleki, vol. 1-2 (Utrecht, 1784), Ep. I, 53.

5. *Jana Kochanowskiego, Dzieła wszystkie*. Wydanie Pomnikowe (The complete works of Jan Kochanowski) vol. 3, ed. Józef Przyborowski (Warsaw, 1884), pp. 14-16.

6. Ivan Esih, *Hrvatska Revija* 2 (1932): 711. Stanisław Kot, "Jana Kochanowskiego podróże i studia zagraniczne," (Jan Kochanowski's foreign travels and studies) in *Studia staropolskie*. Księga ku czci Aleksandra Brücknera (Cracow, 1928), pp. 413-414.

7. *Jana Kochanowskiego, Dzieła wszystkie*, p. 198.

8. Ibid., pp. 220-222.

9. Ibid., pp. 139-144.

10. Tadeusz Ulewicz, *Oddziaływanie europejskie Jana Kochanowskiego* (European influence of Jan Kochanowski) (Wrocław: Ossolineum, 1976), pp. 33-35.

11. Ante Kadić, "Ignjat Durđević, Croatian Baroque Writer", *Journal of Croatian Studies* 18-19 (1977-78): 92-97. Ignat Durđević, *Piesni razlike* (Various songs) (Zagreb: Matica hrvatska, 1971) p. 35.

12. Josip Hamm quotes Durđević's verses on Kochanowski and argues that perhaps they do not refer to the Polish writer but to the great Ivan Gundulić who used to live in Konavle (therefore *"konavoski pjesnik"*), a community not far from Dubrovnik. Though in Durđević's poem the transition from the Dubrovnik authors to Kochanowski is quick and unexpected, nevertheless, the second verse indicating the poet's Polish origin (*"gdi od leške rodjen krvi"*) can refer only to Kochanowski. Hamm had demonstrated a solid knowledge of Durđević's manuscripts and indicated that in the translations of the penitential Psalms there is a greater affinity between Kochanowski and Gundulić than with Durđević, but he himself has concluded that the reading *"konavoski"* was less probable (Josip Hamm, "Kochanowski kod Južnih Slavena," (Kochanowski among the South Slavs) in *Polsko-Jugosłowiańskie stosunki literackie*, ed. Jerzy Śliziński) (Wrocław: Ossolineum 1972), pp. 27-38.

13. Ulewicz, pp. 6-17.

14. *Jana Kochanowskiego, Dzieła wszystkie*, p. 58.

15. "Slavonac, sikući u šumi drva, namiri se na jednoga Satira."

16. *Djela M.. Reljkovića. Stari pisci hrvatski* (The works of M.A. Reljković. Old Croatian writers), vol. 23 (Zagreb, 1916).

17. Tomo Matić, "Neue Beitrage uber M.A. Reljković," in *Archiv für Slavische Philologie* 32 (1911): 166-168.

18. Tomo Matić, *Iz hrvatske književne baštine* (From the Croatian literary inheritance), ed. J. Pupačić (Zagreb: Matica Hrvatska, 1970), p. 301.

428   Ante Kadić

19. Ivan Esih, "Poljski i hrvatski *Satir ili divlji čovjek*" (The Polish and Croatian *Satyr or the Wild Man*) in *Hrvatsko Kolo*, 9 (1927-28): 166-181.

20. Krešimir Georgijevic, *Hrvatska književnost od 16. do 18. stoljeća u Sjevernoj Hrvatskoj i Bosni* (Croatian literature from the sixteenth to the eighteenth centuries in North Croatia and Bosnia) (Zagreb: Matica Hrvatska, 1969), pp. 244-245.

21. Stojan Subotin, "Wokół zagadnień wpływu Jana Kochanowskiego na *Satyra* M.A. Reljkovićia." (About the influence of Jan Kochanowski on M.A. Reljković) in *For Wiktor Weintraub*. (The Hague: Mouton, 1975), pp. 505-514.

Jan Kochanowski: The Model Poet in Eastern Slavic Lectures on Poetics of the Seventeenth and Eighteenth Centuries

Paulina Lewin

O mnie Moskwa i będą wiedzieć Tatarowie,
I róznego mieszkańcy świata Anglikowie;

(About me Moscow will know and the Tatars
And Englishmen, inhabitants of diverse worlds)[1]

Several factors, related one way or another, were to determine the position of Jan Kochanowski, the most eminent poet of the Polish Renaissance, as a model in Eastern Slavic lectures on poetics in the seventeenth and eighteenth centuries. These were lectures delivered in Orthodox ecclesiastical schools of the Polish Commonwealth (the Ukraine and the Grand Duchy of Lithuania), as well as Muscovy which followed the curriculum of Polish Jesuit colleges and academies. Classes in poetics and rhetoric (the so-called *humaniora*) culminated the college education or its equivalent. They were taught in Latin with examples and exercises (*praxes*) in Latin, Polish, Church Slavonic, and the vernacular. As in Jesuit schools, these classes were intended to teach the art of good writing in verse and prose. The lectures on poetics in question, extant in manuscripts, were derived, mainly second or third hand, from such published sources, then being reedited, as Julius Caesar Scaliger, *Poetices libri* VII (1561) Jacobus Pontanus, *Poeticarum institutionum libri* III (1594), and Jacobus Masenius, *Palaestra eloquentiae ligatae* (1654). The lectures reveal that many of the Orthodox professors were not only familiar with the new, Renaissance and baroque, theoretical trends in poetics, but were well-read in ancient and modern Latin poetry and in Polish poetry as well. They knew and cited the Polish Jesuit Maciej Kazimierz Sarbiewski (1530-1584), who wrote in Latin and was called by his contemporaries "the Christian Horace."[2] This was a time when a comparison drawn between a modern poet and an ancient one, a classic, was not simply a courtesy, but first of all a fiducial point, the highest standard of reference to a model.

The very idea of a model poet, formulated by Horace, extensively repeated and exploited in Europe during the time of the Renaissance and later, was brought into the Eastern Slavic culture by school lectures on poetics. In this way the requirement to imitate the language, style, verse structures, genre structures, themes, and ideas of model authors, which was a long-lasting component of the European understanding of the art of poetry "making," started to dominate among the Eastern Slavs as well. Sarbiewski, whom they knew or of whom they had heard, entitled his own lectures on poetics, delivered in Jesuit colleges of Wilno and Połock: *De perfecta poesi, sive Vergilius et Homerus*[3] *De acuto et arguto, sive Seneca et Martialis; De virtutibus et vitiis carminis elegiaci, seu Ovidius; Characteres lyrici, seu Horatius et Pindarus.*[4] In the latter, besides the abundance of quotations from Latin poetry, Sarbiewski quoted in Polish from Kochanowski. This must have been quite a novelty, since the professor felt the need to explain himself by saying that he followed some of his learned colleagues who recently have used examples from poems written in their native tongues: in Italian, French, and Spanish. Introducing Jan Kochanowski's poetry, Sarbiewski calls him "the Orphean genius," the "Polish Horace" who is as good as the Latin one. Comparing him with the Italians Marino, Guido Casoni, Petrarch, Dante, and the French Ronsard, he said that Kochanowski not only is not inferior to them but even superior in the urbanity of his Polish language, the gravity of sentences, the inventiveness and vigor. Their style, when compared to the ancients, seems to be puerile, while Kochanowski displayed the vim and energy of the style of the ancients which is the best of all.[5] This is why, in Sarbiewski's opinion, Kochanowski's poetry presents, a model of inventiveness equal to the ancients, marked by great merit and dignity, of masterly arrangement (*dispositio*), and elegant and easy elocution, that is, in the three main domains of the art of speaking and writing. In some cases, Kochanowski expresses himself even better than Horace and other ancients. Sarbiewski illustrates this several times as, for example, when he compares two excerpts from Horace (Ode 14, I) with Kochanowski's "Lament" VII. Both poets, says Sarbiewski, depict their feelings for a person by addressing inanimate objects which belonged to these persons. Kochanowski, however, does it better.[6]

Kochanowski's poetry was highly regarded in Poland, also during the age of the baroque. Teachers of poetics in the seventeenth century who used his poems cited not only its ancient, classical values, but also its baroque virtue of *varietatis*—plurality and variety of topics, of metrical structures, genres, styles, and moods. Book inventories from the sixteenth, seventeenth, and eighteenth centuries prove that Kochanowski's poetry was read in different social strata of the Polish Commonwealth (by burghers, gentry, and clergy of different denominations) not only in Poland itself, but in the Ukraine and the Grand

Duchy of Lithuania. His poems could be found in lay and religious songbooks as anonymous songs. His poems and short rhymes (*fraszki*) were hand copied by his admirers and by school students, often with divergences (lections)—evidence that they were put down after they had been memorized.

It is true that Sarbiewski's approach to Kochanowski's poetry established the latter's position as a model poet. But seldom was Kochanowski appraised by others according to Sarbiewski's criteria, seldom was he measured from Sarbiewski's viewpoint. Teachers both in Jesuit and Orthodox schools exploited Kochanowski's poetry mainly to explain and to show the variety of verse and stanza structures which could be mastered in Polish and "Slavonic" languages. The poetics they taught were normative. The quantitative structural components of the verse were much easier to apprehend than any other virtues of Kochanowski's art. Characteristically, in 1702 one of the teachers at the Kievan Academy, Hilarion Iaroszewicki,[7] while enumerating the variety of poetic genres which could be written in Polish and Slavonic verses, indicated Kochanowski's achievements with one reservation—that his epigrams, elegies, and other poems do not abound in fictions (*quamvis fictionibus non abundent*),[8] fiction meaning at the time of the baroque a sophisticated play of fancy, plays on thoughts and words. The harmonious mastery of Kochanowski's lyrics that was so highly praised by Sarbiewski in the first half of the seventeenth century did not appeal to the taste of the age of the Eastern Slavic baroque. Professors of poetics and readers of that time looked for other qualities in Kochanowski's art. They fixed the attention of their students first of all upon his skills in versification. And these skills were great, indeed. Maria Dłuska, who has devoted herself to the study of Polish versification, wrote as a conclusion to her own and other scholars' studies on the innovative role of Kochanowski's verse mastery: "Kochanowski changed existing poetics to the core by introducing the enjambement.... With him an impeccable syllabic verse begins, both in whole lines and in their components, and with it a long line of such new length, and combinations as 13 [syllable line] (8 + 5),[9] 11 (4 + 7), 10 (5 + 5), 9 (5 + 4) [a length not used up until then]; and finally the seven [syllable line] without a caesura ... [H]e enriched [Polish] poetics with a new line of a smaller scale than the thirteen [syllable] (7 + 6), namely, 11 (5 + 6), but with the same capacities in genres and literary forms as the former. This meter he used as epic verse, lyric verse, and in tragedy ... [H]e initiated Polish blank verse, and that already in four patterns: 13 (7 + 6), 12 (7 + 5), 11 (5 + 6), and 9 (5 + 4) ... [H]e created a host of new strophic forms. These arose partly thanks to the new verse lines he introduced, partly thanks to the new utilization and new combinations of lines used before him...."[10] The richest in those innovative means is Kochanowski's verse adaptation of the Psalms, *Psałterz Dawidów* (*David's Psalter*),[11] his most popular work—nineteen editions appeared before 1641 (first edition, 1579).

Orthodox schools were founded first in the Ruthenian lands of the Polish Commonwealth as a result of the activities of enlightened Orthodox brotherhoods. The political, religious, and cultural circumstances of the first half of the seventeenth century determined their Latino-Polish orientation. Polish versification was taught there, however, even later, during the times when the Kiev school and other schools of the Ukraine and particularly of Muscovy, which followed the Kievan curriculum, had less need to educate their students in Polish. Notwithstanding these changes, for at least a century before the creation of the Russian syllabotonic metric system, not only the Ukrainians but even the Russians, while writing poetry in the literary languages of the time (i.e., primarily in some variant of Church Slavonic), considered the Polish isosyllabic system as their model. And despite the decisive consequences of Trediakovskij's and Lomonosov's verse reforms, the Polish system was in Russia in use at schools and elsewhere until the seventh decade of the eighteenth century.[12] Therefore, sections on Polish and Slavonic verses appear in many of the poetics courses in question. The most important and influential was the Kiev school. Although the earliest extant Kievan lectures on poetics with sections on Polish verse bear the date 1685, we may assume that in the four preceding decades of the school's existence Polish versification had been taught in Kiev, mainly from manuals and lectures in manuscripts which originated in the Jesuit schools of the Commonwealth. The Ukrainian scholar Vladimir Rezanov described, for instance, a now missing manuscript, *Poetica practica Anno Domini 1648*, containing lectures delivered at the Wilno Jesuit Academy by one of Sarbiewski's successors there and probably used in Kiev. In these lectures Polish verse structures were treated at length, and examples of Polish poetry were given.[13] A manuscript of collected works and notes which were written and copied by Samuel Omeljanovyč Petrovs'kyj-Sytnianovyč, known later (after 1656) as Simeon Polockij, the man who transplanted the syllabic system of the Poles, the Ukrainians, and the Byelorussians to Moscow, bears the same date— 1648. The writer was born in 1629, studied in the Kiev-Mohylean school, then in some Jesuit school, presumably in Wilno, and back in Kiev. It is known that in Kiev he was a student of Lazar Baranovyč, the Orthodox intellectual, who wrote Polish poetry and taught in the Kievan college in the 1640s. Simeon himself, before he moved to Moscow in 1663/64, wrote his poetry mostly in Polish.[14] Like his contemporaries, he too considered Jan Kochanowski to be a model poet. His manuscript mentioned above contains among other works of young Simeon his *Akathistos* to the Holy Virgin, written in Polish verse. The author was faithful to the Orthodox liturgical text, but in those places where Psalms should be sung he cited the first lines of the Psalms in verse with notes "et cetera" and "after Kochanowski." There are no further explanations, obviously because he knew that readers in his Kievan milieu were well-acquainted with Kochanowski's *Psalter*. Among the remnants of Simeon's library was a copy of the Polish book by Łukasz Górnicki, *Dworzanin polski* (The Polish courtier). On the margin of one of its pages in Simeon's own handwriting were written down two lines from Kochanowski's "Song 25", II,[15] with a divergence which probably indicates that the citation was made from memory. To point out Kochanowski's position as a model poet in the Kiev school prior to the extant and dated lectures on poetics, it is worth mentioning that Lazar Baranovyč began one of his books of religious poems published in 1670 with an address to his readers asking them to favor his rhymes even though he could not be compared with Kochanowski.[16]

Simeon Polockij's greatest poetical achievement—his Slavonic verse adaptation of the Psalms, published in 1680 in Moscow—offers the best proof of what Polockij and other, less talented, Kievan students learned in the decades prior to his book on Polish and Slavonic verse, and how they relied upon Jan Kochanowski as a model poet and above all as a master of verse and stanza structures. Polockij himself wrote in one of the prefaces to his *Psalter* that one of the reasons he adapted the Psalms in Slavonic verse was the lack of such an adaptation, which caused people to sing, even in Moscow, sweet Polish Psalms without due understanding of their content. Thus, he ventured to compete with the Poles.[17] Polockij did not mention Kochanowski's name. But his enemies, Patriarch Ioakim and a monk from the Čudov Monastery, Evfimij, while accusing Simeon of heresy, made it clear that the *"Psalter* he published was not that one which had come to us from the Holy Spirit by David's good offices. It was collected by him from Polish books or even taken ready from a certain Jan Kochanowski, a true Latin...."[18] In his detailed comparison of the two authors,[19] Ryszard Łużny established that Polockij aimed to repeat the richness of verse and stanza structures of Kochanowski's *Psalter*. He succeeded to a fair degree. He used all syllabic measures from the 7 to the 14 syllable line and many of the strophic structures: from non-interrupted sequences with a rhyme pattern of a distich or more elaborated irregular sequences to stanzas of six lines, Sapphic strophes, and stanzas built from lines of different lengths arranged in a regular way. Scholars found forty-one combinations in Kochanowski's *Psalter*. Polockij repeated twenty-four of them. The difference came first of all as a result of Polockij's reluctance to use short lines for solemn purposes. In the Psalms where Kochanowski had used them, Polockij applied 11 or 13 syllable lines. In many cases he replaced Kochanowski's distichs with quatrains. Then Polockij used only one type of rhyme—the rhyme of successive lines—even where Kochanowski had rhymed the alternate lines. Polockij followed, however sporadically, Kochanowski's novelty, the enjambement. In conclusion, Łużny states that Polockij's *Psalter* is a verse adaptation of the Orthodox biblical text. He did not follow Kochanowski's style or other artistic devices. Kochanowski's work was for him mainly a model of verse structures.

Our investigation of the extant lectures on poetics in Orthodox Eastern Slavic schools dated from 1671 to 1767 confirm the judgment that for these schools, as for the majority of Jesuit schools of the Commonwealth, Kochanowski was a model poet mainly because of his mastery in verse structures.

Two of the extant Kievan courses on poetics from the seventeenth century contain expanded sections on Polish verse illustrated by the use of Kochanowski's poetry. One is from 1685,[20] the other from 1689.[21] Thus, to show how to master lines of 14 syllables (8 + 6), the teacher in 1685 cited four beginning lines from Kochanowski's poem *Zuzanna*, and Professor Rodowicz in 1689 cited the first lines from the verset "Heth" of "Psalm" 119. In order to demonstrate the 13 syllable line (7 + 6), the following examples were cited in Kiev in 1685: ten lines from Kochanowski's poem *Dziewosłąb* (Matchmaking), which are a Polish adaptation of the ancient myth of King Midas from Ovid's *Metamorphoses*, two stanzas of "Song" 6, II and a fragment of "Lament" VII which has a sequence arrangement 13 (7 + 6) 7aa-13 (7 + 6) 7bb, etc. The song was cited with a divergence, as is the case with many citations from Kochanowski in the poetics in question, testifying that they were delivered from memory. The same teacher cited for the 12 syllable line (7 + 5) the beginning of the second chorus (known also as "Song" 14, II) from Kochanowski's tragedy *Odprawa posłów greckich* (The dismissal of the Greek envoys). Then for the 11 syllable line (5 + 6) he cited the two last quatrains of "Song" 13, II and three quatrains of "Song" 17, I which, by the way, present a phenomenon not very often found in quotations from Kochanowski used in our lectures—one of his innovative achievements, the enjambement.[22] For the 10 syllable line (4 + 6) in 1685 the entire "Song" 2, I built from quatrains was cited, and for the 9 syllable line (5 + 4), unknown before Kochanowski, the first quatrain of "Psalm" 101 was cited in 1689. Eight syllable lines were presented in 1689 by the song of the sixth maiden from the *Pieśń świętojańska o Sobótce* (Song on St. John's Eve) and in 1689 by "Psalm" 142. The 7 syllable lines were illustrated in 1685 by "Song" 24, I and in 1689 by "Psalm" 97; 6 and 5 syllable lines in 1689 by "Psalm" 64 and by one of many of Kochanowski's short occasional poems *fraszki*, "Na zdrowie" (On health) from Book III with an introductory note typical for the lectures: *Ad illa quae sunt 5 syllabarum sit exemplum ex eodem Kochanovio.*

The phenomenon of caesura which should come at the end of a word (*quae debet esse in fine dictionis*) was explained in 1689 by a quotation from "Song" 12, II. The same professor gives as an example of the caesura after the 5th syllable a liberal quotation of the *fraszka* "O koźle" (On the goat), Book II, which has an 11 syllable line (5 + 6). Earlier in 1685, the caesura after the sixth syllable is demonstrated by "Song" 22, I (6 + 5). The same two professors used Kochanowski's poetry to explain the variety of stanza structures. Thus, in the lectures of 1685 "Song" 5, I illustrated the arrangement of a quatrain (6aa 11bb), "Lament" XVI the structure of a minor Sapphic strophe (11aa 11b 5b) and "Song" 14, I the quatrain (11a 7bb 11a). In 1689 a different rhyme arrangment of the same type of line was presented by "Lament" XVIII (11a 7a 7b 11b); a quotation from "Psalm" 35 demonstrated the three line stanza, (11aa 5x), where the last line does not rhyme with any other line of the poem. In the section on Polish verse there we find also two combinations of 13 and 7 syllable lines: from "Song" 9, I (7aa 13bb) and from "Song" 7, II (13a 7a 13b 7b). And finally the teacher in 1689 gives two examples of macaronic verse from Kochanowski's *Carmen macaronicum de eligendo vitae genere.*

At the very end of the seventeenth century and in the eighteenth century Polish verse was taught in Ukrainian schools and in schools of the Muscovite borderlands in Smolensk. Yet at the same time alongside the theory and description of Polish verse the so-called Slavonic verse was examined and taught, eventually to replace the Polish verse for good in many schools. Nevertheless, the impact of Polish versification, i.e., the syllabic system, was so great at the first half of the eighteenth century that in Moscow in 1732, for instance, Professor Kwietnicki, Lomonosov's teacher at the Slavonic-Greek-Latin Academy, while lecturing on the subject of Slavonic verse as different from the Latin, simply transplanted an earlier (1724) Kievan lecture on Polish verse by replacing only the term *carmen polonicum* or *poesis polonica* with *carmen slavonicum* or *poesis slavonica*.[23]

In 1702 Kochanowski's name appeared in Kievan lectures delivered by Hilarion Iaroszewicki[24] in the section on Polish and Slavonic verse. The professor declared that Polish and Slavonic verses serve as well as Latin verses for the composition of epigrams, elegies, epic poems, odes, and dramas, as can be seen in Kochanowski's poetry (*ut patet in Cochanovii poesi*). Then, explaining that syllabic versification requires similar sounds in line cadences (i.e., rhymes), he used as an example the first two lines from Kochanowski's poem *Satyr albo Dziki Mąż* (The Satyr, or the Wild Man) and pointed out that Kochanowski's poetry, his Psalms in particular, demonstrate the art of rhyming successive or alternating lines. In addition, he referred to Kochanowski while explaining that in an 8-syllable line a caesura is not needed.

In 1719 in Kiev[25] only one example of Kochanowski's poetry was used to demonstrate one of the Polish verse patterns—the 13 syllable line in the *fraszka* "Na Matusza" (On Matuš), Book I. Some more quotations were used in 1722.[26] The professor quoted for the 8 syllable line "Song" 15, II, for the 5 syllable line the *fraszka* "Na zdrowie," and for the Sapphic strophe "Song" 10, I. In 1733 Professor Lincewicz (presumably in Kiev)[27] instructed his students to read Kochanowski, most of all his *Psalter*, so as to learn of the varieties of verse structures. And some twenty-five years later Professor Krasnohorski in Smolensk,[28] while teaching Polish and Slavonic versification, cited for the 11 syllable line with alternating rhymes Kochanowski's "Psalm" 61 *in extenso*, for the 7 syllable line three quatrains of "Psalm" 97, and for the 6 syllable line three quatrains of "Psalm" 64.[29]

The influence of Polish verse in the richness of its forms achieved by Kochanowski lasted for the Eastern Slavs some time longer, but the name of the model poet and his poetry disappeared gradually from the pages of the extant lectures in question. There were, however, some uncommon recurrences. Thus, in lectures delivered somewhere in the Ukraine as late as 1767,[30] the section on Polish verse strikingly resembled the one in *Helicon Bivertex 1689*. But even there quotations from Kochanowski were reduced to about a half. And it must be mentioned that the teacher used in other sections of his course examples of modern Russian verse, for instance, from Trediakovskij and Lomonosov, while speaking about Latin and Russian hexameter or about epic poems.

In accordance with the requirement to imitate model poets we find in the above-discussed sections on Polish and Slavonic verse direct imitations of Kochanowski's metrical skills. Thus in 1689, Professor Rodowicz, while explaining a 13 syllable line with a caesura after the seventh syllable, quotes, as was mentioned above, Kochanowski's "Song" 12, II and then three anonymous (perhaps written by himself) Polish fragments. At least one of them is undoubtedly an imitation not only of Kochanowski's verse structure, but also of the topic of the very song on virtue and envy. The imitation reads:

> Cnota sama się ceni, sama jest pozorna,
> Krom fortuny, krom krzeseł wysokich jest gorna.
> Applausy ludzkiemi być głoszona nie żąda,
> Pomocy ani sławy ludzkiej nie wygląda,
> W swych bogactwach jest dumna, bez żadnego strachu
> Patrza na ludzkie rzeczy z wysokiego gmachu.

The same teacher after the quotation of two fragments of Kochanowski's macaronic verse gave three of their imitations. In 1742/43 in Pereiaslav[31] the teacher gave as an example of Polish verse variety the following awkward imitation of Kochanowski's "Song" 10, I:

> Któż mi da skrzydła, któz szybkiemi loty
> W jasnoognistą lextikę Booty
> Wniosszy powoli
> Krążyć pozwoli
> Arktyoskiey sfery wkół przeświętnej tropy
> Wleciawszy w różnych widzieć królestwach Europy?

In the second half of the eighteenth century in bilingual (Latin and Church Slavonic) lectures on poetics[32] a daring procedure was applied for the demonstration of different Polish and, *per analogiam*, Slavonic types of syllabic verse: anonymously cited fragments from Kochanowski's Psalms 87 and 97 and "Songs" 6, II and 7, II were complemented with "newly made" endings. Only the last accomplishment shows some adequate skills. The first stanza of Kochanowski's song is:

> Słońce pali, a ziemia idzie w popiół prawie,
> Świata nie znać w kurzawie;
> Rzeki dnem uciekają,
> A zagorzałe zioła dżdza z nieba wołają.

And the added part reads:

> Płodowiste ogrody wiatrem wysuszone,
> Ogniem grzędy spalone;
> Gdzie ziółka wonne były,
> Tam piaski z ogniem ciepłym twardość rozmnożyły.

In Smolensk in 1752/53 Professor Bazylewicz[33] demonstrated Polish verse with internal rhyme by using an example which happens to be a combined imitation of two of Kochanowski's "Songs" 9, I and 24, I.[34]

Among other literary forms the European Renaissance emphasized the ancient epigram and pronounced Martial its model poet. Its structure was discussed by such acclaimed theoreticians of the time as Robortello, Scaliger, and Minturno. Jacobus Pontanus' manual contributed to the popularization of the genre viewed from positions of the late Renaissance and the baroque which emphasized its conciseness and acuteness. In the seventeenth century the theoreticians and school teachers of the *humaniora* concentrated on problems of acuity and ingenuity and brought forward the witty epigram. Another more pragmatic reason which made the theory and praxis of that genre an important part of Jesuit lectures on poetics was the conviction concerning its suitability and usefulness for the purpose of school training in the art of poetry. Lectures on the epigram always connected that genre with the theory of the baroque conceit, its sources and means. Ancient and Renaissance epigrams were analyzed and demonstrated from this viewpoint. The Orthodox Eastern Slavic schools duplicated that approach and, following Polish Jesuits, found in Kochanowski's poetry models for witty and ingenious epigrams. Already in 1671 in Lwów, presumably in the Orthodox brotherhood school, Kochanowski's *fraszka "Raki"* (Canncrinum), Book I, the title of which comes from a type of verse known as a *palindrome*, a verse that reads forward and backward and in this particular case produces a contrary meaning, was given as an example of an epigram.[35] The same example in the same capacity or as a sample of *poesi curiosa*—artificial, cunning poetry—was repeated many times later on anonymously and with divergences, in Kiev, for instance, in 1689, 1696, 1706/7, 1719/20. Other *fraszki* by Kochanowski, such as *"Epitafium dziecięciu"* (Epitaph for a child), Book I (Kiev, 1689, 1719, 1719/20; Smolensk, 1752/53), *"Nagrobek Adrianowi doktorowi"* (Epitaph for Adrian, the doctor), Book II (Kiev, 1689, 1702, 1719/20, 1737); *"Nagrobek opiłej babie"* (Epitaph for a drunken crone), Book II (Kiev, 1689, 1702); *"Na Ślasę"* (On Slasa), Book I (Kiev, 1695, 1701); *"Epitafium Wysockiemu"* (Epitaph for Wysocki), Book I (Kiev, 1702, 1719/20) were used in the same way. Moreover, *"O doktorze Hiszpanie"* (On the Spanish doctor), *"Na Matusza,"* *"Do Pawełka"* (To little Paul), *"Do Jakuba"* (To Jacob) from Book I, and *"Epitafium Grzegorzowi Podlodowskiemu"* (Epitaph for Gregory Podlodowski), *"Nagrobek koniowi"* (Epitaph for a horse), *"Nagrobek kotowi"* (Epitaph for a cat) from Book II (Kiev, 1689); *"O koźle"* from Book II (Kiev, 1695). Then it became a tradition to quote the fourth and fifth stanza of Kochanowski's *"Song"* 9, I as a witty epigram, as an example of a conceit (*acumen*) *ex contrariis* (Kiev, 1689/90 and 1695; Smolensk, 1652/53). As often happened to a model poet, teachers attributed to Kochanowski epigrams that he never wrote. This was done by Prokopowicz in Kiev in 1705, Gorka in 1706/7, and Konisky in 1746.[36]

As has been emphasized above, at the time in question a model poet was not only supposed to be cited, but to be imitated as well. The students in Orthodox schools were constantly reminded about the need for training, that is, reading, translating, imitating, and varying the models. In 1705 in Kiev

Theofan Prokopowicz devoted a large part of his course to drill this requirement into his students' minds,[37] and so did many others. For instance, in Moscow in 1732 Kwietnicki transformed Sarbiewski's two Latin epigrams (XIV and XXXIV) into Slavonic verses of all possible syllabic measures from the 13 syllable line to the Sapphic strophe to the 4 syllable line, that is, each of them nine times.[38] Kochanowski's poems also served not only as models in connection with different topics of the lectures on poetics, but were used as well for the particular topic of the necessity for and ways of training in the writing of poetry. Thus, a Kievan professor in 1696[39] delivered a special lecture *De imitatione* where he indicated the need to imitate Horace, Seneca, and Jan Kochanowski; in connection with the latter he gave an example of how to do it. He cited the first stanza of Kochanowski's "Song" 10, I and then demonstrated its paraphrase, which, by the way, is rich with enjambements.

> Kto mi da skrzydła? Kto mnie nad obłoki
> Wyniesie? Kędy swe Argus stooki
> Wyprosił oczy, a tak z górnej sfery
> Uwidzę lane ze złota szpalery, etc.

We have seen that later on, in 1742/43, in Pereiaslav, the same song was imitated differently for training in syllabic verse. Then, the above-mentioned combined imitation of two of Kochanowski's "Songs", 9, I and 24, I, which Professor Bazylewicz demonstrated in Smolensk in 1752/53 for the Polish verse with internal rhymes was used several years later, in 1758/59, in the same school, by Professor Krasnohorski as *praxes* of *carmina de pernitiosis mundi illecebris*, that is, as an imitation of the subject-matter of Kochanowski's two poems.[40]

The training in the art of imitation included readings and direct translations of model poems. Professor Iaroszewicki in Kiev in 1702 named model poets for his students, ancient and modern, Latin and Polish, and Jan Kochanowski is one of them. As evidence of the fruitfulness of translation he referred to Sarbiewski's Latin translation of Kochanowski,[41] apparently to "Ode" 5 from Book IV of Sarbiewski's *Lyricorum libri*, which is quite an accurate translation of Kochanowski's "Song" 5, II. Later on in 1722,[42] and in 1736,[43] also in Kiev, both texts were compared and an analysis of the Latin translation was given in a section on training, with a note: *"de exercitatione ex vernaculo stylo in latinum."* And in 1758/59, in Smolensk, Professor Krasnohorski, in a lecture on lyric poetry—its *genus demonstrativum* and one of its genres, *epinicium* (a triumphal ode for the victor)—advised his students to acquaint themselves not only with Sarbiewski's translation, but also with his *"Palinodia ad Parodiam[44] Ioannis Kochanovii." Cum victoria de Turcis parta renuntiaretur ac paulo post Stanislaus Koniecpolius exercituum Regni Poloniarum ductor campestris Scythas prosperis proeliis fudisset"*, i.e., Sarbiewski's "Ode" 6, IV[45] as well. The ode is a retraction (palinode) of the previously translated (as "Ode" 5, IV) "Song" by Kochanowski which mourned the devastation of Podolia by the Turks. The art of imitating the model consisted here in the change of the purpose, the reversal of values:

where Kochanowski spoke about disgrace, Sarbiewski spoke about the fame of the Poles, where Kochanowski set forth the image of the cruel Turks—the predatory wolves, Sarbiewski focused attention on the pursuing hounds—the brave Polish knights.

Professor Gorka in Kiev in 1706/7, while lecturing on the usefulness of learning different creative approaches to the same subject or source, compared two Latin verse paraphrases of Psalm 137 (one of them by the famous neo-Latin poet George Buchanan) with the paraphrase: *"Celeber autem poeta polonicus Ioannes Kochanowski eundem psalmum polonico idiomate sat pulchre ... exposuit."* The same teacher, in a lecture on mournful poetry, recommended *"huius modi exempla threnodiae ... admodum pulchra extant apud polonicum poetam Ioannem Kochanovium vulgo threnii in quibus filiolam suam defunctam Ursulam plangit"* and cited the Polish original "Lament" III. In 1741 his protege, Michail Finicky, a Kievan graduate, lectured on poetics in Gorka's eparchy in the Russian town of Viatka and repeated, to a great degree, Gorka's Kievan lectures.[46] But to satisfy his Russian audience and to prove his own skills, he translated the Polish examples given by Gorka, among them Kochanowski's "Psalm" 137. Concerning the reason for his translation, he said *"Ego tyronibus Rossiacis polonismum ignorantibus carminibus slavonicis id ipsum transversum pono."* He did the same with Kochanowski's "Lament" III.

Kochanowski's *Laments* in the original were used in Kiev in 1719[47] to explain four means to express sorrow in poetry. This is the only case we know where a direct impact of Sarbiewski's treatise, *Characteres lyricii seu Horatius et Pindarus*, can be found in the lectures investigated here. As if following the description of the device called by Sarbiewski *apsychologia*,[48] the Kievan teacher described the way to mourn the beloved deceased while addressing complaints to Death as in Kochanowski's "Lament" IV, and yet another way—while comparing the briefness of life and the cruelty of death ("Lament" V), or another—while speaking to the deceased person's belongings as Kochanowski speaks to his daughter's attire in "Lament" VII (cited also by Sarbiewski), or while addressing the deceased as a transcendent being whom the poet sees as Kochanowski did in "Lament" X. Professors Bazylewicz and Krasnohorski in Smolensk also cited "Laments" VII and V to show the virtues required in an elegy.[49] The above-mentioned Kievan teacher of 1719 recommended Kochanowski's *Carmen macaronicum de eligendo vitae genere* in a different capacity than was done before him in 1689, i.e., not to teach how to make macaronic verses, but to teach how to write satires. And indeed, the poem at that time was treated as such by its readers. Łużny remarks that the Kievan teacher was selective and exploited only such parts of the poem which not only served to illustrate the genre description, but played the required didactic role. With this purpose in mind, he purged the quotations of matters undesirable in a religious school.[50]

Finally, examples from Kochanowski's poetry served in Orthodox Eastern Slavic schools to demonstrate models of rhetorical skills equally needed for the poetic and oratorical art. In lectures on rhetoric delivered in the Moscow Academy in 1713,[51] the teacher explained rhetorical skills using, among others, a Polish quotation *item Kochanovii* which appears to be the last stanza of "Song" 14, I. In 1719/20 in Kiev the teacher uses the fragment from Kochanowski's poem *Dziewosłąb* (the legend of King Midas which was used in 1685 for the 13 syllable line) in another capacity—to explain the hyperbole as a figure of speech, a trope.[52] In 1736/37 the Kievan professor, Barlaam Nowicki, quotes to his students in his class of rhetoric Kochanowski's *fraszka "Nagrobek opiłej babie."*[53]

Thus, in conclusion, we may state that Kochanowski's self-judgment and premonition expressed in his "Song" 24, II which serves as the motto for this essay, itself modeled on Horace's *Ode* 30, III and paraphrased in all times and tongues, found its fulfillment in his position as a model poet in Eastern Slavic Orthodox schools of the seventeenth and eighteenth centuries.

Notes

1. Jan Kochanowski, "Song" 24, II (the Arabic numeral marks the number of the poem and the Roman numeral the number of the book). Translation from Czesław Miłosz, *The History of Polish Literature* (New York-London: Macmillan, 1969), p. 66.

2. In 1623 Sarbiewski was crowned with laurel by Pope Urban VIII for his excellence in poetry. His poems were edited and reedited all over Europe. One of these editions, Antwerp 1632, had a headpiece designed by Rubens. For a detailed account of Sarbiewski's impact on lectures on poetics in Eastern Slavic schools of the seventeenth and eighteenth centuries, see Ryszard Łużny, *Pisarze kręgu Akademii Kijowsko-Mohylańskiej a literatura polska* (Writers of the Kiev Mohylanian Academy circle and Polish literature) (Cracow: Uniwersytet Jagielloński, 1966), passim (hereafter *Pisarze*); Paulina Lewin,*Wykłady poetyki w uczelniach rosyjskich XVIII w. (1722-1774) a tradycje polskie* (Lectures on poetics in Russian schools of the 18th century and Polish traditions) (Wrocław: Ossolineum, 1972) passim (hereafter *Wykłady*); Paulina Lewin, "Teoria akuminu w estetycznej świadomości Wschodniej słowiańszczyzny XVII-XVIII wieku a traktat Sarbiewskiego" (The theory of acumen in the esthetic consciousness of 17th and 18th century Eastern Slavs and Sarbiewski's treatise] in *Literatura staropolska i jej związki europejskie* (Wrocław: Ossolineum, 1973), pp. 309-324.

3. See Maciej Kazimierz Sarbiewski, *O poezji doskonałej czyli Wergiliusz i Homer (De perfecta poesi, sive Vergilius et Homerus)*, ed. Stanisław Skimina, and Marian Plezia, Biblioteka Pisarzów Polskich ser. B, 5. (Wrocław: Ossolineum, 1956).

4. For all three of them see Maciej Kazimierz Sarbiewski, *Wykłady poetyki (Praecepta poetica)* ed. Stanisław Skimina, Biblioteka Pisarzów Polskich ser. B, 5. (Wrocław-Cracow: Ossolineum, 1958), hereafter Sarbiewski.

5. Sarbiewski, p. xxi.

6. Sarbiewski, pp. 69, 47, 38-39, 41. For other confrontations and examples showing Kochanowski's equality with and even superiority to the ancients, see, e.g., pp. 113 and 42.

7. All Ukrainian names are spelled in accordance with the manuscripts they are cited from.

8. Łużny, *Pisarze*, p. 52.

9. The annotation in parenthesis indicates the place of the caesura.

10. Maria Dłuska, "'Kto mi dał skrzydła' ... Poetyka i wiersz Jana Kochanowskiego" ("Who gave me the wings" ... The poetics and the verse of Jan Kochanowski) in *Studia i rozprawy* (Studies and treaties), vol. 2(Cracow: Wydawnictwo Literackie, 1970), pp. 43-44.

11. See Wiktor Weintraub, *Styl Jana Kochanowskiego* (The Style of Jan Kochanowski) (Cracow, 1932).

12. See *Russkaia sillabicheskaia poeziia XVII-XVIII veka* (Russian syllabic poetry of the 17th-18th centuries) (Leningrad, 1970) and for recent discussions: A. A. Il'ushin, "Sillabicheskaia sistema v istorii russkogo stixa" (The syllabic system in the history of Russian poetry) in *Slavianskoe barokko. Istoriko-kul'turnye problemy epoxi* (Slavonic baroque. Historical-cultural problems of the epoch) (Moscow, 1979), pp. 316-334.

13. Vladimir I. Rezanov, *K istorii russkoi dramy. Ekskurs v oblast' teatra jezuitov* (Towards a history of Russian drama. Excursis in the field of the theater of the Jesuits) (Nežyn, 1910), passim.

14. See Łużny, *Pisarze*, pp. 109-128.

15. Łużny, *Pisarze*, p. 19.

16. Łużny, *Pisarze*, p. 129.

17. Simeon Polockij, *Izbrannye sochineniia* ... (Selected works) (Moscow-Leningrad, 1953), p. 213.

18. Cited by I. Serman, "'Psaltyr' ryfmotvornaia Simeona Polockogo i russkaia poeziia XVIII v." ("Psalter in verse" of Simeon Polockij and 18th century Russian poetry) TODRL 18 (1962), p. 216 from "*Osten.*" *Pam'atnik russkoi duxovnoi pis'mennosti XVII v.* (Kazan, 1865), p. 137.

19. Ryszard Łużny, "*Psalterz rymowany* Simeona Połockiego a *Psałterz Dawidów* Jana Kochanowskiego" ("Psalter in verse" of Simeon Polockij and "David's Psalter" of Jan Kochanowski), *Slavia Orientalis* 1, 1962: 3-27.

20. *Fons Castalius in duplices divisus rivulos solatum scilicet et ligatam orationem, Kijovo-Mohilaeanis musis consecratus.* See Łużny, *Pisarze*, pp. 32-35.

21. *Helicon Bivertex seu Poesis Bipartita solutae et ligatae orationis rudimentis instructa et studiosae juventuti in Collegio Kiovo Mohilaeano pro praxi et doctrina data ... sub Reverendo Patre Parthenio Rodowicz.* See Paulina Lewin, "Nieznana poetyka kijowska z XVII wieku" (Unknown Kievan poetics of the 17th century), in *Z dziejów stosunków literackich polsko-ukraińskich* (Wrocław: Ossolineum, 1974), pp. 71-90.

22. Although enjambement was not particularly explained or demonstrated in any of the lectures under investigation, the device was highly valued and widely used at the Kiev school as can be seen, for instance, from the extant school dramas performed there in the seventeenth and eighteenth centuries which were mainly in a local version of Church Slavonic. See Vladimir I. Rezanov, *Drama ukrajins'ka,* (Ukrainian drama) vol. 3-6 (Kiev, 1925- 1929).

23. See Lewin, *Wykłady,* pp. 126-138.

24. *Cedrus Apollinis pharetrati Rossiaco Orphaeo ob bicornem extruendam cytharam bino poëseos ac rhetorices stylo instructam ad concessum perennis gloriae mentibus ac montibus instans in bicolli Kijovo- Mohileano Parnasso erecta* ... See Łużny, *Pisarze* pp. 49-56.

25. *Hymettus extra Atticam duplici tramite neovatibus scandendus sue Poesis bipartita tum ligatae tum solutae orationis praeceptionibus instructa Roxolanaeque iuventuti in Collegio K. M. proposita.* See Łużny, *Pisarze,* pp. 83-87.

26. *Apollo Musaeo Rossiacae Palladis praesidens seu Praecepta poëseos explanas* ... See Łużny, *Pisarze,* pp. 91-92.

442 Paulina Lewin

27. *Liber de arte poëtica, ornatum, modum et numerum ligatae orationis praesentans ad usum sacrae iuventuti Patriae* ... See Łużny, *Pisarze*, p. 91.

28. *Bicollis Parnassus, hoc est bipartita poesis nempe praecepta sua tradens duplicia, tum de soluta, tum de ligata oratione, tradita in usum generosae Roxolanae iuventutis in celebri nec non docto Collegio Smolenscensi* ... See Lewin, *Wykłady*, p. 22.

29. Lewin, *Wykłady*, p. 149-50.

30. *Compendiosa praecepta latinae poëseos in usum iuventuti latini idiomatis studiosae ex variis non improbatis institutionibus poeticis excerpta.* See Paulina Lewin, "Dawne Polonica literackie w archiwach Moskwy i Leningradu" (Old Polish literary texts in the archives of Moscow and Leningrad), *Slavia Orientalis* 1, 1972: 75-76, 79.

31. *Hortus musarum variis ligatae orationis sue artis poëseos modi et principiorum quorundam solutae orationis amplificationibus virens in Parnasseo fidelis collegii Iugopereiaslavo-berloviano ob recreandum Roxolanae iuventutis* ... See Lewin, "Dawne polonica," pp. 75, 78.

32. Exact place, date and title unknown. See Lewin, "Dawne polonica," pp. 75, 78-79.

33. *Structura artis poëticae, in duas classes, scilicet ligatam et solutam orationem divisa, in almo Smoleno-Wiszniowsciano collegio generosae juventuti Roxolanae* ... *aedificata.* See Lewin, *Wykłady*, p. 21.

34. Incipit: "Tylko w świecie, co się plecie jakoby ozdoba, / Mówią ludzie: żyć w obłudzie tej się nam podoba." Lewin, *Wykłady*, p. 150.

35. Łużny, *Pisarze*, p. 32.

36. On Kochanowski's poems in sections on epigram and "artificial" poetry see Łużny, passim; Lewin, "Nieznana poetyka," pp. 79-81.

37. *De arte poetica libri III* in Feofan Prokopovič, *Sochineniia* ... (Works ...) (Moscow-Leningrad, 1961), pp. 229-333.

38. See Lewin, *Wykłady*, pp. 163-168.

39. *Rosa inter spinas seu Ars poëseos suos continens difficultatum aculeos concluso horto Mariae in debitum venerationis cultum dedita atque neopoetis ad carpendum ex ea tam ligati, quam soluti eloquii fructum in Helicone Mohilaeano explicata* ... See Łużny, *Pisarze*, p. 35. Correction of the date, see Lewin, "Nieznana poetyka," pp. 72-73, footnote 12.

40. Lewin, *Wykłady*, pp. 149-150.

41. Łużny, *Pisarze*, p. 56.

42. *Apollo Musaeo Rossiacae Palladis praesidens seu Praecepta poëseos explanans* ... See Łużny, *Pisarze*, p. 91

43. *Via lectanea in* ... *Academiae K-M. Z. proposita.* See Łużny, *Pisarze*, p. 91.

44. It should be remembered that "parodia" meant not mockery at that time but translation or imitation.

45. Lewin, *Wykłady*, p. 142.

46. Both lectures bear the same title: *Idea artis poëseos ad usum et institutionem studiosae iuventutis Roxolanae tradita.* See Paulina Lewin, "Rosyjskie tłumaczenia z Jana Kochanowskiego (pierwsza połowa XVIII w.)" [Russian translations of Jan Kochanowski (the first half of the eighteenth century)] in *Miscelanea staropolskie* vol. 4 (Wrocław: Ossolineum, 1972), pp. 81-85.

47. Łużny, *Pisarze*, p. 84.

48. Sarbiewski, pp. 40-43.

49. Lewin, *Wykłady*, p. 149.

50. Łużny, *Pisarze*, pp. 83-84.

51. *Catena bipiramidalis Tulliana eloguentia Athenis rhetoricorum praeceptorum solidata columnis ac diverso tum oratoriae eruditionis, tum selectiorum apophtegmatum distincta decore in Moschocaesareo Atheneo neorhetoribus reserata* ... See Lewin, ''Dawne polonica,'' pp. 73, 78.

52. *Parnassus alias [?] Apollinis Cithara nobis exercitium poëticum in Collegio traditum et explicatum* ... See Łużny, *Pisarze,* pp. 90- 91.

53. Lewin, ''Dawne polonica,'' pp. 74-75, 79.

Contributors

CZESŁAW MIŁOSZ, Polish poet, novelist, essayist, literary critic, and translator, Professor of Slavic Literatures at the University of California, and recipient of the Nobel Prize for Literature in 1980.

JERZY AXER is Professor of Classics at the University of Warsaw. His principal fields of study are Latin textology and textual criticism in both ancient Roman literature, especially Cicero and Horace and Renaissance literature. In Old Polish literature he has specialized in Kochanowski, Jesuit theatre, Renaissance epistolography and Italo-Polish relations in the sixteenth century.

His published titles include: *Mowa Cicerona w obronie aktora komediowego Roscjusza*. (Cicero's speech in defense of the comic actor Roscius) (Wrocław: Ossolineum, 1976); *The Style and the Composition of Cicero's Speech "Pro Q. Roscio Comeodo"* (Warsaw: University of Warsaw, 1980). His critical editions include: Joncre Johannes, *Tragoedia Boleslaus Secundus Furens*. (Wratislaviae: Ossolineum, 1972); Jerzy z Tyczyna, *Georgii Ticinii ad Martinum Cromerum Epistulae* (a. 1554-1585). (Wratislaviae: Ossolineum, 1975); Cicero Marcus Tullius, *M. Tulli Ciceronis scripta quae manserunt omnia*. (Lipsciae: Bibliotheca Teubneriana, 1976, Fasc. 9); Jerzy z Tyczyna, *Georgii Ticinii ad principes Radziwiłł Epistulae (a.1567-1585)*. (Wratislaviae: Ossolineum, 1980). Among his articles are: " 'Aratus'—Miejsce poematu w twórczości Jana Kochanowskiego" ("Aratus"— The place of the poem in the work of Jan Kochanowski) in *Jan Kochanowski i epoka renesansu*, ed. Teresa Michałowska (Warsaw: PWN, 1984); "Rola kryptocytatów z literatury łacińskiej w polskojęzycznej twórczości Kochanowskiego" (The function of Crypto-quotations from the Latin literature in Jan Kochanowski's Polish-language works) in *Jan Kochanowski i kultura odrodzenia* ed. Zdzisław Libera, and Maciej Żurowski (Warsaw: PWN, 1985). He is co-author of the commentaries in Jan Kochanowski. *Dzieła wszystkie*. Wydanie Sejmowe t. 2, *Treny* (Jan Kochanowski. The Complete Works. The Sejm Edition. vol. 2, *The Laments*) (Wrocław: Ossolineum, 1983).

TERESA BAŁUK-ULEWICZOWA is a lecturer in the Department of English Philology at Jagiellonian University. Her principal field of study is Wawrzyniec

Goślicki. She also does research in the field of Polish-English cultural relations in the sixteenth and seventeenth centuries.

Her articles include: "Z zagadnień kariery anglosaskiej Wawrzyńca Goślickiego" (On the problem of the Anglo-Saxon career of Wawrzyniec Goślicki), *Silva Rerum* (1981); "Sir Robert Filmer i jego obraz ustroju Polski w angielskiej literaturze politycznej XVII wieku" (Sir Robert Filmer and his image of the Polish political system in English political literature of the seventeenth century), *Ruch Literacki* 24 (1983), z. 5 (140). *"De optimo senatore"* Wawrzyńca Goślickiego i *jego oddziaływanie w Anglii* (Wawrzyniec Goślicki's "De optimo senatore" and its influence in England) (in print).

JAN BIAŁOSTOCKI is professor of Art History and Director of the Institute of History of Art at the University of Warsaw and is also Curator of Foreign Art at the National Museum in Warsaw. He is a member of the Polish Academy of Sciences. He has held many visiting professorships both in Europe and the United States; He holds memberships in major European academies of art. He is the author of numerous books and articles in his fields of research: the history of art, especially European painting, 15th-18th centuries, the theory of art, iconography in painting, as well as particular studies of Dürer as a writer and theorist of art, Poussin as a theorist of classicism, Rubens, Rembrandt, and Renaissance sepulchral art.

Among his books are: *Pięć wieków myśli o sztuce. Studia i rozprawy z dziejów teorii i historii sztuki.* (Five centuries of thought on art. Studies and essays on the history of theory and the history of art) 2nd edition (Warsaw: PWN, 1976); *Teoria i twórczość. O tradycji i inwencji w teorii sztuki i ikonografii* (Theory and creativity. On tradition and invention in the theory of art and iconography) (Poznań: PWN, 1961); *Sztuka cenniejsza niż złoto. Opowieść o sztuce europejskiej naszej ery* (Art more valuable than gold. The story of European art of our era) 2 volumes 3rd. edition (Warsaw: PWN, 1969); *Sztuka i myśl humanistyczna. Studia z dziejów sztuki i myśli o sztuce* (Art and humanist thought. Essays on the history of art and thought about art) (Warsaw: PIW, 1966); *Spätmittelalter und beginnende Neuzeit* (Berlin: Propyläen, 1972); *The Art of the Renaissance in Eastern Europe. Bohemia-Hungary-Poland* (Oxford: Oxford Univ. Press, 1976); *Refleksje i syntezy ze świata sztuki* (Reflections and synthesis from the world of art) 2nd edition (Warsaw: PWN, 1987); *Historia sztuki wśród nauk humanistycznych* (History of art in the humanities) (Wrocław: Ossolineum, 1980); *Stil und Ikonographie. Studien zur Kunstwissenschaft*, 2nd edition (Köln: Verlag der Kunst, 1981).

PAULINA BUCHWALD-PELCOWA is Professor of Polish Literature and of the History of Books at Warsaw University and at the National Library in Warsaw where she is head of the Department of Old Books. Her main field of study is Polish literature of the sixteenth to eighteenth centuries and the history of Polish printing.

Her publications include the following books: *Satyra czasów saskich* (The satire in Saxon times) (Wrocław: Ossolineum, 1969); *Katalog starych druków Biblioteki Kórnickiej cz. II* (A Catalog of old printings in the Kórnik Library. Part 2) (Wrocław: Ossolineum, 1969); *Aleksander Augezdecki* (Wrocław: Ossolineum, 1972); *Emblematy w drukach polskich i Polski dotyczących XVI-XVIII w.* (Emblems in Polish printings and in printings concerning Poland in the 16th-18th centuries) (Wrocław: Ossolineum, 1981). Among her articles are: "Historia książki a historia literatury" (The history of the book and the history of literature) in *Dawna książka i kultura* (Wrocław: Ossolineum, 1975); "Stare i nowe w czasach saskich" (The old and the new in Saxon times) in *Problemy literatury staropolskiej*, Series 3, ed. Janusz Pelc (Wrocław: Ossolineum, 1978); "Nieznane pierwsze wydanie 'Pieśni trzech' Jana Kochanowskiego" (An unknown first edition of Jan Kochanowski's "Three Songs") in *Acta Universitatis Nicolai Copernici*, no. 100 (Toruń, 1979); and "Dynamika staropolskich wydań dzieł Jana Kochanowskiego" (The dynamics of the Old Polish editions of the works of Jan Kochanowski) in *Rocznik Świętokrzyski*, vol. 9 (1981). She has also edited facsimile reproductions of the first editions of works of Jan Kochanowski, Szymon Szymonowicz, and Mikołaj Sęp Szarzyński.

SAMUEL FISZMAN is Professor of Slavic Languages and Literatures at Indiana University and formerly professor of the University of Warsaw and of the Polish Academy of Sciences. He has published works dealing with Polish literature in the periods of the Renaissance and romanticism, specializing in Mickiewicz and in Polish-Russian and Polish-West European cultural relations.

His published titles include: *Mickiewicz w Rosji* (Mickiewicz in Russia) (Warsaw: PIW, 1949); *Z problematyki pobytu Adama Mickiewicza w Rosji* (On the question of Adam Mickiewicz's stay in Russia) (Warsaw: PIW, 1956); *Archiwalia Mickiewiczowskie* (Mickiewicz archival materials) (Wrocław: Ossolineum, 1962); *A. Puszkin. "Jeździec Miedziany"* (Aleksandr Pushkin. "The Bronze Horseman") Biblioteka Narodowa (Wrocław: Ossolineum, 1967); *Polonica of the 15th - 20th Centuries in the Libraries of Indiana University* (Bloomington: Polish Studies Center, 1978); *Polish Renaissance in its European Context: An Exhibition of Rare Books* (Bloomington: Polish Studies Center and Lilly Library, 1982). Among his articles are: "Materiały mickiewiczowskie w paryskich Archives Nationales" (Mickiewicz materials in the Paris Archives Nationales) *Pamiętnik Literacki* 4 (1965); "O polsko-rosyjskich stosunkach literackich 1800-1830" (On Polish-Russian literary relations in the period 1800-1830) in *O wzajemnych powiązaniach literackich polsko-rosyjskich* (Wrocław: Ossolineum, 1968); "Nowe aspekty badań nad rolą polskiej kultury w rozwoju kultury rosyjskiej w wieku XVII" (New aspects of research on the role of Polish culture in the development of Russian culture in the seventeenth century) in *For Wiktor Weintraub* (The Hague: Mouton, 1975); "The Comparative Aspects in Adam Mickiewicz's Lectures on Slavic Literatures," *The Polish Review* 1 (1981); "Jan Kochanowski w świecie języka angielskiego" (Jan Kochanowski in the English speaking world) in *Jan Kochanowski. Epoka-Twórczość-Recepcja*, ed. Janusz Pelc et. al. (Lublin: Wyd. Lubelskie, 1988).

MIECZYSŁAW GIERGIELEWICZ was a professor of Polish Literature at the University of Pennsylvania at Philadelphia. He has also held professorships at the Polish University in Exile, London, at Alliance College in Cambridge Springs, PA, and at the University of California at Berkeley.

He was a specialist in Polish versification, its history and development, and in the verse of individual poets. His published works include: *Drogi Mickiewicza* (Mickiewicz's roads) (London: Światowy Związek Polaków z Zagranicy, 1945); *Rym i wiersz* (Rhyme and verse) (London: Polski Uniwersytet na Obczyźnie, 1957); "Twórczość poetycka" (Poetry) in *Literatura polska na obczyźnie* vol. 1 (London, 1964); *Henryk Sienkiewicz* (New York: Twayne Publishers, 1968); *Introduction to Polish versification* (Philadelphia: University of Pennsylvania Press, 1970); and *Studia i spotkania* (Studies and literary meetings) (Warsaw: PIW, 1984). Among his articles are: "Krasiński in the English-speaking World," in *Zygmunt Krasiński, An International Tribute* (New York, 1964); "Henryk Sienkiewicz's American Resonance," in *Antemurale*, Institutum Historicum Polonicum Romae (1966). Together with Ludwik Krzyżanowski he edited *Polish Civilization. Essays and Studies* (New York: New York University Press, 1979).

ALEKSANDER GIEYSZTOR is professor of Polish Medieval History and Historical Auxilliary Sciences at the University of Warsaw. He has been the Director of the Institute of History at the University of Warsaw (1955-75), and has served as Vice-Rector of the University of Warsaw (1956-59). He served as the President of the Polish Academy of Sciences from 1981-83, and since 1981 is Director of the Royal Castle in Warsaw. He is a Member of the Polish Academy of Sciences and a member of many Academies among them, a Corresponding Fellow of the Medieval Academy of America. He has held the position of visiting professor at many European and American univeristies.

In addition to numerous articles, his published works include: *Władza Karola Wielkiego w opinii współczesnej* (The reign of Charlemagne in contemporary opinion) (Warsaw: Nakł. Tow. Naukowego Warszawskiego, 1938); *Zarys nauk pomocniczych historii* (Outline of historical auxilliary sciences) 3rd expanded edition in cooperation with Stanisław Herbst (Warsaw: Akademicka Spółdzielnia Wydawnicza, 1948); *Ze studiów nad genezą wypraw krzyżowych-Encyklika Sergiusza IV, 1009-1012* (Studies on the genesis of the Crusades—the encyclical of Sergius IV, 1009-1012) (Warsaw: Nakł. Tow. Naukowego Warszawskiego, 1948); *La porte de bronze à Gniezno: document d'histoire de Pologne au XIIe siècle* (Rome: A. Signorelli, 1959); *Kultura Śląska między IX a XIII wiekiem* (Silesian culture between the 9th and 13th centuries) (Katowice: Śląsk, 1960); *La Pologne et l'Europe au Moyen Age* (Warsaw: PWN, 1963); *Societa e cultura nell'alto medioevo polacco* (Wrocław: Ossolineum, 1965); *Zarys dziejów pisma łacińskiego* (An outline of the history of the Latin script) (Warsaw: PWN, 1973); *Dzieje Płocka* (The history of Płock), 2nd edition (Płock: Tow. Naukowe Płockie, 1978); *Mitologia Słowian* (The mythology of the Slavic people) (Warsaw: Wydaw. Artystyczne i Filmowe, 1982). He has co-authored the *History of Poland*, 2nd edition (Warsaw: PWN, 1979); (with Stanisław Herbst and Bogusław Leśnodorski) *A Thousand Years of Poland* (Warsaw: Interpress, 1976); and with Michał Walicki and Jan Zachwatowicz, *Sztuka polska przedromańska i romańska do schyłku XIII wieku* (Polish pre-Romanesque and Romanesque art to the close of the 13th century) (Warsaw: PWN, 1971).

ERNA HILFSTEIN is an Affiliate of the Graduate Center of the City University of New York. She has authored and co-authored (with Edward Rosen) several articles and reviews. She is also translator of articles on Copernicus and on the history of science. Among her published works are: *Starowolski's Biographies of Copernicus* in the series *Studia Copernicana XXI* (Wrocław: Ossolineum, 1980). She has edited (together with Paweł Czartoryski and Frank Grande) *Science and History* in the series *Studia Copernicana XVI, Studies in Honor of Edward Rosen* (Wrocław: Ossolineum, 1978). Her articles include: "Bernardino Baldi and His Two Biographies of Copernicus," *The Polish Review* (1979), 24; "Sebastian Petrycy, A Polish Renaissance Scholar," *Paideia*, vol. 3, 1982.

ANTE KADIĆ is professor of Slavic Languages and Literatures at Indiana University. He is a specialist on contemporary Yugoslav literature and culture. He is a member of many scholarly organizations, including the American Renaissance Association and the Croatian Academy in America. He has lectured throughout the United States and Europe.

In addition to his many articles, he has published the books: *Modern Yugoslav Literature: An Anthology with Biographical Sketches* (Berkeley: University of California, 1956); *A Croatian Reader with Vocabulary* (The Hague: Mouton, 1960); *Contemporary Serbian Literature* (The Hague: Mouton, 1964); *From Croatian Renaissance to Yugoslav Socialism, Essays* (The Hague: Mouton, 1969); *Contemporary Croatian Literature* (The Hague: Mouton, 1969); *Juraj Križanić, 1618-1683: Russophile and Ecumenic Visionary*, A Symposium (The Hague: Mouton, 1976); *Kranjčević's Jesus on the Barricades* (Columbus, Ohio: Slavica Publishers, 1978); *The Traditions of Freedom in Croatian Literature. Essays* (Bloomington, IN, Croatian Alliance, 1983).

TYMOTEUSZ KARPOWICZ is professor of Polish literature at the University of Illinois at Chicago Circle. He has taught Polish literature at the University of Wrocław. He began his writing career in the field of the short story, but he is best known for his poetry and drama. His poetry is collected in the volumes: *Żywe wymiary* (Living dimensions), 1948; *Kamienna muzyka* (Stone music), 1958; *Znak równania* (Equation sign), 1960; *W imię znaczenia* (In the name of the meaning), 1962; *Trudny las* (Difficult Forest), 1964; and *Odwrócone światło* (Reversed light), 1972. His plays apperaed in *Dramaty zebrane* (Collected dramas) (Wrocław: Ossolineum, 1975). In the field of criticism, he has published the book *Poezja niemożliwa: modele Leśmianowskiej wyobraźni* (Impossible poetry: Patterns of Leśmian imagination) (Wrocław: Ossolineum, 1975). His articles include: "Naked Poetry," *Polish Review* 21:1-2 (1976); and "Art: A Bridge to the Impossible," *Polish Review* 26:2 (1981).

JERZY KŁOCZOWSKI is professor of medieval history and culture at Catholic University of Lublin. His principal field of study is the social, religious, and cultural history of Poland, with a special emphasis on the Middle Ages. He has served as Vice-Chairman of the Commission of Intellectual Comparative History of Churches, and has served as visiting lecturer in Europe and the United States. His many published titles include: *Dominikanie polscy na Śląsku w XIII-XVI w* (Polish Dominicans in Silesia in the 13th and 14th centuries) (Lublin: Tow. Nauk. Katolickiego Uniwersytetu Lubelskiego, 1956); *Wspólnoty chrześciańskie. Grupy zycia wspólnego w chrześcijaństwie zachodnim od starożytności do XV wieku* (Christian communities, Groups of common life in Western Christianity from antiquity to the 15th century) (Cracow: Znak, 1964); *Sources franco-polonaises d'histoire religieuse* (Paris: Centre de recherche d'histoire religieuse, 1975); *L'essor de l'Europe Centrale-Orientales aux 14-15 s., Peuples et Civilisations* (Paris: Presses Universitaires de France, 1983); *Europa słowiańska i jej rozwój w XIV-XV w.* (Slavic Europe and its development in the 14th-15th centuries) (Warsaw: PIW, 1984); *Dzieje chrześcijaństwa polskiego* (History of Polish christianity) 2 vols. (Paris: Nasza Rodzina. Éditions du dialogue, 1987-88). He is the editor and a contributor to *Kościół w Polsce. Studia nad historią Kościoła Katolickiego w Polsce* (The Church in Poland. Study on the history of the Catholic Church in Poland), vols. 1 and 2 (Cracow: Znak, 1960-70). He is also editor and co-author of *Studia nad historią dominikanów w Polsce 1222-1972* (Studies on the history of the Dominicans in Poland 1222-1972) vols. 1-2 (Warsaw: Wydawnictwo Polskiej Prowincji Dominikanów, 1975-76); *Chrześcijaństwo w Polsce. Zarys przemian 966-1945* (Christianity in Poland. Outline of changes 966 to 1945) (Lublin: Tow. Nauk. Katolickiego Uniwersytetu Lubelskeigo, 1980); *Zarys dziejów Kościoła katolickiego w Polsce* (A history of the Catholic Church in Poland) (Cracow: Znak, 1986); *The Christian Community of Medieval Poland* (Wrocław: Ossolineum, 1981); *Storia del Cristianesimo in Polonia* (Bologna: Centro Studi Europa Orientale, 1980); and *Histoire religieuse de la Pologne* (Paris: Centurion, 1987).

PAUL W. KNOLL is Professor of History at the University of Southern California. His principal fields of study are the history of the West Slavs, particularly of Poland, in the 14th and 15th centuries and the history of late medieval universities, especially the University of Cracow. His publications include: *The Rise of the Polish Monarchy: Piast Poland in East Central Europe, 1320-1370* (Chicago: Univ. of Chicago Press, 1972); with Bogdan Deresiewicz and Daniel S. Buczek, *Saint Stanislaw, Bishop of Cracow* (Santa Barbara, CA: Polish American Historical Association, 1979). Among his articles are: "The Arts Faculty at the University of Cracow at the End of the Fifteenth Century," in Robert Westman, ed., *The Copernican Achievement 1473-1973* (Berkeley and Los Angeles, 1973); "Learning in Late Piast Poland," *Proceedings of the American Philosophical Society*, 120 no. 2 (April 1976); "The Papacy at Avignon and University Foundations," in *The Church in a Changing Society* (Uppsala, Sweden, 1979); "Jan Długosz, 1480-1980," *The Polish Review*, 27:1-2, (1982); "The University of Cracow and the Conciliar Movement," in J. M. Kittelson and Pamela J.Transue, ed., *Rebirth, Reform and Resilience: Universities in Transition 1300-1700* (Columbus, Ohio: Ohio State University Press, 1984).

JERZY R. KRZYŻANOWSKI is Professor of Slavic and East European Languages and Literatures at Ohio State University and also a novelist and translator. His books include: *Ernest Hemingway* (Warsaw: Wiedza Powszechna, 1963); *A Modern Polish Reader* (with Sigmund S. Birkenmayer) (Pennsylvania State University, 1970); *Władysław Stanisław Reymont* (New York: Twayne Publishers, 1972); *Legenda Samosierry i inne prace krytyczne* (The legend of Samosierra and other critical studies) (Warsaw: Czytelnik, 1986); *Generał. Opowieść o Leopoldzie Okulickim* (The General. A story about Leopold Okulicki) (London: Odnowa, 1980); *Diana. Powieść* (Diana. A novel) (New York: Bicentennial Publishing Corp., 1987). Among his numerous articles are: "On the History of *Ashes and Diamonds*," *Slavic and East European Journal* 15:3 (1971); "Prus's *The Doll*: an ironic novel," *Russian and Slavic Literature*, ed. R. Freeborn (Cambridge, Mass: Slavica, 1976); "The Land of No Salvation." *The Polish Review* 23:2 (1978); "A Paradise Lost? The Image of *kresy* in Contemporary Polish Literature," *American Contributions to the Eighth International Congress of Slavists*, vol. 2, ed., Victor Terras (Columbus, Ohio: Slavica, 1978); and "Prus- batalista," (Prus, the battle-scene writer) *Pamiętnik Literacki* 52:4 (1979).

PAULINA LEWIN is visiting lecturer in the Department of Slavic Langauges and Literatures at Harvard University, and visiting scholar at Harvard Ukrainian Research Institute. She has taught at the University of Warsaw. Her books and articles have dealt with East Slavic literatures, especially poetics and drama, Old Polish and Old Russian literature, and Polish- Russian literary relations from the sixteenth to the eighteenth centuries.

Among her published works are the following books: *Intermedia wschodnio-słowiańskie XVI-XVIII w.* (East Slavic Interludes of the 16th and 18th Centuries) (Wrocław: Ossolineum, 1967), and *Wykłady poetyki w uczelniach rosyjskich XVIII w. (1772-1774) a tradycje polskie* (Lectures on the theory of poetic art in Russian schools in the 18th century and Polish traditions) (Wrocław: Ossolineum, 1972). Among her many articles, the following should be mentioned: "Teoria akuminu w estetycznej świadomości wschodniej Słowiańszczyzny XVII-XVIII wieku a traktat Sarbiewskiego," (The Acumen Theory in East Slavic aesthetic consciousness in the seventeenth and eighteenth centuries and Sarbiewski's Treatise) in *Literatura staropolska i jej związki europejskie* (Wrocław: Ossolineum, 1973); "Literatura staropolska a literatury wschodniosłowiańskie" (Old Polish literature and the East Slavic literatures) in *Literatura staropolska w kontekście europejskim* (Wrocław: Ossolineum, 1977); and "The Ukrainian Popular Religious Stage of the 17th and 18th Centuries on the Territory of the Polish Commonwealth," *Harvard Ukrainian Studies* 1:3 (1977).

MARIA RENATA MAYENOWA was a professor at the Institute of Literary Research of the Polish Academy of Sciences. She is the author of historical and theoretical studies in the field of stylistics, and in particular of structural stylistics, versification, and the history of the Polish language. She was the editor of *Poetyka, zarys encyklopedyczny* (Poetics, an encyclopedic outline), Biblioteka pisarzów polskich (Book series on Polish writers), *Słownik polszczyzny XVI wieku* (Dictionary of sixteenth-century Polish) and she edited and co-authored commentaries of Jan Kochanowski, *Dzieła wszystkie. Wydanie Sejmowe* (Jan Kochanowski. The complete works. Sejm edition) (Wrocław: Ossolineum, 1983-). Among her books are: *Poetyka opisowa. Opis utworu literackiego* (Descriptive poetics. Description of the literary work) (Warsaw: PZWS, 1949); *Walka o język w życiu i literaturze staropolskiej* (Struggle for the language in old Polish life and literature) 2nd edition (Warsaw: PIW, 1955); *O sztuce czytania wierszy* (On the art of reading poetry) (Warsaw: Wiedza Powszechna, 1963); *Poetyka teoretyczna: zagadnienie języka* (Theoretical poetics: the question of language) (Wrocław: Ossolineum, 1974); and *O języku poezji Jana Kochanowskiego* (About the language of Jan Kochanowski's poetry) (Cracow: Wydawnictwo Literackie, 1983). Among her numerous articles the following should be mentioned: "Możliwości i niebezpieczeństwa metod matematycznych w poetyce," (Possibilities and dangers of mathematical methods in poetics) in *Poetyka i matematyka*, ed. M.R. Mayenowa (Warsaw: PIW, 1965); "Accent pattern in Polish syllabic verse," in *Poetics. Poetyka. Poetika*. eds. Roman Jakobson, M.R. Mayenowa, et al. (The Hague: Mouton; Warsaw:PWN, 1966); "Textkohärenz und Rezipiententhaltung." in *Literaturtheoretische Modelle und kommunikatives System. Zur aktuellen Diskussion in der polnischen Literaturwissenschaft.* (Kronberg: Scriptor Verlag, 1974).

ANTONI MĄCZAK is Professor of History at Warsaw University. His principal field of study is social and economic history. He has served as director of the

Institute of History at the University of Warsaw, and has lectured extensively serving as Visiting Professor at many European and American Universities. He is co-editor of the *Przegląd Historyczny*, as well as foreign correspondent for the journal *Social History*. He has published studies of various aspects of Poland's economy in early modern times, including the textile industry, agriculture and foreign trade. He has also co-authored economic and social histories of Poland and a study on the effect of natural resources on European history.

Among his many books are: *Sukiennictwo wielkopolskie XIV-XVII w.* (The textile industry in Great Poland in the 14th to 17th centuries) (Warsaw: PWN, 1955); *Gospodarstwo chłopskie na Żuławach malborskich w początkach XVII w.* (The peasant farm in Zulawy near Malbork at the beginning of the 17th century) (Warsaw: PWN, 1962); *U źródeł nowoczesnej gospodarki europejskiej* (At the sources of Modern European Economy) (Warsaw: PWN, 1967); *Między Gdańskiem a Sundem. Studia nad handlem bałtyckim od połowy XVI do połowy XVII w.* (Between Gdańsk and the Sound. Studies on Baltic trade from the middle of the 16th to the middle of the 17th century) (Warsaw: PWN, 1972); *Życie codzienne w podróżach po Europie w XVI i XVII w.* (Daily life of European travelers in the 16th and 17th centuries) (Warsaw: PWN, 1978); *Rządzący i rządzeni* (Rulers and the ruled) (Warsaw: PIW, 1986). He is editor, coeditor, and co-author of *Społeczeństwo polskie od X do XX w.* (Polish society from the 10th to the 20th century) (Warsaw: Książka i Wiedza, 1979); *Encyklopedia historii gospodarczej Polski* (Encyklopedia of Polish Economic History), 2 volumes (Warsaw: Wiedza Powszechna, 1981); *A Republic of Nobles. Studies in Polish History to 1864*, ed, J.K. Fedorowicz (Cambridge: Cambridge University Press, 1982); *East Central Europe in Transition from the Fourteenth to the Seventeenth Century* (Cambridge: Cambridge University Press, 1985); *Klientelsysteme in Europe der frühen Neuzeit* (München, Oldenburg, 1987).

ADAM MIŁOBĘDZKI is Professor of Art History at Warsaw University. A specialist in the architectural history of Central Europe, such as the Late Gothic, the Renaissiance, and Polish architecture of the 17th century, Renaissance architecture and castles and country houses in their social context, and native architecture in wood. He has lectured both in European and USA universities. His books include: *Zarys dziejów architektury w Polsce* (An outline history of architecture in Poland), now in its 3rd edition (Warsaw: Wiedza Powszechna, 1978); *Architektura polska XVII w.*, (Polish architecture of the 17th century) 2 volumes (Warsaw: PWN, 1980). Among his many articles are: "Architektura i społeczeństwo" (Architecture and society) in *Polska w epoce Odrodzenia. Państwo, społeczeństwo, kultura*, ed. Andrzej Wyczański (Warsaw: Wiedza Powszechna, 1970); "Pałac i zamek renesansowy" (The Renaissance palace and castle) in *Renesans, Sztuka i ideologia*, ed. Tadeusz S. Jaroszewski (Warsaw: PWN, 1976); and "Architektura Królestwa Polskiego w XV w." (Architecture of the Polish Kingdom in the 15th century) in *Sztuka i ideologia XV wieku.*, ed. Piotr Skubiszewski (Warsaw: PWN, 1978).

JANUSZ PELC is Pofessor of the History of Polish Literature at the University of Warsaw, and formerly professor at the Institute of Literary Research at the Polish Academy of Science. He is the editor-in-chief of *Problemy literatury staropolskiej* (Problems of Old Polish literature) and of many other publications in the field of Old Polish studies. He has edited the poetry of Jan Kochanowski, Szymon Szymonowicz, Zbigniew Morsztyn, and many volumes of works connected with the Polish Renaissance.

Among his published works are: *Jan Kochanowski w tradycjach literatury polskiej (od XVI do połowy XVIII wieku)* [Jan Kochanowski in the traditions of Polish literature (from the 16th to the mid-18th centuries)] (Warsaw: PIW, 1965); *Zbigniew Morsztyn—arianin i poeta* (Zbigniew Morsztyn—Arian and poet) (Wrocław: Ossolineum, 1966); *Treny Jana Kochanowskiego* (The Laments of Jan Kochanowski) (Warsaw: Czytelnik, 1969); *Obraz-słowo-znak. Studium o emblematach w literaturze staropolskiej* (Image-word-sign. A study of emblems in Old Polish literature) (Wrocław: Ossolineum, 1973); *Zbigniew Morsztyn na tle poezji polskiej XVII w.* (Zbigniew Morsztyn in the context of 17th century Polish poetry) (Warsaw: Wiedza Powszechna, 1973); *Jan Kochanowski. Szczyt renesansu w literaturze polskiej* (Jan Kochanowski. Zenith of the Renaissance in Polish literature) (Warsaw: PWN, 1980). *Europejskość i polskość literatury naszego renesansu* (The European and Polish context of our Renaissance (Warsaw: Czytelnik, 1984); *Jan Kochanowski le poète de la Renaissance* (Paris: UNESCO, 1986). His numerous articles include: "Polish Literature of the Renaissance Epoch," in *Poland— the land of Copernicus* (Wrocław: Ossolineum, 1971) "Les Métamorphoses de l'emblématique et de l'iconologie à l'époque du baroque," in *Il Barocco fra Italia e Polonia* (Warsaw: PWN, 1977); "Lateinishe Dichtung in Polen des 16. Jahrhunderts," in *Fragen der polnischen Kultur im 16 Jahrhundert*, ed. Rheinhold Olesch, Hans Rothe (Giessen: W.S. Schmitz Verlag, 1980).

EDWARD ROSEN was Professor of the History of Science at City University of new York. His main area of research was in the history of science, particularly on Renaissance science. He was translator and editor of the complete works of Copernicus in English and of studies and articles on Copernicus, Copernican theory, and Copernicus' place in the advancement of science.

Among his most important published works are: *Three Copernican Treatises*, 3rd. edition (New York: Farrar, Straus, and Giroux, 1971); *Johann Kepler's Conversation with Galileo's Sidereal Messenger* (New York: Johnson Reprint Corp., 1965). *Introductions à l'astronomie de Copernic* (co-authored with Henri Hugonnard-Roche and Jean-Pierre Verdet) (Paris: Blanchard, 1975); *Copernicus and the Scientific Revolution* (Malabar, FLA: Robert E. Krieger, 1984). He was editor, translator, and commentator of Johann Kepler's *"Somnium"* (Madison, WI: University of Wisconsin Press, 1967), Nicholas Copernicus. *Complete Works*, 3 volumes (Cracow and Warsaw: PWN, and London: Macmillan, 1972-1985).

Among his numerous articles are: "Renaissance Science as Seen by Burckhardt and His Successors," in *The Renaissance*, T. Melton, ed. (Madison: University of Wisconsin Press, 1961); "The Debt of Classical Physics to Renaissance Astronomers, Particularly Kepler," in *Proceedings of the Tenth International Congress of History of Science* (Paris, 1964); "The Impact of Copernicus on Man's Conception of His Place in the World." *Science and Society: Past, Present, and Future*, Nicholas H. Steneck, ed. (Ann Arbor: Univeristy of Michigan Press, 1975); "The Alfonsine Tables and Copernicus," in *Manuscripta* 20, 1976; "In Defense of Tycho Brahe," *Archive for History of Exact Sciences*, 24:4 (1981).

JANUSZ TAZBIR is Professor of History in the Institute of History at the Polish Academy of Sciences and Director of the Institute. He is also a corresponding member of the Polish Academy of Sciences. He holds the position of editor-in-chief of the annual *Odrodzenie i Reformacja w Polsce* (Renaissance and Reformation in Poland). He has specialized in Polish cultural history, especially the Reformation and Counter Reformation. He is author of studies of the Polish Antitrinitarians, Polish gentry culture, the Reformation and the problem of toleration in Poland.

Among his many published titles are the following books: *Państwo bez stosów* (Warsaw: PIW, 1967), which appeared in English as *A State Without Stakes. Polish Religious Toleration in the Sixteenth and Seventeenth Centuries* (Warsaw: Kościuszko Foundation and PIW, 1973); *Szlachta a konkwistadorzy. Opinia staropolska wobec podboju Ameryki przez Hiszpanię* (Szlachta and conquistadors. Polish opinions of the conquest of America by Spain) (Warsaw: PWN, 1969); *Arianie i katolicy* (Arians and Catholics) (Warsaw: Książka i Wiedza, 1971); *Rzeczpospolita i świat. Studia z dziejów kultury XVII w.* (The Commonwealth and the world. Studies on the culture of the seventeenth century) (Wrocław: Ossolineum, 1971); *Dzieje polskiej tolerancji* (History of Polish tolerance) (Warsaw: Interpress, 1973); *Bracia polscy na wygnaniu. Studia z dziejów emigracji ariańskiej* (The Polish Brethern in exile. Studies on the Antitrinitarian emigration) (Warsaw: PWN, 1977); *Kultura szlachecka w Polsce: rozkwit- upadek-relikty* (The culture of the nobility in Poland: its rise, decline, and remnants). 2nd ed. (Warsaw: Wiedza Powszechna, 1979); *Tradycje tolerancji religijnej w Polsce* (Traditions of religious toleration in Poland) (Warsaw: Książka i Wiedza, 1980); *Myśl polska w nowożytnej kulturze europejskiej* (The Polish thought in modern European culture) (Warsaw: Nasza Księgarnia, 1986); *La République nobiliaire et le monde, Etude sur l'histoire de la culture polonaise à l'époque du baroque* (Wrocław: Ossolineum, 1986).

Among his many articles are: "Die Sozinianer in der zweiten Hälfte des 17. Jahrhunderts," in *Reformation und Frühaufklärung in Polen*, ed. Paul Wrzecionko (Göttingen: Vandenhoeck and Ruprecht, 1977); "Die Polnische Kultur des 16 Jahrhunderts," in *Fragen der polnischen Kultur im 16 Jahrhunderts* (Giessen: W. Schmitz, 1980); "The fate of Polish Protestantism in the Seventeenth Century," in *A Republic of Nobles.* (Cambridge: Cambridge University Press, 1982); and

"Culture of the Baroque in Poland," in *East-Central Europe in Transition*. (Cambridge: Cambridge University Press, 1985)

TADEUSZ ULEWICZ is Professor of Polish Philology at the Jagiellonian University. He is the author of works on Polish literature in the sixteenth century, on Polish-Italian literary relations, and on the history of printing in Poland in the era of the Renaissance. He is also the editor of the new series *Silva Rerum* and of many volumes devoted to the history of Polish literature.

His books include: *Świadomość słowiańska Jana Kochanowskiego. Z zagadnień psychiki polskiego renesansu* (The Slavic consciousness of Jan Kochanowski. On the problem of the mentality of the Polish Renaissance) (Cracow: Nakł. Seminarium Historii Literatury Polskiej Uniwersytetu Jagiellońskiego, 1948), no. 8; *Sarmacja. Studium z problematyki słowiańskiej XV i XVI w.* (Sarmatia, Study in the Slavic issue of the fifteenth and sixteenth centuries) (Cracow: Wydaw. Studium Słowiańskiego Uniw. Jagiellońskiego, 1950); *Oddziaływanie europejskie Jana Kochanowskiego. Od renesansu do romatyzmu* (The European influence of Jan Kochanowski. From the Renaissance to romanticism) (Cracow: PWN, 1970); *Wśród impresorów krakowskich doby renesansu* (Among the Cracow printers of the era of the Renaissance) (Cracow: Wydawnictwo Literackie, 1977); *Petrarca e la Polonia* (Padua: Editrice Antenore, 1982). Among his many articles are: "Il problema de sarmatismo nella cultura e letteratura polacca. Problematica generale e profilo storico," *Ricerche Slavistiche* 13 (Rome, 1961); "Gli scrittori polacchi del Cinquecento nell'ambiente umanistico di Padova e di Venezia," in *Italia, Venezia e Polonia. Tra umanesimo e rinascimento* (Wrocław: Ossolineum, 1967); "L'edizione veneziana del *Breviarium Cracoviense* de 1483," in *Studi slavisitici in ricordo di Carlo Verdiani* (Pisa, 1979); "St. Stanislaus of Szczepanów in Old Polish Literature and Cultur," *Aevum* 14:2 (Milan, 1980); "Jan Kochanowski in the Encyclopaedias," in *Polish Review*, 27:3-4 (1982); "The European Significance of Jan Kochanowski," *Cross Currents* 3 (1984). He has also edited works of Słowacki, Niemcewicz, and several of Kochanowski, including: Jan Kochanowski, *Odprawa posłów greckich* (Jan Kochanowski, *The Dismissal of the Greek Envoys*) (Wrocław: Ossolineum, 1974).

WALDEMAR VOISÉ is professor at the University of Aix-en Provence, formerly Professor of the History of Science at the Institute of the History of Science and Technology of the Polish Academy of Sciences. He has specialized in the history of Copernicanism, the history of utopian thought, Polish West European political thinkers, and social thought in the sixteenth and seventeenth centuries.

His published works include the following books: *Frycza Modrzewskiego nauka o państwie i prawie* (Frycz Modrzewski's teachings about the state and law)

(Warsaw: Książka i Wiedza, 1956); *Początki nowożytnych nauk społecznych. Epoka renesansu, jej narodziny i schyłek* (The beginnings of modern social sciences. The period of the Renaissance, its birth and decline) (Warsaw: Książka i Wiedza, 1962); *Histoire du copernicanisme en douze essais* (Paris: Albin Michel, 1973); *La réflexion presociologique d'Erasme à Montesquieu* (Wrocław: Ossolineum, 1973); *Andrzej Frycz Modrzewski, 1503-1572* (Wrocław: Ossolineum, 1975); and *Europolonica. La Circulation de quelques thèmes polonais à travers l'Europe du XVIe au XVIIIe siècle* (Wrocław: Ossolineum, 1981).

WENCESLAS WAGNER is Professor of Law at the University of Detroit. He is a member of numerous American and international organizations and associations. He has taught law at many American and European, particularly French universities. He has been a frequent lecturer at Polish universities as well. His principle areas of study are comparative law, torts, and federalism. He has authored works on international law, Polish law, and American law.

Among his books are: *Les libertés de l'air* (/Editions—Paris, 1948); *The Federal States and their Judiciary* (The Hague: Mouton, 1959); *International Air Transportation as Affected by State Sovereignty* (Brussels: E. Bruylant, 1970); *Obligations in Polish Law* vol. 2 of Polish Civil Law, ed. by Dominik Lasok (Leiden: Sijthoff, 1974); and *Law in the USA in the Bicentennial Era* (American Assn. of Comparative Study of Law, 1978). He is editor and co-author of *Polish Law Throughout the Ages* (Stanford: Hoover Institute, 1970); co-editor of *Legal Thought in the USA under Contemporary Pressures* (Brussels: E. Bruylant, 1970); and co-editor of *Law in the USA in Social and Technological Revolution* (Brussels: E. Bruylant, 1974).

ANDRZEJ WALICKI is O'Neill Professor at the Department of History at the University of Notre Dame, formerly Head of the Department of Modern Polish Philosophy at the Institute of Philosophy and Sociology of the Polish Academy of Sciences. He has been a Visiting Research Fellow at English, American, and Austrialian universities. His scholarly interests include: Russian nineteenth-century literature, Russian philosophy and social thought (including the history of political, religious, and economic ideas) against the background of the history of Western thought, and Polish philosophical and social thought of the nineteenth and twentieth centuries. In addition to numerous articles and studies, his major publications include: *Osobowość a historia* (Personality and history) (Warsaw: PIW, 1959); *W kręgu konserwatywnej utopii* (Warsaw: PIW, 1964) and its English translation *The Slavophile Controversy* (Oxford: The Clarendon Press, 1975), *The Controversy over Capitalism, Studies in the Social Philosphy of the Russian Populists* (Oxford: The Clarendon Press, 1969), *Filozofia a mesjanism* (Philosophy and messianism) (Warsaw: PIW, 1970); *Stanisław Brzozowski. Dzieje myśli* (Stanisław Brzozowski. An intellectual portrait) (Warsaw: PIW, 1977); *A History of Russian Thought from the Enlightenment to Marxism* (Stanford: Stanford Univeristy

Press, 1980); *Philosophy and Romantic Nationalism. The Case of Poland* (Oxford: Clarendon Press, 1982); *Między filozofią, religią, i polityką* (Between Philosophy, Religion, and Politics) (Warsaw: PWN, 1983); *Polska, Rosja, marksizm* (Poland, Russia, marxism) (Warsaw: Książka i Wiedza, 1983); *Legal philosophies of Russian liberalism* (Oxford: Clarendon Press, 1987). He is editor of and contributor to *Polska myśl filozoficzna i społeczna* (Polish philosophy and social thought) vol. 1 (Warsaw: Książka i Wiedza, 1973); and *Zarys dziejów filozofii polskiej, 1815-1918* (An outline of the history of Polish philosophy, 1815-1918) (Warsaw: PWN, 1982).

WIKTOR WEINTRAUB was professor of Polish Literature at Harvard University. He was a member of the Polich Academy of Sciences. He authored numerous books and articles which cover a wide spectrum of problems in Polish literature from the Renaissance to the present. Jan Kochanowski is the Polish poet to whom he has devoted special attention, returning many times to the various aspects of the work of the Master of Czarnolas. Apart from Kochanowski, Adam Mickiewicz occupies a special place in his research, and he has devoted many studies to the great Romantic poet.

His books include: *Styl Jana Kochanowskiego* (The style of Jan Kochanowski) (Cracow: W.L. Anczyc, 1932); *The Poetry of Adam Mickiewicz* (The Hague: Mouton, 1954); *Literature as Prophecy* (The Hague: Mouton, 1959); *Profecja i profesura* (Prophecy and professorship) (Warsaw: PIW, 1975); *Od Reja do Boya* (From Rej to Boy) (Warsaw: PIW, 1977); *Rzecz czarnoleska* (On Czarnolas) (Cracow: Wydawnictwo Literackie, 1977); and *Poeta i prorok, Rzecz o profetyzmie Mickiewicza* (Poet and prophet, On the prophetism of Mickiewicz) (Warsaw: PIW, 1982). Among his articles are: "Kochanowski's Renaissance Manifesto," *Slavonic and East European Review* 30 (1951); "The Paradoxes of Rej's Biography," *Indiana Slavic Studies* 4 (1967); "The Latin and the Polish Kochanowski: The Two faces of a Poet," *Actes du Ve Congrès de l'Association Internationale de Littérature Comparée* (Belgrade, 1969); "Fraszka in a tragic key; remarks on Kochanowski's 'Lament' IX and 'Fraszki' I, 3" in *To Honor Roman Jakobson. Essays on the Occasion of his Seventieth Birthday* (The Hague: Mouton, 1967); "Kochanowski versus Desportes: A Sixteenth-century French-Polish Poetic Duel," *Symbolae in honorem Georgii Y. Shevelov* (München, 1971/73).

GEORGE HUNTSTON WILLIAMS is Hollis Professor of Harvard Divinity School. He is a church historian and his areas of research are: ecclesiastical and doctrinal history in the fourth, eleventh, and sixteenth centuries; the Reformation in Poland; and the life and thought of Pope John Paul II. He is a Fellow of the American Academy of Arts and Sciences, a past president of the American Society of Church Historians (1957-58), and of the American Society of

Reformation Research (1966-67). He was an observer at the Second Vatican Council (1962-65).

His many books include: *The Norman Anonymous of (circa) 1100 A.D.* (Cambridge, Mass: Harvard University Press, 1951); *Wilderness and Paradise in Christian Thought* (New York: Harper, 1962); *The Radical Reformation* (Philadelphia: Westminster, 1962); *American Universalism: a Bicentennial Historical Essay* (Boston: Beacon, 1976); *The Polish Brethern, 1601-1685*, vols. 1-2 (Missoula, Montana: Univ. of Montana Press, 1978); *Thomas Hooker, writings in England and Holland, 1626-1633* (co-authored with Norman Pettit) (Cambridge, Mass.: Harvard Univ. Press, 1975); *The Mind of John Paul II: Origins of his Thought and Action* (New York: Seabury Press, 1981); and *The Contours of Church and State in the Thought of John Paul II* (Waco, Texas: Baylor Univ. Press, 1982).

Among his numerous articles the following should be mentioned: "Erasmianism in Poland," *The Polish Review* 22 (1977); "The Polish Lithuanian Calvin," *Festschrift for Ford Lewis Battles* ed. Brian A. Gerrish (Pittsburgh, 1979); "Stanislas Hosius," and "Peter Skarga," in *Shapers of Religious Traditions in Germany, Switzerland, and Poland 1560-1600* ed. by Jill Raitt (New Haven, 1981).

ANDRZEJ WRÓBLEWSKI is a professor of physics at Warsaw University. He has served as Director of the Institute of Experimental Physics of the Physics Dept. at Warsaw University. He also teaches the history of Physics. He is a corresponding member of the Polish Academy of Sciences and is a member of the Polish Physical Society. He works in the field of experimental physics of elementary particles and is the author of numerous papers dealing primarily with the mechanism of particle production in high energy collisions. He is co-author of an introductory physics text used in Polish universities. In the area of the history of physics, he has dealt with the pseudo-history of science and a variety of subjects ranging from Galileo to famous errors in recent physics.

His publications include: *Wstęp do fizyki* (Introduction to physics), co-author with Janusz A. Zakrzewski (Warsaw: PWN, 1976); *Z powrotem na ziemię. Spór o pochodzenie cywilizacji ludzkich* (Back to earth. Debate on the origin of human civilization), editor and author of introduction (Warsaw: PWN, 1980). In his research area in the history of physics, he has published *Prawda i mity w fizyce* (Truth and myths in physics) (Wrocław: Ossolineum, 1982). He is also chief of the scientific committee for *Encyklopedia fizyki współczesnej* (Encyclopedia of contemporary physics) (Warsaw: PWN, 1982).

Index